Moral Philosophy

DICKENSON BOOKS OF RELATED INTEREST

Problems of Moral Philosophy: An Introduction, Second Edition
  edited by Paul W. Taylor

Reason and Responsibility: Readings in Some Basic Problems of Philosophy, Third Edition
  edited by Joel Feinberg

Philosophy of Law
  edited by Joel Feinberg and Hyman Gross

The Logic of Grammar
  edited by Donald Davidson and Gilbert H. Harman

Philosophical Problems of Causation
  edited by Tom L. Beauchamp

Individual Conduct and Social Norms
  by Rolf Sartorius

Freedom and Authority: An Introduction to Social and Political Philosophy
  edited by Thomas Schwartz

Principles of Ethics: An Introduction
  by Paul W. Taylor

Man in Conflict: Traditions in Social and Political Thought
  by Louis I. Katzner

Metaphysics: An Introduction
  by Keith Campbell

Understanding Moral Philosophy
  edited by James Rachels

Morality in the Modern World
  edited by Lawrence Habermehl

A Preface to Philosophy
  by Mark Woodhouse

A Guide Through the Theory of Knowledge
  by Adam Morton

Moral Philosophy

Classic Texts and Contemporary Problems

edited by

Joel Feinberg
The Rockefeller University

Henry West
Macalester College

DICKENSON PUBLISHING COMPANY, INC.,
ENCINO, CALIFORNIA AND BELMONT, CALIFORNIA

ISBN-0-8221-0196-3

Library of Congress Catalog Card Number: 76-52735

Printed in the United States of America

Printing (last digit): 9 8 7 6 5 4 3 2 1

Cover by Mark Kochan

CONTENTS

PART **VI** EGOISM AND THE ETHICS OF CHARACTER

THE DICKENSON SERIES IN PHILOSOPHY

Philosophy, said Aristotle, begins in wonder—wonder at the phenomenon of self-awareness, wonder at the infinitude of time, wonder that there should be anything at all. Wonder in turn gives rise to a kind of natural puzzlement: How can mind and body interact? How is it possible that there can be free will in a world governed by natural laws? How can moral judgments be shown to be true?

Philosophical perplexity about such things is a familiar and unavoidable phenomenon. College students who have experienced it and taken it seriously are, in a way, philosophers already, well before they come in contact with the theories and arguments of specialists. The good philosophy teacher, therefore, will not present his subject as some esoteric discipline unrelated to ordinary interests. Instead he will appeal directly to the concerns that already agitate the student, the same concerns that agitated Socrates and his companions and serious thinkers ever since.

It is impossible to be a good teacher of philosophy, however, without being a genuine philosopher oneself. Authors of the Dickenson Series in Philosophy are no exceptions to this rule. In many cases their textbooks are original studies of problems and systems of philosophy, with their own views boldly expressed and defended with argument. Their books are at once contributions to philosophy itself and models of original thinking to emulate and criticize.

That equally competent philosophers often disagree with one another is a fact to be exploited, not concealed. Dickenson anthologies bring together essays by authors of widely differing outlook. This diversity is compounded by juxtaposition, wherever possible, of classical essays with leading contemporary materials. The student who is shopping for a world outlook of his own has a large and representative selection to choose among, and the chronological arrangements, as well as the editor's introduction, can often give him a sense of historical development. Some Dickenson anthologies treat a single group of interconnected problems. Others are broader, dealing with a whole branch of philosophy, or representative problems from various branches of philosophy. In both types of collections, essays with opposed views on precisely the same questions are included to illustrate the argumentative give and take which is the lifeblood of philosophy.

Joel Feinberg
Series Editor

PREFACE FOR THE INSTRUCTOR

This collection is intended by its editors to be a highly flexible teaching instrument lending itself to a variety of equally valid pedagogic uses. An instructor whose approach is more systematic or historical than piecemeal might prefer to concentrate on the three classic texts of Part I, assigning individual essays from the other Parts of the book as supplementary treatments by twentieth century writers of problems or themes that have their locus classicus in Aristotle, Kant, or Mill. On the other hand, an instructor whose primary interest is in problems rather than systems of moral philosophy might assign relevant sections of the classic texts to be interspersed among the articles in the Parts of the book organized by problems. For example, all or part of Mill's *Utilitarianism* relates vitally to Part II on "Intrinsic Value," perhaps to be read after Bentham or Huxley, and before Mitchell's critical article; and much of Aristotle can be thought of as belonging in the nonhedonistic section of Part II along with Epictetus and Nietzche, for Aristotle's "self-realization theory" is perhaps the leading historical alternative to hedonism. Similarly, Kant's theory of the unique value of a "good will" similar in spirit to the teachings of stoicism could be taught as an independent entry in Part II among the alternatives to hedonism.

In like manner, the problem-oriented instructor can exercise the option to begin with either normative or metaethical problems. For those who wish to confront head-on the widespread scepticism and relativism of beginning students, Part V, "The Role of Reason in Ethics," would be the place to begin. Those who would prefer to stimulate metaethical interest indirectly could begin with the normative questions of Parts II and III, urging their students to reason and argue about actual moral issues first, holding their metaethical puzzlement at least partly in suspension, before turning to the philosophical puzzles about knowledge, truth, and objectivity that are discussed in Part V. Much can be said for both of these pedagogic strategies; the choice should be the instructor's.

Moral Philosophy

Part I   Three Classical Theories

Moral philosophy is an intellectual discipline with a long history. Perhaps the best way to define it is to characterize the problems it aims to solve and the questions it tries to answer. The problems of moral philosophy, it should be emphasized, are *philosophical* problems. None of them is susceptible of solution, even in principle, by use of the experimental or mathematical methods of science. Scientists, of course, are also concerned with moral questions: discovering means to assigned ends; describing the moral views of individuals, societies, and cultures; and predicting the course and direction of moral change. But none of these types of inquiry is peculiarly philosophical.

At least some of the inquiries of the moral philosopher do not even have the appearance of impeccable neutrality that characterizes the scientist's interests in moral questions. Very often the moral philosopher is impelled to jump into the moral arena and take a stand about some controversial practical question that divides his fellow citizens into contending factions. One may take a stand, as a philosopher, on such issues as the moral permissibility of abortion, euthanasia, "free love," capital punishment, or experiments on animals. A philosopher is not likely to claim any special pipeline to the truth about such matters. Indeed, moral philosophers themselves, no less than other people, tend to disagree with one another. What characterizes their approach and makes their views especially worthy of respect, is that philosophers come to their conclusions on such issues as the result of careful argument from more general principles, and try to render their conclusions consistent with other moral judgments by finding analogies and differences between cases. The philosopher no more than the lawmaker can tolerate vagueness and inconsistency.

The American philosopher John Dewey has argued with considerable plausibility that both in the development of the individual person and in the history of the race, moral thought begins in *conflict*. Not long after children learn how to make moral judgments they find themselves in ethical disagreement with their peers. In adolescence, the discovery is commonly made that some of one's own moral convictions are in conflict, as when one thinks that one kind of action is right and another kind of action is wrong, and yet one cannot find any clearly relevant differences between them; or when a person finds that the case for the rightness of a given act is balanced equally by the case for the wrongness of that act, so that he or she cannot decide what to do, being in a sense in conflict with himself. Such instances of moral perplexity very naturally lead to a more general (and philosophical) perplexity about morals. The way to resolve personal or interpersonal conflict between specific judgments is to trace them to the more general maxims and principles from which they are thought to follow, until finally one arrives at the highest level of generality, that of ultimate or "first principles." If, for example, two people in ethical disagreement can discover that they share the same first principle or principles, then they can hope to resolve their ethical disagreement rationally by concentrating on the factual disagreement that must account for the persistence of their conflict despite their agreement on basic principles. But what if they should learn instead that they disagree also in their basic ethical principles? Is there any point in reasoning together further about the matter? That is a genuinely philosophical question about morals.

Similarly, reflective persons, upon acquiring an experience of cultural diversity, may come to question whether reason can demonstrate the superiority of one nation's (tribe's, church's, historical civilization's) moral code to another's. Even if conflicts within a code can be rationally resolved, there may yet be conflicts between whole codes that have little in common. This may lead to a search (as it did among the Ancient Athenians who had read Herodotus and heard the reports of seamen and commercial travelers returning from distant lands) for transcultural first principles that can be used to compare and evaluate the conflicting moralities of diverse social groups. Again, the search may lead to skepticism ("no one can ever know what is really right") or to relativism ("the truth of moral principles is always relative to the system of which they are a part, and conflicting systems cannot be compared, or are 'equally true' "), or it may lead the investigators to a formulation and defense of a first principle that must, they believe, hold true in all ages and cultures.

Many philosophers make a distinction between the questions and problems of *normative ethics* and those of *metaethics*. Answers to normative questions do not purport to be ethically neutral. They *use* ethical terms like "right," "wrong," "good," "bad," "ought," "duty," "obligation," "worthwhile," "proper," "important," "virtuous," "sinful," and so forth, to *make* ethical judgments, to "take a stand." Some normative judgments express decisions ("I ought to do *x* rather than *y*"); some express verdicts or critical judgments ("What Jones did was wrong"); some express appraisals or evaluations ("Personal excellence is more important than happiness," "Jones is a better person than Smith"). Normative judgments of precise specificity, however, are not especially philosophical. It is not the special province of moral philosophers as such simply to make up their own minds about what they ought to do or about what another person's duty is or was, or to pass judgment about the conduct or character of a specific person or persons at a precisely dated moment in history. Very specific normative judgments are important to moral philosophers, at best, as raw data for their inquiries, or as logical byproducts of their conclusions. Rather they are concerned to formulate and defend normative judgments of greater generality: general rules of conduct, maxims, precepts, and especially ultimate principles when these are thought possible. Even judgments of intermediate generality (we can call them "maxims") are not properly philosophical when they are merely affirmed and collected without elaboration and supporting argument. A kind of handbook in which one could look up the answer to all moral and practical problems, and find a list of duties in their order of priority, as well as a set of comparative evaluations of various states of affairs and traits of character, would be a work of *casuistry,* not of moral philosophy.

Moral philosophers when engaged in normative ethics typically ask such questions as "What is the ultimate standard of right conduct?" They aim not simply to tell us which acts are right and which acts are wrong but rather what makes right acts right and what makes wrong acts wrong. They seek what one writer has called "the right-making characteristic," that property (or properties) common and peculiar to all right acts in virtue of which they are right, and their statement of that characteristic will itself be a criterion distinguishing right from wrong and indifferent acts. Similarly, moral philosophers will not merely list things that are good and things that are bad. Instead they will distinguish between things that are *instrumentally good,* that is, things whose value derives from their being means to other things, and things that are *intrinsically good,* that is, valuable for their own sakes, as ends in themselves quite apart from their consequences. They will not merely list the things that they think are intrinsically good; rather they will ask what there is about them that makes them intrinsically good. Their answers will be a statement of the "good-making characteristic" in the form of a perfectly general criterion, or first principle, of value. Various philosophers have posed their normative questions about value in different but similar ways. Some have endeavored to discover what there is that is ultimately worthwhile; others have depicted in a general way "the good life"; others have sought "the meaning of life" (or in William James's somewhat more precise terms: "What makes a life worth living?"); others, making Aristotle's assumption that every species has its own characteristic good consisting in the fulfillment of its own distinctive natural propensities, seek to learn what is "the good for man."

The questions of metaethics as interpreted by many moral philosophers, on the other hand, do seek answers that are themselves morally neutral. These are philosophical questions *about* normative ethics that do not themselves call for answers in normative terms. In doing metaethics moral philosophers discuss, interpret, and analyze ethical terms without actually *using* them to make personal ethical judgments. They will ask whether it is possible to resolve ethical disagreements rationally or whether disputants must sometimes despair of resolving their disputes short of rhetorical tricks, violence, and other extrarational methods. Are normative judgments supportable by evidence? If so, what sorts of information can count as evidence for and against them? The answer to the question about evidence will depend at least in part on what we understand normative judgments to mean, and this matter in turn will lead moral philosophers to propose definitions for normative terms (or in some cases to deny that useful definitions are possible). Again, philosophers are doing metaethics when they inquire whether any forms of ethical skepticism or relativism can be shown to be correct or incorrect, when they ask whether normative principles can be deduced logically from factual premises, whether normative ethics can in principle become a science, or just how distinctively *moral* normative judgments (for example, "Jones is a virtuous man," "You ought to keep your promise") can be distinguished from normative judgments that have nothing to do with morality ("Harvard has a good football team," "You really ought to try oat crispies for breakfast").

Still other topics, some of which are not easy to classify in terms of the simple categories of normative ethics and metaethics, are commonly treated in works of moral philosophy. There are questions of "moral psychology," for example, which have a direct bearing on general normative issues. What motivation can be provided to persons to be moral when self-interest seems to incline them in the contrary direction? Does morality always "pay off" in the end or does it require of us genuine personal sacrifices? Human nature being what it is, can people be motivated to do what they believe is contrary to their own interests? Then there are questions, both analytic and normative, about specific moral concepts and the special moral contexts in which they have application, for example rights, claims, and deserts, equality and distributive justice, punishment and retributive justice. There are questions about specific personal excellences, for example courage, benevolence, and prudence; about specific personal ideals, for example autonomy, integrity, and authenticity; and about the means and aims of moral education. The subject matter of moral philosophy is very nearly as wide as the practical side of human experience, and as various as the appraisals, verdicts, and decisions of ordinary life.

The selections in this anthology are primarily arranged by problems. Part II, "Intrinsic Value: What Makes a Life Worthwhile?" consists of essays on general normative problems about value, in particular, articles giving answers to the question, "What kinds of things are intrinsically good and bad?" The materials in Part III, "Right and Wrong: Principles of Conduct," are concerned with general normative questions about right conduct, especially the question "What is the standard of right conduct?" or "What is the right-making characteristic?" Part IV, "Rights, Justice, and Punishment," contains discussions of the important ethical concepts of rights and justice, how they relate to each other and to other ethical concepts, and how they apply in the special contexts in which economic benefits and burdens are distributed among a population and in which criminals are brought to punishment. This section contains both metaethical materials (analyzing, clarifying, inter-relating concepts) and normative ones (applying those concepts in the form of general ethical principles to economic distributions and criminal punishments.) The problems discussed in Part V, "The Role of Reason in Ethics," are predominantly metaethical. The essays inquire into the meaning of ethical judgments, how they can be supported (if at all) by evidence, and whether they can be known to be true. Part VI, "Egoism and the Ethics of Character," deals with questions of both "moral psychology" and motivation, and blame, credit, and the evaluation of character.

An introductory anthology in moral philosophy would be seriously deficient, however, if it were arranged entirely by problems. It would very likely give the beginning student a misleading and lopsided impression of the subject. To avoid this imbalance it is important that a classification by problems be supplemented by a classification by systems, as is done in Part I, "Three Classical Theories." Some of the most important and influential treatments of the problems of moral philosophy have occurred in large books rather than brief articles. It would be misleading, however, and also unfair, to pull individual chapters out of books without including the preceding chapters whose arguments are presupposed, and the following chapters where refinements and qualifications are often made.

Moreover, it is an important intellectual discipline for the student to study whole systems as opposed to fragmentary parts, to grasp their organizing plans and supporting structures, to see how the parts fit together to make a whole, to separate out the unproved assumptions and obiter dicta, and to construct and evaluate formal arguments that spread, link by link, over the major part of a book. A solution to a given problem may presuppose the solution to another one which in turn presupposes the solution to still another, so that one's initial inquiry may lead along a circuitous trail into a tangle of subsidiary questions before the basic question that led into the detour may again be considered. Any systematic philosopher, then, must initially put her or his philosophical problems into a kind of "order of presupposition," so that basic questions are linked up in a clear and orderly way with the technical questions (often less interesting in themselves) whose solutions they presuppose. This task of logical organization is an important part of the philosophical enterprise. There is, after all, a sense in which no part of a great philosophical text can be properly appreciated until the work as a whole is fully understood. The treatments of individual problems are not easily isolable.

Some classical works of moral philosophy (most notably those included in Part I) are so important for their treatment of certain individual problems that no useful study of those problems is possible without their inclusion among the readings. No section of a book organized by problems could contain materials on virtue without including Aristotle, on duty without including Kant, or on happiness without including Mill. And yet the contributions by these philosophers to these particular topics occur as parts of their systematic treatises, and are not fully and fairly understandable outside those more comprehensive works. That is by itself a very good reason for including as substantial portions of those treatises as is consistent with space limitations in a collection with an orientation primarily to problems.

This book, therefore, is organized both by problems and by systems with major portions of three "classic texts" constituting Part I. This arrangement permits a great deal of flexibility in the order in which instructors might assign readings. A systems-oriented teacher might assign the systematic works first with various "side trips" to discussions of particular problems at appropriate places in the texts. A problem-oriented instructor might begin with the problems sections, fitting the classic texts, either in whole or in part, into appropriate slots in the particular discussions.

The three classic works—Aristotle's *Nicomachean Ethics,* Immanuel Kant's *Fundamental Principles of the Metaphysic of Morals,* and John Stuart Mill's *Utilitarianism*—were selected for two reasons. First, they are very probably the most widely read and influential of all the treatises of moral philosophy in the Western literature. It is hard indeed to conceive of any college course in ethics in which these writings are not read or studied in some fashion. Second, the writers represent three very different approaches to their common subject. Great philosophers in different periods, or in different traditions, give emphasis to different problems. Not only do they give conflicting answers to the same questions, but they address themselves to subtly different questions. Moral philosophy at first glance may not even seem quite the same subject as treated, for example, by Plato and Bentham, or by Aristotle and Kant. Although there are common strands among the classic texts, the total collection of questions treated may seem to have a somewhat miscellaneous character, with the problems engrossing one classic writer largely neglected by the others.

The three classic writers included in Part I have each employed a different model for his subject.[1] Aristotle's model is *education.* Ethics, on his conception, is a "branch of politics," and the basic task of those who make and administer laws is to design and promote the institutions that will permit each citizen to live the best life he or she can, and as far as possible, to achieve his or her individual good. The moral philosopher's main concern should be to determine the "good for man," and the methods for teaching citizens how to achieve that good. Aristotle looks at the whole subject of moral philosophy from the perspective of the moral educator. Moreover, Aristotle's system is the prime example of what is often called an "ethics of character" as opposed to an "ethics of conduct." There is little discussion in his book of normative principles, maxims, rules, and judgments, and little concern with the actual content of duties and obligations. The primary moral concern Aristotle shares with his reader is neither "What should I do?" nor "What things are most worth having?" but rather "What kind of person is it most worth being?" When moral educators have a detailed answer to that question and also understand the mechanisms by which excellences and flaws of character are acquired, they are in a position to turn to the study of politics and questions of institutional design. The job of the state, Aristotle believes, is not to try to make citizens happy, but rather to make them good; then with a little luck, happiness will come as an unsought dividend. One of Aristotle's most basic concepts is *areté,* a word misleadingly translated as "virtue," but better rendered as "excellence" or "excellence of character." Aristotle clearly meant "personal excellences" to define a class much wider than the class of "moral virtues," for he includes not only such excellences as justice, benevolence,

---

[1] What follows has been influenced by some very astute observations in Bernard Mayo's *Ethics and the Moral Life* (New York: St. Martin's Press, 1958), pp. 200–218.

temperance, and courage, but also "proper pride" (or "large-souledness"), and even the likes of cheerfulness and genuine wittiness.

One of the leading models for Immanuel Kant's approach, like that of the Hebrew moralists, Roman Stoics, and ecclesiastical jurists who preceded him, is *law,* and if Aristotle is best understood as a theorist of moral education, Kant can best be interpreted as a theorist of "the moral law." The object of the work included here is to establish "the supreme principle of morality," and to derive that principle not from the diverse and variable psychological characteristics of human beings, not from the particular rules of various human codes and cultures, but from impersonal reason itself, which is a universal and invariant element in all human beings, indeed in all conceivable "rational beings." Such a rational principle is binding on the will of rational beings in just the way the rules of logic and mathematics are binding on our belief. If we believe that all men are mortal and that Socrates is a man, then we *must* believe that Socrates is mortal. Since we *are* rational, we have no choice but to do as reason commands; the deliverances of reason are "categorical imperatives." One can ask why one is bound to obey the laws of the state, or the rules of a given code, but one cannot ask why one must conform to a rational principle, whether theoretical or practical (moral). Just insofar as one *is* a rational being one has "no choice." A supreme rational principle of morality, then, would be necessarily and universally true (Kant's term is "a priori"), and automatically binding on the will of a rational being. In the latter respect, it is one and the same as a kind of *law,* and its deliverances impose on us an unconditional *duty* of obedience. But insofar as our wills are free, and our psychological natures incline us to act against reason, the possibility of disobedience is always present, and the good person (morally and properly speaking) is one who can swim against the current of natural disposition and conform his or her will to rational law.

Perhaps the most apt model for John Stuart Mill's system of moral philosophy is the science of *economics.* (Indeed, Mill himself was one of the leading political economists of the nineteenth century.) Economics studies the production and distribution of economic goods, that is, goods on which a price tag can be put. From the (relatively) narrow economic point of view, the more wealth produced by an economic system, the better off are the persons who live within the system. In typical modern states, at any rate, it is in virtually everybody's interest that the "pie" they all share be as large as possible so that even those relatively unlucky persons who receive the smaller shares will have enough to meet their basic needs and then some. Money, of course, has no "real value" in itself. It is the perfect example of a mere "instrumental good," valuable only for what it can produce. If we could form an adequate conception, in contrast, of genuinely intrinsic values, then it would be possible to produce a plausible moral system on the economic model. Instead of such a principle as "Whatever increases the gross national product is good," we could say "Whatever promotes the thing that is good as an end in itself (call it 'x' for the moment) is good, and the more x the better." Instead of saying that acts are right if and only if they lead, directly or indirectly, to an increase in the gross national product, we can say that acts are right insofar as they promote x (the good) and wrong insofar as they promote y (intrinsic harm or evil). Conducibility to xness, then, is the right-making characteristic.

What then *is* the moral analogue of wealth, the one kind of thing that is good or worth having not merely as a means but entirely for its own sake? Mill, like Bentham before him, thought the answer obvious: happiness. Thus he thought it part of the moral philosopher's job to formulate rules and "second-ary principles" that will lead to as much happiness all around (or *utility,* to use the word with more hardboiled economic flavor) as possible. Moral philoso-phy then becomes the economics of happiness. Unlike Kant, who begins with the basic ideas of law and duty, and then derives a conception of value from them ("Nothing," he wrote, "can possibly be conceived . . . which can be called good without qualification except a *good will"*), Mill starts with a conception of intrinsic value (happiness) and derives duties and rules of right conduct from it. Kant's approach, with its insistence on the logical priority of duty, is often called *deontological* (from the Greek word for duty); Mill's opposite procedure by which duties are derived from a prior and independent conception of intrinsic values, is often called *teleological* (from the Greek word for "end" or purpose). Both Mill and Aristotle, in quite different ways, are teleological, since both find the ultimate rationale for morality (for rules of conduct in Mill's case, for education in the virtues in Aristotle's) not in the inherently rational form of certain moral principles but in some purpose lying beyond morality, a maximal balance of pleasure over pain for Mill, energetic self-fulfillment (*eudaemonia*) for Aristotle.

A few brief remarks about the classical texts are in order. The date of original publication of a text is normally given; however, for Aristotle's *Nicomachean Ethics,* this cannot be done, for the work was not composed by Aristotle as a *book,* in any usual sense, nor ever published by him. Aristotle was in the later stages of his life the director of the Lyceum in Athens, a school which has been called "the first true university."[2] Many of his major works, including the *Nicomachean Ethics,* were originally his outlines for plans of studies, or his own lecture notes, or perhaps in some cases, even notes taken at his lectures by his students. Aristotle bequeathed his personal library includ-ing his own unpublished notes and manuscripts on papyrus rolls to his successor who in time passed them on to others, until finally they came to rest in the damp and moldy cellar of a family that was determined to hold on to them until their resale price would rise and then somehow forgot them altogether. There they remained in a literally moth-eaten state of decay for at least 150 years, until a wealthy book collector learned of them and purchased them in the first century B.C. His library in turn was captured by the Roman general Sulla in 86 B.C., and shipped to Rome and the protection of a reputable library. When the *Nicomachean Ethics* was finally "published," well over two centuries after its author's death, it was in an unavoidably inaccurate version, and included interpolations of words by later editors (who knew nothing of philosophy) into the gaps caused by torn and eroded places in the original scrolls, and additional errors made by careless scribes. Later scholars, how-ever, purged the manuscript of obvious mistakes, and we now have a "book," not altogether free of gaps and inconsistencies, but no worse in those respects than the classroom lectures even of the most inspired teachers. The student reader then is well advised to remember that he or she is "listening" to a lecture by one of history's greatest teachers, and not reading a deliberately composed dogmatic treatise.

Immanuel Kant's *Grundlegung zur Metaphysik der Sitten,* translated here as "*Fundamental Principles of the Metaphysic of Morals"* but often referred to by scholars simply as "the *Grundlegung*" or "the Groundwork," was published in

[2] J. A. K. Thomson, *The Ethics of Aristotle* (Harmondsworth, Middlesex: Penguin Books, Ltd., 1955), p. 16.

1785, four years after Kant had published his famous *Critique of Pure Reason*. In the latter work, Kant gives an analysis of the grounds and limits of the "theoretical knowledge" we get from science and mathematics. He was especially concerned to explain how what he called "synthetic a priori knowledge" is possible: how general propositions about the world can be necessarily true and known to be such independently of corroborating sense experience, for example the propositions of geometry and the knowledge that all our future experience will be governed by laws of cause and effect. The *Grundlegung* represents Kant's first consideration of analogous questions about the ground and nature of our "practical knowledge," that is, our knowledge of what we ought to do. (Kant never doubts for a moment that the ordinary person has such knowledge.) All he attempts to do in this brief book is to lay the foundations (the "groundwork") for the systematic development of his whole moral theory which followed in his *Critique of Practical Reason* (1788), and the *Metaphysic of Morals* (1797). In these latter works, and also in his *Lectures on Ethics* from which selections are included in Part Three of this collection, Kant considers in his own way many of the questions that preoccupied Aristotle and Mill, but in the *Grundlegung* he grapples with the ethical question he thought presupposed by all the others (in this differing from Aristotle but not from Mill), namely, "What is the supreme principle of morality?" He says in the Preface that this question "alone constitutes a study complete in itself and one which ought to be kept apart from every other moral investigation."

John Stuart Mill's *Utilitarianism* was first published in three separate installments in *Fraser's Magazine* in 1861, and then reprinted as a book in 1863. The word "utilitarianism" (if not the essential tenets of the doctrine that bore that name) was apparently invented by Jeremy Bentham in his *Introduction to the Principles of Morals and Legislation* in 1789 (a selection from which is included in Part Two of this volume). Mill's eminent father James Mill had been a friend and collaborator of Bentham, and John Stuart Mill while still a child was taught by his father the Benthamite moral theory. Bentham had been an abrasive, uncompromising political polemicist. His utilitarianism was widely condemned as a "Godless doctrine" and a "pig-philosophy," derived from a low and contemptuous conception of human nature, and devoid of any element of nobility. Mill's aim in publishing *Utilitarianism* was to soften and revise Bentham's theory, and rebut or evade the charges of its opponents. His style is elegant; his manner is conciliatory; his aim is to persuade friends, rather than to rout enemies. In the course of the book elements have no doubt been introduced that do not sit well together (most critics are agreed on that point), but Mill's exposition nevertheless remains the most useful statement of the utilitarian doctrine for the student, and the most widely read and studied.

1. NICOMACHEAN ETHICS

Aristotle

BOOK I.

THE END

1. Every art and every kind of inquiry, and likewise every act and purpose, seems to aim at some good: and so it has been well said that the good is that at which everything aims.

But a difference is observable among these aims or ends. What is aimed at is sometimes the exercise of a faculty, sometimes a certain result beyond that exercise. And where there is an end beyond the act, there the result is better than the exercise of the faculty.

Now since there are many kinds of actions and many arts and sciences, it follows that there are many ends also; e.g. health is the end of medicine, ships of shipbuilding, victory of the art of war, and wealth of economy.

But when several of these are subordinated to some one art or science,—as the making of bridles and other trappings to the art of horsemanship, and this in turn, along with all else that the soldier does, to the art of war, and so on,—then the end of the master-art is always more desired than the ends of the subordinate arts, since these are pursued for its sake. And this is equally true whether the end in view be the mere exercise of a faculty or something beyond that, as in the above instances.

2. If then in what we do there be some end which we wish for on its own account, choosing all the others as means to this, but not every end without exception as means to something else (for so we should go on *ad infinitum,* and desire would be left void and objectless),—this evidently will be the good or the best of all things. And surely from a practical point of view it much concerns us to know this good; for then, like archers shooting at a definite mark, we shall be more likely to attain what we want.

From *The Nicomachean Ethics of Aristotle,* translated by F. H. Peters, 10 edition, 1906. First edition of this translation, 1881. Books I (all but Chapter 6), II–V, X.

If this be so, we must try to indicate roughly what it is, and first of all to which of the arts or sciences it belongs.

It would seem to belong to the supreme art or science, that one which most of all deserves the name of master-art or master-science.

Now Politics[1] seems to answer to this description. For it prescribes which of the sciences a state needs, and which each man shall study, and up to what point; and to it we see subordinated even the highest arts, such as economy, rhetoric, and the art of war.

Since then it makes use of the other practical sciences, and since it further ordains what men are to do and from what to refrain, its end must include the ends of the others, and must be the proper good of man.

For though this good is the same for the individual and the state, yet the good of the state seems a grander and more perfect thing both to attain and to secure; and glad as one would be to do this service for a single individual, to do it for a people and for a number of states is nobler and more divine.

This then is the aim of the present inquiry, which is a sort of political inquiry.[2]

3. We must be content if we can attain to so much precision in our statement as the subject before us admits of; for the same degree of accuracy is no more to be expected in all kinds of reasoning than in all kinds of handicraft.

Now the things that are noble and just (with which Politics deals) are so various and so uncertain, that some think these are merely conventional and not natural distinctions.

There is a similar uncertainty also about what is good, because good things often do people harm: men have before now been ruined by wealth, and have lost their lives through courage.

Our subject, then, and our data being of this nature, we must be content if we can indicate the truth roughly and in outline, and if, in dealing with matters that are not amenable to immutable laws, and reasoning from premises that are but probable, we can arrive at probable conclusions.

The reader, on his part, should take each of my statements in the same spirit; for it is the mark of an educated man to require, in each kind of inquiry, just so much exactness as the subject admits of: it is equally absurd to accept probable reasoning from a mathematician, and to demand scientific proof from an orator.

But each man can form a judgment about what he knows, and is called "a good judge" of that—of any special matter when he has received a special education therein, "a good judge" (without any qualifying epithet) when he has received a universal education. And hence a young man is not qualified to be a student of Politics; for he lacks experience of the affairs of life, which form the data and the subject-matter of Politics.

Further, since he is apt to be swayed by his feelings, he will derive no benefit from a study whose aim is not speculative but practical.

But in this respect young in character counts the same as young in years; for the young man's disqualification is not a matter of time, but is due to the fact that feeling rules his life and directs all his desires. Men of this character turn the knowledge they get to no account in practice, as we see with those we call incontinent; but those who direct their desires and actions by reason will gain much profit from the knowledge of these matters.

So much then by way of preface as to the student, and the spirit in which he must accept what we say, and the object which we propose to ourselves.

4. Since—to resume—all knowledge and all purpose aims at some good, what is this which we say is the aim of Politics; or, in other words, what is the highest of all realizable goods?

As to its name, I suppose nearly all men are agreed; for the masses and the men of culture alike declare that it is happiness, and hold that to "live well" or to "do well" is the same as to be "happy."

But they differ as to what this happiness is, and the masses do not give the same account of it as the philosophers.

The former take it to be something palpable and plain, as pleasure or wealth or fame; one man holds it to be this, and another that, and often the same man is of different minds at dif-

ferent times,—after sickness it is health, and in poverty it is wealth; while when they are impressed with the consciousness of their ignorance, they admire most those who say grand things that are above their comprehension.

Some philosophers, on the other hand, have thought that, beside these several good things, there is an "absolute" good which is the cause of their goodness.

As it would hardly be worth while to review all the opinions that have been held, we will confine ourselves to those which are most popular, or which seem to have some foundation in reason.

But we must not omit to notice the distinction that is drawn between the method of proceeding from your starting-points or principles, and the method of working up to them. Plato used with fitness to raise this question, and to ask whether the right way is from or to your starting-points, as in the race-course you may run from the judges to the boundary, or *vice versa*.

Well, we must start from what is known.

But "what is known" may mean two things: "what is known to us," which is one thing, or "what is known" simply, which is another.

I think it is safe to say that *we* must start from what is known to *us*.

And on this account nothing but a good moral training can qualify a man to study what is noble and just—in a word, to study questions of Politics. For the undemonstrated fact is here the starting-point, and if this undemonstrated fact be sufficiently evident to a man, he will not require a "reason why." Now the man who has had a good moral training either has already arrived at starting-points or principles of action, or will easily accept them when pointed out. But he who neither has them nor will accept them may hear what Hesiod says[3]—

"The best is he who of himself doth know;
Good too is he who listens to the wise;
But he who neither knows himself nor heeds
The words of others, is a useless man."

5. Let us now take up the discussion at the point from which we digressed.

It seems that men not unreasonably take their notions of the good or happiness from the lives actually led, and that the masses who are the least refined suppose it to be pleasure, which is the reason why they aim at nothing higher than the life of enjoyment.

For the most conspicuous kinds of life are three: this life of enjoyment, the life of the statesman, and, thirdly, the contemplative life.

The mass of men show themselves utterly slavish in their preference for the life of brute beasts, but their views receive consideration because many of those in high places have the tastes of Sardanapalus.

Men of refinement with a practical turn prefer honour; for I suppose we may say that honour is the aim of the statesman's life.

But this seems too superficial to be the good we are seeking: for it appears to depend upon those who give rather than upon those who receive it; while we have a presentiment that the good is something that is peculiarly a man's own and can scarce be taken away from him.

Moreover, these men seem to pursue honour in order that they may be assured of their own excellence,—at least, they wish to be honoured by men of sense, and by those who know them, and on the ground of their virtue or excellence. It is plain, then, that in their view, at any rate, virtue or excellence is better than honour; and perhaps we should take this to be the end of the statesman's life, rather than honour.

But virtue or excellence also appears too incomplete to be what we want; for it seems that a man might have virtue and yet be asleep or be inactive all his life, and, moreover, might meet with the greatest disasters and misfortunes; and no one would maintain that such a man is happy, except for argument's sake. But we will not dwell on these matters now, for they are sufficiently discussed in the popular treatises.

The third kind of life is the life of contemplation: we will treat of it further on.

As for the money-making life, it is something quite contrary to nature; and wealth evidently is not the good of which we are in search, for it is merely useful as a means to something else. So we might rather take pleasure and virtue or excellence to be ends than wealth; for they are chosen on their own account. But it seems that not even they are the end, though much breath has been wasted in attempts to show that they are.

*　　*　　*

7. Leaving these matters, then, let us return once more to the question, what this good can be of which we are in search.

It seems to be different in different kinds of action and in different arts,—one thing in medicine and another in war, and so on. What then is the good in each of these cases? Surely that for the sake of which all else is done. And that in medicine is health, in war is victory, in building is a house,—a different thing in each different case, but always, in whatever we do and in whatever we choose, the end. For it is always for the sake of the end that all else is done.

If then there be one end of all that man does, this end will be the realizable good,—or these ends, if there be more than one.

By this generalization our argument is brought to the same point as before. This point we must try to explain more clearly.

We see that there are many ends. But some of these are chosen only as means, as wealth, flutes, and the whole class of instruments. And so it is plain that not all ends are final.

But the best of all things must, we conceive, be something final.

If then there be only one final end, this will be what we are seeking,—or if there be more than one, then the most final of them.

Now that which is pursued as an end in itself is more final than that which is pursued as means to something else, and that which is never chosen as means than that which is chosen both as an end in itself and as means, and that is strictly final which is always chosen as an end in itself and never as means.

Happiness seems more than anything else to answer to this description: for we always choose it for itself, and never for the sake of something else; while honour and pleasure and reason, and all virtue or excellence, we choose partly indeed for themselves (for, apart from any result, we should choose each of them), but partly also for the sake of happiness, supposing that they will help to make us happy. But no one chooses happiness for the sake of these things, or as a means to anything else at all.

We seem to be led to the same conclusion when we start from the notion of self-sufficiency.

The final good is thought to be self-sufficing [or all-sufficing]. In applying this term we do not regard a man as an individual leading a solitary life, but we also take account of parents, children, wife, and, in short, friends and fellow-citizens generally, since man is naturally a social being. Some limit must indeed be set to this; for if you go on to parents and descendants and friends of friends, you will never come to a stop. But this we will consider further on: for the present we will take self-sufficing to mean what by itself makes life desirable and in want of nothing. And happiness is believed to answer to this description.

And further, happiness is believed to be the most desirable thing in the world, and that not merely as one among other good things: if it were merely one among other good things [so that other things could be added to it], it is plain that the addition of the least of other goods must make it more desirable; for the addition becomes a surplus of good, and of two goods the greater is always more desirable.

Thus it seems that happiness is something final and self-sufficing, and is the end of all that man does.

But perhaps the reader thinks that though no one will dispute the statement that happiness is the best thing in the world, yet a still more precise definition of it is needed.

This will best be gained, I think, by asking, What is the function of man? For as the goodness and the excellence of a piper or a sculptor, or the practiser of any art, and generally of those who have any function or business to do, lies in that function, so man's good would seem to lie in his function, if he has one.

But can we suppose that, while a carpenter and a cobbler has a function and a business of his own, man has no business and no function assigned him by nature? Nay, surely as his several members, eye and hand and foot, plainly have each his own function, so we must suppose that man also has some function over and above all these.

What then is it?

Life evidently he has in common even with the plants, but we want that which is peculiar to him. We must exclude, therefore, the life of mere nutrition and growth.

Next to this comes the life of sense; but this too he plainly shares with horses and cattle and all kinds of animals.

There remains then the life whereby he acts—the life of his rational nature, with its two sides or divisions, one rational as obeying reason, the other rational as having and exercising reason.

But as this expression is ambiguous, we must be understood to mean thereby the life that consists in the exercise of the faculties; for this seems to be more properly entitled to the name.

The function of man, then, is exercise of his vital faculties [or soul] on one side in obedience to reason, and on the other side with reason.

But what is called the function of a man of any profession and the function of a man who is good in that profession are generically the same, e.g. of a harper and of a good harper; and this holds in all cases without exception, only that in the case of the latter his superior excellence at his work is added; for we say a harper's function is to harp, and a good harper's to harp well.

(Man's function then being, as we say, a kind of life—that is to say, exercise of his faculties and action of various kinds with reason—the good man's function is to do this well and beautifully [or nobly]. But the function of anything is done well when it is done in accordance with the proper excellence of that thing.)

If this be so the result is that the good of man is exercise of his faculties in accordance with excellence or virtue, or, if there be more than one, in accordance with the best and most complete virtue.

But there must also be a full term of years for this exercise; for one swallow or one fine day does not make a spring, nor does one day or any small space of time make a blessed or happy man.

This, then, may be taken as a rough outline of the good; for this, I think, is the proper method —first to sketch the outline, and then to fill in the details. But it would seem that, the outline once fairly drawn, any one can carry on the work and fit in the several items which time reveals to us or helps us to find. And this indeed is the way in which the arts and sciences have grown; for it requires no extraordinary genius to fill up the gaps.

We must bear in mind, however, what was said above, and not demand the same degree of accuracy in all branches of study, but in each case so much as the subject-matter admits of and as is proper to that kind of inquiry. The carpenter and the geometer both look for the right angle, but in different ways: the former only wants such an approximation to it as his work requires, but the latter wants to know what constitutes a right angle, or what is its special quality; his aim is to find out the truth. And so in other cases we must follow the same course, lest we spend more time on what is immaterial than on the real business in hand.

Nor must we in all cases alike demand the reason why; sometimes it is enough if the undemonstrated fact be fairly pointed out, as in the case of the starting-points or principles of a science. Undemonstrated facts always form the first step or starting-point of a science; and these starting-points or principles are arrived at some in one way, some in another—some by induction, others by perception, others again by some kind of training. But in each case we must try to apprehend them in the proper way, and do our best to define them clearly; for they have great influence upon the subsequent course of an inquiry. A good start is more than half the race, I think, and our starting-point or principle, once found, clears up a number of our difficulties.

8. We must not be satisfied, then, with examining this starting-point or principle of ours as a conclusion from our data, but must also view it in its relation to current opinions on the subject; for all experience harmonizes with a true principle, but a false one is soon found to be incompatible with the facts.

Now, good things have been divided into three classes, external goods on the one hand, and on the other goods of the soul and goods of the body; and the goods of the soul are commonly said to be goods in the fullest sense, and more good than any other.

But "actions and exercises of the vital faculties or soul" may be said to be "of the soul." So our account is confirmed by this opinion, which is both of long standing and approved by all who busy themselves with philosophy.

But, indeed, we secure the support of this opinion by the mere statement that certain actions and exercises are the end; for this implies that it is to be ranked among the goods of the soul, and not among external goods.

Our account, again, is in harmony with the common saying that the happy man lives well and does well; for we may say that happiness, according to us, is a living well and doing well.

And, indeed, all the characteristics that men expect to find in happiness seem to belong to happiness as we define it.

Some hold it to be virtue or excellence, some prudence, others a kind of wisdom; others, again, hold it to be all or some of these, with the addition of pleasure, either as an ingredient or as a necessary accompaniment; and some even include external prosperity in their account of it.

Now, some of these views have the support of many voices and of old authority; others have few voices, but those of weight; but it is probable that neither the one side nor the other is entirely wrong, but that in some one point at least, if not in most, they are both right.

First, then, the view that happiness is excellence or a kind of excellence harmonizes with our account; for "exercise of faculties in accordance with excellence" belongs to excellence.

But I think we may say that it makes no small difference whether the good be conceived as the mere possession of something, or as its use—as a mere habit or trained faculty, or as the exercise of that faculty. For the habit or faculty may be present, and yet issue in no good result, as when a man is asleep, or in any other way hindered from his function; but with its exercise this is not possible, for it must show itself in acts and in good acts. And as at the Olympic games it is not the fairest and strongest who receive the crown, but those who contend (for among these are the victors), so in life, too, the winners are those who not only have all the excellences, but manifest these in deed.

And, further, the life of these men is in itself pleasant. For pleasure is an affection of the soul, and each man takes pleasure in that which he is said to love,—he who loves horses in horses, he who loves sight-seeing in sight-seeing, and in the same way he who loves justice in acts of justice, and generally the lover of excellence or virtue in virtuous acts or the manifestation of excellence.

And while with most men there is a perpetual conflict between the several things in which they find pleasure, since these are not naturally pleasant, those who love what is noble take pleasure in that which is naturally pleasant. For the manifestations of excellence are naturally pleasant, so that they are both pleasant to them and pleasant in themselves.

Their life, then, does not need pleasure to be added to it as an appendage, but contains pleasure in itself.

Indeed, in addition to what we have said, a man is not good at all unless he takes pleasure in noble deeds. No one would call a man just who did not take pleasure in doing justice, nor generous who took no pleasure in acts of generosity, and so on.

If this be so, the manifestations of excellence will be pleasant in themselves. But they are also both good and noble, and that in the highest degree—at least, if the good man's judgment about them is right, for this is his judgment.

Happiness, then, is at once the best and noblest and pleasantest thing in the world, and these are not separated, as the Delian inscription would have them to be:—

"What is most just is noblest, health is best,
   Pleasantest is to get your heart's desire."

For all these characteristics are united in the best exercises of our faculties; and these, or some one of them that is better than all the others, we identify with happiness.

But nevertheless happiness plainly requires external goods too, as we said; for it is impossible, or at least not easy, to act nobly without some furniture of fortune. There are many things that can only be done through instruments, so to speak, such as friends and wealth and political influence: and there are some things whose absence takes the bloom off our happiness, as good birth, the blessing of children, personal beauty; for a man is not very likely to be happy if he is very ugly in person, or of low birth, or alone in the world, or childless, and perhaps still less if he has worthless children or friends, or has lost good ones that he had.

As we said, then, happiness seems to stand in need of this kind of prosperity; and so some identify it with good fortune, just as others identify it with excellence.

9. This has led people to ask whether happiness is attained by learning, or the formation of habits, or any other kind of training, or comes by some divine dispensation or even by chance.

Well, if the Gods do give gifts to men, happiness is likely to be among the number, more likely, indeed, than anything else, in proportion as it is better than all other human things.

This belongs more properly to another branch of inquiry; but we may say that even if it is not heaven-sent, but comes as a consequence of virtue or some kind of learning or training, still it seems to be one of the most divine things in the world; for the prize and aim of virtue would appear to be better than anything else and something divine and blessed.

Again, if it is thus acquired it will be widely accessible; for it will then be in the power of all except those who have lost the capacity for excellence to acquire it by study and diligence.

And if it be better that men should attain happiness in this way rather than by chance, it is reasonable to suppose that it is so, since in the sphere of nature all things are arranged in the best possible way, and likewise in the sphere of art, and of each mode of causation, and most of all in the sphere of the noblest mode of causation. And indeed it would be too absurd to leave what is noblest and fairest to the dispensation of chance.

But our definition itself clears up the difficulty; for happiness was defined as a certain kind of exercise of the vital faculties in accordance with excellence or virtue. And of the remaining goods [other than happiness itself], some must be present as necessary conditions, while others are aids and useful instruments to happiness. And this agrees with what we said at starting. We then laid down that the end of the art political is the best of all ends; but the chief business of that art is to make the citizens of a certain character—that is, good and apt to do what is noble. It is not without reason, then, that we do not call an ox, or a horse, or any brute happy; for none of them is able to share in this kind of activity.

For the same reason also a child is not happy; he is as yet, because of his age, unable to do such things. If we ever call a child happy, it is because we hope he will do them. For, as we said, happiness requires not only perfect excellence or virtue, but also a full term of years for its exercise. For our circumstances are liable to many changes and to all sorts of chances, and it is possible that he who is now most prosperous will in his old age meet with great disasters, as is told of Priam in the tales of Troy; and a man who is thus used by fortune and comes to a miserable end cannot be called happy.

10. Are we, then, to call no man happy as long as he lives, but to wait for the end, as Solon said?

And, supposing we have to allow this, do we mean that he actually is happy after he is dead? Surely that is absurd, especially for us who say that happiness is a kind of activity or life.

But if we do not call the dead man happy, and if Solon meant not this, but that only then could we safely apply the term to a man, as being now beyond the reach of evil and calamity, then here too we find some ground for objection. For it is thought that both good and evil may in some sort befall a dead man (just as they may befall a living man, although he is unconscious of them), *e.g.* honours rendered to him, or the reverse of these, and again the prosperity or the misfortune of his children and all his descendants.

But this, too, has its difficulties; for after a man has lived happily to a good old age, and ended as he lived, it is possible that many changes may befall him in the persons of his descendants, and that some of them may turn out good and meet with the good fortune they deserve, and others the reverse.. It is evident too that the degree in which the descendants are related to their ancestors may vary to any extent. And it would be a strange thing if the dead man were to change with these changes and become happy and miserable by turns. But it would also be strange to suppose that the dead are not affected at all, even for a limited time, by the fortunes of their posterity.

But let us return to our former question; for its solution will, perhaps, clear up this other difficulty.

The saying of Solon may mean that we ought to look for the end and then call a man happy, not because he now is, but because he once was happy.

But surely it is strange that when he is happy we should refuse to say what is true of him, because we do not like to apply the term to living men in view of the changes to which they are liable, and because we hold happiness to be something that endures and is little liable to

change, while the fortunes of one and the same man often undergo many revolutions: for, it is argued, it is plain that, if we follow the changes of fortune, we shall call the same man happy and miserable many times over, making the happy man "a sort of chameleon and one who rests on no sound foundation."

We reply that it cannot be right thus to follow fortune. For it is not in this that our weal or woe lies; but, as we said, though good fortune is needed to complete man's life, yet it is the excellent employment of his powers that constitutes his happiness, as the reverse of this constitutes his misery.

But the discussion of this difficulty leads to a further confirmation of our account. For nothing human is so constant as the excellent exercise of our faculties. The sciences themselves seem to be less abiding. And the highest of these exercises are the most abiding, because the happy are occupied with them most of all and most continuously (for this seems to be the reason why we do not forget how to do them).

The happy man, then, as we define him, will have this required property of permanence, and all through life will preserve his character; for he will be occupied continually, or with the least possible interruption, in excellent deeds and excellent speculations; and, whatever his fortune be, he will take it in the noblest fashion, and bear himself always and in all things suitably, since he is truly good and "foursquare without a flaw."

But the dispensations of fortune are many, some great, some small. The small ones, whether good or evil, plainly are of no weight in the scale; but the great ones, when numerous, will make life happier if they be good; for they help to give a grace to life themselves, and their use is noble and good; but, if they be evil, will enfeeble and spoil happiness; for they bring pain, and often impede the exercise of our faculties.

But nevertheless true worth shines out even here, in the calm endurance of many great misfortunes, not through insensibility, but through nobility and greatness of soul. And if it is what a man does that determines the character of his life, as we said, then no happy man will become miserable; for he will never do what is hateful and base. For we hold that the man who is truly good and wise will bear with dignity whatever fortune sends, and will always make the best of his circumstances, as a good general will turn the forces at his command to the best account, and a good shoemaker will make the best shoe that can be made out of a given piece of leather, and so on with all other crafts.

If this be so, the happy man will never become miserable, though he will not be truly happy if he meets with the fate of Priam.

But yet he is not unstable and lightly changed: he will not be moved from his happiness easily, nor by any ordinary misfortunes, but only by many heavy ones; and after such, he will not recover his happiness again in a short time, but if at all, only in a considerable period, which has a certain completeness, and in which he attains to great and noble things.

We shall meet all objections, then, if we say that a happy man is "one who exercises his faculties in accordance with perfect excellence, being duly furnished with external goods, not for any chance time, but for a full term of years:" to which perhaps we should add, "and who shall continue to live so, and shall die as he lived," since the future is veiled to us, but happiness we take to be the end and in all ways perfectly final or complete.

If this be so, we may say that those living men are blessed or perfectly happy who both have and shall continue to have these characteristics, but happy as men only.

11. Passing now from this question to that of the fortunes of descendants and of friends generally, the doctrine that they do not affect the departed at all seems too cold and too much opposed to popular opinion. But as the things that happen to them are many and differ in all sorts of ways, and some come home to them more and some less, so that to discuss them all separately would be a long, indeed an endless task, it will perhaps be enough to speak of them in general terms and in outline merely.

Now, as of the misfortunes that happen to a man's self, some have a certain weight and influence on his life, while others are of less moment, so is it also with what happens to any of his friends. And, again, it always makes much more difference whether those who are affected by an occurrence are alive or dead than it does

whether a terrible crime in a tragedy be enacted on the stage or merely supposed to have already taken place. We must therefore take these differences into account, and still more, perhaps, the fact that it is a doubtful question whether the dead are at all accessible to good and ill. For it appears that even if anything that happens, whether good or evil, does come home to them, yet it is something unsubstantial and slight to them if not in itself; or if not that, yet at any rate its influence is not of that magnitude or nature that it can make happy those who are not, or take away their happiness from those that are.

It seems then—to conclude—that the prosperity, and likewise the adversity, of friends does affect the dead, but not in such a way or to such an extent as to make the happy unhappy, or to do anything of the kind.

12. These points being settled, we may now inquire whether happiness is to be ranked among the goods that we praise, or rather among those that we revere; for it is plainly not a mere potentiality, but an actual good.

What we praise seems always to be praised as being of a certain quality and having a certain relation to something. For instance, we praise the just and the courageous man, and generally the good man, and excellence or virtue, because of what they do or produce; and we praise also the strong or the swift-footed man, and so on, because he has a certain gift or faculty in relation to some good and admirable thing.

This is evident if we consider the praises bestowed on the Gods. The Gods are thereby made ridiculous by being made relative to man; and this happens because, as we said, a thing can only be praised in relation to something else.

If, then, praise be proper to such things as we mentioned, it is evident that to the best things is due, not praise, but something greater and better, as our usage shows; for the Gods we call blessed and happy, and "blessed" is the term we apply to the most god-like men.

And so with good things: no one praises happiness as he praises justice, but calls it blessed, as something better and more divine.

On these grounds Eudoxus is thought to have based a strong argument for the claims of pleasure to the first prize: for he maintained that the fact that it is not praised, though it is a good thing, shows that it is higher than the goods we praise, as God and the good are higher; for these are the standards by reference to which we judge all other things,—giving praise to excellence or virtue, since it makes us apt to do what is noble, and passing encomiums on the results of virtue, whether these be bodily or psychical.

But to refine on these points belongs more properly to those who have made a study of the subject of encomiums; for us it is plain from what has been said that happiness is one of the goods which we revere and count as final.

And this further seems to follow from the fact that it is a starting-point or principle: for everything we do is always done for its sake; but the principle and cause of all good we hold to be something divine and worthy of reverence.

13. Since happiness is an exercise of the vital faculties in accordance with perfect virtue or excellence, we will now inquire about virtue or excellence; for this will probably help us in our inquiry about happiness.

And indeed the true statesman seems to be especially concerned with virtue, for he wishes to make the citizens good and obedient to the laws. Of this we have an example in the Cretan and the Lacedaemonian lawgivers, and any others who have resembled them. But if the inquiry belongs to Politics or the science of the state, it is plain that it will be in accordance with our original purpose to pursue it.

The virtue or excellence that we are to consider is, of course, the excellence of man; for it is the good of man and the happiness of man that we started to seek. And by the excellence of man I mean excellence not of body, but of soul; for happiness we take to be an activity of the soul.

If this be so, then it is evident that the statesman must have some knowledge of the soul, just as the man who is to heal the eye or the whole body must have some knowledge of them, and that the more in proportion as the science of the state is higher and better than medicine. But all educated physicians take much pains to know about the body.

As statesmen [or students of Politics], then we must inquire into the nature of the soul, but in so doing we must keep our special purpose in view and go only so far as that requires; for to go into minuter detail would be too laborious for the present undertaking.

Now, there are certain doctrines about the soul which are stated elsewhere with sufficient precision, and these we will adopt.

Two parts of the soul are distinguished, an irrational and a rational part.

Whether these are separated as are the parts of the body or any divisible thing, or whether they are only distinguishable in thought but in fact inseparable, like concave and convex in the circumference of a circle, makes no difference for our present purpose.

Of the irrational part, again, one division seems to be common to all things that live, and to be possessed by plants—I mean that which causes nutrition and growth; for we must assume that all things that take nourishment have a faculty of this kind, even when they are embryos, and have the same faculty when they are full grown; at least, this is more reasonable than to suppose that they then have a different one.

The excellence of this faculty, then, is plainly one that man shares with other beings, and not specifically human.

And this is confirmed by the fact that in sleep this part of the soul, or this faculty, is thought to be most active, while the good and the bad man are undistinguishable when they are asleep (whence the saying that for half their lives there is no difference between the happy and the miserable; which indeed is what we should expect; for sleep is the cessation of the soul from those functions in respect of which it is called good or bad), except that they are to some slight extent roused by what goes on in their bodies, with the result that the dreams of the good man are better than those of ordinary people.

However, we need not pursue this further, and may dismiss the nutritive principle, since it has no place in the excellence of man.

But there seems to be another vital principle that is irrational, and yet in some way partakes of reason. In the case of the continent and of the incontinent man alike we praise the reason or the rational part, for it exhorts them rightly and urges them to do what is best; but there is plainly present in them another principle besides the rational one, which fights and struggles against the reason. For just as a paralyzed limb, when you will to move it to the right, moves on the contrary to the left, so is it with the soul; the incontinent man's impulses run counter to his reason. Only whereas we see the refractory member in the case of the body, we do not see it in the case of the soul. But we must nevertheless, I think, hold that in the soul too there is something beside the reason, which opposes and runs counter to it (though in what sense it is distinct from the reason does not matter here).

It seems, however, to partake of reason also, as we said: at least, in the continent man it submits to the reason; while in the temperate and courageous man we may say it is still more obedient; for in him it is altogether in harmony with the reason.

The irrational part, then, it appears, is twofold. There is the vegetative faculty, which has no share of reason; and the faculty of appetite or of desire in general, which in a manner partakes of reason or is rational as listening to reason and submitting to its sway,—rational in the sense in which we speak of rational obedience to father or friends, not in the sense in which we speak of rational apprehension of mathematical truths. But all advice and all rebuke and exhortation testify that the irrational part is in some way amenable to reason.

If then we like to say that this part, too, has a share of reason, the rational part also will have two divisions: one rational in the strict sense as possessing reason in itself, the other rational as listening to reason as a man listens to his father.

Now, on this division of the faculties is based the division of excellence; for we speak of intellectual excellences and of moral excellences; wisdom and understanding and prudence we call intellectual, liberality and temperance we call moral virtues or excellences. When we are speaking of a man's moral character we do not say that he is wise or intelligent, but that he is gentle or temperate. But we praise the wise man, too, for his habit of mind or trained faculty; and a habit or trained faculty that is praiseworthy is what we call an excellence or virtue.

BOOK II.
MORAL VIRTUE.

1. Excellence, then, being of these two kinds, intellectual and moral, intellectual excellence owes its birth and growth mainly to instruction,

and so requires time and experience, while moral excellence is the result of habit or custom (ἔθος), and has accordingly in our language received a name formed by a slight change from ἔθος.[4]

From this it is plain that none of the moral excellences or virtues is implanted in us by nature; for that which is by nature cannot be altered by training. For instance, a stone naturally tends to fall downwards, and you could not train it to rise upwards, though you tried to do so by throwing it up ten thousand times, nor could you train fire to move downwards, nor accustom anything which naturally behaves in one way to behave in any other way.

The virtues,[5] then, come neither by nature nor against nature, but nature gives the capacity for acquiring them, and this is developed by training.

Again, where we do things by nature we get the power first, and put this power forth in act afterwards: as we plainly see in the case of the senses; for it is not by constantly seeing and hearing that we acquire those faculties, but, on the contrary, we had the power first and then used it, instead of acquiring the power by the use. But the virtues we acquire by doing the acts, as is the case with the arts too. We learn an art by doing that which we wish to do when we have learned it; we become builders by building, and harpers by harping. And so by doing just acts we become just, and by doing acts of temperance and courage we become temperate and courageous.

This is attested, too, by what occurs in states; for the legislators make their citizens good by training; i.e. this is the wish of all legislators, and those who do not succeed in this miss their aim, and it is this that distinguishes a good from a bad constitution.

Again, both the moral virtues and the corresponding vices result from and are formed by the same acts; and this is the case with the arts also. It is by harping that good harpers and bad harpers alike are produced: and so with builders and the rest; by building well they will become good builders, and bad builders by building badly. Indeed, if it were not so, they would not want anybody to teach them, but would all be born either good or bad at their trades. And it is just the same with the virtues also. It is by our conduct in our intercourse with other men that we become just or unjust, and by acting in circumstances of danger, and training ourselves to feel fear or confidence, that we become courageous or cowardly. So, too, with our animal appetites and the passion of anger; for by behaving in this way or in that on the occasions with which these passions are concerned, some become temperate and gentle, and others profligate and ill-tempered. In a word, acts of any kind produce habits or characters of the same kind.

Hence we ought to make sure that our acts be of a certain kind; for the resulting character varies as they vary. It makes no small difference, therefore, whether a man be trained from his youth up in this way or in that, but a great difference, or rather all the difference.

2. But our present inquiry has not, like the rest, a merely speculative aim; we are not inquiring merely in order to know what excellence or virtue is, but in order to become good; for otherwise it would profit us nothing. We must ask therefore about these acts, and see of what kind they are to be; for, as we said, it is they that determine our habits or character.

First of all, then, that they must be in accordance with right reason is a common characteristic of them, which we shall here take for granted, reserving for future discussion[6] the question what this right reason is, and how it is related to the other excellences.

But let it be understood, before we go on, that all reasoning on matters of practice must be in outline merely, and not scientifically exact: for, as we said at starting, the kind of reasoning to be demanded varies with the subject in hand; and in practical matters and questions of expediency there are no invariable laws, any more than in questions of health.

And if our general conclusions are thus inexact, still more inexact is all reasoning about particular cases; for these fall under no system of scientifically established rules or traditional maxims, but the agent must always consider for himself what the special occasion requires, just as in medicine or navigation.

But though this is the case we must try to render what help we can.

First of all, then, we must observe that, in matters of this sort, to fall short and to exceed are alike fatal. This is plain (to illustrate what we cannot see by what we can see) in the case of strength and health. Too much and too little exercise alike destroy strength, and to take too much meat and drink, or to take too little, is equally ruinous to health, but the fitting amount produces and increases and preserves them. Just so, then, is it with temperance also, and courage, and the other virtues. The man who shuns and fears everything and never makes a stand, becomes a coward; while the man who fears nothing at all, but will face anything, becomes foolhardy. So, too, the man who takes his fill of any kind of pleasure, and abstains from none, is a profligate, but the man who shuns all (like him whom we call a "boor") is devoid of sensibility. Thus temperance and courage are destroyed both by excess and defect, but preserved by moderation.

But habits or types of character are not only produced and preserved and destroyed by the same occasions and the same means, but they will also manifest themselves in the same circumstances. This is the case with palpable things like strength. Strength is produced by taking plenty of nourishment and doing plenty of hard work, and the strong man, in turn, has the greatest capacity for these. And the case is the same with the virtues: by abstaining from pleasure we become temperate, and when we have become temperate we are best able to abstain. And so with courage: by habituating ourselves to despise danger, and to face it, we become courageous; and when we have become courageous, we are best able to face danger.

3. The pleasure or pain that accompanies the acts must be taken as a test of the formed habit or character.

He who abstains from the pleasures of the body and rejoices in the abstinence is temperate, while he who is vexed at having to abstain is profligate; and again, he who faces danger with pleasure, or, at any rate, without pain, is courageous, but he to whom this is painful is a coward.

For moral virtue or excellence is closely concerned with pleasure and pain. It is pleasure that moves us to do what is base, and pain that moves us to refrain from what is noble. And therefore, as Plato says, man needs to be so trained from his youth up as to find pleasure and pain in the right objects. This is what sound education means.

Another reason why virtue has to do with pleasure and pain, is that it has to do with actions and passions or affections; but every affection and every act is accompanied by pleasure or pain.

The fact is further attested by the employment of pleasure and pain in correction; they have a kind of curative property, and a cure is effected by administering the opposite of the disease.

Again, as we said before, every type of character [or habit or formed faculty] is essentially relative to, and concerned with, those things that form it for good or for ill; but it is through pleasure and pain that bad characters are formed —that is to say, through pursuing and avoiding the wrong pleasures and pains, or pursuing and avoiding them at the wrong time, or in the wrong manner, or in any other of the various ways of going wrong that may be distinguished.

And hence some people go so far as to define the virtues as a kind of impassive or neutral state of mind. But they err in stating this absolutely, instead of qualifying it by the addition of the right and wrong manner, time, etc.

We may lay down, therefore, that this kind of excellence [*i.e.* moral excellence] makes us do what is best in matters of pleasure and pain, while vice or badness has the contrary effect. But the following considerations will throw additional light on the point.

There are three kinds of things that move us to choose, and three that move us to avoid them: on the one hand, the beautiful or noble, the advantageous, the pleasant; on the other hand, the ugly or base, the hurtful, the painful. Now, the good man is apt to go right, and the bad man to go wrong, about them all, but especially about pleasure: for pleasure is not only common to man with animals, but also accompanies all pursuit or choice; since the noble, and the advantageous also, are pleasant in idea.

Again, the feeling of pleasure has been fostered in us all from our infancy by our training, and has thus become so engrained in our life that it can scarce be washed out.[7] And, indeed, we all more or less make pleasure our test in judging of actions. For this reason too, then, our whole inquiry must be concerned with these matters; since to be pleased and pained in the right or the wrong way has great influence on our actions.

Again, to fight with pleasure is harder than to fight with wrath (which Heraclitus says is hard), and virtue, like art, is always more concerned with what is harder; for the harder the task the better is success. For this reason also, then, both [moral] virtue or excellence and the science of the state must always be concerned with pleasures and pains; for he that behaves rightly with regard to them will be good, and he that behaves badly will be bad.

We will take it as established, then, that [moral] excellence or virtue has to do with pleasures and pains; and that the acts which produce it develop it, and also, when differently done, destroy it; and that it manifests itself in the same acts which produced it.

4. But here we may be asked what we mean by saying that men can become just and temperate only by doing what is just and temperate: surely, it may be said, if their acts are just and temperate, they themselves are already just and temperate, as they are grammarians and musicians if they do what is grammatical and musical.

We may answer, I think, firstly, that this is not quite the case even with the arts. A man may do something grammatical [or write something correctly] by chance, or at the prompting of another person: he will not be grammatical till he not only does something grammatical, but also does it grammatically [or like a grammatical person], *i.e.* in virtue of his own knowledge of grammar.

But, secondly, the virtues are not in this point analogous to the arts. The products of art have their excellence in themselves, and so it is enough if when produced they are of a certain quality; but in the case of the virtues, a man is not said to act justly or temperately [or like a just or temperate man] if what he does merely be of a certain sort—he must also be in a certain state of mind when he does it; *i.e.,* first of all he must know what he is doing; secondly, he must choose it, and choose it for itself; and, thirdly, his act must be the expression of a formed and stable character. Now, of these conditions, only one, the knowledge, is necessary for the possession of any art; but for the possession of the virtues knowledge is of little or no avail, while the other conditions that result from repeatedly doing what is just and temperate are not a little important, but all-important.

The thing that is done, therefore, is called just or temperate when it is such as the just or temperate man would do; but the man who does it is not just or temperate, unless he also does it in the spirit of the just or the temperate man.

It is right, then, to say that by doing what is just a man becomes just, and temperate by doing what is temperate, while without doing thus he has no chance of ever becoming good.

But most men, instead of doing thus, fly to theories, and fancy that they are philosophizing and that this will make them good, like a sick man who listens attentively to what the doctor says and then disobeys all his orders. This sort of philosophizing will no more produce a healthy habit of mind than this sort of treatment will produce a healthy habit of body.

5. We have next to inquire what excellence or virtue is.

A quality of the soul is either (1) a passion or emotion, or (2) a power or faculty, or (3) a habit or trained faculty; and so virtue must be one of these three. By (1) a passion or emotion we mean appetite, anger, fear, confidence, envy, joy, love, hate, longing, emulation, pity, or generally that which is accompanied by pleasure or pain; (2) a power or faculty is that in respect of which we are said to be capable of being affected in any of these ways, as, for instance, that in respect of which we are able to be angered or pained or to pity; and (3) a habit or trained faculty is that in respect of which we are well or ill regulated or disposed in the matter of our afflictions; as, for instance, in the matter of being angered, we are ill regulated if we are too violent or too slack, but if we are moderate in our anger we are well regulated. And so with the rest.

Now, the virtues are not emotions, nor are the vices—(1) because we are not called good or bad in respect of our emotions, but are called so in respect of our virtues or vices; (2) because we are neither praised nor blamed in respect of our emotions (a man is not praised for being afraid or angry, nor blamed for being angry simply, but for being angry in a particular way), but we are praised or blamed in respect of our virtues or vices; (3) because we may be angered or frightened without deliberate choice, but the virtues are a kind of deliberate choice, or at least are impossible without it; and (4) because in respect of our emotions we are said to be moved, but in respect of our virtues and vices we are not said to be moved, but to be regulated or disposed in this way or in that.

For these same reasons also they are not powers or faculties; for we are not called either good or bad for being merely capable of emotion, nor are we either praised or blamed for this. And further, while nature gives us our powers or faculties, she does not make us either good or bad. (This point, however, we have already treated.)

If, then, the virtues be neither emotions nor faculties, it only remains for them to be habits or trained faculties.

6. We have thus found the genus to which virtue belongs; but we want to know, not only that it is a trained faculty, but also what species of trained faculty it is.

We may safely assert that the virtue or excellence of a thing causes that thing both to be itself in good condition and to perform its function well. The excellence of the eye, for instance, makes both the eye and its work good; for it is by the excellence of the eye that we see well. So the proper excellence of the horse makes a horse what he should be, and makes him good at running, and carrying his rider, and standing a charge.

If, then, this holds good in all cases, the proper excellence or virtue of man will be the habit or trained faculty that makes a man good and makes him perform his function well.

How this is to be done we have already said, but we may exhibit the same conclusion in another way, by inquiring what the nature of this virtue is.

Now, if we have any quantity, whether continuous or discrete, it is possible to take either a larger [or too large], or a smaller [or too small], or an equal [or fair] amount, and that either absolutely or relatively to our own needs.

By an equal or fair amount I understand a mean amount, or one that lies between excess and deficiency.

By the absolute mean, or mean relatively to the thing itself, I understand that which is equidistant from both extremes, and this is one and the same for all.

By the mean relatively to us I understand that which is neither too much nor too little for us; and this is not one and the same for all.

For instance, if ten be larger [or too large] and two be smaller [or too small], if we take six we take the mean relatively to the thing itself [or the arithmetical mean]; for it exceeds one extreme by the same amount by which it is exceeded by the other extreme: and this is the mean in arithmetical proportion.

But the mean relatively to us cannot be found in this way. If ten pounds of food is too much for a given man to eat, and two pounds too little, it does not follow that the trainer will order him six pounds: for that also may perhaps be too much for the man in question, or too little; too little for Milo, too much for the beginner. The same holds true in running and wrestling.

And so we may say generally that a master in any art avoids what is too much and what is too little, and seeks for the mean and chooses it—not the absolute but the relative mean.

If, then, every art or science perfects its work in this way, looking to the mean and bringing its work up to this standard (so that people are wont to say of a good work that nothing could be taken from it or added to it, implying that excellence is destroyed by excess or deficiency, but secured by observing the mean; and good artists, as we say, do in fact keep their eyes fixed on this in all that they do), and if virtue, like nature, is more exact and better than any art, it follows that virtue also must aim at the mean—virtue of course meaning moral virtue or excellence; for it has to do with passions and actions, and it is these that admit of excess and deficiency and the mean. For instance, it is possible to feel fear, confidence, desire, anger, pity, and generally to be affected pleasantly and painfully, either too much or too little, in either case wrongly; but to be thus affected at the right times, and on the right occasions, and towards the right persons, and with the right object, and in the right fashion, is the mean course and the best course, and these are characteristics of virtue. And in the same way our outward acts also admit of excess and deficiency, and the mean or due amount.

Virtue, then, has to deal with feelings or passions and with outward acts, in which excess is wrong and deficiency also is blamed, but the mean amount is praised and is right—both of which are characteristics of virtue.

Virtue, then, is a kind of moderation ($\mu\epsilon\sigma\acute{o}\tau\eta\varsigma$ $\tau\iota\varsigma$), inasmuch as it aims at the mean or moderate amount ($\tau\grave{o}$ $\mu\acute{\epsilon}\sigma\sigma\nu$).

Again, there are many ways of going wrong (for evil is infinite in nature, to use a Pythagorean figure, while good is finite), but only one way of going right; so that the one is easy and the other hard—easy to miss the mark and hard to hit. On this account also, then, excess and deficiency are characteristic of vice, hitting the mean is characteristic of virtue:

"Goodness is simple, ill takes any shape."

Virtue, then, is a habit or trained faculty of choice, the characteristic of which lies in moderation or observance of the mean relatively to the persons concerned, as determined by reason, *i.e.* by the reason by which the prudent man would determine it. And it is a moderation, firstly, inasmuch as it comes in the middle or mean between two vices, one on the side of excess, the other on the side of defect; and, secondly, inasmuch as, while these vices fall short of or exceed the due measure in feeling and in action, it finds and chooses the mean, middling, or moderate amount.

Regarded in its essence, therefore, or according to the definition of its nature, virtue is a moderation or middle state, but viewed in its relation to what is best and right it is the extreme of perfection.

But it is not all actions nor all passions that admit of moderation; there are some whose very names imply badness, as malevolence, shamelessness, envy, and, among acts, adultery, theft, murder. These and all other like things are blamed as being bad in themselves, and not merely in their excess or deficiency. It is impossible therefore to go right in them; they are always wrong: rightness and wrongness in such things (*e.g.* in adultery) does not depend upon whether it is the right person and occasion and manner, but the mere doing of any one of them is wrong.

It would be equally absurd to look for moderation or excess or deficiency in unjust cowardly or profligate conduct; for then there would be moderation in excess or deficiency, and excess in excess, and deficiency in deficiency.

The fact is that just as there can be no excess or deficiency in temperance or courage because the mean or moderate amount is, in a sense, an extreme, so in these kinds of conduct also there can be no moderation or excess or deficiency, but the acts are wrong however they be done. For, to put it generally, there cannot be moderation in excess or deficiency, nor excess or deficiency in moderation.

7. But it is not enough to make these general statements [about virtue and vice]: we must go on and apply them to particulars [*i.e.* to the several virtues and vices]. For in reasoning about matters of conduct general statements are too vague, and do not convey so much truth as particular propositions. It is with particulars that conduct is concerned: our statements, therefore, when applied to these particulars, should be found to hold good.

These particulars then [*i.e.* the several virtues and vices and the several acts and affections with which they deal], we will take from the following table.

Moderation in the feelings of fear and confidence is courage: of those that exceed, he that exceeds in fearlessness has no name (as often happens), but he that exceeds in confidence is foolhardy, while he that exceeds in fear, but is deficient in confidence, is cowardly.

Moderation in respect of certain pleasures and also (though to a less extent) certain pains is temperance, while excess is profligacy. But defectiveness in the matter of these pleasures is hardly ever found, and so this sort of people also have as yet received no name: let us put them down as "void of sensibility."

In the matter of giving and taking money, moderation is liberality, excess and deficiency are prodigality and illiberality. But both vices exceed and fall short in giving and taking in contrary ways: the prodigal exceeds in spending, but falls short in taking; while the illiberal man exceeds in taking, but falls short in spending. (For the present we are but giving an outline or summary, and aim at nothing more; we shall

afterwards treat these points in greater detail.)

But, besides these, there are other dispositions in the matter of money: there is a moderation which is called magnificence (for the magnificent is not the same as the liberal man: the former deals with large sums, the latter with small), and an excess which is called bad taste or vulgarity, and a deficiency which is called meanness; and these vices differ from those which are opposed to liberality: how they differ will be explained later.

With respect to honour and disgrace, there is a moderation which is high-mindedness, an excess which may be called vanity, and a deficiency which is little-mindedness.

But just as we said that liberality is related to magnificence, differing only in that it deals with small sums, so here there is a virtue related to high-mindedness, and differing only in that it is concerned with small instead of great honours. A man may have a due desire for honour, and also more or less than a due desire: he that carries this desire to excess is called ambitious, he that has not enough of it is called unambitious, but he that has the due amount has no name. There are also no abstract names for the characters, except "ambition," corresponding to ambitious. And on this account those who occupy the extremes lay claim to the middle place. And in common parlance, too, the moderate man is sometimes called ambitious and sometimes unambitious, and sometimes the ambitious man is praised and sometimes the unambitious. Why this is we will explain afterwards; for the present we will follow out our plan and enumerate the other types of character.

In the matter of anger also we find excess and deficiency and moderation. The characters themselves hardly have recognized names, but as the moderate man is here called gentle, we will call his character gentleness; of those who go into extremes, we may take the term wrathful for him who exceeds, with wrathfulness for the vice, and wrathless for him who is deficient, with wrathlessness for his character.

Besides these, there are three kinds of moderation, bearing some resemblance to one another, and yet different. They all have to do with intercourse in speech and action, but they differ in that one has to do with the truthfulness of this intercourse, while the other two have to do with its pleasantness—one of the two with pleasantness in matters of amusement, the other with pleasantness in all the relations of life. We must therefore speak of these qualities also in order that we may the more plainly see how, in all cases, moderation is praiseworthy, while the extreme courses are neither right nor praiseworthy, but blamable.

In these cases also names are for the most part wanting, but we must try, here as elsewhere, to coin names ourselves, in order to make our argument clear and easy to follow.

In the matter of truth, then, let us call him who observes the mean a true [or truthful] person, and observance of the mean truth [or truthfulness]: pretence, when it exaggerates, may be called boasting, and the person a boaster; when it understates, let the names be irony and ironical.

With regard to pleasantness in amusement, he who observes the mean may be called witty, and his character wittiness; excess may be called buffoonery, and the man a buffoon; while boorish may stand for the person who is deficient, and boorishness for his character.

With regard to pleasantness in the other affairs of life, he who makes himself properly pleasant may be called friendly, and his moderation friendliness; he that exceeds may be called obsequious if he have no ulterior motive, but a flatterer if he has an eye to his own advantage; he that is deficient in this respect, and always makes himself disagreeable, may be called a quarrelsome or peevish fellow.

Moreover, in mere emotions[8] and in our conduct with regard to them, there are ways of observing the mean; for instance, shame (αἰδώς), is not a virtue, but yet the modest (αἰδήμων) man is praised. For in these matters also we speak of this man as observing the mean, of that man as going beyond it (as the shamefaced man whom the least thing makes shy), while he who is deficient in the feeling, or lacks it altogether, is called shameless; but the term modest (αἰδήμων) is applied to him who observes the mean.

Righteous indignation, again, hits the mean between envy and malevolence. These have to do with feelings of pleasure and pain at what happens to our neighbours. A man is called righteously indignant when he feels pain at the sight of undeserved prosperity, but your envious man goes beyond him and is pained by the sight of any one in prosperity, while the malevolent man is so far from being pained that he actually exults in the misfortunes of his neighbours.

But we shall have another opportunity of discussing these matters.

As for justice, the term is used in more senses than one; we will, therefore, after disposing of the above questions, distinguish these various senses, and show how each of these kinds of justice is a kind of moderation.

And then we will treat of the intellectual virtues in the same way.

8. There are, as we said, three classes of disposition, viz. two kinds of vice, one marked by excess, the other by deficiency, and one kind of virtue, the observance of the mean. Now, each is in a way opposed to each, for the extreme dispositions are opposed both to the mean or moderate disposition and to one another, while the moderate disposition is opposed to both the extremes. Just as a quantity which is equal to a given quantity is also greater when compared with a less, and less when compared with a greater quantity, so the mean or moderate dispositions exceed as compared with the defective dispositions, and fall short as compared with the excessive dispositions, both in feeling and in action; e.g. the courageous man seems foolhardy as compared with the coward, and cowardly as compared with the foolhardy; and similarly the temperate man appears profligate in comparison with the insensible, and insensible in comparison with the profligate man; and the liberal man appears prodigal by the side of the illiberal man, and illiberal by the side of the prodigal man.

And so the extreme characters try to displace the mean or moderate character, and each represents him as falling into the opposite extreme, the coward calling the courageous man foolhardly, the foolhardy calling him coward, and so on in other cases.

But while the mean and the extremes are thus opposed to one another, the extremes are strictly contrary to each other rather than to the mean; for they are further removed from one another than from the mean, as that which is greater than a given magnitude is further from that which is less, and that which is less is further from that which is greater, than either the greater or the less is from that which is equal to the given magnitude.

Sometimes, again, an extreme, when compared with the mean, has a sort of resemblance to it, as foolhardiness to courage, or prodigality to liberality; but there is the greatest possible dissimilarity between the extremes.

Again, "things that are as far as possible removed from each other" is the accepted definition of contraries, so that the further things are removed from each other the more contrary they are.

In comparison with the mean, however, it is sometimes the deficiency that is the more opposed, and sometimes the excess; e.g. foolhardiness, which is excess, is not so much opposed to courage as cowardice, which is deficiency; but insensibility, which is lack of feeling, is not so much opposed to temperance as profligacy, which is excess.

The reasons for this are two. One is the reason derived from the nature of the matter itself: since one extreme is, in fact, nearer and more similar to the mean, we naturally do not oppose it to the mean so strongly as the other; e.g. as foolhardiness seems more similar to courage and nearer to it, and cowardice more dissimilar, we speak of cowardice as the opposite rather than the other: for that which is further removed from the mean seems to be more opposed to it.

This, then, is one reason, derived from the nature of the thing itself. Another reason lies in ourselves: and it is this—those things to which we happen to be more prone by nature appear to be more opposed to the mean: e.g. our natural inclination is rather towards indulgence in pleasure, and so we more easily fall into profligate than into regular habits: those courses, then, in which we are more apt to run to great lengths are spoken of as more opposed to the mean; and thus profligacy, which is an excess, is more opposed to temperance than the deficiency is.

9. We have sufficiently explained, then, that moral virtue is moderation or observance of the mean, and in what sense, viz. (1) as holding a middle position between two vices, one on the side of excess, and the other on the side of deficiency, and (2) as aiming at the mean or moderate amount both in feeling and in action.

And on this account it is a hard thing to be good; for finding the middle or the mean in each case is a hard thing, just as finding the middle or centre of a circle is a thing that is not within the power of everybody, but only of him who has the requisite knowledge.

Thus any one can be angry—that is quite easy; any one can give money away or spend it: but to do these things to the right person, to the right extent, at the right time, with the right object, and in the right manner, is not what everybody can do, and is by no means easy; and that is the reason why right doing is rare and praiseworthy and noble.

He that aims at the mean, then, should first of all strive to avoid that extreme which is more opposed to it, as Calypso[9] bids Ulysses—

"Clear of these smoking breakers keep thy ship."

For of the extremes one is more dangerous, the other less. Since then it is hard to hit the mean precisely, we must "row when we cannot sail," as the proverb has it, and choose the least of two evils; and that will be best effected in the way we have described.

And secondly we must consider, each for himself, what we are most prone to—for different natures are inclined to different things—which we may learn by the pleasure or pain we feel. And then we must bend ourselves in the opposite direction; for by keeping well away from error we shall fall into the middle course, as we straighten a bent stick by bending it the other way.

But in all cases we must be especially on our guard against pleasant things, and against pleasure; for we can scarce judge her impartially. And so, in our behaviour towards her, we should imitate the behaviour of the old counsellors towards Helen, and in all cases repeat their saying: if we dismiss her we shall be less likely to go wrong.

This then, in outline, is the course by which we shall best be able to hit the mean.

But it is a hard task, we must admit, especially in a particular case. It is not easy to determine, for instance, how and with whom one ought to be angry, and upon what grounds, and for how long; for public opinion sometimes praises those who fall short, and calls them gentle, and sometimes applies the term manly to those who show a harsh temper.

In fact, a slight error, whether on the side of excess or deficiency, is not blamed, but only a considerable error; for then there can be no mistake. But it is hardly possible to determine by reasoning how far or to what extent a man must err in order to incur blame; and indeed matters that fall within the scope of perception never can be so determined. Such matters lie within the region of particulars, and can only be determined by perception.

So much then is plain, that the middle character is in all cases to be praised, but that we ought to incline sometimes towards excess, sometimes towards deficiency; for in this way we shall most easily hit the mean and attain to right doing.

BOOK III.

CHAPTERS 1–5. THE WILL.

1. Virtue, as we have seen, has to do with feelings and actions. Now, praise[10] or blame is given only to what is voluntary; that which is involuntary receives pardon, and sometimes even pity.

It seems, therefore, that a clear distinction between the voluntary and the involuntary is necessary for those who are investigating the nature of virtue, and will also help legislators in assigning rewards and punishments.

That is generally held to be involuntary which is done under compulsion or through ignorance.

"Done under compulsion" means that the cause is external, the agent or patient contributing nothing towards it; as, for instance, if he were carried somewhere by a whirlwind or by men whom he could not resist.

But there is some question about acts done in order to avoid a greater evil, or to obtain some noble end; e.g. if a tyrant were to order you to do something disgraceful, having your parents or children in his power, who were to live if you did

it, but to die if you did not—it is a matter of dispute whether such acts are involuntary or voluntary.

Throwing a cargo overboard in a storm is a somewhat analogous case. No one voluntarily throws away his property if nothing is to come of it,[11] but any sensible person would do so to save the life of himself and the crew.

Acts of this kind, then, are of a mixed nature, but they more nearly resemble voluntary acts. For they are desired or chosen at the time when they are done, and the end or motive of an act is that which is in view at the time. In applying the terms voluntary and involuntary, therefore, we must consider the state of the agent's mind at the time. Now, he wills the act at the time; for the cause which sets the limbs going lies in the agent in such cases and where the cause lies in the agent, it rests with him to do or not to do.

Such acts, then, are voluntary, though in themselves [or apart from these qualifying circumstances] we may allow them to be involuntary; for no one would choose anything of this kind on its own account.

And, in fact, for actions of this sort men are sometimes praised,[12] e.g. when they endure something disgraceful or painful in order to secure some great and noble result, but in the contrary case they are blamed; for no worthy person would endure the extremity of disgrace when there was no noble result in view, or but a trifling one.

But in some cases we do not praise, but pardon, i.e. when a man is induced to do a wrong act by pressure which is too strong for human nature and which no one could bear. Though there are some cases of this kind, I think, where the plea of compulsion is inadmissible,[13] and where, rather than do the act, a man ought to suffer death in its most painful form; for instance, the circumstances which "compelled" Alemæon in Euripides, to kill his mother seem absurd.

It is sometimes hard to decide whether we ought to do this deed to avoid this evil, or whether we ought to endure this evil rather than do this deed; but it is still harder to abide by our decisions: for generally the evil which we wish to avoid is something painful, the deed we are pressed to do is something disgraceful; and hence we are blamed or praised according as we do or do not suffer ourselves to be compelled.

What kinds of acts, then, are to be called compulsory?

I think our answer must be that, in the first place, when the cause lies outside and the agent has no part in it, the act is called, without qualification, "compulsory" [and therefore involuntary]; but that, in the second place, when an act that would not be voluntarily done for its own sake is chosen now in preference to this given alternative, the cause lying in the agent, such an act must be called "involuntary in itself," or "in the abstract," but "now, and in preference to this alternative, voluntary." But an act of the latter kind is rather of the nature of a voluntary act: for acts fall within the sphere of particulars; and here the particular thing that is done is voluntary.

It is scarcely possible, however, to lay down rules for determining which of two alternatives is to be preferred; for there are many differences in the particular cases.

It might, perhaps, be urged that acts whose motive is something pleasant or something noble are compulsory, for here we are constrained by something outside us.

But if this were so, all our acts would be compulsory; for these are the motives of every act of every man.[14]

Again, acting under compulsion and against one's will is painful, but action whose motive is something pleasant or noble involves pleasure.[15] It is absurd, then, to blame things outside us instead of our own readiness to yield to their allurements, and, while we claim our noble acts as our own, to set down our disgraceful actions to "pleasant things outside us."

Compulsory, then, it appears, is that of which the cause is external, the person compelled contributing nothing thereto.

What is done through ignorance is always "not-voluntary," but is "involuntary"[16] when the agent is pained afterwards and sorry when he finds what he has done.[17] For when a man, who has done something through ignorance, is not vexed at what he has done, you cannot indeed say that he did it voluntarily, as he did not know what he was doing, but neither can you say that he did it involuntarily or unwillingly, since he is not sorry.

A man who has acted through ignorance, then, if he is sorry afterwards, is held to have done the deed involuntarily or unwillingly; if he is not sorry afterwards we may say (to mark the distinction) he did the deed "not-voluntarily;" for, as the case is different, it is better to have a distinct name.

Acting through ignorance, however, seems to be different from acting in ignorance. For instance, when a man is drunk or in a rage he is not thought to act through ignorance, but through intoxication or rage, and yet not knowingly, but *in* ignorance.

Every vicious man, indeed, is ignorant of[18] what ought to be done and what ought not to be done, and it is this kind of error that makes men unjust and bad generally. But the term "involuntary" is not properly applied to cases in which a man is ignorant of what is fitting.[19] The ignorance that makes an act involuntary is not this ignorance of the principles which should determine preference (this constitutes vice),—not, I say, this ignorance of the universal (for we blame a man for this), but ignorance of the particulars, of the persons and things affected by the act. These are the grounds of pity and pardon; for he who is ignorant of any of these particulars acts involuntarily.

It may be as well, then, to specify what these particulars are, and how many. They are—first, the doer; secondly, the deed; and, thirdly, the object or person affected by it; sometimes also that wherewith (e.g. the instrument with which) it is done, and that for the sake of which it is done (e.g. for protection), and the way in which it is done (e.g. gently or violently.)

Now, a man cannot (unless he be mad) be ignorant of all these particulars; for instance, he evidently cannot be ignorant of the doer: for how can he not know himself?

But a man may be ignorant of what he is doing; e.g. a man who has said something will sometimes plead that the words escaped him unawares, or that he did not know that the subject was forbidden (as Æschylus pleaded in the case of the Mysteries); or a man might plead that when he discharged the weapon he only intended to show the working of it, as the prisoner did in the catapult case. Again, a man might mistake his son for an enemy, as Merope does, or a sharp spear for one with a button, or a heavy stone for a pumice-stone. Again, one might kill a man with a drug intended to save him, or hit him hard when one wished merely to touch him (as boxers do when they spar with open hands).

Ignorance, then, being possible with regard to all these circumstances, he who is ignorant of any of them is held to have acted involuntarily, and especially when he is ignorant of the most important particulars; and the most important seem to be the persons affected and the result.

Besides this, however, the agent must be grieved and sorry for what he has done, if the act thus ignorantly committed is to be called involuntary [not merely not-voluntary].

But now, having found that an act is involuntary when done under compulsion or through ignorance, we may conclude that a voluntary act is one which is originated by the doer with knowledge of the particular circumstances of the act.

For I venture to think that it is incorrect to say that acts done through anger or desire are involuntary.

In the first place, if this be so we can no longer allow that any of the other animals act voluntarily, nor even children.

Again, does the saying mean that none of the acts which we do through desire or anger are voluntary, or that the noble ones are voluntary and the disgraceful ones involuntary? Interpreted in the latter sense, it is surely ridiculous, as the cause of both is the same. If we take the former interpretation, it is absurd, I think, to say that we ought to desire a thing, and also to say that its pursuit is involuntary; but, in fact, there are things at which we ought to be angry, and things which we ought to desire, e.g. health and learning.

Again, it seems that what is done unwillingly is painful, while what is done through desire is pleasant.

Again, what difference is there, in respect of involuntariness, between wrong deeds done upon calculation and wrong deeds done in anger? Both alike are to be avoided, but the unreasoning passions or feelings seem to belong to the man just as much as does the reason, so that the acts that are done under the impulse of anger or desire are also the man's acts.[20] To make such actions involuntary, therefore, would be too absurd.

2. Now that we have distinguished voluntary from involuntary acts, our next task is to discuss choice or purpose. For it seems to be most intimately connected with virtue, and to be a surer test of character than action itself.

It seems that choosing is willing, but that the two terms are not identical, willing being the wider. For children and other animals have will, but not choice or purpose; and acts done upon the spur of the moment are said to be voluntary, but not to be done with deliberate purpose.

Those who say that choice is appetite, or anger, or wish, or an opinion of some sort, do not seem to give a correct account of it.

In the first place, choice is not shared by irrational creatures, but appetite and anger are.

Again, the incontinent man acts from appetite and not from choice or purpose, the continent man from purpose and not from appetite.

Again, appetite may be contrary to purpose, but one appetite can not be contrary to another appetite.[21]

Again, the object of appetite [or aversion] is the pleasant or the painful, but the object of purpose [as such] is neither painful nor pleasant.

Still less can purpose be anger ($\theta\nu\mu\sigma\varsigma$); for acts done in anger seem to be least of all done of purpose or deliberate choice.

Nor yet is it wish, though it seem very like; for we cannot purpose or deliberately choose the impossible, and a man who should say that he did would be thought a fool; but we may wish for the impossible, e.g. to escape death.

Again, while we may wish what never could be effected by our own agency (e.g. the success of a particular actor or athlete), we never purpose or deliberately choose such things, but only those that we think may be effected by our own agency.

Again, we are more properly said to wish the end, to choose the means; e.g. we wish to be healthy, but we choose what will make us healthy: we wish to be happy, and confess the wish, but it would not be correct to say we purpose or deliberately choose to be happy; for we may say roundly that purpose or choice deals with what is in our power.

Nor can it be opinion; for, in the first place, anything may be matter of opinion—what is unalterable and impossible no less than what is in our power; and, in the second place, we distinguish opinion according as it is true or false, not according as it is good or bad, as we do with purpose or choice.

We may say, then, that purpose is not the same as opinion in general; nor, indeed, does any one maintain this.

But, further, it is not identical with a particular kind of opinion. For our choice of good or evil makes us morally good or bad, holding certain opinions does not.

Again, we choose to take or to avoid a good or evil thing; we opine what its nature is, or what it is good for, or in what way; but we cannot opine to take or to avoid.

Again, we commend a purpose for its rightness or correctness, an opinion for its truth.

Again, we choose a thing when we know well that it is good; we may have an opinion about a thing of which we know nothing.

Again, it seems that those who are best at choosing are not always the best at forming opinions, but that some who have an excellent judgment fail, through depravity, to choose what they ought.

It may be said that choice or purpose must be preceded or accompanied by an opinion or judgment; but this makes no difference: our question is not that, but whether they are identical.

What, then, is choice or purpose, since it is none of these?

It seems, as we said, that what is chosen or purposed is willed, but that what is willed is not always chosen or purposed.

The required differentia, I think, is "after previous deliberation." For choice or purpose implies calculation and reasoning. The name itself, too, seems to indicate this, implying that something is chosen before or in preference to other things.[22]

3. Now, as to deliberation, do we deliberate about everything, and may anything whatever be matter for deliberation, or are there some things about which deliberation is impossible?

By "matter for deliberation" we should understand, I think, not what a fool or a maniac, but what a rational being would deliberate about.

Now, no one deliberates about eternal or unalterable things, e.g. the system of the heavenly bodies, or the incommensurability of the side and the diagonal of a square.

Again, no one deliberates about things which change, but always change in the same way (whether the cause of change be necessity, or nature, or any other agency), e.g. the solstices and the sunrise;[23] nor about things that are quite irregular, like drought and wet; nor about matters of chance, like the finding of a treasure.

Again, even human affairs are not always matter of deliberation; e.g. what would be the best constitution for Scythia is a question that no Spartan would deliberate about.

The reason why we do not deliberate about these things is that none of them are things that we can ourselves effect.

But the things that we do deliberate about are matters of conduct that are within our control. And these are the only things that remain; for besides nature and necessity and chance, the only remaining cause of change is reason and human agency in general. Though we must add that men severally deliberate about what they can themselves do.

A further limitation is that where there is exact and absolute knowledge, there is no room for deliberation; e.g. writing: for there is no doubt how the letters should be formed.

We deliberate, then, about things that are brought about by our own agency, but not always in the same way; e.g. about medicine and money-making, and about navigation more than about gymnastic, inasmuch as it is not yet reduced to so perfect a system, and so on; but more about matters of art than matters of science, as there is more doubt about them.

Matters of deliberation, then, are matters in which there are rules that generally hold good, but in which the result cannot be predicted, i.e. in which there is an element of uncertainty. In important matters we call in advisers, distrusting our own powers of judgment.

It is not about ends, but about means that we deliberate. A physician does not deliberate whether he shall heal, nor an orator whether he shall persuade, nor a statesman whether he shall make a good system of laws, nor a man in any other profession about his end; but, having the proposed end in view, we consider how and by what means this end can be attained; and if it appear that it can be attained by various means, we further consider which is the easiest and best; but if it can only be attained by one means, we consider how it is to be attained by this means, and how this means itself is to be secured, and so on, until we come to the first link in the chain of causes, which is last in the order of discovery.

For in deliberation we seem to inquire and to analyze in the way described, just as we analyze a geometrical figure in order to learn how to construct it[24] (and though inquiry is not always deliberation—mathematical inquiry, for instance, is not—deliberation is always inquiry); that which is last in the analysis coming first in the order of construction.

If we come upon something impossible, we give up the plan; e.g. if it needs money, and money cannot be got: but if it appear possible, we set to work. By possible I mean something that can be done by *us;* and what can be done by our friends can in a manner be done by us; for it is we who set our friends to work.

Sometimes we have to find out instruments, sometimes how to use them; and so on with the rest: sometimes we have to find out what agency will produce the desired effect, sometimes how or through whom this agency is to be set at work.

It appears, then, that a man, as we have already said, originates his acts; but that he deliberates about that which he can do himself, and that what he does is done for the sake of something else.[25] For he cannot deliberate about the end, but about the means to the end; nor, again, can he deliberate about particular facts, e.g. whether this be a loaf, or whether it be properly baked: these are matters of immediate perception. And if he goes on deliberating for ever he will never come to a conclusion.

But the object of deliberation and the object of choice or purpose are the same, except that the latter is already fixed and determined; when we say, "this is chosen" or "purposed," we mean that it has been selected after deliberation. For we always stop in our inquiry how to do a thing when we have traced back the chain of causes to ourselves, and to the commanding part of ourselves; for this is the part that chooses.

This may be illustrated by the ancient constitutions which Homer describes; for there the kings announce to the people what they have chosen.

Since, then, a thing is said to be chosen or purposed when, being in our power, it is desired after deliberation, choice or purpose may be defined as deliberate desire for something in our power; for we first deliberate, and then, having made our decision thereupon, we desire in accordance with deliberation.

Let this stand, then, for an account in outline of choice or purpose, and of what it deals with, viz. means to ends.

4. Wish, we have already said, is for the end; but whereas some hold that the object of wish is the good others hold that it is what seems good.

Those who maintain that the object of wish[26] is the good have to admit that what those wish for who choose wrongly is not object of wish (for if so it would be good; but it may so happen that it was bad); on the other hand, those who maintain that the object of wish is what seems good have to admit that there is nothing which is naturally object of wish, but that each wishes for what seems good to him—different and even contrary things seeming good to different people.

As neither of these alternatives quite satisfies us, perhaps we had better say that the good is the real object of wish (without any qualifying epithet), but that what seems good is object of wish to each man. The good man, then, wishes for the real object of wish; but what the bad man wishes for may be anything whatever; just as, with regard to the body, those who are in good condition find those things healthy that are really healthy, while those who are diseased find other things healthy (and it is just the same with things bitter, sweet, hot, heavy, etc): for the good or ideal man judges each case correctly, and in each case what is true seems true to him.

For, corresponding to each of our trained faculties, there is a special form of the noble and the pleasant, and perhaps there is nothing so distinctive of the good or ideal man as the power he has of discerning these special forms in each case, being himself, as it were, their standard and measure.

What misleads people seems to be in most cases pleasure; it seems to be a good thing, even when it is not. So they choose what is pleasant as good, and shun pain as evil.

5. We have seen that, while we wish for the end, we deliberate upon and choose the means thereto.

Actions that are concerned with means, then, will be guided by choice, and so will be voluntary.

But the acts in which the virtues are manifested are concerned with means.[27]

Therefore virtue depends upon ourselves:

and vice likewise. For where it lies with us to do, it lies with us not to do. Where we can say no, we can say yes. If then the doing a deed, which is noble, lies with us, the not doing it, which is disgraceful, lies with us; and if the not doing, which is noble, lies with us, the doing, which is disgraceful, also lies with us. But if the doing and likewise the not doing of noble or base deeds lies with us, and if this is, as we found, identical with being good or bad, then it follows that it lies with us to be worthy or worthless men.

And so the saying—

"None would be wicked, none would not be blessed,"

seems partly false and partly true: no one indeed is blessed against his will; but vice is voluntary.

If we deny this, we must dispute the statements made just now, and must contend that man is not the originator and the parent of his actions, as of his children.

But if those statements commend themselves to us, and if we are unable to trace our acts to any other sources than those that depend upon ourselves, then that whose source is within us must itself depend upon us and be voluntary.

This seems to be attested, moreover, by each one of us in private life, and also by the legislators; for they correct and punish those that do evil (except when it is done under compulsion, or through ignorance for which the agent is not responsible), and honour those that do noble deeds, evidently intending to encourage the one sort and discourage the other. But no one encourages us to do that which does not depend on ourselves, and which is not voluntary: it would be useless to be persuaded not to feel heat or pain or hunger and so on, as we should feel them all the same.

I say "ignorance for which the agent is not responsible," for the ignorance itself is punished by the law, if the agent appear to be responsible for his ignorance, *e.g.* for an offence committed in a fit of drunkenness the penalty is doubled: for the origin of the offence lies in the man himself; he might have avoided the intoxication, which was the cause of his ignorance. Again, ignorance of any of the ordinances of the law, which a man ought to know and easily can know, does not avert punishment. And so in other cases, where ignorance seems to be the result of negligence, the offender is punished, since it lay with him to remove this ignorance; for he might have taken the requisite trouble.

It may be objected that it was the man's character not to take the trouble.

We reply that men are themselves responsible for acquiring such a character by a dissolute life, and for being unjust or profligate in consequence of repeated acts of wrong, or of spending their time in drinking and so on. For it is repeated acts of a particular kind that give a man a particular character.

This is shown by the way in which men train themselves for any kind of contest or performance: they practise continually.

Not to know, then, that repeated acts of this or that kind produce a corresponding character or habit, shows an utter want of sense.

Moreover, it is absurd to say that he who acts unjustly does not wish to be unjust, or that he who behaves profligately does not wish to be profligate.

But if a man knowingly does acts which must make him unjust, he will be voluntarily unjust; though it does not follow that, if he wishes it, he can cease to be unjust and be just, any more than he who is sick can, if he wishes it, be whole. And it may be that he is voluntarily sick, through living incontinently and disobeying the doctor. At one time, then, he had the option not to be sick, but he no longer has it now that he has thrown away his health. When you have discharged a stone it is no longer in your power to call it back; but nevertheless the throwing and casting away of that stone rests with you; for the beginning of its flight depended upon you.[28]

Just so the unjust or the profligate man at the beginning was free not to acquire this character, and therefore he is voluntarily unjust or profligate; but now that he has acquired it, he is no longer free to put it off.

But it is not only our mental or moral vices that are voluntary; bodily vices also are sometimes voluntary, and then are censured. We do not censure natural ugliness, but we do censure that which is due to negligence and want of exercise. And so with weakness and infirmity: we should never reproach a man who was born blind, or had lost his sight in an illness or by a blow—we should rather pity him; but we should all censure a man who had blinded himself by excessive drinking or any other kind of profligacy.

We see, then, that of the vices of the body it is those that depend on ourselves that are censured, while those that do not depend on ourselves are not censured. And if this be so, then in other fields also those vices that are blamed must depend upon ourselves.

Some people may perhaps object to this.

"All men," they may say, "desire that which appears good to them, but cannot control this appearance; a man's character, whatever it be, decides what shall appear to him to be the end."

If, I answer, each man be in some way responsible for his habits or character, then in some way he must be responsible for his appearance also.

But if this be not the case, then a man is not responsible for, or is not the cause of, his own evil doing, but it is through ignorance of the end that he does evil, fancying that thereby he will secure the greatest good: and the striving towards the true end does not depend on our own choice, but a man must be born with a gift of sight, so to speak, if he is to discriminate rightly and to choose what is really good: and he is truly well-born who is by nature richly endowed with this gift; for, as it is the greatest and the fairest gift, which we cannot acquire or learn from another, but must keep all our lives just as nature gave it to us, to be well and nobly born in this respect is to be well-born in the truest and completest sense.

Now, granting this to be true, how will virtue be any more voluntary than vice?

For whether it be nature or anything else that determines what shall appear to be the end, it is determined in the same way for both alike, for the good man as for the bad, and both alike refer all their acts of whatever kind to it.

And so whether we hold that it is not merely nature that decides what appears to each to be the end (whatever that be), but that the man himself contributes something; or whether we hold that the end is fixed by nature, but that virtue is voluntary, inasmuch as the good man voluntarily takes the steps to that end—in either case vice will be just as voluntary as virtue; for self is active in the bad man just as much as in the good man, in choosing the particular acts at least, if not in determining the end.

If then, as is generally allowed, the virtues are voluntary (for we do, in fact, in some way help to make our character, and, by being of a certain character, give a certain complexion to our idea of the end), the vices also must be voluntary; for all this applies equally to them.

We have thus described in outline the nature of the virtues in general, and have said that they are forms of moderation or modes of observing the mean, and that they are habits or trained faculties, and that they show themselves in the performance of the same acts which produce them, and that they depend on ourselves and are voluntary, and that they follow the guidance of right reason. But our particular acts are not voluntary in the same sense as our habits: for we are masters of our acts from beginning to end when we know the particular circumstances; but we are masters of the beginnings only of our habits or characters, while their growth by gradual steps is imperceptible, like the growth of disease. Inasmuch, however, as it lay with us to employ or not to employ our faculties in this way, the resulting characters are on that account voluntary.

Now let us take up each of the virtues again in turn, and say what it is, and what its subject is, and how it deals with it; and in doing this, we shall at the same time see how many they are. And, first of all, let us take courage.

BOOK III.

CHAPTER 6–END OF BOOK V. THE SEVERAL MORAL VIRTUES AND VICES

6. We have already said that courage is moderation or observance of the mean with respect to feelings of fear and confidence.

Now, fear evidently is excited by fearful things, and these are, roughly speaking, evil things; and so fear is sometimes defined as "expectation of evil."

Fear, then, is excited by evil of any kind, e.g. by disgrace, poverty, disease, friendlessness, death; but it does not appear that every kind gives scope for courage. There are things which we actually ought to fear, which it is noble to fear and base not to fear, e.g. disgrace. He who fears disgrace is an honourable man, with a due sense of shame, while he who fears it not is shameless (though some people stretch the word courageous so far as to apply it to him; for he has a certain resemblance to the courageous man, courage also being a kind of fearlessness). Poverty, perhaps, we ought not to fear, nor disease, nor generally those things that are not the result of vice, and do not depend upon ourselves. But still to be fearless in regard to these things is not strictly courage; though here also the term is sometimes applied in virtue of a certain resemblance. There are people, for instance, who, though cowardly in the presence of the dangers of war, are yet liberal and bold in the spending of money.

On the other hand, a man is not to be called cowardly for fearing outrage to his children or his wife, or for dreading envy and things of that kind, nor courageous for being unmoved by the prospect of a whipping.

In what kind of terrors, then, does the courageous man display his quality? Surely in the greatest; for no one is more able to endure what is terrible. But of all things the most terrible is death; for death is our limit, and when a man is once dead it seems that there is no longer either good or evil for him.

It would seem, however, that even death does not on all occasions give scope for courage, *e.g.* death by water or by disease.

On what occasions then? Surely on the noblest occasions: and those are the occasions which occur in war; for they involve the greatest and the noblest danger.

This is confirmed by the honours which courage receives in free states and at the hands of princes.

The term courageous, then, in the strict sense, will be applied to him who fearlessly faces an honourable death and all sudden emergencies which involve death; and such emergencies mostly occur in war.

Of course the courageous man is fearless in the presence of illness also, and at sea, but in a different way from the sailors; for the sailors, because of their experience, are full of hope when the landsmen are already despairing of their lives and filled with aversion at the thought of such a death.

Moreover, the circumstances which especially call out courage are those in which prowess may be displayed, or in which death is noble; but in these forms of death there is neither nobility nor room for prowess.

7. Fear is not excited in all men by the same things, but yet we commonly speak of fearful things that surpass man's power to face. Such things, then, inspire fear in every rational man. But the fearful things that a man may face differ in importance and in being more or less fearful (and so with the things that inspire confidence). Now, the courageous man always keeps his presence of mind (so far as a man can). So though he will fear these fearful things, he will endure them as he ought and as reason bids him, for the sake of that which is noble; for this is the end or aim of virtue.

But it is possible to fear these things too much or too little, and again to take as fearful what is not really so. And thus men err sometimes by fearing the wrong things, sometimes by fearing in the wrong manner or at the wrong time, and so on.

And all this applies equally to things that inspire confidence.

He, then, that endures and fears what he ought from the right motive, and in the right manner, and at the right time, and similarly feels confidence, is courageous.

For the courageous man regulates both his feeling and his action according to the merits of each case and as reason bids him.

But the end or motive of every manifestation of a habit or exercise of a trained faculty is the end or motive of the habit or trained faculty itself.

Now, to the courageous man courage is essentially a fair or noble thing.

Therefore the end or motive of his courage is also noble; for everything takes its character from its end.

It is from a noble motive, therefore, that the courageous man endures and acts courageously in each particular case.[29]

Of the characters that run to excess, he that exceeds in fearlessness has no name (and this is often the case, as we have said before); but a man would be either a maniac or quite insensible to pain who should fear nothing, not even earthquakes and breakers, as they say is the case with the Celts.

He that is over-confident in the presence of fearful things is called foolhardy. But the foolhardy man is generally thought to be really a braggart, and to pretend a courage which he has not: at least he wishes to seem what the courageous man really is in the presence of danger;

so he imitates him when he can. And so your foolhardy man is generally a coward at bottom: he blusters to long as he can do so safely, but returns tail when real danger comes.

He that is over-confident in the presence of fearful things is called foolhardy. But the foolhardy man is generally thought to be really a braggart, and to pretend a courage which he has not: at least he wishes to seem what the courageous man really is in the presence of danger; so he imitates him when he can. And so your foolhardy man is generally a coward at bottom: he blusters so long as he can do so safely, but turns tail when real danger comes.

He who is over-fearful is a coward; for he fears what he ought not, and as he ought not, etc.

He is also deficient in confidence; but his character rather displays itself in excess of fear in the presence of pain.

The coward is also despondent, for he is frightened at everything. But it is the contrary with the courageous man; for confidence implies hopefulness.

Thus the coward and the foolhardy and the courageous man display their characters in the same circumstances, behaving differently under them: for while the former exceed or fall short, the latter behaves moderately and as he ought; and while the foolhardy are precipitate and eager before danger comes, but fall away in its presence, the courageous are keen in action, but quiet enough beforehand.

Courage then, as we have said, is observance of the mean with regard to things that excite confidence or fear, under the circumstances which we have specified, and chooses its course and sticks to its post because it is noble to do so, or because it is disgraceful not to do so.

But to seek death as a refuge from poverty, or love, or any painful thing, is not the act of a brave man, but of a coward. For it is effeminacy thus to fly from vexation; and in such a case death is accepted not because it is noble, but simply as an escape from evil.

8. Courage proper, then, is something of this sort. But besides this there are five other kinds of courage so called.

First, "political courage," which most resembles true courage.

Citizens seem often to face dangers because of legal pains and penalties on the one hand, and honours on the other. And on this account the people seem to be most courageous in those states where cowards are disgraced and brave men honoured.

This, too, is the kind of courage which inspires Homer's characters, *e.g.* Diomede and Hector.

"Polydamas will then reproach me first,"[30]

says Hector; and so Diomede:

"Hector one day will speak among his folk
And say, 'The son of Tydeus at my hand—' "[31]

This courage is most like that which we described above, because its impulse is a virtuous one, viz. a sense of honour ($\alpha\iota\delta\omega\varsigma$), and desire for a noble thing (glory), and aversion to reproach, which is disgraceful.

We might, perhaps, put in the same class men who are forced to fight by their officers; but they are inferior, inasmuch as what impels them is not a sense of honour, but fear, and what they shun is not disgrace, but pain. For those in authority compel them in Hector's fashion—

"Whoso is seen to skulk and skirk the fight
Shall nowise save his carcase from the dogs."[32]

And the same thing is done by commanders who order their men to stand, and flog them if they run, or draw them up with a ditch in their rear, and so on: all alike, I mean, employ compulsion.

But a man ought to be courageous, not under compulsion, but because it is noble to be so.

Secondly, experience in this or that matter is sometimes thought to be a sort of courage; and this indeed is the ground of the Socratic notion that courage is knowledge.

This sort of courage is exhibited by various persons in various matters, but notably by regular troops in military affairs; for it seems that in war there are many occasions of groundless alarm, and with these the regulars are better acquainted; so they appear to be courageous, simply because the other troops do not understand the real state of the case.

Again, the regular troops by reason of their experience are more efficient both in attack and defence; for they are skilled in the use of their weapons, and are also furnished with the best kind of arms for both purposes. So they fight with the advantage of armed over unarmed men, or of trained over untrained men; for in athletic contests also it is not the bravest men that can fight best, but those who are strongest and have their bodies in the best order.

But these regular troops turn cowards whenever the danger rises to a certain height and they find themselves inferior in numbers and equipment; then they are the first to fly, while the citizen-troops stand and are cut to pieces, as happened at the temple of Hermes.[33] For the citizens deem it base to fly, and hold death preferable to saving their lives on these terms; but the regulars originally met the danger only because they fancied they were stronger, and run away when they learn the truth, fearing death more than disgrace. But that is not what we mean by courageous.

Thirdly, people sometimes include rage within the meaning of the term courage.

Those who in sheer rage turn like wild beasts on those who have wounded them are taken for courageous, because the courageous man also is full of rage; for rage is above all things eager to rush on danger; so we find in Homer, "Put might into his rage," and "roused his wrath and rage," and "fierce wrath breathed through his nostrils," and "his blood boiled." For all these expressions seem to signify the awakening and the bursting out of rage.

The truly courageous man, then, is moved to act by what is noble, rage helping him: but beasts are moved by pain, *i.e.* by blows or by fear; for in a wood or a marsh they do not attack man. And so beasts are not courageous, since it is pain and rage that drives them to rush on danger, without foreseeing any of the terrible consequences. If this be courage, then asses must be called courageous when they are hungry; for though you beat them they will not leave off eating. Adulterers also are moved to do many bold deeds by their lust.

Being driven to face danger by pain or rage, then, is not courage proper. However, this kind of courage, whose impulse is rage, seems to be the most natural, and, when deliberate purpose and the right motive are added to it, to become real courage.

Again, anger is a painful state, the act of revenge is pleasant; but those who fight from these motives [*i.e.* to avoid the pain or gain the plea-sure] may fight well, but are not courageous: for they do not act because it is noble to act so, or as reason bids, but are driven by their passions; though they bear some resemblance to the courageous man.

Fourthly, the sanguine man is not properly called courageous: he is confident in danger because he has often won and has defeated many adversaries. The two resemble one another, since both are confident; but whereas the courageous man is confident for the reasons specified above, the sanguine man is confident because he thinks he is superior and will win without receiving a scratch. (People behave in the same sort of way when they get drunk; for then they become sanguine.) But when he finds that this is not the case, he runs away; while it is the character of the courageous man, as we saw, to face that which is terrible to a man even when he sees the danger, because it is noble to do so and base not to do so.

And so (it is thought) it needs greater courage to be fearless and cool in sudden danger than in danger that has been foreseen; for behaviour in the former case must be more directly the outcome of formed character, since it is less dependent on preparation. When we see what is coming we may choose to meet it, as the result of calculation and reasoning, but when it comes upon us suddenly we must choose according to our character.

Fifthly, those who are unaware of their danger sometimes appear to be courageous, and in fact are not very far removed from the sanguine persons we last spoke of, only they are inferior in that they have not necessarily any opinion of themselves, which the sanguine must have. And so while the latter hold their ground for some time, the former, whose courage was due to a false belief, run away the moment they perceive or suspect that the case is different; as the Argives did when they engaged the Spartans under the idea that they were Sicyonians.[34]

Thus we have described the character of the courageous man, and of those who are taken for courageous.

But there is another point to notice.

9. Courage is concerned, as we said, with feelings both of confidence and of fear, yet it is not equally concerned with both, but more with occasions of fear: it is the man who is cool and behaves as he ought on such occasions that is

called courageous, rather than he who behaves thus on occasions that inspire confidence.

And so, as we said, men are called courageous for enduring painful things.

Courage, therefore, brings pain, and is justly praised; for it is harder to endure what is painful than to abstain from what is pleasant.

I do not, of course, mean to say that the end of courage is not pleasant, but that it seems to be hidden from view by the attendant circumstances, as is the case in gymnastic contests also. Boxers, for instance, have a pleasant end in view, that for which they strive, the crown and the honours; but the blows they receive are grievous to flesh and blood, and painful, and so are all the labours they undergo; and as the latter are many, while the end is small, the pleasantness of the end is hardly apparent.

If, then, the case of courage is analogous, death and wounds will be painful to the courageous man and against his will, but he endures them because it is noble to do so or base not to do so.

And the more he is endowed with every virtue, and the happier he is, the more grievous will death be to him; for life is more worth living to a man of his sort than to any one else, and he deprives himself knowingly of the very best things; and it is painful to do that. But he is no less courageous because he feels this pain; nay, we may say he is even more courageous, because in spite of it he chooses noble conduct in battle in preference to those good things.

Thus we see that the rule that the exercise of a virtue is pleasant[35] does not apply to all the virtues, except in so far as the end is attained.

Still there is, perhaps, no reason why men of this character should not be less efficient as soldiers than those who are not so courageous, but have nothing good to lose; for such men are reckless of risk, and will sell their lives for a small price.

Here let us close our account of courage; it will not be hard to gather an outline of its nature from what we have said.

10. After courage, let us speak of temperance, for these two seem to be the virtues of the irrational parts of our nature.

We have already said that temperance is moderation or observance of the mean with regard to

pleasures (for it is not concerned with pains so much, nor in the same manner); profligacy also manifests itself in the same field.

Let us now determine what kind of pleasures there are.

First, let us accept as established the distinction between the pleasures of the body and the pleasures of the soul, such as the pleasures of gratified ambition or love of learning.

When he who loves honour or learning is delighted by that which he loves, it is not his body that is affected, but his mind. But men are not called either temperate or profligate for their behaviour with regard to these pleasures; nor for their behaviour with regard to any other pleasures that are not of the body. For instance, those who are fond of gossip and of telling stories, and spend their days in trifles, are called babblers, but not profligate; nor do we apply this term to those who are pained beyond measure at the loss of money or friends.

Temperance, then, will be concerned with the pleasures of the body, but not with all of these even: for those who delight in the use of their eyesight, in colours and forms and painting, are not called either temperate or profligate; and yet it would seem that it is possible to take delight in these things too as one ought, and also more or less than one ought.

And so with the sense of hearing: a man is never called profligate for taking an excessive delight in music or in acting, nor temperate for taking a proper delight in them.

Nor are these terms applied to those who delight (unless it be accidentally) in smells. We do not say that those who delight in the smell of fruit or roses or incense are profligate, but rather those who delight in the smell of unguents and savoury dishes; for the profligate delights in these smells because they remind him of the things that he lusts after.

You may, indeed, see other people taking delight in the smell of food when they are hungry; but only a profligate takes delight in such smells [constantly], as he alone is [constantly] lusting after such things.

The lower animals, moreover, do not get pleasure through these senses, except accidentally. It is not the scent of a hare that delights a dog, but the eating of it; only the announcement comes through his sense of smell. The lion rejoices not in the lowing of the ox, but in the devouring of him; but as the lowing announces that the ox is near, the lion appears to delight in the sound itself. So also, it is not seeing a stag or a wild goat that pleases him, but the anticipation of a meal.

Temperance and profligacy, then, have to do with those kinds of pleasure which are common to the lower animals, for which reason they seem to be slavish and brutal; I mean the pleasures of touch and taste.

Taste, however, seems to play but a small part here, or perhaps no part at all. For it is the function of taste to distinguish flavours, as is done by wine-tasters and by those who season dishes; but it is by no means this discrimination of objects that gives delight (to profligates, at any rate), but the actual enjoyment of them, the medium of which is always the sense of touch, alike in the pleasures of eating, of drinking, and of sexual intercourse.

And hence a certain gourmand wished that his throat were longer than a crane's, thereby implying that his pleasure was derived from the sense of touch.

That sense, then, with which profligacy is concerned is of all senses the commonest or most widespread; and so profligacy would seem to be deservedly of all vices the most censured, inasmuch as it attaches not to our human, but to our animal nature.

To set one's delight in things of this kind, then, and to love them more than all things, is brutish.

And further, the more manly sort even of the pleasures of touch are excluded from the sphere of profligacy, such as the pleasures which the gymnast finds in rubbing and the warm bath; for the profligate does not cultivate the sense of touch over his whole body, but in certain parts only.

11. Now, of our desires or appetites some appear to be common to the race, others to be individual and acquired.

Thus the desire of food is natural [or common to the race]; every man when he is in want desires meat or drink; or sometimes both, and sexual intercourse, as Homer says, when he is young and vigorous.

But not all men desire to satisfy their wants in this or that particular way, nor do all desire the same things; and therefore such desire appears to be peculiar to ourselves, or individual.

Of course it is also partly natural: different people are pleased by different things, and yet there are some things which all men like better than others.

Firstly, then, in the matter of our natural or common desires but few err, and that only on one side, viz. on the side of excess; e.g. to eat or drink of whatever is set before you till you can hold no more is to exceed what is natural in point of quantity, for natural desire or appetite is for the filling of our want simply. And so such people are called "belly-mad," implying that they fill their bellies too full.

It is only utterly slavish natures that acquire this vice.

Secondly, with regard to those pleasures that are individual [i.e. which attend the gratification of our individual desires] many people err in various ways.

Whereas people are called fond of this or that because they delight either in wrong things, or to an unusual degree, or in a wrong fashion, profligates exceed in all these ways. For they delight in some things in which they ought not to delight (since they are hateful things), and if it be right to delight in any of these things they delight in them more than is right and more than is usual.

It is plain, then, that excess in these pleasures is profligacy, and is a thing to be blamed.

But in respect of the corresponding pains the case is not the same here as it was with regard to courage: a man is not called temperate for bearing them, and profligate for not bearing them; but the profligate man is called profligate for being more pained than he ought at not getting certain pleasant things (his pain being caused by his pleasure[36]), and the temperate man is called temperate because the absence of these pleasant things or the abstinence from them is not painful to him.

The profligate, then, desires all pleasant things or those that are most intensely pleasant, and is led by his desire so as to choose these in preference to all other things. And so he is constantly pained by failing to get them and by lusting after them: for all appetite involves pain; but it seems a strange thing to be pained for the sake of pleasure.

People who fall short in the matter of pleasure, and take less delight than they ought in these things, are hardly found at all; for this sort of insensibility is scarcely in human nature. And indeed even the lower animals discriminate kinds of food, and delight in some and not in others; and a being to whom nothing was pleasant, and who found no difference between one thing and another, would be very far removed from being a man. We have no name for such a being, because he does not exist.

But the temperate man observes the mean in these things. He takes no pleasure in those things that the profligate most delights in (but rather disdains them), nor generally in the wrong things, nor very much in any of these things,[37] and when they are absent he is not pained, nor does he desire them, or desires them but moderately, not more than he ought, nor at the wrong time, etc.; but those things which, being pleasant, at the same time conduce to health and good condition, he will desire moderately and in the right manner, and other pleasant things also, provided they are not injurious, or incompatible with what is noble, or beyond his means; for he who cares for them then, cares for them more than is fitting, and the temperate man is not apt to do that, but rather to be guided by right reason.

12. Profligacy seems to be more voluntary than cowardice.

For a man is impelled to the former by pleasure, to the latter by pain; but pleasure is a thing we choose, while pain is a thing we avoid. Pain puts us beside ourselves and upsets the nature of the sufferer, while pleasure has no such effect. Profligacy, therefore, is more voluntary.

Profligacy is for these reasons more to be blamed than cowardice, and for another reason too, viz. that it is easier to train one's self to behave rightly on these occasions [*i.e.* those in which profligacy is displayed]; for such occasions are constantly occurring in our lives, and the training involves no risk; but with occasions of fear the contrary is the case.

Again, it would seem that the habit of mind or character called cowardice is more voluntary than the particular acts in which it is exhibited. It is not painful to be a coward, but the occasions which exhibit cowardice put men beside themselves through fear of pain, so that they throw away their arms and altogether disgrace themselves; and hence these particular acts are even thought to be compulsory.

In the case of the profligate, on the contrary, the particular acts are voluntary (for they are done with appetite and desire), but the character itself less so; for no one desires to be a profligate.

The term "profligacy" we apply also to childish faults,[38] for they have some sort of resemblance. It makes no difference for our present purpose which of the two is named after the other, but it is plain that the later is named after the earlier.

And the metaphor, I think, is not a bad one: what needs "chastening" or "correction"[39] is that which inclines to base things and which has great powers of expansion. Now, these characteristics are nowhere so strongly marked as in appetite and in childhood; children too [as well as the profligate] live according to their appetites, and the desire for pleasant things is most pronounced in them. If then this element be not submissive and obedient to the governing principle, it will make great head: for in an irrational being the desire for pleasant things is insatiable and ready to gratify itself in any way, and the gratification of the appetite increases the natural tendency, and if the gratifications are great and intense they even thrust out reason altogether. The gratifications of appetite, therefore, should be moderate and few, and appetite should be in no respect opposed to reason (this is what we mean by submissive and "chastened"), but subject to reason as a child should be subject to his tutor.

And so the appetites of the temperate man should be in harmony with his reason; for the aim of both is that which is noble: the temperate man desires what he ought, and as he ought, and when he ought; and this again is what reason prescribes.

This, then, may be taken as an account of temperance.

BOOK IV.

THE SAME–Continued.

1. Liberality, of which we will next speak, seems

to be moderation in the matter of wealth. What we commend in a liberal man is his behaviour, not in war, nor in those circumstances in which temperance is commended, nor yet in passing judgment, but in the giving and taking of wealth, and especially in the giving—wealth meaning all those things whose value can be measured in money.

But both prodigality and illiberality are at once excess and defect in the matter of wealth.

Illiberality always means caring for wealth more than is right; but prodigality sometimes stands for a combination of vices. Thus incontinent people, who squander their money in riotous living, are called prodigals. And so prodigals are held to be very worthless individuals, as they combine a number of vices.

But we must remember that this is not the proper use of the term; for the term "prodigal" (ἄσωτος) is intended to denote a man who has one vice, viz. that of wasting his substance: for he is ἄσωτος, or "prodigal," who is destroyed through his own fault, and the wasting of one's substance is held to be a kind of destruction of one's self, as one's life is dependent upon it. This, then, we regard as the proper sense of the term "prodigality."

Anything that has a use may be used well or ill.

Now, riches is abundance of useful things (τὰ χρήσιμα).

But each thing is best used by him who has the virtue that is concerned with that thing.

Therefore he will use riches best who has the virtue that is concerned with wealth[40] (τὰ χρήματα), i.e. the liberal man.

Now, the ways of using wealth are spending and giving, while taking and keeping are rather the ways of acquiring wealth. And so it is more distinctive of the liberal man to give to the right people than to take from the right source and not to take from the wrong source. For it is more distinctive of virtue to do good to others than to have good done to you, and to act nobly than not to act basely: but it is plain that doing good and acting nobly go with the giving, while having good done to you and not acting basely go with the taking.

Again, we are thankful to him who gives, not to him who does not take; and so also we praise the former rather than the latter.

Again, it is easier not to take than to give; for

we are more inclined to be too stingy with our own goods than to take another's.

Again, it is those who give that are commonly called liberal; while those who abstain from taking are not praised for their liberality especially, but rather for their justice; and those who take are not praised at all.

Again, of all virtuous characters the liberal man is perhaps the most beloved, because he is useful; but his usefulness lies in his giving.

But virtuous acts, we said, are noble, and are done for the sake of that which is noble. The liberal man, therefore, like the others, will give with a view to, or for the sake of, that which is noble, and give rightly; i.e. he will give the right things to the right persons at the right times—in short, his giving will have all the characteristics of right giving.

Moreover, his giving will be pleasant to him, or at least painless; for virtuous acts are always pleasant or painless—certainly very far from being painful.

He who gives to the wrong persons, or gives from some other motive than desire for that which is noble, is not liberal, but must be called by some other name.

Nor is he liberal who gives with pain; for that shows that he would prefer[41] the money to the noble action, which is not the feeling of the liberal man.

The liberal man, again, will not take from wrong sources; for such taking is inconsistent with the character of a man who sets no store by wealth.

Nor will he be ready to beg a favour; for he who confers benefits on others is not usually in a hurry to receive them.

But from right sources he will take (e.g. from his own property), not as if there were anything noble in taking, but simply as a necessary condition of giving. And so he will not neglect his property, since he wishes by means of it to help others. But he will refuse to give to any casual person, in order that he may have wherewithal to give to the right persons, at the right times, and where it is noble to give.

It is very characteristic of the liberal man[42] to go even to excess in giving, so as to leave too little for himself; for disregard of self is part of his character.

In applying the term liberality we must take

account of a man's fortune; for it is not the amount of what is given that makes a gift liberal, but the liberal habit or character of the doer; and this character proportions the gift to the fortune of the giver. And so it is quite possible that the giver of the smaller sum may be the more liberal man, if his means be smaller.

Those who have inherited a fortune seem to be more liberal than those who have made one; for they have never known want; and all men are particularly fond of what themselves have made, as we see in parents and poets.

It is not easy for a liberal man to be rich, as he is not apt to take or to keep, but is apt to spend, and cares for money not on its own account, but only for the sake of giving it away.

Hence the charge often brought against fortune, that those who most deserve wealth are least blessed with it. But this is natural enough; for it is just as impossible to have wealth without taking trouble about it, as it is to have anything else.

Nevertheless the liberal man will not give to the wrong people, nor at the wrong times; for if he did, he would no longer be displaying true liberality, and, after spending thus, would not have enough to spend on the right occasions. For, as we have already said, he is liberal who spends in proportion to his fortune, on proper objects, while he who exceeds this is prodigal. And so princes[43] are not called prodigal, because it does not seem easy for them to exceed the measure of their possessions in gifts and expenses.

Liberality, then, being moderation in the giving and taking of wealth, the liberal man will give and spend the proper amount on the proper objects, alike in small things and in great, and that with pleasure; and will also take the proper amount from the proper sources. For since the virtue is moderation in both giving and taking, the man who has the virtue will do both rightly. Right taking is consistent with right giving, but any other taking is contrary to it. Those givings and takings, then, that are consistent with one another are found in the same person, while those that are contrary to one another manifestly are not.

But if a liberal man happen to spend anything in a manner contrary to what is right and noble, he will be pained, but moderately and in due measure; for it is a characteristic of virtue to be pleased and pained on the right occasions and in due measure.

The liberal man, again, is easy to deal with in money matters; it is not hard to cheat him, as he does not value wealth, and is more apt to be vexed at having failed to spend where he ought, than to be pained at having spent where he ought not—the sort of man that Simonides would not commend.[44]

The prodigal, on the other hand, errs in these points also; he is not pleased on the right occasions nor in the right way, nor pained: but this will be clearer as we go on.

We have already said that both prodigality and illiberality are at once excess and deficiency, in two things, viz. giving and taking (expenditure being included in giving). Prodigality exceeds in giving and in not taking, but falls short in taking; illiberality falls short in giving, but exceeds in taking—in small things, we must add.

Now, the two elements of prodigality are not commonly united in the same person:[45] it is not easy for a man who never takes to be always giving; for private persons soon exhaust their means of giving, and it is to private persons that the name is generally applied.[46]

A prodigal of this kind [i.e. in whom both the elements are combined], we must observe, would seem to be not a little better than an illiberal man. For he is easily cured by advancing years and by lack of means, and may come to the middle course. For he has the essential points of the liberal character; he gives and abstains from taking, though he does neither well nor as he ought. If then he can be trained to this, or if in any other way this change in his nature can be effected, he will be liberal; for then he will give to whom he ought, and will not take whence he ought not. And so he is generally thought to be not a bad character; for to go too far in giving and in not taking does not show a vicious or ignoble nature so much as a foolish one.

A prodigal of this sort, then, seems to be much better than an illiberal man, both for the reasons already given, and also because the former does good to many, but the latter to no one, not even to himself.

But most prodigals, as has been said, not only give wrongly, but take from wrong sources, and are in this respect illiberal. They become grasping because they wish to spend, but cannot readily do so, as their supplies soon fail. So they are compelled to draw from other sources. At the same time, since they care nothing for what is noble, they will take quite recklessly from any source whatever; for they long to give, but care not a whit how the money goes or whence it comes.

And so their gifts are not liberal; for they are not noble, nor are they given with a view to that which is noble, nor in the right manner. Sometimes they enrich those who ought to be poor, and will give nothing to men of well-regulated character, while they give a great deal to those who flatter them, or furnish them with any other pleasure. And thus the greater part of them are profligates; for, being ready to part with their money, they are apt to lavish it on riotous living, and as they do not shape their lives with a view to that which is noble, they easily fall away into the pursuit of pleasure.

The prodigal, then, if he fail to find guidance, comes to this, but if he get training he may be brought to the moderate and right course.

But illiberality is incurable; for old age and all loss of power seems to make men illiberal.

It also runs in the blood more than prodigality; the generality of men are more apt to be fond of money than of giving.

Again, it is far-reaching, and has many forms; for there seem to be many ways in which one can be illiberal.

It consists of two parts—deficiency in giving, and excess of taking; but it is not always found in its entirety; sometimes the parts are separated, and one man exceeds in taking, while another falls short in giving. Those, for instance, who are called by such names as niggardly, stingy, miserly, all fall short in giving, but do not covet other people's goods, or wish to take them.

Some are impelled to this conduct by a kind of honesty, or desire to avoid what is disgraceful—I mean that some of them seem, or at any rate profess, to be saving, in order that they may never be compelled to do anything disgraceful; e.g. the cheeseparer[47] (and those like him), who is so named because of the extreme lengths to which he carries his unwillingness to give.

But others are moved to keep their hands from their neighbours' goods only by fear, believing it to be no easy thing to take the goods of others, without having one's own goods taken in turn; so they are content with neither taking nor giving.

Others, again, exceed in the matter of taking so far as to make any gain they can in any way whatever, e.g. those who ply debasing trades, brothel-keepers and such like, and usurers who lend out small sums at a high rate. For all these make money from improper sources to an improper extent.

The common characteristic of these last seems to be the pursuit of base gain; for all of them endure reproach for the sake of gain, and that a small gain. For those who make improper gains in improper ways on a large scale are not called illiberal, e.g. tyrants who sack cities and pillage temples; they are rather called wicked, impious, unjust. The dice-sharper, however, and the man who steals clothes at the bath, or the common thief, are reckoned among the illiberal; for they all make base gains; i.e. both the thief and the sharper ply their trade and endure reproach for gain, and the thief for the sake of his booty endures the greatest dangers, while the sharper makes gain out of his friends, to whom he ought to give. Both then, wishing to make gain in improper ways, are seekers of base gain; and all such ways of making money are illiberal.

But illiberality is rightly called the opposite of liberality; for it is a worse evil than prodigality, and men are more apt to err in this way than in that which we have described as prodigality.

Let this, then, be taken as our account of liberality, and of the vices that are opposed to it.

2. Our next task would seem to be an examination of magnificence. For this also seems to be a virtue that is concerned with wealth.

But it does not, like liberality, extend over the whole field of money transactions, but only over those that involve large expenditure; and in these it goes beyond liberality in largeness. For, as its very name ($\mu\epsilon\gamma\alpha\lambda o\pi\rho\epsilon\pi\epsilon\iota\alpha$) suggests, it is suitable expenditure on a large scale. But the largeness is relative: the expenditure that is suitable for a man who is fitting out a war-ship is not the same as that which is suitable for the chief of a sacred embassy.

What is suitable, then, is relative to the person, and the occasion, and the business on hand. Yet he who spends what is fitting on trifling or moderately important occasions is not called magnificent; *e.g.* the man who can say, in the words of the poet—

"To many a wandering beggar did I give;"

but he who spends what is fitting on great occasions. For the magnificent man is liberal, but a man may be liberal without being magnificent.

The deficiency of this quality is called meanness; the excess of it is called vulgarity, bad taste, etc.; the characteristic of which is not spending too much on proper objects, but spending ostentatiously on improper objects and in improper fashion. But we will speak of them presently.

But the magnificent man is like a skilled artist; he can see what a case requires, and can spend great sums tastefully. For, as we said at the outset, a habit or type of character takes its complexion from the acts in which it issues and the things it produces. The magnificent man's expenses, therefore, must be great and suitable.

What he produces then will also be of the same nature; for only thus will the expense be at once great and suitable to the result.

The result, then, must be proportionate to the expenditure, and the expenditure proportionate to the result, or even greater.

Moreover, the magnificent man's motive in thus spending his money will be desire for that which is noble; for this is the common characteristic of all the virtues.

Further, he will spend gladly and lavishly; for a minute calculation of cost is mean. He will inquire how the work can be made most beautiful and most elegant, rather than what its cost will be, and how it can be done most cheaply.

So the magnificent man must be liberal also; for the liberal man, too, will spend the right amount in the right manner; only, both the amount and the manner being right, magnificence is distinguished from liberality (which has the same sphere of action) by greatness—I mean by actual magnitude of amount spent: and secondly, where the amount spent is the same, the result of the magnificent man's expenditure will be more magnificent.[48]

For the excellence of a possession is not the same as the excellence of a product or work of art: as a possession, that is most precious or estimable which is worth most, *e.g.* gold; as a work of art, that is most estimable which is great and beautiful: for the sight of such a work excites admiration, and a magnificent thing is always admirable; indeed, excellence of work on a great scale is magnificence.

Now, there is a kind of expenditure which is called in a special sense estimable or honourable, such as expenditure on the worship of the gods (*e.g.* offerings, temples, and sacrifices), and likewise all expenditure on the worship of heroes, and again all public service which is prompted by a noble ambition; *e.g.* a man may think proper to furnish a chorus or a war-ship, or to give a public feast, in a handsome style.

But in all cases, as we have said, we must have regard to the person who spends, and ask who he is, and what his means are; for expenditure should be proportionate to circumstances, and suitable not only to the result but to its author.

And so a poor man cannot be magnificent: he has not the means to spend large sums suitably: if he tries, he is a fool; for he spends disproportionately and in a wrong way; but an act must be done in the right way to be virtuous. But such expenditure is becoming in those who have got the requisite means, either by their own efforts or through their ancestors or their connections, and who have birth and reputation, etc.; for all these things give a man a certain greatness and importance.

The magnificent man, then, is properly a man of this sort, and magnificence exhibits itself most properly in expenditure of this kind, as we have said; for this is the greatest and most honourable kind of expenditure: but it may also be displayed on private occasions, when they are such as occur but once in a man's life, *e.g.* a wedding or anything of that kind; or when they are of special interest to the state or the governing classes, *e.g.* receiving strangers and sending them on their way, or making presents to them and returning their presents; for the magnificent man does not lavish money on himself, but on public objects; and gifts to strangers bear some resemblance to offerings to the gods.

But a magnificent man will build his house too in a style suitable to his wealth; for even a fine house is a kind of public ornament. And he will spend money more readily on things that last; for these are the noblest. And on each occasion he will spend what is suitable—which is not the same for gods as for men, for a temple as for a tomb.

And since every expenditure may be great after its kind, great expenditure on a great occasion being most magnificent, and then in a less degree that which is great for the occasion, whatever it be (for the greatness of the result is not the same as the greatness of the expense; *e.g.* the most beautiful ball or the most beautiful bottle that can be got is a magnificent present for a child, though its price is something small and mean), it follows that it is characteristic of the magnificent man to do magnificently that which he does, of whatever kind it be (for such work cannot easily be surpassed), and to produce a result proportionate to the expense.

This, then, is the character of the magnificent man.

The man who exceeds (whom we call vulgar) exceeds, as we said, in spending improperly. He spends great sums on little objects, and makes an unseemly display; *e.g.* if he is entertaining the members of his club, he will give them a wedding feast; if he provides the chorus for a comedy, he will bring his company on the stage all dressed in purple, as they did at Megara. And all this he will do from no desire for what is noble or beautiful, but merely to display his wealth, because he hopes thereby to gain admiration, spending little where he should spend much, and much where he should spend little.

But the mean man will fall short on every occasion, and, even when he spends very large sums, will spoil the beauty of his work by niggardliness in a trifle, never doing anything without thinking twice about it, and considering how it can be done at the least possible cost, and bemoaning even that, and thinking he is doing everything on a needlessly large scale.

Both these characters, then, are vicious, but they do not bring reproach, because they are neither injurious to others nor very offensive in themselves.

3. High-mindedness would seem from its very name (μεγαλοψυχία) to have to do with great things; let us first ascertain what these are.

It will make no difference whether we consider the quality itself, or the man who exhibits the quality.

By a high-minded man we seem to mean one who claims much and deserves much: for he who

claims much without deserving it is a fool; but the possessor of a virtue is never foolish or silly. The man we have described, then, is high-minded.

He who deserves little and claims little is temperate [or modest], but not high-minded: for high-mindedness [or greatness of soul] implies greatness, just as beauty implies stature; small men may be neat and well proportioned, but cannot be called beautiful.

He who claims much without deserving it is vain (though not every one who claims more than he deserves is vain).

He who claims less than he deserves is little-minded, whether his deserts be great or moderate, or whether they be small and he claims still less: but the fault would seem to be greatest in him whose deserts are great; for what would he do if his deserts were less than they are?

The high-minded man, then, in respect of the greatness of his deserts occupies an extreme position, but in that he behaves as he ought, observes the mean; for he claims that which he deserves, while all the others claim too much or too little.

If, therefore, he deserves much and claims much, and most of all deserves and claims the greatest things, there will be one thing with which he will be especially concerned. For desert has reference to external good things. Now, the greatest of external good things we may assume to be that which we render to the gods as their due, and that which people in high stations most desire, and which is the prize appointed for the noblest deeds. But the thing that answers to this description is honour, which, we may safely say, is the greatest of all external goods. Honours and dishonours, therefore, are the field in which the high-minded man behaves as he ought.

And indeed we may see, without going about to prove it, that honour is what high-minded men are concerned with; for it is honour that they especially claim and deserve.

The little-minded man falls short, whether we compare his claims with his own deserts or with what the high-minded man claims for himself.

The vain or conceited man exceeds what is due to himself, though he does not exceed the high-minded man in his claims.[49]

But the high-minded man, as he deserves the

greatest things, must be a perfectly good or excellent man; for the better man always deserves the greater things, and the best possible man the greatest possible things. The really high-minded man, therefore, must be a good or excellent man. And indeed greatness in every virtue or excellence would seem to be necessarily implied in being a high-minded or great-souled man.

It would be equally inconsistent with the high-minded man's character to run away swinging his arms, and to commit an act of injustice; for what thing is there for love of which he would do anything unseemly, seeing that all things are of little account to him?

Survey him point by point and you will find that the notion of a high-minded man that is not a good or excellent man is utterly absurd. Indeed, if he were not good, he could not be worthy of honour; for honour is the prize of virtue, and is rendered to the good as their due.

High-mindedness, then, seems to be the crowning grace, as it were, of the virtues; it makes them greater, and cannot exist without them. And on this account it is a hard thing to be truly high-minded; for it is impossible without the union of all the virtues.

The high-minded man, then, exhibits his character especially in the matter of honours and dishonours and at great honour from good men he will be moderately pleased, as getting nothing more than his due, or even less; for no honour can be adequate to complete virtue; but nevertheless he will accept it, as they have nothing greater to offer him. But honour from ordinary men and on trivial grounds he will utterly despise; for that is not what he deserves. And dishonour likewise he will make light of; for he will never merit it.

But though it is especially in the matter of honours, as we have said, that the high-minded man displays his character, yet he will also observe the mean in his feelings with regard to wealth and power and all kinds of good and evil fortune, whatever may befall him, and will neither be very much exalted by prosperity, nor very much cast down by adversity; seeing that not even honour affects him as if it were a very important thing. For power and wealth are desirable for honour's sake (at least, those who have them wish to gain honour by them). But he

who thinks lightly of honour must think lightly of them also.

And so high-minded men seem to look down upon everything.

But the gifts of fortune also are commonly thought to contribute to high-mindedness. For those who are well born are thought worthy of honour, and those who are powerful or wealthy; for they are in a position of superiority, and that which is superior in any good thing is always held in greater honour. And so these things do make people more high-minded in a sense; for such people find honour from some. But in strictness it is only the good man that is worthy of honour, though he that has both goodness and good fortune is commonly thought to be more worthy of honour. Those, however, who have these good things without virtue, neither have any just claim to great things, nor are properly to be called high-minded; for neither is possible without complete virtue.

But those who have these good things readily come to be supercilious and insolent. For without virtue it is not easy to bear the gifts of fortune becomingly; and so, being unable to bear them, and thinking themselves superior to everybody else, such people look down upon others, and yet themselves do whatever happens to please them. They imitate the high-minded man without being really like him, and they imitate him where they can; that is to say, they do not exhibit virtue in their acts, but they look down upon others. For the high-minded man never looks down upon others without justice (for he estimates them correctly), while most men do so for quite irrelevant reasons.

The high-minded man is not quick to run into petty dangers, and indeed does not love danger, since there are few things that he much values; but he is ready to incur a great danger, and whenever he does so is unsparing of his life, as a thing that is not worth keeping at all costs.

It is his nature to confer benefits, but he is ashamed to receive them; for the former is the part of a superior, the latter of an inferior. And when he has received a benefit, he is apt to confer a greater in return; for thus his creditor will become his debtor and be in the position of a recipient of his favour.

It seems, moreover, that such men remember

the benefits which they have conferred better than those which they have received (for the recipient of a benefit is inferior to the benefactor, but such a man wishes to be in the position of a superior), and that they like to be reminded of the one, but dislike to be reminded of the other; and this is the reason why we read that Thetis would not mention to Zeus the services she had done him, and why the Lacedæmonians, in treating with the Athenians, reminded them of the benefits received by Sparta rather than of those conferred by her.

It is characteristic of the high-minded man, again, never or reluctantly to ask favours, but to be ready to confer them, and to be lofty in his behaviour to those who are high in station and favoured by fortune, but affable to those of the middle ranks; for it is a difficult thing and a dignified thing to assert superiority over the former, but easy to assert it over the latter. A haughty demeanour in dealing with the great is quite consistent with good breeding, but in dealing with those of low estate is brutal, like showing off one's strength upon a cripple.

Another of his characteristics is not to rush in wherever honour is to be won, nor to go where others take the lead, but to hold aloof and to shun an enterprise, except when great honour is to be gained, or a great work to be done—not to do many things, but great things and notable.

Again, he must be open in his hate and in his love (for it is cowardly to dissemble your feelings and to care less for truth than for what people will think of you), and he must be open in word and in deed (for his consciousness of superiority makes him outspoken, and he is truthful except in so far as he adopts an ironical tone in his intercourse with the masses), and he must be unable to fashion his life to suit another, except he be a friend; for that is servile: and so all flatterers or hangers-on of great men are of a slavish nature, and men of low natures become flatterers.

Nor is he easily moved to admiration; for nothing is great to him.

He readily forgets injuries; for it is not consistent with his character to brood on the past, especially on past injuries, but rather to overlook them.

He is no gossip; he will neither talk about himself nor about others; for he cares not that men should praise him, nor that others should be blamed (though, on the other hand, he is not very ready to bestow praise); and so he is not apt to speak evil of others, not even of his enemies, except with the express purpose of giving offence.

When an event happens that cannot be helped or is of slight importance, he is the last man in the world to cry out or to beg for help; for that is the conduct of a man who thinks these events very important.

He loves to possess beautiful things that bring no profit, rather than useful things that pay; for this is characteristic of the man whose resources are in himself.

Further, the character of the high-minded man seems to require that his gait should be slow, his voice deep, his speech measured; for a man is not likely to be in a hurry when there are few things in which he is deeply interested, nor excited when he holds nothing to be of very great importance: and these are the causes of a high voice and rapid movements.

This, then, is the character of the high-minded man.

But he that is deficient in this quality is called little-minded; he that exceeds, vain or conceited.

Now these two also do not seem to be bad—for they do no harm—though they are in error.

For the little-minded man, though he deserves good things, deprives himself of that which he deserves, and so seems to be the worse for not claiming these good things, and for misjudging himself; for if he judged right he would desire what he deserves, as it is good. I do not mean to say that such people seem to be fools, but rather too retiring. But a misjudgment of this kind does seem actually to make them worse; for men strive for that which they deserve, and shrink from noble deeds and employments of which they think themselves unworthy, as well as from mere external good things.

But vain men are fools as well as ignorant of themselves, and make this plain to all the world: for they undertake honourable offices for which they are unfit, and presently stand convicted of incapacity; they dress in fine clothes and put on fine airs and so on; they wish everybody to know of their good fortune; they talk about themselves, as if that were the way to honour.

But little-mindedness is more opposed to high-mindedness than vanity is; for it is both commoner and worse.

High-mindedness, then, as we have said, has to do with honour on a large scale.

4. But it appears (as we said at the outset) that there is also a virtue concerned with honour, which bears the same relation to high-mindedness that liberality bears to magnificence; *i.e.* both the virtue in question and liberality have nothing to do with great things, but cause us to behave properly in matters of moderate or of trifling importance. Just as in the taking and giving of money it is possible to observe the mean, and also to exceed or fall short of it, so it is possible in desire for honour to go too far or not far enough, or, again, to desire honour from the right source and in the right manner.

A man is called ambitious or fond of honour (φιλότιμος) in reproach, as desiring honour more than he ought, and from wrong sources; and a man is called unambitious, or not fond of honour (ἀφιλότιμος) in reproach, as not desiring to be honoured even for noble deeds.

But sometimes a man is called ambitious or fond of honour in praise, as being manly and fond of noble things; and sometimes a man is called unambitious or not fond of honour in praise, as being moderate and temperate (as we said at the outset).

It is plain, then, that there are various senses in which a man is said to be fond of a thing, and that the term fond of honour has not always the same sense, but that as a term of praise it means fonder than most men, and as a term of reproach it means fonder than is right. But, as there is no recognized term for the observance of the mean, the extremes fight, so to speak, for what seems an empty place. But wherever there is excess and defect there is also a mean: and honour is in fact desired more than is right, and less: therefore it may also be desired to the right degree: this character then is praised, being observance of the mean in the matter of honour, though it has no recognized name. Compared with ambition, it seems to be lack of ambition; compared with lack of ambition, it seems to be ambition; compared with both at once, it seems in a way to

be both at once. This, we may observe, also happens in the case of the other virtues. But in this case the extreme characters seem to be opposed to one another [instead of to the moderate character], because the character that observes the mean has no recognized name.

5. Gentleness is moderation with respect to anger. But it must be noted that we have no recognized name for the mean, and scarcely any recognized names for the extremes. And so the term gentleness, which properly denotes an inclination towards deficiency in anger (for which also we have no recognized name), is applied to the mean.

The excess may be called wrathfulness; for the emotion concerned is wrath or anger, though the things that cause it are many and various.

He then who is angry on the right occasions and with the right persons, and also in the right manner, and at the right season, and for the right length of time, is praised; we will call him gentle, therefore, since gentleness is used as a term of praise. For the man who is called gentle wishes not to lose his balance, and not to be carried away by his emotions or passions, but to be angry only in such manner, and on such occasions, and for such period as reason shall prescribe. But he seems to err rather on the side of deficiency; he is loth to take vengeance and very ready to forgive.

But the deficiency—call it wrathlessness or what you will—is censured. Those who are not angered by what ought to anger them seem to be foolish, and so do those who are not angry as and when and with whom they ought to be; for such a man seems to feel nothing and to be pained by nothing, and, as he is never angered, to lack spirit to defend himself. But to suffer one's self to be insulted, or to look quietly on while one's friends are being insulted, shows a slavish nature.

It is possible to exceed in all points, *i.e.* to be angry with persons with whom one ought not, and at things at which one ought not to be angry, and more than one ought, and more quickly, and for a longer time. All these errors, however, are not found in the same person. That would be impossible; for evil is self-destructive, and, if it appears in its entirety, becomes quite unbearable.

So we find that wrathful men get angry very

soon, and with people with whom and at things at which they ought not, and more than they ought; but they soon get over their anger, and that is a very good point in their character. And the reason is that they do not keep in their anger, but, through the quickness of their temper, at once retaliate, and so let what is in them come to light, and then have done with it.

But those who are called choleric are excessively quick-tempered, and apt to be angered at anything and on any occasion; whence the name (ἀκρόχολοι).

Sulky men are hard to appease and their anger lasts long, because they keep it in. For so soon as we retaliate we are relieved: vengeance makes us cease from our anger, substituting a pleasant for a painful state. But the sulky man, as he does not thus relieve himself, bears the burden of his wrath about with him; for no one even tries to reason him out of it, as he does not show it, and it takes a long time to digest one's anger within one's self. Such men are exceedingly troublesome to themselves and their dearest friends.

Lastly, hard (χαλεπός) is the name we give those who are offended by things that ought not to offend them, and more than they ought, and for a longer time, and who will not be appeased without vengeance or punishment.

Of the two extremes the excess is the more opposed to gentleness; for it is commoner (as men are naturally more inclined to vengeance); and a hard-tempered person is worse to live with [than one who is too easy-tempered].

What we said some time ago[50] is made abundantly manifest by what we have just been saying; it is not easy to define how, and with whom, and at what, and for how long one ought to be angry—how far it is right to go, and at what point misconduct begins. He who errs slightly from the right course is not blamed, whether it be on the side of excess or of deficiency; for sometimes we praise those who fall short and call them gentle, and sometimes those who behave hardly are called manly, as being able to rule. But what amount and kind of error makes a man blamable can scarcely be defined; for it depends upon the particular circumstances of each case, and can only be decided by immediate perception.

But so much at least is manifest, that on the one hand the habit which observes the mean is to be praised, i.e. the habit which causes us to be angry with the right persons, at the right things, in the right manner, etc.; and that, on the other hand, all habits of excess or deficiency deserve censure—slight censure if the error be trifling, graver censure if it be considerable, and severe censure if it be great.

It is evident, therefore, that we must strive for the habit which observes the mean.

This then may be taken as our account of the habits which have to do with anger.

6. In the matter of social intercourse, i.e. the living with others and joining with them in conversation and in common occupations, some men show themselves what is called obsequious —those who to please you praise everything, and never object to anything, but think they ought always to avoid giving pain to those whom they meet. Those who take the opposite line, and object to everything and never think for a moment what pain they may give, are called cross and contentious.

It is sufficiently plain that both these habits merit censure, and that the habit which takes the middle course between them is to be commended—the habit which makes a man acquiesce in what he ought and in the right manner, and likewise refuse to acquiesce. This habit or type of character has no recognized name, but seems most nearly to resemble friendliness (φιλία). For the man who exhibits this moderation is the same sort of man that we mean when we speak of an upright friend, except that then affection also is implied. This differs from friendliness in that it does not imply emotion and affection for those with whom we associate; for he who has this quality acquiesces when he ought, not because he loves or hates, but because that is his character. He will behave thus alike to those whom he knows and to those whom he does not know, to those with whom he is intimate and to those with whom he is not intimate, only that in each case he will behave as is fitting; for we are not bound to show the same consideration to strangers as to intimates, nor to take the same care not to pain them.

We have already said in general terms that such a man will behave as he ought in his intercourse with others, but we must add that, while he tries to contribute to the pleasure of others and to avoid giving them pain, he will always be guided by reference to that which is noble and fitting. It seems to be with the pleasures and pains of social intercourse that he is concerned. Now, whenever he finds that it is not noble, or is positively hurtful to himself, to contribute to any of these pleasures, he will refuse to acquiesce and will prefer to give pain. And if the pleasure is such as to involve discredit, and no slight discredit, or some injury to him who is the source of it, while his opposition will give a little pain, he will not acquiesce, but will set his face against it. But he will behave differently according as he is in the company of great people or ordinary people, of intimate friends or mere acquaintances, and so on, rendering to each his due; preferring, apart from other considerations, to promote pleasure, and loth to give pain, but regulating his conduct by consideration of the consequences, if they be considerable —by consideration, I mean, of what is noble and fitting. And thus for the sake of great pleasure in the future he will inflict a slight pain now.

The man who observes the mean, then, is something of this sort, but has no recognized name.

The man who always makes himself pleasant, if he aims simply at pleasing and has no ulterior object in view, is called obsequious; but if he does so in order to get some profit for himself, either in the way of money or of money's worth, he is a flatterer.

But he who sets his face against everything is, as we have already said, cross and contentious.

But the extremes seem here to be opposed to one another [instead of to the mean], because there is no name for the mean.

7. The moderation which lies between boastfulness and irony (which virtue also lacks a name) seems to display itself in almost the same field.

It will be as well to examine these qualities also; for we shall know more about human character, when we have gone through each of its forms; and we shall be more fully assured that the virtues are modes of observing the mean, when we have surveyed them all and found that this is the case with every one of them.

We have already spoken of the characters that are displayed in social intercourse in the matter of pleasure and pain; let us now go on to speak in like manner of those who show themselves truthful or untruthful in what they say and do, and in the pretensions they put forward.

First of all, then, the boaster seems to be fond of pretending to things that men esteem, though he has them not, or not to such extent as he pretends; the ironical man, on the other hand, seems to disclaim what he has, or to depreciate it; while he who observes the mean, being a man who is "always himself" ($\alpha\grave{v}\theta\acute{\epsilon}\kappa\alpha\sigma\tau\acute{o}s$ $\tau\iota s$), is truthful in word and deed, confessing the simple facts about himself, and neither exaggerating nor diminishing them.

Now, each of these lines of conduct may be pursued either with an ulterior object or without one.

When he has no ulterior object in view, each man speaks and acts and lives according to his character.

But falsehood in itself is vile and blamable; truth is noble and praiseworthy in itself.

And so the truthful man, as observing the mean, is praiseworthy, while the untruthful characters are both blamable, but the boastful more than the ironical.

Let us speak then of each of them, and first of the truthful character.

We must remember that we are not speaking of the man who tells the truth in matters of business, or in matters which come within the sphere of injustice and justice (for these matters would belong to another virtue); the man we are considering is the man who in cases where no such important issues are involved is truthful in his speech and in his life, because that is his character.

Such a man would seem to be a good man ($\grave{\epsilon}\pi\iota\epsilon\iota\kappa\acute{\eta}s$). For he who loves truth, and is truthful where nothing depends upon it, will still more surely tell the truth where serious interests are involved; he will shun falsehood as a base thing here, seeing that he shunned it elsewhere, apart from any consequences: but such a man merits praise.

He inclines rather towards under-statement than over-statement of the truth; and this seems to be the more suitable course, since all exaggeration is offensive.

On the other hand, he who pretends to more than he has with no ulterior object [the boaster proper] seems not to be a good character (for if he were he would not take pleasure in falsehood), but to be silly rather than bad.

But of boasters who have an ulterior object, he whose object is reputation or honour is not very severely censured (just as the boaster proper is not), but he whose object is money, or means of making money, is held in greater reproach.

But we must observe that what distinguishes the boaster proper from the other kinds of boasters, is not his faculty of boasting, but his preference for boasting: the boaster proper is a boaster by habit, and because that is his character; just as there is on the one hand the liar proper, who delights in falsehood itself, and on the other hand the liar who lies through desire of honour or gain.

Those who boast with a view to reputation pretend to those things for which a man is commended or is thought happy; those whose motive is gain pretend to those things which are of advantage to others, and whose absence may escape detection, *e.g.* to skill in magic or in medicine. And so it is usually something of this sort that men pretend to and boast of; for the conditions specified are realized in them.

Ironical people, on the other hand, with their depreciatory way of speaking of themselves, seem to be of a more refined character; for their motive in speaking thus seems to be not love of gain, but desire to avoid parade: but what they disclaim seems also[51] to be especially that which men esteem—of which Socrates was an instance.

But those who disclaim petty advantages which they evidently possess are called affected (βαυκοπανουργοι), and are more easily held in contempt. And sometimes this self-depreciation is scarcely distinguishable from boasting, as for instance dressing like a Spartan; for there is something boastful in extreme depreciation as well as in exaggeration.

But those who employ irony in moderation, and speak ironically in matters that are not too obvious and palpable, appear to be men of refinement.

Finally, the boaster seems to be especially the opposite of the truthful man; for he is worse than the ironical man.

8. Again, since relaxation is an element in our life, and one mode of relaxation is amusing conversation, it seems that in this respect also there is a proper way of mixing with others; *i.e.* that there are things that it is right to say, and a right way of saying them: and the same with hearing; though here also it will make a difference what kind of people they are in whose presence you

are speaking, or to whom you are listening.

And it is plain that it is possible in these matters also to go beyond, or to fall short of, the mean.

Now, those who go to excess in ridicule seem to be buffoons and vulgar fellows, striving at all costs for a ridiculous effect, and bent rather on raising a laugh than on making their witticisms elegant and inoffensive to the subject of them. While those who will never say anything laughable themselves, and frown on those who do, are considered boorish and morose. But those who jest gracefully are called witty, or men of ready wit (εὐτράπελοι), as it were ready or versatile men.

For[52] a man's character seems to reveal itself in these sallies or playful movements, and so we judge of his moral constitution by them, as we judge of his body by its movements.

But through the prominence given to ridiculous things, and the excessive delight which most people take in amusement and jesting, the buffoon is often called witty because he gives delight. But that there is a difference, and a considerable difference, between the two is plain from what we have said.

An element in the character that observes the mean in these matters is tact. A man of tact will only say and listen to such things as it befits an honest man and a gentleman to say and listen to; for there are things that it is quite becoming for such a man to say and to listen to in the way of jest, and the jesting of a gentleman differs from that of a man of slavish nature, and the jesting of an educated from that of an uneducated man.

This one may see by the difference between the old comedy and the new: the fun of the earlier writers is obscenity, of the later innuendo; and there is no slight difference between the two as regards decency.

Can good jesting, then, be defined as making jests that befit a gentleman, or that do not pain the hearer, or that even give him pleasure? Nay, surely a jest that gives pleasure to the hearer is something quite indefinite, for different things are hateful and pleasant to different people.

But the things that he will listen to will be of the same sort [as those that he will say, whatever that be]: jests that a man can listen to he can, we think, make himself.

So then there are jests that he will not make [though we cannot exactly define them]; for to make a jest of a man is to vilify him in a way, and the law forbids certain kinds of vilification, and ought perhaps also to forbid certain kinds of jesting.

The refined and gentlemanly man, therefore, will thus regulate his wit, being as it were a law to himself.

This then is the character of him who observes the mean, whether we call him a man of tact or a man of ready wit.

The buffoon, on the other hand, cannot resist an opportunity for a joke, and, if he can but raise a laugh, will spare neither himself nor others, and will say things which no man of refinement would say, and some of which he would not even listen to.

The boor, lastly, is wholly useless for this kind of intercourse; he contributes nothing, and takes everything in ill part. And yet recreation and amusement seem to be necessary ingredients in our life.

In conclusion, then, the modes just described of observing the mean in social life are three in number,[53] and all have to do with conversation or joint action of some kind: but they differ in that one has to do with truth, while the other two are concerned with what is pleasant; and of the two that are concerned with pleasure, one finds its field in our amusements, the other in all other kinds of social intercourse.

9. Shame (αἰδώς) cannot properly be spoken of as a virtue; for it is more like a feeling or emotion than a habit or trained faculty. At least, it is defined as a kind of fear of disgrace, and its effects are analogous to those of the fear that is excited by danger; for men blush when they are ashamed, while the fear of death makes them pale. Both then seem to be in a way physical, which is held to be a mark of a feeling or emotion, rather than of a habit or trained faculty.

Again, it is a feeling which is not becoming at all times of life, but only in youth; it is thought proper for young people to be ready to feel shame, because, as their conduct is guided by their emotions, they often are misled, but are restrained from wrong actions by shame.

And so we praise young men who are ready to feel shame, but no one would praise a man of more advanced years for being apt to be ashamed; for we consider that he ought not to do anything which could make him ashamed of himself.

Indeed, shame is not the part of a good man, since it is occasioned by vile acts (for such acts should not be done: nor does it matter that some acts are really shameful, others shameful in public estimation only; for neither ought to be done, and so a man ought not to be ashamed); it is the part of a worthless man and the result of being such as to do something shameful.

But supposing a man's character to be such that, if he were to do one of these shameful acts, he would be ashamed, it is absurd for him to fancy that he is a good man on that account; for shame is only felt at voluntary acts, and a good man will never voluntarily do vile acts.

At the utmost, shame would be hypothetically good; that is to say, supposing he were to do the act, a good man would be ashamed: but there is nothing hypothetical about the virtues.

Again granting that it is bad to be shameless, or not to be ashamed to do shameful things, it does not therefore follow that it is good to do them and be ashamed of it.

Continence,[54] in the same way, is not a virtue, but something between virtue and vice.

But we will explain this point about continence later;[55] let us now treat of justice.

BOOK V.

THE SAME–CONCLUDED. JUSTICE

1. We now have to inquire about justice and injustice, and to ask what sort of acts they are concerned with, and in what sense justice observes the mean, and what are the extremes whose mean is that which is just. And in this inquiry we will follow the same method as before.

We see that all men intend by justice to signify the sort of habit or character that makes men apt to do what is just, and which further makes them act justly[56] and wish what is just; while by injustice they intend in like manner to signify the sort of character that makes men act unjustly and wish what is unjust. Let us lay this down, then, as an outline to work upon.

We thus oppose justice and injustice, because a habit or trained faculty differs in this respect both from a science and a faculty or power. I mean that whereas both of a pair of opposites come under the same science or power, a habit which produces a certain result does not also produce the opposite result; *e.g.* health produces healthy manifestations only, and not unhealthy; for we say a man has a healthy gait when he walks like a man in health.

[Not that the two opposites are unconnected.] In the first place, a habit is often known by the opposite habit, and often by its causes and results: if we know what good condition is, we can learn from that what bad condition is; and, again, from that which conduces to good condition we can infer what good condition itself is, and conversely from the latter can infer the former. For instance, if good condition be firmness of flesh, it follows that bad condition is flabbiness of flesh, and that what tends to produce firmness of flesh conduces to good condition.

And, in the second place, if one of a pair of opposite terms have more senses than one, the other term will also, as a general rule, have more than one; so that here, if the term "just" have several senses, the term "unjust" also will have several.

And in fact it seems that both "justice" and "injustice" have several senses, but, as the different things covered by the common name are very closely related, the fact that they are different escapes notice and does not strike us, as it does when there is a great disparity—a great difference, say, in outward appearance—as it strikes every one, for instance, that the κλείς (*clavis,* collar-bone) which lies under the neck of an animal is different from the κλείς (*clavis,* key) with which we fasten the door.

Let us then ascertain in how many different senses we call a man unjust.

Firstly, he who breaks the laws is considered unjust, and, secondly, he who takes more than his share, or the unfair man.

Plainly, then, a just man will mean (1) a law-abiding and (2) a fair man.

A just thing then will be (1) that which is in accordance with the law, (2) that which is fair; and the unjust thing will be (1) that which is contrary to law, (2) that which is unfair.

But since the unjust man, in one of the two senses of the word, takes more than his share, the sphere of his action will be good things—not all good things, but those with which good and ill fortune are concerned, which are always good in themselves, but not always good for us—the things that we men pray for and pursue, whereas we ought rather to pray that what is good in itself

may be good for us, while we choose that which is good for us.

But the unjust man does not always take more than his share; he sometimes takes less, viz. of those things which are bad in the abstract; but as the lesser evil is considered to be in some sort good, and taking more means taking more good, he is said to take more than his share. But in any case he is unfair; for this is a wider term which includes the other.

We found that the law-breaker is unjust, and the law-abiding man is just. Hence it follows that whatever is according to law is just in one sense of the word. [And this, we see, is in fact the case;] for what the legislator prescribes is according to law, and is always said to be just.

Now, the laws prescribe about all manner of things, aiming at the common interest of all, or of the best men, or of those who are supreme in the state (position in the state being determined by reference to personal excellence, or to some other such standard); and so in one sense we apply the term just to whatever tends to produce and preserve the happiness of the community, and the several elements of that happiness. The law bids us display courage (as not to leave our ranks, or run, or throw away our arms), and temperance (as not to commit adultery or outrage), and gentleness (as not to strike or revile our neighbours), and so on with all the other virtues and vices, enjoining acts and forbidding them, rightly when it is a good law, not so rightly when it is a hastily improvised one.

Justice, then, in this sense of the word, is complete virtue, with the addition that it is displayed towards others. On this account it is often spoken of as the chief of the virtues, and such that "neither evening nor morning star is so lovely;" and the saying has become proverbial, "Justice sums up all virtues in itself."

It is complete virtue, first of all, because it is the exhibition of complete virtue: it is also complete because he that has it is able to exhibit virtue in dealing with his neighbours, and not merely in his private affairs; for there are many who can be virtuous enough at home, but fail in dealing with their neighbours.

This is the reason why people commend the saying of Bias, "Office will show the man:" for he that is in office *ipso facto* stands in relation to others,[57] and has dealings with them.

This, too, is the reason why justice alone of all

the virtues is thought to be another's good, as implying this relation to others; for it is another's interest that justice aims at—the interest, namely, of the ruler or of our fellow-citizens.

While then the worst man is he who displays vice both in his own affairs and in his dealings with his friends, the best man is not he who displays virtue in his own affairs merely, but he who displays virtue towards others; for this is the hard thing to do.

Justice, then, in this sense of the word, is not a part of virtue, but the whole of it; and the injustice which is opposed to it is not a part of vice, but the whole of it.

How virtue differs from justice in this sense is plain from what we have said; it is one and the same character differently viewed:[58] viewed in relation to others, this character is justice; viewed simply as a certain character, it is virtue.

2. We have now to examine justice in that sense in which it is a part of virtue—for we maintain that there is such a justice—and also the corresponding kind of injustice.

That the word is so used is easily shown. In the case of the other kinds of badness, the man who displays them, though he acts unjustly [in one sense of the word], yet does not take more than his share: for instance, when a man throws away his shield through cowardice, or reviles another through ill temper, or through illiberality refuses to help another with money. But when he takes more than his share, he displays perhaps no one of these vices, nor does he display them all, yet he displays a kind of badness (for we blame him), namely, injustice [in the second sense of the word].

We see, then, that there is another sense of the word injustice, in which it stands for a part of that injustice which is coextensive with badness, and another sense of the word unjust, in which it is applied to a part only of those things to which it is applied in the former sense of "contrary to law."

Again, if one man commits adultery with a view to gain, and makes money by it, and another man does it from lust, with expenditure and loss of money, the latter would not be called grasping, but profligate, while the former would not be called profligate, but unjust [in the narrower sense]. Evidently, then, he would be called unjust because of his gain.

Once more, acts of injustice,[59] in the former sense, are always referred to some particular vice, as if a man commits adultery, to profligacy; if he deserts his comrade in arms, to cowardice; if he strikes another, to anger: but in a case of unjust gain, the act is referred to no other vice than injustice.

It is plain then that, besides the injustice which is coextensive with vice, there is a second kind of injustice, which is a particular kind of vice, bearing the same name[60] as the first, because the same generic conception forms the basis of its definition; *i.e.* both display themselves in dealings with others, but the sphere of the second is limited to such things as honour, wealth, security (perhaps some one name might be found to include all this class) and its motive is the pleasure of gain, while the sphere of the first is coextensive with the sphere of the good man's action.

We have ascertained, then, that there are more kinds of justice than one, and that there is another kind besides that which is identical with complete virtue; we now have to find what it is, and what are its characteristics.

We have already distinguished two senses in which we speak of things as unjust, viz. (1) contrary to law, (2) unfair; and two senses in which we speak of things as just, viz. (1) according to law, (2) fair.

The injustice which we have already considered corresponds to unlawful.

But since unfair is not the same as unlawful, but differs from it as the part from the whole (for unfair is always unlawful, but unlawful is not always unfair), unjust and injustice in the sense corresponding to unfair will not be the same as unjust and injustice in the sense corresponding to unlawful, but different as the part from the whole; for this injustice is a part of complete injustice, and the corresponding justice is a part of complete justice. We must therefore speak of justice and injustice, and of that which is just and that which is unjust, in this limited sense.

We may dismiss, then, the justice which coincides with complete virtue and the corresponding injustice, the former being the exercise of complete virtue towards others, the latter of complete vice.

It is easy also to see how we are to define that which is just and that which is unjust in their corresponding senses [according to law and contrary to law]. For the great bulk, we may say, of the acts which are according to law are the acts which the law commands with a view to complete virtue; for the law orders us to display all the virtues and none of the vices in our lives.

But the acts which tend to produce complete virtue are those of the acts according to law which are prescribed with reference to the education of a man as a citizen. As for the education of the individual as such, which tends to make him simply a good man, we may reserve the question whether it belongs to the science of the state or not; for it is possible that to be a good man is not the same as to be a good citizen of any state whatever.[61]

But of justice as a part of virtue, and of that which is just in the corresponding sense, one kind is that which has to do with the distribution of honour, wealth, and the other things that are divided among the members of the body politic (for in these circumstances it is possible for one man's share to be unfair or fair as compared with another's); and another kind is that which has to give redress in private transactions.

The latter kind is again subdivided; for private transactions are (1) voluntary, (2) involuntary.

"Voluntary transactions or contracts" are such as selling, buying, lending at interest, pledging, lending without interest, depositing, hiring: these are called "voluntary contracts," because the parties enter into them of their own will.

"Involuntary transactions," again, are of two kinds: one involving secrecy, such as theft, adultery, poisoning, procuring, corruption of slaves, assassination, false witness; the other involving open violence, such as assault, seizure of the person, murder, rape, maiming, slander, contumely.

3. The unjust man [in this limited sense of the word], we say, is unfair, and that which is unjust is unfair.

Now, it is plain that there must be a mean which lies between what is unfair on this side and on that. And this is that which is fair or equal; for any act that admits of a too much and a too little admits also of that which is fair.

If then that which is unjust be unfair, that which is just will be fair, which indeed is admitted by all without further proof.

But since that which is fair or equal is a mean between two extremes, it follows that what is just will be a mean.

But equality or fairness implies two terms at least.[62]

It follows, then, that that which is just is both a mean quantity and also a fair amount relatively to something else and to certain persons—in other words, that, on the one hand, as a mean quantity it implies certain other quantities, i.e. a more and a less; and, on the other hand, as an equal or fair amount it involves two quantities,[63] and as a just amount it involves certain persons.

That which is just, then, implies four terms at least: two persons to whom justice is done, and two things.

And there must be the same "equality" [i.e. the same ratio] between the persons and the things: as the things are to one another, so must the persons be. For if the persons be not equal, their shares will not be equal; and this is the source of disputes and accusations, when persons who are equal do not receive equal shares, or when persons who are not equal receive equal shares.

This is also plainly indicated by the common phrase "according to merit." For in distribution all men allow that what is just must be according to merit or worth of some kind, but they do not all adopt the same standard of worth; in democratic states they take free birth as the standard,[64] in oligarchic states they take wealth, in others noble birth, and in the true aristocratic state virtue or personal merit.

We see, then, that that which is just is in some sort proportionate. For not abstract numbers only, but all things that can be numbered, admit of proportion; proportion meaning equality of ratios, and requiring four terms at least.

That discrete proportion[65] requires four terms is evident at once. Continuous proportion also requires four terms: for in it one term is employed as two and is repeated; for instance, $\frac{a}{b} = \frac{b}{c}$. The term b then is repeated; and so, counting b twice over, we find that the terms of the proportion are four in number.

That which is just, then, requires that there be four terms at least, and that the ratio between the two pairs be the same, i.e. that the persons stand to one another in the same ratio as the things.

Let us say, then, $\frac{a}{b} = \frac{c}{d}$, or *alternando* $\frac{a}{c} = \frac{b}{d}$.

The sums of these new pairs then will stand to one another in the original ratio $\left[i.e. \ \frac{a + c}{b + d} = \frac{a}{b} \text{ or } \frac{c}{d} \right]$

But these are the pairs which the distribution joins together;[66] and if the things be assigned in this manner, the distribution is just.

This joining, then, of a to c and of b to d is that which is just in distribution; and that which is just in this sense is a mean quantity, while that which is unjust is that which is disproportionate; for that which is proportionate is a mean quantity, but that which is just is, as we said, proportionate.

This proportion is called by the mathematicians a geometrical proportion; for it is when four terms are in geometrical proportion that the sum [of the first and third] is to the sum [of the second and fourth] in the original ratio [of the first to the second or the third to the fourth].

But this proportion [as applied in justice] cannot be a continuous proportion; for one term cannot represent both a person and a thing.

That which is just, then, in this sense is that which is proportionate; but that which is unjust is that which is disproportionate. In the latter case one quantity becomes more or too much, the other less or too little. And this we see in practice; for he who wrongs another gets too much, and he who is wronged gets too little of the good in question: but of the evil conversely; for the lesser evil stands in the place of good when compared with the greater evil: for the lesser evil is more desirable than the greater, but that which is desirable is good, and that which is more desirable is a greater good.

This then is one form of that which is just.

4. It remains to treat of the other form, viz. that which is just in the way of redress, the sphere of which is private transactions, whether voluntary or involuntary.

This differs in kind from the former.

For that which is just in the distribution of a common stock of good things is always in accordance with the proportion above specified (even when it is a common fund that has to be divided, the sums which the several participants take must bear the same ratio to one another as the sums they have put in), and that which is unjust in the corresponding sense is that which violates this proportion.

But that which is just in private transactions[67] is indeed fair or equal in some sort, and that which is unjust is unfair or unequal; but the proportion to be observed here is not a geometrical proportion as above, but an arithmetical one.

For it makes no difference whether a good man defrauds a bad one, or a bad man a good one, nor whether a man who commits an adultery be a good or a bad man; the law looks only to the difference created by the injury, treating the parties themselves as equal, and only asking whether the one has done, and the other suffered, injury or damage.

That which is unjust, then, is here something unequal [or unfair] which the judge tries to make equal [or fair]. For even when one party is struck and the other strikes, or one kills and the other is killed, that which is suffered and that which is done may be said to be unequally or unfairly divided; the judge then tries to restore equality by the penalty or loss which he inflicts upon the offender, subtracting it from his gain.

For in such cases, though the terms are not always quite appropriate, we generally talk of the doer's "gain" (*e.g.* the striker's) and the sufferer's "loss;" but when the suffering has been assessed by the court, what the doer gets is called "loss" or penalty, and what the sufferer gets is called "gain."

What is fair or equal, then, is a mean between more or too much and less or too little; but gain and loss are both more or too much and less or too little in opposite ways, *i.e.* gain is more or too much good and less or too little evil, and loss the opposite of this.

And in the mean between them, as we found, lies that which is equal or fair, which we say is just.

That which is just in the way of redress, then, is the mean between loss and gain.

When disputes arise, therefore, men appeal to the judge:[68] and an appeal to the judge is an appeal to that which is just; for the judge is intended to be as it were a living embodiment of that which is just; and men require of a judge that he shall be moderate [or observe the mean], and sometimes even call judges "mediators"

($\mu\epsilon\sigma\iota\delta\iotaο\upsilon\varsigma$), signifying that if they get the mean they will get that which is just.

That which is just, then, must be a sort of mean, if the judge be a "mediator."

But the judge restores equality; it is as if he found a line divided into two unequal parts, and were to cut off from the greater that by which it exceeds the half, and to add this to the less.

But when the whole is equally divided, the parties are said to have their own, each now receiving an equal or fair amount.

But the equal or fair amount is here the *arithmetic* mean between the more or too much and the less or too little. And so it is called δίκαιον (just) because there is equal division (δίχα); δίκαιον being in fact equivalent to δίχαιον, and δικαστής (judge) to διχαστής.

If you cut off a part from one of two equal lines and add it to the other, the second is now greater than the first by two such parts (for if you had only cut off the part from the first without adding it to the second, the second would have been greater by only one such part); the second exceeds the mean by one such part, and the mean also exceeds the first by one.

Thus we can tell how much to take away from him who has more or too much, and how much to add to him who has less or too little: to the latter's portion must be added that by which it falls short of the mean, and from the former's portion must be taken away that by which it exceeds the mean.

To illustrate this, let AA', BB', CC' be three equal lines:—

```
A      E               A'
_____

B                      B'
_____

D   C   Z              C'
_____
```

From AA' let AE be cut off; and let CD [equal to AE] be added to CC'; then the whole D CC' exceeds EA' by CD and CZ [equal to AE or CD], and exceeds BB' by CD.

And this[69] holds good not only in geometry, but in the arts also; they could not exist unless that which is worked upon received an impression corresponding in kind and quantity and quality to the exertions of the artist.

But these terms, "loss" and "gain," are borrowed from voluntary exchange. For in voluntary exchange having more than your own is called gaining, and having less than you started with is called losing (in buying and selling, I mean, and in the other transactions in which the law allows free play); but when the result to each is neither more nor less but the very same amount with which he started, then they say that they have their own, and are neither losers nor gainers. That which is just, then, is a mean between a gain and a loss, which are both contrary to the intention,[70] and consists in having after the transaction the equivalent of that which you had before it.

5. Some people, indeed, go so far as to think that simple requital is just. And so the Pythagoreans used to teach; for their definition of what is just was simply that what a man has done to another should be done to him.

But this simple requital does not correspond either with that which is just in distribution or with that which is just in the way of redress (though they try to make out that this is the meaning of the Rhadamanthine rule—

"To suffer that which thou hast done is just");

for in many cases it is quite different. For instance, if an officer strike a man, he ought not to be struck in return; and if a man strike an officer, he ought not merely to be struck, but to be punished.

Further, it makes a great difference whether what was done to the other was done with his consent or against it.

But it is true that, in the interchange of services, this is the rule of justice that holds society together, viz. requital—but proportionate requital, and not simple repayment of equals for equals. For the very existence of a state depends upon proportionate return. If men have suffered evil, they seek to return it; if not, if they cannot requite an injury, we count their condition slavish. And again, if men have received good, they seek to repay it: for otherwise there is no exchange of services; but it is by this exchange that we are bound together in society.

This is the reason why we set up a temple of the graces [charities, χάριτες] in sight of all men, to remind them to repay that which they receive; for this is the special characteristic of charity or grace. We ought to return the good offices of those who have been gracious to us, and then again to take the lead in good offices towards them.

But proportionate interchange is brought about by "cross conjunction."

For instance, let A stand for a builder, B for a shoemaker, C for a house, D for shoes.

The builder then must take some of the shoemaker's work, and give him his own work in exchange.

Now, the desired result will be brought about if requital take place after proportionate equality has first been established.

If this be not done, there is no equality, and intercourse becomes impossible; for there is no reason why the work of the one should not be worth more than the work of the other. Their work, then, must be brought to an equality [or appraised by a common standard of value].

This is no less true of the other arts and professions [than of building and shoemaking]; for they could not exist if that which the patient [client or consumer] receives did not correspond in quantity and quality with that which the agent [artist or producer] does or produces.

For it is not between two physicians that exchange of services takes place, but between a physician and a husbandman, and generally between persons of different professions and of unequal worth; these unequal persons, then, have to be reduced to equality [or measured by a common standard].

All things or services, then, which are to be exchanged must be in some way reducible to a common measure.

For this purpose money was invented, and serves as a medium of exchange; for by it we can measure everything, and so can measure the superiority and inferiority of different kinds of work—the number of shoes, for instance, that is equivalent to a house or to a certain quantity of food.

What is needed then is that so many shoes shall bear to a house (or a measure of corn) the same ratio that a builder [or a husbandman] bears to a shoemaker. For unless this adjustment be effected, no dealing or exchange of services can take place; and it cannot be effected unless the things to be exchanged can be in some way made equal.

We want, therefore, some one common measure of value, as we said before.

This measure is, in fact, the need for each other's services which holds the members of a society together; for if men had no needs, or no common needs, there would either be no exchange, or a different sort of exchange from that which we know.

But money has been introduced by convention as a kind of substitute for need or demand; and this is why we call it νόμισμα, because its value is derived, not from nature, but from law (νόμος), and can be altered or abolished at will.

Requital then will take place after the wares have been so equated [by the adjustment of prices] that the quantity of shoemaker's work bears to the quantity of husbandman's work [which exchanges for it] the same ratio that husbandman bears to shoemaker.[71] But this adjustment must be made[72] not at the time of exchange (for then one of the two parties would get both the advantages[73]), but while they are still in possession of their own wares; if this be done, they are put on an equal footing and can make an exchange, because this kind of equality can be established between them.

If A stand for a husbandman and C for a certain quantity of his work (or corn), B will stand for a shoemaker, and D for that quantity of shoemaker's work that is valued as equal to C.

If they could not requite each other in this way, interchange of services would be impossible.

That it is our need which forms, as it were, a common bond to hold society together, is seen from the fact that people do not exchange unless they are in need of one another's services (each party of the services of the other, or at least one party of the service of the other), as when that which one has, e.g. wine, is needed by other people who offer to export corn in return. This article, then [the corn to be exported], must be made equal [to the wine that is imported].

But even if we happen to want nothing at the moment, money is a sort of guarantee that we shall be able to make an exchange at any future time when we happen to be in need; for the man who brings money must always be able to take goods in exchange.

Money is, indeed, subject to the same conditions as other things: its value is not always the same; but still it tends to be more constant than the value of anything else.

Everything, then, must be assessed in money; for this enables men always to exchange their services, and so makes society possible.

Money, then, as a standard, serves to reduce things to a common measure, so that equal amounts of each may be taken; for there would be no society if there were no exchange, and no exchange if there were no equality, and no equality if it were not possible to reduce things to a common measure.

In strictness, indeed, it is impossible to find any common measure for things so extremely diverse; but our needs give a standard which is sufficiently accurate for practical purposes.

There must, then, be some one common symbol for this, and that a conventional symbol; so we call it money ($\nu\acute{o}\mu\iota\sigma\mu\alpha$, $\nu\acute{o}\mu o\varsigma$). Money makes all things commensurable, for all things are valued in money. For instance, let A stand for a house, B for ten minae, C for a bed; and let $A = \dfrac{B}{2}$, taking a house to be worth or equal to five minae, and let C (the bed) $= \dfrac{B}{10}$. We see at once, then, how many beds are equal to one house, viz. five.

It is evident that, before money came into use, all exchange must have been of this kind: it makes no difference whether you give five beds for a house, or the value of five beds.

Thus we have described that which is unjust and that which is just. And now that these are determined, we can see that doing justice is a mean between doing and suffering injustice; for the one is having too much, and the other too little, or less than one's due.

We see also that the virtue justice is a kind of moderation or observance of the mean, but not quite in the same way as the virtues hitherto spoken of. It does indeed choose a mean, but both the extremes fall under the single vice injustice.[74]

We see also that justice is that habit in respect of which the just man is said to be apt to do deliberately that which is just; that is to say, in dealings between himself and another (or between two other parties), to apportion things, not so that he shall get more or too much, and his neighbour less or too little, of what is desirable, and conversely with what is disadvantageous, but so that each shall get his fair, that is, his proportionate share, and similarly in dealings between two other parties.

Injustice, on the contrary, is the character which chooses what is unjust, which is a disproportionate amount, that is, too much and too little of what is advantageous and disadvantageous respectively.

Thus injustice, as we say, is both an excess and a deficiency, in that it chooses both an excess and a deficiency—in one's own affairs choosing excess of what is, as a general rule, advantageous, and deficiency of what is disadvantageous; in the affairs of others making a similarly disproportionate assignment, though in which way the proportion is violated will depend upon circumstances.

But of the two sides of the act of injustice, suffering is a lesser wrong than doing the injustice.

Let this, then, be accepted as our account, in general terms, of the nature of justice and injustice respectively, and of that which is just and that which is unjust.

6. But since it is possible for a man to do an act of injustice without yet being unjust, what acts of injustice are there, such that the doing of them stamps a man at once as unjust in this or that particular way, e.g. as a thief, or an adulterer, or a robber?

Perhaps we ought to reply that there is no such difference in the acts.[75] A man might commit adultery, knowing what he was about, and yet be acting not from a deliberate purpose at all, but from a momentary passion. In such a case, then, a man acts unjustly, but is not unjust; e.g. is not a thief though he commits a theft, and is not an adulterer though he commits adultery, and so on.[76]

We have already explained the relation which requital bears to that which is just. But we must not fail to notice that what we are seeking is at once that which is just simply [or without any qualifying epithet], and that which is just in a state or between citizens.[77] Now, this implies men who associate together in order to supply their deficiencies, being free men, and upon a footing of equality, either absolute or proportionate.

Between those who are not upon this footing, then, we cannot speak of that which is just as between citizens (though there is something that can be called just metaphorically). For the term just cannot be properly applied, except where men have a law to appeal to,[78] and the existence of law implies the existence of injustice; for the administration of the law is the discrimination of what is just from what is unjust.

But injustice implies an act of injustice (though an act of injustice does not always imply injustice) which is taking too much of the goods and too little of the evils of life. And so we do not allow an individual to rule over us, but reason or law; for an individual is apt thus to take more for himself, and to become a tyrant.

The magistrate's function, then, is to secure that which is just, and if that which is just, then that which is equal or fair. But it seems that he gets no advantage from his office, if he is just (for he does not take a larger share of the good things of life, except when that larger share is proportionate to his worth; he works, therefore, in the interests of others, which is the reason why justice is sometimes called "another's good," as we remarked before).[79] Some salary, therefore, must be given him, and this he receives in the shape of honours and privileges; and it is when magistrates are not content with these that they make themselves tyrants.

That which is just as between master and slave, or between father and child, is not the same as this, though like. We cannot speak (without qualification) of injustice towards what is part of one's self—and a man's chattels and his children (until they are of a certain age and are separated from their parent) are as it were a part of him—for no one deliberately chooses to injure himself; so that a man cannot be unjust towards himself.

We cannot speak in this case, then, of that which is unjust, or of that which is just as between citizens; for that, we found, is according to law, and subsists between those whose situation implies law, i.e., as we found, those who participate equally or fairly in governing and being governed.

The term just, therefore, is more appropriate to a man's relations to his wife than to his relations to his children and his chattels, and we do speak in this sense of that which is just in a family; but even this is not the same as that which is just between citizens.[80]

7. Now, of that which is just as between citizens, part is natural, part is conventional. That is

natural which has the same validity everywhere, and does not depend on our accepting or rejecting it; that is conventional which at the outset may be determined in this way or in that indifferently, but which when once determined is no longer indifferent; e.g. that a man's ransom be a mina, or that a sacrifice consist of a goat and not of two sheep; and, again, those ordinances which are made for special occasions, such as the sacrifice to Brasidas [at Amphipolis], and all ordinances that are of the nature of a decree.

Now, there are people who think that what is just is always conventional, because that which is natural is invariable, and has the same validity everywhere, as fire burns here and in Persia, while that which is just is seen to be not invariable.

But this is not altogether true, though it is true in a way. Among the gods, indeed, we may venture to say it is not true at all; but of that which is just among us part is natural, though all is subject to change. Though all is subject to change, nevertheless, I repeat, part is natural and part not.

Nor is it hard to distinguish, among things that may be other than they are, that which is natural from that which is not natural but dependent on law or convention, though both are alike variable. In other fields we can draw the same distinction; we say, for instance, that the right hand is naturally the stronger, though in any man the left may become equally strong.

And so, of that which is just, that part which is conventional and prescribed with a view to a particular end[81] varies as measures vary; for the measures of wine and of corn are not everywhere the same, but larger where the dealers buy, and smaller where they sell.[82] So I say that which is just not by nature but merely by human ordinance is not the same everywhere, any more than constitutions are everywhere the same, though there is but one constitution that is naturally the best everywhere.

The terms "just" and "lawful" in each of their several senses stand for universal notions which embrace a number of particulars; i.e. the acts are many, but the notion is one, for it is applied to all alike.

"That which is unjust," we must notice, is different from "an act of injustice," and "that which is just" from "an act of justice:" for a thing is unjust either by nature or by ordinance; but this same thing when done is called "an act of injustice," though before it was done it could only be called unjust. And so with "an act of justice" (δικαίωμα); though in the latter case we rather employ δικαιοπράγημα as the generic term, and restrict δικαίωμα to the correction of an act of injustice. But as to the several species of acts of justice and injustice, we must postpone for the present the inquiry into their nature and number and the ground which they cover.

8. Now that we have ascertained what is just and what is unjust, we may say that a man acts unjustly or justly when he does these things voluntarily; but when he does them involuntarily, he does not, strictly speaking, act either unjustly or justly, but only "accidentally," i.e. he does a thing which happens to be just or unjust.[83] For whether an act is or is not to be called an act of injustice (or of justice) depends upon whether it is voluntary or involuntary; for if it be voluntary the agent is blamed, and at the same time the act becomes an act of injustice: so something unjust may be done, and yet it may not be an act of injustice, i.e. if this condition of voluntariness be absent.

By a voluntary act I mean, as I explained before, anything which, being within the doer's control, is done knowingly (i.e. with knowledge of the person, the instrument, and the result; e.g. the person whom and the instrument with which he is striking, and the effect of the blow), without the intervention at any point of accident or constraint; e.g. if another take your hand and with it strike a third person, that is not a voluntary act of yours, for it was not within your control; again, the man you strike may be your father, and you may know that it is a man, or perhaps that it is one of the company, that you are striking but not know that it is your father; and it must be understood that the same distinction is to be made with regard to the result, and, in a word, to the whole act. That then which either is done in ignorance, or, though not done in ignorance, is not under our control, or is done under compulsion, is involuntary; besides which, there are many natural processes in which we knowingly take an active or a passive part, which cannot be called either voluntary or involuntary, such as growing old and dying.

An accidentally unjust act and an accidentally just act are equally possible; e.g. a man might restore a deposit against his will for fear of con-sequences, and then you could not say that he did what was just or acted justly except accidentally;[84] and, similarly, a man who against his will was forcibly prevented from restoring a deposit would be said only accidentally to act unjustly or to do that which is unjust.

Voluntary acts, again, are divided into (1) those that are done of set purpose, and (2) those that are done without set purpose; i.e. (1) those that are done after previous deliberation, and (2) those that are done without previous deliberation.

Now, there are three ways in which we may hurt our neighbour. Firstly, a hurt done in ignorance is generally called a mistake when there is a misconception as to the person affected, or the thing done, or the instrument, or the result; e.g. I may not think to hit, or not to hit with this instrument, or not to hit this person, or not to produce this effect, but an effect follows other than that which was present to my mind; I may mean to inflict a prick, not a wound, or not to wound the person whom I wound, or not to deal a wound of this kind.

But [if we draw the distinction more accurately] when the hurt comes about contrary to what might reasonably be expected, it may be called a mishap: but when, though it is not contrary to what might reasonably be expected, there is still no vicious intention, it is a mistake; for a man makes a mistake when he sets the train of events in motion,[85] but he is unfortunate when an external agency interferes.[86]

Secondly, when the agent acts with knowledge but without previous deliberation, it is an act of injustice; e.g. when he is impelled by anger or any of the other passions to which man is necessarily or naturally subject. In doing such hurt and committing such errors, the doer acts unjustly and the acts are acts of injustice, though they are not such as to stamp him as unjust or wicked; for the hurt is not done out of wickedness.

But, thirdly, when it is done of set purpose, the doer is unjust and wicked.

On this account acts done in anger are rightly held not to be done of malice aforethought; for he who gave the provocation began it, not he who did the deed in a passion.

Again, in such cases as this last, what men dispute about is usually not whether the deed was done or not, but what the justice of the case is; for it is an apparent injustice that stirs the assailant's wrath. There is a difference between cases of this kind and disputes about contracts: in the latter the question is a question of fact, and one or other of the parties must be a vicious character, unless his memory be at fault; but in these cases they agree about the facts, but differ as to which side is in the right (whereas the deliberate aggressor knows very well the rights of the case), so that the one thinks that he is wronged, while the other thinks differently.

But if a man hurt another of set purpose, he acts unjustly, and acts of injustice (*i.e.* violations of what is proportionate and fair), when so done, stamp the doer as an unjust character.

In like manner a man is a just character when he of set purpose acts justly; but he is said to act justly if he merely do voluntarily that which is just.

Of involuntary injuries, on the other hand, some are pardonable, some unpardonable. Errors that are committed not merely in ignorance but by reason of ignorance are pardonable; but those that are committed not through ignorance but rather in ignorance, through some unnatural or inhuman passion, are not pardonable.

9. But it may be doubted whether we have sufficiently explained what it is to suffer and to do injustice. First of all, are these terms applicable to such a case as that which is described in those strange verses of Euripides?

"A. I slew my mother: that is all my tale.
P. But say, did both or neither will the deed?"

Is it really possible, I mean, to suffer injustice [or be wronged] voluntarily? or is suffering injustice always involuntary, as doing injustice is always voluntary?

Again, is suffering injustice always one way or the other (as doing injustice is always voluntary), or is it sometimes voluntary and sometimes involuntary?

Similarly with regard to having justice done to you: doing justice is always voluntary [as doing injustice is], so that one might expect that there is the same relation in both cases between the active and the passive, and that suffering injustice and having justice done to you are either both voluntary or both involuntary. But it would surely be absurd to maintain, even with regard to

having justice done to you, that it is always voluntary; for some that have justice done to them certainly do not will it.

Again we may raise the question in this [more general] form: Can a man who has that which is unjust done to him always be said to suffer injustice [or be wronged]? or are there further conditions necessary for suffering as there are for doing injustice?

Both what I do and what I suffer may be (as we saw) "accidentally" just; and so also it may be "accidentally" unjust: for doing that which is unjust is not identical with doing injustice, nor is suffering that which is unjust the same as suffering injustice; and similarly with doing justice and having justice done to you. For to have injustice done to you implies some one that does injustice, and to have justice done to you implies some one that does justice.

But if to do injustice means simply to hurt a man voluntarily, and voluntarily means with knowledge of the person, the instrument, and the manner, then the incontinent man, who voluntarily hurts himself, will voluntarily suffer injustice, and it will be possible for a man to do injustice to himself—the possibility of which last is also one of the questions in dispute.

Again, a man might, through incontinence, voluntarily suffer himself to be hurt by another also acting voluntarily; so that in this case also a man might voluntarily suffer injustice.

I think rather that the above definition is incorrect, and that to "hurting with knowledge of the person, the instrument, and the manner," we must add "against his wish." If we define it so, then a man may voluntarily be hurt and suffer that which is unjust, but cannot voluntarily have injustice done to him. (For no one *wishes* to be hurt,—even the incontinent man does not wish it, but acts contrary to his wish. No one wishes for anything that he does not think good; what the incontinent man does is not that which he thinks he ought to do.) But he that gives, as Glaucus gives to Diomede in Homer—

"Gold for his bronze, fivescore kine's worth for nine,"

does not suffer injustice; for the giving rests with him, but suffering injustice does not rest with one's self; there must be some one to do injustice.

It is plain, then, that suffering injustice cannot be voluntary.

There are still two questions that we purposed to discuss: (1) Is it the man who assigns or the man who receives a disproportionately large share that does injustice? (2) Is it possible to do injustice to yourself?

In the former case, *i.e.* if he who assigns and not he who receives the undue share does injustice, then if a man knowingly and voluntarily gives too much to another and too little to himself, he does injustice to himself. And this is what moderate persons are often thought to do; for the equitable man is apt to take less than his due. But the case is hardly so simple: it may be that he took a larger share of some other good, *e.g.* of good fame or of that which is intrinsically noble.

Again, the difficulty may be got over by reference to our definition of doing injustice; for in this case nothing is done to the man against his wish, so that no injustice is done him, but at most only harm.

It is plain, moreover, that the man who makes the unjust award does injustice, but not always he who gets more than his share; for a man does not always do injustice when we can say of what he does that it is unjust, but only when we can say that he voluntarily does that which is unjust; and that we can only say of the prime mover in the action, which in this case is the distributor and not the receiver.

Again, there are many senses of the word "do," and in a certain sense an inanimate instrument, or my hand, or again my slave under my orders, may be said to slay; but though these may be said to do what is unjust, they cannot be said to act unjustly or to do an act of injustice.

Again, if a man unwittingly gives unjust judgment, he does not commit injustice in the sense of contravening that which is just according to law, nor is his judgment unjust in this sense, but in a certain sense it is unjust; for there is a difference between that which is just according to law and that which is just in the primary sense of the word: but if he knowingly gives unjust judgment, he is himself grasping at more than his share, in the shape either of favour with one party or vengeance on the other. The judge, then, who gives unjust judgment on these grounds, takes more than his due, quite as much

as if he received a share of the unjust award; for even in the latter case a judge who awards a piece of land would receive, not land, but money.

Men fancy that as it is in their power to act unjustly, so it is an easy matter to be just. But it is not so. To lie with your neighbour's wife, or to strike your neighbour, or to pass certain coins from your hand to his is easy enough, and always within your power, but to do these acts as the outcome of a certain character is not an easy matter, nor one which is always within your power.[87]

Similarly men think that to know what is just and what is unjust needs no great wisdom, since any one can inform himself about those things which the law prescribes (though these things are only accidentally, not essentially, just): but to know how these acts must be done and how these distributions must be made in order to be just,—that indeed is a harder matter than to know what conduces to health; though that is no easy matter. It is easy enough to know the meaning of honey, and wine, and hellebore, and cautery, and the knife, but to know how, and to whom, and when they must be applied in order to produce health, is so far from being easy that to have this knowledge is to be a physician.

For the same reason, some people think that the just man is as able to act unjustly as justly, for he is not less but rather more capable than another of performing the several acts, *e.g.* of lying with a woman or of striking a blow, as the courageous man is rather more capable than another of throwing away his shield and turning his back and running away anywhere. But to play the coward or to act unjustly means not merely to do such an act (though the doer might be said "accidentally" to act unjustly), but to do it in a certain frame of mind; just as to act the part of a doctor and to heal does not mean simply to apply the knife or not to apply it, to give or to withold a drug, but to do this in a particular fashion.

Justice, lastly, implies persons who participate in those things that, generally speaking, are good, but who can have too much or too little of them. For some—for the gods perhaps—no amount of them is too much; and for others—for the incurably vicious—no amount is beneficial, they are always hurtful; but for the rest of mankind they are useful within certain limits: justice, therefore, is essentially human.

10. We have next to speak of equity and of that which is equitable, and to inquire how equity is related to justice, and that which is equitable to that which is just. For, on consideration, they do not seem to be absolutely identical, nor yet generically different. At one time we praise that which is equitable and the equitable man, and even use the word metaphorically as a term of praise synonymous with good, showing that we consider that the more equitable a thing is the better it is. At another time we reflect and find it strange that what is equitable should be praiseworthy, if it be different from what is just; for, we argue, if it be something else, either what is just is not good, or what is equitable is not good; if both be good, they are the same.

These are the reflections which give rise to the difficulty about what is equitable. Now, in a way, they are all correct and not incompatible with one another; for that which is equitable, though it is better than that which is just (in one sense of the word), is yet itself just, and is not better than what is just in the sense of being something generically distinct from it. What is just, then, and what is equitable are generically the same, and both are good, though what is equitable is better.

But what obscures the matter is that though what is equitable is just, it is not identical with, but a correction of, that which is just according to law.

The reason of this is that every law is laid down in general terms, while there are matters about which it is impossible to speak correctly in general terms. Where, then, it is necessary to speak in general terms, but impossible to do so correctly, the legislator lays down that which holds good for the majority of cases, being quite aware that it does not hold good for all.

The law, indeed, is none the less correctly laid down because of this defect; for the defect lies not in the law, nor in the lawgiver, but in the nature of the subject-matter, being necessarily involved in the very conditions of human action.

When, therefore, the law lays down a general rule, but a particular case occurs which is an exception to this rule, it is right, where the legislator fails and is in error through speaking without qualification, to make good this deficiency, just as the lawgiver himself would do if he were present, and as he would have provided in the law itself if the case had occurred to him.

What is equitable, then, is just, and better than what is just in one sense of the word—not better than what is absolutely just, but better than that which fails through its lack of qualification. And the essence of what is equitable is that it is an amendment of the law, in those points where it fails through the generality of its language.

The reason why the law does not cover all cases is that there are matters about which it is impossible to lay down a law, so that they require a special decree. For that which is variable needs a variable rule, like the leaden rule employed in the Lesbian style of masonry; as the leaden rule has no fixed shape, but adapts itself to the outline of each stone, so is the decree adapted to the occasion.

We have ascertained, then, what the equitable course is, and have found that it is just, and also better than what is just in a certain sense of the word. And after this it is easy to see what the equitable man is: he who is apt to choose such a course and to follow it, who does not insist on his rights to the damage of others, but is ready to take less than his due, even when he has the law to back him, is called an equitable man; and this type of character is called equitableness, being a sort of justice, and not a different kind of character.

11. The foregoing discussion enables us to answer the question whether it be possible or not for a man to act unjustly to himself.

That which is just in one sense of the word we found to be those manifestations of the several virtues which the law prescribes: *e.g.* the law does not order a man to kill himself; and what the law does not order it forbids: and, further, when a man, contrary to the law, voluntarily inflicts hurt without provocation, he acts unjustly (voluntarily meaning with knowledge of the person and the instrument). Now, the man who kills himself in a rage voluntarily acts thus against right reason and does what the law forbids: he acts unjustly therefore.

But unjustly to whom? To the state surely, not to himself; for he suffers voluntarily, but no one can have an injustice done him voluntarily. And upon this ground the state actually punishes him, *i.e.* it pronounces a particular kind of disfranchisement upon the man who destroys himself, as one who acts unjustly towards the state.

Again, if we take the word unjust in the other sense, in which it is used to designate not general badness, but a particular species of vice, we find that in this sense also it is impossible to act unjustly to one's self. (This, we found, is different from the former sense of the word: the unjust man in this second sense is bad in the same way as the coward is bad, *i.e.* as having a particular form of vice, not as having a completely vicious character, nor do we mean to say that he displays a completely vicious character when we say that he acts unjustly). For if it were possible, it would be possible for the same thing at the same time to be taken from and added to the same person. But this is impossible; and, in fact, a just deed or an unjust deed always implies more persons than one.

Further, an act of injustice, besides being voluntary, if not deliberate, must be prior to hurt received (for he who, having received some hurt, repays the same that he received is not held to act unjustly); but he who hurts himself suffers that very hurt at the same time that he inflicts it.

Again, if it were possible for a man to act unjustly to himself, it would be possible to suffer injustice voluntarily.

Further, a man cannot act unjustly without doing an act of injustice of some particular kind; but no one commits adultery with his own wife, or burglariously breaks through his own walls, or steals his own property.

But the whole question about acting unjustly to one's self is settled (without going into detail) by the answer we gave[88] to the question whether a man could voluntarily suffer injustice.

(It is plain that to suffer and to do injustice are both bad, for the one is to get less and the other more than the mean amount, which corresponds to what is healthy in medicine, or to what promotes good condition in gymnastics: but, though both are bad, to do injustice is the worse; for to do injustice is blamable and implies vice (either completely formed vice, what we call vice simply, or else that which is on the way to become vice; for a voluntary act of injustice does not always imply injustice), but to have injustice done to you is no token of a vicious and unjust character.

In itself, then, to be unjustly treated is less bad, but there is nothing to prevent its being accidentally the greater evil. Science, however, does not concern itself with these accidents, but calls a pleurisy a greater malady than a stumble; and yet the latter might, on occasion, accidentally become the greater, as, for instance, if a stumble were to cause you to fall and be caught or slain by the enemy.)

Though we cannot apply the term just to a man's behaviour towards himself, yet we can apply it metaphorically and in virtue of a certain resemblance to the relations between certain parts of a man's self—not, however, in all senses of the word just, but in that sense in which it is applied to the relations of master and slave, or husband and wife; for this is the sort of relation that exists between the rational and the irrational parts of the soul.

And it is this distinction of parts that leads people to fancy that there is such a thing as injustice to one's self: one part of a man can have something done to it by another part contrary to its desires: and so they think that the term just can be applied to the relations of these parts to one another, just as to the relations of ruler and ruled.[89]

We may now consider that we have concluded our examination of justice and the other moral virtues.

BOOK X.

CHAPTERS 1–5, PLEASURE

1. Our next business, I think, should be to treat of pleasure. For pleasure seems, more than anything else, to have an intimate connection with our nature; which is the reason why, in educating the young, we use pleasure and pain as the rudders of their course. Moreover, delight in what we ought to delight in, and hatred of what we ought to hate, seem to be of the utmost importance in the formation of a virtuous character; for these feelings pervade the whole of life, and have power to draw a man to virtue and happiness, as we choose what pleases, and shun what pains us.

And it would seem that the discussion of these matters is especially incumbent on us, since there is much dispute about them. There are people who say that the good is pleasure, and there are people who say, on the contrary, that pleasure is altogether bad—some, perhaps, in the conviction that it is really so, others because they think it has a good effect on men's lives to assert that pleasure is a bad thing, even though it be not; for the generality of men, they say, incline this way, and are slaves to their pleasures, so that they ought to be pulled in the opposite direction: for thus they will be brought into the middle course.

But I cannot think that it is right to speak thus. For assertions about matters of feeling and conduct carry less weight than actions; and so, when assertions are found to be at variance with palpable facts, they fall into contempt, and bring the truth also into discredit. Thus, when a man who speaks ill of pleasure is seen at times to desire it himself, he is thought to show by the fact of being attracted by it that he really considers all pleasure desirable; for the generality of men are not able to draw fine distinctions. It seems, then, that true statements are the most useful, for practice as well as for theory; for, being in harmony with facts, they gain credence, and so incline those who understand them to regulate their lives by them. But enough of this: let us now go through the current opinions about pleasure.

2. Eudoxus thought pleasure was the good, because he saw that all beings, both rational and irrational, strive after it; but in all cases, he said, that which is desirable[90] is the good, and that which is most desirable is best: the fact, then, that all beings incline to one and the same thing indicates that this is the best thing for all (for each being finds out what is good for itself—its food, for instance); but that which is good for all, and which all strive after, is the good.

The statements of Eudoxus were accepted rather because of the excellence of his character than on their own account; for he seemed to be a remarkably temperate man; and so people thought that it was not from love of pleasure that he spoke thus, but that what he said really was the fact.

Eudoxus also thought that his point could be proved no less clearly by the argument from the opposite of pleasure:—pain is, in itself, an object of aversion to all beings; therefore its opposite is desirable for all.

Again, he argued, that is most desirable which we choose, not on account of something else, but for its own sake: but this is admitted to be the case with pleasure; for we never ask a man for his motive in taking pleasure, it being understood that pleasure is in itself desirable.

Again, he argued that any good thing whatsoever is made more desirable by the addition of pleasure, e.g. just or temperate conduct; but it can only be by the good that the good is increased.

Now, this last argument seems indeed to show that pleasure is a good thing, but not that it is one whit better than any other good thing; for any good thing is more desirable with the addition of another good thing than by itself.

Nay, Plato actually employs a similar argument to show that pleasure is not the good. "The pleasant life," he says, "is more desirable with wisdom than without: but if the combination of the two be better, pleasure itself cannot be the good; for no addition can make the good more desirable." And it is equally evident that, if any other thing be made more desirable by the addition of one of the class of things that are good in themselves, that thing cannot be the good. What good is there, then, which is thus incapable of addition, and at the same time such that men can participate in it? For that is the sort of good that we want.

But those who maintain, on the contrary, that what all desire is not good, surely talk nonsense. What all men think, that, we say, is true. And to him who bids us put no trust in the opinion of mankind, we reply that we can scarce put greater trust in his opinion. If it were merely irrational creatures that desired these things, there might be something in what he says; but as rational beings also desire them, how can it be anything but nonsense? Indeed, it may be that even in inferior beings there is some natural principle of good stronger than themselves, which strives after their proper good.

Again, what the adversaries of Eudoxus say about his argument from the nature of the opposite of pleasure, does not seem to be sound. They say that, though pain be bad, yet it does not follow that pleasure is good; for one bad thing may be opposed to another bad thing, and both to a third thing which is different from either.[91] Now, though this is not a bad remark, it does not hold true in the present instance. For if both were bad, both alike ought to be shunned, or if neither were bad, neither should be shunned, or, at least, one no more than the other: but, as it is, men evidently shun the one as bad and choose the other as good; they are, in fact, therefore, opposed to one another in this respect.

3. Again, even though pleasure is not a quality, it does not follow that it is not a good thing. The exercise of virtue, happiness itself, is not a quality.

It is objected, again, that the good is determinate, while pleasure is indeterminate, because it admits of a more and a less.

Now, if they say this because one may be more or less pleased, then the same thing may be said of justice and the other virtues; for it is plain that, with regard to them, we speak of people as being and showing themselves more or less virtuous: some men are more just and more brave than others, and it is possible to act more or less justly and temperately.

But if they mean that one pleasure may be more or less of a pleasure than another, I suspect that they miss the real reason when they say it is because some are pure and some are mixed. Why should it not be the same with pleasure as with health, which, though something determinate, yet allows of more and less? For the due proportion of elements [which constitutes health] is not the same for all, nor always the same for the same person, but may vary within certain limits without losing its character, being now more and now less truly health. And it may be the same with pleasure.

Again, assuming that the good is complete, while motion and coming into being are incomplete, they try to show that pleasure is a motion and a coming into being.

But they do not seem to be right even in saying that it is a motion: for every motion seems necessarily to be quick or slow, either absolutely, as the motion of the universe, or relatively; but pleasure is neither quick nor slow. It is, indeed, possible to be quickly pleased, as to be quickly angered; the feeling, however, cannot be quick, even relatively, as can walking and growing, etc. The passage to a state of pleasure, then, may be quick or slow, but the exercise of the power, i.e. the feeling of pleasure, cannot be quick.

Again, how can pleasure be a coming into being?

It seems that it is not possible for anything to come out of just anything, but what a thing comes out of, that it is resolved into. Pain, then, must be the dissolution of that whose coming into being is pleasure. Accordingly, they maintain that pain is falling short of the normal state, pleasure its replenishment.

But these are bodily processes. If, then, pleasure be the replenishment of the normal state, that in which the replenishment takes place, i.e. the body, must be that which is pleased. But this does not seem to be the case. Pleasure, therefore, is not a replenishment, but while the process of replenishment is going on we may be pleased, and while the process of exhaustion is going on we may be pained.

This view of pleasure seems to have been suggested by the pleasures and pains connected with nutrition; for there it is true that we come into a state of want, and, after previous pain, find pleasure in replenishment. But this is not the case with all pleasures; for there is no previous pain involved in the pleasures of the mathematician, nor among the sensuous pleasures in those of smell, nor, again, in many kinds of sights and sounds, nor in memories and hopes. What is there, then, of which these pleasures are the becoming? Here there is nothing lacking that can be replenished.

To those, again, who [in order to show that pleasure is not good] adduce the disgraceful kinds of pleasure we might reply that these things are not pleasant. Though they be pleasant to ill-conditioned persons, we must not therefore hold them to be pleasant *except* to them; just as we do not hold that to be wholesome, or sweet, or bitter, which is wholesome, sweet, or bitter to the sick man, or that to be white which appears white to a man with ophthalmia.

Or, again, we might reply that these pleasures are desirable, but not when derived from these sources, just as it is desirable to be rich, but not at the cost of treachery, and desirable to be in health, but not at the cost of eating any kind of abominable food.

Or we might say that the pleasures are

specifically different. The pleasures derived from noble sources are different from those derived from base sources, and it is impossible to feel the just man's pleasure without being just, or the musical man's pleasure without being musical, and so on with the rest.

The distinction drawn between the true friend and the flatterer seems to show either that pleasure is not good, or else that pleasures differ in kind. For the former in his intercourse is thought to have the good in view, the latter pleasure: and while we blame the latter, we praise the former as having a different aim in his intercourse.

Again, no one would choose to live on condition of having a child's intellect all his life, though he were to enjoy in the highest possible degree all the pleasures of a child; nor choose to gain enjoyment by the performance of some extremely disgraceful act, though he were never to feel pain.

There are many things, too, which we should care for, even though they brought no pleasure, as sight, memory, knowledge, moral and intellectual excellence. Even if we grant that pleasure necessarily accompanies them, this does not affect the question; for we should choose them even if no pleasure resulted from them.

It seems to be evident, then, that pleasure is not the good, nor are all pleasures desirable, but that some are desirable, differing in kind, or in their sources, from those that are not desirable. Let this be taken then as a sufficient account of the current opinions about pleasure and pain.

4. As to the nature or quality of pleasure, we shall more readily discover it if we make a fresh start as follows:—

Vision seems to be perfect or complete at any moment; for it does not lack anything which can be added afterwards to make its nature complete. Pleasure seems in this respect to resemble vision; for it is something whole and entire, and it would be impossible at any moment to find a pleasure which would become complete by lasting longer.

Therefore pleasure is not a motion; for every motion requires time and implies an end (e.g. the motion of building), and is complete when the desired result is produced—either in the whole time therefore, or in this final moment of it. But during the progress of the work all the motions are incomplete, and specifically different from the whole motion and from each other; the fitting together of the stones is different from the fluting of the pillar, and both from the building of the temple. The building of the temple is complete; nothing more is required for the execution of the plan. But the building of the foundation and of the triglyph are incomplete; for each is the building of a part only. These motions, then, are specifically different from one another, and it is impossible to find a motion whose nature is complete at any moment—it is complete, if at all, only in the whole time.

It is the same also with walking and the other kinds of locomotion. For though all locomotion is a motion from one place to another, yet there are distinct kinds of locomotion, as flying, walking, leaping, etc. Nay, not only so, but even in walking itself there are differences, for the whence and whither are not the same in the entire course and in a portion of the course, or in this portion and in that, nor is crossing this line the same as crossing that; for you do not cross a line simply, but a line that is in a given place, and this line is in a different place from that. I must refer to my other works for a detailed discussion of motion; but it seems that it is not complete at any moment, but that its several parts are incomplete, and that they are specifically different from one another, the whence and whither being a specific difference.

Pleasure, on the other hand, is complete in its nature at any moment. It is evident, therefore, that these two must be distinct from each other, and that pleasure must be one of the class of whole and complete things. And this would also seem to follow from the fact that though duration is necessary for motion, it is not necessary for pleasure—for a momentary pleasure is something whole and entire.

From these considerations it is plain that they are wrong in saying that pleasure is a motion or a coming into being. For these terms are not applied to every thing, but only to those things that are divisible into parts and are not wholes. We cannot speak of the coming into being of vision, or of a mathematical point, or of unity; nor is any one of them a motion or a coming into being. And these terms are equally inapplicable to pleasure; for it is something whole and entire.

Every sense exercises itself upon its proper object, and exercises itself completely when it is in good condition and the object is the noblest of those that fall within its scope (for the complete exercise of a faculty seems to mean this; and we may assume that it makes no difference whether we speak of the sense, or of the sensitive subject as exercising itself): of each sense, then, we may say that the exercise is best when on the one side you have the finest condition, and on the other the highest of the objects that fall within the scope of this faculty.

But this exercise of the faculty will be not only the most complete, but also the pleasantest: for the exercise of every sense is attended with pleasure, and so is the exercise of reason and the speculative faculty; and it is pleasantest when it is most complete, and it is most complete when the faculty is well-trained and the object is the best of those that fall under this faculty.

And, further, the pleasure completes the exercise of the faculty. But the pleasure completes it in a different way from that in which the object and the faculty of sense complete it, when both are as they should be; just as health causes healthy activities in a different way from that in which the physician causes them.

(That the exercise of every sense is accompanied by pleasure is evident: we speak of pleasant sights and pleasant sounds.

It is evident also that the pleasure is greatest when both the faculty and that upon which it is exercised are as good as they can be: when this is the case both with the object of sense and the sentient subject, there will always be pleasure, so long, that is, as you have the subject to act and the object to be acted upon.)

Now, the pleasure makes the exercise complete not as the habit or trained faculty[92] does, being already present in the subject, but as a sort of super-added completeness, like the grace of youth.[93]

So long, then, as both the object of thought or of sense and the perceptive or contemplative subject are as they ought to be, so long will there be pleasure in the exercise; for so long as the object to be acted upon and the subject that is able to act remain the same, and maintain the same relation to each other, the result must be the same.

How is it, then, that we are incapable of continuous pleasure? Perhaps the reason is that we become exhausted; for no human faculty is capable of continuous exercise. Pleasure, then, also cannot be continuous; for it is an accom-

paniment of the exercise of faculty. And for the same reason some things please us when new, but afterwards please us less. For at first the intellect is stimulated and exercises itself upon them strenuously, just as we strain our eyes to look hard at something; but after a time the exertion ceases to be so intense, and becomes relaxed; and so the pleasure also loses its keenness.

The desire for pleasure we should expect to be shared by all men, seeing that all desire to live.

For life is an exercise of faculties, and each man exercises the faculties he most loves upon the things he most loves; e.g. the musical man exercises his hearing upon melodies, and the studious man exercises his intellect upon matters of speculation, and so on with the rest.

But pleasure completes the exercise of faculties, and therefore life, which men desire.

Naturally, therefore, men desire pleasure too; for each man finds in it the completion of his life, which is desirable.

But whether we desire life for the sake of pleasure, or pleasure for the sake of life, is a question which we may dismiss for the present. For the two seem to be joined together, and not to admit of separation: without exercise of faculties there is no pleasure, and every such exercise is completed by pleasure.

5. And from this it seems to follow that pleasures differ in kind, since specifically different things we believe to be completed by specifically different things. For this seems to be the case with the products both of nature and of art, as animals and trees, paintings, sculptures, houses, and furniture. Similarly, then, we believe that exercises of faculty which differ in kind are completed by things different in kind.

But the exercises of the intellectual faculties are specifically different from the exercises of the senses, and the several kinds of each from one another; therefore the pleasures which complete them are also different.

The same conclusion would seem to follow from the close connection that exists between each pleasure and the exercise of faculty which it completes. For the exercise is increased by its proper pleasure; e.g. people are more likely to understand any matter, and to go to the bottom of it, if the exercise is pleasant to them. Thus, those who delight in geometry become geometricians, and understand all the propositions better than others; and similarly, those who are fond of music, or of architecture, or of anything else, make progress in that kind of work, because they delight in it. The pleasures, then, help to increase the exercise; but that which helps to increase it must be closely connected with it: but when things are specifically different from one another, the things that are closely connected with them must also be specifically different.

The same conclusion follows perhaps still more clearly from the fact that the exercise of one faculty is impeded by the pleasure proper to another; *e.g.* a lover of the flute is unable to attend to an argument if he hears a man playing, since he takes more delight in flute-playing than in his present business; the pleasure of the flute-player, therefore, hinders the exercise of the reason.

The same result follows in other cases, too, whenever a man is exercising his faculties on two things at a time; the pleasanter business thwarts the other, and, if the difference in pleasantness be great, thwarts it more and more, even to the extent of suppressing it altogether. Thus, when anything gives us intense delight, we cannot do anything else at all, and when we do a second thing, we do not very much care about the first; and so people who eat sweetmeats in the theatre do this most of all when the actors are bad.

Since its proper pleasure heightens the exercise of a faculty, making it both more prolonged and better, while pleasure from another source spoils it, it is evident that there is a great difference between these two pleasures. Indeed, pleasure from another source has almost the same effect as pain from the activity itself. For the exercise of a faculty is spoilt by pain arising from it; as happens, for instance, when a man finds it disagreeable and painful to write or to calculate; for he stops writing in the one case and calculating in the other, since the exercise is painful. The exercise of a faculty, then, is affected in opposite ways by its proper pleasure and its proper pain; and by "proper" I mean that which is occasioned by the exercise itself. But pleasure from another source, we have already said, has almost the same effect as its proper pain; *i.e.* it interferes with the exercise of the faculty, though not to the same extent.

Again, as the exercises of our faculties differ in goodness and badness, and some are to be desired and some to be shunned, while some are indifferent, so do the several pleasures differ; for each exercise has its proper pleasure. The pleasure which is proper to a good activity, then, is good, and that which is proper to one that is not good is bad: for the desire of noble things is laudable, and the desire of base things is blamable; but the pleasures which accompany the exercises of our faculties belong to them even more than the desires do, since the latter are distinct both in time and in nature, while the former are almost coincident in time, and so hard to distinguish from them that it is a matter of debate whether the exercise be not identical with the pleasure.

It seems, however, that the pleasure is not the same as the act of thinking or of feeling; that is impossible: but the fact that the two are inseparable makes some people fancy that they are identical.

As, then, the exercises of the faculties vary, so do their respective pleasures. Sight is purer than touch, hearing and smell than taste[94]: there is a corresponding difference, therefore, between their pleasures; and the pleasures of the intellect are purer than these pleasures of sense, and some of each kind are purer than others.

Each kind of being, again, seems to have its proper pleasure, as it has its proper function,— viz. the pleasure which accompanies the exercise of its faculties or the realization of its nature. And a separate consideration of the several kinds of animals will confirm this: the pleasures of a horse, a dog, and a man are all different—as Heraclitus says, a donkey would prefer hay to gold; for there is more pleasure in fodder than in gold to a donkey.

The pleasures of specifically different beings, then, are specifically different; and we might naturally suppose that there would be no specific difference between the pleasures of beings of the same species. And yet there is no small difference, in the pleasures of men at least: what pleases this man pains that; what is grievous and hateful to one is pleasant and lovable to another. This occurs in the case of sweet things, too: a man in a fever has a different notion of what is sweet from a man in health; and a feeble man's notion of what is hot is different from that of a robust man. And the like occurs in other matters also.

But in all matters of this kind we hold that

things *are* what they appear to be to the perfect man.

Now, if this opinion is correct, as we hold it to be—if, that is, in every case the test is virtue, or the good man as such—then what appears to him to be pleasure will be pleasure, and what he delights in will be pleasant.

If what is disagreeable to him appears pleasant to another, we need not be astonished; for there are many ways in which men are corrupted and perverted: such things, however, are not pleasant, but only pleasant to these men with their disposition. It is plain, then, that we must not allow the confessedly base pleasures to be pleasures at all, except to corrupt men.

But of the pleasures that are considered good, which or what kind are to be called the proper pleasures of man? We cannot be in doubt if we know what are the proper exercises of his faculties; for the proper pleasures are their accompaniments. Whether, then, the exercise of faculties proper to the complete and happy man be one or many, the pleasures that complete that exercise will be called pleasures of man in the full meaning of the words, and the others in a secondary sense and with a fraction of that meaning, just as is the case with the exercises of the faculties.

CHAPTERS 6–9. CONCLUSION.

6. Now that we have discussed the several kinds of virtue and friendship and pleasure, it remains to give a summary account of happiness, since we assume that it is the end of all that man does. And it will shorten our statement if we first recapitulate what we have said above.

We said that happiness is not a habit or trained faculty. If it were, it would be within the reach of a man who slept all his days and lived the life of a vegetable, or of a man who met with the greatest misfortunes. As we cannot accept this conclusion, we must place happiness in some exercise of faculty, as we said before. But as the exercises of faculty are sometimes necessary (*i.e.* desirable for the sake of something else), sometimes desirable in themselves, it is evident that happiness must be placed among those that are desirable in themselves, and not among those that are desirable for the sake of something else: for happiness lacks nothing; it is sufficient in itself.

Now, the exercise of faculty is desirable in itself when nothing is expected from it beyond itself.

Of this nature are held to be (1) the manifestations of excellence; for to do what is noble and excellent must be counted desirable for itself: and (2) those amusements which please us; for they are not chosen for the sake of anything else,—indeed, men are more apt to be injured than to be benefited by them, through neglect of their health and fortunes.

Now, most of those whom men call happy have recourse to pastimes of this sort. And on this account those who show a ready wit in such pastimes find favour with tyrants; for they make themselves pleasant in that which the tyrant wants, and what he wants is pastime. These amusements, then, are generally thought to be elements of happiness, because princes employ their leisure in them. But such persons, we may venture to say, are no criterion. For princely rank does not imply the possession of virtue or of reason, which are the sources of all excellent exercise of faculty. And if these men, never having tasted pure and refined pleasure, have recourse to the pleasures of the body, we should not on that account think these more desirable; for children also fancy that the things which they value are better than anything else. It is only natural, then, that as children differ from men in their estimate of what is valuable, so bad men should differ from good.

As we have often said, therefore, that is truly valuable and pleasant which is so to the perfect man. Now, the exercise of those trained faculties which are proper to him is what each man finds most desirable; what the perfect man finds most desirable, therefore, is the exercise of virtue.

Happiness, therefore, does not consist in amusement, and indeed it is absurd to suppose that the end is amusement, and that we toil and moil all our life long for the sake of amusing ourselves. We may say that we choose everything for the sake of something else, excepting only happiness; for it is the end. But to be serious and to labour for the sake of amusement seems silly and utterly childish; while to amuse ourselves in order that we may be serious, as Anacharsis says, seems to be right; for amusement is a sort of recreation, and we need recreation because we are unable to work continuously.

Recreation, then, cannot be the end; for it is taken as a means to the exercise of our faculties.

Again, the happy life is thought to be that which exhibits virtue; and such a life must be serious and cannot consist in amusement.

Again, it is held that things of serious importance are better than laughable and amusing things, and that the better the organ or the man, the more important is the function; but we have already said that the function or exercise of that which is better is higher and more conducive to happiness.

Again, the enjoyment of bodily pleasures is within the reach of anybody, of a slave no less than the best of men; but no one supposes that a slave can participate in happiness, seeing that he cannot participate in the proper life of man. For indeed happiness does not consist in pastimes of this sort, but in the exercise of virtue, as we have already said.

7. But if happiness be the exercise of virtue, it is reasonable to suppose that it will be the exercise of the highest virtue; and that will be the virtue or excellence of the best part of us.

Now, that part or faculty—call it reason or what you will—which seems naturally to rule and take the lead, and to apprehend things noble and divine—whether it be itself divine, or only the divinest part of us—is the faculty the exercise of which, in its proper excellence, will be perfect happiness.

That this consists in speculation or contemplation we have already said.

This conclusion would seem to agree both with what we have said above, and with known truths.

This exercise of faculty must be the highest possible; for the reason is the highest of our faculties, and of all knowable things those that reason deals with are the highest.

Again, it is the most continuous; for speculation can be carried on more continuously than any kind of action whatsoever.

We think too that pleasure ought to be one of the ingredients of happiness; but of all virtuous exercises it is allowed that the pleasantest is the exercise of wisdom.[95] At least philosophy[96] is thought to have pleasures that are admirable in purity and steadfastness; and it is reasonable to suppose that the time passes more pleasantly with those who possess, than with those who are seeking knowledge.

Again, what is called self-sufficiency will be most of all found in the speculative life. The necessaries of life, indeed, are needed by the wise man as well as by the just man and the rest; but, when these have been provided in due quantity, the just man further needs persons towards whom, and along with whom, he may act justly; and so does the temperate and the courageous man and the rest; while the wise man is able to speculate even by himself, and the wiser he is the more is he able to do this. He could speculate better, we may confess, if he had others to help him, but nevertheless he is more self-sufficient than anybody else.

Again, it would seem that this life alone is desired solely for its own sake; for it yields no result beyond the contemplation, but from the practical activities we get something more or less besides action.

Again, happiness is thought to imply leisure; for we toil in order that we may have leisure, as we make war in order that we may enjoy peace. Now, the practical virtues are exercised either in politics or in war; but these do not seem to be leisurely occupations:—

War, indeed, seems to be quite the reverse of leisurely; for no one chooses to fight for fighting's sake, or arranges a war for that purpose: he would be deemed a bloodthirsty villain who should set friends at enmity in order that battles and slaughter might ensue.

But the politician's life also is not a leisurely occupation, and, beside the practice of politics itself, it brings power and honours, or at least happiness, to himself and his fellow-citizens, which is something different from politics; for we [who are asking what happiness is] also ask what politics is, evidently implying that it is something different from happiness.

If, then, the life of the statesman and the soldier, though they surpass all other virtuous exercises in nobility and grandeur, are not leisurely occupations, and aim at some ulterior end, and are not desired merely for themselves, but the exercise of the reason seems to be superior in seriousness (since it contemplates truth), and to aim at no end beside itself, and to have its proper pleasure (which also helps to increase the exercise), and further to be self-sufficient, and leisurely, and inexhaustible (as far as anything human can be), and to have all the other characteristics that are ascribed to happiness, it follows that the exercise of reason will be the complete happiness of man, *i.e.* when a complete term of days is added; for nothing incomplete can be admitted into our idea of happiness.

But a life which realized this idea would be something more than human; for it would not be the expression of man's nature, but of some divine element in that nature—the exercise of which is as far superior to the exercise of the other kind of virtue [*i.e.* practical or moral virtue], as this divine element is superior to our compound human nature.[97]

If then reason be divine as compared with man, the life which consists in the exercise of reason will also be divine in comparison with human life. Nevertheless, instead of listening to those who advise us as men and mortals not to lift our thoughts above what is human and mortal, we ought rather, as far as possible, to put off our mortality and make every effort to live in the exercise of the highest of our faculties; for though it be but a small part of us, yet in power and value it far surpasses all the rest.

And indeed this part would even seem to constitute our true self, since it is the sovereign and the better part. It would be strange, then, if a man were to prefer the life of something else to the life of his true self.

Again, we may apply here what we said above —for every being that is best and pleasantest which is naturally proper to it. Since, then, it is the reason that in the truest sense is the man, the life that consists in the exercise of the reason is the best and pleasantest for man—and therefore the happiest.

8. The life that consists in the exercise of the other kind of virtue is happy in a secondary sense; for the manifestations of moral virtue are emphatically human [not divine]. Justice, I mean, and courage, and the other moral virtues are displayed in our relations towards one another by the observance, in every case, of what is due in contracts and services, and all sorts of outward acts, as well as in our inward feelings. And all these seem to be emphatically human affairs.

Again, moral virtue seems, in some points, to be actually a result of physical constitution, and in many points to be closely connected with the passions.

Again, prudence is inseparably joined to moral virtue, and moral virtue to prudence, since the moral virtues determine the principles of prudence,[98] while prudence determines what is right in morals.

But the moral virtues, being bound up with the passions, must belong to our compound nature; and the virtues of the compound nature are emphatically human. Therefore the life which manifests them, and the happiness which consists in this, must be emphatically human.

But the happiness which consists in the exercise of the reason is separate from the lower nature. (So much we may be allowed to assert about it: a detailed discussion is beyond our present purpose.)

Further, this happiness would seem to need but a small supply of external goods, certainly less than the moral life needs. Both need the necessaries of life to the same extent, let us say; for though, in fact, the politician takes more care of his person than the philosopher, yet the difference will be quite inconsiderable. But in what they need for their activities there will be a great difference. Wealth will be needed by the liberal man, that he may act liberally; by the just man, that he may discharge his obligations (for a mere wish cannot be tested,—even unjust people pretend a wish to act justly); the courageous man will need strength if he is to execute any deed of courage; and the temperate man liberty of indulgence,—for how else can he, or the possessor of any other virtue, show what he is?

Again, people dispute whether the purpose or the action be more essential to virtue, virtue being understood to imply both. It is plain, then, that both are necessary to completeness. But many things are needed for action, and the greater and nobler the action, the more is needed.

On the other hand, he who is engaged in speculation needs none of these things for his *work;* nay, it may even be said that they are a hindrance to speculation: but as a man living with other men, he chooses to act virtuously; and so he will need things of this sort to enable him to behave like a man.

That perfect happiness is some kind of speculative activity may also be shown in the following way:—

It is always supposed that the gods are, of all beings, the most blessed and happy; but what kind of actions shall we ascribe to them? Acts of justice? Surely it is ridiculous to conceive the gods engaged in trade and restoring deposits, and so on. Or the acts of the courageous character who endures fearful things and who faces danger because it is noble to do so? Or acts of liberality? But to whom are they to give? And is it not absurd to suppose that they have money or anything of that kind? And what could acts of temperance mean with them? Surely it would be an insult to praise them for having no evil desires. In short, if we were to go through the whole list, we should find that all action is petty and unworthy of the gods.

And yet it is universally supposed that they live, and therefore that they exert their powers; for we cannot suppose that they lie asleep like Endymion.

Now, if a being lives, and action cannot be ascribed to him, still less production, what remains but contemplation? It follows, then, that the divine life, which surpasses all others in blessedness, consists in contemplation.

Of all modes of human activity, therefore, that which is most akin to this will be capable of the greatest happiness.

And this is further confirmed by the fact that the other animals do not participate in happiness, being quite incapable of this kind of activity. For the life of the gods is entirely blessed, and the life of man is blessed just so far as he attains to some likeness of this kind of activity; but none of the other animals are happy, since they are quite incapable of contemplation.

Happiness, then, extends just so far as contemplation, and the more contemplation the more happiness is there in a life,—not accidentally, but as a necessary accompaniment of the contemplation; for contemplation is precious in itself.

Our conclusion, then, is that happiness is a kind of speculation or contemplation.

But as we are men we shall need external good fortune also: for our nature does not itself provide all that is necessary for contemplation; the body must be in health, and supplied with food, and otherwise cared for. We must not, however, suppose that because it is impossible to be happy without external good things, therefore a man who is to be happy will want many things or much. It is not the superabundance of good things that makes a man independent, or enables him to act; and a man may do noble deeds,

though he be not ruler of land and sea. A moderate equipment may give you opportunity for virtuous action (as we may easily see, for private persons seem to do what is right not less, but rather more, than princes), and so much as gives this opportunity is enough; for that man's life will be happy who has virtue and exercises it.

Solon too, I think, gave a good description of the happy man when he said that, in his opinion, he was a man who was moderately supplied with the gifts of fortune, but had done the noblest deeds, and lived temperately; for a man who has but modest means may do his duty.

Anaxagoras also seems to have held that the happy man was neither a rich man nor a prince; for he said that he should not be surprised if the happy man were one whom the masses could hardly believe to be so; for they judge by the outside, which is all they can appreciate.

The opinions of the wise, then, seem to agree with our theory. But though these opinions carry some weight, the test of truth in matters of practice is to be found in the facts of life; for it is in them that the supreme authority resides. The theories we have advanced, therefore, should be tested by comparison with the facts of life; and if they agree with the facts they should be accepted, but if they disagree they should be accounted mere theories.

But, once more, the man who exercises his reason and cultivates it, and has it in the best condition, seems also to be the most beloved of heaven. For if the gods take any care for men, as they are thought to do, it is reasonable to suppose that they delight in that which is best in man and most akin to themselves (*i.e.* the reason), and that they requite those who show the greatest love and reverence for it, as caring for that which is dear to themselves and doing rightly and nobly. But it is plain that all these points are found most of all in the wise man. The wise man, therefore, is the most beloved of heaven; and therefore, we may conclude, the happiest.

In this way also, therefore, the wise man will be happier than any one else.

9. Now that we have treated (sufficiently, though summarily) of these matters, and of the virtues, and also of friendship and pleasure, are we to suppose that we have attained the end we proposed? Nay, surely the saying holds good,

that in practical matters the end is not a mere speculative knowledge of what is to be done, but rather the doing of it. It is not enough to know about virtue, then, but we must endeavour to possess it and to use it, or to take any other steps that may make us good.

Now, if theories had power of themselves to make us good, "many great rewards would they deserve" as Theognis says, and such ought we to give; but in fact it seems that though they are potent to guide and to stimulate liberal-minded young men, and though a generous disposition, with a sincere love of what is noble, may by them be opened to the influence of virtue, yet they are powerless to turn the mass of men to goodness. For the generality of men are naturally apt to be swayed by fear rather than by reverence, and to refrain from evil rather because of the punishment that it brings than because of its own foulness. For under the guidance of their passions they pursue the pleasures that suit their nature and the means by which those pleasures may be obtained, and avoid the opposite pains, while of that which is noble and truly pleasant they have not even a conception, as they have never tasted it.

What theories or arguments, then, can bring such men as these to order? Surely it is impossible, or at least very difficult, to remove by any argument what has long been ingrained in the character. For my part, I think we must be well content if we can get some modicum of virtue when all the circumstances are present that seem to make men good.

Now, what makes men good is held by some to be nature, by others habit [or training], by others instruction.

As for the goodness that comes by nature, it is plain that it is not within our control, but is bestowed by some divine agency on certain people who truly deserve to be called fortunate.

As for theory or instruction, I fear that it cannot avail in all cases, but that the hearer's soul must be prepared by training it to feel delight and aversion on the right occasions, just as the soil must be prepared if the seed is to thrive. For if he lives under the sway of his passions, he will not listen to the arguments by which you would dissuade him, nor even understand them. And when he is in this state, how can you change his mind by argument? To put it roundly, passion seems to yield to force only, and not to reason. The character, then, must be already[99] formed, so as to be in some way akin to virtue, loving what is noble and hating what is base.

But to get right guidance from youth up in the road to virtue is hard, unless we are brought up under suitable laws; for to live temperately and regularly is not pleasant to the generality of men, especially to the young. Our nurture, then, should be prescribed by law, and our whole way of life; for it will cease to be painful as we get accustomed to it. And I venture to think that it is not enough to get proper nurture and training when we are young, but that as we ought to carry on the same way of life after we are grown up, and to confirm these habits, we need the intervention of the law in these matters also, and indeed, to put it roundly, in our whole life. For the generality of men are more readily swayed by compulsion than by reason, and by fear of punishment than by desire for what is noble.

For this reason, some hold that the legislator should, in the first instance, invite the people and exhort them to be virtuous because of the nobility of virtue, as those who have been well trained will listen to him; but that when they will not listen, or are of less noble nature, he should apply correction and punishment, and banish utterly those who are incorrigible. For the good man, who takes what is noble as his guide, will listen to reason, but he who is not good, whose desires are set on pleasure, must be corrected by pain like a beast of burden. And for this reason, also, they say the pains to be applied must be those that are most contrary to the pleasures which the culprit loves.

As we have said, then, he who is to be good must be well nurtured and trained, and thereafter must continue in a like excellent way of life, and must never, either voluntarily or involuntarily, do anything vile; and this can only be effected if men live subject to some kind of reason and proper regimen, backed by force.

Now, the paternal rule has not the requisite force or power of compulsion, nor has the rule of any individual, unless he be a king or something like one; but the law has a compulsory power, and at the same time is a rational ordinance proceeding from a kind of prudence or reason. And whereas we take offence at individuals who oppose our inclinations, even though their opposition is right, we do not feel aggrieved when the law bids us do what is right.

But Sparta is the only, or almost the only, state where the legislator seems to have paid attention to the nurture and mode of life of the citizens. In most states these matters are entirely neglected, and each man lives as he likes, ruling wife and children in Cyclopean fashion.

It would be best, then, that the regulation of these matters should be undertaken and properly carried out by the state; but as the state neglects it, it would seem that we should each individually help our own children or friends on the road to virtue, and should have the power or at least the will to do this.

Now, it would seem from what has been said that to enable one to do this the best plan would be to learn how to legislate. For state training is carried on by means of laws, and is good when the laws are good; but it would seem to make no difference whether the laws be written or unwritten, or whether they regulate the education of one person or many, any more than it does in the case of music, or gymnastics, or any other course of training. For as in the state that prevails which is ordained by law and morality, so in the household that which is ordained by the word of the father of the family and by custom prevails no less, or even more, because of the ties of kinship and of obligation; for affection and obedience are already implanted by nature in the members of the family.

Moreover, in spite of what has just been said, individual treatment is better than treatment by masses, in education no less than in medicine. As a general rule, repose and fasting are good for a fever patient, but in a particular case they may not be good. A teacher of boxing, I suppose, does not recommend every one to adopt the same style. It would seem, then, that individuals are educated more perfectly under a system of private education; for then each gets more precisely what he needs.

But you will best be able to treat an individual case (whether you are a doctor, or a trainer, or anything else) when you know the general rule, "Such and such a thing is good for all men," or "for all of a certain temperament;" for science is said to deal, and does deal, with that which is common to a number of individuals.

I do not mean to deny that it may be quite possible to treat an individual well, even without any scientific knowledge, if you know precisely by experience the effect of particular causes upon him, just as some men seem to be able to treat themselves better than any doctor, though they would be quite unable to prescribe for another person.

But, nevertheless, I venture to say that if a man wishes to master any art, or to gain a scientific knowledge of it, he must advance to its general principles, and make himself acquainted with them in the proper method; for, as we have said, it is with universal propositions that the sciences deal.

And so I think that he who wishes to make men better by training (whether many or few) should try to acquire the art or science of legislation, supposing that men may be made good by the agency of law. For fairly to mould the character of any person that may present himself is not a thing that can be done by anybody, but (if at all) only by him who has knowledge, just as is the case in medicine and other professions where careful treatment and prudence are required.

Our next business, then, I think, is to inquire from whom or by what means we are to learn the science or art of legislation.

"As we learn the other arts," it will be said,— "i.e. from the politicians who practise it: for we found that legislation is a part of politics."

But I think the case is not quite the same with politics as with the other sciences and arts. For in other cases it is plain that the same people communicate the art and practise it, as physicians and painters do. But in the case of politics, while the sophists profess to teach the art, it is never they that practise it, but the statesmen. And the statesmen would seem to act by some instinctive faculty, proceeding empirically rather than by reasoning. For it is plain that they never write or speak about these matters (though perhaps that were better than making speeches in the courts or the assembly), and have never communicated the art to their sons or to any of their friends. And yet we might expect that they would have done so if they could; for they could have left no better legacy to their country, nor have chosen anything more precious than this power as a possession for themselves, and, therefore, for those dearest to them.

Experience, however, seems, we must allow, to be of great service here; for otherwise people would never become statesmen by familiarity with politics. Those who wish for a knowledge of statesmanship, then, seem to need experience [as well as theory].

But those sophists who profess to teach statesmanship seem to be ludicrously incapable of fulfilling their promises: for, to speak roundly, they do not even know what it is or what it deals with. If they did know, they would not make it identical with rhetoric, or inferior to it, nor would they think it was easy to frame a system of laws when you had made a collection of the most approved of existing laws. "It is but a matter of picking out the best," they say, ignoring the fact that this selection requires understanding, and that to judge correctly is a matter of the greatest difficulty here, as in music. Those who have special experience in any department can pass a correct judgment upon the result, and understand how and by what means it is produced, and what combinations are harmonious; but those who have no special experience must be content if they are able to say whether the result is good or bad—as, for instance, in the case of painting. Now, laws are the work or result, so to speak, of statesmanship. How then could a collection of laws make a man able to legislate, or to pick out the best of the collection?

Even the art of healing, it seems, can not be taught by compendia. And yet the medical compendia try to tell you not only the remedies, but how to apply them, and how to treat the several classes of patients, distinguishing them according to their temperament. But all this, though it may be serviceable to those who have experi-

ence, would seem to be quite useless to those who know nothing of medicine.

So also, I think we may say, collections of laws and constitutions may be very serviceable to those who are able to examine them with a discriminating eye, and to judge whether an ordinance is good or bad, and what ordinances agree with one another; but if people who have not the trained faculty go through such compendia, they cannot judge properly (unless indeed a correct judgment comes of itself), though they may perhaps sharpen their intelligence in these matters.

Since then our predecessors have left this matter of legislation uninvestigated, it will perhaps be better ourselves to inquire into it, and indeed into the whole question of the management of a state, in order that our philosophy of human life may be completed to the best of our power.

Let us try, then, first of all, to consider any valuable utterances that our predecessors have made upon this or that branch of the subject; and then, looking at our collection of constitutions, let us inquire what things tend to preserve or destroy states, and what things tend to preserve or destroy the several kinds of constitution, and what are the causes of the good government of some states and the misgovernment of others: for when we have got an insight into these matters we shall, I think, be better able to see what is the best kind of constitution, and what is the best arrangement of each of the several kinds; that is to say, what system of laws and customs is best suited to each.

Let us begin then.[100]————

NOTES

1. To Aristotle Politics is a much wider term than to us; it covers the whole field of human life, since man is essentially social (7, G); it has to determine (1) what is the good?—the question of this treatise (§ 9)—and (2) what can law do to promote this good?—the question of the sequel, which is specially called "The Politics;" cf. X. 9.

2. i.e. covers a part of the ground only: see preceding note.

3. "Works and Days," 291–295.

4. ἔθος, custom; ηθος, character; ἠθικὴ ἀρετή, moral excellence: we have no similar sequence, but the Latin mos, mores, from which "morality" comes, covers both ἔθος and ηθος.

5. It is with the moral virtues that this and the three following books are exclusively concerned, the discussion of the intellectual virtues being postponed to Book VI. ἀρεταί is often used in these books, without any epithet, for "moral virtues," and perhaps is so used here.

6. In Book VI.

7. Actions and the accompanying feelings of pleasure and pain have so grown together, that it is impossible to separate the former and judge them apart: cf. X. 4, II.

8. i.e. which do not issue in act like those hitherto mentioned.

9. Hom., Od., xii. 101–110, and 219–220: Calypso should be Circe.

10. It must be remembered that "virtue" is synonymous with "praiseworthy habit;" I. 13, 20; II. 9, 9.

11. ἁπλῶς, "without qualification:" no one chooses loss of property simply, but loss of property with saving of life is what all sensible people would choose.

12. Which shows that the acts are regarded as voluntary.

13. οὐκ ἔστιν ἀναγκασθῆναι, "compulsion is impossible." If the act was compulsory it was not my act, I cannot be blamed: there are some acts, says Aristotle, for which we could not forgive a man, for which, whatever the circumstances, we must blame him; therefore no circumstances can compel him, or compulsion is impossible. The

argument is, in fact, "I ought not, therefore I can not (am able not to do it),"—like Kant's, "I ought, therefore I can." But, if valid at all, it is valid universally, and the conclusion should be that the body only can be compelled, and not the will— that a compulsory act is impossible.

14.   Therefore, strictly speaking, a "compulsory act" is a contradiction in terms; the real question is, "What is an act?"

15.   Therefore, since these are the motives of every act, all voluntary action involves pleasure. If we add "when successful," this quite agrees with Aristotle's theory of pleasure in Books VII and X.

16.   i.e. not merely "not-willed," but done "unwillingly," or "against the agent's will." Unfortunately our usage recognizes no such distinction between "not-voluntary" and "involuntary."

17.   ἐν μεταμελείᾳ, lit. "when the act involves change of mind." This, under the circumstances, can only mean that the agent who willed the act, not seeing the true nature of it at the time, is sorry afterwards, when he comes to see what he has done.

18.   i.e. forms a wrong judgment; cf. ἡ μοχθηρία διαψεύδεσθαι ποιεῖ περὶ τὰς πρακτικὰς ἀρχάς, VI. 12, 10: not that the vicious man does not know that such a course is condemned by society, but he does not assent to society's rules—adopts other maxims contrary to them.

19.   τὸ συμφέρον, what conduces to a given end, expedient. The meaning of the term varies with the end in view: here the end in view is the supreme end, happiness: τὸ συμφέρον, then, means here the rule of conduct to which, in a given case, the agent must conform in order to realize this end: cf. II. 2. 3.

20.   Reason can modify action only by modifying feeling. Every action issues from a feeling or passion (πάθος), which feeling (and therefore the resultant action) is mine (the outcome of my character, and therefore imputable to me), whether it be modified by reason (deliberation, calculation) or no.

21.   Two appetites may pull two different, but not contrary ways (ἐναντιοῦται): that which not merely diverts but restrains me from satisfying an appetite must be desire of a different kind, e.g. desire to do what is right. Ἐπιθυμία is used loosely in cap. 1 for desire (ὄρεξις), here more strictly for appetite, a species of desire, purpose (προαίρεσις) being another species: cf. infra, 3. 10.

22.   προαίρεσις, lit. "choosing before." Our "preference" exactly corresponds here, but unfortunately cannot always be employed.

23.   These are instances of "necessity;" a tree grows by "nature," i.e. by its own natural powers.

24.   If we have to construct a geometrical figure, we first "suppose it done," then analyze the imagined figure in order to see the conditions which it implies and which imply it, and continue the chain till we come to some thing (drawing of some lines) which we already know how to do.

25.   Cf. III. 2, 9, and 5, 1, and X. 7, 5. There is no real inconsistency between this and the doctrine that the end of life is life, that the good act is to be chosen for its own sake (II. 4, 3), because it is noble (III. 7, 13): for the end is not outside the means; happiness or the perfect life is the complete system of these acts, and the real nature of each act is determined by its relation to this system; to choose it as a means to this end is to choose it for itself.

26.   βουλητόν. This word hovers between two senses, (1) wished for, (2) to be wished for, just as αἱρετόν hovers between (1) desired, (2) desirable. The difficulty, as here put, turns entirely upon the equivocation; but at bottom lies the fundamental question, whether there be a common human nature, such that we can say, "This kind of life is man's real life."

27.   Each virtuous act is desired and chosen as a means to realizing a particular virtue, and this again is desired as a part or constituent of, and so as a means to, that perfect self-realization which is happiness: cf. 3, 15.

28.   My act is mine, and does not cease to be mine because I would undo it if I could; and so, further, since we made the habits whose bonds we cannot now unloose, we are responsible, not merely for the acts which made them, but also for the acts which they now produce "in spite of us:" what constrains us is ourselves.

29.   The courageous man desires the courageous act for the same reason for which he desires the virtue itself, viz. simply because it is noble: see note on § 2.

30.   11, xxii. 200.

31.   Ibid., viii. 148, 149.

32.   Ibid, xv. 348, ii. 391.

33.   Outside Corouea, when the town was betrayed, in the Sacred War.

34.   The incident is narrated by Xenophon, Ilell., iv. 10.

35.   Cf. I. 8, 10, f.

36.   Cf. VII. 14, 2: "the opposite of this excessive pleasure ni.e. going without a wrong pleasurem is not pain, except to the man who sets his heart on this excessive pleasure."

37.   i.e. the pleasures of taste and touch.

38.   Of course the English term is not so used.

39.   κόλασις, chastening; ἀκόλαστος, unchastened, incorrigible, profligate.

40.   The connection is plainer in the original, because τὰ χρήματα, "wealth," is at once seen to be identical with τὰ χρήσιμα, "useful things," and connected with χρεία, "use."

41.   Were it not for some extraneous consideration, e.g. desire to stand well with his neighbours.

42.   This is strictly a departure from the virtue; but Aristotle seems often to pass insensibly from the abstract ideal of a virtue to its imperfect embodiment in a complex character. Cf. infra. cap. 3.

43.   No single English word can convey the associations of the Greek τύραννος, a monarch who has seized absolute power, not necessarily one who abuses it.

44.   See Stewart.

45.   i.e. in men of some age and fixed character; they often coexist in very young men, he says, but cannot possibly coexist for long.

46.   As he has already said in effect, supra, § 23.

47.   Lit. "cummin-splitter."

48.   A worthy expenditure of £100,000 would be magnificent from its mere amount; but even £100 may be spent in a magnificent manner (by a man who can afford it), e.g. in buying a rare engraving for a public collection: cf. § 17 and 18.

49.   For that is impossible.

50.   II. 9 7.

51.   The things that the boaster pretends to are also the things that the ironical man disclaims.

52.   What follows explains why all these terms have a specific moral meaning.

53.   Friendliness, truthfulness, wit.

54.   The continent man desires the evil which he ought not to desire, and so is not good; but he does not do it, and so is not bad: thus continence also might be called "hypothetically good"; granting the evil desire (which excludes goodness proper), the best thing is to master it.

55.   Book VII.

56.   A man may "do that which is just" without "acting justly:" cf. supra, II. 4, 3, and infra, cap. 8.

57.   While his children are regarded as parts of him, and even his wife is not regarded as an independent person: cf. infra, 6, 8.

58. Or "differently manifested:" the phrase is used in both senses.

59. This is not merely a repetition of what has been said in § 2: acts of injustice (2) are there distinguished from acts of injustice (1) by the motive (gain), here by the fact that they are referred to no other vice than injustice.

60. Before (1, 7) the two kinds of injustice were called ὁμώνυμα, i.e. strictly, "things that have nothing in common but the name;" here they are called συνώνυμα, "different things bearing a common name because they belong to the same genus," as a man and an ox are both called animals: cf. Categ. I. 1.

61. The two characters coincide perfectly only in the perfect state: cf. Pol. III. 4, 1276^b 16 f.

62. If this amount be equal, it must be equal to something else; if my share is fair, I must be sharing with one other person at least.

63. A's share and B's.

64. Counting all free men as equals entitled to equal shares.

65. e.g. $\frac{a}{b}$ v $\frac{c}{d}$

66. Assigning or joining certain quantities of goods (c and d) to certain persons (a and b).

67. In the way of redress, as given by the law-courts: later on (cap. 5) he gives as an after-thought the kind of justice which ought to regulate buying and selling, etc.

68. The δικασταί at Athens combined the functions of judge and jury.

69. The point to be illustrated is, that in these private transactions what one man gains is equal to what the other loses, so that the penalty that will restore the balance can be exactly measured.

70. For the aim of trade is neither profit nor loss, but fair exchange, i.e. exchange (on the principle laid down in ch. 5) which leaves the position of the parties as the state fixed it (by distributive justice, ch. 3). But when in the private transactions of man with man this position is disturbed, i.e. whenever either unintentionally, by accident or negligence, or intentionally, by force or fraud, one has bettered his position at the expense of another, corrective justice steps in to redress the balance.

71. c.g. suppose the husbandman is twice as good a man as the shoemaker, then, if the transaction is to follow the universal rule of justice and leave their relative position unaltered, in exchange for a certain quantity of husbandman's work the shoemaker must give twice as much of his own. The price, that is, of corn and shoes must be so adjusted that, if a quarter of corn sell for 50s. and three pair of shoes sell for the same sum, the three pair of shoes must represent twice as much labour as the quarter of corn. Aristotle speaks loosely of the ratio between the shoes and the corn, etc., but as their value is ex hypothesei the same, and as the relative size, weight, and number of articles is quite accidental (e.g. we might as well measure the corn by bushels or by pounds), the ratio intended can only be the ratio between the quantities of labour. He omits to tell us that these quantities must be measured by time, but the omission is easily supplied. He omits also to tell us how the relative-worth of the persons is to be measured, but he has already said all that is necessary in 3, 7.

72. Lit. "they must be reduced to proportion," i.e., in strictness, the four terms (two persons and two things).

73. i.e. have his superiority counted twice over. His (e.g. the husbandman's) superiority over the other party (the shoemaker) has been already taken into account in fixing the price of a quarter of corn as equal to three pairs of shoes: this is one advantage which is fairly his; but it would be plainly unfair if, at the time of exchange, the husbandman were to demand 50s. worth of shoes for 25s. worth of corn, on the ground that he was twice as good a man.

74. The mean which justice aims at (the just thing, the due share of goods) lies between two extremes, too much and too little; so far justice is analogous to the other virtues: but whereas in other fields these two extremes are chosen by different and opposite characters (e.g. the cowardly and the foolhardy), the character that chooses too much is here the same as that which chooses too little,—too much for himself or his friend, too little for his enemy. (The habitual choice of too little for oneself is neglected as impossible). Cf. 11. 6, especially § 15–16.

75. It is in the state of mind of the doer that the difference lies, not in the particular things done: cf. infra, cap. 8.

76. This passage, cap. 6, §§ 1, 2, seems to have quite a natural connection with what goes before, though the discussion is not carried on here, but in cap. 8. Again, the discussion which begins with the words πῶς μὲν ουν, cap. 6, § 3, though it has no connection with § 2, comes naturally enough after the end of cap. 5, τὸ ἁπλῶς δίκαιον corresponding to τοῦ δικαίου καὶ ἀδίκου καθόλου. We have, then, two discussions, both growing out of and attached to the discussion which closes with the end of cap. 5, but not connected with each other. If the author had revised the work, he would, no doubt, have fitted these links together; but as he omitted to do so, it is useless for us to attempt, by any rearrangement of the links, to secure the close connection which could only be effected by forging them anew.

77. These are not two distinct kinds of justice; justice proper, he means to say, implies a state.

78. Only the citizen in an ancient state could appeal to the law in his own person; the non-citizen could only sue through a citizen.

79. Supra, 1, 17.

80. Which alone is properly just.

81. τὸ ξυμφέρον, which is usually rendered "expedient," means simply that which conduces to any desired end; as the end varies, then, so will the expedient vary: cf. III. 1, 15, note.

82. e.g. the wine-merchant may buy in the cask what he sells in bottle (Stewart).

83. Cf. § 4.

84. i.e. he willed the act not as just, but as a means of avoiding the painful consequences; the justice of it, therefore, was not part of the essence of the act to him, was not among the qualities of the act which moved him to choose it, or, in Aristotle's language, was "accidental."

85. which leads by a natural, though by him unforeseen, sequence to his neighbour's hurt: negligence, or error of judgment.

86. and gives a fatal termination to an act that would ordinarily be harmless: accident.

87. You can always do the acts if you want to do them, i.e. if you will them; but you cannot at will do them in the spirit of a just or an unjust man; for character is the result of a series of acts of will: cf. supra, III. 5, 22. The contradiction between this and III. 5, 2, is only apparent: we are responsible for our character, though we cannot change it at a moment's notice.

88. Supra, cap. 9.

89. Whereas, says Aristotle, we cannot speak at all of justice or injustice to one's self, and it is only by way of metaphor that we can apply the terms even to the relations of parts of the self—not strictly, since the parts are not persons.

90. τὸ αἱρετὸν covers, as no English word can, the transition from desired to desirable.

91. The neutral state, neither pleasure nor pain, which they hold to be good.

92. As already remarked, there is no one English word which includes these various senses of ἕξις, (1) habit of

body, (2) moral habit or character, (3) intellectual habit or trained faculty.

93.   At other periods of life the various organs of the body may perform their functions completely, but in youth this is accompanied by an inexpressible charm which all other ages lack.

The only analogy between pleasure and the doctor is that both "complete the activity" from outside: medicines alter the functions; pleasure, like beauty, does not alter them, but is an added perfection.

94.   Sight and touch are classed together on the one hand, and hearing, smell, and taste on the other, because, while the announcements of all the senses are, in the first instance, of secondary qualities (colours, sounds, etc.), it is mainly from the announcements of sight and touch that we advance to the knowledge of the mathematical properties or primary qualities (number, figure, motion, etc.).

95.   ἡ κατὰ τὴν σοφίαν ἐνέργεια, the contemplation of absolute truth.

96.   The search for this truth.

97.   *i.e.* our nature as moral agents, as compounds of reason and desire.

98.   *i.e.* the principles of morals cannot be proved, but are accepted without proof by the man whose desires are properly trained. *Cf. supra,* 1. 4, 6.

99.   Before theory or instruction can be any use. *Cf.* I. 4, 6.

100.   The work to which this conclusion forms a preface is the Politics of Aristotle, still extant, but in an incomplete state.

2.   FUNDAMENTAL PRINCIPLES OF THE METAPHYSICS OF MORALS

Immanuel Kant

PREFACE

Ancient Greek philosophy was divided into three sciences: Physics, Ethics, and Logic. This division is perfectly suitable to the nature of the thing; and the only improvement that can be made in it is to add the principle on which it is based, so that we may both satisfy ourselves of its completeness, and also be able to determine correctly the necessary subdivisions.

All rational knowledge is either *material* or *formal:* the former considers some object, the latter is concerned only with the form of the understanding and of the reason itself, and with the universal laws of thought in general without distinction of its objects. Formal philosophy is called Logic. Material philosophy, however, which has to do with determinate objects and the laws to which they are subject, is again two-

From *Kant's Critique of Practical Reason and Other Works on the Theory of Ethics,* translated by Thomas Kingsmill Abbott, 6th edition, 1909. First edition of this translation 1873. *Fundamental Principles of the Metaphysics of Morals,* a translation of *Grundlegung zur Metaphysik der Sitten,* first published in 1785. Preface, First Section, and Second Section.

fold; for these laws are either laws of *nature* or of *freedom.* The science of the former is Physics, that of the latter, Ethics; they are also called *natural philosophy* and *moral philosophy* respectively.

Logic cannot have any empirical part; that is, a part in which the universal and necessary laws of thought should rest on grounds taken from experience; otherwise it would not be logic, *i.e.* a canon for the understanding or the reason, valid for all thought, and capable of demonstration. Natural and moral philosophy, on the contrary, can each have their empirical part, since the former has to determine the laws of nature as an object of experience; the latter the laws of the human will, so far as it is affected by nature: the former, however, being laws according to which everything does happen; the latter, laws according to which everything ought to happen. Ethics, however, must also consider the conditions under which what ought to happen frequently does not.

We may call all philosophy *empirical,* so far as it is based on grounds of experience: on the other hand, that which delivers its doctrines from *à priori* principles alone we may call *pure* philosophy. When the latter is merely formal, it is *logic;* if it is restricted to definite objects of the understanding, it is *metaphysic.*

In this way there arises the idea of a twofold metaphysic—a *metaphysic of nature* and a *metaphysic of morals.* Physics will thus have an empirical and also a rational part. It is the same with Ethics; but here the empirical part might have the special name of *practical anthropology,* the name *morality* being appropriated to the rational part.

All trades, arts, and handiworks have gained by division of labour, namely, when, instead of one man doing everything, each confines himself to a certain kind of work distinct from others in the treatment it requires, so as to be able to perform it with greater facility and in the greatest perfection. Where the different kinds of work are not so distinguished and divided, where everyone is a jack-of-all-trades, there manufactures remain still in the greatest barbarism. It might deserve to be considered whether pure philosophy in all its parts does not require a man specially devoted to it, and whether it would not be better for the whole business of science if those who, to please the tastes of the public, are wont to blend the rational and empirical elements together, mixed in all sorts of proportions unknown to themselves, and who call themselves independent thinkers, giving the name of minute philosophers to those who apply themselves to the rational part only—if these, I say, were warned not to carry on two employments together which differ widely in the treatment they demand, for each of which perhaps a special talent is required, and the combination of which in one person only produces bunglers. But I only ask here whether the nature of science does not require that we should always carefully separate the empirical from the rational part, and prefix to Physics proper (or empirical physics) a metaphysic of nature, and to practical anthropology a metaphysic of morals, which must be carefully cleared of everything empirical, so that we may know how much can be accomplished by pure reason in both cases, and from what sources it draws this its *à priori* teach-

ing, and that whether the latter inquiry is conducted by all moralists (whose name is legion), or only by some who feel a calling thereto.

As my concern here is with moral philosophy, I limit the question suggested to this: Whether it is not of the utmost necessity to construct a pure moral philosophy, perfectly cleared of everything which is only empirical, and which belongs to anthropology? for that such a philosophy must be possible is evident from the common idea of duty and of the moral laws. Everyone must admit that if a law is to have moral force, *i.e.* to be the basis of an obligation, it must carry with it absolute necessity; that, for example, the precept, "Thou shalt not lie," is not valid for men alone, as if other rational beings had no need to observe it; and so with all the other moral laws properly so called; that, therefore, the basis of obligation must not be sought in the nature of man, or in the circumstances in the world in which he is placed, but *à priori* simply in the conceptions of pure reason; and although any other precept which is founded on principles of mere experience may be in certain respects universal, yet in as far as it rests even in the least degree on an empirical basis, perhaps only as to a motive, such a precept, while it may be a practical rule, can never be called a moral law.

Thus not only are moral laws with their principles essentially distinguished from every other kind of practical knowledge in which there is anything empirical, but all moral philosophy rests wholly on its pure part. When applied to man, it does not borrow the least thing from the knowledge of man himself (anthropology), but gives laws *à priori* to him as a rational being. No doubt these laws require a judgment sharpened by experience, in order on the one hand to distinguish in what cases they are applicable, and on the other to procure for them access to the will of the man, and effectual influence on conduct; since man is acted on by so many inclinations that, though capable of the idea of a practical pure reason, he is not so easily able to make it effective *in concreto* in his life.

A metaphysic of morals is therefore indispensably necessary, not merely for speculative reasons, in order to investigate the sources of the practical principles which are to be found *à priori* in our reason, but also because morals themselves are liable to all sorts of corruption, as long as we are without that clue and supreme canon by which to estimate them correctly. For in order that an action should be morally good, it is not enough that it *conform* to the moral law, but it must also be done *for the sake of the law,* otherwise that conformity is only very contingent and uncertain; since a principle which is not moral, although it may now and then produce actions conformable to the law, will also often produce actions which contradict it. Now it is only in a pure philosophy that we can look for the moral law in its purity and genuineness (and, in a practical matter, this is of the utmost consequence): we must, therefore, begin with pure philosophy (metaphysic), and without it there cannot be any moral philosophy at all. That which mingles these pure principles with the empirical does not deserve the name of philosophy (for what distinguishes philosophy from common rational knowledge is, that it treats in separate sciences what the latter only comprehends confusedly); much less does it deserve that of moral philosophy, since by this confusion it even spoils the purity of morals themselves, and conteracts its own end.

Let it not be thought, however, that what is here demanded is already extant in the propædeutic prefixed by the celebrated Wolf[1] to his moral philosophy, namely, his so-called *general practical philosophy,* and that, therefore, we have not to strike into an entirely new field. Just because it was to be a general practical philosophy, it has not taken into consideration a will of any particular kind—say one which should be determined solely from *à priori* principles without any empirical motives, and which we might call a pure will, but volition in general, with all the actions and conditions which belong to it in this general signification. By this it is distinguished from a metaphysic of morals, just as general logic, which treats of the acts and canons of thought *in general,* is distinguished from transcendental philosophy, which treats of the particular acts and canons of *pure* thought, *i.e.* that whose cognitions are altogether *à priori.* For the metaphysic of morals has to examine the idea and the principles of a possible *pure* will, and not the acts and conditions of human volition generally, which for the most part are drawn from psychology. It is true that moral laws and duty are spoken of in the general practical philosophy (contrary indeed to all fitness). But this is no objection, for in this respect also the authors of that science remain true to their idea of it; they do not distinguish the motives which are prescribed as such by reason alone altogether *à priori,* and which are properly moral, from the empirical motives which the understanding raises to general conceptions merely by comparison of experiences; but without noticing the difference of their sources, and looking on them all as homogeneous, they consider only their greater or less amount. It is in this way they frame their notion of *obligation,* which, though anything but moral, is all that can be asked for in a philosophy which passes no judgment at all on the origin of all possible practical concepts, whether they are *à priori,* or only *à posteriori.*

Intending to publish hereafter a metaphysic of morals, I issue in the first instance these fundamental principles. Indeed there is properly no other foundation for it than the *critical examination of a pure practical reason;* just as that of metaphysics is the critical examination of the pure speculative reason, already published. But in the first place the former is not so absolutely necessary as the latter, because in moral concerns human reason can easily be brought to a high degree of correctness and completeness, even in the commonest understanding, while on the contrary in its theoretic but pure use it is wholly dialectical; and in the second place if the critique of a pure practical reason is to be complete, it must be possible at the same time to show its identity with the speculative reason in a common principle, for it can ultimately be only one and the same reason which has to be distinguished merely in its application. I could not, however, bring it to such completeness here, without introducing considerations of a wholly different kind, which would be perplexing to the reader. On this account I have adopted the title of *Fundamental Principles of the Metaphysic of Morals* instead of that of a *Critical Examination of the pure practical reason.*

But in the third place, since a metaphysic of morals, in spite of the discouraging title, is yet capable of being presented in a popular form, and one adapted to the common understanding, I find it useful to separate from it this preliminary treatise on its fundamental principles, in order that I may not hereafter have need to introduce these necessarily subtle discussions into a book of a more simple character.

The present treatise is, however, nothing more than the investigation and establishment of *the supreme principle of morality,* and this alone constitutes a study complete in itself, and one which ought to be kept apart from every other moral investigation. No doubt my conclusions on this weighty question, which has hitherto been very unsatisfactorily examined, would receive much light from the application of the same principle to the whole system, and would be greatly confirmed by the adequacy which it exhibits throughout; but I must forego this advantage; which indeed would be after all more gratifying than useful, since the easy applicability of a principle and its apparent adequacy give no very certain proof of its soundness, but rather inspire a certain partiality, which prevents us from examining and estimating it strictly in itself, and without regard to consequences.

I have adopted in this work the method which I think most suitable, proceeding analytically from common knowledge to the determination of its ultimate principle, and again descending synthetically from the examination of this principle and its sources to the common knowledge in which we find it employed. The division will, therefore, be as follows:—

1. *First section.*—Transition from the common rational knowledge of morality to the philosophical.

2. *Second section.*—Transition from popular moral philosophy to the metaphysic of morals.

3. *Third section.*—Final step from the metaphysic of morals to the critique of the pure practical reason.

FIRST SECTION

TRANSITION FROM THE COMMON RATIONAL KNOWLEDGE OF MORALITY TO THE PHILOSOPHICAL

Nothing can possibly be conceived in the world, or even out of it, which can be called good, without qualification, except a Good Will. Intelligence, wit, judgment, and the other *talents* of the mind, however they may be named, or courage, resolution, perseverance, as qualities of temperament, are undoubtedly good and de-

sirable in many respects; but these gifts of nature may also become extremely bad and mischievous if the will which is to make use of them, and which, therefore, constitutes what is called *character,* is not good. It is the same with the *gifts of fortune.* Power, riches, honour, even health, and the general well-being and contentment with one's condition which is called *happiness,* inspire pride, and often presumption, if there is not a good will to correct the influence of these on the mind, and with this also to rectify the whole principle of acting, and adapt it to its end. The sight of a being who is not adorned with a single feature of a pure and good will, enjoying unbroken prosperity, can never give pleasure to an impartial rational spectator. Thus a good will appears to constitute the indispensable condition even of being worthy of happiness.

There are even some qualities which are of service to this good will itself, and may facilitate its action, yet which have no intrinsic unconditional value, but always presuppose a good will, and this qualifies the esteem that we justly have for them, and does not permit us to regard them as absolutely good. Moderation in the affections and passions, self-control, and calm deliberation are not only good in many respects, but even seem to constitute part of the intrinsic worth of the person; but they are far from deserving to be called good without qualification, although they have been so unconditionally praised by the ancients. For without the principles of a good will, they may become extremely bad; and the coolness of a villain not only makes him far more dangerous, but also directly makes him more abominable in our eyes than he would have been without it.

A good will is good not because of what it performs or effects, not by its aptness for the attainment of some proposed end, but simply by virtue of the volition, that is, it is good in itself, and considered by itself is to be esteemed much higher than all that can be brought about by it in favour of any inclination, nay, even of the sum-total of all inclinations. Even if it should happen that, owing to special disfavour of fortune, or the niggardly provision of a step-motherly nature, this will should wholly lack power to accomplish its purpose, if with its greatest efforts it should yet achieve nothing, and there should remain only the good will (not, to be sure, a mere wish, but the summoning of all means in our power), then, like a jewel, it would still shine by its own light, as a thing which has its whole value in itself. Its usefulness or fruitlessness can neither add to nor take away anything from this value. It would be, as it were, only the setting to enable us to handle it the more conveniently in common commerce, or to attract to it the attention of those who are not yet connoisseurs, but not to recommend it to true connoisseurs, or to determine its value.

There is, however, something so strange in this idea of the absolute value of the mere will, in which no account is taken of its utility, that notwithstanding the thorough assent of even common reason to the idea, yet a suspicion must arise that it may perhaps really be the product of mere high-flown fancy, and that we may have misunderstood the purpose of nature in assigning reason as the governor of our will. Therefore we will examine this idea from this point of view.

In the physical constitution of an organized being, that is, a being adapted suitably to the purposes of life, we assume it as a fundamental principle that no organ for any purpose will be found but what is also the fittest and best adapted for that purpose. Now in a being which has reason and a will, if the proper object of nature were its *conservation,* its *welfare,* in a word, its *happiness,* then nature would have hit upon a very bad arrangement in selecting the reason of the creature to carry out this purpose. For all the actions which the creature has to perform with a view to this purpose, and the whole rule of its conduct, would be far more surely prescribed to it by instinct, and that end would have been attained thereby much more certainly than it ever can be by reason. Should reason have been communicated to this favoured creature over and above, it must only have served it to contemplate the happy constitution of its nature, to admire it, to congratulate itself thereon, and to feel thankful for it to the beneficent cause, but not that it should subject its desires to that weak and delusive guidance, and meddle bunglingly with the purpose of nature. In a word, nature would have taken care that reason should not break forth into *practical exercise,* nor have the presumption, with its weak insight, to think out for itself the plan of happiness, and of the means of attaining it. Nature would not only have taken on herself the choice of the ends, but also of the means, and with wise foresight would have entrusted both to instinct.

And, in fact, we find that the more a cultivated reason applies itself with deliberate purpose to the enjoyment of life and happiness, so much the more does the man fail of true satisfaction. And from this circumstance there arises in many, if they are candid enough to confess it, a certain degree of *misology,* that is, hatred of reason, especially in the case of those who are most experienced in the use of it, because after calculating all the advantages they derive, I do not say from the invention of all the arts of common luxury, but even from the sciences (which seem to them to be after all only a luxury of the understanding), they find that they have, in fact, only brought more trouble on their shoulders, rather than gained in happiness; and they end by envying, rather than despising, the more common stamp of men who keep closer to the guidance of mere instinct, and do not allow their reason much influence on their conduct. And this we must admit, that the judgment of those who would very much lower the lofty eulogies of the advantages which reason gives us in regard to the happiness and satisfaction of life, or who would even reduce them below zero, is by no means morose or ungrateful to the goodness with which the world is governed, but that there lies at the root of these judgments the idea that our existence has a different and far nobler end, for which, and not for happiness, reason is properly intended, and which must, therefore, be regarded as the supreme condition to which the private ends of man must, for the most part, be postponed.

For as reason is not competent to guide the will with certainty in regard to its objects and the satisfaction of all our wants (which it to some extent even multiples), this being an end to which an implanted instinct would have led with much greater certainty; and since, nevertheless, reason is imparted to us as a practical faculty, *i.e.* as one which is to have influence on the *will,* therefore, admitting that nature generally in the distribution of her capacities has adapted the means to the end, its true destination must be to produce a *will,* not merely good as a *means* to something else, but *good in itself,* for which reason was absolutely necessary. This will then, though not indeed the sole and complete good, must be the supreme good and the condition of every other, even of the desire of happiness. Under these circumstances, there is nothing inconsistent with the wisdom of nature in the fact that the cultivation of the reason, which is requisite for the first and unconditional purpose, does in many ways interfere, at least in this life, with the attainment of the second, which is always conditional, namely, happiness. Nay, it may even reduce it to nothing, without nature thereby failing of her purpose. For reason recognizes the establishment of a good will as its highest practical destination, and in attaining this purpose is capable only of a satisfaction of its own proper kind, namely, that from the attainment of an end, which end again is determined by reason only, notwithstanding that this may involve many a disappointment to the ends of inclination.

We have then to develop the notion of a will which deserves to be highly esteemed for itself, and is good without a view to anything further, a notion which exists already in the sound natural understanding, requiring rather to be cleared up than to be taught, and which in estimating the value of our actions always takes the first place, and constitutes the condition of all the rest. In order to do this, we will take the notion of duty, which includes that of a good will, although implying certain subjective restrictions and hindrances. These, however, far from concealing it, or rendering it unrecognizable, rather bring it out by contrast, and make it shine forth so much the brighter.

I omit here all actions which are already recognized as inconsistent with duty, although they may be useful for this or that purpose, for with these the question whether they are done *from duty* cannot arise at all, since they even conflict with it. I also set aside those actions which really conform to duty, but to which men have *no* direct *inclination,* performing them because they are impelled thereto by some other inclination. For in this case we can readily distinguish whether the action which agrees with duty is done *from duty,* or from a selfish view. It is much harder to make this distinction when the action accords with duty, and the subject has besides a *direct* inclination to it. For example, it is always a matter of duty that a dealer should not overcharge an inexperienced purchaser; and wherever there is much commerce the prudent tradesman does not overcharge, but keeps a fixed price for everyone, so that a child buys of him as well as any other. Men are thus *honestly* served; but this is not enough to make us believe that the tradesman has so acted from duty and from principles of honesty: his own advantage required it; it is out of the question in this case to suppose that he might besides have a direct inclination in favour of the buyers, so that, as it were, from love he should give no advantage to one over another. Accordingly the action was done neither from duty nor from direct inclination, but merely with a selfish view.

On the other hand, it is a duty to maintain one's life; and, in addition, everyone has also a direct inclination to do so. But on this account the often anxious care which most men take for it has no intrinsic worth, and their maxim has no moral import. They preserve their life *as duty requires,* no doubt, but not *because duty requires.* On the other hand, if adversity and hopeless sorrow have completely taken away the relish for life; if the unfortunate one, strong in mind, indignant at his fate rather than desponding or dejected, wishes for death, and yet preserves his life without loving it—not from inclination or fear, but from duty—then his maxim has a moral worth.

To be beneficent when we can is a duty; and besides this, there are many minds so sympathetically constituted that, without any other motive of vanity or self-interest, they find a pleasure in spreading joy around them, and can take delight in the satisfaction of others so far as it is their own work. But I maintain that in such a case an action of this kind, however proper, however amiable it may be, has nevertheless no true moral worth, but is on a level with other inclinations, *e.g.* the inclination to honour, which, if it is happily directed to that which is in fact of public utility and accordant with duty, and consequently honourable, deserves praise and encouragement, but not esteem. For the maxim lacks the moral import, namely, that such actions be done *from duty,* not from inclination. Put the case that the mind of that philanthropist was clouded by sorrow of his own, extinguishing all sympathy with the lot of others, and that while he still has the power to benefit others in distress, he is not touched by their trouble because he is absorbed with his own; and now suppose that he tears himself out of this dead insensibility, and performs the action without any inclination to it, but simply from duty, then first has his action its genuine moral worth. Further still; if nature has put little sympathy in the heart of this or that man; if he, supposed to be an upright man, is by temperament cold and indifferent to the sufferings of others, perhaps because in respect of his own he is provided with the special gift of patience and fortitude, and supposes, or even requires, that others should have the same—and such a man would certainly not be the meanest product of nature—but if nature had not specially framed him for a philanthropist, would he not still find in himself a source from whence to give himself a far higher worth than that of a good-natured temperament could be? Unquestionably. It is just in this that the moral worth of the character is brought out which is incomparably the highest of all, namely, that he is beneficent, not from inclination, but from duty.

To secure one's own happiness is a duty, at least indirectly; for discontent with one's condition, under a pressure of many anxieties and amidst unsatisfied wants, might easily become a great *temptation to transgression of duty.* But here again, without looking to duty, all men have already the strongest and most intimate inclination to happiness, because it is just in this idea that all inclinations are combined in one total. But the precept of happiness is often of such a sort that it greatly interferes with some inclinations, and yet a man cannot form any definite and certain conception of the sum of satisfaction of all of them which is called happiness. It is not then to be wondered at that a single inclination, definite both as to what it promises and as to the time within which it can be gratified, is often able to overcome such a fluctuating idea, and that a gouty patient, for instance, can choose to enjoy what he likes, and to suffer what he may, since, according to his calculation, on this occasion at least, he has [only] not sacrificed the enjoyment of the present moment to a possibly mistaken expectation of a happiness which is supposed to be found in health. But even in this case, if the general desire for happiness did not influence

his will, and supposing that in his particular case health was not a necessary element in this calculation, there yet remains in this, as in all other cases, this law, namely, that he should promote his happiness not from inclination but from duty, and by this would his conduct first acquire true moral worth.

It is in this manner, undoubtedly, that we are to understand those passages of Scripture also in which we are commanded to love our neighbour, even our enemy. For love, as an affection, cannot be commanded, but beneficence for duty's sake may: even though we are not impelled to it by any inclination—nay, are even repelled by a natural and unconquerable aversion. This is *practical* love, and not *pathological*—a love which is seated in the will, and not in the propensions of sense—in principles of action and not of tender sympathy; and it is this love alone which can be commanded.

The second[2] proposition is: That an action done from duty derives its moral worth, *not from the purpose* which is to be attained by it, but from the maxim by which it is determined, and therefore does not depend on the realization of the object of the action, but merely on the *principle of volition* by which the action has taken place, without regard to any object of desire. It is clear from what precedes that the purposes which we may have in view in our actions, or their effects regarded as ends and springs of the will, cannot give to actions any unconditional or moral worth. In what, then, can their worth lie, if it is not to consist in the will and in reference to its expected effect? It cannot lie anywhere but in the *principle of the will* without regard to the ends which can be attained by the action. For the will stands between its *à priori* principle, which is formal, and its *à posteriori* spring, which is material, as between two roads, and as it must be determined by something, it follows that it must be determined by the formal principle of volition when an action is done from duty, in which case every material principle has been withdrawn from it.

The third proposition, which is a consequence of the two preceding, I would express thus: *Duty is the necessity of acting from respect for the law.* I may have *inclination* for an object as the effect of my proposed action, but I cannot have *respect* for it, just for this reason, that it is an effect and not an energy of will. Similarly, I cannot have respect for inclination, whether my own or another's; I can at most, if my own, approve it; if another's, sometimes even love it; *i.e.* look on it as favourable to my own interest. It is only what is connected with my will as a principle, by no means as an effect—what does not subserve my inclination, but overpowers it, or at least in case of choice excludes it from its calculation—in other words, simply the law of itself, which can be an object of respect, and hence a command. Now an action done from duty must wholly exclude the influence of inclination, and with it every object of the will, so that nothing remains which can determine the will except objectively the *law,* and subjectively *pure respect* for this practical law, and consequently the maxim[3] that I should follow this law even to the thwarting of all my inclinations.

Thus the moral worth of an action does not lie in the effect expected from it, nor in any principle of action which requires to borrow its motive from this expected effect. For all these effects—aggreeableness of one's condition, and even the promotion of the happiness of others—could have been also brought about by other causes, so that for this there would have been no need of the will of a rational being; whereas it is in this alone that the supreme and unconditional good can be found. The pre-eminent good which we call moral can therefore consist in nothing else than *the conception of law* in itself, *which certainly is only possible in a rational being,* in so far as this conception, and not the expected effect, determines the will. This is a good which is already present in the person who acts accordingly, and we have not to wait for it to appear first in the result.[4]

But what sort of law can that be, the conception of which must determine the will, even without paying any regard to the effect expected from it, in order that this will may be called good absolutely and without qualification? As I have deprived the will of every impulse which could arise to it from obedience to any law, there remains nothing but the universal conformity of its actions to law in general, which alone is to serve the will as a principle, *i.e.* I am never to act otherwise than so *that I could also will that my maxim should become a universal law.* Here, now, it is the simple conformity to law in general,

without assuming any particular law applicable to certain actions, that serves the will as its principle, and must so serve it, if duty is not to be a vain delusion and a chimerical notion. The common reason of men in its practical judgments perfectly coincides with this, and always has in view the principle here suggested. Let the question be, for example: May I when in distress make a promise with the intention not to keep it? I readily distinguish here between the two significations which the question may have: Whether it is prudent, or whether it is right, to make a false promise? The former may undoubtedly often be the case. I see clearly indeed that it is not enough to extricate myself from a present difficulty by means of this subterfuge, but it must be well considered whether there may not hereafter spring from this lie much greater inconvenience than that from which I now free myself, and as, with all my supposed *cunning,* the consequences cannot be so easily foreseen but that credit once lost may be much more injurious to me than any mischief which I seek to avoid at present, it should be considered whether it would not be more *prudent* to act herein according to a universal maxim, and to make it a habit to promise nothing except with the intention of keeping it. But it is soon clear to me that such a maxim will still only be based on the fear of consequences. Now it is a wholly different thing to be truthful from duty, and to be so from apprehension of injurious consequences. In the first case, the very notion of the action already implies a law for me; in the second case, I must first look about elsewhere to see what results may be combined with it which would affect myself. For to deviate from the principle of duty is beyond all doubt wicked; but to be unfaithful to my maxim of prudence may often be very advantageous to me, although to abide by it is certainly safer. The shortest way, however, and an unerring one, to discover the answer to this question whether a lying promise is consistent with duty, is to ask myself, Should I be content that my maxim (to extricate myself from difficulty by a false promise) should hold good as a universal law, for myself as well as for others? and should I be able to say to myself, "Every one may make a deceitful promise when he finds himself in a difficulty from which he cannot otherwise extricate himself"? Then I presently become aware that while I can will the lie, I can by no means will that lying should be a universal law. For with such a law there would be no promises at all, since it would be in vain to allege my intention in regard to my future actions to those who would not believe this allegation, or if they over-hastily did so, would pay me back in my own coin. Hence my maxim, as soon as it should be made a universal law, would necessarily destroy itself.

I do not, therefore, need any far-reaching penetration to discern what I have to do in order that my will may be morally good. Inexperienced in the course of the world, incapable of being prepared for all its contingencies, I only ask myself: Canst thou also will that thy maxim should be a universal law? If not, then it must be rejected, and that not because of a disadvantage accruing from it to myself or even to others, but because it cannot enter as a principle into a possible universal legislation, and reason extorts from me immediate respect for such legislation. I do not indeed as yet *discern* on what this respect is based (this the philosopher may inquire), but at least I understand this, that it is an estimation of the worth which far outweighs all worth of what is recommended by inclination, and that the necessity of acting from *pure* respect for the practical law is what constitutes duty, to which every other motive must give place, because it is the condition of a will being good *in itself,* and the worth of such a will is above everything.

Thus, then, without quitting the moral knowledge of common human reason, we have arrived at its principle. And although, no doubt, common men do not conceive it in such an abstract and universal form, yet they always have it really before their eyes, and use it as the standard of their decision. Here it would be easy to show how, with this compass in hand, men are well able to distinguish, in every case that occurs, what is good, what bad, conformably to duty or inconsistent with it, if, without in the least teaching them anything new, we only, like Socrates, direct their attention to the principle they themselves employ; and that, therefore, we do not need science and philosophy to know what we should do to be honest and good, yea, even wise and virtuous. Indeed we might well have conjectured beforehand that the knowledge of what every man is bound to do, and therefore also to

know, would be within the reach of every man, even the commonest.[5] Here we cannot forbear admiration when we see how great an advantage the practical judgment has over the theoretical in the common understanding of men. In the latter, if common reason ventures to depart from the laws of experience and from the perceptions of the senses, it falls into mere inconceivabilities and self-contradictions, at least into a chaos of uncertainty, obscurity, and instability. But in the practical sphere it is just when the common understanding excludes all sensible springs from practical laws that its power of judgment begins to show itself to advantage. It then becomes even subtle, whether it be that it chicanes with its own conscience or with other claims respecting what is to be called right, or whether it desires for its own instruction to determine honestly the worth of actions; and, in the latter case, it may even have as good a hope of hitting the mark as any philosopher whatever can promise himself. Nay, it is almost more sure of doing so, because the philosopher cannot have any other principle, while he may easily perplex his judgment by a multitude of considerations foreign to the matter, and so turn aside from the right way. Would it not therefore be wiser in moral concerns to acquiesce in the judgment of common reason, or at most only to call in philosophy for the purpose of rendering the system of morals more complete and intelligible, and its rules more convenient for use (especially for disputation), but not so as to draw off the common understanding from its happy simplicity, or to bring it by means of philosophy into a new path of inquiry and instruction?

Innocence is indeed a glorious thing, only, on the other hand, it is very sad that it cannot well maintain itself, and is easily seduced. On this account even wisdom—which otherwise consists more in conduct than in knowledge—yet has need of science, not in order to learn from it, but to secure for its precepts admission and permanence. Against all the commands of duty which reason represents to man as so deserving of respect, he feels in himself a powerful counterpoise in his wants and inclinations, the entire satisfaction of which he sums up under the name of happiness. Now reason issues its commands unyieldingly, without promising anything to the inclinations, and, as it were, with disregard and contempt for these claims, which are so impetuous, and at the same time so plausible, and which will not allow themselves to be suppressed by any command. Hence there arises a natural *dialectic,* i.e. a disposition, to argue against these strict laws of duty and to question their validity, or at least their purity and strictness; and, if possible, to make them more accordant with our wishes and inclinations, that is to say, to corrupt them at their very source, and entirely to destroy their worth—a thing which even common practical reason cannot ultimately call good.

Thus is the *common reason of man* compelled to go out of its sphere, and to take a step into the field of a *practical philosophy,* not to satisfy any speculative want (which never occurs to it as long as it is content to be mere sound reason), but even on practical grounds, in order to attain in it information and clear instruction respecting the source of its principle, and the correct determination of it in opposition to the maxims which are based on wants and inclinations, so that it may escape from the perplexity of opposite claims, and not run the risk of losing all genuine moral principles through the equivocation into which it easily falls. Thus, when practical reason cultivates itself, there insensibly arises in it a dialectic which forces it to seek aid in philosophy, just as happens to it in its theoretic use; and in this case, therefore, as well as in the other, it will find rest nowhere but in a thorough critical examination of our reason.

SECOND SECTION

TRANSITION FROM POPULAR MORAL PHILOSOPHY TO THE METAPHYSIC OF MORALS

If we have hitherto drawn our notion of duty from the common use of our practical reason, it is by no means to be inferred that we have treated it as an empirical notion. On the contrary, if we attend to the experience of men's conduct, we meet frequent and, as we ourselves allow, just complaints that one cannot find a single certain example of the disposition to act from pure duty. Although many things are done in *conformity* with what *duty* prescribes, it is nevertheless always doubtful whether they are done strictly *from duty,* so as to have a moral worth. Hence there have at all times been philosophers who have altogether denied that this disposition actually exists at all in human actions, and have ascribed everything to a more or less refined self-love. Not that they have on that account questioned the soundness of the conception of morality; on the contrary, they spoke with sincere regret of the frailty and corruption of human nature, which though noble enough to take as its rule an idea so worthy of respect, is yet too weak to follow it, and employs reason, which ought to give it the law only for the purpose of providing for the interest of the inclinations, whether singly or at the best in the greatest possible harmony with one another.

In fact, it is absolutely impossible to make out by experience with complete certainty a single case in which the maxim of an action, however right in itself, rested simply on moral grounds and on the conception of duty. Sometimes it happens that with the sharpest self-examination we can find nothing beside the moral principle of duty which could have been powerful enough to move us to this or that action and to so great a sacrifice; yet we cannot from this infer with certainty that it was not really some secret impulse of self-love, under the false appearance of duty, that was the actual determining cause of the will. We like then to flatter ourselves by falsely taking credit for a more noble motive; whereas in fact we can never, even by the strictest examination, get completely behind the secret springs of action; since, when the question is of moral worth, it is not with the actions which we see that we are concerned, but with those inward principles of them which we do not see.

Moreover, we cannot better serve the wishes of those who ridicule all morality as a mere chimera of human imagination overstepping itself from vanity, than by conceding to them that notions of duty must be drawn only from experience (as from indolence, people are ready to think is also the case with all other notions); for this is to prepare for them a certain triumph. I am willing to admit out of love of humanity that even most of our actions are correct, but if we look closer at them we everywhere come upon the dear self which is always prominent, and it is this they have in view, and not the strict command of duty which would often require self-denial. Without being an enemy of virtue, a cool observer, one that does not mistake the wish for good, however lively, for its reality, may sometimes doubt whether true virtue is actually found anywhere in the world, and this especially as years increase and the judgment is partly made wiser by experience, and partly also more acute in observation. This being so, nothing can secure us from falling away altogether from our ideas of duty, or maintain in the soul a well-grounded respect for its law, but the clear conviction that although there should never have been actions which really sprang from such pure sources, yet whether this or that takes place is not at all the question; but that reason of itself, independent on all experience, ordains what ought to take place, that accordingly actions of which perhaps the world has hitherto never given an example, the feasibility even of which might be very much doubted by one who founds everything on experience, are nevertheless inflexibly commanded by reason; that, *ex. gr.,* even though there might never yet have been a sincere friend, yet not a whit the less is pure sincerity in friendship required of every man, because, prior to all experience, this duty is involved as duty in the idea of a reason determining the will by *à priori* principles.

When we add further that, unless we deny that the notion of morality has any truth or reference to any possible object, we must admit that its law must be valid, not merely for men, but for all *rational creatures generally,* not merely under certain contingent conditions or with exceptions, but *with absolute necessity,* then it is clear that no experience could enable us to infer even the possibility of such apodictic laws. For with what right could we bring into unbounded respect as a universal precept for every rational nature that which perhaps holds only under the contingent conditions of humanity? Or how could laws of the determination of *our* will be regarded as laws of the determination of the will of rational beings generally, and for us only as such, if they were merely empirical, and did not take their origin wholly *à priori* from pure but practical reason?

Nor could anything be more fatal to morality than that we should wish to derive it from examples. For every example of it that is set before me must be first itself tested by principles of morality, whether it is worthy to serve as an original

example, *i.e.* as a pattern, but by no means can it authoritatively furnish the conception of morality. Even the Holy One of the Gospels must first be compared with our ideal of moral perfection before we can recognize Him as such; and so He says of Himself, "Why call ye Me [whom you see] good; none is good [the model of good] but God only [whom ye do not see]?" But whence have we the conception of God as the supreme good? Simply from the *idea* of moral perfection, which reason frames *à priori,* and connects inseparably with the notion of a free will. Imitation finds no place at all in morality, and examples serve only for encouragement, *i.e.* they put beyond doubt the feasibility of what the law commands, they make visible that which the practical rule expresses more generally, but they can never authorize us to set aside the true original which lies in reason, and to guide ourselves by examples.

If then there is no genuine supreme principle of morality but what must rest simply on pure reason, independent on all experience, I think it is not necessary even to put the question, whether it is good to exhibit these concepts in their generality (*in abstracto*) as they are established *à priori* along with the principles belonging to them, if our knowledge is to be distinguished from the *vulgar,* and to be called philosophical. In our times indeed this might perhaps be necessary; for if we collected votes, whether pure rational knowledge separated from everything empirical, that is to say, metaphysic of morals, or whether popular practical philosophy is to be preferred, it is easy to guess which side would preponderate.

This descending to popular notions is certainly very commendable, if the ascent to the principles of pure reason has first taken place and been satisfactorily accomplished. This implies that we first *found* Ethics on Metaphysics, and then, when it is firmly established, procure a *hearing* for it by giving it a popular character. But it is quite absurd to try to be popular in the first inquiry, on which the soundness of the principles depends. It is not only that this proceeding can never lay claim to the very rare merit of a true *philosophical popularity,* since there is no art in being intelligible if one renounces all thoroughness of insight; but also it produces a disgusting medley of compiled observations and half-reasoned principles. Shallow pates enjoy this because it can be used for every-day chat, but the sagacious find in it only confusion, and being unsatisfied and unable to help themselves, they turn away their eyes, while philosophers, who see quite well through this delusion, are little listened to when they call men off for a time from this pretended popularity, in order that they might be rightfully popular after they have attained a definite insight.

We need only look at the attempts of moralists in that favourite fashion, and we shall find at one time the special constitution of human nature (including, however, the idea of a rational nature generally), at one time perfection, at another happiness, here moral sense, there fear of God, a little of this, and a little of that, in marvellous mixture, without its occurring to them to ask whether the principles of morality are to be sought in the knowledge of human nature at all (which we can have only from experience); and, if this is not so, if these principles are to be found altogether *à priori* free from everything empirical, in pure rational concepts only, and nowhere else, not even in the smallest degree; then rather to adopt the method of making this a separate inquiry, as pure practical philosophy, or (if one may use a name so decried) as metaphysic of morals,[6] to bring it by itself to completeness, and to require the public, which wishes for popular treatment, to await the issue of this undertaking.

Such a metaphysic of morals, completely isolated, not mixed with any anthropology, theology, physics, or hyperphysics, and still less with occult qualities (which we might call hypophysical), is not only an indispensable substratum of all sound theoretical knowledge of duties, but is at the same time a desideratum of the highest importance to the actual fulfilment of their precepts. For the pure conception of duty, unmixed with any foreign addition of empirical attractions, and, in a word, the conception of the moral law, exercises on the human heart, by way of reason alone (which first becomes aware with this that it can of itself be practical), an influence so much more powerful than all other springs[7] which may be derived from the field of experience, that in the consciousness of its worth, it despises the latter, and can by degrees become their master; whereas a mixed ethics, compounded partly of motives drawn from feelings and inclinations, and partly also of

conceptions of reason, must make the mind waver between motives which cannot be brought under any principle, which lead to good only by mere accident, and very often also to evil.

From what has been said, it is clear that all moral conceptions have their seat and origin completely *à priori* in the reason, and that, moreover, in the commonest reason just as truly as in that which is in the highest degree speculative; that they cannot be obtained by abstraction from any empirical, and therefore merely contingent knowledge; that it is just this purity of their origin that makes them worthy to serve as our supreme practical principle, and that just in proportion as we add anything empirical, we detract from their genuine influence, and from the absolute value of actions; that it is not only of the greatest necessity, in a purely speculative point of view, but is also of the greatest practical importance, to derive these notions and laws from pure reason, to present them pure and unmixed, and even to determine the compass of this practical or pure rational knowledge, *i.e.* to determine the whole faculty of pure practical reason; and, in doing so, we must not make its principles dependent on the particular nature of human reason, though in speculative philosophy this may be permitted, or may even at times be necessary; but since moral laws ought to hold good for every rational creature, we must derive them from the general concept of a rational being. In this way, although for its *application* to man morality has need of anthropology, yet, in the first instance, we must treat it independently as pure philosophy, *i.e.* as metaphysic, complete in itself (a thing which in such distinct branches of science is easily done); knowing well that unless we are in possession of this, it would not only be vain to determine the moral element of duty in right actions for purposes of speculative criticism, but it would be impossible to base morals on their genuine principles, even for common practical purposes, especially of moral instruction, so as to produce pure moral dispositions, and to engraft them on men's minds to the promotion of the greatest possible good in the world.

But in order that in this study we may not merely advance by the natural steps from the common moral judgment (in this case very worthy of respect) to the philosophical, as has been already done, but also from a popular philosophy, which goes no further than it can reach by groping with the help of examples, to metaphysic (which does not allow itself to be checked by anything empirical, and as it must measure the whole extent of this kind of rational knowledge, goes as far as ideal conceptions, where even examples fail us), we must follow and clearly describe the practical faculty of reason, from the general rules of its determination to the point where the notion of duty springs from it.

Everything in nature works according to laws. Rational beings alone have the faculty of acting according *to the conception* of laws, that is according to principles, *i.e.* have a *will.* Since the deduction of actions from principles requires *reason,* the will is nothing but practical reason. If reason infallibly determines the will, then the actions of such a being which are recognized as objectively necessary are subjectively necessary also, *i.e.* the will is a faculty to choose *that only* which reason independent on inclination recognizes as practically necessary, *i.e.* as good. But if reason of itself does not sufficiently determine the will, if the latter is subject also to subjective conditions (particular impulses) which do not always coincide with the objective conditions; in a word, if the will does not *in itself* completely accord with reason (which is actually the case with men), then the actions which objectively are recognized as necessary are subjectively contingent, and the determination of such a will according to objective laws is *obligation,* that is to say, the relation of the objective laws to a will that is not thoroughly good is conceived as the determination of the will of a rational being by principles of reason, but which the will from its nature does not of necessity follow.

The conception of an objective principle, in so far as it is obligatory for a will, is called a command (of reason), and the formula of the command is called an Imperative.

All imperatives are expressed by the word *ought* [or *shall*], and thereby indicate the relation of an objective law of reason to a will, which from its subjective constitution is not necessarily determined by it (an obligation). They say that something would be good to do or to forbear, but they say it to a will which does not always do a thing because it is conceived to be good to do it. That is practically *good,* however, which determines the will by means of the conceptions of reason, and consequently not from subjective causes, but objectively, that is on principles which are valid for every rational being as such. It is distinguished from the *pleasant,* as that which influences the will only by means of sensation from merely subjective causes, valid only for the sense of this or that one, and not as a principle of reason, which holds for every one.[8]

A perfectly good will would therefore be equally subject to objective laws (viz. laws of good), but could not be conceived as *obliged* thereby to act lawfully, because of itself from its subjective constitution it can only be determined by the conception of good. Therefore no imperatives hold for the Divine will, or in general for a *holy* will; *ought* is here out of place, because the volition is already of itself necessarily in unison with the law. Therefore imperatives are only formulæ to express the relation of objective laws of all volition to the subjective imperfection of the will of this or that rational being, *e.g.* the human will.

Now all *imperatives* command either *hypothetically* or *categorically.* The former represent the practical necessity of a possible action as means to something else that is willed (or at least which one might possibly will). The categorical imperative would be that which represented an action as necessary of itself without reference to another end, *i.e.,* as objectively necessary.

Since every practical law represents a possible action as good, and on this account, for a subject who is practically determinable by reason, necessary, all imperatives are formulae determining an action which is necessary according to the principle of a will good in some respects. If now the action is good only as a means *to something else,* then the imperative is *hypothetical;* if it is conceived as good *in itself* and consequently as being necessarily the principle of a will which of itself conforms to reason, then it is *categorical.*

Thus the imperative declares what action possible by me would be good, and presents the practical rule in relation to a will which does not forthwith perform an action simply because it is good, whether because the subject does not always know that it is good, or because, even if it know this, yet its maxims might be opposed to the objective principles of practical reason.

Accordingly the hypothetical imperative only says that the action is good for some purpose, *possible* or *actual*. In the first case it is a Problematical, in the second an Assertorial practical principle. The categorical imperative which declares an action to be objectively necessary in itself without reference to any purpose, *i.e.* without any other end, is valid as an Apodictic (practical) principle.

Whatever is possible only by the power of some rational being may also be conceived as a possible purpose of some will; and therefore the principles of action as regards the means necessary to attain some possible purpose are in fact infinitely numerous. All sciences have a practical part, consisting of problems expressing that some end is possible for us, and of imperatives directing how it may be attained. These may, therefore, be called in general imperatives of Skill. Here there is no question whether the end is rational and good, but only what one must do in order to attain it. The precepts for the physician to make his patient thoroughly healthy, and for a poisoner to ensure certain death, are of equal value in this respect, that each serves to effect its purpose perfectly. Since in early youth it cannot be known what ends are likely to occur to us in the course of life, parents seek to have their children taught a *great many things,* and provide for their *skill* in the use of means for all sorts of arbitrary ends, of none of which can they determine whether it may not perhaps hereafter be an object to their pupil, but which it is at all events *possible* that he might aim at; and this anxiety is so great that they commonly neglect to form and correct their judgment on the value of the things which may be chosen as ends.

There is *one* end, however, which may be assumed to be actually such to all rational beings (so far as imperatives apply to them, viz. as dependent beings), and, therefore, one purpose which they not merely *may* have, but which we may with certainty assume that they all actually *have* by a natural necessity, and this is *happiness.* The hypothetical imperative which expresses the practical necessity of an action as means to the advancement of happiness is Assertorial. We are not to present it as necessary for an uncertain and merely possible purpose, but for a purpose which we may presuppose with certainty and *à priori* in every man, because it belongs to his being. Now skill in the choice of means to his own greatest well-being may be called *prudence,*[9]

in the narrowest sense. And thus the imperative which refers to the choice of means to one's own happiness, *i.e.* the precept of prudence, is still always *hypothetical;* the action is not commanded absolutely, but only as means to another purpose.

Finally, there is an imperative which commands a certain conduct immediately, without having as its condition any other purpose to be attained by it. This imperative is Categorical. It concerns not the matter of the action, or its intended result, but its form and the principle of which it is itself a result; and what is essentially good in it consists in the mental disposition, let the consequence be what it may. This imperative may be called that of Morality.

There is a marked distinction also between the volitions on these three sorts of principles in the *dissimilarity* of the obligation of the will. In order to mark this difference more clearly, I think they would be most suitably named in their order if we said they are either *rules* of skill, or *counsels* of prudence, or *commands (laws)* of morality. For it is *law* only that involves the conception of an *unconditional* and objective necessity, which is consequently universally valid; and commands are laws which must be obeyed, that is, must be followed, even in opposition to inclination. *Counsels,* indeed, involve necessity, but one which can only hold under a contingent subjective condition, viz. they depend on whether this or that man reckons this or that as part of his happiness; the categorical imperative, on the contrary, is not limited by any condition, and as being absolutely, although practically, necessary, may be quite properly called a command. We might also call the first kind of imperatives *technical* (belonging to art), the second *pragmatic*[10] (to welfare), the third *moral* (belonging to free conduct generally, that is, to morals).

Now arises the question, how are all these imperatives possible? This question does not seek to know how we can conceive the accomplishment of the action which the imperative ordains, but merely how we can conceive the obligation of the will which the imperative expresses. No special explanation is needed to show how an imperative of skill is possible. Whoever wills the end, wills also (so far as reason decides his conduct) the means in his power which are indispensably necessary thereto. This proposition is, as regards the volition, analytical; for, in willing an object as my effect, there is already thought the causality of myself as an acting cause, that is to say, the use of the means; and the imperative educes from the conception of volition of an end the conception of actions necessary to this end. Synthetical propositions must no doubt be employed in defining the means to a proposed end; but they do not concern the principle, the act of the will, but the object and its realization. *Ex. gr.,* that in order to bisect a line on an unerring principle I must draw from its extremities two intersecting arcs; this no doubt is taught by mathematics only in synthetical propositions; but if I know that it is only by this process that the intended operation can be performed, then to say that if I fully will the operation, I also will the action required for it, is an analytical proposition; for it is one and the same thing to conceive something as an effect which I can produce in a certain way, and to conceive myself as acting in this way.

If it were only equally easy to give a definite conception of happiness, the imperatives of prudence would correspond exactly with those of skill, and would likewise be analytical. For in this case as in that, it could be said, whoever wills the end, wills also (according to the dictate of reason necessarily) the indispensable means thereto which are in his power. But, unfortunately, the notion of happiness is so indefinite that although every man wishes to attain it, yet he never can say definitely and consistently what it is that he really wishes and wills. The reason of this is that all the elements which belong to the notion of happiness are altogether empirical, *i.e.* they must be borrowed from experience, and nevertheless the idea of happiness requires an absolute whole, a maximum of welfare in my present and all future circumstances. Now it is impossible that the most clear-sighted and at the same time most powerful being (supposed finite) should frame to himself a definite conception of what he really wills in this. Does he will riches, how much anxiety, envy, and snares might he not thereby draw upon his shoulders? Does he will knowledge and discernment, perhaps it might prove to be only an eye so much the sharper to show him so much the more fearfully the evils that are now concealed from him, and that cannot be avoided, or to impose more

wants on his desires, which already give him concern enough. Would he have long life? who guarantees to him that it would not be a long misery? would he at least have health? how often has uneasiness of the body restrained from excesses into which perfect health would have allowed one to fall? and so on. In short, he is unable, on any principle, to determine with certainty what would make him truly happy; because to do so he would need to be omniscient. We cannot therefore act on any definite principles to secure happiness, but only on empirical counsels, *ex. gr.* of regimen, frugality, courtesy, reserve, etc., which experience teaches do, on the average, most promote well-being. Hence it follows that the imperatives of prudence do not, strictly speaking, command at all, that is, they cannot present actions objectively as practically *necessary;* that they are rather to be regarded as counsels (*consilia*) than percepts (*præscepta*) of reason, that the problem to determine certainly and universally what action would promote the happiness of a rational being is completely insoluble, and consequently no imperative respecting it is possible which should, in the strict sense, command to do what makes happy; because happiness is not an ideal of reason but of imagination, resting solely on empirical grounds, and it is vain to expect that these should define an action by which one could attain the totality of a series of consequences which is really endless. This imperative of prudence would, however, be an analytical proposition if we assume that the means to happiness could be certainly assigned; for it is distinguished from the imperative of skill only by this, that in the latter the end is merely possible, in the former it is given; as, however, both only ordain the means to that which we suppose to be willed as an end, it follows that the imperative which ordains the willing of the means to him who wills the end is in both cases analytical. Thus there is no difficulty in regard to the possibility of an imperative of this kind either.

On the other hand, the question, how the imperative of *morality* is possible, is undoubtedly one, the only one, demanding a solution, as this is not at all hypothetical, and the objective necessity which it presents cannot rest on any hypothesis, as is the case with the hypothetical imperatives. Only here we must never leave out of consideration that we *cannot* make out *by any example,* in other words empirically, whether there is such an imperative at all; but it is rather to be feared that all those which seem to be categorical may yet be at bottom hypothetical. For instance, when the precept is: Thou shalt not promise deceitfully; and it is assumed that the necessity of this is not a mere counsel to avoid some other evil, so that it should mean: Thou shalt not make a lying promise, lest if it become known thou shouldst destroy thy credit, but that an action of this kind must be regarded as evil in itself, so that the imperative of the prohibition is categorical; then we cannot show with certainty in any example that the will was determined merely by the law, without any other spring of action, although it may appear to be so. For it is always possible that fear of disgrace, perhaps also obscure dread of other dangers, may have a secret influence on the will. Who can prove by experience the non-existence of a cause when all that experience tells us is that we do not perceive it? But in such a case the so-called moral imperative, which as such appears to be categorical and unconditional, would in reality be only a pragmatic precept, drawing our attention to our own interests, and merely teaching us to take these into consideration.

We shall therefore have to investigate *à priori* the possibility of a categorical imperative, as we have not in this case the advantage of its reality being given in experience, so that [the elucidation of] its possibility should be requisite only for its explanation, not for its establishment. In the meantime it may be discerned beforehand that the categorical imperative alone has the purport of a practical law: all the rest may indeed be called *principles* of the will but not laws, since whatever is only necessary for the attainment of some arbitrary purpose may be considered as in itself contingent, and we can at any time be free from the precept if we give up the purpose: on the contrary, the unconditional command leaves the will no liberty to choose the opposite; consequently it alone carries with it that necessity which we require in a law.

Secondly, in the case of this categorical imperative or law of morality, the difficulty (of discerning its possibility) is a very profound one. It is an *à priori* synthetical practical proposition,[11] and as there is so much difficulty in discerning the possibility of speculative propositions of this kind, it may readily be supposed that the difficulty will be no less with the practical.

In this problem we will first inquire whether the mere conception of a categorical imperative may not perhaps supply us also with the formula of it, containing the proposition which alone can be a categorical imperative; for even if we know the tenor of such an absolute command, yet how it is possible will require further special and laborious study, which we postpone to the last section.

When I conceive a hypothetical imperative, in general I do not know beforehand what it will contain until I am given the condition. But when I conceive a categorical imperative, I know at once what it contains. For as the imperative contains besides the law only the necessity that the maxims[12] shall conform to this law, while the law contains no conditions restricting it, there remains nothing but the general statement that the maxim of the action should conform to a universal law, and it is this conformity alone that the imperative properly represents as necessary.[13]

There is therefore but one categorical imperative, namely, this: *Act only on that maxim whereby thou canst at the same time will that it should become a universal law.*

Now if all imperatives of duty can be deduced from this one imperative as from their principle, then, although it should remain undecided whether what is called duty is not merely a vain notion, yet at least we shall be able to show what we understand by it and what this notion means.

Since the universality of the law according to which effects are produced constitutes what is properly called *nature* in the most general sense (as to form), that is the existence of things so far as it is determined by general laws, the imperative of duty may be expressed thus: *Act as if the maxim of thy action were to become by thy will a universal law of nature.*

We will now enumerate a few duties, adopting the usual division of them into duties to ourselves and to others, and into perfect and imperfect duties.[14]

1. A man reduced to despair by a series of misfortunes feels wearied of life, but is still so far in possession of his reason that he can ask himself whether it would not be contrary to his duty to himself to take his own life. Now he inquires

whether the maxim of his action could become a universal law of nature. His maxim is: From self-love I adopt it as a principle to shorten my life when its longer duration is likely to bring more evil than satisfaction. It is asked then simply whether this principle founded on self-love can become a universal law of nature. Now we see at once that a system of nature of which it should be a law to destroy life by means of the very feeling whose special nature it is to impel to the improvement of life would contradict itself, and therefore could not exist as a system of nature; hence that maxim cannot possibly exist as a universal law of nature, and consequently would be wholly inconsistent with the supreme principle of all duty.[15]

2. Another finds himself forced by necessity to borrow money. He knows that he will not be able to repay it, but sees also that nothing will be lent to him, unless he promises stoutly to repay it in a definite time. He desires to make this promise, but he has still so much conscience as to ask himself: Is it not unlawful and inconsistent with duty to get out of a difficulty in this way? Suppose, however, that he resolves to do so, then the maxim of his action would be expressed thus: When I think myself in want of money, I will borrow money and promise to repay it, although I know that I never can do so. Now this principle of self-love or of one's own advantage may perhaps be consistent with my whole future welfare; but the question now is, Is it right? I change then the suggestion of self-love into a universal law, and state the question thus: How would it be if my maxim were a universal law? Then I see at once that it could never hold as a universal law of nature, but would necessarily contradict itself. For supposing it to be a universal law that everyone when he thinks himself in a difficulty should be able to promise whatever he pleases, with the purpose of not keeping his promise, the promise itself would become impossible, as well as the end that one might have in view in it, since no one would consider that anything was promised to him, but would ridicule all such statements as vain pretences.

3. A third finds in himself a talent which with the help of some culture might make him a useful man in many respects. But he finds himself in comfortable circumstances, and prefers to indulge in pleasure rather than to take pains in enlarging and improving his happy natural ca-

pacities. He asks, however, whether his maxim of neglect of his natural gifts, besides agreeing with his inclination to indulgence, agrees also with what is called duty. He sees then that a system of nature could indeed subsist with such a universal law although men (like the South Sea islanders) should let their talents rest, and resolve to devote their lives merely to idleness, amusement, and propagation of their species— in a word, to enjoyment; but he cannot possibly *will* that this should be a universal law of nature, or be implanted in us as such by a natural instinct. For, as a rational being, he necessarily wills that his faculties be developed, since they serve him, and have been given him, for all sorts of possible purposes.

4. A fourth, who is in prosperity, while he sees that others have to contend with great wretchedness and that he could help them, thinks: What concern is it of mine? Let everyone be as happy as Heaven pleases, or as he can make himself; I will take nothing from him nor even envy him, only I do not wish to contribute anything to his welfare or to his assistance in distress! Now no doubt if such a mode of thinking were a universal law, the human race might very well subsist, and doubtless even better than in a state in which everyone talks of sympathy and good-will, or even takes care occasionally to put it into practice, but, on the other side, also cheats when he can, betrays the rights of men, or otherwise violates them.. But although it is possible that a universal law of nature might exist in accordance with that maxim, it is impossible to *will* that such a principle should have the universal validity of a law of nature. For a will which resolved this would contradict itself, inasmuch as many cases might occur in which one would have need of the love and sympathy of others, and in which, by such a law of nature, sprung from his own will, he would deprive himself of all hope of the aid he desires.

These are a few of the many actual duties, or at least what we regard as such, which obviously fall into two classes on the one principle that we have laid down. We must be *able to will* that a maxim of our action should be a universal law. This is the canon of the moral appreciation of the action generally. Some actions are of such a character that their maxim cannot without contradiction be even *conceived* as a universal law of nature, far from it being possible that we should *will* that it *should* be so. In others this intrinsic impossibility is not found, but still it is impossible to *will* that their maxim should be raised to the universality of a law of nature, since such a will would contradict itself. It is easily seen that the former violate strict or rigorous (inflexible) duty; the latter only laxer (meritorious) duty. Thus it has been completely shown by these examples how all duties depend as regards the nature of the obligation (not the object of the action) on the same principle.

If now we attend to ourselves on occasion of any transgression of duty, we shall find that we in fact do not will that our maxim should be a universal law, for that is impossible for us; on the contrary, we will that the opposite should remain a universal law, only we assume the liberty of making an *exception* in our own favour or (just for this time only) in favour of our inclination. Consequently if we considered all cases from one and the same point of view, namely, that of reason, we should find a contradiction in our own will, namely, that a certain principle should be objectively necessary as a universal law, and yet subjectively should not be universal, but admit of exceptions. As, however, we at one moment regard our action from the point of view of a will wholly conformed to reason, and then again look at the same action from the point of view of a will affected by inclination, there is not really any contradiction, but an antagonism of inclination to the precept of reason, whereby the universality of the principle is changed into a mere generality, so that the practical principle of reason shall meet the maxim half way. Now, although this cannot be justified in our own impartial judgment, yet it proves that we do really recognize the validity of the categorical imperative and (with all respect for it) only allow ourselves a few exceptions, which we think unimportant and forced from us.

We have thus established at least this much, that if duty is a conception which is to have any import and real legislative authority for our actions, it can only be expressed in categorical, and not at all in hypothetical imperatives. We have also, which is of great importance, exhibited clearly and definitely for every practical application the content of the categorical imperative, which must contain the principle of all duty if there is such a thing at all. We have not yet, however, advanced so far as to prove *à priori* that

there actually is such an imperative, that there is a practical law which commands absolutely of itself, and without any other impulse, and that the following of this law is duty.

With the view of attaining to this it is of extreme importance to remember that we must not allow ourselves to think of deducing the reality of this principle from the *particular attributes of human nature.* For duty is to be a practical, unconditional necessity of action; it must therefore hold for all rational beings (to whom an imperative can apply at all), and *for this reason only* be also a law for all human wills. On the contrary, whatever is deduced from the particular natural characteristics of humanity, from certain feelings and propensions,[16] nay, even, if possible, from any particular tendency proper to human reason, and which need not necessarily hold for the will of every rational being; this may indeed supply us with a maxim, but not with a law; with a subjective principle on which we may have a propension and inclination to act, but not with an objective principle on which we should be *enjoined* to act, even though all our propensions, inclinations, and natural dispositions were opposed to it. In fact, the sublimity and intrinsic dignity of the command in duty are so much the more evident, the less the subjective impulses favour it and the more they oppose it, without being able in the slightest degree to weaken the obligation of the law or to diminish its validity.

Here then we see philosophy brought to a critical position, since it has to be firmly fixed, notwithstanding that it has nothing to support it in heaven or earth. Here it must show its purity as absolute director of its own laws, not the herald of those which are whispered to it by an implanted sense or who knows what tutelary nature. Although these may be better than nothing, yet they can never afford principles dictated by reason, which must have their source wholly *à priori* and thence their commanding authority, expecting everything from the supremacy of the law and the due respect for it nothing from inclination, or else condemning the man to self-contempt and inward abhorrence.

Thus every empirical element is not only quite incapable of being an aid to the principle of morality, but is even highly prejudicial to the purity of morals; for the proper and inestimable worth of an absolutely good will consists just in this, that the principle of action is free from all influence of contingent grounds, which alone experience can furnish. We cannot too much or too often repeat our warning against this lax and even mean habit of thought which seeks for its principle amongst empirical motives and laws; for human reason in its weariness is glad to rest on this pillow, and in a dream of sweet illusions (in which, instead of Juno, it embraces a cloud) it substitutes for morality a bastard patched up from limbs of various derivation, which looks like anything one chooses to see in it; only not like virtue to one who has once beheld her in her true form.[17]

The question then is this: Is it a necessary law *for all rational beings* that they should always judge of their actions by maxims of which they can themselves will that they should serve as universal laws? If it is so, then it must be connected (altogether *à priori*) with the very conception of the will of a rational being generally. But in order to discover this connexion we must, however reluctantly, take a step into metaphysic, although into a domain of it which is distinct from speculative philosophy, namely, the metaphysic of morals. In a practical philosophy, where it is not the reasons of what *happens* that we have to ascertain, but the laws of what *ought to happen,* even although it never does, *i.e.* objective practical laws, there it is not necessary to inquire into the reasons why anything pleases or displeases, how the pleasure of mere sensation differs from taste, and whether the latter is distinct from a general satisfaction of reason; on what the feeling of pleasure or pain rests, and how from it desires and inclinations arise, and from these again maxims by the co-operation of reason: for all this belongs to an empirical psychology, which would constitute the second part of physics, if we regard physics as the *philosophy* of nature, so far as it is based on *empirical laws.* But here we are concerned with objective practical laws, and consequently with the relation of the will to itself so far as it is determined by reason alone, in which case whatever has reference to anything empirical is necessarily excluded; since if *reason of itself alone* determines the conduct (and it is the possibility of this that we are now investigating), it must necessarily do so *à priori.*

The will is conceived as a faculty of determin-ing oneself to action *in accordance with the conception of certain laws.* And such a faculty can be found only in rational beings. Now that which serves the will as the objective ground of its self-determination is the *end,* and if this is assigned by reason alone, it must hold for all rational beings. On the other hand, that which merely contains the ground of possibility of the action of which the effect is the end, this is called the *means.* The subjective ground of the desire is the *spring,* the objective ground of the volition is the *motive;* hence the distinction between subjective ends which rest on springs, and objective ends which depend on motives valid for every rational being. Practical principles are *formal* when they abstract from all subjective ends; they are *material* when they assume these, and therefore particular springs of action. The ends which a rational being proposes to himself at pleasure as *effects* of his actions (material ends) are all only relative, for it is only their relation to the particular desires of the subject that gives them their worth, which therefore cannot furnish principles universal and necessary for all rational beings and for every volition, that is to say practical laws. Hence all these relative ends can give rise only to hypothetical imperatives.

Supposing, however, that there were something *whose existence* has *in itself* an absolute worth, something which, being *an end in itself,* could be a source of definite laws, then in this and this alone would lie the source of a possible categorical imperative, *i.e.* a practical law.

Now I say: man and generally any rational being *exists* as an end in himself, *not merely as a means* to be arbitrarily used by this or that will, but in all his actions, whether they concern himself or other rational beings, must be always regarded at the same time as an end. All objects of the inclinations have only a conditional worth; for if the inclinations and the wants founded on them did not exist, then their object would be without value. But the inclinations themselves being sources of want are so far from having an absolute worth for which they should be desired, that, on the contrary, it must be the universal wish of every rational being to be wholly free from them. Thus the worth of any object which is *to be acquired* by our action is always conditional. Beings whose existence depends not on our will but on nature's, have nevertheless, if they are not rational beings, only a relative value as means, and are therefore called *things*; rational beings, on the contrary, are called *persons,* because their very nature points them out as ends in themselves, that is as something which must not be used merely as means, and so far therefore restricts freedom of action (and is an object of respect). These, therefore, are not merely subjective ends whose existence has a worth *for us* as an effect of our action, but *objective ends,* that is things whose existence is an end in itself: an end moreover for which no other can be substituted, which they should subserve *merely* as means, for otherwise nothing whatever would possess *absolute worth*; but if all worth were conditioned and therefore contingent, then there would be no supreme practical principle of reason whatever.

If then there is a supreme practical principle or, in respect of the human will, a categorical imperative, it must be one which, being drawn from the conception of that which is necessarily an end for everyone because it is *an end in itself,* constitutes an *objective* principle of will, and can therefore serve as a universal practical law. The foundation of this principle is: *rational nature exists as an end in itself.* Man necessarily conceives his own existence as being so: so far then this is a *subjective* principle of human actions. But every other rational being regards its existence similarly, just on the same rational principle that holds for me[18]: so that it is at the same time an objective principle, from which as a supreme practical law all laws of the will must be capable of being deduced. Accordingly the practical imperative will be as follows: *So act as to treat humanity, whether in thine own person or in that of any other, in every case as an end withal, never as means only.* We will now inquire whether this can be practically carried out.

To abide by the previous examples:

Firstly, under the head of necessary duty to oneself: He who contemplates suicide should ask himself whether his action can be consistent with the idea of humanity *as an end in itself.* If he destroys himself in order to escape from painful circumstances, he uses a person merely as *a mean* to maintain a tolerable condition up to the end of life. But a man is not a thing, that is to say, something which can be used merely as means, but must in all his actions be always considered as an end in himself. I cannot, therefore, dispose in any way of a man in my own person so as to mutilate him, to damage or kill him. (It belongs to ethics proper to define this principle more precisely, so as to avoid all misunderstanding, *e.g.* as to the amputation of the limbs in order to preserve myself; as to exposing my life to danger with a view to preserve it, etc. This question is therefore omitted here.)

Secondly, as regards necessary duties, or those of strict obligation, towards others; he who is thinking of making a lying promise to others will see at once that he would be using another man *merely as a mean,* without the latter containing at the same time the end in himself. For he whom I propose by such a promise to use for my own purposes cannot possibly assent to my mode of acting towards him, and therefore cannot himself contain the end of this action. This violation of the principle of humanity in other men is more obvious if we take in examples of attacks on the freedom and property of others. For then it is clear that he who transgresses the rights of men intends to use the person of others merely as means, without considering that as rational beings they ought always to be esteemed also as ends, that is, as beings who must be capable of containing in themselves the end of the very same action.[19]

Thirdly, as regards contingent (meritorious) duties to oneself; it is not enough that the action does not violate humanity in our own person as an end in itself, it must also *harmonize with* it. Now there are in humanity capacities of greater perfection which belong to the end that nature has in view in regard to humanity in ourselves as the subject: to neglect these might perhaps be consistent with the *maintenance* of humanity as an end in itself, but not with the *advancement* of this end.

Fourthly, as regards meritorious duties towards others: the natural end which all men have is their own happiness. Now humanity might indeed subsist, although no one should contribute anything to the happiness of others, provided he did not intentionally withdraw anything from it; but after all, this would only harmonize negatively, not positively, with *humanity as an end in itself,* if everyone does not also endeavour, as far as in him lies, to forward the ends of others. For the ends of any subject which is an end in himself, ought as far as possible to be *my* ends also, if that conception is to have its *full* effect with me.

This principle, that humanity and generally every rational nature is *an end in itself* (which is the supreme limiting condition of every man's freedom of action), is not borrowed from experience, *firstly,* because it is universal, applying as it does to all rational beings whatever, and experience is not capable of determining anything about them; *secondly,* because it does not present humanity as an end to men (subjectively), that is as an object which men do of themselves actually adopt as an end; but as an objective end, which must as a law constitute the supreme limiting condition of all our subjective ends, let them be what we will; it must therefore spring from pure reason. In fact the objective principle of all practical legislation lies (according to the first principle) in *the rule* and its form of universality which makes it capable of being a law (say, *e.g.,* a law of nature); but the *subjective* principle is in the *end*; now by the second principle the subject of all ends is each rational being inasmuch as it is an end in itself. Hence follows the third practical principle of the will, which is the ultimate condition of its harmony with the universal practical reason, viz.: the idea of *the will of every rational being as a universally legislative will.*

On this principle all maxims are rejected which are inconsistent with the will being itself universal legislator. Thus the will is not subject simply to the law, but so subject that it must be regarded *as itself giving the law,* and on this ground only, subject to the law (of which it can regard itself as the author).

In the previous imperatives, namely, that based on the conception of the conformity of actions to general laws, as in a *physical system of nature,* and that based on the universal *prerogative* of rational beings as *ends* in themselves —these imperatives just because they were conceived as categorical, excluded from any share in their authority all admixture of any interest as a spring of action; they were, however, only *assumed* to be categorical, because such an assumption was necessary to explain the conception of duty. But we could not prove independently that there are practical propositions which command categorically, nor can it be proved in this section; one thing, however, could be done, namely, to indicate in the imperative itself by some determinate expression, that in the case of volition from duty all interest is renounced, which is the specific criterion of categorical as distinguished from hypothetical imperatives. This is done in the present (third) formula of the principle, namely, in the idea of the will of every rational being as a *universally legislating will.*

For although a will *which is subject to laws* may be attached to this law by means of an interest, yet a will which is itself a supreme lawgiver so far as it is such cannot possibly depend on any interest, since a will so dependent would itself still need another law restricting the interest of its self-love by the condition that it should be valid as universal law.

Thus the *principle* that every human will is *a will which in all its maxims gives universal laws,*[20] provided it be otherwise justified, would be very *well adapted* to be the categorical imperative, in this respect, namely, that just because of the idea of universal legislation it is *not based on any interest,* and therefore it alone among all possible imperatives can be *unconditional.* Or still better, converting the proposition, if there is a categorical imperative (*i.e.,* a law for the will of every rational being), it can only command that everything be done from maxims of one's will regarded as a will which could at the same time will that it should itself give universal laws, for in that case only the practical principle and the imperative which it obeys are unconditional, since they cannot be based on any interest.

Looking back now on all previous attempts to discover the principle of morality, we need not wonder why they all failed. It was seen that man was bound to laws by duty, but it was not observed that the laws to which he is subject are *only those of his own giving,* though at the same time they are *universal,* and that he is only bound to act in conformity with his own will; a will, however, which is designed by nature to give universal laws. For when one has conceived man only as subject to a law (no matter what), then this law required some interest, either by way of attraction or constraint, since it did not originate as a law from *his own* will, but this will was according to a law obliged by *something else* to act in a certain manner. Now by this necessary consequence all the labour spent in finding a supreme principle of *duty* was irrevocably lost. For men never elicited duty, but only a necessity of acting from a certain interest. Whether this interest was private or otherwise, in any case the imperative must be conditional, and could not by any means be capable of being a moral command. I will therefore call this the principle of *Autonomy* of the will, in contrast with every other which I accordingly reckon as *Heteronomy.*[21]

The conception of every rational being as one which must consider itself as giving in all the maxims of its will universal laws, so as to judge itself and its actions from this point of view—this conception leads to another which depends on it and is very fruitful, namely, that of a *kingdom of ends.*

By a *kingdom* I understand the union of different rational beings in a system by common laws. Now since it is by laws that ends are determined as regards their universal validity, hence, if we abstract from the personal differences of rational beings, and likewise from all the content of their private ends, we shall be able to conceive all ends combined in a systematic whole (including both rational beings as ends in themselves, and also the special ends which each may propose to himself), that is to say, we can conceive a kingdom of ends, which on the preceding principles is possible.

For all rational beings come under the *law* that each of them must treat itself and all others *never merely as means,* but in every case *at the same time as ends in themselves.* Hence results a systematic union of rational beings by common objective laws, *i.e.,* a kingdom which may be called a kingdom of ends, since what these laws have in view is just the relation of these beings to one another as ends and means. It is certainly only an ideal.

A rational being belongs as a *member* to the kingdom of ends when, although giving universal laws in it, he is also himself subject to these laws. He belongs to it *as sovereign* when, while giving laws, he is not subject to the will of any other.

A rational being must always regard himself as giving laws either as member or as sovereign in a kingdom of ends which is rendered possible by the freedom of will. He cannot, however, maintain the latter position merely by the maxims of his will, but only in case he is a completely independent being without wants and with unrestricted power adequate to his will.

Morality consists then in the reference of all action to the legislation which alone can render a kingdom of ends possible. This legislation must be capable of existing in every rational being, and of emanating from his will, so that the principle of this will is, never to act on any maxim which could not without contradiction be also a universal law, and accordingly always so to act *that the will could at the same time regard itself as giving in its maxims universal laws.* If now the maxims of rational beings are not by their own nature coincident with this objective principle, then the necessity of acting on it is called practical necessitation, i.e. *duty.* Duty does not apply to the sovereign in the kingdom of ends, but it does to every member of it and to all in the same degree.

The practical necessity of acting on this principle, *i.e.* duty, does not rest at all on feelings, impulses, or inclinations, but solely on the relation of rational beings to one another, a relation in which the will of a rational being must always be regarded as *legislative,* since otherwise it could not be conceived as *an end in itself.* Reason then refers every maxim of the will, regarding it as legislating universally, to every other will and also to every action towards oneself; and this not on account of any other practical motive or any future advantage, but from the idea of the *dignity* of a rational being, obeying no law but that which he himself also gives.

In the kingdom of ends everything has either Value or Dignity. Whatever has a value can be replaced by something else which is *equivalent;* whatever, on the other hand, is above all value, and therefore admits of no equivalent, has a dignity.

Whatever has reference to the general inclinations and wants of mankind has a *market value;* whatever, without presupposing a want, corresponds to a certain taste, that is to a satisfaction in the mere purposeless play of our faculties, has a *fancy value;* but that which constitutes the condition under which alone anything can be an end in itself, this has not merely a relative worth, *i.e.* value, but an intrinsic worth, that is *dignity.*

Now morality is the condition under which alone a rational being can be an end in himself, since by this alone it is possible that he should be a legislating member in the kingdom of ends. Thus morality, and humanity as capable of it, is that which alone has dignity. Skill and diligence in labour have a market value; wit, lively imagination, and humour, have fancy value; on the other hand, fidelity to promises, benevolence from principle (not from instinct), have an intrinsic worth. Neither nature nor art contains anything which in default of these it could put in their place, for their worth consists not in the effects which spring from them, not in the use and advantage which they secure, but in the disposition of mind, that is, the maxims of the will which are ready to manifest themselves in such actions, even though they should not have the desired effect. These actions also need no recommendation from any subjective taste or sentiment, that they may be looked on with immediate favour and satisfaction: they need no immediate propension or feeling for them; they exhibit the will that performs them as an object of an immediate respect, and nothing but reason is required to *impose* them on the will; not to *flatter* it into them, which, in the case of duties, would be a contradiction. This estimation therefore shows that the worth of such a disposition is dignity, and places it infinitely above all value, with which it cannot for a moment be brought into comparison or competition without as it were violating its sanctity.

What then is it which justifies virtue or the morally good disposition, in making such lofty claims? It is nothing less than the privilege it secures to the rational being of participating in the giving of universal laws, by which it qualifies him to be a member of a possible kingdom of ends, a privilege to which he was already destined by his own nature as being an end in himself, and on that account legislating in the kingdom of ends; free as regards all laws of physical nature, and obeying those only which he himself gives, and by which his maxims can belong to a system of universal law, to which at the same time he submits himself. For nothing has any worth except what the law assigns it. Now the legislation itself which assigns the worth of everything must for that very reason possess dignity, that is an unconditional incomparable worth; and the word *respect* alone supplies a becoming expression for the esteem which a rational being must have for it. *Autonomy* then is the basis of the dignity of human and of every rational nature.

The three modes of presenting the principle of morality that have been adduced are at bottom only so many formulae of the very same law, and each of itself involves the other two. There is, however, a difference in them, but it is rather subjectively than objectively practical, intended namely to bring an idea of the reason nearer to intuition (by means of a certain analogy), and thereby nearer to feeling. All maxims, in fact, have—

1. A *form*, consisting in universality; and in this view the formula of the moral imperative is expressed thus, that the maxims must be so chosen as if they were to serve as universal laws of nature.

2. A *matter*, [22] namely, an end, and here the formula says that the rational being, as it is an end by its own nature and therefore an end in itself, must in every maxim serve as the condition limiting all merely relative and arbitrary ends.

3. A *complete characterisation* of all maxims by means of that formula, namely, that all maxims ought by their own legislation to harmonize with a possible kingdom of ends as with a kingdom of nature. [23] There is a progress here in the order of the categories of *unity* of the form of the will (its universality), *plurality* of the matter (the objects, *i.e.* the ends), and *totality* of the system of these. In forming our moral *judgment* of actions it is better to proceed always on the strict method, and start from the general formula of the categorical imperative: *Act according to a maxim which can at the same time make itself a universal law.* If, however, we wish to gain an *entrance* for the moral law, it is very useful to bring one and the same action under the three specified conceptions, and thereby as far as possible to bring it nearer to intuition.

We can now end where we started at the beginning, namely, with the conception of a will unconditionally good. *That will* is *absolutely good* which cannot be evil—in other words, whose maxim, if made a universal law, could never contradict itself. This principle, then, is its supreme law: Act always on such a maxim as thou canst at the same time will to be a universal law; this is the sole condition under which a will can never contradict itself; and such an imperative is categorical. Since the validity of the will as a universal law for possible actions is analogous to the universal connexion of the existence of things by general laws, which is the formal notion of nature in general, the categorical imperative can also be expressed thus: *Act on maxims which can at the same time have for their object themselves as universal laws of nature.* Such then is the formula of an absolutely good will.

Rational nature is distinguished from the rest of nature by this, that it sets before itself an end. This end would be the matter of every good will. But since in the idea of a will that is absolutely good without being limited by any condition (of attaining this or that end) we must abstract wholly from every end *to be effected* (since this would make every will only relatively good), it follows that in this case the end must be conceived, not as an end to be effected, but as an *independently* existing end. Consequently it is conceived only negatively, *i.e.,* as that which we must never act against, and which, therefore, must never be regarded merely as means, but must in every volition be esteemed as an end likewise. Now this end can be nothing but the subject of all possible ends, since this is also the subject of a possible absolutely good will; for such a will cannot without contradiction be postponed to any other object. This principle: So act in regard to every rational being (thyself and others), that he may always have place in thy maxim as an end in himself, is accordingly essentially identical with this other: Act upon a maxim which, at the same time, involves its own universal validity for every rational being. For that in using means for every end I should limit my maxim by the condition of its holding good as a law for every subject, this comes to the same thing as that the fundamental principle of all maxims of action must be that the subject of all ends, *i.e.,* the rational being himself, be never employed merely as means, but as the supreme condition restricting the use of all means, that is in every case as an end likewise.

It follows incontestably that, to whatever laws any rational being may be subject, he being an end in himself must be able to regard himself as also legislating universally in respect of these same laws, since it is just this fitness of his maxims for universal legislation that distinguishes him as an end in himself; also it follows that this implies his dignity (prerogative) above all mere physical beings, that he must always take his maxims from the point of view which regards himself, and likewise every other rational being,

as lawgiving beings (on which account they are called persons). In this way a world of rational beings (*mundus intelligibilis*) is possible as a kingdom of ends, and this by virtue of the legislation proper to all persons as members. Therefore every rational being must so act as if he were by his maxims in every case a legislating member in the universal kingdom of ends. The formal principle of these maxims is: So act as if thy maxim were to serve likewise as the universal law (of all rational beings). A kingdom of ends is thus only possible on the analogy of a kingdom of nature, the former, however, only by maxims, that is self-imposed rules, the latter only by the laws of efficient causes acting under necessitation from without. Nevertheless, although the system of nature is looked upon as a machine, yet so far as it has reference to rational beings as its ends, it is given on this account the name of a kingdom of nature. Now such a kingdom of ends would be actually realized by means of maxims conforming to the canon which the categorical imperative prescribes to all rational beings, *if they were universally followed.* But although a rational being, even if he punctually follows this maxim himself, cannot reckon upon all others being therefore true to the same, nor expect that the kingdom of nature and its orderly arrangements shall be in harmony with him as a fitting member, so as to form a kingdom of ends to which he himself contributes, that is to say, that it shall favour his expectation of happiness, still that law: Act according to the maxims of a member of a merely possible kingdom of ends legislating in it universally, remains in its full force, inasmuch as it commands categorically. And it is just in this that the paradox lies; that the mere dignity of man as a rational creature, without any other end or advantage to be attained thereby, in other words, respect for a mere idea, should yet serve as an inflexible precept of the will, and that it is precisely in this independence of the maxim on all such springs of action that its sublimity consists; and it is this that makes every rational subject worthy to be a legislative member in the kingdom of ends: for otherwise he would have to be conceived only as subject to the physical law of his wants. And although we should suppose the kingdom of nature and the kingdom of ends to be united under one sovereign, so that the latter kingdom thereby ceased to be a mere idea and acquired true reality, then it would no doubt gain the accession of a strong spring, but by no means any increase of its intrinsic worth. For this sole absolute lawgiver must, notwithstanding this, be always conceived as estimating the worth of rational beings only by their disinterested behaviour, as prescribed to themselves from that idea [the dignity of man] alone. The essence of things is not altered by their external relations, and that which, abstracting from these, alone constitutes the absolute worth of man, is also that by which he must be judged, whoever the judge may be, and even by the Supreme Being. *Morality,* then, is the relation of actions to the autonomy of the will, that is, to the potential universal legislation by its maxims. An action that is consistent with the autonomy of the will is *permitted;* one that does not agree therewith is *forbidden.* A will whose maxims necessarily coincide with the laws of autonomy is a *holy* will, good absolutely. The dependence of a will not absolutely good on the principle of autonomy (moral necessitation) is obligation. This, then, cannot be applied to a holy being. The objective necessity of actions from obligation is called *duty.*

From what has just been said, it is easy to see how it happens that although the conception of duty implies subjection to the law, we yet ascribe a certain *dignity* and sublimity to the person who fulfils all his duties. There is not, indeed, any sublimity in him, so far as he is *subject* to the moral law; but inasmuch as in regard to that very law he is likewise a *legislator,* and on that account alone subject to it, he has sublimity. We have also shown above that neither fear nor inclination, but simply respect for the law, is the spring which can give actions a moral worth. Our own will, so far as we suppose it to act only under the condition that its maxims are potentially universal laws, this ideal will which is possible to us is the proper object of respect; and the dignity of humanity consists just in this capacity of being universally legislative, though with the condition that it is itself subject to this same legislation.

The Autonomy of the Will as the Supreme Principle of Morality.

Autonomy of the will is that property of it by which it is a law to itself (independently on any property of the objects of volition). The principle of autonomy then is: Always so to choose that the same volition shall comprehend the maxims of our choice as a universal law. We cannot prove that this practical rule is an imperative, *i.e.,* that the will of every rational being is necessarily bound to it as a condition, by a mere analysis of the conceptions which occur in it, since it is a synthetical proposition; we must advance beyond the cognition of the objects to a critical examination of the subject, that is of the pure practical reason, for this synthetic proposition which commands apodictically must be capable of being cognized wholly *à priori.* This matter, however, does not belong to the present section. But that the principle of autonomy in question is the sole principle of morals can be readily shown by mere analysis of the conceptions of morality. For by this analysis we find that its principle must be a categorical imperative, and that what this commands is neither more nor less than this very autonomy.

Heteronomy of the Will as the Source of all spurious Principles of Morality.

If the will seeks the law which is to determine it *anywhere else* than in the fitness of its maxims to be universal laws of its own dictation, consequently if it goes out of itself and seeks this law in the character of any of its objects, there always results *heteronomy.* The will in that case does not give itself the law, but it is given by the object through its relation to the will. This relation, whether it rests on inclination or on conceptions of reason, only admits of hypothetical imperatives: I ought to do something *because I wish for something else.* On the contrary, the moral, and therefore categorical, imperative says: I ought to do so and so, even though I should not wish for anything else. *Ex. gr.,* the former says: I ought not to lie if I would retain my reputation; the latter says: I ought not to lie although it should not bring me the least discredit. The latter therefore must so far abstract from all objects that they shall have no *influence* on the will, in order that practical reason (will) may not be restricted to administering an interest not belonging to it, but may simply show its own commanding authority as the supreme legislation. Thus, *ex. gr.,* I ought to endeavour to promote the happiness of others, not as if its realization involved any concern of mine (whether by immediate inclination or by any satisfaction indirectly gained through reason), but simply because a maxim which excludes it cannot be comprehended as a universal law in one and the same volition.

CLASSIFICATION

Of all Principles of Morality which can be founded on the Conception of Heteronomy.

Here as elsewhere human reason in its pure use, so long as it was not critically examined, has first tried all possible wrong ways before it succeeded in finding the one true way.

All principles which can be taken from this point of view are either *empirical* or *rational.* The *former,* drawn from the principle of *happiness,* are built on physical or moral feelings; the *latter,* drawn from the principle of *perfection,* are built either on the rational conception of perfection as a possible effect, or on that of an independent perfection (the will of God) as the determining cause of our will.

Empirical principles are wholly incapable of serving as a foundation for moral laws. For the universality with which these should hold for all rational beings without distinction, the unconditional practical necessity which is thereby imposed on them is lost when their foundation is taken from the *particular constitution of human nature,* or the accidental circumstances in which it is placed. The principle of *private happiness,* however, is the most objectionable, not merely because it is false, and experience contradicts the supposition that prosperity is always proportioned to good conduct, nor yet merely because it contributes nothing to the establishment of morality—since it is quite a different thing to make a prosperous man and a good man, or to make one prudent and sharp-sighted for his own interests, and to make him virtuous—but because the springs it provides for morality are such as rather undermine it and destroy its sublimity, since they put the motives to virtue and to vice in the same class, and only teach us to make a better calculation, the specific difference between virtue and vice being entirely extinguished. On the other hand, as to moral feeling, this supposed special sense,[24] the appeal to it is indeed superficial when those who cannot *think* believe that *feeling* will help them out, even in what concerns general laws: and besides,

feelings which naturally differ infinitely in degree cannot furnish a uniform standard of good and evil, nor has anyone a right to form judgments for others by his own feelings: nevertheless this moral feeling is nearer to morality and its dignity in this respect, that it pays virtue the honour of ascribing to her *immediately* the satisfaction and esteem we have for her, and does not, as it were, tell her to her face that we are not attached to her by her beauty but by profit.

Amongst the *rational* principles of morality, the ontological conception of *perfection,* notwithstanding its defects, is better than the theological conception which derives morality from a Divine absolutely perfect will. The former is, no doubt, empty and indefinite, and consequently useless for finding in the boundless field of possible reality the greatest amount suitable for us; moreover, in attempting to distinguish specifically the reality of which we are now speaking from every other, it inevitably tends to turn in a circle, and cannot avoid tacitly presupposing the morality which it is to explain; it is nevertheless preferable to the theological view, first, because we have no intuition of the Divine perfection, and can only deduce it from our own conceptions, the most important of which is that of morality, and our explanation would thus be involved in a gross circle; and, in the next place, if we avoid this, the only notion of the Divine will remaining to us is a conception made up of the attributes of desire of glory and dominion, combined with the awful conceptions of might and vengeance, and any system of morals erected on this foundation would be directly opposed to morality.

However, if I had to choose between the notion of the moral sense and that of perfection in general (two systems which at least do not weaken morality, although they are totally incapable of serving as its foundation), then I should decide for the latter, because it at least withdraws the decision of the question from the sensibility and brings it to the court of pure reason; and although even here it decides nothing, it at all events preserves the indefinite idea (of a will good in itself) free from corruption, until it shall be more precisely defined.

For the rest I think I may be excused here from a detailed refutation of all these doctrines; that would only be superfluous labour, since it is so easy, and is probably so well seen even by those whose office requires them to decide for one of those theories (because their hearers would not tolerate suspension of judgment). But what interests us more here is to know that the prime foundation of morality laid down by all these principles is nothing but heteronomy of the will, and for this reason they must necessarily miss their aim.

In every case where an object of the will has to be supposed, in order that the rule may be prescribed which is to determine the will, there the rule is simply heteronomy; the imperative is conditional, namely, *if* or *because* one wishes for this object, one should act so and so: hence it can never command morally, that is categorically. Whether the object determines the will by means of inclination, as in the principle of private happiness, or by means of reason directed to objects of our possible volition generally, as in the principle of perfection, in either case the will never determines itself *immediately* by the conception of the action, but only by the influence which the foreseen effect of the action has on the will; *I ought to do something, on this account, because I wish for something else;* and here there must be yet another law assumed in me as its subject, by which I necessarily will this other thing, and this law again requires an imperative to restrict this maxim. For the influence which the conception of an object within the reach of our faculties can exercise on the will of the subject in consequence of its natural properties, depends on the nature of the subject, either the sensibility (inclination and taste), or the understanding and reason, the employment of which is by the peculiar constitution of their nature attended with satisfaction. It follows that the law would be, properly speaking, given by nature, and as such, it must be known and proved by experience, and would consequently be con-

tingent, and therefore incapable of being an apodictic practical rule, such as the moral rule must be. Not only so, but it is *inevitably only heteronomy;* the will does not give itself the law, but it is given by a foreign impulse by means of a particular natural constitution of the subject adapted to receive it. An absolutely good will, then, the principle of which must be a categorical imperative, will be indeterminate as regards all objects, and will contain merely the *form of volition* generally, and that as autonomy, that is to say, the capability of the maxims of every good will to make themselves a universal law, is itself the only law which the will of every rational being imposes on itself, without needing to assume any spring or interest as a foundation.

How such a synthetical practical à priori *proposition is possible,* and why it is necessary, is a problem whose solution does not lie within the bounds of the metaphysic of morals; and we have not here affirmed its truth, much less professed to have a proof of it in our power. We simply showed by the development of the universally received notion of morality that an autonomy of the will is inevitably connected with it, or rather is its foundation. Whoever then holds morality to be anything real, and not a chimerical idea without any truth, must likewise admit the principle of it that is here assigned. This section, then, like the first, was merely analytical. Now to prove that morality is no creation of the brain, which it cannot be if the categorical imperative and with it the autonomy of the will is true, and as an *à priori* principle absolutely necessary, this supposes the *possibility of a synthetic use of pure practical reason,* which, however, we cannot venture on without first giving a critical examination of this faculty of reason. In the concluding section we shall give the principal outlines of this critical examination as far as is sufficient for our purpose.

NOTES

1.   [Johann Christian Von Wolf (1679–1754) was the author of treatises on philosophy, mathematics, etc., which were for a long time the standard text-books in the German Universities. His philosophy was founded on that of Leibnitz.]

2.   [The first proposition was that to have moral worth an action must be done from duty.]

3.   A *maxim* is the subjective principle of volition. The objective principle (*i.e.* that which would also serve subjec-

tively as a practical principle to all rational beings if reason had full power over the faculty of desire) is the practical *law*.

4.   It might be here objected to me that I take refuge behind the word *respect* in an obscure feeling, instead of giving a distinct solution of the question by a concept of the reason. But although respect is a feeling, it is not a feeling *received* through influence, but is *self-wrought* by a rational concept, and, therefore, is specifically distinct from all feelings of the former kind, which may be referred either to

inclination or fear. What I recognize immediately as a law for me, I recognize with respect. This merely signifies the consciousness that my will is *subordinate* to a law, without the intervention of other influences on my sense. The immediate determination of the will be the law, and the consciousness of this, is called *respect,* so that this is regarded as an *effect* of the law on the subject, and not as the *cause* of it. Respect is properly the conception of a worth which thwarts my self-love. Accordingly it is something which is considered neither as an object of inclination nor of fear, although it has something analogous to both. The *object* of respect is the *law* only, and that, the law which we impose on *ourselves,* and yet recognize as necessary in itself. As a law, we are subjected to it without consulting self-love; as imposed by us on ourselves, it is a result of our will. In the former aspect it has an analogy to fear, in the latter to inclination. Respect for a person is properly only respect for the law (of honesty, etc.) of which he gives us an example. Since we also look on the improvement of our talents as a duty, we consider that we see in a person of talents, as it were, the *example of a law* (viz. to become like him in this by exercise), and this constitutes our respect. All so-called moral *interest* consists simply in *respect* for the law.

5. [Compare the note to the preface to the *Critique of the Practical Reason,* p. 111. A specimen of Kant's proposed application of the Socratic method may be found in Mr. Semple's translation of the *Metaphysic of Ethics,* p. 290.]

6. Just as pure mathematics are distinguished from applied, pure logic from applied, so if we choose we may also distinguish pure philosophy of morals (metaphysic) from applied (viz. applied to human nature). By this designation we are also at once reminded that moral principles are not based on properties of human nature, but must subsist *à priori* of themselves, while from such principles practical rules must be capable of being deduced for every rational nature, and accordingly for that of man.

7. I have a letter from the late excellent Sulzer, in which he asks me what can be the reason that moral instruction, although containing much that is convincing for the reason, yet accomplishes so little? My answer was postponed in order that I might make it complete. But it is simply this, that the teachers themselves have not got their own notions clear, and when they endeavour to make up for this by raking up motives of moral goodness from every quarter, trying to make their physic right strong, they spoil it. For the commonest understanding shows that if we imagine, on the one hand, an act of honesty done with steadfast mind, apart from every view to advantage of any kind in this world or another, and even under the greatest temptations of necessity or allurement, and, on the other hand, a similar act which was affected, in however low a degree, by a foreign motive, the former leaves far behind and eclipses the second; it elevates the soul, and inspires the wish to be able to act in like manner oneself. Even moderately young children feel this impression, and one should never represent duties to them in any other light.

8. The dependence of the desires on sensations is called inclination, and this accordingly always indicates a *want.* The dependence of a contingently determinable will on principles of reason is called an *interest.* This, therefore, is found only in the case of a dependent will which does not always of itself conform to reason; in the Divine will we cannot conceive any interest. But the human will can also *take an interest* in a thing without therefore acting *from interest.* The former signifies the *practical* interest in the action, the latter the *pathological* in the object of the action. The former indicates only dependence of the will on principles of reason in themselves; the second, dependence on principles of reason for the sake of inclination, reason supplying only the practical

rules how the requirement of the inclination may be satisfied. In the first case the action interests me; in the second the object of the action (because it is pleasant to me). We have seen in the first section that in an action done from duty we must look not to the interest in the object, but only to that in the action itself, and in its rational principle (viz. the law).

9. The word *prudence* is taken in two senses: in the one it may bear the name of knowledge of the world, in the other that of private prudence. The former is a man's ability to influence others so as to use them for his own purposes. The latter is the sagacity to combine all these purposes for his own lasting benefit. This latter is properly that to which the value even of the former is reduced, and when a man is prudent in the former sense, but not in the latter, we might better say of him that he is clever and cunning, but, on the whole, imprudent. [Compare on the difference between *klug* and *gescheu* here alluded to, *Anthropologie,* § 45, ed. Schubert, p. 110.]

10. It seems to me that the proper signification of the word *pragmatic* may be most accurately defined in this way. For *sanctions* [see *Cr. of Pract. Reas.,* p. 271] are called pragmatic which flow properly, not from the law of the states as necessary enactments, but from *precaution* for the general welfare. A history is composed pragmatically when it teaches *prudence,* i.e. instructs the world how it can provide for its interests better, or at least as well as the men of former time.

11. I connect the act with the will without presupposing any condition resulting from any inclination, but *à priori,* and therefore necessarily (thought only objectively, *i.e.* assuming the idea of a reason possessing full power over all subjective motives). This is accordingly a practical proposition which does not deduce the willing of an action by mere analysis from another already presupposed (for we have not such a perfect will), but connects it immediately with the conception of the will of a rational being, as something not contained in it.

12. A maxim is a subjective principle of action, and must be distinguished from the *objective principle,* namely, practical law. The former contains the practical rule set by reason according to the conditions of the subject (often its ignorance or its inclinations), so that it is the principle on which the subject *acts;* but the law is the objective principle valid for every rational being, and is the principle on which it *ought to act* that is an imperative.

13. [I have no doubt that "den" in the original before "Imperativ" is a misprint for "der," and have translated accordingly. Mr. Semple has done the same. The editions that I have seen agree in reading "den," and Mr. Barni so translates. With this reading, it is the conformity that presents the imperative as necessary.]

14. It must be noted here that I reserve the division of duties for a future *metaphysic of morals;* so that I give it here only as an arbitrary one (in order to arrange my examples). For the rest, I understand by a perfect duty one that admits no exception in favour of inclination, and then I have not merely external but also internal perfect duties. This is contrary to the use of the word adopted in the schools; but I do not intend to justify it here, as it is all one for my purpose whether it is admitted or not. [*Perfect* duties are usually understood to be those which can be enforced by external law; *imperfect,* those which cannot be enforced. They are also called respectively *determinate* and *indeterminate, officio juris* and *officio virtutis.*]

15. [On suicide cf. further *Metaphysik der Sitten,* p. 274.]

16. [Kant distinguishes "Hang *(propensio)*" from "Neigung *(inclinatio)*" as follows:—"Hang" is a predisposition to the desire of some enjoyment; in other words, it is the subjective possibility of excitement of a certain desire which

precedes the conception of its object. When the enjoyment has been experienced, it produces a "Neigung" (inclination) to it, which accordingly is defined "habitual sensible desire." —*Anthropologie,* §§ 72, 79; *Religion,* p. 31.]

17.   To behold virtue in her proper form is nothing else but to contemplate morality stripped of all admixture of sensible things and of every spurious ornament of reward or self-love. How much she then eclipses everything else that appears charming to the affections, every one may readily perceive with the least exertion of his reason, if it be not wholly spoiled for abstraction.

18.   This proposition is here stated as a postulate. The ground of it will be found in the concluding section.

19.   Let it not be thought that the common: *quod tibi non vis fieri, etc.,* could serve here as the rule or principle. For it is only a deduction from the former, though with several limitations; it cannot be a universal law, for it does not contain the principle of duties to oneself, nor of the duties of benevolence to others (for many a one would gladly consent that others should not benefit him, provided only that he might be excused from showing benevolence to them), nor finally that of duties of strict obligation to one another, for on this principle the criminal might argue against the judge who punishes him, and so on.

20.   I may be excused from adducing examples to elucidate this principle, as those which have already been used to elucidate the categorical imperative and its formula would all serve for the like purpose here.

21.   [Cp. *Critical Examination of Practical Reason,* p. 184.]

22.   [The reading "Maxime," which is that both of Rosenkranz and Hartenstein, is obviously an error for "Materie."]

23.   Teleology considers nature as a kingdom of ends; Ethics regards a possible kingdom of ends as a kingdom of nature. In the first case, the kingdom of ends is a theoretical idea, adopted to explain what actually is. In the latter it is a practical idea, adopted to bring about that which is not yet, but which can be realized by our conduct, namely, if it conforms to this idea.

24.   I class the principle of moral feeling under that of happiness, because every empirical interest promises to contribute to our well-being by the agreeableness that a thing affords, whether it be immediately and without a view to profit, or whether profit be regarded. We must likewise, with Hutcheson, class the principle of sympathy with the happiness of others under his assumed moral sense.

3.   *UTILITARIANISM*

John Stuart Mill

CHAPTER I. GENERAL REMARKS

There are few circumstances among those which make up the present condition of human knowledge more unlike what might have been expected, or more significant of the backward state in which speculation on the most important subjects still lingers, than the little progress which has been made in the decision of the controversy respecting the criterion of right and wrong. From the dawn of philosophy, the question concerning the *summum bonum,* or, what is the same thing, concerning the foundation of morality, has been accounted the main problem in speculative thought, has occupied the most gifted intellects and divided them into sects and schools carrying on a vigorous warfare against one another. And after more than two thousand years the same discussions continue, philosophers are still ranged under the same contending banners, and neither thinkers nor mankind at large seem nearer to being unanimous on the

From John Stuart Mill, *Utilitarianism,* first published 1861. Chapters 1, 2, 4, 5.

subject than when the youth Socrates listened to the old Protagoras and asserted (if Plato's dialogue be grounded on a real conversation) the theory of utilitarianism against the popular morality of the so-called sophist.

It is true that similar confusion and uncertainty and, in some cases, similar discordance exist respecting the first principles of all the sciences, not excepting that which is deemed the most certain of them—mathematics, without much impairing, generally indeed without impairing at all, the trustworthiness of the conclusions of those sciences. An apparent anomaly, the explanation of which is that the detailed doctrines of a science are not usually deduced from, nor depend for their evidence upon, what are called its first principles. Were it not so, there would be no science more precarious, or whose conclusions were more insufficiently made out, than algebra, which derives none of its certainty from what are commonly taught to learners as its elements, since these, as laid down by some of its most eminent teachers, are as full of fictions as English law, and of mysteries as theology. The truths which are ultimately accepted as the first principles of a science are really the last results of metaphysical analysis practiced on the elementary notions with which the science is conversant; and their relation to the science is not that of foundations to an edifice, but of roots to a tree, which may perform their office equally well though they be never dug down to and exposed to light. But though in science the particular truths precede the general theory, the contrary might be expected to be the case with a practical art, such as morals or legislation. All action is for the sake of some end, and rules of action, it seems natural to suppose, must take their whole character and color from the end to which they are subservient. When we engage in a pursuit, a clear and precise conception of what we are pursuing would seem to be the first thing we need, instead of the last we are to look forward to. A test of right and wrong must be the means, one would think, of ascertaining what is right or wrong, and not a consequence of having already ascertained it.

The difficulty is not avoided by having recourse to the popular theory of a natural faculty, a sense of instinct, informing us of right and wrong. For—besides that the existence of such a moral instinct is itself one of the matters in dispute—those believers in it who have any pretensions to philosophy have been obliged to abandon the idea that it discerns what is right or wrong in the particular case in hand, as our other senses discern the sight or sound actually present. Our moral faculty, according to all those of its interpreters who are entitled to the name of thinkers, supplies us only with the general principles of moral judgments; it is a branch of our reason, not of our sensitive faculty, and must be looked to for the abstract doctrines of morality, not for perception of it in the concrete. The intuitive, no less than what may be termed the inductive, school of ethics insists on the necessity of general laws. They both agree that the morality of an individual action is not a question of direct perception, but of the application of a law to an individual case. They recognize also, to a great extent, the same moral laws, but differ as to their evidence and the source from which they derive their authority. According to

the one opinion, the principles of morals are evident *a priori,* requiring nothing to command assent except that the meaning of the terms be understood. According to the other doctrine, right and wrong, as well as truth and falsehood, are questions of observation and experience. But both hold equally that morality must be deduced from principles; and the intuitive school affirm as strongly as the inductive that there is a science of morals. Yet they seldom attempt to make out a list of the *a priori* principles which are to serve as the premises of the science; still more rarely do they make any effort to reduce those various principles to one first principle or common ground of obligation. They either assume the ordinary precepts of morals as of *a priori* authority, or they lay down as the common groundwork of those maxims some generality much less obviously authoritative than the maxims themselves, and which has never succeeded in gaining popular acceptance. Yet to support their pretensions there ought either to be some one fundamental principle or law at the root of all morality, or, if there be several, there should be a determinate order of precedence among them; and the one principle, or the rule for deciding between the various principles when they conflict, ought to be self-evident.

To inquire how far the bad effects of this deficiency have been mitigated in practice, or to what extent the moral beliefs of mankind have been vitiated or made uncertain by the absence of any distinct recognition of an ultimate standard, would imply a complete survey and criticism of past and present ethical doctrine. It would, however, be easy to show that whatever steadiness or consistency these moral beliefs have attained has been mainly due to the tacit influence of a standard not recognized. Although the nonexistence of an acknowledged first principle has made ethics not so much a guide as a consecration of men's actual sentiments, still, as men's sentiments, both of favor and of aversion, are greatly influenced by what they suppose to be the effects of things upon their happiness, the principle of utility, or, as Bentham latterly called it, the greatest happiness principle, has had a large share in forming the moral doctrines even of those who most scornfully reject its authority. Nor is there any school of thought which refuses to admit that the influence of actions on happiness is a most material and even predominant consideration in many of the details of morals, however unwilling to acknowledge it as the fundamental principle of morality and the source of moral obligation. I might go much further and say that to all those *a priori* moralists who deem it necessary to argue at all, utilitarian arguments are indispensable. It is not my present purpose to criticize these thinkers; but I cannot help referring, for illustration, to a systematic treatise by one of the most illustrious of them, the *Metaphysics of Ethics* by Kant. This remarkable man, whose system of thought will long remain one of the landmarks in the history of philosophical speculation, does, in the treatise in question, lay down a universal first principle as the origin and ground of moral obligation; it is this: "So act that the rule on which thou actest would admit of being adopted as a law by all rational beings." But when he begins to deduce from this precept any of the actual duties of morality, he fails, almost grotesquely, to show that there would be any contradiction, any logical (not to say physical) impossibility, in the adoption by all rational beings of the most outrageously immoral rules of conduct. All he shows is that the *consequences* of their universal adoption would be such as no one would choose to incur.

On the present occasion, I shall, without further discussion of the other theories, attempt to contribute something toward the understanding and appreciation of the "utilitarian" or "happiness" theory, and toward such proof as it is susceptible of. It is evident that this cannot be proof in the ordinary and popular meaning of the term. Questions of ultimate ends are not amenable to direct proof. Whatever can be proved to be good must be so by being shown to be a means to something admitted to be good without proof. The medical art is proved to be good by its conducing to health; but how is it possible to prove that health is good? The art of music is good, for the reason, among others, that it produces pleasure; but what proof is it possible to give that pleasure is good? If, then, it is asserted that there is a comprehensive formula, including all things which are in themselves good, and that whatever else is good is not so as an end but as a means, the formula may be

accepted or rejected, but is not a subject of what is commonly understood by proof. We are not, however, to infer that its acceptance or rejection must depend on blind impulse or arbitrary choice. There is a larger meaning of the word "proof," in which this question is as amenable to it as any other of the disputed questions of philosophy. The subject is within the cognizance of the rational faculty; and neither does that faculty deal with it solely in the way of intuition. Considerations may be presented capable of determining the intellect either to give or withhold its assent to the doctrine; and this is equivalent to proof.

We shall examine presently of what nature are these considerations; in what manner they apply to the case, and what rational grounds, therefore, can be given for accepting or rejecting the utilitarian formula. But it is a preliminary condition of rational acceptance or rejection that the formula should be correctly understood. I believe that the very imperfect notion ordinarily formed of its meaning is the chief obstacle which impedes its reception, and that, could it be cleared even from only the grosser misconceptions, the question would be greatly simplified and a large proportion of its difficulties removed. Before, therefore, I attempt to enter into the philosophical grounds which can be given for assenting to the utilitarian standard, I shall offer some illustrations of the doctrine itself, with the view of showing more clearly what it is, distinguishing it from what it is not, and disposing of such of the practical objections to it as either originate in, or are closely connected with, mistaken interpretations of its meaning. Having thus prepared the ground, I shall afterwards endeavor to throw such light as I can call upon the question considered as one of philosophical theory.

CHAPTER II. WHAT UTILITARIANISM IS

A passing remark is all that needs be given to the ignorant blunder of supposing that those who stand up for utility as the test of right and wrong use the term in that restricted and merely colloquial sense in which utility is opposed to pleasure. An apology is due to the philosophical opponents of utilitarianism for even the momentary appearance of confounding them with anyone capable of so absurd a misconception; which is the more extraordinary, inasmuch as the contrary accusation, of referring everything to pleasure, and that, too, in its grossest form, is another of the common charges against utilitarianism: and, as has been pointedly remarked by an able writer, the same sort of persons, and often the very same persons, denounce the theory "as impracticably dry when the word 'utility' precedes the word 'pleasure,' and as too practicably voluptuous when the word 'pleasure' precedes the word 'utility.' " Those who know anything about the matter are aware that every writer, from Epicurus to Bentham, who maintained the theory of utility meant by it, not something to be contradistinguished from pleasure, but pleasure itself, together with exemption from pain; and instead of opposing the useful to the agreeable or the ornamental, have always declared that the useful means these, among other things. Yet the common herd, including the herd of writers, not only in newspapers and periodicals, but in books of weight and pretension, are perpetually falling into this shallow mistake. Having caught up the word "utilitarian," while knowing nothing whatever about it but its sound, they habitually express by it the rejection or the neglect of pleasure in some of its forms: of beauty, of ornament, or of amusement. Nor is the term thus ignorantly misapplied solely in disparagement, but occasionally in compliment, as though it implied superiority to frivolity and the mere pleasures of the moment. And this perverted use is the only one in which the word is popularly known, and the one from which the new generation are acquiring their sole notion of its meaning. Those who introduced the word, but who had for many years discontinued it as a distinctive appellation, may well feel themselves called upon to resume it if by doing so they can hope to contribute anything toward rescuing it from this utter degradation.[1]

The creed which accepts as the foundation of morals "utility" or the "greatest happiness principle" holds that actions are right in proportion as they tend to promote happiness; wrong as they tend to produce the reverse of happiness. By happiness is intended pleasure and the absence of pain; by unhappiness, pain and the privation of pleasure. To give a clear view of the moral standard set up by the theory, much more requires to be said; in particular, what things it includes in the ideas of pain and pleasure, and to what extent this is left an open question. But these supplementary explanations do not affect the theory of life on which this theory of morality is grounded—namely, that pleasure and freedom from pain are the only things desirable as ends; and that all desirable things (which are as numerous in the utilitarian as in any other scheme) are desirable either for pleasure inherent in themselves or as means to the promotion of pleasure and the prevention of pain.

Now such a theory of life excites in many minds, and among them in some of the most estimable in feeling and purpose, inveterate dislike. To suppose that life has (as they express it) no higher end than pleasure—no better and nobler object of desire and pursuit—they designate as utterly mean and groveling, as a doctrine worthy only of swine, to whom the followers of Epicurus were, at a very early period, contemptuously likened; and modern holders of the doctrine are occasionally made the subject of equally polite comparisons by its German, French, and English assailants.

When thus attacked, the Epicureans have always answered that it is not they, but their accusers, who represent human nature in a degrading light, since the accusation supposes human beings to be capable of no pleasures except those of which swine are capable. If this supposition were true, the charge could not be gainsaid, but would then be no longer an imputation; for if the sources of pleasure were precisely the same to human beings and to swine, the rule of life which is good enough for the one would be good enough for the other. The comparison of the Epicurean life to that of beasts is felt as degrading, precisely because a beast's pleasures do not satisfy a human being's conceptions of happiness. Human beings have faculties more elevated than the animal appetites and, when once made conscious of them, do not regard anything as happiness which does not include their gratification. I do not, indeed, consider the Epicureans to have been by any means faultless in drawing out their scheme of consequences from the utilitarian principle. To do this in any sufficient manner, many Stoic, as well as Christian, elements require to be included. But there is no known Epicurean theory of life which does not assign to the pleasures of the intellect, of the feelings and imagination, and of the moral sentiments a much higher value as pleasures than to those of mere sensation. It must be admitted, however, that utilitarian writers in general have placed the superiority of mental over bodily pleasures chiefly in the greater permanency, safety, uncostliness, etc., of the former—that is, in their circumstantial advantages rather than in their intrinsic nature. And on all these points utilitarians have fully proved their case; but they might have taken the other and, as it may be called, higher ground with entire consistency. It is quite compatible with the principle of utility to recognize the fact that some kinds of pleasure are more desirable and more valuable than others. It would be absurd that, while in estimating all other things quality is considered as well as quantity, the estimation of pleasure should be supposed to depend on quantity alone.

If I am asked what I mean by difference of quality in pleasures, or what makes one pleasure more valuable than another, merely as a pleasure, except its being greater in amount, there is but one possible answer. Of two pleasures, if there be one to which all or almost all who have experience of both give a decided preference, irrespective of any feeling of moral obligation to prefer it, that is the more desirable pleasure. If one of the two is, by those who are competently acquainted with both, placed so far above the other that they prefer it, even though knowing it to be attended with a greater amount of discontent, and would not resign it for any quantity of the other pleasure which their nature is capable of, we are justified in ascribing to the preferred enjoyment a superiority in quality so far outweighing quantity as to render it, in comparison, of small account.

Now it is an unquestionable fact that those who are equally acquainted with and equally capable of appreciating and enjoying both do give a most marked preference to the manner of existence which employs their higher faculties. Few human creatures would consent to be changed into any of the lower animals for a promise of the fullest allowance of a beast's pleasures; no intelligent human being would consent to be a fool, no instructed person would be an ignoramus, no person of feeling and conscience would be selfish and base, even though they should be persuaded that the fool, the dunce, or the rascal is better satisfied with his lot than they are with theirs. They would not resign what they possess more than he for the most complete satisfaction of all the desires which they have in common with him. If they ever fancy they would, it is only in cases of unhappiness so extreme that to escape from it they would exchange their lot for almost any other, however undesirable in their own eyes. A being of higher faculties requires more to make him happy, is capable probably of more acute suffering, and certainly accessible to it at more points, than one of an inferior type; but in spite of these liabilities, he can never really wish to sink into what he feels to be a lower grade of existence. We may give what explanation we please of this unwillingness; we may attribute it to pride, a name which is given indiscriminately to some of the most and to some of the least estimable feelings of which mankind are capable; we may refer it to the love of liberty and personal independence, an appeal to which was with the Stoics one of the most effective means for the inculcation of it; to the love of power or to the love of excitement, both of which do really enter into and contribute to it; but its most appropriate appellation is a sense of dignity, which all human beings possess in one form or other, and in some, though by no means in exact, proportion to their higher faculties, and which is so essential a part of the happiness of those in whom it is strong that nothing which conflicts with it could be otherwise than momentarily an object of desire to them. Whoever supposes that this preference takes place at a sacrifice of happiness—that the superior being, in anything like equal circumstances, is not happier than the inferior—confounds the two very different ideas of happiness and content. It is indisputable that the being whose capacities of enjoyment are low has the greatest chance of having them fully satisfied; and a highly endowed being will always feel that any happiness which he can look for, as the world is constituted, is imperfect. But he can learn to bear its imperfections, if they are at all bearable; and they will not make him envy the being who is indeed unconscious of the imperfections, but only because he feels not at all the good which those imperfections qualify. It is better to be a human being dissatisfied than a pig satisfied; better to be Socrates dissatisfied than a fool satisfied. And if the fool, or the pig, are of a different opinion, it is because they only know their own side of the question. The other party to the comparison knows both sides.

It may be objected that many who are capable of the higher pleasures occasionally, under the influence of temptation, postpone them to the lower. But this is quite compatible with a full appreciation of the intrinsic superiority of the higher. Men often, from infirmity of character, make their election for the nearer good, though they know it to be the less valuable; and this no less when the choice is between two bodily pleasures than when it is between bodily and mental. They pursue sensual indulgences to the injury of health, though perfectly aware that health is the greater good. It may be further objected that many who begin with youthful enthusiasm for everything noble, as they advance in years, sink into indolence and selfishness. But I do not believe that those who undergo this very common change voluntarily choose the lower description of pleasures in preference to the higher. I believe that, before they devote themselves exclusively to the one, they have already become incapable of the other. Capacity for the nobler feelings is in most natures a very tender plant, easily killed, not only by hostile influences, but by mere want of sustenance; and in the majority of young persons it speedily dies away if the occupations to which their position in life has devoted them, and the society into which it has thrown them, are not favorable to keeping that higher capacity in exercise. Men lose their high aspirations as they lose their intellectual tastes, because they have not time or opportunity for indulging them; and they addict themselves to inferior pleasures, not because they deliberately prefer them, but because they are either the only ones to which they have access or the only ones which they are any longer capable of enjoying. It may be questioned whether anyone who has remained equally susceptible to both classes of pleasures ever knowingly and calmly preferred the lower, though many, in all ages, have broken down in an ineffectual attempt to combine both.

From this verdict of the only competent judges, I apprehend there can be no appeal. On a question which is the best worth having of two pleasures, or which of two modes of existence is the most grateful to the feelings, apart from its moral attributes and from its consequences, the judgment of those who are qualified by knowledge of both, or, if they differ, that of the majority among them, must be admitted as final. And there needs be the less hesitation to accept this judgment respecting the quality of pleasures, since there is no other tribunal to be referred to even on the question of quantity. What means are there of determining which is the acutest of two pains, or the intensest of two pleasurable sensations, except the general suffrage of those who are familiar with both? Neither pains nor pleasures are homogeneous, and pain is always heterogeneous with pleasure. What is there to decide whether a particular pleasure is worth purchasing at the cost of a particular pain, except the feelings and judgment of the experienced? When, therefore, those feelings and judgment declare the pleasures derived from the higher faculties to be preferable *in kind,* apart from the question of intensity, to those of which the animal nature, disjoined from the higher faculties, is susceptible, they are entitled on this subject to the same regard.

I have dwelt on this point as being a necessary part of a perfectly just conception of utility or happiness considered as the directive rule of human conduct. But it is by no means an indispensable condition to the acceptance of the utilitarian standard; for that standard is not the agent's own greatest happiness, but the greatest amount of happiness altogether; and if it may possibly be doubted whether a noble character is always the happier for its nobleness, there can be no doubt that it makes other people happier, and that the world in general is immensely a gainer by it. Utilitarianism, therefore, could only attain its end by the general cultivation of nobleness of character, even if each individual were only benefited by the nobleness of others, and his own, so far as happiness is concerned, were a sheer deduction from the benefit. But the bare enunciation of such an absurdity as this last renders refutation superfluous.

According to the greatest happiness principle, as above explained, the ultimate end, with reference to and for the sake of which all other things are desirable—whether we are considering our own good or that of other people—is an existence exempt as far as possible from pain, and as rich as possible in enjoyments, both in point of quantity and quality; the test of quality and the rule for measuring it against quantity being the preference felt by those who, in their opportunities of experience, to which must be added their habits of self-consciousness and self-observation, are best furnished with the means of comparison. This, being according to the utilitarian opinion the end of human action, is necessarily also the standard of morality, which may accordingly be defined "the rules and precepts for human conduct," by the observance of which an existence such as has been described might be, to the greatest extent possible, secured to all mankind; and not to them only, but, so far as the nature of things admits, to the whole sentient creation.

Against this doctrine, however, arises another class of objectors who say that happiness, in any form, cannot be the rational purpose of human life and action; because, in the first place, it is unattainable; and they contemptuously ask, What right hast thou to be happy?—a question which Mr. Carlyle clinches by the addition, What right, a short time ago, hadst thou even *to be?* Next they say that men can do *without* happiness; that all noble human beings have felt this, and could not have become noble but by learning the lesson of *Entsagen,* or renunciation; which lesson, thoroughly learned and submitted to, they affirm to be the beginning and necessary condition of all virtue.

The first of these objections would go to the root of the matter were it well founded; for if no happiness is to be had at all by human beings, the attainment of it cannot be the end of morality or of any rational conduct. Though, even in that case, something might still be said for the utilitarian theory, since utility includes not solely the pursuit of happiness, but the prevention or mitigation of unhappiness; and if the former aim be chimerical, there will be all the greater scope and more imperative need for the latter, so long at least as mankind think fit to live and do not take refuge in the simultaneous act of suicide recommended under certain conditions by Novalis. When, however, it is thus positively asserted to be impossible that human life should be happy, the assertion, if not something like a

verbal quibble, is at least an exaggeration. If by happiness be meant a continuity of highly pleasurable excitement, it is evident enough that this is impossible. A state of exalted pleasure lasts only moments or in some cases, and with some intermissions, hours or days, and is the occasional brilliant flash of enjoyment, not its permanent and steady flame. Of this the philosophers who have taught that happiness is the end of life were as fully aware as those who taunt them. The happiness which they meant was not a life of rapture, but moments of such, in an existence made up of few and transitory pains, many and various pleasures, with a decided predominance of the active over the passive, and having as the foundation of the whole not to expect more from life than it is capable of bestowing. A life thus composed, to those who have been fortunate enough to obtain it, has always appeared worthy of the name of happiness. And such an existence is even now the lot of many during some considerable portion of their lives. The present wretched education and wretched social arrangements are the only real hindrance to its being attainable by almost all.

The objectors perhaps may doubt whether human beings, if taught to consider happiness as the end of life, would be satisfied with such a moderate share of it. But great numbers of mankind have been satisfied with much less. The main constituents of a satisfied life appear to be two, either of which by itself is often found sufficient for the purpose: tranquillity and excitement. With much tranquillity, many find that they can be content with very little pleasure; with much excitement, many can reconcile themselves to a considerable quantity of pain. There is assuredly no inherent impossibility of enabling even the mass of mankind to unite both, since the two are so far from being incompatible that they are in natural alliance, the prolongation of either being a preparation for, and exciting a wish for, the other. It is only those in whom indolence amounts to a vice that do not desire excitement after an interval of repose; it is only those in whom the need of excitement is a disease that feel the tranquillity which follows excitement dull and insipid, instead of pleasurable in direct proportion to the excitement which preceded it. When people who are tolerably fortunate in their outward lot do not find in life sufficient enjoyment to make it valuable to them, the cause generally is caring for nobody but themselves. To those who have neither public nor private affections, the excitements of life are much curtailed, and in any case dwindle in value as the time approaches when all selfish interests must be terminated by death; while those who leave after them objects of personal affection, and especially those who have also cultivated a fellow-feeling with the collective interests of mankind, retain as lively an interest in life on the eve of death as in the vigor of youth and health. Next to selfishness, the principal cause which makes life unsatisfactory is want of mental cultivation. A cultivated mind—I do not mean that of a philosopher, but any mind to which the fountains of knowledge have been opened, and which has been taught, in any tolerable degree, to exercise its faculties—finds sources of inexhaustible interest in all that surrounds it: in the objects of nature, the achievements of art, the imaginations of poetry, the incidents of history, the ways of mankind, past and present, and their prospects in the future. It is possible, indeed, to become indifferent to all this, and that too without having exhausted a thousandth part of it, but only when one has had from the beginning no moral or human interest in these things and has sought in them only the gratification of curiosity.

Now there is absolutely no reason in the nature of things why an amount of mental culture sufficient to give an intelligent interest in these objects of contemplation should not be the inheritance of everyone born in a civilized country. As little is there an inherent necessity that any human being should be a selfish egotist, devoid of every feeling or care but those which center in his own miserable individuality. Something far superior to this is sufficiently common even now, to give ample earnest of what the human species may be made. Genuine private affections and a sincere interest in the public good are possible, though in unequal degrees, to every rightly brought up human being. In a world in which there is so much to interest, so much to enjoy, and so much also to correct and improve, everyone who has this moderate amount of moral and intellectual requisites is capable of an existence which may be called enviable; and unless such a person, through bad

laws or subjection to the will of others, is denied the liberty to use the sources of happiness within his reach, he will not fail to find this enviable existence, if he escape the positive evils of life, the great sources of physical and mental suffering—such as indigence, disease, and the unkindness, worthlessness, or premature loss of objects of affection. The main stress of the problem lies, therefore, in the contest with these calamities from which it is a rare good fortune entirely to escape; which, as things now are, cannot be obviated, and often cannot be in any material degree mitigated. Yet no one whose opinion deserves a moment's consideration can doubt that most of the great positive evils of the world are in themselves removable, and will, if human affairs continue to improve, be in the end reduced within narrow limits. Poverty, in any sense implying suffering, may be completely extinguished by the wisdom of society combined with the good sense and providence of individuals. Even that most intractable of enemies, disease, may be indefinitely reduced in dimensions by good physical and moral education and proper control of noxious influences, while the progress of science holds out a promise for the future of still more direct conquests over this detestable foe. And every advance in that direction relieves us from some, not only of the chances which cut short our own lives, but, what concerns us still more, which deprive us of those in whom our happiness is wrapt up. As for vicissitudes of fortune and other disappointments connected with worldly circumstances, these are principally the effect either of gross imprudence, of ill-regulated desires, or of bad or imperfect social institutions. All the grand sources, in short, of human suffering are in a great degree, many of them almost entirely, conquerable by human care and effort; and though their removal is grievously slow—though a long succession of generations will perish in the breach before the conquest is completed, and this world becomes all that, if will and knowledge were not wanting, it might easily be made—yet every mind sufficiently intelligent and generous to bear a part, however small and inconspicuous, in the endeavor will draw a noble enjoyment from the contest itself, which he would not for any bribe in the form of selfish indulgence consent to be without.

And this leads to the true estimation of what is said by the objectors concerning the possibility and the obligation of learning to do without happiness. Unquestionably it is possible to do without happiness; it is done involuntarily by nineteen-twentieths of mankind, even in those parts of our present world which are least deep in barbarism; and it often has to be done voluntarily by the hero or the martyr, for the sake of something which he prizes more than his individual happiness. But this something, what is it, unless the happiness of others or some of the requisites of happiness? It is noble to be capable of resigning entirely one's own portion of happiness, or chances of it; but, after all, this self-sacrifice must be for some end; it is not its own end; and if we are told that its end is not happiness but virtue, which is better than happiness, I ask, would the sacrifice be made if the hero or martyr did not believe that it would earn for others immunity from similar sacrifices? Would it be made if he thought that his renunciation of happiness for himself would produce no fruit for any of his fellow creatures, but to make their lot like his and place them also in the condition of persons who have renounced happiness? All honor to those who can abnegate for themselves the personal enjoyment of life when by such renunciation they contribute worthily to increase the amount of happiness in the world; but he who does it or professes to do it for any other purpose is no more deserving of admiration than the ascetic mounted on his pillar. He may be an inspiriting proof of what men *can* do, but assuredly not an example of what they *should*.

Though it is only in a very imperfect state of the world's arrangements that anyone can best serve the happiness of others by the absolute sacrifice of his own, yet, so long as the world is in that imperfect state, I fully acknowledge that the readiness to make such a sacrifice is the highest virtue which can be found in man. I will add that in this condition of the world, paradoxical as the assertion may be, the conscious ability to do without happiness gives the best prospect of realizing such happiness as is attainable. For nothing except that consciousness can raise a person above the chances of life by making him feel that, let fate and fortune do their worst, they have not power to subdue him; which, once felt, frees him from excess of anxiety concerning the evils of life and enables him, like many a Stoic in the worst times of the Roman Empire, to cultivate in tranquillity the sources of satisfaction accessible to him, without concerning himself about the uncertainty of their duration any more than about their inevitable end.

Meanwhile, let utilitarians never cease to claim the morality of self-devotion as a possession which belongs by as good a right to them as either to the Stoic or to the Transcendentalist. The utilitarian morality does recognize in human beings the power of sacrificing their own greatest good for the good of others. It only refuses to admit that the sacrifice is itself a good. A sacrifice which does not increase or tend to increase the sum total of happiness, it considers as wasted. The only self-renunciation which it applauds is devotion to the happiness, or to some of the means of happiness, of others, either of mankind collectively or of individuals within the limits imposed by the collective interests of mankind.

I must again repeat what the assailants of utilitarianism seldom have the justice to acknowledge, that the happiness which forms the utilitarian standard of what is right in conduct is not the agent's own happiness but that of all concerned. As between his own happiness and that of others, utilitarianism requires him to be as strictly impartial as a disinterested and benevolent spectator. In the golden rule of Jesus of Nazareth, we read the complete spirit of the ethics of utility. "To do as you would be done by," and "to love your neighbor as yourself," constitute the ideal perfection of utilitarian morality. As the means of making the nearest approach to this ideal, utility would enjoin, first, that laws and social arrangements should place the happiness or (as, speaking practically, it may be called) the interest of every individual as nearly as possible in harmony with the interest of the whole; and, secondly, that education and opinion, which have so vast a power over human character, should so use that power as to establish in the mind of every individual an indissoluble association between his own happiness and the good of the whole, especially between his own happiness and the practice of such modes of conduct, negative and positive, as regard for the universal happiness prescribes; so that not only he may be unable to conceive the possibility of happiness to himself, consistently with conduct opposed to the general good, but also that a direct impulse to promote the general good may be in every individual one of the habitual motives of action, and the sentiments connected therewith may fill a large and prominent place in every human being's sentient existence. If the impugners of the utilitarian morality represented it to their own minds in this its true character, I know not what recommendation possessed by any other morality they could possibly affirm to be wanting to it; what more beautiful or more exalted developments of human nature any other ethical system can be supposed to foster, or what springs of action, not accessible to the utilitarian, such systems rely on for giving effect to their mandates.

The objectors to utilitarianism cannot always be charged with representing it in a discreditable light. On the contrary, those among them who entertain anything like a just idea of its disinterested character sometimes find fault with its standard as being too high for humanity. They say it is exacting too much to require that people shall always act from the inducement of promoting the general interests of society. But this is to mistake the very meaning of a standard of morals and confound the rule of action with the motive of it. It is the business of ethics to tell us what are our duties, or by what test we may know them; but no system of ethics requires that the sole motive of all we do shall be a feeling of duty; on the contrary, ninety-nine hundredths of all our actions are done from other motives, and rightly so done if the rule of duty does not condemn them. It is the more unjust to utilitarianism that this particular misapprehension should be made a ground of objection to it, inasmuch as utilitarian moralists have gone beyond almost all others in affirming that the motive has nothing to do with the morality of the action, though much with the worth of the agent. He who saves a fellow creature from drowning does what is morally right, whether his motive be duty or the hope of being paid for his trouble; he who betrays the friend that trusts him is guilty of a crime, even if his object be to serve another friend to whom he is under greater obligations.[2] But to speak only of actions done from the motive of duty, and in direct obedience to principle: it is a misapprehension of the utilitarian mode of

thought to conceive it as implying that people should fix their minds upon so wide a generality as the world, or society at large. The great majority of good actions are intended not for the benefit of the world, but for that of individuals, of which the good of the world is made up; and the thoughts of the most virtuous man need not on these occasions travel beyond the particular persons concerned, except so far as is necessary to assure himself that in benefiting them he is not violating the rights, that is, the legitimate and authorized expectations, of anyone else. The multiplication of happiness is, according to the utilitarian ethics, the object of virtue. The occasions on which any person (except one in a thousand) has it in his power to do this on an extended scale—in other words, to be a public benefactor—are but exceptional; and on these occasions alone is he called on to consider public utility; in every other case, private utility, the interest or happiness of some few persons, is all he has to attend to. Those alone the influence of whose actions extends to society in general need concern themselves habitually about so large an object. In the case of abstinences indeed—of things which people forbear to do from moral considerations, though the consequences in the particular case might be beneficial—it would be unworthy of an intelligent agent not to be consciously aware that the action is of a class which, if practiced generally, would be generally injurious, and that this is the ground of the obligation to abstain from it. The amount of regard for the public interest implied in this recognition is no greater than is demanded by every system of morals, for they all enjoin to abstain from whatever is manifestly pernicious to society.

The same considerations dispose of another reproach against the doctrine of utility, founded on a still grosser misconception of the purpose of a standard of morality and of the very meaning of the words "right" and "wrong." It is often affirmed that utilitarianism renders men cold and unsympathizing; that it chills their moral feelings toward individuals; that it makes them regard only the dry and hard consideration of the consequences of actions, not taking into their moral estimate the qualities from which those actions emanate. If the assertion means that they do not allow their judgment respecting the rightness or wrongness of an action to be influenced by their opinion of the qualities of the person who does it, this is a complaint not against utilitarianism, but against any standard of morality at all; for certainly no known ethical standard decides an action to be good or bad because it is done by a good or a bad man, still less because done by an amiable, a brave, or a benevolent man, or the contrary. These considerations are relevant, not to the estimation of actions, but of persons; and there is nothing in the utilitarian theory inconsistent with the fact that there are other things which interest us in persons besides the rightness and wrongness of their actions. The Stoics, indeed, with the paradoxical misuse of language which was part of their system, and by which they strove to raise themselves above all concern about anything but virtue, were fond of saying that he who has that has everything; that he, and only he, is rich, is beautiful, is a king. But no claim of this description is made for the virtuous man by the utilitarian doctrine. Utilitarians are quite aware that there are other desirable possessions and qualities besides virtue, and are perfectly willing to allow to all of them their full worth. They are also aware that a right action does not necessarily indicate a virtuous character, and that actions which are blamable often proceed from qualities entitled to praise. When this is apparent in any particular case, it modifies their estimation, not certainly of the act, but of the agent. I grant that they are, notwithstanding, of opinion that in the long run the best proof of a good character is good actions; and resolutely refuse to consider any mental disposition as good of which the predominant tendency is to produce bad conduct. This makes them unpopular with many people, but it is an unpopularity which they must share with everyone who regards the distinction between right and wrong in a serious light; and the reproach is not one which a conscientious utilitarian need be anxious to repel.

If no more be meant by the objection than that many utilitarians look on the morality of actions, as measured by the utilitarian standards, with too exclusive a regard, and do not lay sufficient stress upon the other beauties of character which go toward making a human being lovable or admirable, this may be admitted. Utilitarians who have cultivated their moral feelings, but not their sympathies, nor their artistic per-

ceptions, do fall into this mistake; and so do all other moralists under the same conditions. What can be said in excuse for other moralists is equally available for them, namely, that, if there is to be any error, it is better that it should be on that side. As a matter of fact, we may affirm that among utilitarians, as among adherents of other systems, there is every imaginable degree of rigidity and of laxity in the application of their standard; some are even puritanically rigorous, while others are as indulgent as can possibly be desired by sinner or by sentimentalist. But on the whole, a doctrine which brings prominently forward the interest that mankind have in the repression and prevention of conduct which violates the moral law is likely to be inferior to no other in turning the sanctions of opinion against such violations. It is true, the question "What does violate the moral law?" is one on which those who recognize different standards of morality are likely now and then to differ. But difference of opinion on moral questions was not first introduced into the world by utilitarianism, while that doctrine does supply, if not always an easy, at all events a tangible and intelligible, mode of deciding such differences.

It may not be superfluous to notice a few more of the common misapprehensions of utilitarian ethics, even those which are so obvious and gross that it might appear impossible for any person of candor and intelligence to fall into them; since persons, even of considerable mental endowment, often give themselves so little trouble to understand the bearings of any opinion against which they entertain a prejudice, and men are in general so little conscious of this voluntary ignorance as a defect that the vulgarest misunderstandings of ethical doctrines are continually met with in the deliberate writings of persons of the greatest pretensions both to high principle and to philosophy. We not uncommonly hear the doctrine of utility inveighed against as a *godless* doctrine. If it be necessary to say anything at all against so mere an assumption, we may say that the question depends upon what idea we have formed of the moral character of the Deity. If it be a true belief that God desires, above all things, the happiness of his creatures, and that this was his purpose in their creation, utility is not only not a godless doctrine, but more profoundly religious than any other. If it be meant that utilitarianism does not recognize the revealed will of God as the supreme law of morals, I answer that a utilitarian who believes in the perfect goodness and wisdom of *God* necessarily believes that whatever God has thought fit to reveal on the subject of morals must fulfill the requirements of utility in a supreme degree. But others besides utilitarians have been of opinion that the Christian revelation was intended, and is fitted, to inform the hearts and minds of mankind with a spirit which should enable them to find for themselves what is right, and incline them to do it when found, rather than to tell them, except in a very general way, what it is; and that we need a doctrine of ethics, carefully followed out, to *interpret* to us the will of God. Whether this opinion is correct or not, it is superfluous here to discuss; since whatever aid religion, either natural or revealed, can afford to ethical investigation is as open to the utilitarian moralist as to any other. He can use it as the testimony of God to the usefulness or hurtfulness of any given course of action by as good a right as others can use it for the indication of a transcendental law having no connection with usefulness or with happiness.

Again, utility is often summarily stigmatized as an immoral doctrine by giving it the name of "expediency," and taking advantage of the popular use of that term to contrast it with principle. But the expedient, in the sense in which it is opposed to the right, generally means that which is expedient for the particular interest of the agent himself; as when a minister sacrifices the interests of his country to keep himself in place. When it means anything better than this, it means that which is expedient for some immediate object, some temporary purpose, but which violates a rule whose observance is expedient in a much higher degree. The expedient, in this sense, instead of being the same thing with the useful, is a branch of the hurtful. Thus it would often be expedient, for the purpose of getting over some momentary embarrassment, or attaining some object immediately useful to ourselves or others, to tell a lie. But inasmuch as the cultivation in ourselves of a sensitive feeling on the subject of veracity is one of the most useful, and the enfeeblement of that feeling one of the most hurtful, things to which our conduct can be instrumental; and inasmuch as any, even unin-

tentional, deviation from truth does that much toward weakening the trustworthiness of human assertion, which is not only the principal support of all present social well-being, but the insufficiency of which does more than any one thing that can be named to keep back civilization, virtue, everything on which human happiness on the largest scale depends—we feel that the violation, for a present advantage, of a rule of such transcendent expediency is not expedient, and that he who, for the sake of convenience to himself or to some other individual, does what depends on him to deprive mankind of the good, and inflict upon them the evil, involved in the greater or less reliance which they can place in each other's word, acts the part of one of their worst enemies. Yet that even this rule, sacred as it is, admits of possible exceptions is acknowledged by all moralists; the chief of which is when the withholding of some fact (as of information from a malefactor, or of bad news from a person dangerously ill) would save an individual (especially an individual other than oneself) from great and unmerited evil, and when the withholding can only be effected by denial. But in order that the exception may not extend itself beyond the need, and may have the least possible effect in weakening reliance on veracity, it ought to be recognized and, if possible, its limits defined; and, if the principle of utility is good for anything, it must be good for weighing these conflicting utilities against one another and marking out the region within which one or the other preponderates.

Again, defenders of utility often find themselves called upon to reply to such objections as this—that there is not time, previous to action, for calculating and weighing the effects of any line of conduct on the general happiness. This is exactly as if anyone were to say that it is impossible to guide our conduct by Christianity because there is not time, on every occasion on which anything has to be done, to read through the Old and New Testaments. The answer to the objection is that there has been ample time, namely, the whole past duration of the human species. During all that time mankind have been learning by experience the tendencies of actions; on which experience all the prudence as well as all the morality of life are dependent. People talk as if the commencement of this course of experience had hitherto been put off, and as if, at the moment when some man feels tempted to meddle with the property or life of another, he had to begin considering for the first time whether murder and theft are injurious to human happiness. Even then I do not think that he would find the question very puzzling; but, at all events, the matter is now done to his hand. It is truly a whimsical supposition that, if mankind were agreed in considering utility to be the test of morality, they would remain without any agreement as to what *is* useful, and would take no measures for having their notions on the subject taught to the young and enforced by law and opinion. There is no difficulty in proving any ethical standard whatever to work ill if we suppose universal idiocy to be conjoined with it; but on any hypothesis short of that, mankind must by this time have acquired positive beliefs as to the effects of some actions on their happiness; and the beliefs which have thus come down are the rules of morality for the multitude, and for the philosopher until he has succeeded in finding better. That philosophers might easily do this, even now, on many subjects; that the received code of ethics is by no means of divine right; and that mankind have still much to learn as to the effects of actions on the general happiness, I admit or rather earnestly maintain. The corollaries from the principle of utility, like the precepts of every practical art, admit of indefinite improvement, and, in a progressive state of the human mind, their improvement is perpetually going on. But to consider the rules of morality as improvable is one thing; to pass over the intermediate generalization entirely and endeavor to test each individual action directly by the first principle is another. It is a strange notion that the acknowledgment of a first principle is inconsistent with the admission of secondary ones. To inform a traveler respecting the place of his ultimate destination is not to forbid the use of landmarks and direction-posts on the way. The proposition that happiness is the end and aim of morality does not mean that no road ought to be laid down to that goal, or that persons going thither should not be advised to take one direction rather than another. Men really ought to leave off talking a kind of nonsense on this subject, which they would neither talk nor listen to on other matters of practical concernment. Nobody argues that the art of navigation is not founded on astronomy because sailors cannot wait to calculate the Nautical Almanac. Being rational creatures, they go to sea with it ready calculated; and all rational creatures go out upon the sea of life with their minds made up on the common questions of right and wrong, as well as on many of the far more difficult questions of wise and foolish. And this, as long as foresight is a human quality, it is to be presumed they will continue to do. Whatever we adopt as the fundamental principle of morality, we require subordinate principles to apply it by; the impossibility of doing without them, being common to all systems, can afford no argument aganst any one in particular; but gravely to argue as if no such secondary principles could be had, and as if mankind had remained till now, and always must remain, without drawing any general conclusions from the experience of human life is as high a pitch, I think, as absurdity has ever reached in philosophical controversy.

The remainder of the stock arguments against utilitarianism mostly consist in laying to its charge the common infirmities of human nature, and the general difficulties which embarrass conscientious persons in shaping their course through life. We are told that a utilitarian will be apt to make his own particular case an exception to moral rules, and, when under temptation, will see a utility in the breach of a rule, greater than he will see in its observance. But is utility the only creed which is able to furnish us with excuses for evil-doing and means of cheating our own conscience? They are afforded in abundance by all doctrines which recognize as a fact in morals the existence of conflicting considerations, which all doctrines do that have been believed by sane persons. It is not the fault of any creed, but of the complicated nature of human affairs, that rules of conduct cannot be so framed as to require no exceptions, and that hardly any kind of action can safely be laid down as either always obligatory or always condemnable. There is no ethical creed which does not temper the rigidity of its laws by giving a certain latitude, under the moral responsibility of the agent, for accommodation to peculiarities of circumstances; and under every creed, at the opening thus made, self-deception and dishonest casuistry get in. There exists no moral system under which there do not arise unequivocal cases of conflicting obligation. These are the real difficulties, the knotty points both in the theory of ethics and in the conscientious guidance of personal conduct. They are overcome practically, with greater or with less success, according to the intellect and virtue of the individual; but it can hardly be pretended that anyone will be the less qualified for dealing with them, from possessing an ultimate standard to which conflicting rights and duties can be referred. If utility is the ultimate source of moral obligations, utility may be invoked to decide between them when their demands are incompatible. Though the application of the standard may be difficult, it is better than none at all; while in other systems, the moral laws all claiming independent authority, there is no common umpire entitled to interfere between them; their claims to precedence one over another rest on little better than sophistry, and, unless determined, as they generally are, by the unacknowledged influence of consideration of utility, afford a free scope for the action of personal desires and partialities. We must remember that only in these cases of conflict between secondary principles is it requisite that first principles should be appealed to. There is no case of moral obligation in which some secondary principle is not involved; and if only one, there can seldom be any real doubt which one it is, in the mind of any person by whom the principle itself is recognized.

CHAPTER III. OF THE ULTIMATE SANCTION OF THE PRINCIPLE OF UTILITY

The question is often asked, and properly so, in regard to any supposed moral standard, What is its sanction? what are the motives to obey it? or, more specifically, what is the source of its obligation? whence does it derive its binding force? It is a necessary part of moral philosophy to provide the answer to this question, which, though frequently assuming the shape of an objection to the utilitarian morality, as if it had some special applicability to that above others, really arises in regard to all standards. It arises, in fact, whenever a person is called on to *adopt* a standard or refer morality to any basis on which he has not been accustomed to rest it. For the customary morality, that which education and opinion have consecrated, is the only one which presents itself to the mind with the feeling of being *in itself* obligatory; and, when a person is asked to believe that this morality *derives* its obligation from some general principle round which custom has not thrown the same halo, the assertion is to him a paradox: the supposed corollaries seem to have a more binding force than the original theorem; the superstructure seems to stand better without than with what is represented as its foundation. He says to himself, "I feel that I am bound not to rob or murder, betray or deceive, but why am I bound to promote the general happiness? If my own happiness lies in something else, why may I not give that the preference?"

If the view adopted by the utilitarian philosophy of the nature of the moral sense be correct, this difficulty will always present itself, until the influences which form moral character have taken the same hold of the principle which they have taken of some of the consequences, until, by the improvement of education, the feeling of unity with our fellow creatures shall be (what it cannot be denied that Christ intended it to be) as deeply rooted in our character and, to our own consciousness, as completely a part of our nature, as the horror of crime is in an ordinarily well brought up young person. In the mean time, however, the difficulty has no peculiar application to the doctrine of utility, but is inherent in every attempt to analyze morality, and reduce it to principles, which, unless the principle is already in men's minds invested with as much sacredness as any of its applications, always seems to divest them of a part of their sanctity.

The principle of utility either has, or there is no reason why it might not have, all the sanctions which belong to any other system of morals. Those sanctions are either external or internal. Of the external sanctions it is not necessary to speak at any length. They are the hope of favor and the fear of displeasure from our fellow creatures, or from the Ruler of the universe, along with whatever we may have of sympathy or affection for them or of love and awe of him, inclining us to do his will independently of selfish consequences. There is evidently no reason why all these motives for observance should not attach themselves to the utilitarian morality as completely and as powerfully as to any other. Indeed, those of them which refer to our fellow creatures are sure to do so, in proportion to the amount of general intelligence; for, whether there be any other ground of moral obligation than the general happiness or not, men do desire happiness and, however imperfect may be their own practice, they desire and commend all conduct in others towards themselves by which they think their happiness is promoted. With regard to the religious motive, if men believe, as most profess to do, in the goodness of God, those who think that conduciveness to the general happiness is the essence, or even only the criterion of good, must necessarily believe that it is also that which God approves. The whole force, therefore, of external reward and punishment, whether physical or moral, and whether proceeding from God or from our fellow men, together with all that the capacities of human nature admit of disinterested devotion to either, become available to enforce the utilitarian morality, in proportion as that morality is recognized, and the more powerfully, the more the appliances of education and general cultivation are bent to the purpose.

So far as to external sanctions. The internal sanction of duty, whatever our standard of duty may be, is one and the same—a feeling in our own mind, a pain, more or less intense, attendant on violation of duty, which, in properly cultivated moral natures, rises in the more serious cases into shrinking from it as an impossibility. This feeling, when disinterested, and connecting itself with the pure idea of duty and not with some particular form of it, or with any of the merely accessory circumstances, is the essence of Conscience; though in that complex phenomenon, as it actually exists, the simple fact is, in general, all incrusted over with collateral associations, derived from sympathy, from love, and still more from fear, from all the forms of religious feeling, from the recollections of childhood, and of all our past life, from self-esteem, desire of the esteem of others, and occasionally even self-abasement. This extreme complication is, I apprehend, the origin of the sort of mystical character which, by a tendency of the human mind of which there are many other examples, is apt to be attributed to the idea of moral obligation, and which leads people to believe that the idea cannot possibly attach itself to any other objects than those which, by a supposed mysterious law, are found in our present experience to excite it. Its binding force, however, consists in the existence of a mass of feeling which must be broken through in order to do what violates our standard of right, and which, if we do nevertheless violate that standard, will probably have to be encountered afterwards in the form of remorse. Whatever theory we have of the nature or origin of conscience, this is what essentially constitutes it.

The ultimate sanction, therefore, of all morality (external motives apart) being a subjective feeling in our own minds, I see nothing embarrassing, to those whose standard is utility, in the question, What is the sanction of that particular standard? We may answer, The same as of all other moral standards—the conscientious feelings of mankind. Undoubtedly this sanction has no binding efficacy on those who do not possess the feelings it appeals to, but neither will these persons be more obedient to any other moral principle than to the utilitarian one. On them, morality of any kind has no hold but through the external sanctions. Meanwhile the feelings exist—a fact in human nature, the reality of which, and the great power with which they are capable of acting on those in whom they have been duly cultivated, are proved by experience. No reason has ever been shown why they may not be cultivated to as great intensity in connection with the utilitarian as with any other rule of morals.

There is, I am aware, a disposition to believe that a person who sees in moral obligation a transcendental fact, an objective reality belonging to the province of "things in themselves," is likely to be more obedient to it than one who believes it to be entirely subjective, having its seat in human consciousness only. But, whatever a person's opinion may be on this point of ontology, the force he is really urged by is his own subjective feeling and is exactly measured by its strength. No one's belief that Duty is an objective reality is stronger than the belief that God is so, yet the belief in God, apart from the expectation of actual reward and punishment, only operates on conduct through, and in proportion to, the subjective religious feeling. The sanction, so far as it is disinterested, is always in the mind itself; and the notion, therefore, of the transcendental moralists must be that this sanction will not exist *in* the mind, unless it is believed to have its root out of the mind, and that if a person is able to say to himself, "This which is restraining me, and which is called my conscience, is only a feeling in my own mind," he may possibly draw the conclusion that, when the feeling ceases, the obligation ceases, and that, if he find the feeling inconvenient, he may disregard it and endeavor to get rid of it. But is this danger confined to the utilitarian morality? Does the belief that moral obligation has its seat outside the mind make the feeling of it too strong to be got rid of? The fact is so far otherwise that all moralists admit and lament the ease with which, in the generality of minds, conscience can be silenced or stifled. The question, Need I obey my conscience? is quite as often put to themselves by persons who never heard of the principle of utility as by its adherents. Those whose conscientious feelings are so weak as to allow of their asking this question, if they answer it affirmatively, will not do so because they believe in the transcendental theory but because of the external sanctions.

It is not necessary, for the present purpose, to decide whether the feeling of duty is innate or implanted. Assuming it to be innate, it is an open question to what objects it naturally attaches itself, for the philosophic supporters of that theory are now agreed that the intuitive perception is of principles of morality and not of the details. If there be any thing innate in the matter, I see no reason why the feeling which is innate should not be that of regard to the pleasures and pains of others. If there is any principle of morals which is intuitively obligatory, I should say it must be that. If so, the intuitive ethics would coincide with the utilitarian, and there would be no further quarrel between them. Even as it is, the intuitive moralists, though they believe that there are other intuitive moral obligations, do already believe this to be one, for they unanimously hold that a large *portion* of morality turns upon the consideration due to the interests of our fellow creatures. Therefore, if the belief in the transcendental origin of moral obligation gives any additional efficacy to the internal sanction, it appears to me that the utilitarian principle has already the benefit of it.

On the other hand, if, as is my own belief, the moral feelings are not innate but acquired, they are not for that reason the less natural. It is natural to man to speak, to reason, to build cities, to cultivate the ground, though these are acquired faculties. The moral feelings are not indeed a part of our nature, in the sense of being in any perceptible degree present in all of us, but this, unhappily, is a fact admitted by those who believe the most strenuously in their transcendental origin. Like the other acquired capacities above referred to, the moral faculty, if not a part of our nature, is a natural outgrowth from it, capable like them, in a certain small degree, of springing up spontaneously, and susceptible of being brought by cultivation to a high degree of development. Unhappily, it is also susceptible, by a sufficient use of the external sanctions and of the force of early impressions, of being cultivated in almost any direction, so that there is hardly any thing so absurd or so mischievous that it may not, by means of these influences, be made to act on the human mind with all the authority of conscience. To doubt that the same potency might be given by the same means to the principle of utility, even if it had no foundation in human nature, would be flying in the face of all experience.

But moral associations which are wholly of artificial creation, when intellectual culture goes on, yield by degrees to the dissolving force of analysis; and if the feeling of duty, when associated with utility, would appear equally arbitrary, if there were no leading department of our nature, no powerful class of sentiments, with which that association would harmonize, which would make us feel it congenial, and incline us not only to foster it in others (for which we have abundant interested motives), but also to cherish it in ourselves, if there were not, in short, a natural basis of sentiment for utilitarian morality —it might well happen that this association also, even after it had been implanted by education, might be analyzed away.

But there *is* this basis of powerful natural sentiment, and this it is, which, when once the general happiness is recognized as the ethical standard, will constitute the strength of the utilitarian morality. This firm foundation is that of the social feelings of mankind: the desire to be in unity with our fellow creatures, which is already a powerful principle in human nature, and happily one of those which tend to become stronger, even without express inculcation from the influences of advancing civilization. The social state is at once so natural, so necessary, and so habitual to man, that except in some unusual circumstances, or by an effort of voluntary abstraction, he never conceives himself otherwise than as a member of a body, and this association is riveted more and more as mankind are further removed from the state of savage independence. Any condition, therefore, which is essential to a state of society, becomes more and more an inseparable part of every person's conception of the state of things which he is born into, and which is the destiny of a human being. Now, society between human beings, except in the relation of master and slave, is manifestly impossible on any other footing than that the interests of all are to be consulted. Society between equals can only exist on the understanding that the interests of all are to be regarded equally. And since, in all states of civilization, every person except an absolute monarch has equals, every one is obliged to live on these terms with somebody, and in every age, some advance is made towards a state in which it will be impossible to live permanently on other terms with anybody. In this way, people grow up unable to conceive as possible to them a state of total disregard of other people's interests. They are under a necessity of conceiving themselves as at least abstaining from all the grosser injuries, and (if only for their own protection) living in a state of constant protest against them. They are also familiar with the fact of cooperating with others, and proposing to themselves a collective, not an individual, interest as the aim (at least for the time being) of their actions. So long as they are cooperating, their ends are identified with those of others; there is at least a temporary feeling that the interests of others are their own interests. Not only does all strengthening of social ties, and all healthy growth of society, give to each individual a stronger personal interest in practically consulting the welfare of others; it also leads him to identify his *feelings* more and more with their good, or at least with an ever greater degree of practical consideration for it. He comes, as though instinctively, to be conscious of himself as a being who *of course* pays regard to others. The good of others becomes to him a thing naturally and necessarily to be attended to, like any of the physical conditions of

our existence. Now, whatever amount of this feeling a person has, he is urged by the strongest motives, both of interest and of sympathy, to demonstrate it and, to the utmost of his power, encourage it in others, and, even if he has none of it himself, he is as greatly interested as any one else that others should have it. Consequently, the smallest germs of the feeling are laid hold of and nourished by the contagion of sympathy and the influences of education, and a complete web of corroborative association is woven round it by the powerful agency of the external sanctions. This mode of conceiving ourselves and human life, as civilization goes on, is felt to be more and more natural. Every step in political improvement renders it more so, by removing the sources of opposition of interest and leveling those inequalities of legal privilege between individuals or classes, owing to which there are large portions of mankind whose happiness it is still practicable to disregard. In an improving state of the human mind, the influences are constantly on the increase which tend to generate in each individual a feeling of unity with all the rest, which, if perfect, would make him never think of or desire any beneficial condition for himself, in the benefits of which they are not included. If we now suppose this feeling of unity to be taught as a religion, and the whole force of education, of institutions, and of opinion directed, as it once was in the case of religion, to make every person grow up from infancy surrounded on all sides both by the profession and the practice of it, I think that no one who can realize this conception will feel any misgiving about the sufficiency of the ultimate sanction for the Happiness morality. To any ethical student who finds the realization difficult, I recommend, as a means of facilitating it, the second of M. Comte's two principal works, the *Traité de Politique Positive*. I entertain the strongest objections to the system of politics and morals set forth in that treatise; but I think it has superabundantly shown the possibility of giving to the service of humanity, even without the aid of belief in a Providence, both the psychological power and the social efficacy of a religion, making it take hold of human life, and color all thought, feeling, and action, in a manner of which the greatest ascendancy ever exercised by any religion may be but a type and foretaste, and of which the danger is, not that it should be insufficient, but that it should be so excessive as to interfere unduly with human freedom and individuality.

Neither is it necessary to the feeling which constitutes the binding force of the utilitarian morality on those who recognize it, to wait for those social influences which would make its obligation felt by mankind at large. In the comparatively early state of human advancement in which we now live, a person cannot indeed feel that entireness of sympathy with all others which would make any real discordance in the general direction of their conduct in life impossible, but already a person in whom the social feeling is at all developed cannot bring himself to think of the rest of his fellow-creatures as struggling rivals with him for the means of happiness, whom he must desire to see defeated in their object in order that he may succeed in his. The deeply rooted conception which every individual even now has of himself as a social being tends to make him feel it one of his natural wants that there should be harmony between his feelings and aims and those of his fellow creatures. If differences of opinion and of mental culture make it impossible for him to share many of their actual feelings—perhaps make him denounce and defy those feelings—he still needs to be conscious that his real aim and theirs do not conflict, that he is not opposing himself to what they really wish for—namely, their own good—but is, on the contrary, promoting it. This feeling in most individuals is much inferior in strength to their selfish feelings, and is often wanting altogether. But to those who have it, it possesses all the characters of a natural feeling. It does not present itself to their minds as a superstition of education, or a law despotically imposed by the power of society, but as an attribute which it would not be well for them to be without. This conviction is the ultimate sanction of the greatest-happiness morality. This it is which makes any mind of well-developed feelings work with, and not against, the outward motives to care for others, afforded by what I have called the external sanctions, and when those sanctions are wanting, or act in an opposite direction, constitutes in itself a powerful internal binding force, in proportion to the sensitiveness and thoughtfulness of the character; since few but those whose mind is a moral blank could bear to

lay out their course of life on the plan of paying no regard to others, except so far as their own private interest compels.

CHAPTER IV. OF WHAT SORT OF PROOF THE PRINCIPLE OF UTILITY IS SUSCEPTIBLE

It has already been remarked that questions of ultimate ends do not admit of proof, in the ordinary acceptation of the term. To be incapable of proof by reasoning is common to all first principles, to the first premises of our knowledge, as well as to those of our conduct. But the former, being matters of fact, may be the subject of a direct appeal to the faculties which judge of fact —namely, our senses and our internal consciousness. Can an appeal be made to the same faculties on questions of practical ends? Or by what other faculty is cognizance taken of them?

Questions about ends are, in other words, questions what things are desirable. The utilitarian doctrine is that happiness is desirable, and the only thing desirable, as an end; all other things beings only desirable as means to that end. What ought to be required of this doctrine, what conditions is it requisite that the doctrine should fulfill—to make good its claim to be believed?

The only proof capable of being given that an object is visible is that people actually see it. The only proof that a sound is audible is that people hear it; and so of the other sources of our experience. In like manner, I apprehend, the sole evidence it is possible to produce that anything is desirable is that people do actually desire it. If the end which the utilitarian doctrine proposes to itself were not, in theory and in practice, acknowledged to be an end, nothing could ever convince any person that it was so. No reason can be given why the general happiness is desirable, except that each person, so far as he believes it to be attainable, desires his own happiness. This, however, being a fact, we have not only all the proof which the case admits of, but all which it is possible to require, that happiness is a good, that each person's happiness is a good to that person, and the general happiness, therefore, a good to the aggregate of all persons. Happiness has made out its title as *one* of the ends of conduct and, consequently, one of the criteria of morality.

But it has not, by this alone, proved itself to be the sole criterion. To do that, it would seem, by the same rule, necessary to show, not only that people desire happiness, but that they never desire anything else. Now it is palpable that they do desire things which, in common language, are decidedly distinguished from happiness. They desire, for example, virtue and the absence of vice no less really than pleasure and the absence of pain. The desire of virtue is not as universal, but it is as authentic a fact as the desire of happiness. And hence the opponents of the utilitarian standard deem that they have a right to infer that there are other ends of human action besides happiness, and that happiness is not the standard of approbation and disapprobation.

But does the utilitarian doctrine deny that people desire virtue, or maintain that virtue is not a thing to be desired? The very reverse. It maintains not only that virtue is to be desired, but that it is to be desired disinterestedly, for itself. Whatever may be the opinion of utilitarian moralists as to the original conditions by which virtue is made virtue, however they may believe (as they do) that actions and dispositions are only virtuous because they promote another end than virtue, yet this being granted, and it having been decided, from considerations of this description, what *is* virtuous, they not only place virtue at the very head of the things which are good as means to the ultimate end, but they also recognize as a psychological fact the possibility of its being, to the individual, a good in itself, without looking to any end beyond it; and hold that the mind is not in a right state, not in a state conformable to utility, not in the state most conducive to the general happiness, unless it does love virtue in this manner—as a thing desirable in itself, even although, in the individual instance, it should not produce those other desirable consequences which it tends to produce, and on account of which it is held to be virtue. This opinion is not, in the smallest degree, a departure from the happiness principle. The ingredients of happiness are very various, and each of them is desirable in itself, and not merely when considered as swelling an aggregate. The principle of utility does not mean that any given pleasure, as music, for instance, or any given exemption from pain, as for example health, is to be looked upon as means to a collective something termed happiness, and to be desired on that account. They are desired and desirable in and for themselves; besides being means, they are a part of the end. Virtue, according to the utilitarian doctrine, is not naturally and originally part of the end, but it is capable of becoming so; and in those who live it disinterestedly it has become so, and is desired and cherished, not as a means to happiness, but as a part of their happiness.

To illustrate this further, we may remember that virtue is not the only thing originally a means, and which if it were not a means to anything else would be and remain indifferent, but which by association with what it is a means to comes to be desired for itself, and that too with the utmost intensity. What, for example, shall we say of the love of money? There is nothing originally more desirable about money than about any heap of glittering pebbles. Its worth is solely that of the things which it will buy; the desires for other things than itself, which it is a means of gratifying. Yet the love of money is not only one of the strongest moving forces of human life, but money is, in many cases, desired in and for itself; the desire to possess it is often stronger than the desire to use it, and goes on increasing when all the desires which point to ends beyond it, to be compassed by it, are falling off. It may, then, be said truly that money is desired not for the sake of an end, but as part of the end. From being a means to happiness, it has come to be itself a principal ingredient of the individual's conception of happiness. The same may be said of the majority of the great objects of human life: power, for example, or fame, except that to each of these there is a certain amount of immediate pleasure annexed, which has at least the semblance of being naturally inherent in them—a thing which cannot be said of money. Still, however, the strongest natural attraction, both of power and of fame, is the immense aid they give to the attainment of our other wishes; and it is the strong association thus generated between them and all our objects of desire which gives to the direct desire of them the intensity it often assumes, so as in some characters to surpass in strength all other desires. In these cases the means have become a part of the end, and a more important part of it than any of the things which they are means to. What was once desired as an instrument for the attainment of happiness has come to be desired for its own sake. In being desired for its own sake it is, however, desired as *part* of happiness. The person is made, or thinks he would be made, happy by its mere possession; and is made unhappy by failure to obtain it. The desire of it is not a different thing from the desire of happiness any more than the love of music or the desire of health. They are included in happiness. They are some of the elements of which the desire of happiness is made up. Happiness is not an abstract idea but a concrete whole; and these are some of its parts. And the utilitarian standard sanctions and approves their being so. Life would be a poor thing, very ill provided with sources of happiness, if there were not this provision of nature by which things originally indifferent, but conducive to, or otherwise associated with, the satisfaction of our primitive desires, become in themselves sources of pleasure more valuable than the primitive pleasures, both in permanency, in the space of human existence that they are capable of covering, and even in intensity.

Virtue, according to the utilitarian conception, is a good of this description. There was no original desire of it, or motive to it, save its conduciveness to pleasure, and especially to protection from pain. But through the association thus formed it may be felt a good in itself, and desired as such with as great intensity as any other good; and with this difference between it and the love of money, of power, or of fame—that all of these may, and often do, render the individual noxious to the other members of the society to which he belongs, whereas there is nothing which makes him so much a blessing to them as the cultivation of the disinterested love of virtue. And consequently, the utilitarian standard, while it tolerates and approves those other acquired desires, up to the point beyond which they would be more injurious to the general happiness than promotive of it, enjoins and requires the cultivation of the love of virtue up to the greatest strength possible, as being above all things important to the general happiness.

It results from the preceding considerations that there is in reality nothing desired except happiness. Whatever is desired otherwise than as a means to some end beyond itself, and ultimately to happiness, is desired as itself a part of happiness, and is not desired for itself until it has

become so. Those who desire virtue for its own sake desire it either because the consciousness of it is a pleasure, or because the consciousness of being without it is a pain, or for both reasons united; as in truth the pleasure and pain seldom exist separately, but almost always together—the same person feeling pleasure in the degree of virtue attained, and pain in not having attained more. If one of these gave him no pleasure, and the other no pain, he would not love or desire virtue, or would desire it only for the other benefits which it might produce to himself or to persons whom he cared for.

We have now, then, an answer to the question, of what sort of proof the principle of utility is susceptible. If the opinion which I have now stated is psychologically true—if human nature is so constituted as to desire nothing which is not either a part of happiness or a means of happiness—we can have no other proof, and we require no other, that these are the only things desirable. If so, happiness is the sole end of human action, and the promotion of it the test by which to judge of all human conduct; from whence it necessarily follows that it must be the criterion of morality, since a part is included in the whole.

And now to decide whether this is really so, whether mankind do desire nothing for itself but that which is a pleasure to them, or of which the absence is a pain, we have evidently arrived at a question of fact and experience, dependent, like all similar questions, upon evidence. It can only be determined by practiced self-consciousness and self-observation, assisted by observation of others. I believe that these sources of evidence, impartially consulted, will declare that desiring a thing and finding it pleasant, aversion to it and thinking of it as painful, are phenomena entirely inseparable or, rather, two parts of the same phenomenon—in strictness of language, two different modes of naming the same psychological fact; that to think of an object as desirable (unless for the sake of its consequences) and to think of it as pleasant are one and the same thing; and that to desire anything except in proportion as the idea of it is pleasant is a physical and metaphysical impossibility.

So obvious does this appear to me that I expect it will hardly be disputed; and the objection made will be, not that desire can possibly be directed to anything ultimately except pleasure and exemption from pain, but that the will is a different thing from desire; that a person of confirmed virtue or any other person whose purposes are fixed carries out his purposes without any thought of the pleasure he has in contemplating them or expects to derive from their fulfillment, and persists in acting on them, even though these pleasures are much diminished by changes in his character or decay of his passive sensiblities, or are outweighed by the pains which the pursuit of the purposes may bring upon him. All this I fully admit and have stated it elsewhere as positively and emphatically as anyone. Will, the active phenomenon, is a different thing from desire, the state of passive sensibility, and, though originally an offshoot from it, may in time take root and detach itself from the parent stock, so much so that in the case of a habitual purpose, instead of willing the thing because we desire it, we often desire it only because we will it. This, however, is but an instance of that familiar fact, the power of habit, and is nowise confined to the case of virtuous actions. Many indifferent things which men originally did from a motive of some sort they continue to do from habit. Sometimes this is done unconsciously, the consciousness coming only after the action; at other times with conscious volition, but volition which has become habitual and is put in operation by the force of habit, in opposition perhaps to the deliberate preference, as often happens with those who have contracted habits of vicious or hurtful indulgence. Third and last comes the case in which the habitual act of will in the individual instance is not in contradiction to the general intention prevailing at other times, but in fulfillment of it, as in the case of the person of confirmed virtue and of all who pursue deliberately and consistently any determinate end. The distinction between will and desire thus understood is an authentic and highly important psychological fact; but the fact consists solely in this—that will, like all other parts of our constitution, is amenable to habit, and that we may will from habit what we no longer desire for itself, or desire only because we will it. It is not the less true that will, in the beginning, is entirely produced by desire, including in that term the repelling influence of pain as well as the attractive one of pleasure. Let us take into consideration no longer the person

who has a confirmed will to do right, but him in whom that virtuous will is still feeble, conquerable by temptation, and not to be fully relied on; by what means can it be strengthened? How can the will to be virtuous, where it does not exist in sufficient force, be implanted or awakened? Only by making the person *desire* virtue—by making him think of it in a pleasurable light, or of its absence in a painful one. It is by associating the doing right with pleasure, or the wrong with pain, or by eliciting and impressing and bringing home to the person's experience the pleasure naturally involved in the one or the pain in the other, that it is possible to call forth that will to be virtuous which, when confirmed, acts without any thought of either pleasure or pain. Will is the child of desire, and passes out of the dominion of its parent only to come under that of habit. That which is the result of habit affords no presumption of being intrinsically good; and there would be no reason for wishing that the purpose of virtue should become independent of pleasure and pain were it not that the influence of the pleasurable and painful associations which prompt to virtue is not sufficiently to be depended on for unerring constancy of action until it has acquired the support of habit. Both in feeling and in conduct, habit is the only thing which imparts certainty; and it is because of the importance to others of being able to rely absolutely on one's feelings and conduct, and to oneself of being able to rely on one's own, that the will to do right ought to be cultivated into this habitual independence. In other words, this state of the will is a means to good, not intrinsically a good; and does not contradict the doctrine that nothing is a good to human beings but in so far as it is either itself pleasurable or a means of attaining pleasure or averting pain.

But if this doctrine be true, the principle of utility is proved. Whether it is so or not must now be left to the consideration of the thoughtful reader.

CHAPTER V. ON THE CONNECTION BETWEEN JUSTICE AND UTILITY

In all ages of speculation one of the strongest obstacles to the reception of the doctrine that utility or happiness is the criterion of right and wrong has been drawn from the idea of justice. The powerful sentiment and apparently clear perception which that word recalls with a rapidity and certainty resembling an instinct have seemed to the majority of thinkers to point to an inherent quality in things; to show that the just must have an existence in nature as something absolute, generically distinct from every variety of the expedient and, in idea, opposed to it, though (as is commonly acknowledged) never, in the long run, disjoined from it in fact.

In the case of this, as of our other moral sentiments, there is no necessary connection between the question of its origin and that of its binding force. That a feeling is bestowed on us by nature does not necessarily legitimate all its promptings. The feeling of justice might be a peculiar instinct, and might yet require, like our other instincts, to be controlled and enlightened by a higher reason. If we have intellectual instincts leading us to judge in a particular way, as well as animal instincts that prompt us to act in a particular way, there is no necessity that the former should be more infallible in their sphere than the latter in theirs; it may as well happen that wrong judgments are occasionally suggested by those, as wrong actions by these. But though it is one thing to believe that we have natural feelings of justice, and another to acknowledge them as an ultimate criterion of conduct, these two opinions are very closely connected in point of fact. Mankind are always predisposed to believe that any subjective feeling, not otherwise accounted for, is a revelation of some objective reality. Our present object is to determine whether the reality to which the feeling of justice corresponds is one which needs any such special revelation, whether the justice or injustice of an action is a thing intrinsically peculiar and distinct from all its other qualities or only a combination of certain of those qualities presented under a peculiar aspect. For the purpose of this inquiry it is practically important to consider whether the feeling itself, of justice and injustice, is *sui generis* like our sensations of color and taste or a derivative feeling formed by a combination of others. And this it is the more essential to examine, as people are in general willing enough to allow that objectively the dictates of justice coincide with a part of the field of general expediency; but inasmuch

as the subjective mental feeling of justice is different from that which commonly attaches to simple expediency, and, except in the extreme cases of the latter, is far more imperative in its demands, people find it difficult to see in justice only a particular kind or branch of general utility, and think that its superior binding force requires a totally different origin.

To throw light upon this question, it is necessary to attempt to ascertain what is the distinguishing character of justice, or of injustice; what is the quality, or whether there is any quality, attributed in common to all modes of conduct designated as unjust (for justice, like many other moral attributes, is best defined by its opposite), and distinguishing them from such modes of conduct as are disapproved, but without having that particular epithet of disapprobation applied to them. If in everything which men are accustomed to characterize as just or unjust some one common attribute or collection of attributes is always present, we may judge whether this particular attribute or combination of attributes would be capable of gathering round it a sentiment of that peculiar character and intensity by virtue of the general laws of our emotional constitution, or whether the sentiment is inexplicable and requires to be regarded as a special provision of nature. If we find the former to be the case, we shall, in resolving this question, have resolved also the main problem; if the latter, we shall have to seek for some other mode of investigating it.

To find the common attributes of a variety of objects, it is necessary to begin by surveying the objects themselves in the concrete. Let us therefore advert successively to the various modes of action and arrangements of human affairs which are classed, by universal or widely spread opinion, as just or as unjust. The things well known to excite the sentiments associated with those names are of a very multifarious character. I shall pass them rapidly in review, without studying any particular arrangement.

In the first place, it is mostly considered unjust to deprive anyone of his personal liberty, his property, or any other thing which belongs to him by law. Here, therefore, is one instance of the application of the terms ";ust" and "unjust" in a perfectly definite sense, namely, that it is just to respect, unjust to violate, the *legal rights* of anyone. But this judgment admits of several exceptions, arising from the other forms in which the notions of justice and injustice present themselves. For example, the person who suffers the deprivation may (as the phrase is) have *forfeited* the rights which he is so deprived of—a case to which we shall return presently. But also—

Secondly, the legal rights of which he is deprived may be rights which *ought* not to have belonged to him; in other words, the law which confers 'on him these rights may be a bad law. When it is so or when (which is the same thing for our purpose) it is supposed to be so, opinions will differ as to the justice or injustice of infringing it. Some maintain that no law, however bad, ought to be disobeyed by an individual citizen; that his opposition to it, if shown at all, should only be shown in endeavoring to get it altered by competent authority. This opinion (which condemns many of the most illustrious benefactors of mankind, and would often protect pernicious institutions against the only weapons which, in the state of things existing at the time, have any chance of succeeding against them) is defended by those who hold it on grounds of expediency, principally on that of the importance to the common interest of mankind, of maintaining inviolate the sentiment of submission to law. Other persons, again, hold the directly contrary opinion that any law, judged to be bad, may blamelessly be disobeyed, even though it be not judged to be unjust but only inexpedient, while others would confine the license of disobedience to the case of unjust laws; but, again, some say that all laws which are inexpedient are unjust, since every law imposes some restriction on the natural liberty of mankind, which restriction is an injustice unless legitimated by tending to their good. Among these diversities of opinion it seems to be universally admitted that there may be unjust laws, and that law, consequently, is not the ultimate criterion of justice, but may give to one person a benefit, or impose on another an evil, which justice condemns. When, however, a law is thought to be unjust, it seems always to be regarded as being so in the same way in which a breach of law is unjust, namely, by infringing somebody's right, which, as it cannot in this case be a legal right, receives a different appellation

and is called a moral right. We may say, therefore, that a second case of injustice consists in taking or withholding from any person that to which he has a *moral right*.

Thirdly, it is universally considered just that each person should obtain that (whether good or evil) which he *deserves,* and unjust that he should obtain a good or be made to undergo an evil which he does not deserve. This is, perhaps, the clearest and most emphatic form in which the idea of justice is conceived by the general mind. As it involves the notion of desert, the question arises what constitutes desert? Speaking in a general way, a person is understood to deserve good if he does right, evil if he does wrong; and in a more particular sense, to deserve good from those to whom he does or has done good, and evil from those to whom he does or has done evil. The precept of returning good for evil has never been regarded as a case of the fulfillment of justice, but as one in which the claims of justice are waived, in obedience to other considerations.

Fourthly, it is confessedly unjust to *break faith* with anyone: to violate an engagement, either express or implied, or disappoint expectations raised by our own conduct, at least if we have raised those expectations knowingly and voluntarily. Like the other obligations of justice already spoken of, this one is not regarded as absolute, but as capable of being overruled by a stronger obligation of justice on the other side, or by such conduct on the part of the person concerned as is deemed to absolve us from our obligation to him and to constitute a *forfeiture* of the benefit which he has been led to expect.

Fifthly, it is, by universal admission, inconsistent with justice to be *partial*—to show favor or preference to one person over another in matters to which favor and preference do not properly apply. Impartiality, however, does not seem to be regarded as a duty in itself, but rather as instrumental to some other duty; for it is admitted that favor and preference are not always censurable, and, indeed, the cases in which they are condemned are rather the exception than the rule. A person would be more likely to be blamed than applauded for giving his family or friends no superiority in good offices over strangers when he could do so without violating any other duty; and no one thinks it unjust to seek one person in preference to another as a friend, connection, or companion. Impartiality where rights are concerned is of course obligatory, but this is involved in the more general obligation of giving to everyone his right. A tribunal, for example, must be impartial because it is bound to award, without regard to any other consideration, a disputed object to the one of two parties who has the right to it. There are other cases in which impartiality means being solely influenced by desert, as with those who, in the capacity of judges, preceptors, or parents, administer reward and punishment as such. There are cases, again, in which it means being solely influenced by consideration for the public interest, as in making a selection among candidates for a government employment. Impartiality, in short, as an obligation of justice, may be said to mean being exclusively influenced by the considerations which it is supposed ought to influence the particular case in hand, and resisting solicitation of any motives which prompt to conduct different from what those considerations would dictate.

Nearly allied to the idea of impartiality is that of *equality,* which often enters as a component part both into the conception of justice and into the practice of it, and, in the eyes of many persons, constitutes its essence. But in this, still more than in any other case, the notion of justice varies in different persons, and always conforms in its variations to their notion of utility. Each person maintains that equality is the dictate of justice, except where he thinks that expediency requires inequality. The justice of giving equal protection to the rights of all is maintained by those who support the most outrageous inequality in the rights themselves. Even in slave countries it is theoretically admitted that the rights of the slave, such as they are, ought to be as sacred as those of the master, and that a tribunal which fails to enforce them with equal strictness is wanting in justice; while, at the same time, institutions which leave to the slave scarcely any rights to enforce are not deemed unjust because they are not deemed inexpedient. Those who think that utility requires distinctions of rank do not consider it unjust that riches and social privileges should be unequally dispensed; but those who think this inequality inexpedient think it unjust also. Whoever thinks

that government is necessary sees no injustice in as much inequality as is constituted by giving to the magistrate powers not granted to other people. Even among those who hold leveling doctrines, there are differences of opinion about expediency. Some communists consider it unjust that the produce of the labor of the community should be shared on any other principle than that of exact equality; others think it just that those should receive most whose wants are greatest; while others hold that those who work harder, or who produce more, or whose services are more valuable to the community, may justly claim a larger quota in the division of the produce. And the sense of natural justice may be plausibly appealed to in behalf of every one of these opinions.

Among so many diverse applications of the term "justice," which yet is not regarded as ambiguous, it is a matter of some difficulty to seize the mental link which holds them together, and on which the moral sentiment adhering to the term essentially depends. Perhaps, in this embarrassment, some help may be derived from the history of the word, as indicated by its etymology.

In most if not in all languages, the etymology of the word which corresponds to "just" points distinctly to an origin connected with the ordinances of law. *Justum* is a form of *jussum,* that which has been ordered. *Dikaion* comes directly from *dike,* a suit at law. *Recht,* from which came *right* and *righteous,* is synonymous with law. The courts of justice, the administration of justice, are the courts and the administration of law. *La justice,* in French, is the established term for judicature. I am not committing the fallacy, imputed with some show of truth to Horne Tooke, of assuming that a word must still continue to mean what it originally meant. Etymology is slight evidence of what the idea now signified is, but the very best evidence of how it sprang up. There can, I think, be no doubt that the *idée mère,* the primitive element, in the formation of the notion of justice was conformity to law. It constituted the entire idea among the Hebrews, up to the birth of Christianity; as might be expected in the case of a people whose laws attempted to embrace all subjects on which precepts were required, and who believed those laws to be a direct emanation from the Supreme Being. But other nations, and in particular the Greeks and Romans, who knew that their laws had been made originally, and still continued to be made, by men, were not afraid to admit that those men might make bad laws; might do, by law, the same things, and from the same motives, which if done by individuals without the sanction of law would be called unjust. And hence the sentiment of injustice came to be attached, not to all violations of law, but only to violations of such laws as *ought* to exist, including such as ought to exist but do not, and to laws themselves if supposed to be contrary to what ought to be law. In this manner the idea of law and of its injunctions was still predominant in the notion of justice, even when the laws actually in force ceased to be accepted as the standard of it.

It is true that mankind consider the idea of justice and its obligations as applicable to many things which neither are, nor is it desired that they should be, regulated by law. Nobody desires that laws should interfere with the whole detail of private life; yet everyone allows that in all daily conduct a person may and does show himself to be either just or unjust. But even here, the idea of the breach of what ought to be law still lingers in a modified shape. It would always give us pleasure, and chime in with our feelings of fitness, that acts which we deem unjust should be punished, though we do not always think it expedient that this should be done by the tribunals. We forego that gratification on account of incidental inconveniences. We should be glad to see just conduct enforced and injustice repressed, even in the minutest details, if we were not, with reason, afraid of trusting the magistrate with so unlimited an amount of power over individuals. When we think that a person is bound in justice to do a thing, it is an ordinary form of language to say that he ought to be compelled to do it. We should be gratified to see the obligation enforced by anybody who had the power. If we see that its enforcement by law would be inexpedient, we lament the impossibility, we consider the impunity given to injustice as an evil, and strive to make amends for it by bringing a strong expression of our own and the public disapprobation to bear upon the offender. Thus the idea of legal constraint is still the generating idea of the notion of justice, though undergoing several transformations be-

fore that notion as it exists in an advanced state of society becomes complete.

The above is, I think, a true account, as far as it goes, of the origin and progressive growth of the idea of justice. But we must observe that it contains as yet nothing to distinguish that obligation from moral obligation in general. For the truth is that the idea of penal sanction, which is the essence of law, enters not only into the conception of injustice, but into that of any kind of wrong. We do not call anything wrong unless we mean to imply that a person ought to be punished in some way or other for doing it—if not by law, by the opinion of his fellow creatures; if not by opinion, by the reproaches of his own conscience. This seems the real turning point of the distinction between morality and simple expediency. It is a part of the notion of duty in every one of its forms that a person may rightfully be compelled to fulfill it. Duty is a thing which may be *exacted* from a person, as one exacts a debt. Unless we think that it may be exacted from him, we do not call it his duty. Reasons of prudence, or the interest of other people, may militate against actually exacting it, but the person himself, it is clearly understood, would not be entitled to complain. There are other things, on the contrary, which we wish that people should do, which we like or admire them for doing, perhaps dislike or despise them for not doing, but yet admit that they are not bound to do; it is not a case of moral obligation; we do not blame them, that is, we do not think that they are proper objects of punishment. How we come by these ideas of deserving and not deserving punishment will appear, perhaps, in the sequel; but I think there is no doubt that this distinction lies at the bottom of the notions of right and wrong; that we call any conduct wrong, or employ, instead, some other term of dislike or disparagement, according as we think that the person ought, or ought not, to be punished for it; and we say it would be right to do so and so, or merely that it would be desirable or laudable, according as we would wish to see the person whom it concerns compelled, or only persuaded and exhorted, to act in that manner.

This, therefore, being the characteristic difference which marks off, not justice, but morality in general from the remaining provinces of expediency and worthiness, the character is still to be sought which distinguishes justice from other branches of morality. Now it is known that ethical writers divide moral duties into two classes, denoted by the ill-chosen expressions, duties of perfect and of imperfect obligation; the latter being those in which, though the act is obligatory, the particular occasions of performing it are left to our choice, as in the case of charity or beneficence, which we are indeed bound to practice but not toward any definite person, nor at any prescribed time. In the more precise language of philosophic jurists, duties of perfect obligation are those duties in virtue of which a correlative *right* resides in some person or persons; duties of imperfect obligation are those moral obligations which do not give birth to any right. I think it will be found that this distinction exactly coincides with that which exists between justice and the other obligations of morality. In our survey of the various popular acceptations of justice, the term appeared generally to involve the idea of a personal right—a claim on the part of one or more individuals, like that which the law gives when it confers a proprietary or other legal right. Whether the injustice consists in depriving a person of a possession, or in breaking faith with him, or in treating him worse than he deserves, or worse than other people who have no greater claims—in each case the supposition implies two things: a wrong done, and some assignable person who is wronged. Injustice may also be done by treating a person better than others; but the wrong in this case is to his competitors, who are also assignable persons. It seems to me that this feature in the case—a right in some person, correlative to the moral obligation—constitutes the specific difference between justice and generosity or beneficence. Justice implies something which it is not only right to do, and wrong not to do, but which some individual person can claim from us as his moral right. No one has a moral right to our generosity or beneficence because we are not morally bound to practice those virtues toward any given individual. And it will be found with respect to this as to every correct definition that the instances which seem to conflict with it are those which most confirm it. For if a moralist attempts, as some have done, to make out that mankind generally, though not any given individual, have a right to all the good we can do

them, he at once, by that thesis, includes generosity and beneficence within the category of justice. He is obliged to say that our utmost exertions are *due* to our fellow creatures, thus assimilating them to a debt; or that nothing less can be a sufficient *return* for what society does for us, thus classing the case as one of gratitude; both of which are acknowledged cases of justice, and not of the virtue of beneficence; and whoever does not place the distinction between justice and morality in general, where we have now placed it, will be found to make no distinction between them at all, but to merge all morality in justice.

Having thus endeavored to determine the distinctive elements which enter into the composition of the idea of justice, we are ready to enter on the inquiry whether the feeling which accompanies the idea is attached to it by a special dispensation of nature, or whether it could have grown up, by any known laws, out of the idea itself; and, in particular, whether it can have originated in considerations of general expediency.

I conceive that the sentiment itself does not arise from anything which would commonly or correctly be termed an idea of expediency, but that, though the sentiment does not, whatever is moral in it does.

We have seen that the two essential ingredients in the sentiment of justice are the desire to punish a person who has done harm and the knowledge or belief that there is some definite individual or individuals to whom harm has been done.

Now it appears to me that the desire to punish a person who has done harm to some individual is a spontaneous outgrowth from two sentiments, both in the highest degree natural and which either are or resemble instincts: the impulse of self-defence and the feeling of sympathy.

It is natural to resent and to repel or retaliate any harm done or attempted against ourselves or against those with whom we sympathize. The origin of this sentiment it is not necessary here to discuss. Whether it be an instinct or a result of intelligence, it is, we know, common to all animal nature; for every animal tries to hurt those who have hurt, or who it thinks are about to hurt, itself or its young. Human beings, on this point, only differ from other animals in two particulars. First, in being capable of sympathizing, not solely with their offspring, or, like some of the more noble animals, with some superior animal who is kind to them, but with all human, and even with all sentient, beings; secondly, in having a more developed intelligence, which gives a wider range to the whole of their sentiments, whether self-regarding or sympathetic. By virtue of his superior intelligence, even apart from his superior range of sympathy, a human being is capable of apprehending a community of interest between himself and the human society of which he forms a part, such that any conduct which threatens the security of the society generally is threatening to his own, and calls forth his instinct (if instinct it be) of self-defense. The same superiority of intelligence, joined to the power of sympathizing with human beings generally, enables him to attach himself to the collective idea of his tribe, his country, or mankind in such a manner that any act hurtful to them raises his instinct of sympathy and urges him to resistance.

The sentiment of justice, in that one of its elements which consists of the desire to punish, is thus, I conceive, the natural feeling of retaliation or vengeance, rendered by intellect and sympathy applicable to those injuries, that is, to those hurts, which wound us through, or in common with, society at large. This sentiment, in itself, has nothing moral in it; what is moral is the exclusive subordination of it to the social sympathies, so as to wait on and obey their call. For the natural feeling would make us resent indiscriminately whatever anyone does that is disagreeable to us; but, when moralized by the social feeling, it only acts in the directions conformable to the general good: just persons resenting a hurt to society, though not otherwise a hurt to themselves, and not resenting a hurt to themselves, however painful, unless it be of the kind which society has a common interest with them in the repression of.

It is no objection against this doctrine to say that, when we feel our sentiment of justice outraged, we are not thinking of society at large or of any collective interest, but only of the individual case. It is common enough, certainly, though the reverse of commendable, to feel resentment merely because we have suffered pain; but a

person whose resentment is really a moral feeling, that is, who considers whether an act is blamable before he allows himself to resent it—such a person, though he may not say expressly to himself that he is standing up for the interest of society, certainly does feel that he is asserting a rule which is for the benefit of others as well as for his own. If he is not feeling this, if he is regarding the act solely as it affects him individually, he is not consciously just: he is not concerning himself about the justice of his actions. This is admitted even by anti-utilitarian moralists. When Kant (as before remarked) propounds as the fundamental principle of morals, "So act that thy rule of conduct might be adopted as a law by all rational beings," he virtually acknowledges that the interest of mankind collectively, or at least of mankind indiscriminately, must be in the mind of the agent when conscientiously deciding on the morality of the act. Otherwise he uses words without a meaning; for that a rule even of utter selfishness could not *possibly* be adopted by all rational beings—that there is any insuperable obstacle in the nature of things to its adoption—cannot be even plausibly maintained. To give any meaning to Kant's principle, the sense put upon it must be that we ought to shape our conduct by a rule which all rational beings might adopt *with benefit to their collective interest.*

To recapitulate: the idea of justice supposes two things—a rule of conduct and a sentiment which sanctions the rule. The first must be supposed common to all mankind and intended for their good. The other (the sentiment) is a desire that punishment may be suffered by those who infringe the rule. There is involved, in addition, the conception of some definite person who suffers by the infringement, whose rights (to use the expression appropriated to the case) are violated by it. And the sentiment of justice appears to me to be the animal desire to repel or retaliate a hurt or damage to oneself or to those with whom one sympathizes, widened so as to include all persons, by the human capacity of enlarged sympathy and the human conception of intelligent self-interest. From the latter elements the feeling derives its morality; from the former, its peculiar impressiveness and energy of self-assertion.

I have, throughout, treated the idea of a *right* residing in the injured person and violated by the injury, not as a separate element in the composition of the idea and sentiment, but as one of the forms in which the other two elements clothe themselves. These elements are a hurt to some assignable person or persons, on the one hand, and a demand for punishment, on the other. An examination of our own minds, I think, will show that these two things include all that we mean when we speak of violation of a right. When we call anything a person's right, we mean that he has a valid claim on society to protect him in the possession of it, either by the force of law or by that of education and opinion. If he has what we consider a sufficient claim, on whatever account, to have something guaranteed to him by society, we say that he has a right to it. If we desire to prove that anything does not belong to him by right, we think this done as soon as it is admitted that society ought not to take measures for securing it to him, but should leave him to chance or to his own exertions. Thus a person is said to have a right to what he can earn in fair professional competition, because society ought not to allow any other person to hinder him from endeavoring to earn in that manner as much as he can. But he has not a right to three hundred a year, though he may happen to be earning it; because society is not called on to provide that he shall earn that sum. On the contrary, if he owns ten thousand pounds three-per-cent stock, he *has* a right to three hundred a year because society has come under an obligation to provide him with an income of that amount.

To have a right, then, is, I conceive, to have something which society ought to defend me in the possession of. If the objector goes on to ask why it ought, I can give him no other reason than general utility. If that expression does not seem to convey a sufficient feeling of the strength of the obligation, nor to account for the peculiar energy of the feeling, it is because there goes to the composition of the sentiment, not a rational only but also an animal element—the thirst for retaliation; and this thirst derives its intensity, as well as its moral justification, from the extraordinarily important and impressive kind of utility which is concerned. The interest involved is that of security, to everyone's feelings the most vital of all interests. All other earthly benefits are needed by one person, not needed by another; and many of them can, if necessary, be cheerfully foregone or replaced by something else; but security no human being can possibly do without; on it we depend for all our immunity from evil and for the whole value of all and every good, beyond the passing moment, since nothing but the gratification of the instant could be of any worth to us if we could be deprived of everything the next instant by whoever was momentarily stronger than ourselves. Now this most indispensable of all necessaries, after physical nutriment, cannot be had unless the machinery for providing it is kept unintermittedly in active play. Our notion, therefore, of the claim we have on our fellow creatures to join in making safe for us the very groundwork of our existence gathers feelings around it so much more intense than those concerned in any of the more common cases of utility that the difference in degree (as is often the case in psychology) becomes a real difference in kind. The claim assumes that character of absoluteness, that apparent infinity and incommensurability with all other considerations which constitute the distinction between the feeling of right and wrong and that of ordinary expediency and inexpediency. The feelings concerned are so powerful, and we count so positively on finding a responsive feeling in others (all being alike interested) that *ought* and *should* grow into *must,* and recognized indispensability becomes a moral necessity, analogous to physical, and often not inferior to it in binding force.

If the preceeding analysis, or something resembling it, be not the correct account of the notion of justice—if justice be totally independent of utility, and be a standard *per se,* which the mind can recognize by simple introspection of itself—it is hard to understand why that internal oracle is so ambiguous, and why so many things appear either just or unjust, according to the light in which they are regarded.

We are continually informed that utility is an uncertain standard, which every different person interprets differently, and that there is no safety but in the immutable, ineffaceable, and unmistakable dictates of justice, which carry their evidence in themselves and are independent of the fluctuations of opinion. One would suppose from this that on questions of justice there could be no controversy; that, if we take that for our rule, its application to any given case could leave us in as little doubt as a mathematical demonstration. So far is this from being the fact that there is as much difference of opinion, and as much discussion, about what is just as about what is useful to society. Not only have different nations and individuals different notions of justice, but in the mind of one and the same individual, justice is not some one rule, principle, or maxim, but many which do not always coincide in their dictates, and, in choosing between which, he is guided either by some extraneous standard or by his own personal predilections.

For instance, there are some who say that it is unjust to punish anyone for the sake of example to others, that punishment is just only when intended for the good of the sufferer himself. Others maintain the extreme reverse, contending that to punish persons who have attained years of discretion, for their own benefit, is despotism and injustice, since, if the matter at issue is solely their own good, no one has a right to control their own judgment of it; but that they may justly be punished to prevent evil to others, this being the exercise of the legitimate right of self-defense. Mr. Owen, again, affirms that it is unjust to punish at all, for the criminal did not make his own character; his education and the circumstances which surrounded him have made him a criminal, and for these he is not responsible. All these opinions are extremely plausible; and so long as the question is argued as one of justice simply, without going down to the principles which lie under justice and are the source of its authority, I am unable to see how any of these reasoners can be refuted. For in truth every one of the three builds upon rules of justice confessedly true. The first appeals to the acknowledged injustice of singling out an individual and making him a sacrifice, without his consent, for other people's benefit. The second relies on the acknowledged justice of self-defense and the admitted injustice of forcing one person to conform to another's notions of what constitutes his good. The Owenite invokes the admitted principle that it is unjust to punish anyone for what he cannot help. Each is triumphant so long as he is not compelled to take into consideration any other maxims of justice

than the one he has selected; but as soon as their several maxims are brought face to face, each disputant seems to have exactly as much to say for himself as the others. No one of them can carry out his own notion of justice without trampling upon another equally binding. These are difficulties; they have always been felt to be such; and many devices have been invented to turn rather than to overcome them. As a refuge from the last of the three, men imagined what they called the freedom of the will—fancying that they could not justify punishing a man whose will is in a thoroughly hateful state unless it be supposed to have come into that state through no influence of anterior circumstances. To escape from the other difficulties, a favorite contrivance has been the fiction of a contract whereby at some unknown period all the members of society engaged to obey the laws and consented to be punished for any disobedience to them, thereby giving to their legislators the right, which it is assumed they would not otherwise have had, of punishing them, either for their own good or for that of society. This happy thought was considered to get rid of the whole difficulty and to legitimate the infliction of punishment, in virtue of another received maxim of justice, *volenti non fit injuria*—that is not unjust which is done with the consent of the person who is supposed to be hurt by it. I need hardly remark that, even if the consent were not a mere fiction, this maxim is not superior in authority to the others which it is brought in to supersede. It is, on the contrary, an instructive specimen of the loose and irregular manner in which supposed principles of justice grow up. This particular one evidently came into use as a help to the coarse exigencies of courts of law, which are sometimes obliged to be content with very uncertain presumptions, on account of the greater evils which would often arise from any attempt on their part to cut finer. But even courts of law are not able to adhere consistently to the maxim, for they allow voluntary engagements to be set aside on the ground of fraud, and sometimes on that of mere mistake or misinformation.

Again, when the legitimacy of inflicting punishment is admitted, how many conflicting conceptions of justice come to light in discussing the proper apportionment of punishments to offenses. No rule on the subject recommends itself so strongly to the primitive and spontaneous sentiment of justice as the *lex talionis,* an eye for an eye and a tooth for a tooth. Though this principle of the Jewish and of the Mohammedan law has been generally abandoned in Europe as a practical maxim, there is, I suspect, in most minds, a secret hankering after it; and when retribution accidentally falls on an offender in that precise shape, the general feeling of satisfaction evinced bears witness how natural is the sentiment to which this repayment in kind is acceptable. With many, the test of justice in penal infliction is that the punishment should be proportioned to the offense, meaning that it should be exactly measured by the moral guilt of the culprit (whatever be their standard for measuring moral guilt), the consideration what amount of punishment is necessary to deter from the offense having nothing to do with the question of justice, in their estimation; while there are others to whom that consideration is all in all, who maintain that it is not just, at least for man, to inflict on a fellow creature, whatever may be his offenses, any amount of suffering beyond the least that will suffice to prevent him from repeating, and others from imitating, his misconduct.

To take another example from a subject already once referred to. In co-operative industrial association, is it just or not that talent or skill should give a title to superior remuneration? On the negative side of the question it is argued that whoever does the best he can deserves equally well, and ought not in justice to be put in a position of inferiority for no fault of his own; that superior abilities have already advantages more than enough, in the admiration they excite, the personal influence they command, and the internal sources of satisfaction attending them, without adding to these a superior share of the world's goods; and that society is bound in justice rather to make compensation to the less favored for this unmerited inequality of advantages than to aggrevate it. On the contrary side it is contended that society receives more from the more efficient laborer; that, his services being more useful, society owes him a larger return for them; that a greater share of the joint result is actually his work, and not to allow his claim to it is a kind of robbery; that, if he is only to receive as much as others, he

can only be justly required to produce as much, and to give a smaller amount of time and exertion, proportioned to his superior efficiency. Who shall decide between these appeals to conflicting principles of justice? Justice has in this case two sides to it, which it is impossible to bring into harmony, and the two disputants have chosen opposite sides; the one looks to what it is just that the individual should receive, the other to what it is just that the community should give. Each, from his own point of view, is unanswerable; and any choice between them, on grounds of justice, must be perfectly arbitrary. Social utility alone can decide the preference.

How many, again, and how irreconcilable are the standards of justice to which reference is made in discussing the repartition of taxation. One opinion is that payment to the state should be in numerical proportion to pecuniary means. Others think that justice dictates what they term graduated taxation—taking a higher percentage from those who have more to spare. In point of natural justice a strong case might be made for disregarding means altogether, and taking the same absolute sum (whenever it could be got) from everyone; as the subscribers to a mess or to a club all pay the same sum for the same privileges, whether they can all equally afford it or not. Since the protection (it might be said) of law and government is afforded to and is equally required by all, there is no injustice in making all buy it at the same price. It is reckoned justice, not injustice, that a dealer should charge to all customers the same price for the same article, not a price varying according to their means of payment. This doctrine, as applied to taxation, finds no advocates because it conflicts so strongly with man's feelings of humanity and of social expediency; but the principle of justice which it invokes is as true and as binding as those which can be appealed to against it. Accordingly it exerts a tacit influence on the line of defense employed for other modes of assessing taxation. People feel obliged to argue that the state does more for the rich man than for the poor, as a justification for its taking more from them, though this is in reality not true, for the rich would be far better able to protect themselves, in the absence of law or government, than the poor, and indeed would probably be successful in converting the poor into their slaves. Others, again, so far defer to the same conception of justice as to maintain that all should pay an equal capitation tax for the protection of their persons (these being of equal value to all), and an unequal tax for the protection of property, which is unequal. To this others reply that the all of one man is as valuable to him as the all of another. From these confusions there is no other mode of extrication than the utilitarian.

Is, then, the difference between the just and the expedient a merely imaginary distinction? Have mankind been under a delusion in thinking that justice is a more sacred thing than policy, and that the latter ought only to be listened to after the former has been satisfied? By no means. The exposition we have given of the nature and origin of the sentiment recognizes a real distinction; and no one of those who profess the most sublime contempt for the consequences of actions as an element in their morality attaches more importance to the distinction than I do. While I dispute the pretensions of any theory which sets up an imaginary standard of justice not grounded on utility, I account the justice which is grounded on utility to be the chief part, and incomparably the most sacred and binding part, of all morality. Justice is a name for certain classes of moral rules which concern the essentials of human well-being more nearly, and are therefore of more absolute obligation, than any other rules for the guidance of life; and the notion which we have found to be of the essence of the idea of justice—that of a right residing in an individual—implies and testifies to this more binding obligation.

The moral rules which forbid mankind to hurt one another (in which we must never forget to include wrongful interference with each other's freedom) are more vital to human well-being than any maxims, however important, which only point out the best mode of managing some department of human affairs. They have also the peculiarity that they are the main element in determining the whole of the social feelings of mankind. It is their observance which alone preserves peace among human beings; if obedience to them were not the rule, and disobedience the exception, everyone would see in everyone else an enemy against whom he must be perpetually guarding himself. What is hardly less important, these are the precepts which mankind have the strongest and the most direct inducements for impressing upon one another. By merely giving to each other prudential instruction or exhortation, they may gain, or think they gain, nothing; in inculcating on each other the duty of positive beneficence, they have an unmistakable interest, but far less in degree; a person may possibly not need the benefits of others, but he always needs that they should not do him hurt. Thus the moralities which protect every individual from being harmed by others, either directly or by being hindered in his freedom of pursuing his own good, are at once those which he himself has most at heart and those which he has the strongest interest in publishing and enforcing by word and deed. It is by a person's observance of these that his fitness to exist as one of the fellowship of human beings is tested and decided; for on that depends his being a nuisance or not to those with whom he is in contact. Now it is these moralities primarily which compose the obligations of justice. The most marked cases of injustice, and those which give the tone to the feeling of repugnance which characterizes the sentiment, are acts of wrongful aggression or wrongful exercise of power over someone; the next are those which consist in wrongfully withholding from him something which is his due—in both cases inflicting on him a positive hurt, either in the form of direct suffering or of the privation of some good which he had reasonable ground, either of a physical or of a social kind, for counting upon.

The same powerful motives which command the observance of these primary moralities enjoin the punishment of those who violate them; and as the impulses of self-defense, of defense of others, and of vengeance are all called forth against such persons, retribution, or evil for evil, becomes closely connected with the sentiment of justice, and is universally included in the idea. Good for good is also one of the dictates of justice; and this, though its social utility is evident, and though it carries with it a natural human feeling, has not at first sight that obvious connection with hurt or injury which, existing in the most elementary cases of just and unjust, is the source of the characteristic intensity of the sentiment. But the connection, though less obvious, is not less real. He who accepts benefits and denies a return of them when needed inflicts a real hurt by disappointing one of the most natural and reasonable of expectations, and one which he must at least tacitly have encouraged, otherwise the benefits would seldom have been conferred. The important rank, among human evils and wrongs, of the disappointment of expectation is shown in the fact that it constitutes the principal criminality of two such highly immoral acts as a breach of friendship and a breach of promise. Few hurts which human beings can sustain are greater, and none wound more, than when that on which they habitually and with full assurance relied fails them in the hour of need; and few wrongs are greater than this mere withholding of good; none excite more resentment, either in the person suffering or in a sympathizing spectator. The principle, therefore, of giving to each what they deserve, that is, good for good as well as evil for evil, is not only included within the idea of justice as we have defined it, but is a proper object of that intensity of sentiment which places the just in human estimation above the simply expedient.

Most of the maxims of justice current in the world, and commonly appealed to in its transactions, are simply instrumental to carrying into effect the principles of justice which we have now spoken of. That a person is only responsible for what he has done voluntarily, or could voluntarily have avoided, that it is unjust to condemn any person unheard; that the punishment ought to be proportioned to the offense, and the like, are maxims intended to prevent the just principle of evil for evil from being perverted to the infliction of evil without that justification. The greater part of these common maxims have come into use from the practice of courts of justice, which have been naturally led to a more complete recognition and elaboration than was likely to suggest itself to others, of the rules necessary to enable them to fulfill their double function—of inflicting punishment when due, and of awarding to each person his right.

That first of judicial virtues, impartiality, is an obligation of justice, partly for the reason last mentioned, as being a necessary condition of the fulfillment of other obligations of justice. But this is not the only source of the exalted rank, among human obligations, of those maxims of equality and impartiality, which, both in popular estimation and in that of the most enlightened,

are included among the precepts of justice. In one point of view, they may be considered as corollaries from the principles already laid down. If it is a duty to do to each according to his deserts, returning good for good, as well as repressing evil by evil, it necessarily follows that we should treat all equally well (when no higher duty forbids) who have deserved equally well of *us,* and that society should treat all equally well who have deserved equally well of *it,* that is, who have deserved equally well absolutely. This is the highest abstract standard of social and distributive justice, toward which all institutions and the efforts of all virtuous citizens should be made in the utmost possible degree to converge. But this great moral duty rests upon a still deeper foundation, being a direct emanation from the first principle of morals, and not a mere logical corollary from secondary or derivative doctrines. It is involved in the very meaning of utility, or the greatest happiness principle. That principle is a mere form of words without rational signification unless one person's happiness, supposed equal in degree (with the proper allowance made for kind), is counted for exactly as much as another's. Those conditions being supplied, Bentham's dictum, "everybody to count for one, nobody for more than one," might be written under the principle of utility as an explanatory commentary.[3] The equal claim of everybody to happiness, in the estimation of the moralist and of the legislator, involves an equal claim to all the means of happiness except in so far as the inevitable conditions of human life and the general interest in which that of every individual is included set limits to the maxim: and those limits ought to be strictly construed. As every other maxim of justice, so this is by no means applied or held applicable universally; on the contrary, as I have already remarked, it bends to every person's ideas of social expediency. But in whatever case it is deemed applicable at all, it is held to be the dictate of justice. All persons are deemed to have a *right* to equality of treatment, except when some recognized social expediency requires the reverse. And hence all social inequalities which have ceased to be considered expedient assume the character, not of simple inexpediency, but of injustice, and appear so tyrannical that people are apt to wonder how they ever could have been tolerated—forgetful that they themselves, perhaps, tolerate other inequalities under an equally mistaken notion of expediency, the correction of which would make that which they approve seem quite as monstrous as what they have at last learned to condemn. The entire history of social improvement has been a series of transitions by which one custom or institution after another, from being a supposed primary necessity of social existence, has passed into the rank of a universally stigmatized injustice and tyranny. So it has been with the distinctions of slaves and freemen, nobles and serfs, patricians and plebeians; and so it will be, and in part already is, with the aristocracies of color, race, and sex.

It appears from what has been said that justice is a name for certain moral requirements which, regarded collectively, stand higher in the scale of social utility, and are therefore of more paramount obligation, than any others, though particular cases may occur in which some other social duty is so important as to overrule any of the general maxims of justice. Thus, to save a life, it may not only be allowable, but a duty, to steal or take by force the necessary food or medicine, or to kidnap and compel to officiate the only qualified medical practitioner. In such cases, as we do not call anything justice which is not a virtue, we usually say, not that justice must give way to some other moral principle, but that what is just in ordinary cases is, by reason of that other principle, not just in the particular case.

By this useful accommodation of language, the character of indefeasibility attributed to justice is kept up, and we are saved from the necessity maintaining that there can be laudable injustice.

The considerations which have not been adduced resolve, I conceive, the only real difficulty in the utilitarian theory of morals. It has always been evident that all cases of justice are also cases of expediency; the difference is in the peculiar sentiment which attaches to the former, as contradistinguished from the latter. If this characteristic sentiment has been sufficiently accounted for; if there is no necessity to assume for it any peculiarity of origin; if it is simply the natural feeling of resentment, moralized by being made coextensive with the demands of social good; and if this feeling not only does but ought to exist in all the classes of cases to which the idea of justice corresponds—that idea no longer presents itself as a stumbling block to the utilitarian ethics. Justice remains the appropriate name for certain social utilities which are vastly more important, and therefore more absolute and imperative, than any others are as a class (though not more so than others may be in particular cases); and which, therefore, ought to be, as well as naturally are, guarded by a sentiment, not only different in degree, but also in kind; distinguished from the milder feeling which attaches to the mere idea of promoting human pleasure or convenience at once by the more definite nature of its commands and by the sterner character of its sanctions.

NOTES

1. The author of this essay has reason for believing himself to be the first person who brought the word "utilitarian" into use. He did not invent it, but adopted it from a passing expression in Mr. Gait's *Annals of the Parish.* After using it as a designation for several years, he and others abandoned it from a growing dislike to anything resembling a badge or watchword of sectarian distinction. But as a name for one single opinion, not a set of opinions—to denote the recognition of utility as a standard, not any particular way of applying it—the term supplies a want in the language, and offers, in many cases, a convenient mode of avoiding tiresome circumlocution.

2. An opponent, whose intellectual and moral fairness it is a pleasure to acknowledge (the Rev. J. Llewellyn Davies), has objected to this passage, saying, "Surely the rightness or wrongness of saving a man from drowning does depend very much upon the motive with which it is done. Suppose that a tyrant, when his enemy jumped into the sea to escape from him, saved him from drowning simply in order that he might inflict upon him more exquisite tortures, would it tend to

clearness to speak of that rescue as 'a morally right action'? Or suppose again, according to one of the stock illustrations of ethical inquiries, that a man betrayed a trust received from a friend, because the discharge of it would fatally injure that friend himself or someone belonging to him, would utilitarianism compel one to call the betrayal 'a crime' as much as if it had been done from the meanest motive?"

I submit that he who saves another from drowning in order to kill him by torture afterwards does not differ only in motive from him who does the same thing from duty or benevolence; the act itself is different. The rescue of the man is, in the case supposed, only the necessary first step of an act far more atrocious than leaving him to drown would have been. Had Mr. Davies said, "The rightness or wrongness of saving a man from drowning does depend very much"—not upon the motive, but—"upon the *intention*," no utilitarian would have differed from him. Mr. Davies, by an oversight too common not to be quite venial, has in this case confounded the very different ideas of Motive and Intention. There is no point which utilitarian thinkers (and Bentham pre-eminently) have taken more pains to illustrate than this. The morality of the action depends entirely upon the intention—that is, upon what the agent *wills to do*. But the motive, that is, the feeling which makes him will so to do, if it makes no difference in the act, makes none in the morality: though it makes a great difference in our moral estimation of the agent, especially if it indicates a good or a bad habitual *disposition*—a bent of character from which useful, or from which hurtful actions are likely to arise.

[The foregoing note appeared in the second (1864) edition of *Utilitarianism* but was dropped in succeeding ones.]

3.   This implication, in the first principle of the utilitarian scheme, of perfect impartiality between persons is regarded by Mr. Herbert Spencer (in his *Social Statics*) as a disproof of the pretensions of utility to be a sufficient guide to right; since (he says) the principle of utility presupposes the anterior principle that everybody has an equal right to happiness. It may be more correctly described as supposing that equal amounts of happiness are equally desirable, whether felt by the same or different persons. This, however, is not a *pre*-supposition, not a premise needful to support the principle of utility, but the very principle itself; for what is the principle of utility if it be not that "happiness" and "desirable" are synonymous terms? If there is any anterior principle implied, it can be no other than this, that the truths of arithmetic are applicable to the valuation of happiness, as of all other measurable quantities.

(Mr. Herbert Spencer, in a private communication on the subject of the preceding note, objects to being considered an opponent of utilitarianism and states that he regards happiness as the ultimate end of morality; but deems that end only partially attainable by empirical generalizations from the observed results of conduct, and completely attainable only by deducing, from the laws of life and the conditions of existence, what kinds of action necessarily tend to produce happiness, and what kinds to produce unhappiness. With the exception of the word "necessarily," I have no dissent to express from this doctrine; and (omitting that word) I am not aware that any modern advocate of utilitarianism is of a different opinion. Bentham, certainly, to whom in the *Social Statics* Mr. Spencer particularly referred, is, least of all writers, chargeable with unwillingness to deduce the effect of actions on happiness from the laws of human nature and the universal conditions of human life. The common charge against him is of relying too exclusively upon such deductions and declining altogether to be bound by the generalizations from specific experience which Mr. Spencer thinks that utilitarians generally confine themselves to. My own opinion (and, as I collect, Mr. Spencer's) is that in ethics, as in all other branches of scientific study, the consilience of the results of both these processes, each corroborating and verifying the other, is requisite to give to any general proposition the kind and degree of evidence which constitutes scientific proof.)

SUGGESTIONS FOR FURTHER READING

A. OTHER PRIMARY SOURCES

Aristotle, *Eudemian Ethics*, translated by H. Rackham (London: William Heinemann Ltd., "The Loeb Classical Library," 1952); translated by J. Solomon in *The Works of Aristotle*, edited by W. D. Ross (Oxford: Clarendon Press, 1925).

_____ , *Magna Moralia*, translated by St. George Stock in *The Works of Aristotle*, edited by W. D. Ross (Oxford: Clarendon Press, 1925).

_____ , *Politics*, various translations and editions.

Kant, Immanuel, *Critique of Practical Reason*, translated by Lewis W. Beck (Chicago: The University of Chicago Press, 1949); translated by T. K. Abbott, 6th edition (London: Longmans, 1909/1967).

_____ , *Lectures on Ethics*, translated by Louis Infield (London: Methuen & Co., Ltd., 1930; reprinted, New York: Harper and Row, 1963).

_____ , *Metaphysics of Morals*, Part II, translated by J. Ellington as *The Metaphysical Principles of Virtue* (New York: Library of Liberal Arts, 1964), and translated by Mary Gregor as *The Doctrine of Virtue* (New York: Harper Torchbooks, 1964).

Mill, John Stuart, *On Liberty*, various editions.

_____ , "Remarks on Bentham's Philosophy," "Blakey's History of Moral Science," "Sedgwick's Discourse," "Bentham," and "Whewell on Moral Philosophy," reprinted in *Collected Works of John Stuart Mill*, Vol. X: *Essays on Ethics, Religion and Society*, edited by J. M. Robson (Toronto: University of Toronto Press, 1969).

_____ , *A System of Logic*, Book VI, Chapter XII, published as *On the Logic of the Moral Sciences* (Indianapolis: The Bobbs-Merrill Company, Inc., 1965).

_____ , *Representative Government*, various editions.

_____ , *The Subjection of Women*, various editions.

Schneewind, J. B. (editor), *Mill's Ethical Writings* (New York: The Macmillan Company, 1965).

B. COMMENTARIES: ARISTOTLE

Aquinas, St. Thomas, *Commentary on Aristotle's Nicomachean Ethics*, 2 vols., translated by C. I. Litzinger (Chicago: Henry Regnery Company, 1964).

Hardie, W. F. R., *Aristotle's Ethical Theory* (Oxford: Oxford University Press, 1968).

_____ , "The Final Good in Aristotle's Ethics," *Philosophy*, Vol. 40 (1965), pp. 277–295.

Joachim, H. H., *Aristotle: The Nicomachean Ethics* (Oxford: Clarendon Press, 1951).

Ross, W. D., *Aristotle*, 5th edition (Oxford: Oxford University Press, 1968).

Stewart, J. A., *Notes on the Nicomachean Ethics of Aristotle,* 2 vols. (Oxford: Clarendon Press, 1892).

Walsh, J. J., and Shapiro, H. L. (editors), *Aristotle's Ethics:* Issues and Interpretations (Belmont, Calif.: Wadsworth Publishing Company, Inc., 1967).

Williams, B. A. O., "Aristotle on the Good," *Philosophical Quarterly,* Vol. 12 (1962), pp. 289–296.

C. COMMENTARIES: KANT

Acton, H. B., *Kant's Moral Philosophy* (London: Macmillan and Company, 1970).

Beck, L. W., *A Commentary on Kant's Critique of Practical Reason* (Chicago: University of Chicago Press, 1960).

Broad, C. D., *Five Types of Ethical Theory* (London: Routledge & Kegan Paul, 1930), Chapter V.

Duncan, A. R. C., *Practical Reason and Morality* (Edinburgh: Thomas Nelson & Sons Ltd., 1957).

Field, G. C., *Moral Theory* (London: Methuen and Co., Ltd., 1921), Part I.

Gregory, Mary, *The Laws of Freedom* (Oxford: Oxford University Press, 1963).

Harrison, J., "Kant's Four Examples of the First Formulation of the Categorical Imperative," *Philosophical Quarterly,* Vol. VII (1957), pp. 50–62.

Hutchings, Patrick A., *Kant on Absolute Value* (Detroit: Wayne State University Press, 1972).

Jones, W. T., *Morality and Freedom in the Philosophy of Kant* (London: Oxford University Press, 1940).

Murphy, Jeffrie G., *Kant: The Philosophy of Right* (New York: St. Martin's Press, 1970), Chapters 2 and 3.

Nell, Onora, *Acting on Principle, An Essay on Kantian Ethics* (New York and London: Columbia University Press, 1975).

Paton, H. J., *The Categorical Imperative* (Chicago: The University of Chicago Press, 1948).

Ross, W. D., *Kant's Ethical Theory* (Oxford: Oxford University Press, 1963).

Teale, A. E., *Kantian Ethics* (London: Oxford University Press, 1951).

Ward, Keith, *The Development of Kant's View of Ethics* (Oxford: Basil Blackwell, 1972).

Williams, T. C., *The Concept of the Categorical Imperative* (Oxford: Oxford University Press, 1968).

Wolff, R. P., *Kant: A Collection of Critical Essays* (Garden City, New York: Doubleday, 1967), Part Two.

D. COMMENTARIES: MILL

Bradley, F. H., *Ethical Studies,* 2nd edition (Oxford: Clarendon Press, 1927), pp. 64–81.

Dryer, D. P., "Mill's Utilitarianism," *Collected Works of John Stuart Mill,* Vol. X: *Essays on Ethics, Religion and Society,* edited by J. M. Robson (Toronto: University of Toronto Press, 1969), pp. *lxiii–cxiii.*

Gorovitz, Samuel (editor), *Utilitarianism: with Critical Essays* (Indianapolis: Bobbs-Merrill, 1971). This thick paperback volume contains the complete text of Mill's *Utilitarianism* and a large number of interpretive and critical essays by many writers on Mill's theory and utilitarianism in general. It includes essays by Hall, Urmson, and others.

Hall, Everett W., "The 'Proof' of Utility in Bentham and Mill," *Ethics,* Vol. 60 (1949), pp. 1–18.

McNeilly, F. S., "Pre-moral Appraisals," *Philosophical Quarterly,* Vol. 8 (1958), pp. 97–111.

Martin, Rex, "A Defense of Mill's Qualitative Hedonism," *Philosophy,* Vol. 47 (1972), pp. 140–151.

Moore, G. E., *Principia Ethica* (Cambridge: Cambridge University Press, 1959; first edition, 1903), pp. 64–81.

Raphael, D. D., "Fallacies in and about Mill's Utilitarianism," *Philosophy,* Vol. 30 (1955), pp. 344–357.

Schneewind, J. B. (editor), *Mill: A Collection of Critical Essays* (New York: Doubleday and Company, 1968). This volume reprints many essays including those by Hall and Urmson listed here and contains an original one: Mandelbaum, Maurice, "Two Moot Issues in Mill's *Utilitarianism.*"

Seth, J., "Alleged Fallacies in Mill's *Utilitarianism,*" *The Philosophical Review,* Vol. 17 (1908), pp. 469–488.

Smith, James M., and Sosa, Ernest (editors), *Mill's Utilitarianism: Text and Criticism* (Belmont, Calif.: Wadsworth Publishing Company, Inc., 1969). In addition to Mill's text, this volume reprints critical commentaries by Moore, Urmson, Bradley, and others, and contains an original essay by Ernest Sosa entitled "Mill's *Utilitarianism.*"

Sutherland, J., "An Alleged Gap in Mill's *Utilitarianism,*" *Mind,* Vol. XI (1886), pp. 597–599.

Urmson, J. O., "The Interpretation of the Moral Philosophy of J. S. Mill," *Philosophical Quarterly,* Vol. 3 (1953), pp. 33–39.

Wellman, Carl, "A Reinterpretation of Mill's Proof," *Ethics,* Vol. 69 (1959), pp. 268–276.

West, Henry R., "Reconstructing Mill's Proof of the Principle of Utility," *Mind,* Vol. 81 (1972), pp. 256–257.

Part II Intrinsic Value:
What Makes a Life Worthwhile?

"**W**hat ultimately makes life worthwhile?" or, as Aristotle asks it, "What is the highest of all realizable goods?" are questions fundamental to moral philosophy. When we make choices, we implicitly show that we value one thing more than another. Whether we are concerned with living our own lives wisely or treating others as we would like to be treated ourselves, we need a set of values, criteria for what is good and bad in life.

Three distinctions are useful in pursuing the question before us. A first is the distinction between *intrinsic* value and *instrumental* value. A second is the distinction between intrinsic value and *moral* value. A third is the distinction between something being *valued* and its being *valuable* (between *being held to be* of value and *being* of value).

Many of the things we desire or whose possession we value are regarded merely as means to something else. Money is a standard example: the possession of money is not an end in itself, except perhaps for the miser, but is valued for the useful possessions it will buy and the security and power it brings. In other cases we may regard things as desirable or undesirable in themselves. The pleasure of eating an ice cream cone or the pain of a toothache seem to be of this sort. This is the basis for the distinction between things which are instrumentally good and bad, things whose value derives from their being means to other things; and things which are intrinsically good and bad, that is, valuable for their own sakes, as ends in themselves quite apart from their consequences. In developing a theory of value, the moral philosopher is interested in what is intrinsically valuable. If something is valued merely as a means to a further end, its value is derivative, and the wisdom of securing the means is dependent upon the wisdom of obtaining the end. At the same time, we must recognize that things may have both intrinsic and instrumental value. Going to the dentist may be painful in itself but instrumental in avoiding greater pain at a later time. Also, something may be the cause of more than one effect and the effects may have contrary values. Going to war may result in a nation's maintaining or expanding its territory, but it also results in the loss of many lives. When it is debated whether the end justifies the means, these complications must be taken into account. A further complication is that the "thing" which is judged valuable or not must be properly analyzed. Eating an ice cream cone is not valuable in itself unless it is a pleasurable experience; so some philosophers say it is the *pleasure* of eating an ice cream cone which is intrinsically valuable and the act of eating is merely a necessary condition for that pleasure. Even if the necessary condition does not occur before the pleasure, it may still be regarded as merely a means of having the pleasure and the pleasure be regarded as a consequence, in spite of their simultaneity. Some disputes about intrinsic value turn out to be disputes about the proper analysis of some whole which is mutually agreed to be of value. The dispute is as to which constituent of that whole is the constituent which has intrinsic value.

A second distinction is between intrinsic value and moral value. Various kinds of things can be said to be called good in themselves, for example, experiences, actions, or virtues. Some experiences which we have been calling intrinsically good, such as the pleasure of eating an ice cream cone, seem to have little moral significance; so the concept of what is morally good and what is intrinsically good seem to be distinct concepts. Furthermore, the distinction between what is intrinsically and merely instrumentally good may arise in the moral sphere, as in Kant's distinction between the good will, which is morally good in itself, not because of what it performs or effects, and qualities such as self-control and calm deliberation, which are of service to this good will and therefore deserve our esteem, but which have no intrinsic value since they could also aid in villainy. For Kant the good will is not the sole and complete good, but since it is the supreme good and the condition of every other, he would deny that there is any independently intrinsically good thing, not even happiness.

On the other hand, John Stuart Mill regards his moral theory as grounded in a "theory of life" as to what is good as an end, namely, that pleasure and freedom from pain are the only things desirable as ends. According to Mill, actions are right in proportion as they tend to promote pleasure, wrong as they tend to produce pain, and this rightness and wrongness takes on moral significance if the consequences of the actions are important enough that a person ought to be compelled to do the action or compelled to refrain from the action by punishment or moral censure.

Kant's and Mill's views represent two extreme views of the role of consequences in the assessment of morally right and wrong acts. On Kant's view, consequences have no significance. He is a pure "formalist" (since morality depends on the act's conformity to reason) or *deontologist* (from the Greek word for "duty"), attempting to base the rightness of an action entirely upon the will's conformity to duty, regardless of outcome. For Mill, consequences are all important, and Mill points out that on his view "the motive has nothing to do with the morality of the action, though much with the worth of the agent."[1] Mill is thus a pure "consequentialist" or *teleologist* (from the Greek word for "end" or "goal"). Mill labeled his position "Utilitarianism," so consequentialistic views are often regarded as varieties of utilitarianism. In its classical form the utility of an action was regarded as the degree to which it produced pleasure or the avoidance of pain. Some recent philosophers, including the British philosopher G. E. Moore, have called themselves utilitarians although holding a theory of intrinsic value according to which things other than pleasure, such as knowledge, virtue, justice, beauty, or love are also of intrinsic value. Such a view has been labeled "ideal utilitarianism," since the utility of an action is the maximization of these various ideals.

For Kant, intrinsic value is found by identifying the conditions for a good will, and intrinsically good actions are those which are necessary in order to conform to a good will. For consequentialists, however, a theory of intrinsic value is premoral. One develops a theory of what makes life worth living before one can determine what acts are right and wrong. Even without being purely consequentialistic, however, a moral theory may have a consequentialistic element which presupposes a theory of intrinsic value. The position of W. D. Ross,[2] for example, is pluralistic, recognizing some duties which are not based on consequences, while recognizing others which are. His duties of beneficence and nonmaleficence require that, other thing being equal, we benefit others if we can and we not harm others if we can avoid it. This requires that we have criteria for benefit and harm, that is, that we have a theory of intrinsic value.

A third important distinction is that between something being *valued* and its actually being *valuable,* between something being desired and its being desirable. This is obvious in the case of instrumental values. If I desire a college education as a means of making more money, I may be mistaken in my choice of the means. Some other type of training or experience may be more valuable as a means to that goal. If I desire to be rich in order to be happy, I may find myself disappointed; even if I am successful in achieving the means, I may find myself frustrated in failing to achieve the end. With regard to intrinsic values,

---

[1] *Utilitarianism,* Chapter II, included in Part I of this volume.
[2] A selection from Ross is included in Part III of this volume, pp. 302–307.

however, the distinction is more difficult to sustain. Since intrinsic values are ultimate, not derived from any further values, there may be a point at which there is no longer any test for their correctness and so the question whether what is valued is actually valuable may be untestable and therefore meaningless. Without denying that such a point may be reached, it is possible to point to some considerations which provide a method for the evaluation of "ultimate" values and thus for the viability of the distinction between something's being valued and its being valuable, even when it is a question of intrinsic value. One consideration is consistency. If my values are inconsistent with one another, or if they are inconsistent with facts about the universe which are well established, there is reason for rethinking them. A second consideration is the reliability of any factual evidence upon which my value system is based. If science were to change its claims about the nature of the universe, or if any religious suppositions were different, would that make a difference in my value judgments? Another consideration is the degree of analysis that has gone into my judgments of intrinsic value. Maybe I have taken as intrinsic something that is only of instrumental value. Perhaps I have not made an important distinction which needs to be made or have made one which should not be made. Perhaps I have not recognized the implications of my position, and when such implications are recognized see that there are inconsistences in my position. Finally, perhaps I hold the values I do by default, in the absence of any viable alternative. Faced with alternative systems, I may be led to give mine up, even if none is proved or disproved. The importance of the distinction between the valued and the valuable is not that there are agreed upon criteria for testing one's values, but that we are doing normative ethics. What is of intrinsic value is not simply what someone regards as such. A philosophical theory of intrinsic value must seem a plausible theory in the light of arguments and counterarguments, evidence and counterevidence, analysis and counteranalysis, and in comparison with alternative theories.

When we begin to reflect upon the question, "What is worthwhile in life?" we may think that there are lots of things, even many kinds of things: various character traits which can be summed up under Aristotle's term "virtue," such as trustworthiness or loyalty, and the self-respect which accompanies these; to be successful at what one undertakes, whatever it is, and the sense of achievement which accompanies that; to have friends, to love and be loved; to be intelligent and well-informed—the list could go on and on. When we reflect further, however, asking if these would be valuable even if they never had any good consequences, we may be able to shorten the list. Perhaps some of these are worthwhile because they usually have good consequences; perhaps, however, they would be worthwhile even if they didn't. This is the problem of intrinsic value.

John Stuart Mill holds the position that pleasure and pain are the only things of intrinsic value, all other things being valuable only as means to the production of pleasure or the avoidance of pain. This theory is call *hedonism* (from the Greek word for "pleasure") and is an appealing theory because of its simplicity. It also draws support from the degree to which actions are motivated by pleasure and avoidance of pain. The theory that *all* actions are motivated by pleasure and avoidance of pain is called "psychological hedonism" and is not the same as "ethical hedonism," the theory that pleasure and pain are the only things of intrinsic value. People are often motivated in directions which are contrary to their best interests, so motivation is not an infallible sign of value. Furthermore, psychological hedonism is usually the view that one pursues only his or her own pleasure, while Mill's ethical doctrine is that pleasure is intrinsically valuable wherever it occurs, in one's own life or in that of another. But if psychological hedonism is true, it can be used as a strong argument in support of ethical hedonism, as is shown in Chapter IV of Mill's *Utilitarianism.*

If pleasure and pain could be quantified, then a "hedonic calculus" would be possible. In determining the value of an act, one could add up all the quantities of pleasure which would be produced, subtract the quantities of pain which would be produced, and the balance would be the value of the act. By comparing one act with its alternatives, one would thus be able to calculate what would be the best thing to do. This approach is put forward by Jeremy Bentham in a selection from *Introduction to the Principles of Morals and Legislation,* the first of the readings in this section. Notice that he believes that pleasures are derived from many sources, from a good name, from power, from piety, and so forth, as well as from the senses. He believes, however, that the pleasure derived from these diverse sources is a common denominator which makes them commensurable. A life worth living is one in which the series of conscious states which make up life are such that the quantity of pleasure is greater than the quantity of pain. The highest of realizable goods is the life in which the net amount of pleasure (quantity of pleasure minus quantity of pain) is maximized.

Critics have argued that pleasure and pain cannot be quantified and, when derived from different sorts of experience or when occurring in the experience of different persons, are incommensurable; but it should be remembered that every day we do in fact make crude comparisons of quantities of pleasure and pain. We have an injection of pain-killer at the dentist because we believe the pain of the injection will be less than the pain being prevented. We sometimes choose one way of spending our spare time rather than another because we believe it will be more enjoyable, and the two activities may be quite dissimilar. We make judgments which affect other people guessing, but nevertheless judging, as to the greater or lesser quantity of pleasure and pain involved.

Some different objections to hedonism are found in Aristotle's *Ethics,* especially in Book I and Book X. Among other arguments, he puts forth the claim that there are many things we should care for, even if they brought no pleasure, such as sight, memory, knowledge, moral and intellectual excellence. The issue depends upon the analysis of the value of such things, whether they are to be valued entirely for the pleasure and avoidance of pain which normally accompanies them or whether they are valuable independently. Suppose that sight was always slightly discomforting. Would we then see it as having intrinsic value and wish to use our sight even when it had no practical or aesthetic purposes, or would we come to regard it as of merely instrumental value? Aristotle's analysis is an alternative to hedonism, since he concludes that pleasure is only one good, not the sole good and not the highest good. On his view, the activity of reason in its proper way is the highest good, although it, like the proper functioning of any organ, will be accompanied by pleasure as a by-product, and, being the highest faculty, will be accompanied by the most pleasure.

Suppose we accept the hedonist view and try to imagine a society which successfully achieves the maximum of pleasure and the minimum of pain possible. What would it be like? Aldous Huxley, in the novel *Brave New World,* pictures such a society. In this society, the family has been eliminated; fetuses are nurtured in test tubes, immunized from all diseases, conditioned to function properly so that there is no discrepency between what one ought to do and what one does. Everything is organized so that society functions without conflict and with abundant opportunity for pleasurable sensation. The euphoric drug *soma* is used to avoid any depression in life or pain in dying. The merits of such a society are debated in the novel in a confrontation between a "Savage," a man who grew up on an American Indian reservation that has not yet been brought into civilization, and the Controller, the director of the society. Part of their discussion is found in the selection contained in this section.

If one finds the hedonistic paradise of *Brave New World* disappointing, or even revolting, a possible reply is that Huxley is overemphasizing the purely sensual sources of pleasures and pains. In *Brave New World* there is very little creativity, very little sense of personal achievement, and no depth of emotion. There is no pleasure derived from friendship or love except of a most superficial sort; there is no pleasure derived from moral achievement, for everyone is conditioned to do what she or he ought to do without any temptation to do otherwise. Perhaps *Brave New World* is not a hedonistic paradise after all because in eliminating sources of pain it has also eliminated many sources of pleasure. John Stuart Mill's reply to the objection that hedonistic utilitarianism is worthy only of swine is to point out that humans are capable of much "higher" pleasures than swine and persons qualified by experience of both the higher and the lower prefer the higher because of their qualitative superiority. In taking this position, Mill has been accused of deserting hedonism, of appealing to some other standard of value. Dorothy Mitchell's article, "Mill's Theory of Value," discusses these charges and presents an interpretation of Mill which seeks to defend him as a consistent hedonist, as well as to defend his essay against other charges, especially those concerning his "proof" in chapter IV.

A final selection on hedonism from "Hedonistic and Nonhedonistic Utilitarianism," by J. J. C. Smart, discusses how much practical ethics is likely to be affected by the question of the recognition of qualitatively higher pleasures. Smart finds the issue dramatized by the possibility of artificial stimulation of pleasure centers of the brain, as has apparently been done in research on rats. This raises many of the challenges of *Brave New World* in an acute way, since electrode brain stimulation (or its analogue of pleasure derived from drugs) could be realized by an individual in society today. It also is a challenge to Mill's assertion that qualified persons consistently prefer higher pleasures. The electrode addict has presumably experienced normal and artificially stimulated pleasures and prefers the latter.

Two nonhedonistic views are represented by selections from Epictetus (The *Enchiridron*), and from Nietzsche. Epictetus, living at the time of the Roman empire, belonged to a tradition in philosophy known as Stoicism, the central tenet of which was for human beings to make their lives harmonious with nature and to accept with tranquility whatever fortunes or misfortunes are outside of their control. Some aspects of the teachings of Epictetus can be given a hedonistic interpretation. If people limit personal desires to those things which are within their power, they will avoid pains of frustration and disappointment which could be greater than any pleasure of fulfilment. But Epictetus places a value upon virtue, on doing the duties imposed by one's relations (brother, son, neighbor, citizen, and so forth) which does not appear based upon any possible hedonic calculation. He bases it upon what will keep one's will conformable to nature.

The selections from Nietzsche, *Thus Spake Zarathustra* and *Explanatory Notes, Beyond Good and Evil,* and *The Antichrist,* show his explicit rejection and even contempt for hedonism and for the ideals of reason and virtue as well. Creativity, power, and passion are Nietzsche's ultimate values.

H. W.

4. *INTRODUCTION TO THE PRINCIPLES OF MORALS AND LEGISLATION*

Jeremy Bentham

CHAPTER I. OF THE PRINCIPLE OF UTILITY

1. Nature has placed mankind under the governance of two sovereign masters, *pain* and *pleasure.* It is for them alone to point out what we ought to do, as well as to determine what we shall do. On the one hand the standard of right and wrong, on the other the chain of causes and effects, are fastened to their throne. They govern us in all we do, in all we say, in all we think: every effort we can make to throw off our subjection, will serve but to demonstrate and confirm it. In words a man may pretend to abjure their empire: but in reality he will remain subject to it all the while. The *principle of utility*[1] recognises this subjection, and assumes it for the foundation of that system, the object of which is to rear the fabric of felicity by the hands of reason and of law. Systems which attempt to question it, deal in sounds instead of sense, in caprice instead of reason, in darkness instead of light.

But enough of metaphor and declamation: it is not by such means that moral science is to be improved.

2. The principle of utility is the foundation of the present work: it will be proper therefore at the outset to give an explicit and determinate account of what is meant by it. By the principle[2] of utility is meant that principle which approves or disapproves of every action whatsoever, according to the tendency which it appears to have to augment or diminish the happiness of the party whose interest is in question: or, what is

the same thing in other words, to promote or to oppose that happiness. I say of every action whatsoever; and therefore not only of every action of a private individual, but of every measure of government.

3. By utility is meant that property in any object, whereby it tends to produce benefit, advantage, pleasure, good, or happiness, (all this in the present case comes to the same thing) or (what comes again to the same thing) to prevent the happening of mischief, pain, evil, or unhappiness to the party whose interest is considered: if that party be the community in general, then the happiness of the community: if a particular individual, then the happiness of that individual.

4. The interest of the community is one of the most general expressions that can occur in the phraseology of morals: no wonder that the meaning of it is often lost. When it has a meaning, it is this. The community is a fictitious *body,* composed of the individual persons who are considered as constituting as it were its *members.* The interest of the community then is, what?—the sum of the interests of the several members who compose it.

5. It is in vain to talk of the interest of the community, without understanding what is the interest of the individual.[3] A thing is said to promote the interest, or to be *for* the interest, of an individual, when it tends to add to the sum total of his pleasures: or, what comes to the same thing, to diminish the sum total of his pains.

6. An action then may be said to be conformable to the principle of utility, or, for short-

From Jeremy Bentham, *An Introduction to the Principles of Morals and Legislation.* First publication 1789 (printed, though not published, in 1780. New edition published in 1823. Chapters I–V.

ness sake, to utility, (meaning with respect to the community at large) when the tendency it has to augment the happiness of the community is greater than any it has to diminish it.

7. A measure of government (which is but a particular kind of action, performed by a particular person or persons) may be said to be conformable to or dictated by the principle of utility, when in like manner the tendency which it has to augment the happiness of the community is greater than any which it has to diminish it.

8. When an action, or in particular a measure of government, is supposed by a man to be conformable to the principle of utility, it may be convenient, for the purposes of discourse, to imagine a kind of law or dictate, called a law or dictate of utility: and to speak of the action in question, as being conformable to such law or dictate.

9. A man may be said to be a partisan of the principle of utility, when the approbation or disapprobation he annexes to any action, or to any measure, is determined by, and proportioned to the tendency which he conceives it to have to augment or to diminish the happiness of the community: or in other words, to its conformity or unconformity to the laws or dictates of utility.

10. Of an action that is conformable to the principle of utility, one may always say either that it is one that ought to be done, or at least that it is not one that ought not to be done. One may say also, that it is right it should be done; at least that it is not wrong it should be done: that it is a right action; at least that it is not a wrong action. When thus interpreted, the words *ought,* and *right* and *wrong,* and others of that stamp, have a meaning: when otherwise, they have none.

11. Has the rectitude of this principle been ever formally contested? It should seem that it had, by those who have not known what they have been meaning. Is it susceptible of any direct proof? It should seem not: for that which is used to prove every thing else, cannot itself be proved: a chain of proofs must have their commencement somewhere. To give such proof is as impossible as it is needless.

12. Not that there is or ever has been that human creature breathing, however stupid or perverse, who has not on many, perhaps on most occasions of his life, deferred to it. By the natural constitution of the human frame, on most occasions of their lives men in general embrace this principle, without thinking of it: if not for the ordering of their own actions, yet for the trying of their own actions, as well as of those of other men. There have been, at the same time, not many, perhaps, even of the most intelligent, who have been disposed to embrace it purely and without reserve. There are even few who have not taken some occasion or other to quarrel with it, either on account of their not understanding always how to apply it, or on account of some prejudice or other which they were afraid to examine into, or could not bear to part with. For such is the stuff that man is made of: in principle and in practice, in a right track and in a wrong one, the rarest of all human qualities is consistency.

13. When a man attempts to combat the principle of utility, it is with reasons drawn, without his being aware of it, from that very principle itself.[4] His arguments, if they prove any thing, prove not that the principle is *wrong,* but that, according to the applications he supposes to be made of it, it is *misapplied.* Is it possible for a man to move the earth? Yes; but he must first find out another earth to stand upon.

14. To disprove the propriety of it by arguments is impossible; but, from the causes that have been mentioned, or from some confused or partial view of it, a man may happen to be disposed not to relish it. Where this is the case, if he thinks the settling of his opinions on such a subject worth the trouble, let him take the following steps, and at length, perhaps, he may come to reconcile himself to it.

(1) Let him settle with himself, whether he would wish to discard this principle altogether; if so, let him consider what it is that all his reasonings (in matters of politics especially) can amount to?

(2) If he would, let him settle with himself, whether he would judge and act without any principle, or whether there is any other he would judge and act by?

(3) If there be, let him examine and satisfy himself whether the principle he thinks he has found is really any separate intelligible principle; or whether it be not a mere principle in words, a

kind of phrase, which at bottom expresses neither more nor less than the mere averment of his own unfounded sentiments; that is, what in another person he might be apt to call *caprice?*

(4) If he is inclined to think that his own approbation or disapprobation, annexed to the idea of an act, without any regard to its consequences, is a sufficient foundation for him to judge and act upon, let him ask himself whether his sentiment is to be a standard of right and wrong, with respect to every other man, or whether every man's sentiment has the same privilege of being a standard to itself?

(5) In the first case, let him ask himself whether his principle is not despotical, and hostile to all the rest of human race?

(6) In the second case, whether it is not anarchical, and whether at this rate there are not as many different standards of right and wrong as there are men? and whether even to the same man, the same thing, which is right today, may not (without the least change in its nature) be wrong to-morrow? and whether the same thing is not right and wrong in the same place at the same time? and in either case, whether all argument is not at an end? and whether, when two men have said, 'I like this,' and 'I don't like it,' they can (upon such a principle) have any thing more to say?

(7) If he should have said to himself, No: for that the sentiment which he proposes as a standard must be grounded on reflection, let him say on what particulars the reflection is to turn? if on particulars having relation to the utility of the act, then let him say whether this is not deserting his own principle, and borrowing assistance from that very one in opposition to which he sets it up: or if not on those particulars, on what other particulars?

(8) If he should be for compounding the matter, and adopting his own principle in part, and the principle of utility in part, let him say how far he will adopt it?

(9) When he has settled with himself where he will stop, then let him ask himself how he justifies to himself the adopting it so far? and why he will not adopt it any farther?

(10) Admitting any other principle than the principle of utility to be a right principle, a principle that it is right for a man to pursue; admitting (what is not true) that the word *right* can

have a meaning without reference to utility, let him say whether there is any such thing as a *motive* that a man can have to pursue the dictates of it: if there is, let him say what that motive is, and how it is to be distinguished from those which enforce the dictates of utility: if not, then lastly let him say what it is this other principle can be good for?

CHAPTER II. OF PRINCIPLES ADVERSE TO THAT OF UTILITY

1. If the principle of utility be a right principle to be governed by, and that in all cases, it follows from what has been just observed, that whatever principle differs from it in any case must necessarily be a wrong one. To prove any other principle, therefore, to be a wrong one, there needs no more than just to show it to be what it is, a principle of which the dictates are in some point or other different from those of the principle of utility: to state it is to confute it.

2. A principle may be different from that of utility in two ways: 1. By being constantly opposed to it: this is the case with a principle which may be termed the principle of *asceticism*. 2. By being sometimes opposed to it, and sometimes not, as it may happen: this is the case with another, which may be termed the principle of *sympathy* and *antipathy*.

3. By the principle of asceticism I mean that principle, which, like the principle of utility, approves or disapproves of any action, according to the tendency which it appears to have to augment or diminish the happiness of the party whose interest is in question; but in an inverse manner: approving of actions in as far as they tend to diminish his happiness; disapproving of them in as far as they tend to augment it.

4. It is evident that any one who reprobates any the least particle of pleasure, as such, from whatever source derived, is *pro tanto* a partisan of the principle of asceticism. It is only upon that principle, and not from the principle of utility, that the most abominable pleasure which the vilest of malefactors ever reaped from his crime would be to be reprobated, if it stood alone. The case is, that it never does stand alone; but is necessarily followed by such a quantity of pain (or, what comes to the same thing, such a chance for a certain quantity of pain) that the pleasure in

comparison of it, is as nothing: and this is the true and sole, but perfectly sufficient, reason for making it a ground for punishment.

5. There are two classes of men of very different complexions, by whom the principle of asceticism appears to have been embraced; the one a set of moralists, the other a set of religionists. Different accordingly have been the motives which appear to have recommended it to the notice of these different parties. Hope, that is the prospect of pleasure, seems to have animated the former: hope, the aliment of philosophic pride: the hope of honour and reputation at the hands of men. Fear, that is the prospect of pain, the latter: fear, the offspring of superstitious fancy: the fear of future punishment at the hands of a splenetic and revengeful Deity. I say in this case fear: for of the invisible future, fear is more powerful than hope. These circumstances characterize the two different parties among the partisans of the principle of asceticism; the parties and their motives different, the principle the same.

6. The religious party, however, appear to have carried it farther than the philosophical: they have acted more consistently and less wisely. The philosophical party have scarcely gone farther than to reprobate pleasure: the religious party have frequently gone so far as to make it a matter of merit and of duty to court pain. The philosophical party have hardly gone farther than the making pain a matter of indifference. It is no evil, they have said: they have not said, it is a good. They have not so much as reprobated all pleasure in the lump. They have discarded only what they have called the gross; that is, such as are organical, or of which the origin is easily traced up to such as are organical: they have even cherished and magnified the refined. Yet this, however, not under the name of pleasure: to cleanse itself from the sordes of its impure original, it was necessary it should change its name: the honourable, the glorious, the reputable, the becoming, the *honestum,* the *decorum,* it was to be called: in short, any thing but pleasure.

7. From these two sources have flowed the doctrines from which the sentiments of the bulk of mankind have all along received a tincture of this principle; some from the philosophical, some from the religious, some from both. Men

of education more frequently from the philosophical, as more suited to the elevation of their sentiments: the vulgar more frequently from the superstitious, as more suited to the narrowness of their intellect, undilated by knowledge: and to the abjectness of their condition, continually open to the attacks of fear. The tinctures, however, derived from the two sources, would naturally intermingle, insomuch that a man would not always know by which of them he was most influenced: and they would often serve to corroborate and enliven one another. It was this conformity that made a kind of alliance between parties of a complexion otherwise so dissimilar: and disposed them to unite upon various occasions against the common enemy, the partisan of the principle of utility, whom they joined in branding with the odious name of Epicurean.

8. The principle of asceticism, however, with whatever warmth it may have been embraced by its partisans as a rule of private conduct, seems not to have been carried to any considerable length, when applied to the business of government. In a few instances it has been carried a little way by the philosophical party: witness the Spartan regimen. Though then, perhaps, it may be considered as having been a measure of security: and an application, though a precipitate and perverse application, of the principle of utility. Scarcely in any instances, to any considerable length, by the religious: for the various monastic orders, and the societies of the Quakers, Dumplers, Moravians, and other religionists, have been free societies, whose regimen no man has been astricted to without the intervention of his own consent. Whatever merit a man may have thought there would be in making himself miserable, no such notion seems ever to have occurred to any of them, that it may be a merit, much less a duty, to make others miserable: although it should seem, that if a certain quantity of misery were a thing so desirable, it would not matter much whether it were brought by each man upon himself, or by one man upon another. It is true, that from the same source from whence, among the religionists, the attachment to the principle of asceticism took its rise, flowed other doctrines and practices, from which misery in abundance was produced in one man by the instrumentality of another: witness the holy wars, and the per-

secutions for religion. But the passion for producing misery in these cases proceeded upon some special ground: the exercise of it was confined to persons of particular descriptions: they were tormented, not as men, but as heretics and infidels. To have inflicted the same miseries on their fellow-believers and fellow-sectaries, would have been as blameable in the eyes even of these religionists, as in those of a partisan of the principle of utility. For a man to give himself a certain number of stripes was indeed meritorious: but to give the same number of stripes to another man, not consenting, would have been a sin. We read of saints, who for the good of their souls, and the mortification of their bodies, have voluntarily yielded themselves a prey to vermin: but though many persons of this class have wielded the reins of empire, we read of none who have set themselves to work, and made laws on purpose, with a view of stocking the body politic with the breed of highwaymen, housebreakers, or incendiaries. If at any time they have suffered the nation to be preyed upon by swarms of idle pensioners, or useless placemen, it has rather been from negligence and imbecility, than from any settled plan for oppressing and plundering of the people. If at any time they have sapped the sources of national wealth, by cramping commerce, and driving the inhabitants into emigration, it has been with other views, and in pursuit of other ends. If they have declaimed against the pursuit of pleasure, and the use of wealth, they have commonly stopped at declamation: they have not, like Lycurgus, made express ordinances for the purpose of banishing the precious metals. If they have established idleness by a law, it has been not because idleness, the mother of vice and misery, is itself a virtue, but because idleness (say they) is the road to holiness. If under the notion of fasting, they have joined in the plan of confining their subjects to a diet, thought by some to be of the most nourishing and prolific nature, it has been not for the sake of making them tributaries to the nations by whom that diet was to be supplied, but for the sake of manifesting their own power, and exercising the obedience of the people. If they have established, or suffered to be established, punishments for the breach of celibacy, they have done no more than comply with the petitions of those deluded rigorists, who, dupes to the ambitious and deep-laid policy of their rulers, first laid themselves under that idle obligation by a vow.

9. The principle of asceticism seems originally to have been the reverie of certain hasty speculators, who having perceived, or fancied, that certain pleasures, when reaped in certain circumstances, have, at the long run, been attended with pains more than equivalent to them, took occasion to quarrel with every thing that offered itself under the name of pleasure. Having then got thus far, and having forgot the point which they set out from, they pushed on, and went so much further as to think it meritorious to fall in love with pain. Even this, we see, is at bottom but the principle of utility misapplied.

10. The principle of utility is capable of being consistently pursued; and it is but tautology to say, that the more consistently it is pursued, the better it must ever be for human-kind. The principle of asceticism never was, nor ever can be, consistently pursued by any living creature. Let but one tenth part of the inhabitants of this earth pursue it consistently, and in a day's time they will have turned it into a hell.

11. Among principles adverse to that of utility, that which at this day seems to have most influence in matters of government, is what may be called the principle of sympathy and antipathy. By the principle of sympathy and antipathy, I mean that principle which approves or disapproves of certain actions, not on account of their tending to augment the happiness, nor yet on account of their tending to diminish the happiness of the party whose interest is in question, but merely because a man finds himself disposed to approve or disapprove of them: holding up that approbation or disapprobation as a sufficient reason for itself, and disclaiming the necessity of looking out for any extrinsic ground. Thus far in the general department of morals: and in the particular department of politics, measuring out the quantum (as well as determining the ground) of punishment, by the degree of the disapprobation.

12. It is manifest, that this is rather a principle in name than in reality: it is not a positive principle of itself, so much as a term employed to signify the negation of all principle. What one expects to find in a principle is something that

points out some external consideration, as a means of warranting and guiding the internal sentiments of approbation and disapprobation: this expectation is but ill fulfilled by a proposition, which does neither more nor less than hold up each of those sentiments as a ground and standard for itself.

13. In looking over the catalogue of human actions (says a partisan of this principle) in order to determine which of them are to be marked with the seal of disapprobation, you need but to take counsel of your own feelings: whatever you find in yourself a propensity to condemn, is wrong for that very reason. For the same reason it is also meet for punishment: in what proportion it is adverse to utility, or whether it be adverse to utility at all, is a matter that makes no difference. In that same *proportion* also is it meet for punishment: if you hate much, punish much: if you hate little, punish little: punish as you hate. If you hate not at all, punish not at all: the fine feelings of the soul are not to be overborne and tyrannized by the harsh and rugged dictates of political utility.

14. The various systems that have been formed concerning the standard of right and wrong, may all be reduced to the principle of sympathy and antipathy. One account may serve for all of them. They consist all of them in so many contrivances for avoiding the obligation of appealing to any external standard, and for prevailing upon the reader to accept of the author's sentiment or opinion as a reason and that a sufficient one for itself. The phrases different, but the principle the same.

15. It is manifest, that the dictates of this principle will frequently coincide with those of utility, though perhaps without intending any such thing. Probably more frequently than not: and hence it is that the business of penal justice is carried on upon that tolerable sort of footing upon which we see it carried on in common at this day. For what more natural or more general ground of hatred to a practice can there be, than the mischievousness of such practice? What all men are exposed to suffer by, all men will be disposed to hate. It is far yet, however, from being a constant ground: for when a man suffers, it is not always that he knows what it is he suffers by. A man may suffer grievously, for instance, by a new tax, without being able to trace up the cause of his sufferings to the injustice of some

neighbour, who has eluded the payment of an old one.

16. The principle of sympathy and antipathy is most apt to err on the side of severity. It is for applying punishment in many cases which deserve none: in many cases which deserve some, it is for applying more than they deserve. There is no incident imaginable, be it ever so trivial, and so remote from mischief, from which this principle may not extract a ground of punishment. Any difference in taste: any difference in opinion: upon one subject as well as upon another. No disagreement so trifling which perseverance and altercation will not render serious. Each becomes in the other's eyes an enemy, and, if laws permit, a criminal. This is one of the circumstances by which the human race is distinguished (not much indeed to its advantage) from the brute creation.

17. It is not, however, by any means unexampled for this principle to err on the side of lenity. A near and perceptible mischief moves antipathy. A remote and imperceptible mischief, though not less real, has no effect. Instances in proof of this will occur in numbers in the course of the work. It would be breaking in upon the order of it to give them here.

18. It may be wondered, perhaps, that in all this while no mention has been made of the *theological* principle; meaning that principle which professes to recur for the standard of right and wrong to the will of God. But the case is, this is not in fact a distinct principle. It is never any thing more or less than one or other of the three before-mentioned principles presenting itself under another shape. The *will* of God here meant cannot be his revealed will, as contained in the sacred writings: for that is a system which nobody ever thinks of recurring to at this time of day, for the details of political administration: and even before it can be applied to the details of private conduct, it is universally allowed, by the most eminent divines of all persuasions, to stand in need of pretty ample interpretations; else to what use are the works of those divines? And for the guidance of these interpretations, it is also allowed, that some other standard must be assumed. The will then which is meant on this occasion, is that which may be called the *presumptive* will: that is to say, that which is presumed to be his will on account of the conformity of its dictates to those of some other

principle. What then may be this other principle? it must be one or other of the three mentioned above: for there cannot, as we have seen, be any more. It is plain, therefore, that, setting revelation out of the question, no light can ever be thrown upon the standard of right and wrong, by any thing that can be said upon the question, what is God's will. We may be perfectly sure, indeed, that whatever is right is conformable to the will of God: but so far is that from answering the purpose of showing us what is right, that it is necessary to know first whether a thing is right, in order to know from thence whether it be conformable to the will of God.

19. There are two things which are very apt to be confounded, but which it imports us carefully to distinguish:—the motive or cause, which, by operating on the mind of an individual, is productive of any act: and the ground or reason which warrants a legislator, or other by-stander, in regarding that act with an eye of approbation. When the act happens, in the particular instance in question, to be productive of effects which we approve of, much more if we happen to observe that the same motive may frequently be productive, in other instances, of the like effects, we are apt to transfer our approbation to the motive itself, and to assume, as the just ground for the approbation we bestow on the act, the circumstance of its originating from that motive. It is in this way that the sentiment of antipathy has often been considered as a just ground of action. Antipathy, for instance, in such or such a case, is the cause of an action which is attended with good effects: but this does not make it a right ground of action in that case, any more than in any other. Still farther. Not only the effects are good, but the agent sees beforehand that they will be so. This may make the action indeed a perfectly right action: but it does not make antipathy a right ground of action. For the same sentiment of antipathy, if implicitly deferred to, may be, and very frequently is, productive of the very worst effects. Antipathy, therefore, can never be a right ground of action. No more, therefore, can resentment, which, as will be seen more particularly hereafter, is but a modification of antipathy. The only right ground of action, that can possibly subsist, is, after all, the consideration of utility, which, if it is a right principle of action, and of approbation, in any one case, is so in every other. Other principles in abundance,

that is, other motives, may be the reasons why such and such an act *has* been done: that is, the reasons or causes of its being done: but it is this alone that can be the reason why it might or ought to have been done. Antipathy or resentment requires always to be regulated, to prevent its doing mischief: to be regulated by what? always by the principle of utility. The principle of utility neither requires nor admits of any other regulator than itself.

CHAPTER III. OF THE FOUR SANCTIONS OR SOURCES OF PAIN AND PLEASURE

1. It has been shown that the happiness of the individuals, of whom a community is composed, that is their pleasures and their security, is the end and the sole end which the legislator ought to have in view: the sole standard, in conformity to which each individual ought, as far as depends upon the legislator, to be *made* to fashion his behaviour. But whether it be this or any thing else that is to be *done,* there is nothing by which a man can ultimately be *made* to do it, but either pain or pleasure. Having taken a general view of these two grand objects (viz. pleasure, and what comes to the same thing, immunity from pain) in the character of *final* causes; it will be necessary to take a view of pleasure and pain itself, in the character of *efficient* causes or means.

2. There are four distinguishable sources from which pleasure and pain are in use to flow: considered separately, they may be termed the *physical,* the *political,* and *moral,* and the *religious:* and inasmuch as the pleasures and pains belonging to each of them are capable of giving a binding force to any law or rule of conduct, they may all of them be termed *sanctions.*[5]

3. If it be in the present life, and from the ordinary course of nature, not purposely modified by the interposition of the will of any human being, nor by any extraordinary interposition of any superior invisible being, that the pleasure or the pain takes place or is expected, it may be said to issue from or to belong to the *physical sanction.*

4. If at the hands of a *particular* person or set of persons in the community, who under names correspondent to that of *judge,* are chosen for the particular purpose of dispensing it, according to the will of the sovereign or supreme ruling

power in the state, it may be said to issue from the *political sanction*.

5. If at the hands of such *chance* persons in the community, as the party in question may happen in the course of his life to have concerns with, according to each man's spontaneous disposition, and not according to any settled or concerted rule, it may be said to issue from the *moral* or *popular sanction*.[6]

6. If from the immediate hand of a superior invisible being, either in the present life, or in a future, it may be said to issue from the *religious sanction*.

7. Pleasures or pains which may be expected to issue from the *physical, political*, or *moral* sanctions, must all of them be expected to be experienced, if ever, in the *present* life: those which may be expected to issue from the *religious* sanction, may be expected to be experienced either in the *present* life or in a *future*.

8. Those which can be experienced in the present life, can of course be no others than such as human nature in the course of the present life is susceptible of: and from each of these sources may flow all the pleasures or pains of which, in the course of the present life, human nature is susceptible. With regard to these then (with which alone we have in this place any concern) those of them which belong to any one of those sanctions, differ not ultimately in kind from those which belong to any one of the other three: the only difference there is among them lies in the circumstances that accompany their production. A suffering which befalls a man in the natural and spontaneous course of things, shall be styled, for instance, a *calamity;* in which case, if it be supposed to befall him through any imprudence of his, it may be styled a punishment issuing from the *physical* sanction. Now this same suffering, if inflicted by the law, will be what is commonly called a *punishment;* if incurred for want of any friendly assistance, which the misconduct, or supposed misconduct, of the sufferer has occasioned to be withholden, a punishment issuing from the *moral* sanction; if through the immediate interposition of a particular providence, a punishment issuing from the *religious* sanction.

9. A man's goods, or his person, are consumed by fire. If this happened to him by what is called an accident, it was a *calamity:* if by reason of his

own imprudence (for instance, from his neglecting to put his candle out) it may be styled a punishment of the *physical* sanction: if it happened to him by the sentence of the political magistrate, a punishment belonging to the *political* sanction; that is, what is commonly called a *punishment:* if for want of any assistance which his *neighbour* withheld from him out of some dislike to his *moral* character, a punishment of the *moral* sanction: if by an immediate act of *God's* displeasure, manifested on account of some *sin* committed by him, or through any distraction of mind, occasioned by the dread of such displeasure, a punishment of the *religious* sanction.[7]

10. As to such of the pleasures and pains belonging to the religious sanction, as regard a future life, of what kind these may be we cannot know. These lie not open to our observation. During the present life they are matter only of expectation: and, whether that expectation be derived from natural or revealed religion, the particular kind of pleasure or pain, if it be different from all those which lie open to our observation, is what we can have no idea of. The best ideas we can obtain of such pains and pleasures are altogether unliquidated in point of quality. In what other respects our ideas of them *may* be liquidated will be considered in another place.

11. Of these four sanctions the physical is altogether, we may observe, the ground-work of the political and the moral: so is it also of the religious, in as far as the latter bears relation to the present life. It is included in each of those other three. This may operate in any case, (that is, any of the pains or pleasures belonging to it may operate) independently of *them:* none of *them* can operate but by means of this. In a word, the powers of nature may operate of themselves; but neither the magistrate, nor men at large, *can* operate, nor is God in the case in question *supposed* to operate, but through the powers of nature.

12. For these four objects, which in their nature have so much in common, it seemed of use to find a common name. It seemed of use, in the first place, for the convenience of giving a name to certain pleasures and pains, for which a name equally characteristic could hardly otherwise have been found: in the second place, for the

sake of holding up the efficacy of certain moral forces, the influence of which is apt not to be sufficiently attended to. Does the political sanction exert an influence over the conduct of mankind? The moral, the religious sanctions do so too. In every inch of his career are the operations of the political magistrate liable to be aided or impeded by these two foreign powers: who, one or other of them, or both, are sure to be either his rivals or his allies. Does it happen to him to leave them out in his calculations? he will be sure almost to find himself mistaken in the result. Of all this we shall find abundant proofs in the sequel of this work. It behoves him, therefore, to have them continually before his eyes; and that under such a name as exhibits the relation they bear to his own purposes and designs.

CHAPTER IV. VALUE OF A LOT OF PLEASURE OR PAIN, HOW TO BE MEASURED

1. Pleasures then, and the avoidance of pains, are the *ends* which the legislator has in view: it behoves him therefore to understand their *value*. Pleasures and pains are the *instruments* he has to work with: it behoves him therefore to understand their force, which is again, in another point of view, their value.

2. To a person considered *by himself,* the value of a pleasure or pain considered *by itself,* will be greater or less, according to the four following circumstances[8]:

    1. Its *intensity.*
    2. Its *duration.*
    3. Its *certainty* or *uncertainty.*
    4. Its *propinquity* or *remoteness.*

3. These are the circumstances which are to be considered in estimating a pleasure or a pain considered each of them by itself. But when the value of any pleasure or pain is considered for the purpose of estimating the tendency of any *act* by which it is produced, there are two other circumstances to be taken into the account; these are,

    5. Its *fecundity,* or the chance it has of being followed by sensations of the *same* kind: that is, pleasures, if it be a pleasure: pains, if it be a pain.

6. Its *purity,* or the chance it has of *not* being followed by sensations of the *opposite* kind: that is, pains, if it be a pleasure: pleasures, if it be a pain.

These two last, however, are in strictness scarcely to be deemed properties of the pleasure or the pain itself; they are not, therefore, in strictness to be taken into the account of the value of that pleasure or that pain. They are in strictness to be deemed properties only of the act, or other event, by which such pleasure or pain has been produced; and accordingly are only to be taken into the account of the tendency of such act or such event.

4. To a *number* of persons, with reference to each of whom the value of a pleasure or a pain is considered, it will be greater or less, according to seven circumstances: to wit, the six preceding ones; viz.

    1. Its *intensity.*
    2. Its *duration.*
    3. Its *certainty* or *uncertainty.*
    4. Its *propinquity* or *remoteness.*
    5. Its *fecundity.*
    6. Its *purity.*

And one other; to wit:

    7. Its *extent;* that is, the number of persons to whom it *extends;* or (in other words) who are affected by it.

5. To take an exact account then of the general tendency of any act, by which the interests of a community are affected, proceed as follows. Begin with any one person of those whose interests seem most immediately to be affected by it: and take an account,

    1. Of the value of each distinguishable *pleasure* which appears to be produced by it in the *first* instance.

    2. Of the value of each *pain* which appears to be produced by it in the *first* instance.

    3. Of the value of each pleasure which appears to be produced by it *after* the first. This constitutes the *fecundity* of the first *pleasure* and the *impurity* of the first *pain.*

4. Of the value of each *pain* which appears to be produced by it after the first. This constitutes the *fecundity* of the first *pain,* and the *impurity* of the first pleasure.

5. Sum up all the values of all the *pleasures* on the one side, and those of all the *pains* on the other. The balance, if it be on the side of pleasure, will give the *good* tendency of the act upon the whole, with respect to the interests of that *individual* person; if on the side of pain, the *bad* tendency of it upon the whole.

6. Take an account of the *number* of persons whose interests appear to be concerned; and repeat the above process with respect to each. *Sum up* the numbers expressive of the degrees of *good* tendency, which the act has, with respect to each individual, in regard to whom the tendency of it is *good* upon the whole: do this again with respect to each individual, in regard to whom the tendency of it is *bad* upon the whole. Take the *balance;* which, if on the side of *pleasure,* will give the general *good tendency* of the act, with respect to the total number or community of individuals concerned; if on the side of pain, the general *evil tendency,* with respect to the same community.

6. It is not to be expected that this process should be strictly pursued previously to every moral judgment, or to every legislative or judicial operation. It may, however, be always kept in view: and as near as the process actually pursued on these occasions approaches to it, so near will such process approach to the character of an exact one.

7. The same process is alike applicable to pleasure and pain, in whatever shape they appear: and by whatever denomination they are distinguished: to pleasure, whether it be called *good* (which is properly the cause or instrument of pleasure) or *profit* (which is distant pleasure, or the cause or instrument of distant pleasure,) or *convenience,* or *advantage, benefit, emolument, happiness,* and so forth: to pain, whether it be called *evil,* (which corresponds to *good*) or *mischief,* or *inconvenience,* or *disadvantage,* or *loss,* or *unhappiness,* and so forth.

8. Nor is this a novel and unwarranted, any more than it is a useless theory. In all this there is nothing but what the practice of mankind, wheresoever they have a clear view of their own interest, is perfectly conformable to. An article of property, an estate in land, for instance, is valuable, on what account? On account of the pleasures of all kinds which it enables a man to produce, and what comes to the same thing the pains of all kinds which it enables him to avert. But the value of such an article of property is universally understood to rise or fall according to the length or shortness of the time which a man has in it: the certainty or uncertainty of its coming into possession: and the nearness or remoteness of the time at which, if at all, it is to come into possession. As to the *intensity* of the pleasures which a man may derive from it, this is never thought of, because it depends upon the use which each particular person may come to make of it; which cannot be estimated till the particular pleasures he may come to derive from it, or the particular pains he may come to exclude by means of it, are brought to view. For the same reason, neither does he think of the *fecundity* or *purity* of those pleasures.

Thus much for pleasure and pain, happiness and unhappiness, in *general.* We come now to consider the several particular kinds of pain and pleasure.

CHAPTER V. PLEASURES AND PAINS, THEIR KINDS

1. Having represented what belongs to all sorts of pleasures and pains alike, we come now to exhibit, each by itself, the several sorts of pains and pleasures. Pains and pleasures may be called by one general word, interesting perceptions. Interesting perceptions are either simple or complex. The simple ones are those which cannot any one of them be resolved into more: complex are those which are resolvable into divers simple ones. A complex interesting perception may accordingly be composed either, 1. Of pleasures alone: 2. Of pains alone: or, 3. Of a pleasure or pleasures, and a pain or pains together. What determines a lot of pleasure, for example, to be regarded as one complex pleasure, rather than as divers simple ones, is the nature of the exciting cause. Whatever pleasures

are excited all at once by the action of the same cause, are apt to be looked upon as constituting all together but one pleasure.

2. The several simple pleasures of which human nature is susceptible, seem to be as follows: 1. The pleasures of sense. 2. The pleasures of wealth. 3. The pleasures of skill. 4. The pleasures of amity. 5. The pleasures of a good name. 6. The pleasures of power. 7. The pleasures of piety. 8. The pleasures of benevolence. 9. The pleasures of malevolence. 10. The pleasures of memory. 11. The pleasures of imagination. 12. The pleasures of expectation. 13. The pleasures dependent on association. 14. The pleasures of relief.

3. The several simple pains seem to be as follows: 1. The pains of privation. 2. The pains of the senses. 3. The pains of awkwardness. 4. The pains of enmity. 5. The pains of an ill name. 6. The pains of piety. 7. The pains of benevolence. 8. The pains of malevolence. 9. The pains of the memory. 10. The pains of the imagination. 11. The pains of expectation. 12. The pains dependent on association.[9]

4. (1) The pleasures of sense seem to be as follows: 1. The pleasures of the taste or palate; including whatever pleasures are experienced in satisfying the appetites of hunger and thirst. 2. The pleasure of intoxication. 3. The pleasures of the organ of smelling. 4. The pleasures of the touch. 5. The simple pleasures of the ear; independent of association. 6. The simple pleasures of the eye; independent of association. 7. The pleasure of the sexual sense. 8. The pleasure of health: or, the internal pleasurable feeling or flow of spirits (as it is called,) which accompanies a state of full health and vigour; especially at times of moderate bodily exertion. 9. The pleasures of novelty: or, the pleasures derived from the gratification of the appetite of curiosity, by the application of new objects to any of the senses.[10]

5. (2) By the pleasures of wealth may be meant those pleasures which a man is apt to derive from the consciousness of possessing any article or articles which stand in the list of instruments of enjoyment or security, and more particularly at the time of his first acquiring them; at which time the pleasure may be styled a pleasure of gain or a pleasure of acquisition: at other times a pleasure of possession.

(3) The pleasures of skill, as exercised upon particular objects, are those which accompany the application of such particular instruments of enjoyment to their uses, as cannot be so applied without a greater or less share of difficulty or exertion.[11]

6. (4) The pleasures of amity, or self-recommendation, are the pleasures that may accompany the persuasion of a man's being in the acquisition or the possession of the good-will of such or such assignable person or persons in particular: or, as the phrase is, of being upon good terms with him or them: and as a fruit of it, of his being in a way to have the benefit of their spontaneous and gratuitous services.

7. (5) The pleasures of a good name are the pleasures that accompany the persuasion of a man's being in the acquisition or the possession of the good-will of the world about him; that is, of such members of society as he is likely to have concerns with; and as a means of it, either their love or their esteem, or both: and as a fruit of it, of his being in the way to have the benefit of their spontaneous and gratuitous services. These may likewise be called the pleasures of good repute, the pleasures of honour, or the pleasures of the moral sanction.[12]

8. (6) The pleasures of power are the pleasures that accompany the persuasion of a man's being in a condition to dispose people, by means of their hopes and fears, to give him the benefit of their services: that is, by the hope of some service, or by the fear of some disservice, that he may be in the way to render them.

9. (7) The pleasures of piety are the pleasures that accompany the belief of a man's being in the acquisition or in possession of the good-will or favour of the Supreme Being: and as a fruit of it, of his being in a way of enjoying pleasures to be received by God's special appointment, either in this life, or in a life to come. These may also be called the pleasures of religion, the pleasures of a religious disposition, or the pleasures of the religious sanction.[13]

10. (8) The pleasures of benevolence are the pleasures resulting from the view of any pleasures supposed to be possessed by the beings who may be the objects of benevolence; to wit, the sensitive beings we are acquainted with; under which are commonly included, 1. The Supreme Being. 2. Human beings. 3. Other ani-

mals. These may also be called the pleasures of good-will, the pleasures of sympathy, or the pleasures of the benevolent or social affections.

11. (9) The pleasures of malevolence are the pleasures resulting from the view of any pain supposed to be suffered by the beings who may become the objects of malevolence: to wit, 1. Human beings. 2. Other animals. These may also be styled the pleasures of ill-will, the pleasures of the irascible appetite, the pleasures of antipathy, or the pleasures of the malevolent or dissocial affections.

12. (10) The pleasures of the memory are the pleasures which, after having enjoyed such and such pleasures, or even in some case after having suffered such and such pains, a man will now and then experience, at recollecting them exactly in the order and in the circumstances in which they were actually enjoyed or suffered. These derivative pleasures may of course be distinguished into as many species as there are of original perceptions, from whence they may be copied. They may also be styled pleasures of simple recollection.

13. (11) The pleasures of the imagination are the pleasures which may be derived from the contemplation of any such pleasures as may happen to be suggested by the memory, but in a different order, and accompanied by different groups of circumstances. These may accordingly be referred to any one of the three cardinal points of time, present, past, or future. It is evident they may admit of as many distinctions as those of the former class.

14. (12) The pleasures of expectation are the pleasures that result from the contemplation of any sort of pleasure, referred to time *future,* and accompanied with the sentiment of *belief.* These also may admit of the same distinctions.[14]

15. (13) The pleasures of association are the pleasures which certain objects or incidents may happen to afford, not of themselves, but merely in virtue of some association they have contracted in the mind with certain objects or incidents which are in themselves pleasurable. Such is the case, for instance, with the pleasure of skill, when afforded by such a set of incidents as compose a game of chess. This derives its pleasurable quality from its association partly with the pleasures of skill, as exercised in the production of incidents pleasurable of themselves: partly from its association with the plea-

sures of power. Such is the case also with the pleasure of good luck, when afforded by such incidents as compose the game of hazard, or any other game of chance, when played at for nothing. This derives its pleasurable quality from its association with one of the pleasures of wealth; to wit, with the pleasure of acquiring it.

16. (14) Farther on we shall see pains grounded upon pleasures; in like manner may we now see pleasures grounded upon pains. To the catalogue of pleasures may accordingly be added the pleasures of *relief:* or, the pleasures which a man experiences when, after he has been enduring a pain of any kind for a certain time, it comes to cease, or to abate. These may of course be distinguished into as many species as there are of pains: and may give rise to so many pleasures of memory, of imagination, and of expectation.

17. (1) Pains of privation are the pains that may result from the thought of not possessing in the time present any of the several kinds of pleasures. Pains of privation may accordingly be resolved into as many kinds as there are of pleasures to which they may correspond, and from the absence whereof they may be derived.

18. There are three sorts of pains which are only so many modifications of the several pains of privation. When the enjoyment of any particular pleasure happens to be particularly desired, but without any expectation approaching to assurance, the pain of privation which thereupon results takes a particular name, and is called the pain of *desire,* or of unsatisfied desire.

19. Where the enjoyment happens to have been looked for with a degree of expectation approaching to assurance, and that expectation is made suddenly to cease, it is called a pain of disappointment.

20. A pain of privation takes the name of a pain of regret in two cases: 1. Where it is grounded on the memory of a pleasure, which having been once enjoyed, appears not likely to be enjoyed again: 2. Where it is grounded on the idea of a pleasure, which was never actually enjoyed, nor perhaps so much as expected, but which might have been enjoyed (it is supposed,) had such or such a contingency happened, which, in fact, did not happen.

21. (2) The several pains of the senses seem to be as follows: 1. The pains of hunger and thirst: or the disagreeable sensations produced by the

want of suitable substances which need at times to be applied to the alimentary canal. 2. The pains of the taste: or the disagreeable sensations produced by the application of various substances to the palate, and other superior parts of the same canal. 3. The pains of the organ of smell: or the disagreeable sensations produced by the effluvia of various substances when applied to that organ. 4. The pains of the touch; or the disagreeable sensations produced by the application of various substances to the skin. 5. The simple pains of the hearing: or the disagreeable sensations excited in the organ of that sense by various kinds of sounds: independently (as before,) of association. 6. The simple pains of the sight: or the disagreeable sensations if any such there be, that may be excited in the organ of that sense by visible images, independent of the principle of association. 7.[15] The pains resulting from excessive heat or cold, unless these be referable to the touch. 8. The pains of disease: or the acute and uneasy sensations resulting from the several diseases and indispositions to which human nature is liable. 9. The pain of exertion, whether bodily or mental: or the uneasy sensation which is apt to accompany any intense effort, whether of mind or body.

22. (3)[16] The pains of awkardness are the pains which sometimes result from the unsuccessful endeavour to apply any particular instruments of enjoyment or security to their uses, or from the difficulty a man experiences in applying them.[17]

23. (4) The pains of enmity are the pains that may accompany the persuasion of a man's being obnoxious to the ill-will of such or such an assignable person or persons in particular: or, as the phrase is, of being upon ill terms with him or them: and, in consequence, of being obnoxious to certain pains of some sort or other, of which he may be the cause.

24. (5) The pains of an ill-name, are the pains that accompany the persuasion of a man's being obnoxious, or in a way to be obnoxious to the ill-will of the world about him. These may likewise be called the pains of ill-repute, the pains of dishonour, or the pains of the moral sanction.[18]

25. (6)[19] The pains of piety are the pains that accompany the belief of a man's being obnoxious to the displeasure of the Supreme Being: and in consequence to certain pains to be inflicted by his especial appointment, either in this life or in a life to come. These may also be called the pains of religion; the pains of a religious disposition; or the pains of the religious sanction. When the belief is looked upon as well-grounded, these pains are commonly called religious terrors; when looked upon as ill-grounded, superstitious terrors.[20]

26. (7) The pains of benevolence are the pains resulting from the view of any pains supposed to be endured by other beings. These may also be called the pains of good-will, of sympathy, or the pains of the benevolent or social affections.

27. (8) The pains of malevolence are the pains resulting from the view of any pains supposed to be enjoyed by any beings who happen to be the objects of a man's displeasure. These may also be styled the pains of ill-will, of antipathy, or the pains of the malevolent or dissocial affections.

28. (9) The pains of the memory may be grounded on every one of the above kinds, as well as pains of privation as of positive pains. These correspond exactly to the pleasures of the memory.

29. (10) The pains of the imagination may also be grounded on any one of the above kinds, as well as pains of privation as of positive pains: in other respects they correspond exactly to the pleasures of the imagination.

30. (11) The pains of expectation may be grounded on each one of the above kinds, as well of pains of privation as of positive pains. These may be also termed pains of apprehension.[21]

31. (12) The pains of association correspond exactly to the pleasures of association.

32. Of the above list there are certain pleasures and pains which suppose the existence of some pleasure or pain of some other person, to which the pleasure or pain of the person in question has regard: such pleasures and pains may be termed *extra-regarding*. Others do not suppose any such thing: these may be termed *self-regarding*.[22] The only pleasures and pains of the extra-regarding class are those of benevolence, and those of malevolence: all the rest are self-regarding.[23]

33. Of all these several sorts of pleasures and pains, there is scarce any one which is not liable, on more accounts than one, to come under the consideration of the law. Is an offence committed? it is the tendency which it has to destroy, in such or such persons, some of these pleasures, or to produce some of these pains, that consti-

tutes the mischief of it, and the ground for punishing it. It is the prospect of some of these pleasures, or of security from some of these pains, that constitutes the motive or temptation, it is the attainment of them that constitutes the profit of the offence. Is the offender to be punished? It can be only by the production of one or more of these pains, that the punishment can be inflicted.[24]

NOTES

1.   Note by the Author, July 1822.

To this denomination has of late been added, or substituted, the *greatest happiness* or *greatest felicity* principle: this for shortness, instead of saying at length *that principle* which states the greatest happiness of all those whose interest is in question, as being the right and proper, and only right and proper and universally desirable, end of human action: of human action in every situation, and in particular in that of a functionary or set of functionaries exercising the powers of Government. The word *utility* does not so clearly point to the ideas of *pleasure* and *pain* as the words *happiness* and *felicity* do: nor does it lead us to the consideration of the *number*, of the interests affected; to the *number*, as being the circumstance, which contributes, in the largest proportion, to the formation of the standard here in question: the *standard of right and wrong*, by which alone the propriety of human conduct, in every situation, can with propriety be tried. This want of a sufficiently manifest connexion between the ideas of *happiness* and *pleasure* on the one hand, and the idea of *utility* on the other, I have every now and then found operating, and with but too much efficiency, as a bar to the acceptance, that might otherwise have been given, to this principle.

2.   (Principle) The word principle is derived from the Latin *principium:* which seems to be compounded of the two words *primus,* first, or chief, and *cipium,* a termination which seems to be derived from *capio,* to take, as in *mancipium, municipium;* to which are analogous *auceps, forceps,* and others. It is a term of very vague and very extensive signification: it is applied to any thing which is conceived to serve as a foundation or beginning to any series of operations: in some cases, of physical operations; but of mental operations in the present case.

The principle here in question may be taken for an act of the mind; a sentiment; a sentiment of approbation; a sentiment which, when applied to an action, approves of its utility, as that quality of it by which the measure of approbation or disapprobation bestowed upon it ought to be governed.

3.   (Interest, etc.) Interest is one of those words, which not having any superior *genus,* cannot in the ordinary way be defined.

4.   'The principle of utility, (I have heard it said) is a dangerous principle: it is dangerous on certain occasions to consult it.' This is as much as to say, what? that it is not consonant to utility, to consult utility: in short, that it is *not* consulting it, to consult it.

Addition by the author, July 1822.

Not long after the publication of the Fragment on Government, anno 1776, in which, in the character of an all-comprehensive and all-commanding principle, the principle of *utility* was brought to view, one person by whom observation to the above effect was made was *Alexander Wedderburn,* at that time Attorney or Solicitor General, afterwards successively Chief Justice of the Common Pleas, and Chancellor of England, under the successive titles of Lord Loughborough and Earl of Rosslyn. It was made—not indeed in my hearing, but in the hearing of a person by whom it was almost immediately communicated to me. So far from being self-contradictory, it was a shrewd and perfectly true one. By that distinguished functionary, the state of the Government was thoroughly understood: by the obscure individual, at that time not so much as supposed to be so: his disquisitions had not been as yet applied, with any thing like a comprehensive view, to the field of Constitutional Law, nor therefore to those features of the English Government, by which the greatest happiness of the ruling *one* with or without that of a favoured few, are now so plainly seen to be the only ends to which the course of it has at any time been directed. The *principle of utility* was an appellative, at that time employed—employed by me, as it had been by others, to designate that which, in a more perspicuous and instructive manner, may, as above, be designated by the name of the *greatest happiness principle.* 'This principle (said Wedderburn) is a dangerous one.' Saying so, he said that which, to a certain extent, is strictly true: a principle, which lays down, as the only *right* and justifiable end of Government, the greatest happiness of the greatest number—how can it be denied to be a dangerous one? Dangerous it unquestionably is, to every government which has for its *actual* end or object, the greatest happiness of a certain *one,* with or without the addition of some comparatively small number of others, whom it is matter of pleasure or accommodation to him to admit, each of them, to a share in the concern, on the footing of so many junior partners. *Dangerous* it therefore really was, to the interest—the sinister interest—of all those functionaries, himself included, whose interest it was, to maximize delay, vexation, and expense, in judicial and other modes of procedure, for the sake of the profit, extractable out of the expense. In a Government which had for its end in view the greatest happiness of the greatest number, Alexander Wedderburn might have been Attorney General and then Chancellor: but he would not have been Attorney General with 15,000 a year, nor Chancellor, with a peerage, with a veto upon all justice, with 25,000 a year, and with 500 sinecures at his disposal, under the name of Ecclesiastical Benefices, besides *et ceteras.*

5.   *Sanctio,* in Latin, was used to signify the *act of binding,* and, by a common grammatical transition, *any thing which serves to bind a man:* to wit, to the observance of such or such a mode of conduct. According to a Latin grammarian, the import of the word is derived by rather a far-fetched process (such as those commonly are, and in a great measure indeed must be, by which intellectual ideas are derived from sensible ones) from the word *sanguis,* blood: because, among the Romans, with a view to inculcate into the people a persuasion that such or such a mode of conduct would be rendered obligatory upon a man by the force of what I call the religious sanction (that is, that he would be 'made to suffer by the extraordinary interposition of some superior being, if he failed to observe the mode of conduct in question) certain ceremonies were contrived by the priests: in the course of which ceremonies the blood of victims was made use of.

A sanction then is a source of obligatory powers or *motives:* that is, of *pains* and pleasures; which, according as they are connected with such or such modes of conduct, operate, and are indeed the only things which can operate, as *motives.* See Ch. X (Motives).

6. (Moral Sanction). Better termed *popular,* as more directly indicative of its constituent cause; as likewise of its relation to the more common phrase *public opinion,* in French *opinion publique,* the name there given to that tutelary power, of which of late so much is said, and by which so much is done. The latter appellation is however unhappy and inexpressive; since if *opinion* is material, it is only in virtue of the influence it exercises over action, through the medium of the affections and the will.

7. A suffering conceived to befall a man by the immediate act of God, as above, is often, for shortness sake, called a *judgment:* instead of saying, a suffering inflicted on him in consequence of a special judgment formed, and resolution thereupon taken, by the Deity.

8. These circumstances have since been denominated *elements* or *dimensions* of *value* in a pleasure or a pain.

Not long after the publication of the first edition, the following memoriter verses were framed, in the view of lodging more effectually, in the memory, these points, on which the whole fabric of morals and legislation may be seen to rest.

> *Intense, long, certain, speedy, fruitful, pure—*
> Such marks in *pleasures* and in *pains* endure.
> Such pleasures seek, if *private* be thy end:
> If it be *public,* wide let them *extend.*
> Such *pains* avoid, whichever be thy view:
> If pains *must* come, let them *extend* to few.

9. The catalogue here given, is what seemed to be a complete list of the several simple pleasures and pains of which human nature is susceptible: insomuch, that if, upon any occasion whatsoever, a man feels pleasure or pain, it is either referable at once to some one or other of these kinds, or resolvable into such as are. It might perhaps have been a satisfaction to the reader, to have seen an analytical view of the subject, taken upon an exhaustive plan, for the purpose of demonstrating the catalogue to be what it purports to be, a complete one. The catalogue is in fact the result of such an analysis; which, however, I thought it better to discard at present, as being of too metaphysical a cast, and not strictly within the limits of this design. See Ch. XIII (Cases unmeet) Par. 2. Note.

10. There are also pleasures of novelty, excited by the appearance of new ideas: these are pleasures of the imagination. See infra 13.

11. For instance, the pleasure of being able to gratify the sense of hearing, by singing, or performing upon any musical instrument. The pleasure thus obtained, is a thing superadded to, and perfectly distinguishable from, that which a man enjoys from hearing another person perform in the same manner.

12. See Ch. III (Sanctions).

13. See Ch. III (Sanctions).

14. In contradistinction to these, all other pleasures may be termed pleasures of *enjoyment.*

15. The pleasure of the sexual sense seems to have no positive pain to correspond to it: it has only a pain of privation, or pain of the mental class, the pain of unsatisfied desire. If any positive pain of body result from the want of such indulgence, it belongs to the head of pains of disease.

16. The pleasures of novelty have no positive pains corresponding to them. The pain which a man experiences when he is in the condition of not knowing what to do with himself, that pain, which in French is expressed by a single word *ennui,* is a pain of privation: a pain resulting from the absence, not only of all the pleasures of novelty, but of all kinds of pleasure whatsoever.

The pleasures of wealth have also no positive pains corresponding to them: the only pains opposed to them are pains of privation. If any positive pains result from the want of wealth, they are referable to some other class of positive pains; principally to those of the senses. From the want of food, for instance, result the pains of hunger; from the want of clothing, the pains of cold; and so forth.

17. It may be a question, perhaps, whether this be a positive pain of itself, or whether it be nothing more than a pain of privation, resulting from the consciousness of a want of skill. It is, however, but a question of words, nor does it matter which way it be determined.

18. In as far as a man's fellow-creatures are supposed to be determined by any event not to regard him with any degree of esteem or *good* will, or to regard him with a less degree of esteem or *good* will than they would otherwise; not to do him any sorts of *good* offices, or not to do him so many *good* offices as they would otherwise; the pain resulting from such consideration may be reckoned a pain of privation: as far as they are supposed to regard him with such a degree of aversion or disesteem as to be disposed to do him positive *ill* offices, it may be reckoned a positive pain. The pain of privation, and the positive pain, in this case run one into another indistinguishably.

19. There seem to be no positive pains to correspond to the pleasures of power. The pains that a man may feel from the want or the loss of power, in as far as power is distinguished from all other sources of pleasure, seem to be nothing more than pains of privation.

20. The positive pains of piety, and the pains of privation, opposed to the pleasures of piety, run one into another in the same manner as the positive pains of enmity, or of an ill name, do with respect to the pains of privation, opposed to the pleasures of amity, and those of a good name. If what is apprehended at the hands of God is barely the not receiving pleasure, the pain is of the privative class: if, moreover, actual pain be apprehended, it is of the class of positive pains.

21. In contradistinction to these, all other pains may be termed pains of *sufferance.*

22. See Ch. X (Motives).

23. By this means the pleasures and pains of amity may be the more clearly distinguished from those of benevolence: and on the other hand, those of enmity from those of malevolence. The pleasures and pains of amity and enmity are of the self-regarding cast: those of benevolence and malevolence of the extra-regarding.

24. It would be a matter not only of curiosity, but of some use, to exhibit a catalogue of the several complex pleasures and pains, analyzing them at the same time into the several simple ones, of which they are respectively composed. But such a disquisition would take up too much room to be admitted here. A short specimen, however, for the purpose of illustration, can hardly be dispensed with.

The pleasures taken in at the eye and ear are generally very complex. The pleasures of a country scene, for instance, consist commonly, amongst others, of the following pleasures:

I. Pleasures of the senses

1. The simple pleasures of sight, excited by the perception of agreeable colours and figures, green fields, waving foliage, glistening water, and the like.

2. The simple pleasures of the ear, excited by the perceptions of the chirping of birds, the murmuring of waters, the rustling of the wind among the trees.

3. The pleasures of the smell, excited by the perceptions of the fragrance of flowers, of new-mown hay, or other vegetable substances, in the first stages of fermentation.

4. The agreeable inward sensation, produced by a brisk circulation of the blood, and the ventilation of it in the lungs by a pure air, such as that in the country frequently is in comparison of that which is breathed in towns.

II. Pleasures of the imagination produced by association

1. The idea of the plenty, resulting from the possession of the objects that are in view, and of the happiness arising from it.

2. The idea of the innocence and happiness of the birds, sheep, cattle, dogs, and other gentle or domestic animals.

3. The idea of the constant flow of health, supposed to be enjoyed by all these creatures: a notion which is apt to result from the occasional flow of health enjoyed by the supposed spectator.

4. The idea of gratitude, excited by the contemplation of the all-powerful and beneficent Being, who is looked up to as the author of these blessings.

These four last are all of them, in some measure at least, pleasures of sympathy.

The depriving a man of this group of pleasures is one of the evils apt to result from imprisonment; whether produced by illegal violence, or in the way of punishment, by appointment of the laws.

5. *BRAVE NEW WORLD*

Aldous Huxley

CHAPTER SEVENTEEN

"Art, science—you seem to have paid a fairly high price for your happiness," said the Savage, when they were alone. "Anything else?"

"Well, religion, of course," replied the Controller. "There used to be something called God —before the Nine Years' War. But I was forgetting; you know all about God, I suppose."

"Well . . ." The Savage hesitated. He would have liked to say something about solitude, about night, about the mesa lying pale under the moon, about the precipice, the plunge into shadowy darkness, about death. He would have liked to speak; but there were no words. Not even in Shakespeare.

The Controller, meanwhile, had crossed to the other side of the room and was unlocking a large safe let into the wall between the bookshelves. The heavy door swung open. Rummaging in the darkness within, "It's a subject," he said, "that has always had a great interest for me." He pulled out a thick black volume. "You've never read this, for example."

The Savage took it. "*The Holy Bible, containing the Old and New Testaments,*" he read aloud from the title-page.

"Nor this." It was a small book and had lost its cover.

"*The Imitation of Christ.*"

"Nor this." He handed out another volume.

"*The Varieties of Religious Experience.* By William James."

"And I've got plenty more," Mustapha Mond continued, resuming his seat. "A whole collection of pornographic old books. God in the safe and Ford on the shelves." He pointed with a laugh to his avowed library—to the shelves of books, the racks full of reading-machine bobbins and sound-track rolls.

"But if you know about God, why don't you tell them?" asked the Savage indignantly. "Why don't you give them these books about God?"

"For the same reason as we don't give them *Othello:* they're old; they're about God hundreds of years ago. Not about God now."

"But God doesn't change."

"Men do, though."

"What difference does that make?"

"All the difference in the world," said Mustapha Mond. He got up again and walked to the safe. "There was a man called Cardinal Newman," he said. "A cardinal," he exclaimed parenthetically, "was a kind of Arch-Community-Songster."

" 'I Pandulph, of fair Milan, cardinal,' I've read about them in Shakespeare."

Chapter Seventeen (pp. 276–288) from *Brave New World* by Aldous Huxley. Copyright 1932, 1960 by Aldous Huxley. Reprinted by permission of Harper & Row, Publishers, Inc.

"Of course you have. Well, as I was saying, there was a man called Cardinal Newman. Ah, here's the book." He pulled it out. "And while I'm about it I'll take this one too. It's by a man called Maine de Biran. He was a philosopher, if you know what that was."

"A man who dreams of fewer things than there are in heaven and earth," said the Savage promptly.

"Quite so. I'll read you one of the things he *did* dream of in a moment. Meanwhile, listen to what this old Arch-Community-Songster said." He opened the book at the place marked by a slip of paper and began to read. " 'We are not our own any more than what we possess is our own. We did not make ourselves, we cannot be supreme over ourselves. We are not our own masters. We are God's property. Is it not our happiness thus to view the matter? Is it any happiness or any comfort, to consider that we *are* our own? It may be thought so by the young and prosperous. These may think it a great thing to have everything, as they suppose, their own way —to depend on no one—to have to think of nothing out of sight, to be without the irksomeness of continual acknowledgment, continual prayer, continual reference of what they do to the will of another. But as time goes on, they, as all men, will find that independence was not made for man—that it is an unnatural state— will do for a while, but will not carry us on safely to the end . . .' " Mustapha Mond paused, put down the first book and, picking up the other, turned over the pages. "Take this, for example," he said, and in his deep voice once more began to read: " 'A man grows old; he feels in himself that radical sense of weakness, of listlessness, of discomfort, which accompanies the advance of age; and, feeling thus, imagines himself merely sick, lulling his fears with the notion that this distressing condition is due to some particular cause, from which, as from an illness, he hopes to recover. Vain imaginings! That sickness is old age; and a horrible disease it is. They say that it is the fear of death and of what comes after death that makes men turn to religion as they advance in years. But my own experience has given me the conviction that, quite apart from any such terrors or imaginings, the religious sentiment tends to develop as we grow older; to develop because, as the passions grow calm, as the fancy and sensibilities are less excited and less ex-

citable, our reason becomes less troubled in its working, less obscured by the images, desires and distractions, in which it used to be absorbed; whereupon God emerges as from behind a cloud; our soul feels, sees, turns towards the source of all light; turns naturally and inevitably; for now that all that gave to the world of sensations its life and charm has begun to leak away from us, now that phenomenal existence is no more bolstered up by impressions from within or from without, we feel the need to lean on something that abides, something that will never play us false—a reality, an absolute and everlasting truth. Yes, we inevitably turn to God; for this religious sentiment is of its nature so pure, so delightful to the soul that experiences it, that it makes up to us for all our other losses.' " Mustapha Mond shut the book and leaned back in his chair. "One of the numerous things in heaven and earth that these philosophers didn't dream about was this" (he waved his hand), "us, the modern world. 'You can only be independent of God while you've got youth and prosperity; independence won't take you safely to the end.' Well, we've now got youth and prosperity right up to the end. What follows? Evidently, that we can be independent of God. 'The religious sentiment will compensate us for all our losses.' But there aren't any losses for us to compensate; religious sentiment is superfluous. And why should we go hunting for a substitute for youthful desires, when youthful desires never fail? A substitute for distractions, when we go on enjoying all the old fooleries to the very last? What need have we of repose when our minds and bodies continue to delight in activity? of consolation, when we have *soma?* of something immovable, when there is the social order?"

"Then you think there is no God?"

"No, I think there quite probably is one."

"Then why? . . ."

Mustapha Mond checked him. "But he manifests himself in different ways to different men. In premodern times he manifested himself as the being that's described in these books. Now . . ."

"How does he manifest himself now?" asked the Savage.

"Well, he manifests himself as an absence; as though he weren't there at all."

"That's your fault."

"Call it the fault of civilization. God isn't compatible with machinery and scientific medicine and universal happiness. You must make your choice. Our civilization has chosen machinery and medicine and happiness. That's why I have to keep these books locked up in the safe. They're smut. People would be shocked if . . ."

The Savage interrupted him. "But isn't it *natural* to feel there's a God?"

"You might as well ask if it's natural to do up one's trousers with zippers," said the Controller sarcastically. "You remind me of another of those old fellows called Bradley. He defined philosophy as the finding of bad reason for what one believes by instinct. As if one believed anything by instinct! One believes things because one has been conditioned to believe them. Finding bad reasons for what one believes for other bad reasons—that's philosophy. People believe in God because they've been conditioned to believe in God."

"But all the same," insisted the Savage, "it is natural to believe in God when you're alone—quite alone, in the night, thinking about death . . ."

"But people never are alone now," said Mustapha Mond. "We make them hate solitude; and we arrange their lives so that it's almost impossible for them ever to have it."

The Savage nodded gloomily. At Malpais he had suffered because they had shut him out from the communal activities of the pueblo, in civilized London he was suffering because he could never escape from those communal activities, never be quietly alone.

"Do you remember that bit in *King Lear?*" said the Savage at last. " 'The gods are just and of our pleasant vices make instruments to plague us; the dark and vicious place where thee he got cost him his eyes,' and Edmund answers—you remember, he's wounded, he's dying—'Thou hast spoken right; 'tis true. The wheel has come full circle; I am here.' What about that now? Doesn't there seem to be a God managing things, punishing, rewarding?"

"Well, does there?" questioned the Controller in his turn. "You can indulge in any number of pleasant vices with a freemartin and run no risks of having your eyes put out by your son's mistress. 'The wheel has come full circle; I am here.' But where would Edmund be nowadays?

Sitting in a pneumatic chair, with his arm round a girl's waist, sucking away at his sex-hormone chewing-gum and looking at the feelies. The gods are just. No doubt. But their code of law is dictated, in the last resort, by the people who organize society; Providence takes its cue from men."

"Are you sure?" asked the Savage. "Are you quite sure that the Edmund in that pneumatic chair hasn't been just as heavily punished as the Edmund who's wounded and bleeding to death? The gods are just. Haven't they used his pleasant vices as an instrument to degrade him?"

"Degrade him from what position? As a happy, hard-working, goods-consuming citizen he's perfect. Of course, if you choose some other standard than ours, then perhaps you might say he was degraded. But you've got to stick to one set of postulates. You can't play Electro-magnetic Golf according to the rules of Centrifugal Bumble-puppy."

"But value dwells not in particular will," said the Savage. "It holds his estimate and dignity as well wherein 'tis precious of itself as in the prizer."

"Come, come," protested Mustapha Mond, "that's going rather far, isn't it?"

"If you allowed yourselves to think of God, you wouldn't allow yourselves to be degraded by pleasant vices. You'd have a reason for bearing things patiently, for doing things with courage. I've seen it with the Indians."

"I'm sure you have," said Mustapha Mond. "But then we aren't Indians. There isn't any need for a civilized man to bear anything that's seriously unpleasant. And as for doing things—Ford forbid that he should get the idea into his head. It would upset the whole social order if men started doing things on their own.

"What about self-denial, then? If you had a God, you'd have a reason for self-denial."

"But industrial civilization is only possible when there's no self-denial. Self-indulgence up to the very limits imposed by hygiene and economics. Otherwise the wheels stop turning."

"You'd have a reason for chastity!" said the Savage, blushing a little as he spoke the words.

"But chastity means passion, chastity means neurasthenia. And passion and neurasthenia mean instability. And instability means the end of civilization. You can't have a lasting civilization without plenty of pleasant vices."

"But God's the reason for everything noble and fine and heroic. If you had a God . . ."

"My dear young friend," said Mustapha Mond, "civilization has absolutely no need of nobility or heroism. These things are symptoms of political inefficiency. In a properly organized society like ours, nobody has any opportunities for being noble or heroic. Conditions have got to be thoroughly unstable before the occasion can arise. Where there are wars, where there are divided allegiances, where there are temptations to be resisted, objects of love to be fought for or defended—there, obviously, nobility and heroism have some sense. But there aren't any wars nowadays. The greatest care is taken to prevent you from loving any one too much. There's no such thing as a divided allegiance; you're so conditioned that you can't help doing what you ought to do. And what you ought to do is on the whole so pleasant, so many of the natural impulses are allowed free play, that there really aren't any temptations to resist. And if ever, by some unlucky chance, anything unpleasant should somehow happen, why, there's always *soma* to give you a holiday from the facts. And there's always *soma* to calm your anger, to reconcile you to your enemies, to make you patient and long-suffering. In the past you could only accomplish these things by making a great effort and after years of hard moral training. Now, you swallow two or three half-gramme tablets, and there you are. Anybody can be virtuous now. You can carry at least half your morality about in a bottle. Christianity without tears—that's what *soma* is."

"But the tears are necessary. Don't you remember what Othello said? 'If after every tempest came such calms, may the winds blow till they have wakened death.' There's a story one of the old Indians used to tell us, about the Girl of Mátaski. The young men who wanted to marry her had to do a morning's hoeing in her garden. It seemed easy; but there were flies and mosquitoes, magic ones. Most of the young men simply couldn't stand the biting and stinging. But the one that could—he got the girl."

"Charming! But in civilized countries," said the Controller, "you can have girls without hoeing for them; and there aren't any flies or mosquitoes to sting you. We got rid of them all centuries ago."

The Savage nodded, frowning. "You got rid of them. Yes, that's just like you. Getting rid of everything unpleasant instead of learning to put up with it. Whether 'tis better in the mind to suffer the slings and arrows of outrageous fortune, or to take arms against a sea of troubles and by opposing end them . . . But you don't do either. Neither suffer nor oppose. You just abolish the slings and arrows. It's too easy."

He was suddenly silent, thinking of his mother. In her room on the thirty-seventh floor, Linda had floated in a sea of singing lights and perfumed caresses—floated away, out of space, out of time, out of the prison of her memories, her habits, her aged and bloated body. And Tomakin, ex-Director of Hatcheries and Conditioning, Tomakin was still on holiday—on holiday from humiliation and pain, in a world where he could not hear those words, that derisive laughter, could not see that hideous face, feel those moist and flabby arms round his neck, in a beautiful world . . .

"What you need," the Savage went on, "is something *with* tears for a change. Nothing costs enough here."

("Twelve and a half million dollars," Henry Foster had protested when the Savage told him that. "Twelve and a half million—that's what the new Conditioning Centre cost. Not a cent less.")

"Exposing what is mortal and unsure to all that fortune, death and danger dare, even for an eggshell. Isn't there something in that?" he asked, looking up at Mustapha Mond. "Quite apart from God—though of course God would be a reason for it. Isn't there something in living dangerously?"

"There's a great deal in it," the Controller replied. "Men and women must have their adrenals stimulated from time to time."

"What?" questioned the Savage, uncomprehending.

"It's one of the conditions of perfect health. That's why we've made the V.P.S. treatments compulsory."

"V.P.S.?"

"Violent Passion Surrogate. Regularly once a month. We flood the whole system with adrenin. It's the complete physiological equivalent of fear and rage. All the tonic effects of murdering Desdemona and being murdered by Othello, without any of the inconveniences."

"But I like the inconveniences."

"We don't," said the Controller. "We prefer to do things comfortably."

"But I don't want comfort. I want God, I want poetry, I want real danger, I want freedom, I want goodness. I want sin."

"In fact," said Mustapha Mond, "you're claiming the right to be unhappy."

"All right then," said the Savage defiantly, "I'm claiming the right to be unhappy."

"Not to mention the right to grow old and ugly and impotent; the right to have syphilis and cancer; the right to have too little to eat; the right to be lousy; the right to live in constant apprehension of what may happen to-morrow; the right to catch typhoid; the right to be tortured by unspeakable pains of every kind."

There was a long silence.

"I claim them all," said the Savage at last.

Mustapha Mond shrugged his shoulders. "You're welcome," he said.

6.   MILL'S THEORY OF VALUE

Dorothy Mitchell

Mill's theory of value has been widely attacked. It has been claimed that there is no connection between what is desired, and what is desirable, that his view that some pleasures are better than others is incompatible with his hedonism, and that he commits the fallacy of composition. I shall defend his theory against all these charges and argue that it is both consistent and elegant. The criticism that must be made is that the predicates "is desirable" and "is a better pleasure than" would have an unqualified use only if there were a greater uniformity in what we want and what we enjoy than there seems to be.

I

The essence of Mill's theory of value is the identification of the intrinsically good as the intrinsically desirable, or as that which is desirable for its own sake. The instrumentally good is that which is desirable, not for its own sake, but as a means.

Mill claims that pleasure or happiness is the only thing desirable for its own sake. Pleasure is thus the only good, since it is the only thing desirable for its own sake. If anything other that

pleasure, or happiness, could be shown to be intrinsically desirable, that too would have been shown to be intrinsically good. If Mill is mistaken in thinking that only pleasure or happiness is intrinsically desirable, his account of intrinsic goodness will not have been refuted, but only his claim that pleasure is the only intrinsic good.

Mill holds that pleasure can be shown to be intrinsically good, or intrinsically desirable, but not by "reasoning." ". . . questions of ultimate ends do not admit of proof in the ordinary acceptation of the term. To be incapable of proof by reasoning is common to all first principles. . . ."[1] That is, ultimate principles cannot be proved by being derived from still more ultimate principles. Things which are instrumentally good can be proved to be instrumentally good by showing that they are good as means towards some end, but this method of proof is not available for showing that something is intrinsically good. "The medical art is proved to be good by its conducing to health, but how is it possible to prove that health is good?"[2] To try to show that something is intrinsically good, by showing that it is a good means towards some end, is to fail to understand the distinction between intrinsic and instrumental good.

Mill suggests that we can find out what is desirable for its own sake by finding out what is

From Dorothy Mitchell, "Mill's Theory of Value," *Theoria,* Vol. 36 (1970), pp. 100–115. Reprinted by permission of the editor of *Theoria.*

desired for its own sake. "The only proof capable of being given that an object is visible is that people actually see it, the only proof that a sound is audible is that people hear it, and so of the other sources of our experience . . . the sole evidence it is possible to produce that anything is desirable is that people actually do desire it."[3] Mill's account of the good as the desirable has been allowed because "desirable" has been allowed as a "value term,"[4] but Mill's empirical method for finding out just which things are intrinsically good has not been allowed to pass. G. E. Moore attacks Mill's method on two counts. First, he claims that " 'desirable' does not mean 'able to be desired' as 'visible' means 'able to be seen.' The desirable means simply what ought to be desired; just as the detestable means not what can be, but what ought to be detested and the damnable what deserves to be damned."[5] Secondly, he claims that some desires are bad desires.[6] His argument seems to be that some desires are for things which ought not to be desired, and that therefore not everything which is desired can be desirable, or good. Each of these objections is misconceived.

The second objection misses the point, through failing to distinguish between the morally good and the intrinsically good. (Moore insists on this distinction in propounding his own theory.) Mill does not claim that all ends, desirable in themselves, ought, morally speaking, to be sought after. He claims that the readiness to sacrifice his own happiness to procure the happiness of another is the highest virtue that can be found in man.[7] Moreover, he insists that "the happiness which forms the utilitarian standard of what is right in conduct is not the agent's own happiness but that of all concerned."[8] It is clear then that the criteria for intrinsic goodness and moral rightness are different: for something to be intrinsically good is for it to be desirable for its own sake, for an act to be right is for it to be optimific. For Mill, judgements of moral rightness and wrongness concern the consequences of acts but judgements of intrinsic value do not. It follows that it may be immoral to seek certain ends which are good in themselves. According to Mill, pleasure is intrinsically good, but it would be immoral for a man to seek pleasure which could be obtained only at the cost of pain for others. Sometimes the achieving of an intrinsic good may be incompatible with the achieving of the greatest possible amount of good. Morally speaking, the right thing to do in such circumstances is the act which will achieve the greatest possible amount of good. Mill knows that some goods may have to be given up in order to achieve the greatest possible good: this is apparent in his discussion of the way a utilitarian should bring up his children. Education should be used "to establish in the mind of every individual an indissoluble association between his own happiness and the good of the whole . . . so that . . . he may be unable to conceive the possibility of happiness to himself consistently with conduct opposed to the general good."[9] Utilitarian morality requires that some of the chances of happiness that these children have are to be sacrificed in the interest of achieving the greatest good of the greatest number. Clearly, Mill does not equate the morally good and the intrinsically good. So, one cannot attack his account of the intrinsically good by showing that something which is intrinsically good on his account is not morally good.

Moore's other objection is that Mill has "attempted to establish the identity of good with the desired, by confusing the proper sense of 'desirable,' in which it denotes that which it is good to desire, with the sense it would bear if it were analogous to such words as 'visible.' If 'desirable' is to be identical with 'good' then it must bear one sense: and if it is to be identical with 'desired,' then it must bear quite another sense."[10]

Mill however does not say that "desirable" means "able to be desired." Unfortunately, he does not give an account of the desirable, beyond saying that the only way to establish that something is desirable is to show that it is desired, just as the only way to establish that something is visible is to show that people can see it. With modifications, this claim can be defended.

First, "desirable" does not mean "which ought to be desired" if this means "which it is good to desire," although it may mean "which ought to be desired" in the sense of "which you would expect to be desired." So, if "desirable" is explicated as "which ought to be desired" it has not been shown that "desirable" is an irreducibly evaluative, as opposed to factual, term. To describe a house as a desirable family house is to claim that it is the sort of house one would expect family men to want, not, that it is the sort of house which morally speaking, people ought to want.

There are important parallels between "visible" and "audible" on the one hand, and "desirable" on the other. One is that things which are visible, audible or desirable, are visible, audible, or desirable, relative to a certain group. Normally, to say that something is visible is to say that it could be seen by men without the use of optical instruments. Normally, to say that something is audible is to say that it can be heard by men without the use of amplifying equipment. However, it is also possible to say that something is audible only to houseflies, or visible only through a telescope. Similarly, what is desirable, is desirable relative to a certain group. When it is said that an undesirable family has moved into the neighbourhood, this does not mean that the family is undesirable from its own point of view—it means that the family is undesirable from the point of view of the established residents. Likewise, if an insurgents' manual states that it is desirable that all prisoners should be shot, this does not mean that it is desirable from the point of view of the prisoners that they should be shot.

A second parallel is that the visible, audible, or desirable will be seen, heard, or desired only if certain conditions are fulfilled. For instance, things which are visible to men will be seen only by men whose eyes are open, who are not blind, etc. I suspect that it would be very difficult indeed to list the conditions under which the audible will be heard and the visible seen. Because certain conditions have to be fulfilled before a visible thing will be seen, it is possible for a thing to be visible without ever having been seen. Likewise, it is possible for a desirable thing never to have been desired. A desirable house may fail to be desired if no one knows that it exists. For an existing desirable thing to be desired, someone must know that it exists. Of course, not only things which actually exist are desirable; a life totally devoid of pain and totally given over to enjoyment may be highly desirable. One condition then that must be fulfilled before the desirable will be desired, is that the desirable must be known or believed to exist, or considered possible, or at least conceived of. I shall call this the "knowledge condition."

The claim that the desirable will not necessarily be desired is compatible with Mill's claim that one can find out what is desirable by finding out what is desired, but it is not compatible with his claim that one can find out everything that is desirable by finding out everything that is desired. Since there may be desirable objects and states of affairs that no one knows about or has even conceived of, I consider that, leaving aside all other objections, Mill has not shown that pleasure is the only good. This, of course, does not show that his identification of the good as the desirable is mistaken.

The knowledge condition must be fulfilled before the desirable will be desired. It does not follow that if the knowledge condition is fulfilled the desirable will be desired, since the knowledge condition is not the only condition that has to be fulfilled. Suppose a desirable family house came on the market at a time when no one wanted it. Perhaps at the time every family man had a house he was satisfied with. If that were so, one could not conclude that the house was not desirable, although if no one wanted the house because its rooms were too small, one could conclude that it was not desirable. The difference is that in the second case there was a deficiency in the house which made it not desirable, relative to the class of family men, that is, there was something about the house which made it not the sort of house that such men want, when they want a family-house for the usual purposes.

A desirable family house is the sort of house you would expect a family man to want, although you would not necessarily expect any other sort of person to want it. Moreover, you would not expect every family man to want it, since many men are already satisfied with the houses they have. A desirable family house is the sort of house a family man would want if he was looking for a house for the normal domestic purposes. To put it another way, a desirable family house is the sort of house a man who had the usual interest in family houses, and who was looking for a house to satisfy that interest, would want. The formulation seems to me to be particularly significant, since "good" used instrumentally, means something like "capable of satisfying the usual interest in such things". If this formulation is right, then the conditions under which a man will desire the (instrumentally) desirable are the same as the conditions under which a man will desire the (instrumentally) good. I see this fact as supporting, in an unexpected way, Mill's identification of the good and the desirable.

To sum up, the logic of "desirable" is like that of "visible" and "audible" in at least these respects, that what is desirable is so relative to a particular group, that something can be desirable without being desired, and that certain conditions have to be fulfilled before the desirable will be desired.

There is one important difference. As Gauthier points out, the invisible cannot be seen but the undesirable may be desired.[11] If this is so, how can Mill use the fact that x is desired as evidence for x's desirability? Mill's theory has to be qualified here, but the qualification is minor and in character with other elements in his theory.

We make use of the distinction between *being* desirable and *seeming* desirable. For instance, someone may say that he would like to get into the rat race, and someone else reply that the rat race only seems desirable to those who are not in it, that is, to those who do not know what it is like. Or someone may speak enthusiastically about the life of a shepherd on a Greek island, and someone else reply "If you knew what it would be like you wouldn't find the prospect so desirable" or "If you knew what it would be like you wouldn't want that". The contrast between "being desirable" and "seeming desirable" arises because it is possible to desire something without fully knowing the nature of what it is one desires. Something is only really desirable, relative to a certain group, if members of the group would still want it if they were fully acquainted with its nature. I conclude that Mill will not obtain a list of intrinsic goods by finding out what things people want, not as a means to ends, but for their own sake. A list of "goods" obtained in this way might well include things which are only apparent goods, that is, such a list could well include things which only *seem* desirable. Speaking only of the intrinsically good or the intrinsically desirable, I suggest that a desirable state of affairs is a state of affairs that someone would desire, given that he had full knowledge of its nature. It follows that the way to find out what is desirable is to find out, not what it is that people desire, but what it is that people, *who know what it is that they are desiring,*

desire to get, and to have. This proviso is consistent with the rest of Mill's theory; he uses a similar proviso in setting out the method of distinguishing between the intrinsically good and the intrinsically better.[12]

One can discover some of the things that are desirable by asking those who know the nature of things what they desire. However, this method cannot guarantee that one has discovered everything that is desirable since not every desirable object need be desired, and will not be desired if the appropriate conditions are not fulfilled.

One final criticism must be made. Mill would agree that what is desirable relative to a certain group; the group he is interested in is that of men. However, Mill seems to assume a uniformity of desires which may not exist. Can one assume, as he seems to, that all people, or even all knowledgeable and experienced people, will have the same desires? Unless there is this uniformity of desire amongst those who know what it is that they are desiring, the non-relational sounding predicate "desirable" will be misleading. Unless this uniformity exists it is misleading to make statements such as "Peace is desirable". From the point of view of most of us, peace may be desirable, but some may want war, and know what it is that they are wanting. Of course, some may want war as a means to some other end they have, but could there not be some who want it for its own sake? If this is so, then it is much more accurate to say, not that peace is desirable, but that peace is desirable from the point of view of some and not desirable from the point of view of others. If one is to use the utilitarian calculus, one must have accurate information; the utilitarian should accurately inform himself of the exact number of people to whom peace is a good, and the exact number of people to whom peace is not a good, and then proceed with his calculations.

II

Mill's basic position is that the intrinsically good is the intrinsically desirable, and that the only thing that is intrinsically desirable, is pleasure. He insists, however, that some pleasures are better than others: "there is no known Epicurean theory of life which does not assign to the pleasures of the intellect, of the feelings and imagination, and of the moral sentiments, a much higher value as pleasures than to those of mere sensation".[13] The claim that these pleasures are better in "their intrinsic nature" and that "quality" as well as "quantity" is to be taken into account in evaluating pleasures has been thought to be incompatible with his hedonism. Moore argues that "If we really mean 'Pleasure alone is good as an end', then we must agree with Bentham that 'Quantity of pleasure being equal, pushpin is as good as poetry'."[14] Illustrating his point by an analogy, Moore argues ". . .if colour is our only possible end, as Mill says pleasure is, then there can be no possible reason for preferring one colour to another, red for instance to blue, except that this one is more of a colour than the other. Yet the opposite of this is what Mill is attempting to hold with regard to pleasures. ". . .if you say, as Mill does, that quality of pleasure is to be taken into account, then you are no longer holding that pleasure alone is good as an end, since you imply that something else . . . is also good as an end."[15] Moore is surely right in holding that the consistent hedonist cannot introduce some further criterion of intrinsic goodness, over and above pleasantness. I shall argue that Mill does not do so, and does not need to do so.

Note that Mill's point is not that some pleasures are morally better than others. His claim is that the intellectual pleasures are better as pleasures, not only in quantity, as Bentham claimed, but in quality.

Moore's conclusion is that the consistent hedonist can say that one pleasure is better than another only if he means, that there is more of it. This seems also to be Bentham's assumption and Mill rejects it. He does not introduce some further criterion other than pleasantness to evaluate pleasures by, but he rejects as inadequate Bentham's claim that "the value of a pleasure or pain considered by itself, will be greater or less, according to the four following circumstances:

1. Its intensity,
2. Its duration,
3. Its certainty or uncertainty,
4. Its propinquity or remoteness."[16]

These considerations may be relevant in measuring amounts of pleasure, if that is possible, but amount, as Bentham's scale measures it, is not relevant in assessing pleasures as more or less pleasurable than other pleasures. Mill's point is that "the greater pleasure" does not mean "the greater amount of pleasure".

More specifically, "the greater" pleasure does not mean either "the more intense" or "the longer lasting" pleasure. If I say that it is more fun to dine on the balcony than in the dining room, I mean neither that if we dine on the balcony we will have some experience which will be more intense than the experience we would have if we dined inside, nor that there is some experience which we will have which will last longer if we have it on the balcony. The greatest pleasures are not necessarily the most intense, nor of the longest duration. Bentham's account therefore fails to explain the idea of a greater or better or pleasanter pleasure.

Mill gives a rival account. "If I am asked what I mean by difference of quality in pleasures, or what makes one pleasure more valuable than another, merely as a pleasure, except its being greater in amount, there is but one possible answer. Of two pleasures, if there be one to which all or almost all who have experience of both give a decided preference, irrespective of any feeling of moral obligation to prefer it, that is the more desirable pleasure."[17] On this account the greater pleasure is the one that people who have had experience of both, would choose. If they would choose pleasure A in preference to pleasure B, even if pleasure B was greater in intensity and duration, then pleasure A is the greater pleasure.

Mill therefore rejects, with perfect consistency, the requirement that he evaluate pleasures, as pleasures, only in terms of "amount" of pleasure. His claim that, of two pleasures, the better pleasure is the greater pleasure, shares with Bentham's quantitative view the advantage of not introducing an extraneous criterion of goodness, but it is not itself "quantitative." Note that he does not say that the preference of an experienced man is a *sign* that one pleasure is better than another. He states quite specifically that he is giving an account of what he means by difference in quality in pleasures.

It should now be clear how consistent Mill's remarks about the intrinsic values of certain pleasures are with his theory of value. To be intrinsically good is to be intrinsically desirable, and for one thing to be intrinsically better than another is for it to be intrinsically more desirable, or intrinsically preferable to the other. We discover what is preferable by consulting people's preferences, just as we discover what is desirable by finding out what people desire. In the case of preferability, Mill insists that we count only the preferences of those who have sampled both pleasures; I argued in Part I that a parallel qualification should be added to the method Mill recommends for finding out what is desirable, i.e. that we count only the desires of the knowledgeable and experienced.

Moore, claiming that the person who thinks pleasure alone is good can give no possible reason for preferring one pleasure to another, concludes that if hedonism is true, one pleasure cannot be better than another. However, Moore's objection does not touch Mill, since the hedonist is in no better, and no worse, a position to give a reason for preferring one pleasure to another, than anyone else. If I tell you why I prefer the city to the country, what I am doing is telling you what it is about the city that I like. If I say that I prefer the city because I like to go to the theatre, I am not introducing some criterion of preferability, but telling you exactly what it is that I prefer—places with theatres. My believing that the only thing that is intrinsically good is pleasure, does not prevent me from telling you why I prefer the city, that is, from telling you what it is about the city that I prefer. A non-hedonist could say no more; explaining his preferences would consist in telling us just what it is that he prefers. He may say he prefers one pleasure to another because it leads to the acquiring of knowledge, but then he is not saying which of the two activities he prefers as pleasures, that is, he is not telling us which he finds the greater pleasure, but which he prefers on some other grounds. I conclude that there is no reason for preferring one pleasure to another, purely as pleasure, that a hedonist cannot give. Mill can insist that the only thing that is good in itself is pleasure, and still allow that some pleasures are qualitatively better than others, because he allows that we take pleasure in many different activities, and greater in some than in others.

That it is in a sense impossible to say why you prefer the pleasures you prefer, is quite con-

sistent with Mill's general position. On his view, we cannot say why we want the things that we want for their own sake—the giving of reasons is possible only to explain why we want the things that we want as means to some end. Since according to Mill the only things wanted for their own sake are pleasure and the absence of pain, it follows that to explain that you did something because you enjoy doing that sort of thing, is to come to a logical stopping point of the possibility of giving reasons. The same will hold with explanations of preference. If in answer to the question why I went to the tennis rather than to the cricket, I say that I take more pleasure in watching tennis than in watching cricket, I have come to the end of the chain of appropriate reasons that can be given. This is not to deny that I may go to the tennis for reasons other than to seek pleasure. It is to say that the task of giving reasons comes to an end, if we are discussing the pleasures I prefer, not as a means to some further end but in themselves, when I tell you just what it is that I do prefer.

I conclude that Mill's account is quite consistent. Being a better pleasure does not consist in possessing some special mark. Being a better pleasure consists in being the sort of pleasure that will be chosen by those who know both sorts of pleasure. Being an intrinsic good consists in being intrinsically desirable. Being a high class intrinsic good consists in being preferable to other intrinsic goods.

In order for one pleasure to count as a better or greater pleasure than another, it has to be preferred by all or almost all of those who know both pleasures. The criterion of betterness is not merely majority preference. In this I think Mill is right. Unqualified statements such as "a yellow fever injection hurts more than a typhoid injection" or "it's more pleasant to go to the dentist now than it was before the high speed drill was developed" have a use only because everyone or almost everyone is hurt more by yellow fever injections than by typhoid injections, and finds visits to the dentist less unpleasant than they used to be. Where this near uniformity of reaction does not occur, we have no use for the unqualified "more pleasant" or "more painful." Instead, we specify who finds what more painful or more pleasant. We say things like "most people prefer milk in their tea" or "some people find a mild sunburn not painful." Mill cannot conclude that reading poetry is more pleasant than playing push pin, he can only conclude that some prefer one activity and some the other.

Where there is no uniform preference for pleasurable activity A over pleasurable activity B, the utilitarian would do well to provide his computer with exact information about the percentage who prefer A and the percentage who prefer B. This would be inconvenient, but accurate information of this sort is essential if the utilitarian really does want to know how to maximise pleasure.

III

The third allegation against Mill is that he commits the fallacy of composition. This is said to occur in his attempt to show that the general happiness is desirable. He claims that "No reason can be given why the general happiness is desirable, except that each person, so far as he believes it to be attainable, desires his own happiness. This, however, being a fact, we have not only all the proof that the case admits of, but all that it is possible to require, that happiness is a good, that each person's happiness is a good to that person, and the general happiness therefore a good to the aggregate of persons."[18] The fallacy is said to occur in adding the people, adding the objects of their desire, and ascribing the totality of desires to the totality of people. This however can be done without fallacy. From the premises

> "Bill wants an apple" and
> "Joe wants a pear"

one can conclude

(i)   "Bill and Joe *between them* want an apple and a pear."

One cannot of course conclude

(ii)   "Bill and Joe *each* wants an apple and a pear."

The inference to conclusion (i) is perfectly proper, and is the sort of inference that people in the catering trade must make often. In order to

show that Mill has committed a fallacy, it would be necessary to show that he is trying to establish a conclusion of the second type, i.e. that he is trying to show that the general happiness is a good to each person.

Mill is trying to show that the general happiness is a good. It might be supposed therefore that he might attempt to do this by showing that each person desires the general happiness. However, this interpretation cannot be allowed because Mill makes it quite clear in the text that he does not believe this. Mill believes that many people are selfish and can be induced to do the right thing only by the use of sanctions. He also lays great stress on the need to develop in children feelings of sympathy and regard for others, if the greatest good of the greatest number is to be achieved.

The chapter in which the argument under discussion occurs, is called "Of What Sort of Proof the Principle of Utility is Susceptible" but the arguments in it do not seem to be aimed at a proof of the principle. What is Mill trying to prove? There are three separate questions someone might ask about the principle of utility, and call his asking a demand for proof. First, is the analysis of the right act as the optimific act, correct? I shall call this question the truth question. There is another question which I shall call the motive question. Someone could admit that the right act, morally speaking, is the optimific act, but go on to ask what reason he had to be moral, or what reason he had to do whatever is optimific. He might want to know what reason he could possibly have for doing what was optimific, if it was not in his interest to do so. The third question that could be asked is what I shall call the justification question. Someone might want to know what the good of being moral is, whether there is any good at all to be achieved in this way.

Mill is not trying to answer the truth question in Chapter Four. Nowhere in *Utilitarianism* does he seem concerned to show that his account of moral right and wrong is correct, except to remark that the Utilitarian criterion is the one that men implicitly use, even those who think Utilitarianism to be mistaken.[19] Of course, there is nothing more that can be said in support of an analysis. Mill is certainly not defending his account of moral concepts in Chapter Four. The discussion there is about intrinsic goods, not about the nature of moral obligation. The title of the chapter is misleading.

Moreover, Mill is not trying to answer the motive question. Since he is not, there is no justification for the interpretation that he is trying to give us all a motive for doing the right thing by showing that we all desire the happiness of the greatest number. Mill's answer to the motive question is not that, and it is in a different place. In order to achieve the greatest good of the greatest number, children are to be brought up so that they cannot conceive of themselves being happy if someone else is miserable.[20] So, anyone who is well brought up will be able to answer his own question "What reason have I to do the right thing?" by reminding himself that he wants other people to be happy. Mill discusses the motive question at length in Chapter Three, "Of the Ultimate Sanction of the Principle of Utility."

Mill's concern in Chapter Four is the justification question, "What is the good of morality?," "What is the good of doing the morally right act?". What is the good of that?" is not a philosophical question but an everyday sort of question. In cleaning out a cupboard, one might ask of an object, "What is the good of this?" or even "Is this any good?" One can ask such questions about social practices; for instance, "What is the good of wearing ties in the summer?" or "What is the good of teaching children about the way plants reproduce?". And one can ask such questions about morality. Is any good achieved by people behaving, as they say, morally, or are moralities just sets of useless superstitious practices? [Note that the motive question should not be confused with the justification question. Morality could be useful without being useful to me, and I could be shown the good of morality without being given a reason for being moral.]

Mill's answer to the question "What is the good of morality?" or "What is the good of doing the right thing?" is that morality is a means to the greatest possible amount of good. He is not here trying to show that the right act is the one that is productive of the greatest happiness of the greatest number, but that the greatest happiness of the greatest number is a good, and the greatest possible good. He is trying to show that there is some good to be achieved by having morality, in fact, the greatest possible amount of good. He believes that he has previously shown that each man's happiness is a good to that man, and so his justification of morality is that, since morality aims at the greatest happiness of the greatest number of people,[21] it aims at the maximisation of goods. In order to show this he does not need to show that the greatest good of the greatest number is a good to any particular individual but only that the greatest good of the greatest number is the sum of all goods, or the sum of the greatest possible number of goods which can co-exist.

NOTES

1. J. S. Mill, *Utilitarianism*, Everyman's Library, ch. 4, p. 32.
2. *Ibid.*, ch. 1, p. 4.
3. *Ibid.*, ch. 4, p. 32.
4. For example, see G. E. Moore, *Principia Ethica*, Cambridge University Press, sect. 41.
5. *Ibid.*, sect. 40.
6. *Ibid.*, sect. 40.
7. *Op. cit.*, ch. 2, p. 15.
8. *Ibid.*, ch. 2, p. 10.
9. *Ibid.*, ch. 2, p. 16.
10. *Op. cit.*, sect. 41.
11. Gauthier, *Practical Reasoning*, Oxford University Press, p. 34.
12. See Section II of this paper.
13. *Op. cit.*, ch. 4.
14. *Op. cit.*, ch. 2, p. 7.
15. *Op. cit.*, sect. 48.
16. Bentham, *Principles of Morals and Legislation*, Oxford University Press, ch. 4, sect. II, p. 29.
17. *Op. cit.*, ch. 2, p. 8.
18. *Ibid.*, ch. 4, pp. 32–3.
19. *Op. cit.*, ch. I, p. 3.
20. *Ibid.*, ch. II, p. 16.
21. *Ibid.*, ch. I, p. 2. Mill regards morality as a practical art which has an end.

7. HEDONISTIC AND NONHEDONISTIC UTILITARIANISM

J. J. C. Smart

It is worth while enquiring how much practical ethics is likely to be affected by the possibility of disagreement over the question of Socrates dissatisfied versus the fool satisfied.

'Not very much,' one feels like saying at first. We noted that the most complex and intellectual pleasures are also the most fecund. Poetry elevates the mind, makes one more sensitive, and so harmonizes with various intellectual pursuits, some of which are of practical value. Delight in mathematics is even more obviously, on Benthamite views, a pleasure worth encouraging, for on the progress of mathematics depends the progress of mankind. Even the most hedonistic schoolmaster would prefer to see his boys enjoying poetry and mathematics rather than neglecting these arts for the pleasures of marbles or the tuckshop. Indeed many of the brutish pleasures not only lack fecundity but are actually the reverse of fecund. To enjoy food too much is to end up fat, unhealthy and without zest or vigour. To enjoy drink too much is even worse. In most circumstances of ordinary life the pure hedonist will agree in his practical recommendations with the quasi-ideal utilitarian.

This need not always be so. Some years ago two psychologists, Olds and Milner, carried out some experiments with rats.[1] Through the skull of each rat they inserted an electrode. These electrodes penetrated to various regions of the brain. In the case of some of these regions the rat showed behaviour characteristics of pleasure when a current was passed from the electrode, in others they seemed to show pain, and in others the stimulus seemed neutral. That a stimulus was pleasure-giving was shown by the fact that the

rat would learn to pass the current himself by pressing a lever. He would neglect food and make straight for this lever and start stimulating himself. In some cases he would sit there pressing the lever every few seconds for hours on end. This calls up a pleasant picture of the voluptuary of the future, a bald-headed man with a number of electrodes protruding from his skull, one to give the physical pleasure of sex, one for that of eating, one for that of drinking, and so on. Now is this the sort of life that all our ethical planning should culminate in? A few hours' work a week, automatic factories, comfort and security from disease, and hours spent at a switch, continually electrifying various regions of one's brain? Surely not. Men were made for higher things, one can't help wanting to say, even though one knows that men weren't made for anything, but are the product of evolution by natural selection.

It might be said that the objection to continual sensual stimulation of the above sort is that though it would be pleasant in itself it would be infecund of future pleasures. This is often so with the ordinary sensual pleasures. Excessive indulgence in the physical pleasures of sex may possibly have a debilitating effect and may perhaps interfere with the deeper feelings of romantic love. But whether stimulation by the electrode method would have this weakening effect and whether it would impair the possibility of future pleasures of the same sort is another matter. For example, there would be no excessive secretion of hormones. The whole biochemical mechanism would, almost literally, be short-circuited. Maybe, however, a person who stimulated himself by the electrode method would find it so enjoyable that he would neglect all other pursuits. Maybe if everyone became an electrode operator people would lose interest in everything else and the human race would die out.

From J. J. C. Smart, "An Outline of a System of Utilitarian Ethics," in *Utilitarianism: For and Against*, by J. J. C. Smart and Bernard Williams (Cambridge University Press, 1973), pp. 18–26. Reprinted by permission of Cambridge University Press.

Suppose, however, that the facts turned out otherwise: that a man could (and would) do his full share of work in the office or the factory and come back in the evening to a few hours contented electrode work, without bad after-effects. This would be his greatest pleasure, and the pleasure would be so great intrinsically and so easily repeatable that its lack of fecundity would not matter. Indeed perhaps by this time human arts, such as medicine, engineering, agriculture and architecture will have been brought to a pitch of perfection sufficient to enable most of the human race to spend most of its time electrode operating, without compensating pains of starvation, disease and squalor. Would this be a satisfactory state of society? Would this be the millennium towards which we have been striving? Surely the pure hedonist would have to say that it was.

It is time, therefore, that we had another look at the concept of happiness. Should we say that the electrode operator was really happy? This is a difficult question to be clear about, because the concept of happiness is a tricky one. But whether we should call the electrode operator 'happy' or not, there is no doubt (a) that he would be *contented* and (b) that he would be *enjoying himself*.

Perhaps a possible reluctance to call the electrode operator 'happy' might come from the following circumstance. The electrode operator might be perfectly contented, might perfectly enjoy his electrode operating, and might not be willing to exchange his lot for any other. And we ourselves, perhaps, once we became electrode operators too, could become perfectly contented and satisfied. But nevertheless, as we are now, we just do not want to become electrode operators. We want other things, perhaps to write a book or get into a cricket team. If someone said 'from tomorrow onwards you are going to be forced to be an electrode operator' we should not be pleased. Maybe from tomorrow onwards, once the electrode work had started, we should be perfectly contented, but we are not contented now at the prospect. We are not satisfied at being told that we would be in a certain state from tomorrow onwards, even though we may know that from tomorrow onwards we should be perfectly satisfied. All this is psychologically possible. It is just the obverse of

a situation which we often find. I remember an occasion on which I was suspended by cable car half-way up a precipitous mountain. As the cable car creaked upwards, apparently so flimsily held above the yawning chasm below, I fervently wished that I had never come in it. When I bought the ticket for the cable car I knew that I should shortly be wishing that I had never bought it. And yet I should have been annoyed if I had been refused it. Again, a man may be very anxious to catch a bus, so as to be in time for a dental appointment, and yet a few minutes later, while the drill is boring into his tooth, may wish that he had missed that bus. It is, contrariwise, perfectly possible that I should be annoyed today if told that from tomorrow onwards I should be an electrode addict, even though I knew that from tomorrow onwards I should be perfectly contented.

This, I think, explains part of our hesitancy about whether to call the electrode operator 'happy.' The notion of happiness ties up with that of contentment: to be fairly happy at least involves being fairly contented, though it involves something more as well. Though we should be contented when we became electrode operators, we are not contented now with the prospect that we should become electrode operators. Similarly if Socrates had become a fool he might thereafter have been perfectly contented. Nevertheless if beforehand he had been told that he would in the future become a fool he would have been even more dissatisfied than in fact he was. This is part of the trouble about the dispute between Bentham and Mill. The case involves the possibility of (a) our being contented if we are in a certain state, and (b) our being contented at the prospect of being so contented. Normally situations in which we should be contented go along with our being contented at the prospect of our getting into such situations. In the case of the electrode operator and in that of Socrates and the fool we are pulled two ways at once.

Now to call a person 'happy' is to say more than that he is contented for most of the time, or even that he frequently enjoys himself and is rarely discontented or in pain. It is, I think, in part to express a favourable attitude to the idea of such a form of contentment and enjoyment. That is, for *A* to call *B* 'happy,' *A* must be contented at the prospect of *B* being in his present state of mind and at the prospect of *A* himself, should the opportunity arise, enjoying that sort of state of mind. That is, 'happy' is a word which is mainly descriptive (tied to the concepts of contentment and enjoyment) but which is also partly evaluative. It is because Mill approves of the 'higher' pleasures, e.g. intellectual pleasures, so much more than he approves of the more simple and brutish pleasures, that, quite apart from consequences and side effects, he can pronounce the man who enjoys the pleasures of philosophical discourse as 'more happy' than the man who gets enjoyment from pushpin or beer drinking.

The word 'happy' is not wholly evaluative, for there would be something absurd, as opposed to merely unusual, in calling a man who was in pain, or who was not enjoying himself, or who hardly ever enjoyed himself, or who was in a more or less permanent state of intense dissatisfaction, a 'happy' man. For a man to be happy he must, as a minimal condition, be fairly contented and moderately enjoying himself for much of the time. Once this minimal condition is satisfied we can go on to evaluate various types of contentment and enjoyment and to grade them in terms of happiness. Happiness is, of course, a long-term concept in a way that enjoyment is not. We can talk of a man enjoying himself at a quarter past two precisely, but hardly of a man being happy at a quarter past two precisely. Similarly we can talk of it raining at a quarter past two precisely, but hardly about it being a wet climate at a quarter past two precisely. But happiness involves enjoyment at various times, just as a wet climate involves rain at various times.

To be enjoying oneself, Ryle once suggested, is to be doing what you want to be doing and not to be wanting to do anything else,[2] or, more accurately, we might say that one enjoys oneself the more one wants to be doing what one is in fact doing and the less one wants to be doing anything else. A man will not enjoy a round of golf if (a) he does not particularly want to play golf, or (b) though he wants to play golf there is something else he wishes he were doing at the same time, such as buying the vegetables for his wife, filling in his income tax forms, or listening to a lecture on philosophy. Even sensual pleasures come under the same description. For example the pleasure of eating an ice-cream in-

volves having a certain physical sensation, in a way in which the pleasure of golf or of symbolic logic does not, but the man who is enjoying an ice-cream can still be said to be doing what he wants to do (have a certain physical sensation) and not to be wanting to do anything else. If his mind is preoccupied with work or if he is conscious of a pressing engagement somewhere else, he will not enjoy the physical sensation, however intense it be, or will not enjoy it very much.

The hedonistic ideal would then appear to reduce to a state of affairs in which each person is enjoying himself. Since, as we noted, a dog may, as far as we can tell, enjoy chasing a rat as much as a philosopher or a mathematician may enjoy solving a problem, we must, if we adopt the purely hedonistic position, defend the higher pleasures on account of their fecundity. And that might not turn out to be a workable defense in a world made safe for electrode operators.

To sum up so far, happiness is partly an evaluative concept, and so the utilitarian maxim 'You ought to maximize happiness' is doubly evaluative. There is the possibility of an ultimate disagreement between two utilitarians who differ over the question of pushpin versus poetry, or Socrates dissatisfied versus the fool satisfied. The case of the electrode operator shows that two utilitarians might come to advocate very different courses of actions if they differed about what constituted happiness, and this difference between them would be simply an ultimate difference in attitude. Some other possibilities of the 'science fiction' type will be mentioned briefly below. So I do not wish to say that the difference in ultimate valuation between a hedonistic and a non-hedonistic utilitarian will *never* lead to difference in practice.

Leaving these more remote possibilities out of account, however, and considering the decisions we have to make at present, the question of whether the 'higher' pleasures should be preferred to the 'lower' ones does seem to be of slight practical importance. There are already perfectly good hedonistic arguments for poetry as against pushpin. As has been pointed out, the more complex pleasures are incomparably more fecund than the less complex ones: not only are they enjoyable in themselves but they are a means to further enjoyment. Still less, on the whole, do they lead to disillusionment, physical deterioration or social disharmony. The connoisseur of poetry may enjoy himself no more than the connoisseur of whisky, but he runs no danger of a headache on the following morning. Moreover the question of whether the general happiness would be increased by replacing most of the human population by a bigger population of contented sheep and pigs is not one which by any stretch of the imagination could become a live issue. Even if we thought, on abstract grounds, that such a replacement would be desirable, we should not have the slightest chance of having our ideas generally adopted.

So much for the issue between Bentham and Mill. What about that between Mill and Moore? Could a pleasurable state of mind have no intrinsic value at all, or perhaps even a *negative* intrinsic value?[3] Are there pleasurable states of mind towards which we have an unfavourable attitude, even though we disregard their consequences? In order to decide this question let us imagine a universe consisting of one sentient being only, who falsely believes that there are other sentient beings and that they are undergoing exquisite torment. So far from being distressed by the thought, he takes a great delight in these imagined sufferings. Is this better or worse than a universe containing no sentient being at all? Is it worse, again, than a universe containing only one sentient being with the same beliefs as before but who sorrows at the imagined tortures of his fellow creatures? I suggest, as against Moore, that the universe containing the deluded sadist is the preferable one. After all he is happy, and since there is no other sentient being, what harm can he do? Moore would nevertheless agree that the sadist was happy, and this shows how happiness, though partly an evaluative concept, is also partly not an evaluative concept.

It is difficult, I admit, not to feel an immediate repugnance at the thought of the deluded sadist. If throughout our childhood we have been given an electric shock whenever we had tasted cheese, then cheese would have become immediately distasteful to us. Our repugnance to the sadist arises, naturally enough, because in our universe sadists invariably do harm. If we lived in a universe in which by some extraordinary laws of psychology a sadist was always confounded by his own knavish tricks and invariably did a great deal of good, then we should feel better disposed towards the sadistic mentality. Even if we could de-condition ourselves from feeling an immediate repugnance to a sadist (as we could de-condition ourselves from a repugnance to cheese by going through a course in which the taste of cheese was invariably associated with a pleasurable stimulus) language might make it difficult for us to distinguish an extrinsic distaste for sadism, founded on our distaste for the consequences of sadism, from an immediate distaste for sadism as such. Normally when we call a thing 'bad' we mean indifferently to express a dislike for it in itself or to express a dislike for what it leads to. When a state of mind is sometimes extrinsically good and sometimes extrinsically bad, we find it easy to distinguish between our intrinsic and extrinsic preferences for instances of it, but when a state of mind is always, or almost always, extrinsically bad, it is easy for us to confuse an extrinsic distaste for it with an intrinsic one. If we allow for this, it does not seem so absurd to hold that there are no pleasures which are intrinsically bad. Pleasures are bad only because they cause harm to the person who has them or to other people. But if anyone likes to disagree with me about this I do not feel very moved to argue the point. Such a disagreement about ultimate ends is not likely to lead to any disagreement in practice. For in all actual cases there are sufficient extrinsic reasons for abhorring sadism and similar states of mind. *Approximate* agreement about ultimate ends is often quite enough for rational and co-operative moral discourse. In practical cases the possibility of factual disagreement about what causes produce what effects is likely to be overwhelmingly more important than disagreement in ultimate ends between hedonistic and ideal utilitarians.

NOTES

1.   James Olds and Peter Milner, 'Positive reinforcement produced by electrical stimulation of the septal area and other regions of the rat brain,' *Journal of Comparative and Physiological Psychology* 47 (1954) 419–27. James Olds, 'A preliminary mapping of electrical reinforcing effect in the rat brain,' *ibid.* 49 (1956) 281–5. I. J. Good has also used these results of Olds and Milner in order to discuss ethical hedonism. See his 'A problem for the hedonist,' in I. J. Good (ed.), *The Scientist Speculates* (Heinemann London, 1962). Good takes the possibility of this sort of thing to provide a *reductio ad absurdum* of hedonism.

2.   Gilbert Ryle, *The Concept of Mind* (Hutchison, London, 1949), p. 108.

3.   Cf. G. E. Moore, *Principia Ethica,* pp. 209–10.

8. *THE ENCHIRIDION*

Epictetus

I

There are things which are within our power, and there are things which are beyond our power. Within our power are opinion, aim, desire, aversion, and, in one word, whatever affairs are our own. Beyond our power are body, property, reputation, office, and, in one word, whatever are not properly our own affairs.

Now the things within our power are by nature free, unrestricted, unhindered; but those beyond our power are weak, dependent, restricted, alien. Remember, then, that if you attribute freedom to things by nature dependent and take what belongs to others for your own, you will be hindered, you will lament, you will be disturbed, you will find fault both with gods and men. But if you take for your own only that which is your own and view what belongs to others just as it really is, then no one will ever compel you, no one will restrict you; you will find fault with no one, you will accuse no one, you will do nothing against your will; no one will hurt you, you will not have an enemy, nor will you suffer any harm.

Aiming, therefore, at such great things, remember that you must not allow yourself any inclination, however slight, toward the attainment of the others; but that you must entirely quit some of them, and for the present postpone the rest. But if you would have these, and possess power and wealth likewise, you may miss the latter in seeking the former; and you will certainly fail of that by which alone happiness and freedom are procured.

Seek at once, therefore, to be able to say to every unpleasing semblance, "You are but a semblance and by no means the real thing." And then examine it by those rules which you have; and first and chiefly by this: whether it concerns the things which are within our own power or those which are not; and if it concerns anything beyond our power, be prepared to say that it is nothing to you.

II

Remember that desire demands the attainment of that of which you are desirous; and aversion demands the avoidance of that to which you are averse; that he who fails of the object of his desires is disappointed; and he who incurs the object of his aversion is wretched. If, then, you shun only those undesirable things which you can control, you will never incur anything which you shun; but if you shun sickness, or death, or poverty, you will run the risk of wretchedness. Remove [the habit of] aversion, then, from all things that are not within our power, and apply it to things undesirable which are within our power. But for the present, altogether restrain desire; for if you desire any of the things not within our own power, you must necessarily be disappointed; and you are not yet secure of those which are within our power, and so are legitimate objects of desire. Where it is practically necessary for you to pursue or avoid anything, do even this with discretion and gentleness and moderation.

III

With regard to whatever objects either delight the mind or contribute to use or are tenderly beloved, remind yourself of what nature they are, beginning with the merest trifles: if you have a favorite cup, that it is but a cup of which you are fond of—for thus, if it is broken, you can bear it; if you embrace your child or your wife, that you embrace a mortal—and thus, if either of them dies, you can bear it.

From Epictetus, *The Enchiridion,* translated by Thomas W. Higginson.

IV

When you set about any action, remind yourself of what nature the action is. If you are going to bathe, represent to yourself the incidents usual in the bath—some persons pouring out, others pushing in, others scolding, others pilfering. And thus you will more safely go about this action if you say to yourself, "I will now go to bathe and keep my own will in harmony with nature." And so with regard to every other action. For thus, if any impediment arises in bathing, you will be able to say, "It was not only to bathe that I desired, but to keep my will in harmony with nature; and I shall not keep it thus if I am out of humor at things that happen."

V

Men are disturbed not by things, but by the views which they take of things. Thus death is nothing terrible, else it would have appeared so to Socrates. But the terror consists in our notion of death, that it is terrible. When, therefore, we are hindered or disturbed, or grieved, let us never impute it to others, but to ourselves—that is, to our own views. It is the action of an uninstructed person to reproach others for his own misfortunes; of one entering upon instruction, to reproach himself; and one perfectly instructed, to reproach neither others nor himself.

VI

Be not elated at any excellence not your own. If a horse should be elated, and say, "I am handsome," it might be endurable. But when you are elated and say, "I have a handsome horse," know that you are elated only on the merit of the horse. What then is your own? The use of the phenomena of existence. So that when you are in harmony with nature in this respect, you will be elated with some reason; for you will be elated at some good of your own.

VII

As in a voyage, when the ship is at anchor, if you go on shore to get water, you may amuse yourself with picking up a shellfish or a truffle in your way, but your thoughts ought to be bent toward the ship, and perpetually attentive, lest the captain should call, and then you must leave all these things, that you may not have to be carried on board the vessel, bound like a sheep; thus likewise in life, if, instead of a truffle or shellfish, such a thing as a wife or a child be granted you, there is no objection; but if the captain calls, run to the ship, leave all these things, and never look behind. But if you are old, never go far from the ship, lest you should be missing when called for.

VIII

Demand not that events should happen as you wish; but wish them to happen as they do happen, and you will go on well.

IX

Sickness is an impediment to the body, but not to the will unless itself pleases. Lameness is an impediment to the leg, but not to the will; and say this to yourself with regard to everything that happens. For you will find it to be an impediment to something else, but not truly to yourself.

X

Upon every accident, remember to turn toward yourself and inquire what faculty you have for its use. If you encounter a handsome person, you will find continence the faculty needed; if pain, then fortitude; if reviling, then patience. And when thus habituated, the phenomena of existence will not overwhelm you.

XI

Never say of anything, "I have lost it," but, "I have restored it." Has your child died? It is restored. Has your wife died? She is restored. Has your estate been taken away? That likewise is restored. "But it was a bad man who took it." What is it to you by whose hands he who gave it has demanded it again? While he permits you to possess it, hold it as something not your own, as do travelers at an inn.

XII

If you would improve, lay aside such reasonings as these: "If I neglect my affairs, I shall not have a maintenance; if I do not punish my servant, he will be good for nothing." For it were better to die of hunger, exempt from grief and fear, than to live in affluence with perturbation; and it is better that your servant should be bad than you unhappy.

Begin therefore with little things. Is a little oil spilled or a little wine stolen? Say to yourself, "This is the price paid for peace and tranquility; and nothing is to be had for nothing." And when you call your servant, consider that it is possible he may not come at your call; or, if he does, that he may not do what you wish. But it is not at all desirable for him, and very undesirable for you, that it should be in his power to cause you any disturbance.

XIII

If you would improve, be content to be thought foolish and dull with regard to externals. Do not desire to be thought to know anything; and though you should appear to others to be somebody, distrust yourself. For be assured, it is not easy at once to keep your will in harmony with nature and to secure externals; but while you are absorbed in the one, you must of necessity neglect the other.

XIV

If you wish your children and your wife and your friends to live forever, you are foolish, for you wish things to be in your power which are not so, and what belongs to others to be your own. So likewise, if you wish your servant to be without fault, you are foolish, for you wish vice not to be vice but something else. But if you wish not to be disappointed in your desires, that is in your own power. Exercise, therefore, what is in your power. A man's master is he who is able to confer or remove whatever that man seeks or shuns. Whoever then would be free, let him wish nothing, let him decline nothing, which depends on others; else he must necessarily be a slave.

XV

Remember that you must behave as at a banquet. Is anything brought round to you? Put out your hand and take a moderate share. Does it pass by you? Do not stop it. Is it not yet come? Do not yearn in desire toward it, but wait till it reaches you. So with regard to children, wife, office, riches; and you will some time or other be worthy to feast with the gods. And if you do not so much as take the things which are set before you, but are able even to forego them, then you will not only be worthy to feast with the gods, but to rule with them also. For, by thus doing, Diogenes and Heraclitus, and others like them, deservedly became divine, and were so recognized.

XVI

When you see anyone weeping for grief, either that his son has gone abroad or that he has suffered in his affairs, take care not to be overcome by the apparent evil, but discriminate and be ready to say, "What hurts this man is not this occurrence itself—for another man might not be hurt by it—but the view he chooses to take of it." As far as conversation goes, however, do not disdain to accommodate yourself to him and, if need be, to groan with him. Take heed, however, not to groan inwardly, too.

XVII

Remember that you are an actor in a drama of such sort as the Author chooses—if short, then in a short one; if long, then in a long one. If it be his pleasure that you should enact a poor man, or a cripple, or a ruler, or a private citizen, see that you act it well. For this is your business—to act well the given part, but to choose it belongs to another.

XVIII

When a raven happens to croak unluckily, be not overcome by appearances, but discriminate and say, "Nothing is portended to *me*, either to my paltry body, or property, or reputation, or children, or wife. But to *me* all portents are lucky if I will. For whatsoever happens, it belongs to me to derive advantage therefrom."

XIX

You can be unconquerable if you enter into no combat in which it is not in your own power to conquer. When, therefore, you see anyone eminent in honors or power, or in high esteem on any other account, take heed not to be bewildered by appearances and to pronounce him happy; for if the essence of good consists in things within our own power, there will be no room for envy or emulation. But, for your part, do not desire to be a general, or a senator, or a consul, but to be free; and the only way to this is a disregard of things which lie not within our own power.

XX

Remember that it is not he who gives abuse or blows, who affronts, but the view we take of these things as insulting. When, therefore, anyone provokes you, be assured that it is your own opinion which provokes you. Try, therefore, in the first place, not to be bewildered by appearances. For if you once gain time and respite, you will more easily command yourself.

XXI

Let death and exile, and all other things which appear terrible, be daily before your eyes, but death chiefly; and you will never entertain an abject thought, nor too eagerly covet anything.

XXII

If you have an earnest desire toward philosophy, prepare yourself from the very first to have the multitude laugh and sneer, and say, "He is returned to us a philosopher all at once"; and, "Whence this supercilious look?" Now, for your part, do not have a supercilious look indeed, but keep steadily to those things which appear best to you, as one appointed by God to this particular station. For remember that, if you are persistent, those very persons who at first ridiculed will afterwards admire you. But if you are conquered by them, you will incur a double ridicule.

XXIII

If you ever happen to turn your attention to externals, for the pleasure of anyone, be assured that you have ruined your scheme of life. Be content, then, in everything, with being a philosopher; and if you wish to seem so likewise to anyone, appear so to yourself, and it will suffice you.

XXIV

Let not such considerations as these distress you: "I shall live in discredit and be nobody anywhere." For if discredit be an evil, you can no more be involved in evil through another than in baseness. Is it any business of yours, then, to get power or to be admitted to an entertainment? By no means. How then, after all, is this discredit? And how it is true that you will be nobody anywhere when you ought to be somebody in those things only which are within your own power, in which you may be of the greatest consequence? "But my friends will be unassisted." What do you mean by "unassisted"? They will not have money from you, nor will you make them Roman citizens. Who told you, then, that these are among the things within our own power, and not rather the affairs of others? And who can give to another the things which he himself has not? "Well, but get them, then, that we too may have a share." If I can get them with the preservation of my own honor and fidelity and self-respect, show me the way and I will get them; but if you require me to lose my own proper good, that you may gain what is no good, consider how unreasonable and foolish you are. Besides, which would you rather have, a sum of money or a faithful and honorable friend? Rather assist me, then, to gain this character than require me to do those things by which I may lose it. Well, but my country, say you, as far as depends upon me, will be unassisted. Here, again, what assistance is this you mean? It will not have porticos nor baths of your providing? And what signifies that? Why, neither does a smith provide it with shoes, nor a shoemaker with arms. It is enough if everyone fully performs his own proper business. And were you to supply it with another faithful and honorable citizen, would not he be of use to it? Yes. Therefore neither are you yourself useless to it. "What place, then," say you, "shall I hold in the state?" Whatever you can hold with the preservation of your fidelity and honor. But if, by desiring to be useful to that, you lose these, how can you serve your country when you have become faithless and shameless?

XXV

Is anyone preferred before you at an entertainment, or in courtesies, or in confidential intercourse? If these things are good, you ought to rejoice that he has them; and if they are evil, do not be grieved that you have them not. And remember that you cannot be permitted to rival others in externals without using the same means to obtain them. For how can he who will not haunt the door of any man, will not attend him, will not praise him, have an equal share with him who does these things? You are unjust, then, and unreasonable if you are unwilling to pay the price for which these things are sold, and would have them for nothing. For how much are lettuces sold? An obulus, for instance. If another, then, paying an obulus, takes the lettuces, and you, not paying it, go without them, do not imagine that he has gained any advantage over you. For as he has the lettuces, so you have the obulus which you did not give. So, in the present case, you have not been invited to such a person's entertainment because you have not paid him the price for which a supper is sold. It is sold for praise; it is sold for attendance. Give him, then, the value if it be for your advantage. But if you would at the same time not pay the one, and yet receive the other, you are unreasonable and foolish. Have you nothing, then, in place of the supper? Yes, indeed, you have—not to praise him whom you do not like to praise; not to bear the insolence of his lackeys.

XXVI

The will of nature may be learned from things upon which we are all agreed. As when our neighbor's boy has broken a cup, or the like, we are ready at once to say, "These are casualties that will happen"; be assured, then, that when your own cup is likewise broken, you ought to be affected just as when another's cup was bro-

ken. Now apply this to greater things. Is the child or wife of another dead? There is no one who would not say, "This is an accident of mortality." But if anyone's own child happens to die, it is immediately, "Alas! how wretched am I!" It should be always remembered how we are affected on hearing the same thing concerning others.

XXVII

As a mark is not set up for the sake of missing the aim, so neither does the nature of evil exist in the world.

XXVIII

If a person had delivered up your body to some passer-by, you would certainly be angry. And do you feel no shame in delivering up your own mind to any reviler, to be disconcerted and confounded?

XXIX

In every affair consider what precedes and what follows, and then undertake it. Otherwise you will begin with spirit, indeed, careless of the consequences, and when these are developed, you will shamefully desist. "I would conquer at the Olympic Games." But consider what precedes and what follows, and then, if it be for your advantage, engage in the affair. You must conform to rules, submit to a diet, refrain from dainties; exercise your body, whether you choose it or not, at a stated hour, in heat and cold; you must drink no cold water, and sometimes no wine—in a word, you must give yourself up to your trainer as to a physician. Then, in the combat, you may be thrown into a ditch, dislocate your arm, turn your ankle, swallow an abundance of dust, receive stripes [for negligence], and, after all, lose the victory. When you have reckoned up all this, if your inclination still holds, set about the combat. Otherwise, take notice, you will behave like children who sometimes play wrestlers, sometimes gladiators, sometimes blow a trumpet, and sometimes act a tragedy, when they happen to have seen and admired these shows. Thus you too will be at one time a wrestler, and another a gladiator; now a philosopher, now an orator; but nothing in earnest. Like an ape you mimic all you see, and one thing after another is sure to please you, but is out of favor as soon as it becomes familiar. For you have never entered upon anything considerately; nor after having surveyed and tested the whole matter, but carelessly, and with a halfway zeal. Thus some, when they have seen a philosopher and heard a man speaking like Euphrates— though, indeed, who can speak like him?—have a mind to be philosophers, too. Consider first, man, what the matter is, and what your own nature is able to bear. If you would be a wrestler, consider your shoulders, your back, your thighs; for different persons are made for different things. Do you think that you can act as you do and be a philosopher, that you can eat, drink, be angry, be discontented, as you are now? You must watch, you must labor, you must get the better of certain appetites, must quit your acquaintances, be despised by your servant, be laughed at by those you meet; come off worse than others in everything—in offices, in honors, before tribunals. When you have fully considered all these things, approach, if you please— that is, if, by parting with them, you have a mind to purchase serenity, freedom, and tranquillity. If not, do not come hither; do not, like children, be now a philosopher, then a publican, then an orator, and then one of Caesar's officers. These things are not consistent. You must be one man, either good or bad. You must cultivate either your own reason or else externals; apply yourself either to things within or without you—that is, be either a philosopher or one of the mob.

XXX

Duties are universally measured by relations. Is a certain man your father? In this are implied taking care of him, submitting to him in all things, patiently receiving his reproaches, his correction. But he is a bad father. Is your natural tie, then, to a *good* father? No, but to a father. Is a brother unjust? Well, preserve your own just relation toward him. Consider not what *he* does, but what *you* are to do to keep your own will in a state conformable to nature, for another cannot hurt you unless you please. You will then be hurt when you consent to be hurt. In this manner, therefore, if you accustom yourself to contemplate the relations of neighbor, citizen, com-

mander, you can deduce from each the corresponding duties.

XXXI

Be assured that the essence of piety toward the gods lies in this—to form right opinions concerning them, as existing and as governing the universe justly and well. And fix yourself in this resolution, to obey them, and yield to them, and willingly follow them amidst all events, as being ruled by the most perfect wisdom. For thus you will never find fault with the gods, nor accuse them of neglecting you. And it is not possible for this to be affected in any other way than by withdrawing yourself from things which are not within our own power, and by making good or evil to consist only in those which are. For if you suppose any other things to be either good or evil, it is inevitable that, when you are disappointed of what you wish or incur what you would avoid, you should reproach and blame their authors. For every creature is naturally formed to flee and abhor things that appear hurtful and that which causes them; and to pursue and admire those which appear beneficial and that which causes them. It is impracticable, then, that one who supposes himself to be hurt should rejoice in the person who, as he thinks, hurts him, just as it is impossible to rejoice in the hurt itself. Hence, also, a father is reviled by his son when he does not impart the things which seem to be good; and this made Polynices and Eteocles mutually enemies—that empire seemed good to both. On this account the husbandman reviles the gods; [and so do] the sailor, the merchant, or those who have lost wife or child. For where our interest is, there, too, is piety directed. So that whoever is careful to regulate his desires and aversions as he ought is thus made careful of piety likewise. But it also becomes incumbent on everyone to offer libations and sacrifices and first fruits, according to the customs of his country, purely, and not heedlessly nor negligently; not avariciously, nor yet extravagantly.

XXXII

When you have recourse to divination, remember that you know not what the event will be, and you come to learn it of the diviner; but of what nature it is you knew before coming; at least, if you are of philosophic mind. For if it is among the things not within our own power, it can by no means be either good or evil. Do not, therefore, bring with you to the diviner either desire or aversion—else you will approach him trembling—but first clearly understand that every event is indifferent and nothing to *you,* of whatever sort it may be; for it will be in your power to make a right use of it, and this no one can hinder. Then come with confidence to the gods as your counselors; and afterwards, when any counsel is given you, remember what counselors you have assumed, and whose advice you will neglect if you disobey. Come to divination as Socrates prescribed, in cases of which the whole consideration relates to the event, and in which no opportunities are afforded by reason or any other art to discover the matter in view. When, therefore, it is our duty to share the danger of a friend or of our country, we ought not to consult the oracle as to whether we shall share it with them or not. For though the diviner should forewarn you that the auspices are unfavorable, this means no more than that either death or mutilation or exile is portended. But we have reason within us; and it directs us, even with these hazards, to stand by our friend and our country. Attend, therefore, to the greater diviner, the Pythian God, who once cast out of the temple him who neglected to save his friend.

XXXIII

Begin by prescribing to yourself some character and demeanor, such as you may preserve both alone and in company.

Be mostly silent, or speak merely what is needful, and in few words. We may, however, enter sparingly into discourse sometimes, when occasion calls for it; but let it not run on any of the common subjects, as gladiators, or horse races, or athletic champions, or food, or drink—the vulgar topics of conversation—and especially not on men, so as either to blame, or praise, or make comparisons. If you are able, then, by your own conversation, bring over that of your company to proper subjects; but if you happen to find yourself among strangers, be silent.

Let not your laughter be loud, frequent, or abundant.

Avoid taking oaths, if possible, altogether; at any rate, so far as you are able.

Avoid public and vulgar entertainments; but if ever an occasion calls you to them, keep your attention upon the stretch, that you may not imperceptibly slide into vulgarity. For be assured that if a person be ever so pure himself, yet, if his companion be corrupted, he who converses with him will be corrupted likewise.

Provide things relating to the body no further than absolute need requires, as meat, drink, clothing, house, retinue. But cut off everything that looks toward show and luxury. Before marriage guard yourself with all your ability from unlawful intercourse with women; yet be not uncharitable or severe to those who are led into this, nor boast frequently that you yourself do otherwise.

If anyone tells you that a certain person speaks ill of you, do not make excuses about what is said of you, but answer: "He was ignorant of my other faults, else he would not have mentioned these alone."

It is not necessary for you to appear often at public spectacles; but if ever there is a proper occasion for you to be there, do not appear more solicitous for any other than for yourself—that is, wish things to be only just as they are, and only the best man to win; for thus nothing will go against you. But abstain entirely from acclamations and derision and violent emotions. And when you come away, do not discourse a great deal on what has passed and what contributes nothing to your own amendment. For it would appear by such discourse that you were dazzled by the show.

Be not prompt or ready to attend private recitations; but if you do attend, preserve your gravity and dignity, and yet avoid making yourself disagreeable.

When you are going to confer with anyone, and especially with one who seems your superior, represent to yourself how Socrates or Zeno would behave in such a case, and you will not be at a loss to meet properly whatever may occur.

When you are going before anyone in power, fancy to yourself that you may not find him at home, that you may be shut out, that the doors may not be opened to you, that he may not notice you. If, with all this, it be your duty to go, bear what happens and never say to yourself, "It was not worth so much"; for this is vulgar, and like a man bewildered by externals.

In company, avoid a frequent and excessive mention of your own actions and dangers. For however agreeable it may be to yourself to allude to the risks you have run, it is not equally agreeable to others to hear your adventures. Avoid likewise an endeavor to excite laughter, for this may readily slide you into vulgarity, and, besides, may be apt to lower you in the esteem of your acquaintance. Approaches to indecent discourse are likewise dangerous. Therefore, when anything of this sort happens, use the first fit opportunity to rebuke him who makes advances that way, or, at least, by silence and blushing and a serious look show yourself to be displeased by such talk.

XXXIV

If you are dazzled by the semblance of any promised pleasure, guard yourself against being bewildered by it; but let the affair wait your leisure, and procure yourself some delay. Then bring to your mind both points of time—that in which you shall enjoy the pleasure, and that in which you will repent and reproach yourself, after you have enjoyed it—and set before you, in opposition to these, how you will rejoice and applaud yourself if you abstain. And even though it should appear to you a seasonable gratification, take heed that its enticements and allurements and seductions may not subdue you, but set in opposition to this how much better it is to be conscious of having gained so great a victory.

XXXV

When you do anything from a clear judgment that it ought to be done, never shrink from being seen to do it, even though the world should misunderstand it; for if you are not acting rightly, shun the action itself; if you are, why fear those who wrongly censure you?

XXXVI

As the proposition, "either it is day or it is night," has much force in a disjunctive argument, but none at all in a conjunctive one, so, at a feast, to choose the largest share is very suitable to the bodily appetite, but utterly inconsistent with the social spirit of the entertainment. Remember, then, when you eat with another, not only the value to the body of those things which are set before you, but also the value of proper courtesy toward your host.

XXXVII

If you have assumed any character beyond your strength, you have both demeaned yourself ill in that and quitted one which you might have supported.

XXXVIII

As in walking you take care not to tread upon a nail, or turn your foot, so likewise take care not to hurt the ruling faculty of your mind. And if we were to guard against this in every action, we should enter upon action more safely.

XXXIX

The body is to everyone the proper measure of its possessions, as the foot is of the shoe. If, therefore, you stop at this, you will keep the measure; but if you move beyond it, you must necessarily be carried forward, as down a precipice; as in the case of a shoe, if you go beyond its fitness to the foot, it comes first to be gilded, then purple, and then studded with jewels. For to that which once exceeds the fit measure there is no bound.

XL

Women from fourteen years old are flattered by men with the title of mistresses. Therefore, perceiving that they are regarded only as qualified to give men pleasure, they begin to adorn themselves, and in that to place all their hopes. It is worth while, therefore, to try that they may perceive themselves honored only so far as they appear beautiful in their demeanor and modestly virtuous.

XLI

It is a mark of want of intellect to spend much time in things relating to the body, as to be immoderate in exercises, in eating and drinking, and in the discharge of other animal functions. These things should be done incidentally and our main strength be applied to our reason.

XLII

When any person does ill by you, or speaks ill of you, remember that he acts or speaks from an impression that it is right for him to do so. Now it is not possible that he should follow what appears right to you, but only what appears so to himself. Therefore, if he judges from false appearances, he is the person hurt, since he, too, is the person deceived. For if anyone takes a true proposition to be false, the proposition is not hurt, but only the man is deceived. Setting out, then, from these principles, you will meekly bear with a person who reviles you, for you will say upon every occasion, "It seemed so to him."

XLIII

Everything has two handles: one by which it may be borne, another by which it cannot. If your brother acts unjustly, do not lay hold on the affair by the handle of his injustice, for by that it cannot be borne, but rather by the opposite— that he is your brother, that he was brought up with you; and thus you will lay hold on it as it is to be borne.

XLIV

These reasonings have no logical connection: "I am richer than you, therefore I am your superior." "I am more eloquent than you, therefore I am your superior." The true logical connection is rather this: "I am richer than you, therefore my possessions must exceed yours." "I am more eloquent than you, therefore my style must surpass yours." But you, after all, consist neither in property nor in style.

XLV

Does anyone bathe hastily? Do not say that he does it ill, but hastily. Does anyone drink much wine? Do not say that he does ill, but that he drinks a great deal. For unless you perfectly understand his motives, how should you know if he acts ill? Thus you will not risk yielding to any appearances but such as you fully comprehend.

XLVI

Never proclaim yourself a philosopher, nor make much talk among the ignorant about your principles, but show them by actions. Thus, at an entertainment, do not discourse how people ought to eat, but eat as you ought. For remember that thus Socrates also universally avoided all ostentation. And when persons came to him and desired to be introduced by him to philosophers, he took them and introduced them; so well did he bear being overlooked. So if ever there should be among the ignorant any discussion of principles, be for the most part silent. For there is great danger in hastily throwing out what is undigested. And if anyone tells you that you know nothing, and you are not nettled at it, then you may be sure that you have really entered on your work. For sheep do not hastily throw up the grass to show the shepherds how much they have eaten, but, inwardly digesting their food, they produce it outwardly in wool and milk. Thus, therefore, do you not make an exhibition before the ignorant of your principles, but of the actions to which their digestion gives rise.

XLVII

When you have learned to nourish your body frugally, do not pique yourself upon it; nor, if you drink water, be saying upon every occasion, "I drink water." But first consider how much more frugal are the poor than we, and how much more patient of hardship. If at any time you would inure yourself by exercise to labor and privation, for your own sake and not for the public, do not attempt great feats; but when you are violently thirsty, just rinse your mouth with water, and tell nobody.

XLVIII

The condition and characteristic of a vulgar person is that he never looks for either help or harm from himself, but only from externals. The condition and characteristic of a philosopher is that he looks to himself for all help or harm. The marks of a proficient are that he censures no one, praises no one, blames no one, accuses no one; says nothing concerning himself as being anybody or knowing anything. When he is in any instance hindered or restrained, he accuses himself; and if he is praised, he smiles to himself at the person who praises him; and if he is censured, he makes no defense. But he goes about with the caution of a convalescent, careful of interference with anything that is doing well but not yet quite secure. He restrains desire; he transfers his aversion to those things only which thwart the proper use of our own will; he employs his energies moderately in all directions; if he appears stupid or ignorant, he does not care; and, in a word, he keeps watch over himself as over an enemy and one in ambush.

XLIX

When anyone shows himself vain on being able to understand and interpret the works of Chrysippus, say to yourself: "Unless Chrysippus had written obscurely, this person would have had nothing to be vain of. But what do I desire? To understand nature, and follow her. I ask, then, who interprets her; and hearing that Chrysippus does, I have recourse to him. I do not understand his writings. I seek, therefore, one to interpret *them.*" So far there is nothing to value myself upon. And when I find an interpreter, what remains is to make use of his instructions. This alone is the valuable thing. But if I admire merely the interpretation, what do I become more than a grammarian, instead of a philosopher, except, indeed, that instead of Homer I interpret Chrysippus? When anyone, therefore, desires me to read Chrysippus to him, I rather blush when I cannot exhibit actions that are harmonious and consonant with his discourse.

L

Whatever rules you have adopted, abide by them as laws, and as if you would be impious to transgress them; and do not regard what anyone says of you, for this, after all, is no concern of yours. How long, then, will you delay to demand of yourself the noblest improvements, and in no instance to transgress the judgments of reason? You have received the philosophic principles with which you ought to be conversant; and you have been conversant with them. For what other master, then, do you wait as an excuse for this delay in self-reformation? You are no longer a boy but a grown man. If, therefore, you will be negligent and slothful, and always add procrastination to procrastination, purpose to purpose, and fix day after day in which you will attend to yourself, you will insensibly continue to accomplish nothing and, living and dying, remain of vulgar mind. This instant, then, think yourself worthy of living as a man grown up and a proficient. Let whatever appears to be the best be to you an inviolable law. And if any instance of pain or pleasure, glory or disgrace, be set before you, remember that now is the combat, now the Olympiad comes on, nor can it be put off; and that by one failure and defeat honor may be lost or—won. Thus Socrates became perfect, improving himself by everything, following reason alone. And though you are not yet a Socrates, you ought, however, to live as one seeking to be a Socrates.

9. THUS SPAKE ZARATHUSTRA, THE ANTICHRIST, and BEYOND GOOD AND EVIL

Friedrich Nietzsche

What is the greatest thing ye can experience? It is the hour of great contempt. The hour in which even your happiness becometh loathsome unto you, and so also your reason and virtue.

The hour when ye say: "What good is my happiness! It is poverty and pollution and wretched self-complacency. But my happiness should justify existence itself!"

The hour when ye say: "What good is my reason! Doth it long for knowledge as the lion for his food? It is poverty and pollution and wretched self-complacency!"

The hour when ye say: "What good is my virtue! As yet it hath not made me passionate. How weary I am of my good and my bad! It is all poverty and pollution and wretched self-complacency!"

The hour when ye say: "What good is my justice! I do not see that I am fervour and fuel. The just, however, are fervour and fuel!"

The hour when we say: "What good is my pity! Is not pity the cross on which he is nailed who loveth man? But my pity is not a crucifixion."

Have ye ever spoken thus? Have ye ever cried thus? Ah! would that I had heard you crying thus!

From Friedrich Nietzsche, *Thus Spake Zarathustra,* translated by T. Common, Vol. XI of *The Complete Works of Friedrich Nietzsche,* Oscar Levy, General Editor (Edinburgh: T. N. Foulis, 1909; reissued, New York: Russell & Russell, 1964); *The Antichrist* and *Notes to Zarathustra,* translated by A. M. Ludovici, in Vol. XVI of *The Complete Works of Friedrich Nietzsche,* Oscar Levy, General Editor (Edinburgh: T. N. Foulis, 1911; reissued New York: Russell & Russell, 1964); *Beyond Good and Evil,* translated by Helen Zimmern, Vol XII of *The Complete Works of Friedrich Nietzsche,* Oscar Levy, General Editor (Edinburgh: T. N. Foulis, 1907; reissued New York: Russell & Russell, 1964). Reprinted with permission of Atheneum Publishers, Inc. and George Allen Unwin Ltd.

It is not your sin—it is your self-satisfaction that crieth unto heaven; your very sparingness in sin crieth unto heaven!

Where is the lightning to lick you with its tongue? Where is the frenzy with which ye should be inoculated?

*   *   *

When Zarathustra had spoken these words, he again looked at the people, and was silent. "There they stand," said he to his heart; "there they laugh: they understand me not; I am not the mouth for these ears.

Must one first batter their ears, that they may learn to hear with their eyes? Must one clatter like kettledrums and penitential preachers? Or do they only believe the stammerer?

They have something whereof they are proud. What do they call it, that which maketh them proud? Culture, they call it; it distinguisheth them from the goatherds.

They dislike, therefore, to hear of 'contempt' of themselves. So I will appeal to their pride.

I will speak unto them of the most contemptible thing: that, however, is *the last man!*"

And thus spake Zarathustra unto the people:

It is time for man to fix his goal. It is time for man to plant the germ of his highest hope.

Still is his soil rich enough for it. But that soil will one day be poor and exhausted, and no lofty tree will any longer be able to grow thereon.

Alas! there cometh the time when man will no longer launch the arrow of his longing beyond man—and the string of his bow will have unlearned to whizz!

I tell you: one must still have chaos in one, to give birth to a dancing star. I tell you: ye have still chaos in you.

Alas! There cometh the time when man will no longer give birth to any star. Alas! There cometh the time of the most despicable man, who can no longer despise himself.

Lo! I show you *the last man.*

"What is love? What is creation? What is longing? What is a star?"—so asketh the last man and blinketh.

The earth hath then become small, and on it there hoppeth the last man who maketh everything small. His species is ineradicable like that of the groundflea; the last man liveth longest.

"We have discovered happiness"—say the last men, and blink thereby.

They have left the regions where it is hard to live; for they need warmth. One still loveth one's neighbour and rubbeth against him; for one needeth warmth.

Turning ill and being distrustful, they consider sinful: they walk warily. He is a fool who still stumbleth over stones or men!

A little poison now and then: that maketh pleasant dreams. And much poison at last for a pleasant death.

One still worketh, for work is a pastime. But one is careful lest the pastime should hurt one.

One no longer becometh poor or rich; both are too burdensome. Who still wanteth to rule? Who still wanteth to obey? Both are too burdensome.

No shepherd, and one herd! Every one wanteth the same; every one is equal: he who hath other sentiments goeth voluntarily into the madhouse.

"Formerly all the world was insane,"—say the subtlest of them, and blink thereby.

They are clever and know all that hath happened: so there is no end to their raillery. People still fall out, but are soon reconciled—otherwise it spoileth their stomachs.

They have their little pleasures for the day, and their little pleasures for the night: but they have a regard for health.

"We have discovered happiness,"—say the last men, and blink thereby.—

* * *

The strongest in body and soul are the best— Zarathustra's fundamental proposition—; from them is generated that higher morality of the creator. Man must be regenerated after his own image: this is what he wants, this is his honesty.

* * *

The measure and mean must be found in striving to attain to something beyond mankind: the highest and strongest kind of man must be discovered! The highest tendency must be represented continually in small things:—perfection, maturity, rosy-checked health, mild discharges of power. Just as an artist works, must we apply ourselves to our daily task and bring ourselves to perfection in everything we do. We must be honest in acknowledging our real motives to ourselves, as is becoming in the mighty man.

* * *

What is it which gives a meaning, a value, an importance to things? It is the creative heart which yearns and which created out of this yearning. It created joy and woe. It wanted to sate itself also with woe. Every kind of pain that man or beast has suffered, we must take upon ourselves and bless, and have a goal whereby such suffering would acquire some meaning.

Principal doctrine: the transfiguration of pain into a blessing, and of poison into food, lies in our power. The will to suffering.

* * *

What is good? All that enhances the feeling of power, the Will to Power, and power itself in man. What is bad?—All that proceeds from weakness. What is happiness?—The feeling that power is *increasing,*—that resistance has been overcome.

Not contentment, but more power; not peace at any price, but war; not virtue, but efficiency (virtue in the Renaissance sense, *virtù,* free from all moralic acid). The weak and the botched shall perish: first principle of our humanity. And they ought even to be helped to perish.

What is more harmful than any vice?—Practical sympathy with all the botched and the weak —Christianity.

* * *

Whether it be hedonism, pessimism, utilitarianism, or eudaemonism, all those modes of thinking which measure the worth of things according to *pleasure* and *pain,* that is, according to accompanying circumstances and secondary considerations, are plausible modes of thought and naïvetés, which every one conscious of *creative* powers and an artist's conscience will look down upon with scorn, though not without sympathy. Sympathy for *you!*—to be sure, that is not sympathy as you understand it: it is not sympathy for social "distress," for "society" with its sick and misfortuned, for the hereditarily vicious and defective who lie on the ground around us; still less is it sympathy for the grumbling, vexed, revolutionary slave-classes who strive after power—they call it "freedom." *Our* sympathy is a loftier and furthersighted sympathy:—we see how *man* dwarfs himself, how *you* dwarf him! and there are moments when we view *your* sympathy with an indescribable anguish, when we resist it,—when we regard your seriousness as more dangerous than any kind of levity. You want, if possible—and there is not a more foolish "if possible"—*to do away with suffering;* and we?—it really seems that *we* would rather have it increased and made worse than it has ever been! Well-being, as you understand it—is certainly not a goal; it seems to us an *end;* a condition which at once renders man ludicrous and contemptible—and makes his destruction *desirable!* The discipline of suffering, of *great* suffering—know ye not that it is only *this* discipline that has produced all the elevations of humanity hitherto? The tension of soul in misfortune which communicates to it its energy, its shuddering in view of rack and ruin, its inventiveness and bravery in undergoing, enduring, interpreting, and exploiting misfortune, and whatever depth, mystery, disguise, spirit, artifice, or greatness has been bestowed upon the soul—has it not been bestowed through suffering, through the discipline of great suffering? In man *creature* and *creator* are united: in man there is not only matter, shred, excess, clay, mire, folly, chaos; but there is also the creator, the sculptor, the hardness of the hammer, the divinity of the spectator, and the seventh day—do ye understand this contrast? And that *your* sympathy for the "creature in man" applies to that which has to be fashioned, bruised, forged, stretched, roasted, annealed, refined—to that which must necessarily *suffer,* and *is meant* to suffer? And *our* sympathy—do ye not understand what our *reverse* sympathy applies to, when it resists your sympathy as the worst of all pampering and enervation?—So it is sympathy *against* sympathy!—But to repeat it once more, there are higher problems than the problems of pleasure and pain and sympathy; and all systems of philosophy which deal only with these are naïvetés.

SUGGESTIONS FOR FURTHER READING

A. HEDONISM

Alchian, A. A., "The Meaning of Utility Measurement," *American Economic Review,* Vol. 43 (1953), pp. 26–50.

Aristotle, *Nicomachean Ethics,* Books I and X. Reprinted in Part I of this volume.

Baumgardt, David, *Bentham and the Ethics of Today* (Princeton: Princeton University Press, 1952; reprinted, New York: Octagon Books, Inc., 1966), pp. 167–239, 554–566.

Blake, Ralph, "Why Not Hedonism?" *Ethics,* Vol. 37 (1926–27), pp. 1–18.

Bradley, F. H. *Ethical Studies,* second edition (Oxford: Oxford University Press, 1927), Essay III.

Baylis, Charles A., *Ethics: The Principles of Wise Choice* (New York: Holt, 1958).

Brandt, Richard, *Ethical Theory* (Englewood Cliffs, N. J.: Prentice-Hall, Inc., 1959), Chapters 12 and 13.

Carritt, Edgar F., *Ethical and Political Thinking* (New York: Oxford University Press, 1947), Chapters 7 and 8.

Dewey, John, *Theory of Valuation, International Encyclopedia of Unified Science,* Vol. 2, No. 4 (Chicago: University of Chicago Press, 1939).

Frankena, William K., *Ethics,* second edition (Englewood Cliffs, N. J., Prentice-Hall, Inc., 1973: first edition, 1963), Chapter 5.

Hospers, John, *Human Conduct* (New York: Harcourt, Brace & World, Inc., 1961), Chapter 3.

Huxley, Aldous, *Brave New World Revisited* (New York: Harper & Bros., 1958).

Kenny, Anthony, "Happiness," *Proceedings of the Aris-*

totelian Society, Vol. 66 (1965–66), pp. 93–102. Reprinted in *Moral Concepts,* edited by J. Feinberg (Oxford University Press, 1969).

MacIntyre, Alisdair, "Pleasure as a Reason for Action," *The Monist,* Vol. 49, (1965).

McNaughton, R. M., "A Metrical Conception of Happiness," *Philosophy and Phenomenological Research,* Vol. 14 (1954), pp. 172–183.

Moore, G. E., *Principia Ethica* (Cambridge: Cambridge University Press, 1929), Sections 36–57.

———, *Ethics* (Oxford: Oxford University Press, 1949), Chapters 1, 2.

Nowell-Smith, P. H., *Ethics* (Harmondsworth: Penguin Books, 1954), Chapters 10, 17.

Perry, R. B., *General Theory of Value* (New York: Longmans, Green & Co., 1926), Chapters 21, 22.

Rashdall, Hastings, *The Theory of Good and Evil* (Oxford: Oxford University Press, 1907), Vol. II, Book II, Chapter 1.

Ross, W. D., *The Right and the Good* (New York: Oxford University Press, 1930), Chapter 5.

Sidgwick, Henry, *Methods of Ethics* (London: Macmillan, 1962), Book II, Chapter 3, and Book III, Chapter 14.

Thomas, D. A. Lloyd, "Happiness," *Philosophical Quarterly,* Vol. 18 (1968), pp. 97–113.

Von Wright, Georg, *The Varieties of Goodness* (London: Routledge and Kegan Paul, 1963), Chapters 4 and 5.

Wilson, John, "Happiness," *Analysis,* Vol. 29 (October, 1968), pp. 13–21.

Zink, Sidney, *The Concepts of Ethics* (New York: St. Martin's Press, Inc., Chapters 1–3.

Also see "Suggestions for Further Reading" for Part I of this volume.

B. STOICISM

Blanshard, Brand, *Reason and Goodness* (London: Allen & Unwin, 1961), Chapter 2.

Edelstein, L., *The Meaning of Stoicism* (Cambridge: Harvard University Press, 1966), Chapter 4.

Epictetus, *Discourses,* various editions.

Hicks, R. D., *Stoic and Epicurean* (New York: Russell and Russell, 1962), Chapters 3 and 4.

Hyde, William De Witt, *The Five Great Philosophies of Life,* 2nd edition (New York: The Macmillan Company, 1911; first published, 1904), Chapter 2.

Marcus Aurelius, *The Meditations,* various editions.

Xenakis, J., *Epictetus* (The Hague: Martinus Nijhoff, 1969).

C. NIETZSCHE

Copleston, Frederick, *Friedrich Nietzsche: Philosopher of Culture* (London: Burns Oates & Washbourne Ltd., 1942), Chapters 4 and 5.

Danto, Arthur C., *Nietzsche as Philosopher* (New York: Macmillan 1965).

Hollingdale, R. J., *Nietzsche* (London & Boston: Routledge & Kegan Paul, 1973), Chapter 4.

Kaufman, Walter, *Nietzsche: Philosopher, Psychologist, Antichrist,* 3rd edition (New York: Vintage Books, 1968; first published, 1950), especially Part III.

———, (editor), *The Portable Nietzsche* (New York: Viking Press, 1954).

Nietzsche, Friedrich, *The Genealogy of Morals,* various editions.

———, *The Will to Power,* translated by Walter Kaufman and R. J. Hollingdale (New York: Random House, 1967).

Morgan, G. A., *What Nietzsche Means* (Cambridge, Mass.: Harvard University Press, 1941).

Salter, W. M., *Nietzsche the Thinker* (New York: Holt, Rinehart and Winston, 1917), Chapters 14–27.

Part III Principles of Conduct

The perplexity which generates the philosophical search for ethical principles arises in the choices which one must make in everyday life. Perhaps one is faced with choosing a vocation and, in the quandary, asks, "What is the right thing to do?" Out of this can arise the question, "What would make the decision the correct one?" Perhaps one is tempted to cheat on an examination but remembers being told that this is wrong. Out of this can arise the question, "What makes it wrong?" Perhaps one receives an appeal to support famine relief in Asia. After refusing or making a nominal contribution with a resulting sense of guilt, one perhaps reflects on the question, "Is there a duty to share one's wealth with starving people? And, if so, how much? Until it hurts? Until you yourself are on the brink of starvation? Why or why not?"

These practical questions that arise in daily life are the substance of ethics, which seeks to find ultimate principles for answering them. The moral philosopher as an individual may be interested in developing a consistent ethical system out of pure intellectual curiosity, but if it is a genuine ethical system it will be applicable to both personal decisions and the controversial issues of the day.

There are innumerable specific moral problems which could be used to illustrate the character of "ground-level" moral issues: the morality of abortion, of experiments on fetuses, of invasions of privacy for purposes of national security, of racial discrimination or "reverse" discrimination, or of capital punishment. All of these and others are worthy of discussion, and it is hoped that the reader will reflect upon how the general ethical theories represented in this volume would apply to them. We have chosen to introduce this section with illustrations of specific moral problems drawn from questions of the morality of killing and of sexual morality.

The first two selections, "The Principle of Euthanasia" by Antony Flew and "An Alternative to the Ethic of Euthanasia," by Arthur Dyck, present different views on the morality of euthanasia ("mercy-killing"). Neither of these writers takes the most extreme view possible, and each makes distinctions which have an important bearing upon the analysis of the problem. Among the range of possible attitudes is the extreme position that not only should life never be deliberately terminated, but that all medical measures available should be used to prolong life as long as possible. A more moderate view is that in terminal cases involving extreme suffering, only "ordinary" measures need be taken to prolong life, not extraordinary or "heroic" measures. (This, of course, involves a difficult distinction between ordinary and extraordinary. Is administration of antibiotics "ordinary"?) Another approach is to attempt to distinguish between killing and "letting die," with the former prohibited but the latter permissible in certain cases. Another distinction that is sometimes made is between doing an act with the intention of shortening life, or which "directly" shortens life, and doing an act which has the foreseen "indirect" effect of shortening life but which is done with a different intention, for example, the injection of massive dosages of sedative drugs for the purpose of easing pain, although it is known, but not intended, that this shortens life. Some would argue that the latter act is all right, but not the former.

For those who favor euthanasia under certain conditions, there are a range of circumstances which may be significant in deciding for or against mercy-killing, for example, whether the patient is able to communicate his own wishes or not. If he is, and wishes to die, termination is "voluntary" euthanasia. If he is, and does not wish to die, termination is "involuntary" euthanasia. Some people who would favor the former would oppose the latter; others would justify even the latter in some cases on the grounds that the evolutionary process of selection has made animals, including human beings, fight to stay alive even when it is irrational to do so. If the patient cannot communicate his wishes, the problem is often more difficult. Another dimension of the problem is the probability that the patient may recover. If there is the slightest chance, does this make euthanasia prohibited? Some regard as significant the effects of the patient's illness upon others. If hospital care is pushing the patient's family so deeply into debt that it is ruining life prospects for education, for example, does that make a difference? Finally, and among the most important considerations, is the quality of life of the patient: is it one of a vegetable, or one of excruciating pain, or one of indignity resulting from incapacitation, or merely one of dependence?

Still other dimensions to the problem are the side effects and possible abuse of the practice of euthanasia. Some argue that the practice of euthanasia would greatly lessen confidence in physicians. Others have pointed out that decisions in favor of euthanasia could allow heirs to speed the passing of the fortunes of their aged parents into their own greedy hands, or those in political power to eliminate their enemies. Most advocates of euthanasia have been concerned that there be precautions taken to eliminate mistaken judgment as well as fraud. Usually it is proposed that a board of doctors review each case before a final decision is made. Dyck, in his opposition to euthanasia, makes assumptions as to the kind of community which is possible if the Biblical prohibition, "Thou shalt not kill," is not a foundation stone. This also raises questions about the existence of God, the authority of the Bible, and the interpretation of the Ten Commandments.

The complexity of the preceding discussion of euthanasia is found in nearly all moral problems. The morality of killing in war presents issues ranging from the morality of an individual participating in an on-going war to the morality of war itself. Richard Wasserstrom, in a selection from "On the Morality of War: A Preliminary Inquiry," addresses himself primarily to the latter question, and he finds complexity even there. The morality of war may be thought to depend upon the degree to which the "laws of war" are adhered to, or upon the cause for which the war is fought, or upon whether or not the war is one of aggression or self-defense. All of these are subjected to careful analysis, as is the argument against war on the ground that it results in the death of innocent persons. On the latter point, it turns out to be very difficult to identify who is "innocent," but Wasserstrom nevertheless believes it to be a very powerful argument.

The three readings on sexual ethics reprinted in this section take extremely different points of view. Although David Hume and Immanuel Kant both take what would be regarded as very "conservative" or "old-fashioned" views towards sex, notice that their views do differ substantially and that their supporting arguments are quite different. In a selection from *A Treatise of Human Nature,* Hume justifies modesty and chastity on the grounds that it functions to support paternal participation in child-rearing. He also finds grounds to defend a "double standard" between the male and female sexes. Kant (from *Lectures on Ethics*) sees sexual appetite as intrinsically degrading, the sacrificing of human to animal nature. He has arguments that human beings cannot use themselves as things or allow themselves to be used as things without immorality, and the only relationship in which the body remains united in the whole person in a sexual relationship is in the mutual relationship of matrimony.

Richard Wasserstrom, in "Is Adultery Immoral?" gives different arguments against extramarital sex. Within cultural settings in which sex and affection are customarily connected and in which it is assumed that such affection must be reserved for only one other person, he argues that extramarital sex is immoral because it involves breaking a promise, taking unfair advantage of another, or deception. But Wasserstrom questions whether these customs and assumptions apply to today's youth. Is the connection between sex and affection any longer a custom? And need intimate affection be reserved for only one other person? Is "open marriage," in which there is no assumption of sexual or affectional exclusivity, possible or desirable?

In assessing moral problems, whether they be euthanasia, war, or extramarital sex, the ultimate question is "What makes acts right or wrong?" We react to specific actions with horror or disgust or anger or admiration, but as philosophers we look for general principles in accordance with which these actions and attitudes can be critically assessed and judged appropriate or inappropriate. Classical moral theories, such as those of Aristotle, Kant, and Mill, can be roughly divided between those which base the rightness and wrongness of actions on the consequences of the actions and those which do not. The utilitarians, such as Mill, say explicitly that an act is right as it tends to promote happiness (that is, as it has good consequences) and is wrong as it tends to produce the reverse of happiness (that is, as it has bad consequences). The classical utilitarian theory of intrinsic value attempted to resolve all good consequences ultimately into instances of happiness, which in turn were analyzed as pleasures, and all bad consequences ultimately into instances of the reverse of happiness, which in turn were analyzed as pains, but it is possible to be a consequentialist without adopting the classical utilitarian theory of value. G. E. Moore, for example, held that a right act is one which produces as much good as is possible, but he held that there are many kinds of things which are intrinsically good in addition to pleasure. In Part II of this volume, hedonism and its alternatives as theories of intrinsic value are discussed. Although a theory of intrinsic value may be crucial in deciding the plausibility of a total ethical theory, we can abstract from that issue and compare consequentialism with its alternatives, leaving aside the question of whether pleasures and pains exhaust the list of intrinsically good and bad things or whether the list is more extensive. There are problems inherent in consequentialism regardless of its theory of intrinsic value.

There are also attractive features to consequentialism. It may be that there is greater disagreement among different people as to what acts are right than there is as to what consequences are desirable. If the dispute can be focused on the achievement of agreed upon goals, the choice of means to achieve these may become more amenable to scientific procedure and resolution. Furthermore, the alternative ethics of duty regardless of consequence is counterintuitive. To feel that one must do that action which is one's "duty," even if no one benefits from it, seems a waste of time, and the view that one must do one's duty, even if it hurts everyone affected, seems absurd. Perhaps, then, the entire basis for one's obligations can be found in the good and bad consequences which can be expected to ensue.

Consequentialism is the theory that the end justifies the means. If good consequences result, it appears that whatever means are required to obtain them are justified, which immediately jolts the moral sensitivity of most people. In the selection from *The Prince* by Niccolò Machiavelli, for example, we find him citing with praise the cruelty of Cesare Borgia which united Romagna and brought it to order and obedience. He says the effect of this behavior was far more merciful to the people of the city than that of others who, to avoid cruelty, suffered a city to be torn to pieces by factions. He regards it as well for a prince to seem merciful or faithful and also to be that way, but if it is necessary to be cruel and faithless, he must be able to change. And in the actions of all people, he concludes, there is no tribunal to which we can appeal but results; if these are satisfactory the means will always be judged honorable.

The position of Machiavelli seems the very antithesis of morality. As he himself says, a prince must learn how to be other than good. Deceit, cruelty, faithlessness, and the most horrible atrocities are permitted if necessary to maintain the prince in power. But if we are looking at consequentialism as an ethical doctrine, the end is not the best consequences for the prince or even for a city or nation. Consequentialism in its most plausible form is not egoistic, directed at the best consequences for oneself, nor nationalistic, directed at the best consequences for one's nation. It is universalistic, requiring that an action be justified as having the best consequences for everyone affected. From this perspective, it will be noticed that the means themselves often involve suffering for someone, and that suffering is an end which has to be included in the weighing of the total consequences. If throwing Christians to lions in the arena is to be justified on consequentialist grounds, it must be shown to have the best consequences, including among the consequences the suffering of the Christians and their loss of future life as well as the pleasures of the spectators (and of the lions). If alternative means which involve less suffering can bring about what is otherwise the same end, the means are *not* justified. Another complication is that the means may lead to many ends other than the one in view. One argument for pacifism is that violent means always evoke further violence—what is intended as a war to bring peace to the world inevitably sows the seeds of further violence. Furthermore, actions which in a particular case have good consequences may set precedents for somewhat similar actions which have bad consequences of a much greater magnitude; or, they may have a chain effect requiring other somewhat similar but ultimately unjustified actions. What begins as a "white lie" to avoid embarassing someone may have to be "covered up" with a larger lie until one is living a life of deceit.

Finally, the means may not actually produce the end intended. Unfair campaign practices designed to elect one's candidate may backfire through disclosure and ensure defeat. A breaking-and-entering designed to gather intelligence on an opposition party resulted in the forced resignation of a president. All the results of an action are not certain in advance, and if the means chosen are intrinsically bad, and will occur with certainty if chosen, the certain bad result may outweigh the uncertain good result, even on consequentialist grounds. To the extent that consequences are uncertain, they have to be given less weight in assessing proper choice. The result is a value for the "expected utility" or *expected* good consequences of actions. If there is a choice between A and B, such that A will certainly result in 4 units of good consequences while B has a 50% probability of resulting in 6 units of good consequences, all other results being equal, the "expected" good consequences of A is 4 and of B is 3.

To sum up these remarks, a consequentialist theory should not be oversimplified. It should not just consider the effects of the action upon the agent, but upon everyone affected. It should take into account the total of all consequences, including those inherent in the act itself and including any remote consequences such as those caused by precedents set and the influence of example. It should compare the act with alternatives open to the agent, and it should take into consideration the probability with which various results can be expected.

With all these qualifications, however, consequentialism can still justify actions which are immoral by traditional standards, and it proposes an assessment of the morality of actions which is far from the traditional methods of assessment. This is pointed out by E. F. Carritt, in a selection from *Ethical and Political Thinking* included in this section. According to traditional attitudes towards debts and promises, one has an obligation to pay debts and to keep promises even if there is something better that one can think of doing with one's money and other resources. In case the consequentialist should point out that debt-paying and promise-keeping normally have good consequences, and a particular violation sets a bad precedent, inviting others to violate these useful rules by its example, Carritt gives an example in which the promise is not known to have been made by any other living person, and therefore any influence of the example of its violation is nullified: suppose there is an agreement between two isolated explorers such that one agrees to die for the other's survival if the other will promise to educate his children. Since no living person knows that the promise is made, is it as if the promise had never been made? Another example which runs counter to our moral intuitions is the example of framing and hanging an innocent person to still a violent crime wave. The false belief that one of the criminals has been apprehended may deter a far larger number of deaths of other innocent persons, but it is clearly unjust. Consequentialists may swallow these implications of their theory and say, "So much the worse for moral intuitions which are based on the normal case. In unusual circumstances, one has to do what is necessary to produce the best consequences, and if it really has the best consequences, it is the right thing to do." Other philosophers, however, have sought a more complex consequentialism which does not imply that these acts ought to be done.

The fact that a particular act in particular circumstances may have consequences which acts of that type in other circumstances do not have has led some philosophers to draw a distinction between justifying a rule or practice, such as promise-keeping or punishing only the guilty, and justifying a particular act falling under the rule. Consequentialist considerations may go into deciding which rules to have, or which rules are justified; particular acts may be justified by whether or not they are in conformity with or in violation of justified rules, rather than by whether they, as particular acts, have best consequences. This distinction is explored in the essay by John Rawls in this section, "Two Concepts of Rules." Although Rawls in his other writings does not defend a utilitarian position, in this essay he shows that such a distinction can help bring the requirements imposed by utilitarianism closer to our considered moral judgments. The practice of promise-keeping can be justified on consequentialist grounds as a social structure which enables people to plan their futures with greater certainty, but particular instances of promise-keeping or promise-breaking can require justification not by appeal directly to the principle of utility, but by the requirement that the particular instance conform to the practice of promise-keeping.

The type of consequentialism developed out of the distinction Rawls makes has been labeled "rule utilitarianism" and contrasted to "act utilitarianism," the theory that tests particular acts directly by whether or not they have the best consequences. Various versions of rule utilitarianism are critically discussed and one form defended in Richard B. Brandt's essay, "Some Merits of

One Form of Rule-Utilitarianism." An act utilitarian reply, stating a thesis of the appropriate place of rules in an act utilitarian theory, is given in the selections by J. J. C. Smart from "Rightness and Wrongness of Actions" and "The Place of Rules in Act Utilitarianism."

If consequentialism is found unacceptable in any of its pure or complicated forms, what are the alternatives? Important alternatives are found in Aristotle and Kant, whose writings form the bulk of Part I of this volume and are introduced there. Another alternative is to view consequentialism as a part of morality but not the whole. There may be a plurality of sources of moral obligation, of which the obligation to do things which have good consequences and refrain from doing things which have bad consequences are two, but two among others with which they may be in conflict. W. D. Ross, in "What Makes Right Acts Right?" develops a theory of "prima facie duties" based on the assumption that there are various irreducible right-making or wrong-making characteristics of actions which may be in conflict with each other, and there is no way of saying in general which should take precedence. In addition to having moral significance ultimately based on consequentialist features, he regards actions as having nonderivative moral significance based on their being instances of fidelity, of reparation, of gratitude, of justice, or of self-improvement. To the extent that an action has moral significance from being in one of these categories, it is a prima facie duty and ought to be done if there is no conflict with any other prima facie duty. In case of conflict, his appeal is to the reflections of moral consciousness to indicate which prima facie duty is the most stringent and therefore one's totiresultant or absolute duty.

H. W.

10. *THE PRINCIPLE OF EUTHANASIA*

Antony Flew

1

My particular concern here is to deploy a general moral case for the establishment of a legal right to voluntary euthanasia. The first point to emphasize is that the argument is about *voluntary* euthanasia. Neither I nor any other contributor to the present volume advocates the euthanasia of either the incurably sick or the miserably senile except in so far as this is the strong, constant, and unequivocally expressed wish of the afflicted candidates themselves. Anyone, therefore, who dismisses what is in fact being contended on the gratuitously irrelevant grounds that he could not tolerate compulsory euthanasia, may very reasonably be construed as thereby tacitly admitting inability to meet and to overcome the case actually presented.

Second, my argument is an argument for the establishment of a legal right. What I am urging is that any patient whose condition is hopeless and painful, who secures that it is duly and professionally certified as such, and who himself clearly and continuously desires to die should be enabled to do so: and that he should be enabled to do so without his incurring, or his family incurring, or those who provide or administer the means of death incurring, any legal penalty or stigma whatsoever. To advocate the establishment of such a legal right is not thereby to be committed even to saying that it would always be morally justifiable, must less that it would always be morally obligatory, for any patient to exercise this right if he found himself in a position so to do. For a legal right is not as such necessarily and always a moral right; and hence, *a fortiori,* it is not necessarily and always a moral duty to exercise whatever legal rights you may happen to possess.

This is a vital point. It was—to refer first to an issue now at last happily resolved—crucial to the question of the relegalization in Great Britain of homosexual relations between consenting male adults. Only when it was at last widely grasped, and grasped in its relation to this particular question, could we find the large majorities in both Houses of Parliament by which a liberalizing bill was passed into law. For presumably most members of those majorities not only found the idea of homosexual relations repugnant—as most of us do—but also believed such relations to be morally wrong—as I for one do not. Yet they brought themselves to recognize that neither the repugnance generally felt towards some practice, nor even its actual wrongness if it actually is wrong, by itself constitutes sufficient reason for making or keeping that practice illegal. By the same token it can in the present instance be entirely consistent to urge, both that there ought to be a legal right to voluntary euthanasia, and that it would sometimes or always be morally wrong to exercise that legal right.

Third, the case presented here is offered as a moral one. In developing and defending such a case I shall, of course, have to consider certain peculiarly religious claims. Such claims, however, become relevant here only in so far as they either constitute, or may be thought to constitute, or in so far as they warrant, or may be thought to warrant, conclusions incompatible with those which it is my primary and positive purpose to urge.

Fourth, and finally, this essay is concerned primarily with general principles, not with particular practicalities. I shall not here discuss or—except perhaps quite incidentally—touch upon any questions of comparative detail: questions, for instance, of how a Euthanasia Act ought to be drafted; of what safeguards would need to be incorporated to prevent abuse of the new legal possibilities by those with disreputable reasons for wanting someone else dead; of exactly what and how much should be taken as constituting an unequivocal expression of a clear and constant

Antony Flew, "The Principle of Euthanasia," from *Euthanasia and the Right to Death,* edited by A. B. Downing. Published by Peter Owen, London. Reprinted by permission.

wish; of the circumstances, if any, in which we ought to take earlier calculated expressions of a patient's desires as constituting still adequate grounds for action when at some later time the patient has become himself unable any longer to provide sufficiently sober, balanced, constant and unequivocal expressions of his wishes; and so on.

I propose here as a matter of policy largely to ignore such particular and practical questions. This is not because I foolishly regard them as unimportant, or irresponsibly dismiss them as dull. Obviously they could become of the most urgent interest. Nor yet is it because I believe that my philosophical cloth disqualifies me from contributing helpfully to any down-to-earth discussions. On the contrary, I happen to be one of those numerous academics who are convinced, some of them correctly, that they are practical and businesslike men! The decisive reason for neglecting these vital questions of detail here in, and in favour of, a consideration of the general principle of the legalization of voluntary euthanasia is that they are all secondary to that primary issue. For no such subordinate question can properly arise as relevantly practical until and unless the general principle is conceded. Some of these practical considerations are in any event dealt with by other contributors to this volume.

2

So what can be said in favour of the principle? There are two main, and to my mind decisive, moral reasons. But before deploying these it is worth pausing for a moment to indicate why the onus of proof does not properly rest upon us. It may seem as if it does, because we are proposing a change in the present order of things; and it is up to the man who wants a change to produce the reasons for making whatever change he is proposing. This most rational principle of conservatism is in general sound. But here it comes into conflict with the overriding and fundamental liberal principle. It is up to any person and any institution wanting to prevent anyone from doing anything he wishes to do, or to compel anyone to do anything he does not wish to do, to provide positive good reason to justify interference. The question should therefore be: *not*

'Why should people be given this new legal right?'; *but* 'Why should people in this matter be restrained by law from doing what they want?'

Yet even if this liberal perspective is accepted, as it too often is not, and even if we are able to dispose of any reasons offered in defence of the present legal prohibitions, still the question would arise, whether the present state of the law represents a merely tiresome departure from sound liberal principles of legislation, or whether it constitutes a really substantial evil. It is here that we have to offer our two main positive arguments.

(1) First, there are, and for the foreseeable future will be, people afflicted with incurable and painful diseases who urgently and fixedly want to die quickly. The first argument is that a law which tries to prevent such sufferers from achieving this quick death, and usually thereby forces other people who care for them to watch their pointless pain helplessly, is a very cruel law. It is because of this legal cruelty that advocates of euthanasia sometimes speak of euthanasia as 'mercy-killing.' In such cases the sufferer may be reduced to an obscene parody of a human being, a lump of suffering flesh eased only by intervals of drugged stupor. This, as things now stand, must persist until at last every device of medical skill fails to prolong the horror.

(2) Second, a law which insists that there must be no end to this process—terminated only by the overdue relief of 'death by natural causes'— is a very degrading law. In the present context the full force of this second reason may not be appreciated immediately, if at all. We are so used to meeting appeals to 'the absolute value of human personality,' offered as the would-be knock-down objection to any proposal to legalize voluntary euthanasia, that it has become hard to realize that, in so far as we can attach some tolerably precise meaning to the key phrase, this consideration would seem to bear in the direction precisely opposite to that in which it is usually mistaken to point. For the agonies of prolonged terminal illness can be so terrible and so demoralizing that the person is blotted out in ungovernable nerve reactions. In such cases as this, to meet the patient's longing for death is a means of showing for human personality that respect which cannot tolerate any ghastly tra-

vesty of it. So our second main positive argument, attacking the present state of the law as degrading, derives from a respect for the wishes of the individual person, a concern for human dignity, an unwillingness to let the animal pain disintegrate the man.

Our first main positive argument opposes the present state of the law, and of the public opinion which tolerates it, as cruel. Often and appositely this argument is supported by contrasting the tenderness which rightly insists that on occasion dogs and horses must be put out of their misery, with the stubborn refusal in any circumstances to permit one person to assist another in cutting short his suffering. The cry is raised, 'But people are not animals!' Indeed they are not. Yet this is precisely not a ground for treating people worse than brute animals. Animals are like people, in that they too can suffer. It is for this reason that both can have a claim on our pity and our mercy.[1]

But people are also more than brute animals. They can talk and think and wish and plan. It is this that makes it possible to insist, as we do, that there must be no euthanasia unless it is the firm considered wish of the person concerned. People also can, and should, have dignity as human beings. That is precisely why we are urging that they should be helped and not hindered when they wish to avoid or cut short the often degrading miseries of incurable disease or, I would myself add, of advanced senile decay.

<h1 style="text-align:center">3</h1>

In the first section I explained the scope and limitations of the present chapter. In the second I offered—although only after suggesting that the onus of proof in this case does not really rest on the proposition—my two main positive reasons in favour of euthanasia. It is time now to begin to face, and to try to dispose of, objections. This is the most important phase in the whole exercise. For to anyone with any width of experience and any capacity for compassion the positive reasons must be both perfectly obvious and strongly felt. The crucial issue is whether or not there are decisive, overriding objections to these most pressing reasons of the heart.

(1) Many of the objections commonly advanced, which are often mistaken to be fundamental, are really objections only to a possible specific manner of implementing the principle of voluntary euthanasia. Thus it is suggested that if the law permitted doctors on occasion to provide their patients with means of death, or where necessary to do the actual killing, and they did so, then the doctors who did either of these things would be violating the Hippocratic Oath, and the prestige of and public confidence in the medical profession would be undermined.

As to the Hippocratic Oath, this makes two demands which in the special circumstances we have in mind may become mutually contradictory. They then cannot both be met at the same time. The relevant section reads: 'I will use treatments to help the sick according to my ability and judgment, but never with a view to injury and wrong-doing. I will not give anyone a lethal dose if asked to do so, nor will I suggest such a course.[2] The fundamental undertaking 'to help the sick according to my ability and judgment' may flatly conflict with the further promise not to 'give anyone a lethal dose if asked to do so.' To observe the basic undertaking a doctor may have to break the further promise. The moral would, therefore, appear to be: not that the Hippocratic Oath categorically and unambiguously demands that doctors must have no dealings with voluntary euthanasia; but rather that the possible incompatibility in such cases of the different directives generated by two of its logically independent clauses constitutes a reason for revising that Oath.

As to the supposed threat to the prestige of and to our confidence in the medical profession, I am myself inclined to think that the fears expressed are—in more than one dimension—disproportionate to the realities. But whatever the truth about this the whole objection would bear only against proposals which permitted or required doctors to do, or directly to assist in, the actual killing. This is not something which is essential to the whole idea of voluntary euthanasia, and the British Euthanasia Society's present draft bill is so formulated as altogether to avoid this objection. It is precisely such inessential objections as this which I have undertaken to eschew in this essay, in order to consider simply the general principle.

(2) The first two objections which do really bear on this form a pair. One consists in the con-

tention that there is no need to be concerned about the issue, since in fact there are not any, or not many, patients who when it comes to the point want to die quickly. The other bases the same complacent conclusion on the claim that in fact, in the appropriate cases, doctors already mercifully take the law into their own hands. These two comfortable doctrines are, like many other similarly reassuring bromides, both entirely wrong and rather shabby.

(a) To the first the full reply would probably have to be made by a doctor, for a medical layman can scarcely be in a position to make an estimate of the number of patients who would apply and could qualify for euthanasia.[3] But it is quite sufficient for our immediate purposes to say two things. First, there can be few who have reached middle life, and who have not chosen to shield their sensibilities with some impenetrable carapace of dogma, who cannot recall at least one case of an eager candidate for euthanasia from their own experience—even from their own peacetime experience only. If this statement is correct, as my own inquiries suggest that it is, then the total number of such eager candidates must be substantial. Second, though the need for enabling legalization becomes progressively more urgent the greater the numbers of people personally concerned, I wish for myself to insist that it still matters very much indeed if but one person who would have decided for a quick death is forced to undergo a protracted one.

(b) To the second objection, which admits that there are many cases where euthanasia is indicated, but is content to leave it to the doctors to defy the law, the answer is equally simple. First, it is manifestly not true that all doctors are willing on the appropriate occasions either to provide the means of death or to do the killing. Many, as they are Roman Catholics, are on religious grounds absolutely opposed to doing so. Many others are similarly opposed for other reasons, or by force of training and habit. And there is no reason to believe that among the rest the proportion of potential martyrs is greater than it is in any other secular occupational group. Second, it is entirely wrong to expect the members of one profession as a regular matter of course to jeopardize their whole careers by breaking the criminal law in order to save the rest of us the labour and embarrassment of changing that law.

Here I repeat two points made to me more than once by doctor friends. First, if a doctor were convinced he ought to provide euthanasia in spite of the law, it would often be far harder for him to do so undetected than many laymen think, especially in our hospitals. Second, the present attitude of the medical establishment is such that if a doctor did take the chance, was caught and brought to trial, and even if the jury, as they well might, refused to convict, still he must expect to face complete professional disaster.

(3) The next two objections, which in effect bear on the principle, again form a pair. The first pair had in common the claim that the facts were such that the question of legislative action need not arise. The second pair are alike in that whereas both might appear to be making contentions of fact, in reality we may have in each a piece of exhortation or of metaphysics masquerading as an empirical proposition.

(a) Of this second relevant pair the first suggests that there is no such thing as an incurable disease. This implausible thesis becomes more intelligible, though no more true, when we recall how medical ideologues sometimes make proclamations: 'Modern medicine cannot recognize any such thing as a disease which is incurable'; and the like. Such pronouncements may sound like reports on the present state of the art. It is from this resemblance that they derive their peculiar idiomatic point. But the advance of medicine has not reached a stage where all diseases are curable. And no one seriously thinks that it has. At most this continuing advance has suggested that we need never despair of finding cures *some day*. But this is not at all the same thing as saying, what is simply not true, that *even now* there is no condition which is at any stage incurable. This medical ideologue's slogan has to be construed as a piece of exhortation disguised for greater effect as a paradoxical statement of purported fact. It may as such be instructively compared with certain favourite educationalists' paradoxes: 'We do not teach subjects, we teach children!' or 'There are no bad children, only bad teachers!'

(b) The second objection of this pair is that no one can ever be certain that the condition of any particular patient is indeed hopeless. This is more tricky. For an objection of this form might be given two radically different sorts of content. Yet it would be easy and is common to slide from one interpretation to the other, and back again, entirely unwittingly.

Simply and straightforwardly, such an objection might be made by someone whose point was that judgments of incurability are, as a matter of purely contingent fact, so unreliable that no one has any business to be certain, or to claim to know, that anyone is suffering from an incurable affliction. This contention would relevantly be backed by appealing to the alleged fact that judgments that 'this case is hopeless, *period*' are far more frequently proven to have been mistaken than judgments that, for instance, 'this patient will recover fully, *provided that* he undergoes the appropriate operation.' This naïve objector's point could be made out, or decisively refuted, only by reference to quantitative studies of the actual relative reliabilities and unreliabilities of different sorts of medical judgments. So unless and until such quantitative empirical studies are actually made, and unless and until their results are shown to bear upon the question of euthanasia in the way suggested, there is no grounded and categorical objection here to be met.

But besides this first and straightforwardly empirical interpretation there is a second interpretation of another quite different sort. Suppose someone points to an instance, as they certainly could and well might, where some patient whom all the doctors had pronounced to be beyond hope nevertheless recovers, either as the result of the application of new treatment derived from some swift and unforeseen advance in medical science, or just through nature taking its unexpected course. This happy but chastening outcome would certainly demonstrate that the doctors concerned had on this occasion been mistaken; and hence that, though they had sincerely claimed to know the patient's condition to have been incurable, they had not really known this. The temptation is to mistake it that such errors show that no one ever really knows. It is this perfectly general contention, applied to the particular present case of judgments of incurability, which constitutes the second objection in its second interpretation. The

objector seizes upon the point that even the best medical opinion turns out sometimes to have been wrong (as here). He then urges, simply because doctors thus prove occasionally to have been mistaken (as here) and because it is always —theoretically if not practically—possible that they may be mistaken again the next time, that therefore none of them ever really knows (at least in such cases). Hence, he concludes, there is after all no purchase for the idea of voluntary euthanasia. For this notion presupposes that there are patients recognizably suffering from conditions known to be incurable.

The crux to grasp about this contention is that, notwithstanding that it may be presented and pressed as if it were somehow especially relevant to one particular class of judgments, in truth it applies—if it applies at all—absolutely generally. The issue is thus revealed as not medical but metaphysical. If it follows that if someone is ever mistaken then he never really knows, and still more if it follows that if it is even logically possible that he may be mistaken then he never really knows, then, surely, the consequence must be that none of us ever does know—not *really*. (When a metaphysician says that something is never really such and such, what he really means is that it very often is, *really*.) For it is of the very essence of our cognitive predicament that we do all sometimes make mistakes; while always it is at least theoretically possible that we may. Hence the argument, if it holds at all, must show that knowledge, *real* knowledge, is for all us mortal men for ever unattainable.

What makes the second of the present pair of objections tricky to handle is that it is so easy to pass unwittingly from an empirical to a metaphysical interpretation. We may fail to notice, or noticing may fail convincingly to explain, how an empirical thesis has degenerated into metaphysics, or how metaphysical misconceptions have corrupted the medical judgment. Yet, once these utterly different interpretations have been adequately distinguished, two summary comments should be sufficient.

First, in so far as the objection is purely metaphysical, to the idea that *real* knowledge is possible, it applies absolutely generally; or not at all. It is arbitrary and irrational to restrict it to the examination of the principle of voluntary euthanasia. If doctors never really know, we presumably have no business to rely much upon any of their judgments. And if, for the same metaphysical reasons, there is no knowledge to be had anywhere, then we are all of us in the same case about everything. This may be as it may be, but it is nothing in particular to the practical business in hand.

Second, when the objection takes the form of a pretended refusal to take any decision in matters of life and death on the basis of a judgment which theoretically might turn out to have been mistaken, it is equally unrealistic and arbitrary. It is one thing to claim that judgments of incurability are peculiarly fallible: if that suggestion were to be proved to be correct. It is quite another to claim that it is improper to take vital decisions on the basis of sorts of judgment which either are in principle fallible, or even prove occasionally in fact to have been wrong. It is an inescapable feature of the human condition that no one is infallible about anything, and there is no sphere of life in which mistakes do not occur. Nevertheless we cannot as agents avoid, even in matters of life and death and more than life and death, making decisions to act or to abstain. It is only necessary and it is only possible to insist on ordinarily strict standards of warranted assertability, and on ordinarily exacting rather than obsessional criteria of what is beyond reasonable doubt.

Of course this means that mistakes will sometimes be made. This is in practice a corollary of the uncontested fact that infallibility is not an option. To try to ignore our fallibility is unrealistic, while to insist on remembering it only in the context of the question of voluntary euthanasia is arbitrary. Nor is it either realistic or honourable to attempt to offload the inescapable burdens of practical responsibility, by first claiming that we never really *know,* and then pretending that a decision not to act is somehow a decision which relieves us of all proper responsibility for the outcome.

(4) The two pairs of relevant objections so far considered have both been attempts in different ways to show that the issue does not, or at any rate need not, arise as a practical question. The next concedes that the question does arise and is important, but attempts to dispose of it with the argument that what we propose amounts to the legalization, in certain circumstances, of murder, or suicide or both; and that this cannot be

right because murder and suicide are both gravely wrong always. Now even if we were to concede all the rest it would still not follow, because something is gravely wrong in morals, that there ought to be a law against it; and that we are wrong to try to change the law as it now subsists. We have already urged that the onus of proof must always rest on the defenders of any restriction.

(a) In fact the rest will not do. In the first place, if the law were to be changed as we want, the present legal definition of 'murder' would at the same time have to be so changed that it no longer covered the provision of euthanasia for a patient who had established that it was his legal right. 'Does this mean,' someone may indignantly protest, 'that right and wrong are created by Acts of Parliament?' Emphatically, yes: and equally emphatically, no. Yes indeed, if what is intended is *legal* right and *legal* offence. What is meant by the qualification 'legal' if it is not that these rights are the rights established and sanctioned by the law? Certainly not, if what is intended is *moral* right and *moral* wrong. Some moral rights happen to be at the same time legal rights, and some moral wrongs similarly also constitute offences against the law. But, notoriously, legislatures may persist in denying moral rights; while, as I insisted earlier, not every moral wrong either is or ought to be forbidden and penalized by law.

Well then, if the legal definition of 'murder' can be changed by Act of Parliament, would euthanasia nevertheless be murder, morally speaking? This amounts to asking whether administering euthanasia legally to someone who is incurably ill, and who has continually wanted it, is in all relevant respects similar to, so to speak, a standard case of murder; and whether therefore it is to be regarded morally as murder. Once the structure of the question is in this way clearly displayed it becomes obvious that the cases are different in at least three important respects. First, whereas the murder victim is (typically) killed against his will, a patient would be given or assisted in obtaining euthanasia only if he steadily and strongly desired to die. Second, whereas the murderer kills his victim treating him usually as a mere object for disposal, in euthanasia the object of the exercise would be to save someone, at his own request, from needless suffering, to prevent the degradation of a human person. Third, whereas the murderer by his action defies the law, the man performing euthanasia would be acting according to law, helping another man to secure what the law allowed him.

It may sound as if that third clause goes back on the earlier repudiation of the idea that moral right and wrong are created by Act of Parliament. That is not so. For we are not saying that this action would now be justifiable, or at least not murder morally, simply because it was now permitted by the law; but rather that the change in the law would remove one of possible reasons for moral objection. The point is this: that although the fact that something is enjoined, permitted, or forbidden by law does not necessarily make it right, justifiable, or wrong morally, nevertheless the fact that something is enjoined or forbidden by a law laid down by established authority does constitute one moral reason for obedience. So a doctor who is convinced that the objects of the Euthanasia Society are absolutely right should at least hesitate to take the law into his own hands, not only for prudential but also for moral reasons. For to defy the law is, as it were, to cast your vote against constitutional procedures and the rule of law, and these are the foundations and framework of any tolerable civilized society. (Consider here the injunction posted by some enlightened municipal authorities upon their public litter bins: 'Cast your vote here for a tidy New York!'—or wherever it may be.)

Returning to the main point, the three differences which we have just noticed are surely sufficient to require us to refuse to assimilate legalized voluntary euthanasia to the immoral category of murder. But to insist on making a distinction between legalized voluntary euthanasia and murder is not the same thing as, nor does it by itself warrant, a refusal to accept that both are equally immoral. What an appreciation of these three differences, but crucially of the first, should do is to suggest that we ought to think of such euthanasia as a special case not of murder but of suicide. Let us therefore examine the second member of our third pair of relevant objections.

(b) This objection was that to legalize voluntary euthanasia would be to legalize, in certain conditions, the act of assisting suicide. The question therefore arises: 'Is suicide always morally wrong?'

The purely secular considerations usually advanced and accepted are not very impressive. First, it is still sometimes urged that suicide is unnatural, in conflict with instinct, a breach of the putative law of self-preservation. All arguments of this sort, which attempt directly to deduce conclusions about what *ought* to be from premises stating, or mis-stating, only what *is* are —surely—unsound: they involve what philosophers label, appropriately, the 'Naturalistic Fallacy.' There is also a peculiar viciousness about appealing to what is supposed to be a descriptive law of nature to provide some justification for the prescription to obey that supposed law. For if the law really obtained as a description of what always and unavoidably happens, then there would be no point in prescribing that it should; whereas if the descriptive law does not in fact hold, then the basis of the supposed justification does not exist.[4] Furthermore, even if an argument of this first sort could show that suicide is always immoral, it could scarcely provide a reason for insisting that it ought also to be illegal.

Second, it is urged that the suicide by his act deprives other people of the services which he might have rendered them had he lived longer. This can be a strong argument, especially where the suicide has a clear, positive family or public obligations. It is also an argument which, even in a liberal perspective, can provide a basis for legislation. But it is irrelevant to the circumstances which advocates of the legalization of voluntary euthanasia have in mind. In such circumstances as these, there is no longer any chance of being any use to anyone, and if there is any family or social obligation it must be all the other way—to end your life when it has become a hopeless burden both to yourself and to others.

Third, it is still sometimes maintained that suicide is in effect murder—'self-murder.' To this, offered in a purely secular context, the appropriate and apparently decisive reply would seem to be that by parity of reasoning marriage is really adultery—'own-wife-adultery.' For, surely, the gravamen of both distinctions lies in the differences which such paradoxical assimilations override. It is precisely because suicide is the destruction of oneself (by one's own choice), while murder is the destruction of somebody else (against his wishes), that the former can be, and is, distinguished from the latter.

Yet there is a counter to this own-wife-adultery-move. It begins by insisting, rightly, that sexual relations—which are what is common to both marriage and adultery—are not in themselves wrong: the crucial question is, 'Who with?' It then proceeds to claim that what is common to both murder and suicide is the killing of a human being; and here the questions of 'Which one?' or 'By whom?' are not, morally, similarly decisive. Finally appeal may be made, if the spokesman is a little old-fashioned, to the Sixth Commandment, or if he is in the contemporary swim, to the Principle of the Absolute Sanctity of Human Life.

The fundamental difficulty which confronts anyone making this counter move is that of finding a formulation for his chosen principle about the wrongness of all killing, which is both sufficiently general not to appear merely question-begging in its application to the cases in dispute, and which yet carries no consequences that the spokesman himself is not prepared to accept. Thus, suppose he tries to read the Sixth Commandment as constituting a veto on any killing of human beings. Let us waive here the immediate scholarly objections: that such a reading involves accepting the mistranslation 'Thou shalt not kill' rather than the more faithful 'Thou shalt do no murder'; and that neither the children of Israel nor even their religious leaders construed this as a law forbidding all war and all capital punishment.[5] The question remains whether our spokesman himself is really prepared to say that all killing, without any exception, is morally wrong.

It is a question which has to be pressed, and which can only be answered by each man for himself. Since I cannot give your answer, I can only say that I know few if any people who would sincerely say 'Yes.' But as soon as any exceptions or qualifications are admitted, it becomes excessively difficult to find any presentable principle upon which these can be admitted while still excluding suicide and assistance to suicide in a case of euthanasia. This is not just because, generally, once any exceptions or qualifications have been admitted to any rule it becomes hard or impossible not to allow others. It is because, particularly, the case for excluding suicide and assisting suicide from the scope of any embargo on killing people is so strong that only some absolutely universal rule admitting no

exceptions of any sort whatever could have the force convincingly to override it.

Much the same applies to the appeal to the Principle of the Absolute Sanctity of Human Life. Such appeals were continually made by conservatives—many of them politically not Conservative but Socialist—in opposition to the recent efforts to liberalize the British abortion laws. Such conservatives should be, and repeatedly were, asked whether they are also opponents of all capital punishment and whether they think that it is always wrong to kill in a 'just war.' (In fact none of those in Parliament could honestly have answered 'Yes' to both questions.) In the case of abortion their position could still be saved by inserting the qualification 'innocent,' a qualification traditionally made by cautious moralists who intend to rest on this sort of principle. But any such qualification, however necessary, must make it almost impossible to employ the principle thus duly qualified to proscribe all suicide. It would be extraordinarily awkward and far-fetched to condemn suicide or assisting suicide as 'taking an innocent life.'

Earlier in the present subsection I described the three arguments I have been examining as secular. This was perhaps misleading. For all three are regularly used by religious people: indeed versions of all three are to be found in St Thomas Aquinas's *Summa Theologica,* the third being there explicitly linked with St Augustine's laboured interpretation of the Sixth Commandment to cover suicide.[6] And perhaps the incongruity of trying to make the amended Principle of the Absolute Sanctity of Innocent Human Life yield a ban on suicide is partly to be understood as a result of attempting to derive from secularized premises conclusions which really depend upon a religious foundation. But the next two arguments are frankly and distinctively religious.

The first insists that human beings are God's property: 'It is our duty to take care of God's property entrusted to our charge—our souls and bodies. They belong not to us but to God';[7] 'Whoever takes his own life sins against God, even as he who kills another's slave sins against that slave's master';[8] and 'Suicide is the destruction of the temple of God and a violation of the property rights of Jesus Christ.'[9]

About this I restrict myself to three comments here. First, as it stands, unsupplemented by appeal to some other principle of principles, it must apply, if it applies at all, equally to *all* artificial and intentional shortening *or* lengthening of any human life, one's own *or* that of anyone else. Alone and unsupplemented it would commit one to complete quietism in all matters of life and death; for all interference would be interference with someone else's property. Otherwise one must find further particular moral revelations by which to justify capital punishment, war, medicine, and many other such at first flush impious practices. Second, it seems to presuppose that a correct model of the relation between man and God is that of slave and slave-master, and that respect for God's property ought to be the fundamental principle of morals. It is perhaps significant that it is to this image that St Thomas and the pagan Plato, in attacking suicide, both appeal. This attempt to derive not only theological but all obligations from the putative theological fact of Creation is a commonplace of at least one tradition of moral theology. In this derivation the implicit moral premise is usually that unconditional obedience to a Creator, often considered as a very special sort of owner, is the primary elemental obligation.[10] Once this is made explicit it does not appear to be self-evidently true; nor is it easy to see how a creature in absolute ontological dependence could be the genuinely responsible subject of obligations to his infinite Creator.[11] Third, this objection calls to mind one of the sounder sayings of the sinister Tiberius: 'If the gods are insulted let them see to it themselves.' This remark is obviously relevant only to the question of legalization, not to that of the morality or the prudence of the action itself.

The second distinctively religious argument springs from the conviction that God does indeed see to it Himself, with a penalty of infinite severity. If you help someone to secure euthanasia, 'You are sending him from the temporary and comparatively light suffering of this world to the eternal suffering of hell.' Now if this appalling suggestion could be shown to be true it would provide the most powerful moral reason against helping euthanasia in any way, and for using any legislative means which might save people from suffering a penalty so inconceivably cruel. It would also be the strongest possible prudential reason against 'suiciding oneself.'[12] (Though surely anyone who know-

ingly incurred such a penalty would by that very action prove himself to be genuinely of unsound mind; and hence not *justly* punishable at all. Not that a Being contemplating such unspeakable horrors could be expected to be concerned with justice!)

About this second, peculiarly religious, argument there is, it would seem, little to be done except: either simply to concede that for anyone holding this belief it indeed is reasonable to oppose euthanasia, and to leave it at that; or, still surely conceding this, to attempt to mount a general offensive against the whole system of which it forms a part.

(5) The final objection is one raised, with appropriate modifications, by the opponents of every reform everywhere. It is that even granting that the principle of the reform is excellent it would, if adopted, lead inevitably to something worse; and so we had much better not make any change at all. Thus G. K. Chesterton pronounced that the proponents of euthanasia now seek only the death of those who are a nuisance to themselves, but soon it will be broadened to include those who are a nuisance to others.[13] Such cosy arguments depend on two assumptions: that the supposedly inevitable consequences are indeed evil and substantially worse than the evils the reform would remove; and that the supposedly inevitable consequences really are inevitable consequences.

In the present case we certainly can grant the first assumption, if the consequence supposed is taken to be large-scale legalized homicide in the Nazi manner. But whatever reason is there for saying that this would, much less inevitably must, follow? For there are the best of reasons for insisting that there is a world of difference between legalized voluntary euthanasia and such legalized mass-murder. Only if public opinion comes to appreciate their force will there be any chance of getting the reform we want. Then we should have no difficulty, in alliance doubtless with all our present opponents, in blocking any move to legalize murder which might conceivably arise from a misunderstanding of the case for voluntary euthanasia. Furthermore, it is to the point to remind such objectors that the Nazi atrocities they probably have in mind were in fact not the result of any such reform, but were the work of people who consciously repudiated the whole approach to ethics represented in the argument of the present essay. For this approach is at once human and humanitarian. It is concerned above all with the reduction of suffering; but concerned at the same time with other values too, such as human dignity and respect for

the wishes of the individual person. And always it is insistent that morality should not be 'left in the dominion of vague feeling or inexplicable internal conviction, but should be . . . made a matter of reason and calculation.[14]

NOTES

1. Thus Jeremy Bentham, urging that the legislator must not neglect animal sufferings, insists that the 'question is not "Can they *reason?*" nor "Can they *talk?*" but "Can they *suffer?*" ' (*Principles of Morals and Legislation,* Chap. XVII, *n.*)

2. The Greek text is most easily found in *Hippocrates and the Fragments of Heracleitus,* ed. W. H. S. Jones and E. T. Withington for the Loeb series (Harvard Univ. Pr. and Heinemann), Vol. 1, p. 298. The translation in the present essay is mine.

3. See Downing, pp. 20–1; also pp. 23–4 for his reference to Professor Hinton's work, *Dying* (Pelican, 1967).

4. I have argued this kind of point more fully in *Evolutionary Ethics* (London: Macmillan, 1967). See Chap. IV, 'From *Is* to *Ought.*'

5. See, f.i., Joseph Fletcher, *Morals and Medicine* (1954; Gollancz, 1955), pp. 195–6. I recommend this excellent treatment by a liberal Protestant of a range of questions in moral theology too often left too far from liberal Roman Catholics.

6. Part II: Q. 64, A5. The Augustine reference is to *The City of God,* 1, 20. It is worth comparing, for ancient Judaic attitudes, E. Westermarck's *Origin and Development of the Moral Ideas,* Vol. 1, pp. 246–7.

7. See the Rev. G. J. MacGillivray, 'Suicide and Euthanasia,' p. 10; a widely distributed Catholic Truth Society pamphlet.

8. Aquinas, loc. cit.

9. Koch-Preuss, *Handbook of Moral Theology,* Vol. II, p. 76. This quotation has been taken from Fletcher, op. cit., p. 192.

10. Cf., for convenience, MacGillivray, loc. cit.; and for a Protestant analogue the Bishop of Exeter quoted by P. Nowell-Smith in *Ethics* (Penguin, 1954), pp. 37–8 *n.*

11. I have developed this contention in *God and Philosophy* (Hutchinson, 1966), §§ 2.34 ff.

12. This rather affected-sounding gallicism is adopted deliberately: if you believe, as I do, that suicide is not always and as such wrong, it is inappropriate to speak of 'committing suicide;' just as correspondingly if you believe, as I do not, that (private) profit is wrong, it becomes apt to talk of those who 'commit a profit.'

13. I take this quotation, too, from Fletcher, op, cit., p. 201: it originally appeared in *The Digest* (Dec. 23, 1937). Another, much more recent specimen of this sort of obscurantist flim-flam may be found in Lord Longford's speech to the House of Lords against Mr. David Steel's Abortion Bill as originally passed by the Commons. Lord Longford (formerly Pakenham) urged that if that bill were passed, we might see the day when senile members of their lordships' House were put down willy-nilly.

14. J. S. Mill's essay on Bentham quoted in F. R. Leavis, *Mill on Bentham and Coleridge* (Chatto & Windus, 1950), p. 92.

11. *AN ALTERNATIVE TO THE ETHIC OF EUTHANASIA*

Arthur J. Dyck

Contemporary society and modern medicine face difficult policy decisions. This is illustrated most recently in the Voluntary Euthanasia Act of 1969, submitted for consideration in the British Parliament. The purpose of that act is to provide for "the administration of euthanasia to persons who request it and who are suffering from an irremediable condition" (Downing,

From Arthur Dyck, "An Alternative to the Ethic of Euthanasia," in *To Live and to Let Die,* ed. by R. H. Williams (New York: Springer-Verlag, 1973), pp. 98–112. Reprinted by permission of the publisher.

1971) and to enable such persons to make such a request in advance. For the purposes of that act, euthanasia means "the painless inducement of death" to be administered by a physician, i.e., "a registered medical practitioner."

The declaration that one signs under this act, should one become incurably ill and wish to have euthanasia administered, reads as follows:

If I should at any time suffer from a serious physical illness or impairment reasonably thought in my case to be incurable and expected to cause me severe distress or render me incapable of rational existence, I request the administration of euthanasia at a time or in circumstances to be indicated or specified by me or, if it is apparent that I have become incapable of giving directions, at the discretion of the physician in charge of my case.

In the event of my suffering from any of the conditions specified above, I request that no active steps should be taken . . . to prolong my life or restore me to consciousness.

This declaration is to remain in force unless I revoke it, which I may do at any time. . . .

I wish it to be understood that I have confidence in the good faith of my relatives and physicians, and fear degeneration and indignity far more than I fear premature death.

The ethic by which one justifies making such a declaration has been eloquently expressed by Joseph Fletcher. He speaks of "the right of spiritual beings to use intelligent control over physical nature rather than to submit beastlike to its blind workings." For Fletcher, "Death control, like birth control, is a matter of human dignity. Without it persons become puppets. To perceive this is to grasp the error lurking in the notion—widespread in medical circles—that life as such is the highest good."

Within our society today there are those who agree with the ethic of Joseph Fletcher. They agree also that an ethic that places a supreme value upon life is dominant in the medical profession. In a candid editorial (Cal. Med.), the traditional Western ethic with its affirmation of "the intrinsic worth and equal value of every human life regardless of its stage or condition" and with its roots in the Judaic and Christian heritage, is declared to be the basis for most of our laws and much of our social policy. What is more, the editorial says, "the reverence for each and every human life" is "a keystone of Western medicine and is the ethic which has caused physicians to try to preserve, protect, repair, prolong and enhance every human life which comes under their surveillance." Although this medical editor sees this traditional ethic as still clearly dominant, he is convinced that it is being eroded and that it is being replaced by a new ethic that he believes medicine should accept and applaud. This editor sees the beginning of the new ethic in the increasing acceptance of abortion, the general practice of which is in direct defiance of an ethic that affirms the "intrinsic and equal value for every human life regardless of its stage, condition, or status." For, in the opinion of this editor, human life begins at conception, and abortion is killing. Such killing is to be condoned and embraced by the new ethic.

In the above editorial a case is made for what is called "the quality of life." To increase the quality of life, it is assumed that the traditional Western ethic will necessarily have to be revised or even totally replaced. This, it is argued, is because it "will become necessary and acceptable to place relative rather than absolute values on such things as human lives, the use of scarce resources and the various elements which are to make up the quality of life or of living which is to be sought." On such a view, the new ethic aids medicine in improving the quality of life; the ethic designated as the old ethic, rooted in Judaism and Christianity, is treated as an impediment to medicine's efforts to improve the quality of life. What kind of ethic should guide contemporary decisions regarding sterilization, abortion, and euthanasia—decisions as to who shall live and who shall die? Given the limits of this chapter, we shall discuss and assess the ethic (moral policy) of those who favor a policy of voluntary euthanasia and the ethic (moral policy) of those who oppose it. (Abortion and sterilization are large topics I have discussed in some detail elsewhere [Dyck, 1971].) The term "euthanasia" is used here, exactly as in the Voluntary Euthanasia Act of 1969, to mean "the painless inducement of death."

THE ETHIC OF EUTHANASIA

What then is the ethic that guides those who support legislation like the Voluntary Euthanasia Act of 1969 and its Declaration? The arguments for euthanasia focus upon two humane and significant concerns: compassion for those who are painfully and terminally ill; and concern for the human dignity associated with freedom of choice. Compassion and freedom are values that sustain and enhance the common good. The question here, however, is how these values affect our behavior toward the dying.

The argument for compassion usually occurs in the form of attacking the inhumanity of keeping dying people alive when they are in great pain or when they have lost almost all of their usual functions, particularly when they have lost the ability or will to communicate with others. Thus, someone like Joseph Fletcher cites examples of people who are kept alive in a hopelessly debilitated state by means of the latest medical techniques, whether these be respirators, intravenous feeding, or the like. Often when Fletcher and others are arguing for the legalization of decisions not to intervene in these ways, the point is made that physicians already make decisions to turn off respirators or in other ways fail to use every means to prolong life. It is this allegedly compassionate behavior that the law would seek to condone and encourage.

The argument for compassion is supplemented by an argument for greater freedom for a patient to choose how and when he or she will die. For one thing, the patient should not be subjected to medical treatment to which that patient does not consent. Those who argue for voluntary euthanasia extend this notion by arguing that the choice to withhold techniques that would prolong life is a choice to shorten life. Hence, if one can choose to shorten one's life, why cannot one ask a physician by a simple and direct act of intervention to put an end to one's life? Here it is often argued that physicians already curtail life by means of pain-killing drugs, which in the doses administered, will hasten death. Why should not the law recognize and sanction a simple and direct hastening of death, should the patient wish it?

How do the proponents of euthanasia view the general prohibition against killing? First of all, they maintain that we are dealing here with people who will surely die regardless of the intervention of medicine. They advocate the termination of suffering and the lawful foreshortening of the dying process. Secondly, although the patient is committing suicide, and the physician is an accomplice in such a suicide, both acts are morally justifiable to cut short the suffering of one who is dying.

It is important to be very clear about the precise moral reasoning by which advocates of voluntary euthanasia justify suicide and assisting a suicide. They make no moral dsitinction between those instances when a patient or a physician chooses to have life shortened by failing to accept or use life-prolonging techniques and those instances when a patient or a physician shorten life by employing a death-dealing chem-

ical or instrument. They make no moral distinction between a drug given to kill pain, which also shortens life, and a substance given precisely to shorten life and for no other reason. Presumably these distinctions are not honored, because regardless of the stratagem employed—regardless of whether one is permitting to die or killing directly—the result is the same, the patient's life is shortened. Hence, it is maintained that, if you can justify one kind of act that shortens the life of the dying, you can justify any act that shortens the life of the dying when this act is seen to be willed by the one who is dying. Moral reasoning of this sort is strictly utilitarian; it focuses solely on the consequences of acts, not on their intent.

Even though the reasoning on the issue of compassion is so strictly utilitarian, one is puzzled about the failure to raise certain kinds of questions. A strict utilitarian might inquire about the effect of the medical practice of promoting or even encouraging direct acts on the part of physicians to shorten the lives of their patients. And, in the same vein, a utilitarian might also be very concerned about whether the loosening of constraints on physicians may not loosen the constraints on killing generally. There are two reasons these questions are either not raised or are dealt with rather summarily. First, it is alleged that there is no evidence that untoward consequences would result. And second, the value of freedom is invoked, so that the question of killing becomes a question of suicide and assistance in a suicide.

The appeal to freedom is not strictly a utilitarian argument, at least not for some proponents of voluntary euthanasia. Joseph Fletcher, for example, complains about the foolishness of nature in bringing about situations in which dying is a prolonged process of suffering. He feels strongly that the failure to permit or encourage euthanasia demeans the dignity of persons. Fletcher has two themes here: On the one hand, the more people are able to control the process of nature, the more dignity and freedom they have; on the other hand, people have dignity only insofar as they are able to choose when, how, and why they are to live or to die. For physicians this means also choices as to who is to die, because presumably one cannot assist in the suicide of just any patient who claims to be suffering, or who thinks he or she is dying.

The ethic that defends suicide as a matter of individual conscience and as an expression of human dignity is a very old ethic. Both the Stoics and the Epicureans considered the choice of one's own death as the ultimate expression of human freedom and as an essential component of the dignity that attaches to rational personhood. This willingness to take one's life is an aspect of Stoic courage (Tillich, 1952). A true Stoic could not be manipulated by those who threatened death. When death seemed inevitable, they chose it before someone could inflict it upon them. Human freedom for the Stoics was not complete unless one could also choose death and not compromise oneself for fear of it. All the "heroes" in literature exhibit this kind of Stoic courage in the face of death.

A euthanasia ethic, as exemplified already in ancient Stoicism, contains the following essential presuppositions or beliefs:

1) That an individual's life belongs to that individual to dispose of entirely as he or she wishes;
2) That the dignity that attaches to personhood by reason of the freedom to make moral choices demands also the freedom to take one's own life;
3) That there is such a thing as a life not worth living, whether by reason of distress, illness, physical or mental handicaps, or even sheer despair for whatever reason;
4) That what is sacred or supreme in value is the "human dignity" that resides in man's own rational capacity to choose and control life and death.

This commitment to the free exercise of the human capacity to control life and death takes on a distinct religious aura. Speaking of the death control that amniocentesis makes possible, Robert S. Morrison declares that, "the birth of babies with gross physical and mental handicaps will no longer be left entirely to God, to chance, or to the forces of nature."

AN ETHIC OF BENEMORTASIA

From our account of the ethic of euthanasia, those who oppose voluntary euthanasia would seem to lack compassion for the dying and the courage to affirm human freedom. They appear incompassionate because they oppose what has come to be regarded as synonymous with a good death—namely, a painless and deliberately foreshortened process of dying. The term euthanasia originally meant a painless and happy death with no reference to whether such a death was induced. Although this definition still appears in modern dictionaries, a second meaning of the term has come to prevail: euthanasia now generally means "an act or method of causing death painlessly so as to end suffering" (Webster's New World Dictionary, 1962). In short, it would appear that the advocates of euthanasia, i.e., of *causing* death, are the advocates of a good death, and the advocates of voluntary euthanasia seek for all of us the freedom to have a good death.

Because of this loss of a merely descriptive term for a happy death, it is necessary to invent a term for a happy or good death—namely, benemortasia. The familiar derivatives for this new term are *bene* (good) and *mors* (death). The meaning of "bene" in "benemortasia" is deliberately unspecified so that it does not necessarily imply that a death must be painless and/or induced in order to be good. What constitutes a good or happy death is a disputable matter of moral policy. How then should one view the arguments for voluntary euthanasia? And, if an ethic of euthanasia is unacceptable, what is an acceptable ethic of benemortasia?

An ethic of benemortasia does not stand in opposition to the values of compassion and human freedom. It differs, however, from the ethic of euthanasia in its understanding of how these values are best realized. In particular, certain constraints upon human freedom are recognized and emphasized as enabling human beings to increase compassion and freedom rather than diminish them. For the purposes of this essay, we trace the roots of our ethic of benemortasia to Jewish and Christian sources. This does not mean that such an ethic is confined to those traditions or to persons influenced by them any more than an ethic of euthanasia is confined to its Stoic origins or adherents.

The moral life of Jews and Christians alike is and has been guided by the Decalogue, or Ten Commandments. "Thou shalt not kill" is one of the clear constraints upon human decisions and actions expressed in the Decalogue. It is precisely the nature of this constraint that is at stake in decisions regarding euthanasia.

Modern biblical scholarship has discovered that the Decalogue, or Mosaic Covenant, is in the form of a treaty between a Suzerian and his people (Mendenhall, 1955). The point of such a treaty is to specify the relationship between a ruler and his people, and to set out the conditions necessary to form and sustain community with that ruler. One of the most significant purposes of such a treaty is to specify constraints that members of a community must observe if the community is to be viable at all. Fundamentally, the Decalogue articulates the indispensable prerequisites of the common life.

Viewed in this way the injunction not to kill is part of a total effort to prevent the destruction of the human community. It is an absolute prohibition in the sense that no society can be indifferent about the taking of human life. Any act, insofar as it is an act of taking a human life, is wrong, that is to say, taking a human life is a wrong-making characteristic of actions.

To say, however, that killing is prima facie wrong does not mean that an act of killing may never be justified (Ross, 1930). For example, a person's effort to prevent someone's death may lead to the death of the attacker. However, we can morally justify that act of intervention only because it is an act of saving a life, not because it is an act of taking a life. If it were simply an act of taking a life, it would be wrong.[1]

A further constraint upon human freedom within the Jewish and Christian traditions is articulated in a myth concerning the loss of paradise. The loss of Eden comes at the point where man and woman succumb to the temptation to know good and evil, and to know it in the perfect and ultimate sense in which a perfect and ultimate being would know it (Revised Standard Version of the Bible, 1952). To know who should live and who should die, one would have to know everything about people, including their ultimate destiny. Only God could have such knowledge. Trying to decide who shall live and who shall die is "playing god." It is tragic to "play god" because one does it with such limited and uncertain knowledge of what is good and evil.

This contraint upon freedom has a liberating effect in the practice of medicine. Nothing in Jewish and Christian tradition presumes that a physician has a clear mandate to impose his or her wishes and skills upon patients for the sake of prolonging the length of their dying where those patients are diagnosed as terminally ill and do not wish the interventions of the physician. Thus the freedom of the patient to accept his or her dying and to decide whether he or she is to have any particular kind of medical care is surely enhanced. A patient, who has every reason to believe that he or she is dying, would lose the last vestige of freedom were he or she denied the right to choose the circumstances under which the terminal illness would take its course. Presumably that patient is someone who has not chosen to die, but who does have some choices left as to how the last hours and days will be spent. Interventions, in the form of drugs, drainage tubes, or feeding by injection or whatever, may or may not be what the patient wishes or would find beneficial for these last hours or days. People who are dying have as much freedom as other living persons to accept or to refuse medical treatment when that treatment provides no cure for their ailment. There is nothing in the Jewish or Christian tradition that provides an exact blueprint as to what is the most compassionate thing to do for someone who is dying. Presumably the most compassionate act is to be a neighbor to such a person and to minister to such a person's needs. Depending upon the circumstances, this may or may not include intervention to prolong the process of dying.

Our ethic of benemortasia acknowledges the freedom of patients who are incurably ill to refuse interventions that prolong dying and the freedom of physicians to honor such wishes. However, these actions are not acts of suicide and assisting in suicide. In our ethic of benemortasia, suicide and assisting in suicide are unjustifiable acts of killing. Unlike the ethic of those who would legalize voluntary euthanasia, our ethic makes a moral distinction between acts that *permit* death and acts that *cause* death. As George P. Fletcher notes, one can make a sharp distinction, one that will stand up in law, between "permitting to die" and "causing death." Jewish and Christian tradition, particularly Roman Catholic thought, have maintained this clear distinction between the failure to use extraordinary measures (permitting to die) and direct intervention to bring about death (causing death).[2] A distinction is also drawn between a drug administered to cause death and a drug administered to ease pain which has the added effect of shortening life (see, for example, Smith, 1970).

Why are these distinctions important in instances where permitting to die or causing death both have the effect of shortening life? In both instances there is a failure to try to prolong the life of one who is dying. It is at this point that one must see why consequential reasoning is in itself too narrow, and why it is important also not to limit the discussion of benemortasia to the immediate relationship between a patient and his or her physician.

Where a person is dying of a terminal illness, it is fair to say that no one, including the dying person and his or her physician, has wittingly chosen this affliction and this manner or time of death. The choices that are left to a dying patient, an attendant physician, others who know the patient, and society concern how the last days of the dying person are to be spent.

From the point of view of the dying person, when could his or her decisions be called a deliberate act to end life, the act we usually designate as suicide? Only, it seems to me, when the dying person commits an act that has the immediate intent of ending life and has no other purpose. That act may be to use, or ask the physician to use, a chemical or an instrument that has no other immediate effect than to end the dying person's life. If, for the sake of relieving pain, a dying person chooses drugs administered in potent doses, the intent of this act is not to shorten life, even though it has that effect. It is a choice as to how to live while dying. Similarly, if a patient chooses to forego medical interventions that would have the effect of prolonging his or her life without in any way promising release from death, this also is a choice as to what is the most meaningful way to spend the remainder of life, however short that may be. The choice to use drugs to relieve pain and the choice not to use medical measures that cannot promise a cure for one's dying are no different in principle from the choices we make throughout our lives as to how much we will rest, how hard we will work, how little and how much medical intervention we will seek or tolerate, and the like. For society

or physicians to map out life styles for individuals with respect to such decisions is surely beyond anything that we find in Stoic, Jewish, or Christian ethics. Such intervention in the liberty of individuals is far beyond what is required in any society whose rules are intended to constrain people against harming others.

But human freedom should not be extended to include the taking of one's own life. Causing one's own death cannot generally be justified, even when one is dying. To see why this is so, we have to consider how causing one's death does violence to one's self and harms others.

The person who causes his or her own death repudiates the meaningfulness and worth of his or her own life. To decide to initiate an act that has as its primary purpose to end one's life is to decide that that life has no worth to anyone, especially to oneself. It is an act that ends all choices regarding what one's life and whatever is left of it is to symbolize.

Suicide is the ultimately effective way of shutting out all other people from one's life. Psychologists have observed how hostility for others can be expressed through taking one's own life. People who might want access to the dying one to make restitution, offer reparation, bestow last kindnesses, or clarify misunderstandings are cut off by such an act. Every kind of potentially and actually meaningful contact and relation among persons is irrevocably severed except by means of memories and whatever life beyond death may offer. Certainly for those who are left behind by death, there can remain many years of suffering occasioned by that death. The sequence of dying an inevitable death can be much better accepted than the decision on the part of a dying one that he or she has no worth to anyone. An act that presupposes that final declaration leaves tragic overtones for anyone who participated in even the smallest way in that person's dying.

But the problem is even greater. If in principle a person can take his or her own life whenever he or she no longer finds it meaningful, there is nothing in principle that prevents anyone from taking his or her life, no matter what the circumstances. For if the decision hinges on whether one regards his or her own life as meaningful, anyone can regard his or her own life as meaningless even under circumstances that would appear to be most fortunate and opportune for an abundant life.

What about those who would commit suicide or request euthanasia in order to cease being a "burden" on those who are providing care for them? If it is a choice to accept death by refusing non-curative care that prolongs dying, the freedom to embrace death or give one's life in this way is honored by our ethic of benemortasis. What is rejected is the freedom to cause death whether by suicide or by assisting in one. (Dyke, 1968, distinguishes between *giving* one's life and *taking* one's life.)

How a person dies has a definite meaning for those to whom that person is related. In the first year of bereavement, the rate of death among bereaved relatives of those who die in hospitals is twice that of bereaved relatives of those who die at home; sudden deaths away from hospital and home increase the death rate of the bereaved even more (Lasagna, 1970).

The courage to be, as expressed in Christian and Jewish thought, is more than the overcoming of the fear of death, although it includes that Stoic dimension. It is the courage to accept one's own life as having worth no matter what life may bring, including the threat of death, because that life remains meaningful and is regarded as worthy by God, regardless of what that life may be like.

An ethic of benemortasia stresses what Tillich has called the "courage to be as a part"—namely, the courage to affirm not only oneself, but also one's participation as a self in a universal community of beings. The courage to be as a part recognizes that one is not merely one's own, that one's life is a gift bestowed and protected by the human community and by the ultimate forces that make up the cycle of birth and death. In the cycle of birth and death, there may be suffering, as there is joy, but suffering does not render a life meaningless or worthless. Suffering people need the support of others; suffering people should not be encouraged to commit suicide by their community, or that community ceases to be a community.

This consideration brings us to a further difficulty with voluntary euthanasia and its legalization. Not only does euthanasia involve suicide, but also, if legalized, it sanctions assistance in suicide by physicians. Legislation like the Vol-untary Euthanasia Act of 1969 makes it a duty of the medical profession to take someone else's life for him. Here the principle not to kill is even further eroded and violated by giving the physician the power and the encouragement to decide that someone else's life is no longer worth living. The whole notion that a physician can engage in euthanasia implies acceptance of the principle that another person's life is no longer meaningful enough to sustain, a principle that does not afford protection for the lives of any of the most defenseless, voiceless, or otherwise dependent members of a community. Everyone in a community is potentially a victim of such a principle, particularly among members of racial minorities, the very young, and the very old.

Those who would argue that these consequences of a policy of voluntary euthanasia cannot be predicted fail to see two things: that we have already had an opportunity to observe what happens when the principle that sanctions euthanasia is accepted by a society; and that regardless of what the consequences may be of such acts, the acts themselves are wrong in principle.

With respect to the first point, Leo Alexander's (1949) very careful analysis of medical practices and attitudes of German physicians before and during the reign of Nazism in Germany should serve as a definite warning against the consequences of making euthanasia a public policy. He notes that the outlook of German physicians that led to their cooperation in what became a policy of mass murders,

started with the acceptance of that attitude, basic in the euthanasia movement, that there is such a thing as life not worthy to be lived. This attitude in its early stages concerned itself merely with the severely and chronically sick. Gradually the sphere of those to be included in this category was enlarged to include the socially unproductive, the racially unwanted, and finally all non-Germans. But it is important to realize that the infinitely small wedged-in lever from which this entire trend of mind received its impetus was the attitude toward the nonrehabilitable sick.

Those who reject out of hand any comparison of what happened in Nazi Germany with what we can expect here in the United States should consider current examples of medical practice in this nation. The treatment of mongoloids is a case in point. Now that the notion is gaining acceptance that a fetus diagnosed in the womb as mongoloid can, at the discretion of a couple or the pregnant woman, be justifiably aborted, instances of infanticide in hospitals are being reported. At Johns Hopkins Hospital, for example, an allegedly mongoloid infant whose parents would not permit an operation that is generally successful in securing normal physical health and development, was ordered to have "nothing by mouth," condemning that infant to a death that took 15 days. By any of our existing laws, this was a case of murder, justified on the ground that this particular life was somehow not worth saving. (If one argues that the infant was killed because the parents did not want it, we have in this kind of case an even more radical erosion of our restraints upon killing.)

Someone may argue that the mongoloid was permitted to die, not killed. But this is faulty reasoning. In the case of an infant whose future life and happiness could be reasonably assured through surgery, we are not dealing with someone who is dying and with intervention that has no curative effect. The fact that some physicians refer to this as a case of permitting to die is an ominous portent of the dangers inherent in accepting the principle that a physician or another party can decide for a patient that his or her life is not worth living. Equally ominous is the assumption that this principle, once accepted, can easily be limited to cases of patients for whom no curative intervention is known to exist.

With all the risks that attend changing the physician's role from one who sustains life to one who induces death, one may well ask why physicians should be called upon to assist a suicide?

M. R. Barrington, an advocate of suicide and of voluntary euthanasia, is aware of the difficulty of making this request of physicians and of the necessity for justifying legalization of such requests. She suggests that the role of the physician in assisting suicide is essential, "especially as human frailty requires that it should be open to a patient to ask the doctor to choose a time for the giving of euthanasia that is not known to the patient" (Barrington, 1971). This appeal to "human frailty" is very telling. The hesitation to commit suicide and the ambivalence of the dying about their worth should give one pause before

one signs a declaration that empowers a physician to decide that at some point one can no longer be trusted as competent to judge whether or not one wants to die. Physicians are also frail humans, and mistaken diagnoses, research interests, and sometimes errors of judgment that stem from a desire for organs, are part of the practice of medicine.[3]

Comatose patients pose special problems for an ethic of benemortasia as they do for the advocates of voluntary euthanasia. Where patients are judged to be irreversibly comatose and where sustained efforts have been made to restore such persons to consciousness, no clear case can be made for permitting to die, even though it seems merciful to do so. It seems that the best we can do is to develop some rough social and medical consensus about a reasonable length of time for keeping "alive" a person's organ systems after "brain death" has been decided (Ramsey, 1970). Because of the pressures to do research and to transplant organs, it may also be necessary to employ special patient advocates who are not physicians and nurses. These patient advocates, trained in medical ethics, would function as ombudsmen.

In summary, even if the practice of euthanasia were to be confined to those who voluntarily request an end to their lives, no physician could in good conscience participate in such an act. To decide directly to cause the death of a patient is to abandon a cardinal principle of medical practice—namely, to do no harm to one's patient. The relief of suffering, which is surely a time-honored role for the physician, does not extend to an act that presupposes that the life of a patient who is suffering is not worthy to be lived. As we have argued, not even the patient who is dying can justifiably and unilaterally universalize the principle by which a dying life would be declared to be worthless.

Some readers may remain unconvinced that euthanasia is morally wrong as a general policy. Perhaps what still divides us is what distinguishes a Stoic from a Jewish and Christian way of life. The Stoic heritage declares that my life and my selfhood are my own to dispose of as I see fit and when I see fit. The Jewish and Christian heritage declares that my life and my selfhood are not my own, and are not mine to dispose of as I see fit.

In the words of H. Richard Neibuhr,

I live but do not have the power to live. And further, I may die at any moment, but I am powerless to die. It was not in my power, nor in my parents' power, to elect my *self* into existence. Though they willed a child or consented to it they did not will *me*—this I, thus and so. And so also I now, though I *will* to be no more, cannot elect myself out of existence, if the inscrutable power by which I am, elects otherwise. Though I wish to be mortal, if the power that threw me into being in this mortal destructible body elects me into being again there is nothing I can do about that. I can destroy the life of my body. Can I destroy myself? This remains the haunting question of the literature of suicide and of all the lonely debates of men to whom existence is a burden. Whether they shall wake up again, either here in this life or there in some other mode of being, is beyond their control. We can choose among many alternatives; but the power to choose self-existence or self-extinction is not ours. Men can practice birth-control, not self-creation; they can commit *bio*cide; whether they can commit suicide, self-destruction, remains a question.

Although one has the power to commit biocide, this does not give one the right to do so. Niebuhr views our lives as shaped by our responses to others and their responses to us. All of us are in responsible relations to others. The claim that an act of suicide (biocide) would harm no one else is unrealistic. To try to make that a reality would require an incredibly lonely existence cut off from all ties of friendship, cooperation, and mutual dependence. And in so doing, we would repudiate the value and benefits of altruism.

The other points at which the proponents of euthanasia and the advocates of benemortasia part company concern the perception of the context in which all moral decisions are made. Here again the division has religious overtones. Those who decide for euthanasia seem to accept an ethic which ultimately privatizes and subjectivizes the injunction not to kill. Those who oppose euthanasia see the decision not to kill as one that is in harmony with what is good for everyone, and indeed is an expression of what is required of everyone if goodness is to be pervasive and powerful on earth. Once again, H. Richard Niebuhr has eloquently expressed this latter position:

All my specific and relative evaluations expressed in my interpretations and responses are shaped, guided, and formed by the understanding of good and evil I have *upon the whole*. In distrust of the radical action by which I am, by which my society is, by which this world is, I must find my center of valuation in myself, or in my nation, or in my church, or in my science, or in humanity, or in life. Good and evil in this view mean what is good for me and bad for me; or good and evil for my nation, or good and evil for one of these finite causes, such as mankind, or life or reason. But should it happen that confidence is given to me in the power by which all things are and by which I am; should I learn in the depths of my existence to praise the creative source, . . . all my relative evaluations will be subjected to the continuing and great correction. They will be made to fit into a total process producing good—not what is good for me (though my confidence accepts that as included), nor what is good for man (though that is also included), nor what is good for the development of life (though that also belongs in the picture), but what is good for being, for universal being, or for God, center and source of all existence.

Our ethic of benemortasia has argued for the following beliefs and values:

1) that an individual person's life is not solely at the disposal of that person; every human life is part of the human community that bestows and protects the lives of its members; the possibility of community itself depends upon constraints against taking life;
2) that the dignity that attaches to personhood by reason of the freedom to make moral choices includes the freedom of dying people to refuse noncurative, life-prolonging interventions when one is dying, but does not extend to taking one's life or causing death for someone who is dying;
3) that every life has some worth; there is no such thing as a life not worth living;
4) that the supreme value is goodness itself to which the dying and those who care for the dying are responsible. Religiously expressed the supreme value is God. Less than perfectly good beings, human beings, require constraints upon their decisions regarding those who are dying. No human being or human community can presume to know who deserves to live or to die.

At the same time, we have implied throughout that religion and the Jewish and Christian expressions of it are not obstacles to modern medicine and a better life; rather they help foster humanity's ceaseless quest to preserve and enhance human life on this earth.

NOTES

1. One may be perplexed that societies with their roots in Jewish and Christian traditions have been able to justify capital punishment. If one believes that capital punishment will have a deterrent effect, i.e., will save lives, its justification is at least understandable. We have raised serious doubts in recent years as to its deterrent effect and hence now have good reason to question this practice.

2. See, for example, an excellent discussion by the Protestant Paul Ramsey, *The Patient as Person,* pp. 113–164, which contains many references also to Roman Catholic literature on the care for the dying. For the Jewish views, see the classic text by Immanuel Jakobovits, *Jewish Medical Ethics.* Whereas Jewish law forbids active euthanasia, Jakobovits makes it clear that "Jewish law sanctions and perhaps even demands the withdrawal of any factor—whether extraneous to the patient himself or not—which may artificially delay the demise of the final phase."

3. See Yale Kamisar, "Euthanasia Legislation: Some Non-Religious Objections" for copious documentation of medical error and other aspects of medical practice that would make euthanasia legislation hazardous.

12.   ON THE MORALITY OF WAR

Richard Wasserstrom

Before we examine the moral criteria for assessing war, we must examine the claim that it is not possible to assess war in moral terms. Proponents of this position assert that moral predicates either cannot meaningfully or should not be applied to wars. For want of a better name for this general view, I shall call it moral nihilism in respect to war. If it is correct, there is, of course, no point in going further.

It is apparent that anyone who believes that all moral predicates are meaningless, or that all morality (and not just conventional morality) is a sham and a fraud, will regard the case of the morality of war as an a fortiori case. This is not the position I am interested in considering. Rather the view I call moral nihilism in respect to war is, I think, more interesting in the sense that it is restricted to the case of war. What I have in mind is this: During the controversy over the

From Richard Wasserstrom, "On the Morality of War: A Preliminary Inquiry," *Stanford Law Review,* Vol. 21, No. 6 (June 1969), pp. 1627–1656. Copyright 1969 by the Board of Trustees of Leland Stanford Junior University. The portion included here is from pp. 1636–1656 and comprises Parts II, III, and IV of the article. Reprinted by permission of the *Stanford Law Review.*

rightness of the Vietnam War there have been any number of persons, including a large number in the university, who have claimed that in matters of war (but not in other matters) morality has no place. The war in Vietnam may, they readily concede, be stupid, unwise, or against the best interests of the United States, but it is neither immoral nor unjust—not because it is moral or right, but because these descriptions are *in this context* either naive or meaningless or inapplicable.

Nor is this view limited to the Vietnam war. Consider, for instance, the following passage from a speech given only a few years ago by Dean Acheson:

[T]hose involved in the Cuban crisis of October, 1962, will remember the irrelevance of the supposed moral considerations brought out in the discussions. Judgment centered about the appraisal of dangers and risks, the weighing of the need for decisive and effective action against considerations of prudence; the need to do enough, against the consequences of doing too much. Moral talk did not bear on the problem. Nor did it bear upon the decision of those called upon to advise the President in 1949 whether and with what degree of urgency to press the attempt to produce a thermonuclear weapon. A respected colleague advised me that it would be better that our nation and people should perish rather than be party to a course so evil as producing that weapon. I told him that on the Day of Judgment his view might be confirmed and that he was free to go forth and preach the necessity for salvation. It was not, however, a view which I would entertain as a public servant.[1]

Admittedly, the passage just reproduced is susceptible of different interpretations. Acheson may be putting forward the view that even if moral evaluation is relevant to the "ends" pursued by any country (including our own) it is not relevant to the policies adopted in furtherance of these ends. But at times, at least, he appears to expound a quite different view, namely, that in the realm of foreign affairs moral judgments, as opposed to strategic or prudential ones, are simply misplaced and any attempts at moral assessment misdirected.

Whatever may be the correct exegesis of this text, I want to treat it as illustrative of the position that morality has no place in the assessment of war.[2] There are several things worth considering in respect to such a view. In the first place, the claim that in matters of war morality has no place is ambiguous. To put it somewhat loosely, the claim may be descriptive, or it may be analytic, or it may be prescriptive. Thus, it would be descriptive if it were merely the factual claim that matters relating to war uniformly turn out to be decided on grounds of national interest or expediency rather than by appeal to what is moral.[3] This claim I will not consider further; it is an empirical one better answered by students of American (and foreign) diplomatic relations.

It would be a prescriptive claim were it taken to assert that matters relating to war ought always be decided by appeal to (say) national interest rather than an appeal to the moral point of view. For reasons which have yet to be elucidated, on this view the moral criteria are capable of being employed but it is undesirable to do so. I shall say something more about this view in a moment.[4]

The analytic point is not that morality ought not be used, but rather that it cannot. On this view the statement "The United States is behaving immorally in the way it is waging war in Vietnam" (or, "in waging war in Vietnam") is not wrong but meaningless.

What are we to make of the analytic view? As I have indicated, it could, of course, be advanced simply as an instance of a more sweeping position concerning the general meaninglessness of the moral point of view. What I find particularly interesting, though, is the degree to which this thesis is advanced as a special view about war and not as a part of a more general claim that all morality is meaningless.[5]

I think that there are at least four reasons why this special view may be held. First, the accusation that one's own country is involved in a immoral war is personally very threatening. For one thing, if the accusation is well-founded it may be thought to imply that certain types of socially cooperative behavior are forbidden to the citizen and that other kinds of socially deviant behavior are obligatory upon him. Yet, in a time of war it is following just this sort of dictate that will be treated most harshly by the actor's own government. Hence the morally responsible citizen is put in a most troublesome moral dilemma. If his country is engaged in an immoral war then he may have a duty to oppose and resist; yet opposition and resistance will typically carry extraordinarily severe penalties.

The pressure is, I suspect, simply too great for many of us. We are unwilling to pay the fantastically high personal price that goes with the moral point of view, and we are equally unwilling to plead guilty to this most serious charge of immorality. So we solve the problem by denying the possibility that war can be immoral. The relief is immediate; the moral "heat" is off. If war cannot be immoral, then one's country cannot be engaged in an immoral war, but only a stupid or unwise one. And whatever one's obligation to keep one's country from behaving stupidly or improvidently, they are vastly less stringent and troublesome than obligations imposed by the specter of complicity in an immoral war. We may, however, pay a price for such relief since we obliterate the moral distinctions between the Axis and the Allies in World War II at the same time as the distinctions between the conduct of the United States in 1941–45 and the conduct of the United States in 1967–68 in Vietnam.

Second, I think the view that moral judgments are meaningless sometimes seems plausible because of the differences between personal behavior and the behavior of states. There are not laws governing the behavior of states in the same way in which there are positive laws governing the behavior of citizens. International law is a troublesome notion just because it is both like and unlike our concept of positive law.

Now, how does skepticism about the law-like quality of international law lead to the claim that it is impossible for war to be either moral or immoral? It is far from obvious. Perhaps it is because there is at least one sense of justice that is intimately bound up with the notion of rule-violation; namely, that which relates justice to the following of rules and to the condemnation and punishment of those who break rules. In the absence of positive laws governing the behavior of states, it may be inferred (although I think mistakenly) that it is impossible for states to behave either justly or unjustly.[6] But even if justice can be said to be analyzable solely in terms of following rules, morality certainly cannot. Hence the absence of international laws cannot serve to make the moral appraisal of war impossible.

Third, there is the substantially more plausible view that, in the absence of positive laws *and* in the absence of any machinery by which to punish even the grossest kinds of immorality, an adequate excuse will always exist for behaving immorally. This is one way to take Hobbes' assertion that in the state of nature the natural laws bind in conscience but not in action. Even this view, however, would not render the moral assessment of the behavior of states meaningless; it would only excuse immorality in the absence of effective international law. More importantly, though, it, too, misstates the general understanding of morality in its insistence that morality depends for its *meaning* on the existence of guarantees of moral conformity by others.

Fourth, and still more plausible, is the view that says there can be no moral assessment of war just because there is, by definition, no morality in war. If war is an activity in which anything goes, moral judgments on war are just not possible.

To this there are two responses. To begin with, it is not, as our definitional discussion indicates, a necessary feature of war that it be an activity in which everything is morally permissible. There is a difference between the view

that war is unique because killing and violence are morally permissible in contexts and circumstances where they otherwise would not be and the view that war is unique because everything is morally permissible.

A less absolutist argument for the absurdity of discussing the morality of war might be that at least today the prevailing (although not necessary) conception of war is one that as a practical matter rules out no behavior on moral grounds. After all, if flamethrowers are deemed perfectly permissible, if the bombing of cities is applauded and not condemned, and if thermonuclear weapons are part of the arsenal of each of the major powers, then the remaining moral prohibitions on the conduct of war are sufficiently insignificant to be ignored.

The answer to this kind of an argument requires, I believe, that we distinguish the question of what is moral in war from that of the morality of war or of war generally. I return to this distinction later,[7] but for the present it is sufficient to observe that the argument presented only goes to the question of whether moral judgments can meaningfully be made concerning the *way* in which war is conducted. Paradoxically, the more convincing the argument from war's conduct, the stronger is the moral argument *against* engaging in war at all. For the more it can be shown that engaging in war will inevitably lead to despicable behavior to which no moral predicates are deemed applicable, the more this also constitutes an argument against bringing such a state of affairs into being.[8]

There is still another way to take the claim that in matters of war morality has no place. That is what I have called the prescriptive view: that national interest ought to determine policies in respect to war, not morality. This is surely one way to interpret the remarks of Dean Acheson reproduced earlier. It is also, perhaps, involved in President Truman's defense of the dropping of the atomic bomb on Hiroshima. What he said was this:

Having found the bomb, we have to use it. We have used it against those who attacked us without warning at Pearl Harbor, against those who have starved and beaten and executed American prisoners of war, against those who have abandoned all pretense of obeying international laws of warfare. We have used it in order to shorten the agony of war, in order to save the lives of thousands and thousands of young Americans.[9]

Although this passage has many interesting features, I am concerned only with President Truman's insistence that the dropping of the bomb was justified because it saved the lives "of thousands and thousands of young Americans."

Conceivably, this is merely an elliptical way of saying that on balance fewer lives were lost through the dropping of the bomb and the accelerated cessation of hostilities than through any alternative course of conduct. Suppose, though, that this were not the argument. Suppose, instead, that the justification were regarded as adequate provided only that it was reasonably clear that fewer *American* lives would be lost than through any alternative course of conduct. Thus, to quantify the example, we can imagine someone maintaining that Hiroshima was justified because 20,000 fewer Americans died in the Pacific theater than would have died if the bomb had not been dropped. And this is justified even though 30,000 more Japanese died than would have been killed had the war been fought to an end with conventional means. Thus, even though 10,000 more people died than would otherwise have been the case, the bombing was justified because of the greater number of American lives saved.

On this interpretation the argument depends upon valuing the lives of Americans higher than the lives of persons from other countries. As such, is there anything to be said for the argument? Its strongest statement, and the only one that I shall consider, might go like this: Truman was the President of the United States and as such had an obligation always to choose that course of conduct that appeared to offer the greatest chance of maximizing the interests of the United States.[10] As President, he was obligated to prefer the lives of American soldiers over those from any other country, and he was obligated to prefer them just because they were Americans and he was their President.

Some might prove such a point by drawing an analogy to the situation of a lawyer, a parent, or a corporation executive. A lawyer has a duty to present his client's case in the fashion most calculated to ensure his client's victory; and he has this obligation irrespective of the objective merits of his client's case. Similarly, we are neither surprised nor dismayed when a parent prefers the interests of *his* child over those of other children. A parent *qua* parent is certainly not behaving immorally when he acts so as to secure satisfactions for his child, again irrespective of the objective merits of the child's needs or wants. And, *mutatis mutandis,* a corporate executive has a duty to maximize profits for his company. Thus, as public servants, Dean Acheson and Harry Truman had no moral choice but to pursue those policies that appeared to them to be in the best interest of the United States. And to a lesser degree, all persons *qua* citizens of the United States have a similar, if slightly more attenuated, obligation. Therefore morality has no real place in war.

The analogy, however, must not stop halfway. It is certainly both correct and important to observe that public officials, like parents, lawyers, and corporate executives, do have special moral obligations that are imposed by virtue of the position or role they fill. A lawyer does have a duty to prefer his client's interests in a way that would be improper were the person anyone other than a client. And the same sort of duty, I think, holds for a parent, an executive, a President, and a citizen in their respective roles. The point becomes distorted, however, when it is supposed that such an obligation always, under all circumstances, overrides any and all other obligations that the person might have. The case of the lawyer is instructive. While he has an obligation to attend to his client's interests in very special ways, there are many other things that it is impermissible for the lawyer to do in furtherance of his client's interests—irrespective, this time, of how significantly they might advance that interest.

The case for the President, or for public servants generally, is similar. While the President may indeed have an obligation to prefer and pursue the national interests, this obligation could only be justifiable—could only be a moral obligation—if it were enmeshed in a comparable range of limiting and competing obligations. If we concede that the President has certain obligations to prefer the national interest that no one else has, we must be equally sensitive to the fact that the President also has some of the same obligations to other persons that all other men have—if for no other reason than that all persons have the right to be treated or not treated in certain ways. So, whatever special obligations the President may have cannot by themselves support the view that in war morality ought have no place.

In addition, the idea that one can separate a man's personality from the duties of his office is theoretically questionable and practically unbelievable. Experience teaches that a man cannot personally be guided by moral dictates while abjuring them in public life even if he wants to.

It is also unlikely that a man on becoming President will try to adopt such an approach unless there is something about the office that compels a dual personality. Common sense indicates there is not. If there were, it would mean that the electorate could not purposely choose someone to follow a course not dictated by the "national interest" since, whatever his pre-election promises, the office would reform him.

But the major problem with the national-interest argument is its assumption that the national interest not only is something immutable and knowable but also that it limits national interest to narrowly national concerns. It is parochial to suppose that the American national interest really rules out solicitude for other states in order to encourage international stability.

Finally, national interest as a goal must itself be justified. The United States' position of international importance may have imposed on it a duty of more than national concern. The fact that such a statement has become hackneyed by constant use to justify American interference abroad should not blind us to the fact that it may be viable as an argument for a less aggressive international responsibility.[11]

If we turn now to confront more directly the question of the morality of wars, it is evident that there is a variety of different perspectives from which, or criteria in terms of which, particular wars may be assessed. First, to the extent to which the model of war as a game continues to have a place, wars can be evaluated in terms of the degree to which the laws of war—the rules for initiating and conducting war—are adhered to by the opposing countries. Second, the right-ness or wrongness of wars is often thought to depend very much upon the *cause* for which a war is fought. And third, there is the independent justification for a war that is founded upon an appeal of some kind to a principle of self-defense.

In discussing the degree to which the laws of war are followed or disregarded there are two points that should be stressed. First, a skepticism as to the meaningfulness of any morality *within* war is extremely common. The gnomic statement is Sherman's: "War is hell." The fuller argument depends upon a rejection of the notion of war as a game. It goes something like this. War is the antithesis of law or rules. It is violence, killing and all of the horror they imply. Even if moral distinctions can be made in respect to such things as the initiation and purposes of a war, it is absurd to suppose that moral distinctions can be drawn once a war has begun. All killing is bad, all destruction equally wanton.[12]

Now, there does seem to me to be a fairly simple argument of sorts that can be made in response. Given the awfulness of war, it nonetheless appears plausible to discriminate among degrees of awfulness. A war in which a large number of innocent persons are killed is, all other things being equal, worse than one in which only a few die. A war in which few combatants are killed is, *ceteris paribus,* less immoral than one in which many are killed. And more to the point, perhaps, any unnecessary harm to others is surely unjustifiable. To some degree, at least, the "laws of war" can be construed as attempts to formalize these general notions and to define instances of unnecessary harm to others.[13]

The second criterion, the notion of the cause that can be invoked to justify a war may involve two quite different inquiries. On the one hand, we may intend the sense in which cause refers to the *consequences* of waging war, to the forward-looking criteria of assessment. Thus, when a war is justified as a means by which to make the world safe for democracy, or on the grounds that a failure to fight now will lead to a loss of confidence on the part of one's allies, or as necessary to avoid fighting a larger, more destructive war later, when these sorts of appeals are made, the justification is primarily consequential or forward-looking in character.

Here the distinction between morality and prudence—never a very easy one to maintain in international relations—is always on the verge of collapse. On the other hand, a war may be evaluated through recourse to what may be termed backward-looking criteria. Just as in the case of punishment or blame where what happened in the past is relevant to the justice of punishing or blaming someone, so in the case of war, what has already happened is, on this view, relevant to the justice or rightness of the war that is subsequently waged. The two backward-looking criteria that are most frequently invoked in respect to war are the question of whether the war involved a violation of some prior promise, typically expressed in the form of a treaty or concord.

Two sorts of assertions are often made concerning the role of the treaty in justifying resort to war. First, if a country has entered into a treaty not to go to war and if it violates that treaty, it is to be condemned for, in effect, having broken its promise. And second, if a country has entered into a treaty in which it has agreed to go to war under certain circumstances and if those circumstances come to pass, then the country is at least justified in going to war—although it is not in fact obligated to do so.

Once again, even if we pass over the difficult analytic questions that might be asked about whether countries can promise to do anything and, if they can, what the nature and duration of such promises are, it is clear that treaties can be relevant but not decisive factors. This is so just because it is sometimes right to break our promises and sometimes wrong to keep them. The fact that a treaty is violated at best tends to make a war unjust or immoral in some degree, but it does not necessarily render the war unjustified.[14]

The other backward-looking question, that of aggression, is often resolved by concluding that under no circumstances is the initiation of a war of aggression justified. This is a view that Americans and America have often embraced. Such a view was expounded at Nuremberg by Mr. Justice Jackson when he said:

[T]he wrong for which their [the German] fallen leaders are on trial is not that they lost the war, but that they started it. And we must not allow ourselves to be drawn into a trial of the causes of war, for our position is that no grievances or policies will justify resort to aggressive war. . . . Our position is that whatever grievances a nation may have, however objectionable it finds that *status quo*, aggressive warfare is an illegal means for settling those grievances or for altering those conditions.[15]

A position such as this is typically thought to imply two things: (1) the initiation of war is never justifiable; (2) the warlike response to aggressive war is justifiable. Both views are troublesome.

To begin with, it is hard to see how the two propositions go together very comfortably. Conceivably, there are powerful arguments against the waging of aggressive war. Almost surely, though, the more persuasive of these will depend, at least in part, on the character of war itself—on such things as the supreme importance of human life, or the inevitable injustices committed in every war. If so, then the justifiability of meeting war with war will to that degree be called into question.

To take the first proposition alone, absent general arguments about the unjustifiability of all war, it is hard to see how aggressive war can be ruled out in a wholly a priori fashion. Even if we assume that no problems are presented in determining what is and is not aggression, it is doubtful that the quality of aggression could always be morally decisive in condemning the war. Would a war undertaken to free innocent persons from concentration camps or from slavery always be unjustifiable just because *it was aggressive?* Surely this is to rest too much upon only one of a number of relevant considerations.[16]

From a backward-looking point of view, the claim that a warring response to aggressive war is always justified is even more perplexing. One way to take this claim is to regard it as plain retributivism. A country is justified in fighting back because the aggressor hit first. Since aggression is wrong, it deserves to be thwarted and punished. The difficulty with this position is, in part, that retributivism generally is more plausible as a statement of necessary rather than of sufficient conditions. Thus, it would be one thing to claim that a war was *only* justified if undertaken in response to aggression, but it is quite another thing to assert that a war is justified *provided* it is undertaken in response to aggression. For reasons already stated, I think even this would be unsatisfactory, but it would surely come closer to being right than a view that finds aggression to be a sufficient justification for making war. A number of these issues reappear in the related problem of self-defense as a justification.

In order to understand the force of the doctrine of self-defense when invoked in respect to war, and to assess its degree of legitimate applicability, it is necessary that we look briefly at self-defense as it functions as a doctrine of municipal criminal law. The first thing to notice is that the doctrine of self-defense does not depend upon either typically retributive or typically consequential considerations. Instead, it rests upon the prevention by the intended victim of quite immediate future harm to himself. To be sure, the doctrine is backward-looking in its insistence that an "attack" of some sort be already under way. But the fact that it is not retributive can be seen most clearly from the fact that self-defense cannot be invoked in response to an attack that is over. In the same fashion, the doctrine is forward-looking in its insistence upon the prevention of future harm.

Second, it is by no means clear whether the doctrine can be understood better as a justification or as an excuse. It can be understood to rest upon the notion that one is *entitled* to defend oneself from a serious and imminent attack upon life and limb. Concomitantly, the doctrine can be interpreted to depend upon the proposition that it is a natural, almost unavoidable—and hence excusable—reaction to defend oneself when attacked.

In either case what is important is that we keep in mind two of the respects in which the law qualifies resort to the claim of self-defense. On one hand, the doctrine cannot be invoked successfully if the intended victim could have avoided the encounter through a reasonable escape or retreat unless the attack takes place on one's own property. And on the other hand, the doctrine requires that no more force be employed than is reasonably necessary to prevent the infliction of comparable harm.

Now how does all of this apply to self-defense as a justification for engaging in war? In the first place, to the extent to which the basic doctrine serves as an excuse, the applicability to war seems doubtful. While it may make sense to regard self-defense of one's person as a natural, instinctive response to an attack, it is only a very anthropomorphic view of countries that would lead us to elaborate a comparable explanation here.[17]

In the second place, it is not even clear that self-defense can function very persuasively as a justification. For it to do so it might be necessary, for example, to be able to make out a case that countries die in the same way in which persons do, or that a country can be harmed in the same way in which a person can be. Of course, persons in the country can be harmed and killed by war, and I shall return to this point in a moment, but we can also imagine an attack in which none of the inhabitants of the country will be killed or even physically harmed unless they fight back. But the country, as a separate political entity, might nonetheless disappear. Would we say that this should be regarded as the equivalent of human death? That it is less harmful? More harmful? These are issues to which those who readily invoke the doctrine of self-defense seldom address themselves.

Even if we were to decide, however, that there is no question but that a country is justified in relying upon a doctrine of self-defense that is essentially similar to that which obtains in the criminal law, it would be essential to observe the constraints that follow. Given even the unprovoked aggressive waging of war by one country against another, the doctrine of self-defense could not be invoked by the country so attacked to justify waging unlimited defensive war or insisting upon unconditional surrender. Each or both of these responses might be justifiable, but not simply because a country was wrongly attacked. It would, instead, have to be made out that something analogous to retreat was neither possible nor appropriate, and, even more, that no more force was used than was reasonably necessary to terminate the attack.

There is, to be sure, an answer to this. The restrictions that the criminal law puts upon self-defense are defensible, it could be maintained, chiefly because we have a municipal police force, municipal laws, and courts. If we use no more than reasonable force to repel attacks, we can at least be confident that the attacker will be apprehended and punished and, further, that we live in a society in which this sort of aggressive behavior is deterred by a variety of means. It is the absence of such a context that renders restrictions on an international doctrine of self-defense inappropriate.

I do not think this answer is convincing. It is relevant to the question of what sorts of constraints will be operative on the behavior of persons and countries, but it is not persuasive as to the invocation of *self*-defense as a justification for war. To use more force than is reasonably necessary to defend oneself is, in short, to do more than defend oneself. If such non-self-defensive behavior is to be justified, it must appeal to some different principle or set of principles.

There are, therefore, clearly cases in which a principle of self-defense does appear to justify engaging in a war: at a minimum, those cases in which one's country is attacked in such a way that the inhabitants are threatened with deadly force and in which no more force than is reasonably necessary is employed to terminate the attack.

One might argue, of course, for some of the reasons discussed above, that this is too restrictive a range for the legitimate application of the principle. More specifically, it might be observed that I have provided an unduly restricted account of the cases in which the use of deadly force is permissible in our legal system; namely, to defend certain classes of third parties from attacks threatening serious bodily harm or death, and to prevent the commission of certain felonies. These, clearly, would also have ostensibly important applications to the justifiable use of deadly force in the international setting. I shall return to this point when I discuss the problem of war and the death of innocent persons in part IV. At present, however, I want to consider an argument for refusing to accord any legitimacy whatsoever to an appeal to self-defense. The argument is a version of what can appropriately be called the pacifist position. The formulation I have in mind is found in the writings of the nineteenth-century pacifist, Adin Ballou, and it merits reproduction at some length. What Ballou says is this:

If it [self-defense] be the true method, it must on the whole work well. It must preserve human life and secure mankind against injury, more certainly and effectually than any other possible method. Has it done this? I do not admit it. How happens it that, according to the lowest probable estimate, some fourteen thousand millions of human beings have been slain by human means, in war and otherwise? Here are enough to people eighteen planets like the earth with its present population. What inconceivable miseries must have been endured by these worlds of people and their friends, in the process of those murderous conflicts which extinguished their earthly existence! . . . If this long-trusted method of self-preservation be indeed the best which nature affords to her children, their lot is most deplorable. To preserve what life has been preserved at such a cost, renders life itself a thing of doubtful value. If only a few thousands, or even a few millions, had perished by the two edged sword; if innocence and justice and right had uniformly triumphed; if aggression, injustice, violence, injury and insult, after a few dreadful experiences, had been overawed; if gradually the world had come into wholesome order—a state of truthfulness, justice and peace; if the sword of self-defense had frightened the sword of aggression into its scabbard, there to consume in its rust; then might we admit that the common method of self-preservation was the true one. But now we have ample demonstration that *they who take the sword, perish with the sword*. Is it supposable that if no injured person or party, since the days of Abel, had lifted up a deadly weapon, or threatened an injury against an offending party, there would have been a thousandth part of the murders and miseries which have actually taken place on our earth? Take the worst possible view; resolve all the assailed and injured into the most passive non-resistants imaginable, and let the offenders have unlimited scope to commit all the robberies, cruelties and murders they pleased; would as many lives have been sacrificed, or as much real misery have been experienced by the human race, as have actually resulted from the general method of self-preservation, by personal conflict and resistance of injury with injury? He must be a bold man who affirms it.[18]

What is most interesting about Ballou's argument is that it is, in essence, an empirical one. His claim is not the more typical pacifist claim that there is some principle that directly forbids the use of force even in cases of self-defense. His assertion is rather that the consequences of regarding the use of force as appropriate in self-defensive situations have been disastrous—or, more exactly, worse precisely in terms of the preservation of human life than would have been the case if the use of force even in such circumstances were always deemed impermissible.

It is very difficult to know what to make of such an argument. In particular, it is more difficult than it may appear at first to state the argument coherently. What precisely is Ballou's thesis? Perhaps he is saying something like this: The principle that force may justifiably be used in cases of self-defense tends to be misapplied in practice. Persons almost inevitably tend to overestimate the imminence and severity of a threat of violence to themselves. They use force prematurely and in excess under an invocation of the doctrine of self-defense. And if this is true of persons generally, it is probably even truer of countries in their relations with other countries. The answer, therefore, is to induce persons and countries to forgo the resort to force even in cases of self-defense.

This argument is something of a paradox. If everyone were to accept and consistently to act upon the principle that force ought never to be used, even in cases of self-defense, then there would be nothing to worry about. No one would ever use force at all, and we really would not have to worry about misapplications of the principle of self-defense.

But Ballou's appeal is to persons to give up the principle of self-defense even if others have not renounced even the aggressive resort to force. In other words, Ballou's argument is one for unilateral rather than bilateral pacifism, and that is precisely what makes it so hard to accept. As I have said, Ballou's thesis appears to be an empirical one. He appears to concede that if only some persons renounce the doctrine of self-defense they certainly do not thereby guarantee their own safety from attack. Innocent persons in this position may very well be killed by those who use force freely. Ballou seems to be saying that while this is so, the consequences have been still worse where self-defense has not been abandoned. But there is just no reason to suppose that unilateral pacifism if practiced by an unspecified group of persons would have resulted in fewer rather than more deaths.[19]

Perhaps, though, this is not what Ballou really has in mind. Perhaps instead the main thrust of his argument is as follows: People generally agree that force should not be used except in self-defense. But the evidence indicates that this principle is usually misapplied. Hence, a partial pacifism, restricted to the use of force only in cases of self-defense, is illusory and unsound. Even if all countries agreed never to use force except in self-defense, they would still be so prone to construe the behavior of other countries as imminently threatening that wars would be prevalent and the consequences horrendous. This is the reason why even self-defense cannot be permitted as an exception to pacifism. Everyone and every country should, therefore, renounce self-defense as the one remaining exception to pacifism.

Again there is an element of paradox to the argument. Suppose it looks to country Y as though country X is about to attack it. Ballou would say country Y should not, under the principle of self-defense, prepare to fight back. Of course, if all countries do follow the principle of never using force except in self-defense, this makes good sense because country Y can rely on the fact that country X will not attack first. So there is no need to eliminate the defense of self-defense. But what if country X should in fact attack? Here Ballou's advice is that country Y should still not respond because of the likelihood of misapplying the doctrine of self-defense. Once again the case is simply not convincing. In any particular case it just might be that the doctrine would not be misapplied and that the consequences of not defending oneself would in fact be less desirable than those of resorting to self-defensive force.

In short, the case against a limited doctrine of self-defense cannot, I think, be plausibly made out on grounds such as those urged by Ballou. Although a world without war would doubtless be a better one, it is by no means clear that unilateral abandonment of the doctrine of self-defense would have such beneficial consequences. If there is an argument against war, it must rest on something other than the harms inherent in the doctrine of self-defense.

The strongest argument against war is that which rests upon the connection between the morality of war and the death of innocent persons. The specter of thermonuclear warfare makes examination of this point essential; yet the problem was both a genuine and an urgent one in the pre-atomic days of air warfare, particularly during the Second World War.

The argument based upon the death of innocent persons goes something like this: Even in war innocent persons have a right to life and limb that should be respected. It is no less wrong and no more justifiable to kill innocent persons in war than at any other time. Therefore, if innocent persons are killed in a war, that war is to be condemned.

The argument can quite readily be converted into an attack upon all modern war. Imagine a thoroughly unprovoked attack upon another country—an attack committed, moreover, from the worst of motives and for the most despicable of ends. Assume too, for the moment, that under such circumstances there is nothing immoral about fighting back and even killing those who are attacking. Nonetheless, if in fighting back innocent persons will be killed, the defenders will be acting immorally. However, given any war fought today, innocent persons will inevitably be killed. Therefore, any war fought today will be immoral.

There are a variety of matters that require clarification before the strength of this argument can be adequately assessed. In particular, there are four questions that must be examined: (1) What is meant by "innocence" in this context? (2) Is it plausible to suppose that there are any innocents? (3) Under what circumstances is the death of innocent persons immoral? (4) What is the nature of the connection between the immorality of the killing of innocent persons and the immorality of the war in which this killing occurs?

It is anything but clear what precisely is meant by "innocence" or "the innocent" in an argument such as this. One possibility would be that all noncombatants are innocent. But then, of course, we would have to decide what was meant by "noncombatants." Here we might be tempted to claim that noncombatants are all of those persons who are not in the army—not actually doing the fighting; the combatants are those who are. There are, however, serious problems with this position. For it appears that persons can be noncombatants in this sense and yet indistinguishable in any apparently relevant sense from persons in the army. Thus, civilians may be manufacturing munitions, devising new weapons, writing propaganda, or doing any number of other things that make them indistinguishable from many combatants vis-à-vis their relationship to the war effort.

A second possibility would be to focus upon an individual's causal connection with the attempt to win the war rather than on his status as soldier or civilian. On this view only some noncombatants would be innocent and virtually no

combatants would be. If the causal connection is what is relevant, meaningful distinctions might be made among civilians. One might distinguish between those whose activities or vocations help the war effort only indirectly, if at all, and those whose activities are more plausibly described as directly beneficial. Thus the distinctions would be between a typical grocer or a tailor on the one hand, and a worker in an armaments plant on the other. Similarly, children, the aged, and the infirm would normally not be in a position to play a role causally connected in this way with the waging of war.[20]

There are, of course, other kinds of possible causal connections. In particular, someone might urge that attention should also be devoted to the existence of a causal connection between the individual's civic behavior and the war effort. Thus, for example, a person's voting behavior, or the degree of his political opposition to the government, or his financial contributions to the war effort might all be deemed to be equally relevant to his status as an innocent.

Still a fourth possibility, closely related to those already discussed, would be that interpretation of innocence concerned with culpability rather than causality per se. On this view a person would properly be regarded as innocent if he could not fairly be held responsible for the war's initiation or conduct. Clearly, the notion of culpability is linked in important ways with that of causal connection, but they are by no means identical. So it is quite conceivable, for example, that under some principles of culpability many combatants might not be culpable and some noncombatants might be extremely culpable, particularly if culpability were to be defined largely in terms of state of mind and enthusiasm for the war. Thus, an aged or infirm person who cannot do very much to help the war effort but is an ardent proponent of its aims and objectives might be more culpable (and less innocent in this sense) than a conscriptee who is firing a machine gun only because the penalty for disobeying the command to do so is death.[21]

But we need not propose an airtight definition of "innocence" in order to answer the question of whether, in any war, there will be a substantial number of innocent persons involved. For irrespective of which sense or senses of innocence are ultimately deemed most instructive or important, it does seem clear that there will be a number of persons in any country (children are probably the clearest example) who will meet any test of innocence that is proposed.

The third question enumerated earlier is: Under what circumstances is the death of innocent persons immoral? One possible view is that which asserts simply that it is unimportant which circumstances bring about the death of innocent persons. As long as we know that innocent persons will be killed as a result of war, we know all we need to know to condemn any such war.

Another, and perhaps more plausible, view is that which regards the death of innocent persons as increasingly unjustifiable if it was negligently, recklessly, knowingly, or intentionally brought about. Thus, if a country engages in acts of war with the intention of bringing about the death of children, perhaps to weaken the will of the enemy, it would be more immoral than if it were to engage in acts of war aimed at killing combatants but which through error also kill children.[22]

A different sort of problem arises if someone asks how we are to differentiate the deaths of children in war from, for example, the deaths of children that accompany the use of highways or airplanes in times of peace. Someone might, that is, argue that we permit children to ride in cars on highways and to fly in airplanes even though we *know* that there will be accidents and that as a result of these accidents innocent children will die. And since we know this to be the case, the situation appears to be indistinguishable from that of engaging in acts of war where it is known that the death of children will be a direct, although not intended, consequence.

I think that there are three sorts of responses that can be made to an objection of this sort. In the first place, in a quite straightforward sense the highway does not, typically, cause the death of the innocent passenger; the careless driver or the defective tire does. But it is the intentional bombing of the heavily populated city that does cause the death of the children who live in the city.

In the second place, it is one thing to act where one knows that certain more or less identifiable persons will be killed (say, bombing a troop camp when one knows that those children who live in the vicinity of the camp will also be killed), and quite another thing to engage in conduct in which all one can say is that it can be predicted with a high degree of confidence that over a given period of time a certain number of persons (including children) will be killed. The difference seems to lie partly in the lack of specificity concerning the identity of the persons and partly in the kind of causal connection involved.

In the third place, there is certainly a difference in the two cases in respect to the possibility of deriving benefits from the conduct. That is to say, when a highway is used, one is participating in a system or set of arrangements in which benefits are derived from that use (even though risks, and hence costs, are also involved). It is not easy to see how a similar sort of analysis can as plausibly be proposed in connection with typical acts of war.

The final and most important issue that is raised by the argument concerning the killing of the innocent in time of war is that of the connection between the immorality of the killing of innocent persons and the immorality of the war in which this killing occurs. Writers in the area often fail to discuss the connection.

Miss Anscombe puts the point this way: "[I]t is murderous to attack [the innocent] or make them a target for an attack which [the attacker] judges will help him toward victory. For murder is the deliberate killing of the innocent, whether for its own sake or as a means to some further end."[23] And Father John Ford, in a piece that certainly deserves to be more widely known outside of theological circles, puts the point several different ways: At one place he asserts that noncombatants have a right to live, even in wartime;[24] and at another place he says that "to take the life of an innocent person is always intrinsically wrong,"[25] and at still a third place: "[E]very Catholic theologian would condemn as intrinsically immoral the direct killing of innocent noncombatants."[26]

Now, leaving aside the question of whether Miss Anscombe has defined murder correctly and leaving aside the question of whether Father Ford's three assertions are equivalent expressions, the serious question that does remain is what precisely they mean to assert about the intentional killing of innocent persons in time of war.

There are two very different ambiguities in their statements that have to be worked out. In the first place, we have to determine whether the immorality in question is in their view "absolute" or in some sense "prima facie." And in the second place, we should ask whether the immorality in question is in their view to be predicated of the particular act of intentional killing or of the entire war. To elaborate briefly in turn on each of these two ambiguities: Suppose someone were to claim that it is immoral or wrong to lie. He might mean any one of at least three different things: (1) He might mean that it is *absolutely* immoral to lie. That is to say, he might be claiming that there are no circumstances under which one would be justified in telling a lie and that there are no circumstances under which it would, morally speaking, be better to lie than to tell the truth. (2) Or he might mean that it is prima facie immoral to lie. That is to say, he might be claiming that, absent special, overriding circumstances, it is immoral to lie. On this view, even when these special, overriding circumstances do obtain so that an act of lying is justifiable, it still involves some quantum of immorality. (3) The third possibility is that he might mean that, typically, lying is wrong. As a rule it is immoral to lie, but sometimes it is not. And when it is not, there is nothing whatsoever wrong or immoral about telling a lie.

For the purposes of the present inquiry the differences between (2) and (3) are irrelevant;[27] the differences between a position of absolute immorality and either (2) or (3) are not. The question of the killing of the innocents should similarly fit into the foregoing categories and identical conclusions should obtain, although to some degree the differences among these views and the plausibility of each are affected by the type of activity under consideration. Thus, the absolutist view, (1), may seem very strange and unconvincing when applied to lying or promise-keeping; it may seem less so, though, when applied to murder or torture. Similarly (3) may seem quite sensible when predicated of lying or promise-keeping but patently defective when applied to murder or torture.

In any event the case at hand is that of murder. It is likely that Father Ford and Miss Anscombe mean to assert an absolutist view here—that there are no circumstances under which the intentional killing of innocent persons, even in time of war, can be justified. It is always immoral to do so.[28] At least their arguments are phrased in absolutist terms. If this is the view that they intend to defend, it is, I think, a hard one to

accept. This is so just because it ultimately depends upon too complete a rejection of the relevance of consequences to the moral character of action. It also requires too rigid a dichotomy between acts and omissions. It seems to misunderstand the character of our moral life to claim that, no matter what the consequences, the intentional killing of an innocent person could never be justifiable—even, for example, if a failure to do so would bring about the death of many more innocent persons.

This does not, of course, mean that the argument from the death of the innocent is either irrelevant or unconvincing. It can be understood to be the very convincing claim that the intentional or knowing killing of an innocent person is always prima facie (in sense (2)) wrong. A serious evil is done every time it occurs. Moreover, the severity of the evil is such that there is a strong presumption against its justifiability. The burden, and it is a heavy one, rests upon anyone who would seek to justify behavior that has as a consequence the death of innocent persons.

The second question concerns what we might call the "range" of the predication of immorality. Even if we were to adopt the absolutist view in respect to the killing of the innocent, it would still remain unclear precisely what it was that was immoral. The narrowest view would be that which holds that the particular action—for instance, the intentional killing of a child—is immoral and unjustified. A broader view would be one that holds that the side that engages in such killing is conducting the war immorally. But this too could mean one of two different things.

A moderate view would be that if one is helpless to prevent the death of the innocent, it is appropriate to weigh such a result against such things as the rightness of the cause for which the war is being fought, the offensive or defensive character of the war, and so on. While there is nothing that can justify or excuse the killing of a particular innocent, this does not necessarily mean that, on balance, the total participation in the war by the side in question is to be deemed absolutely immoral or unjustifiable.

A more extreme view would hold that the occurrence of even a single instance of immorality makes the entire act of fighting the war unjustifiable. Thus, the murder of innocent persons is absolutely immoral in not one but two quite different senses.

My own view is that as a theoretical matter an absolutist position is even less convincing here. Given the number of criteria that are relevant to the moral assessment of any war and given the great number of persons involved in and the extended duration of most wars, it would be false to the complexity of the issues to suppose that so immediately simple a solution were possible.

But having said all of this, *the practical,* as opposed to the theoretical, thrust of the argument is virtually unabated. If wars were conducted, or were likely to be conducted, so as to produce only the occasional intentional killing of the innocent, that would be one thing. We could then say with some confidence that on this ground at least wars can hardly be condemned out of hand. Unfortunately, though, mankind no longer lives in such a world and, as a result, the argument from the death of the innocent has become increasingly more convincing. The intentional, or at least knowing, killing of the innocent on a large scale became a practically necessary feature of war with the advent of air warfare. And the genuinely indiscriminate killing of very great numbers of innocent persons is the dominant legacy of the birth of thermonuclear weapons. At this stage the argument from the death of the innocent moves appreciably closer to becoming a decisive objection to war. For even if we reject, as I have argued we should, both absolutist interpretations of the argument, the core of truth that remains is the insistence that in war, no less than elsewhere, the knowing killing of the innocent is an evil that throws up the heaviest of justificatory burdens. My own view is that in any major war that can or will be fought today, none of those considerations that can sometimes justify engaging in war will in fact come close to meeting this burden. But even if I am wrong, the argument from the death of the innocent does, I believe, make it clear both where the burden is and how unlikely it is today to suppose that it can be honestly discharged.

NOTES

1. Acheson, "Ethics in International Relations Today," in M. Raskin and B. Fall (eds.), *The Vietnam Reader* (1965), p. 13.

2. Acheson's view is admittedly somewhat broader than this since it appears to encompass all foreign relations.

3. Such a view could also hold, although it need not, that it would be desirable for matters relating to war to be determined on moral grounds, even though they are not.

4. See notes 9–11 infra and accompanying text.

5. Much of this analysis applies with equal force to what I call the prescriptive view, which is discussed more fully at notes 9–11 infra and accompanying text. Although I refer only to the analytic view, I mean to include them both where appropriate.

6. It is a mistake just because justice is not analyzable solely in terms of rule-following and rule-violating behavior.

One of the genuine puzzles in this whole area is why there is so much talk about *just* and *unjust* wars. Except in this very limited context of the relationship of justice to rules, it appears that the predicates "just" and "unjust" when applied to wars are synonymous with "moral" and "immoral."

7. See notes 12–19 infra and accompanying text.

8. But suppose someone should argue that the same argument applies to the question of *when* and *under what circumstances* to wage war, and that here, too, the only relevant criteria of assessment are prudential or strategic ones. Again, my answer would be that this also constitutes a perfectly defensible and relevant reason for making a moral judgment about the desirability of war as a social phenomenon.

9. Address to the Nation by President Harry S. Truman, Aug. 9, 1945, quoted in R. Tucker, *The Just War* (1960), pp. 21–22, n. 14.

10. Other arguments that might be offered—such as that the President was justified because Japan was the aggressor, or that he was justified because this was essentially an attack on combatants—are discussed at notes 12–19 infra and accompanying text.

11. It is probably a reaction to the parochial view of national interest that makes plausible movements that seek to develop a single world government and a notion of *world* rather than *national* citizenship.

12. This may be what Paul Henri Spaak had in mind when he said: "I must . . . say that the proposal to humanize war has always struck me as hypocrisy. I have difficulty in seeing the difference from a moral and humane point of view between the use of a guided missile of great power which can kill tens and even hundreds of people without regard for age or sex, and which if used repeatedly will kill millions, and the use of an atomic bomb which achieves the same result at the first stroke. Does crime against humanity begin only at the moment when a certain number of innocent people are killed or at the moment when the first one is killed?" Quoted in R. Tucker, supra note 9, pp. 78–79, n. 71.

13. This is the view put forward by Michael Walzer in his piece "Moral Judgment in Time of War," *Dissent,* May–June 1967, p. 284.

I purposely say "to some degree" because there are powerful objections to taking the "laws of war" too seriously, particularly if they are to be construed as laws or even binding rules. . . . More generally, there are at least four respects in which their character as laws seems suspect: (1) There is no authoritative body to make or declare them. (2) The distinctions made by the rules are specious and unconvincing; for example, the use of irregular-shaped bullets and projectiles filled with glass violates our standards of land warfare—see U.S. Dept. of the Army, *The Law of Land Warfare,* art. 34 (Basic Field Manual 27-10, 1956)—but the use of an atomic bomb does not. (3) The sanctions are typically applied only to the losing side. (4) The countries involved tend to regard their own behavior as lawful because falling under some exception or other.

14.   I discuss this distinction between injustice and unjustifiability at notes 23–28 infra and accompanying text.

15.   Quoted in R. Tucker, supra note 9, p. 12.

16.   G. E. M. Anscombe makes the same point in her article "War and Murder," in *Nuclear Weapons–A Catholic Response,* (1961), pp. 45, 47: "The present-day conception of 'aggression,' like so many strongly influential conceptions, is a bad one. Why *must* it be wrong to strike the first blow in a struggle? The only question is, who is in the right."

17.   Such a view certainly exists, however; we talk, for instance, about national pride and honor, insults to a country, etc. One real question is whether this way of thinking ought to be exorcised. In any event, however, countries do not respond "instinctively" in the way in which persons sometimes do, and, hence, the excuse rationale is just not appropriate.

18.   Ballou, "Christian Non-Resistance," in S. Lynd (ed.), *Nonviolence in America: A Documentary History* (1966), pp. 31, 38–39.

19.   Still another argument against unilateral pacifism is, of course, that there are evils other than the destruction of lives. Suppose, for example, that unilateral pacifism would result in fewer deaths but in substantially greater human slavery. It is by no means clear that such would be a morally preferable state of affairs.

20.   For a fuller development of this point see Ford, "The Morality of Obliteration Bombing," *Theological Studies,* Vol. 5 (1944), pp. 261, 280–86.

21.   This discussion hardly exhausts the possible problems involved in making clear the appropriate notion of innocence. I have not, for example, discussed at all the view that culpability is linked with the *cause* for which a war is fought. On this view, innocence might turn much more on the question of which side a person was on than on his connection with or responsibility for waging the war. I do not think this sense of innocence is intended by those who condemn wars that involve the deaths of innocent persons.

Similarly, I have avoided completely a number of difficulties inherent in the problem of culpability for the behavior of one's country. To what degree does the denial of access to adequate information about the war excuse one from culpability in supporting it? Are children who are

taught that their country is always right to be regarded as innocents even though they act on this instruction and assiduously do what they can to aid the war effort? To what degree does the existence of severe penalties for political opposition render ostensibly culpable behavior in fact innocent?

All of these questions arise more directly in connection with the issue of individual responsibility for the behavior of one's country and oneself in time of war. This issue is, as I have indicated, beyond the scope of this Article. As is apparent, however, a number of the relevant considerations are presented once the problem of the death of innocent persons is raised.

22.   There is a substantial body of literature on the problem of the intentionality of conduct in time of war. Discussion has focused chiefly on the plausibility of the Catholic doctrine of "double" or "indirect" effect. See, e.g., P. Ramsey, *War and the Christian Conscience* (1961), pp. 46–59; Anscombe (supra note 16), pp. 57–59; Ford (supra note 20), pp. 289, 290–98.

23.   Anscombe (supra note 16), p. 49.

24.   Ford (supra note 20), p. 269.

25.   *Ibid.,* p. 272.

26.   *Ibid.,* p. 273.

27.   For discussion of the differences between these two positions in other contexts, see Wasserstrom, "The Obligation to Obey the Law," *U.C.L.A. Law Review,* Vol. 10 (1963), pp. 780, 783–85.

28.   I offer this interpretation because the language typically used seems to support it. For example, Miss Anscombe says: "Without understanding of this principle [of double effect], anything can be—and is wont to be—justified, and the Christian teaching that *in no circumstances may one commit murder, adultery, apostasy (to give a few examples) goes by the board.* These absolute prohibitions of Christianity by no means exhaust its ethic; there is a large area where what is just is determined partly by a prudent weighing up of consequences. But the prohibitions are bedrock, and without them the Christian ethic goes to pieces." Anscombe (supra note 16), pp. 57–58 (emphasis added). And it is also consistent with what I take to be the more general Catholic doctrine on the intentional taking of "innocent" life—the absolute prohibition against abortion on just this ground.

13. OF CHASTITY AND MODESTY

David Hume

If any difficulty attend this system concerning the laws of nature and nations, 'twill be with regard to the universal approbation or blame, which follows their observance or transgression, and which some may not think sufficiently explain'd from the general interests of society. To remove, as far as possible, all scruples of this kind, I shall here consider another set of duties, *viz.* the *modesty* and *chastity* which belong to the fair sex: And I doubt not but these virtues will be found to be still more conspicuous instances of the operation of those principles, which I have insisted on.

There are some philosophers, who attack the female virtues with great vehemence, and fancy they have gone very far in detecting popular errors, when they can show, that there is no foundation in nature for all that exterior modesty, which we require in the expressions, and dress, and behaviour of the fair sex. I believe I may spare myself the trouble of insisting on so obvious a subject, and may proceed, without farther preparation, to examine after what manner such notions arise from education, from the voluntary conventions of men, and from the interest of society.

Whoever considers the length and feebleness of human infancy, with the concern which both sexes naturally have for their offspring, will easily perceive, that there must be an union of male and female for the education of the young, and that this union must be of considerable duration. But in order to induce the men to impose on themselves this restraint, and undergo chearfully all the fatigues and expences, to which it subjects them, they must believe, that the children are their own, and that their natural instinct is not directed to a wrong object, when they give a loose to love and tenderness. Now if we examine the structure of the human body, we shall find, that this security is very difficult to be attain'd on our part; and that since, in the copulation of the sexes, the principle of generation goes from the man to the woman, an error may easily take place on the side of the former, tho' it be utterly impossible with regard to the latter. From this trivial and anatomical observation is deriv'd that vast difference betwixt the education and duties of the two sexes.

Were a philosopher to examine the matter *a priori*, he wou'd reason after the following manner. Men are induc'd to labour for the maintenance and education of their children, by the persuasion that they are really their own; and therefore 'tis reasonable, and even necessary, to give them some security in this particular. This security cannot consist entirely in the imposing of severe punishments on any transgressions of conjugal fidelity on the part of the wife; since these public punishments cannot be inflicted without legal proof, which 'tis difficult to meet with in this subject. What restraint, therefore, shall we impose on women, in order to counterbalance so strong a temptation as they have to infidelity? There seems to be no restraint possible, but in the punishment of bad fame or reputation; a punishment, which has a mighty influence on the human mind, and at the same time is inflicted by the world upon surmizes, and conjectures, and proofs, that wou'd never be receiv'd in any court of judicature. In order, therefore, to impose a due restraint on the female sex, we must attach a peculiar degree of shame to their infidelity, above what arises merely from its injustice, and must bestow proportionable praises on their chastity.

But tho' this be a very strong motive to fidelity, our philosopher wou'd quickly discover, that it wou'd not alone be sufficient to that purpose. All human creatures, especially of the female sex, are apt to over-look remote motives in favour of any present temptation: The temptation is here the strongest imaginable: Its approaches are insensible and seducing: And a woman easily finds, or flatters herself she shall find, certain means of securing her reputation,

From David Hume, *A Treatise of Human Nature,* Book III (First published 1740), Part II, Section XII, "Of Chastity and Morality."

and preventing all the pernicious consequences of her pleasures. 'Tis necessary, therefore, that, beside the infamy attending such licences, there shou'd be some preceding backwardness or dread, which may prevent their first approaches, and may give the female sex a repugnance to all expressions, and postures, and liberties, that have an immediate relation to that enjoyment.

Such wou'd be the reasonings of our speculative philosopher: But I am persuaded, that if he had not a perfect knowledge of human nature, he wou'd be apt to regard them as mere chimerical speculations, and wou'd consider the infamy attending infidelity, and backwardness to all its approaches, as principles that were rather to be wish'd than hop'd for in the world. For what means, wou'd he say, of persuading mankind, that the transgressions of conjugal duty are more infamous than any other kind of injustice, when 'tis evident they are more excusable, upon account of the greatness of the temptation? And what possibility of giving a backwardness to the approaches of a pleasure, to which nature has inspir'd so strong a propensity; and a propensity that 'tis absolutely necessary in the end to comply with, for the support of the species?

But speculative reasonings, which cost so much pains to philosophers, are often form'd by the world naturally, and without reflection: As difficulties, which seem unsurmountable in theory, are easily got over in practice. Those, who have an interest in the fidelity of women, naturally disapprove of their infidelity, and all the approaches to it. Those, who have no interest, are carried along with the stream. Education takes possession of the ductile minds of the fair sex in their infancy. And when a general rule of this kind is once establish'd, men are apt to extend it beyond those principles, from which it first arose. Thus batchelors, however debauch'd, cannot chuse but be shock'd with any instance of lewdness or impudence in women. And tho' all these maxims have a plain reference to generation, yet women past child-bearing have no more privilege in this respect, than those who are in the flower of their youth and beauty. Men have undoubtedly an implicit notion, that all those ideas of modesty and decency have a regard to generation; since they impose not the same laws, *with the same force,* on the male sex, where that reason takes not place. The exception is there obvious and extensive, and founded on a remarkable difference, which produces a clear separation and disjunction of ideas. But as the case is not the same with regard to the different ages of women, for this reason, tho' men know, that these notions are founded on the public interest, yet the general rule carries us beyond the original principle, and makes us extend the notions of modesty over the whole sex, from their earliest infancy to their extremest old-age and infirmity.

Courage, which is the point of honour among men, derives its merit, in a great measure, from artifice, as well as the chastity of women; tho' it has also some foundation in nature, as we shall see afterwards.

As to the obligations which the male sex lie under, with regard to chastity, we may observe, that according to the general notions of the world, they bear nearly the same proportion to the obligations of women, as the obligations of the law of nations do to those of the law of nature. 'Tis contrary to the interest of civil society, that men shou'd have an *entire* liberty of indulging their appetites in venereal enjoyment: But as this interest is weaker than in the case of the female sex, the moral obligation, arising from it, must be proportionably weaker. And to prove this we need only appeal to the practice and sentiments of all nations and ages.

14. *DUTIES TOWARDS THE BODY IN RESPECT OF SEXUAL IMPULSE and CRIMINA CARNIS*

Immanuel Kant

DUTIES TOWARDS THE BODY IN RESPECT OF SEXUAL IMPULSE

Amongst our inclinations there is one which is directed towards other human beings. They themselves, and not their work and services, are its Objects of enjoyment. It is true that man has no inclination to enjoy the flesh of another—except, perhaps, in the vengeance of war, and then it is hardly a desire—but none the less there does exist an inclination which we may call an appetite for enjoying another human being. We refer to sexual impulse. Man can, of course, use another human being as an instrument for his service; he can use his hands, his feet, and even all his powers; he can use him for his own purposes with the other's consent. But there is no way in which a human being can be made an Object of indulgence for another except through sexual impulse. This is in the nature of a sense, which we can call the sixth sense; it is an appetite for another human being. We say that a man loves someone when he has an inclination towards another person. If by this love we mean true human love, then it admits of no distinction between types of persons, or between young and old. But a love that springs merely from sexual impulse cannot be love at all, but only appetite. Human love is good-will, affection, promoting the happiness of others and finding joy in their happiness. But it is clear that, when a person loves another purely from sexual desire, none of these factors enter into the love. Far from there being any concern for the happiness of the loved one, the lover, in order to satisfy his desire and still his appetite, may even plunge the loved one into the depths of misery. Sexual love makes of the loved person an Object of appetite; as soon as that appetite has been stilled, the person is cast aside as one casts away a lemon which has been sucked dry. Sexual love can, of course, be combined with human love and so carry with it the characteristics of the latter, but taken by itself and for itself, it is nothing more than appetite. Taken by itself it is a degradation of human nature; for as soon as a person becomes an Object of appetite for another, all motives of moral relationship cease to function, because as an Object of appetite for another a person becomes a thing and can be treated and used as such by every one. This is the only case in which a human being is designed by nature as the Object of another's enjoyment. Sexual desire is at the root of it; and that is why we are ashamed of it, and why all strict moralists, and those who had pretensions to be regarded as saints, sought to suppress and extirpate it. It is true that without it a man would be incomplete; he would rightly believe that he lacked the necessary organs, and this would make him imperfect as a human being; none the less men made pretence on this question and sought to suppress these inclinations because they degraded mankind.

Because sexuality is not an inclination which one human being has for another as such, but is an inclination for the sex of another, it is a principle of the degradation of human nature, in that

From Immanuel Kant, *Lectures in Ethics,* translated by Louis Infield (New York: Harper & Row, 1963), pp. 162–171. Reprinted by permission of Harper & Row, Publishers, Inc.

it gives rise to the preference of one sex to the other, and to the dishonouring of that sex through the satisfaction of desire. The desire which a man has for a woman is not directed towards her because she is a human being, but because she is a woman; that she is a human being is of no concern to the man; only her sex is the object of his desires. Human nature is thus subordinated. Hence it comes that all men and women do their best to make not their human nature but their sex more alluring and direct their activities and lusts entirely towards sex. Human nature is thereby sacrificed to sex. If then a man wishes to satisfy his desire, and a woman hers, they stimulate each other's desire; their inclinations meet, but their object is not human nature but sex, and each of them dishonours the human nature of the other. They make of humanity an instrument for the satisfaction of their lusts and inclinations, and dishonour it by placing it on a level with animal nature. Sexuality, therefore, exposes mankind to the danger of equality with the beasts. But as man has this desire from nature, the question arises how far he can properly make use of it without injury to his manhood. How far may persons allow one of the opposite sex to satisfy his or her desire upon them? Can they sell themselves, or let themselves out on hire, or by some other contract allow use to be made of their sexual faculties? Philosophers generally point out the harm done by this inclination and the ruin it brings to the body or to the commonwealth, and they believe that, except for the harm it does, there would be nothing contemptible in such conduct in itself. But if this were so, and if giving vent to this desire was not in itself abominable and did not involve immorality, then any one who could avoid being harmed by them could make whatever use he wanted of his sexual propensities. For the prohibitions of prudence are never unconditional; and the conduct would in itself be unobjectionable, and would only be harmful under certain conditions. But in point of fact, there is in the conduct itself something which is contemptible and contrary to the dictates of morality. It follows, therefore, that there must be certain conditions under which alone the use of the *facultates sexuales* would be in keeping with morality. There must be a basis for restraining

our freedom in the use we make of our inclinations so that they conform to the principles of morality. We shall endeavour to discover these conditions and this basis. Man cannot dispose over himself because he is not a thing; he is not his own property; to say that he is would be self-contradictory; for in so far as he is a person he is a Subject in whom the ownership of things can be vested, and if he were his own property, he would be a thing over which he could have ownership. But a person cannot be a property and so cannot be a thing which can be owned, for it is impossible to be a person and a thing, the proprietor and the property.

Accordingly, a man is not at his own disposal. He is not entitled to sell a limb, not even one of his teeth. But to allow one's person for profit to be used by another for the satisfaction of sexual desire, to make of oneself an Object of demand, is to dispose over oneself as over a thing and to make of oneself a thing on which another satisfies his appetite, just as he satisfies his hunger upon a steak. But since the inclination is directed towards one's sex and not toward one's humanity, it is clear that one thus partially sacrifices one's humanity and thereby runs a moral risk. Human beings are, therefore, not entitled to offer themselves, for profit, as things for the use of others in the satisfaction of their sexual propensities. In so doing they would run the risk of having their person used by all and sundry as an instrument for the satisfaction of inclination. This way of satisfying sexuality is *vaga libido,* in which one satisfies the inclinations of others for gain. It is possible for either sex. To let one's person out on hire and to surrender it to another for the satisfaction of his sexual desire in return for money is the depth of infamy. The underlying moral principle is that man is not his own property and cannot do with his body what he will. The body is part of the self; in its togetherness with the self it constitutes the person; a man cannot make of his person a thing, and this is exactly what happens in *vaga libido.* This manner of satisfying sexual desire is, therefore, not permitted by the rules of morality. But what of the second method, namely *concubinatus?* Is this also inadmissible? In this case both persons satisfy their desire mutually and there is no idea of gain, but they serve each other only for the satisfaction of sexuality. There appears to be nothing unsuitable in this arrangement, but there is nevertheless one consideration which rules it out. Concubinage consists in one person surrendering to another only for the satisfaction of their sexual desire whilst retaining freedom and rights in other personal respects affecting welfare and happiness. But the person who so surrenders is used as a thing; the desire is still directed only towards sex and not towards the person as a human being. But it is obvious that to surrender part of oneself is to surrender the whole, because a human being is a unity. It is not possible to have the disposal of a part only of a person without having at the same time a right of disposal over the whole person, for each part of a person is integrally bound up with the whole. But concubinage does not give me a right of disposal over the whole person but only over a part, namely the *organa sexualia.* It presupposes a contract. This contract deals only with the enjoyment of a part of the person and not with the entire circumstances of the person. Concubinage is certainly a contract, but it is one-sided; the rights of the two parties are not equal. But if in concubinage I enjoy a part of a person, I thereby enjoy the whole person; yet by the terms of the arrangement I have not the rights over the whole person, but only over a part; I, therefore, make the person into a thing. For that reason this method of satisfying sexual desire is also not permitted by the rules of morality. The sole condition on which we are free to make use of our sexual desire depends upon the right to dispose over the person as a whole—over the welfare and happiness and generally over all the circumstances of that person. If I have the right over the whole person, I have also the right over the part and so I have the right to use that person's *organa sexualia* for the satisfaction of sexual desire. But how am I to obtain these rights over the whole person? Only by giving that person the same rights over the whole of myself. This happens only in marriage. Matrimony is an agreement between two persons by which they grant each other reciprocal rights, each of them undertaking to surrender the whole of their person to the other with a complete right to disposal over it. We can now apprehend by reason how a *commercium sexuale* is possible without degrading humanity and breaking the moral laws. Matrimony is the only condi-

tion in which use can be made of one's sexuality. If one devotes one's person to another, one devotes not only sex but the whole person; the two cannot be separated. If, then, one yields one's person, body and soul, for good and ill and in every respect, so that the other has complete rights over it, and if the other does not similarly yield himself in return and does not extend in return the same rights and privileges, the arrangement is one-sided. But if I yield myself completely to another and obtain the person of the other in return, I win myself back; I have given myself up as the property of another, but in turn I take that other as my property, and so win myself back again in winning the person whose property I have become. In this way the two persons become a unity of will. Whatever good or ill, joy or sorrow befall either of them, the other will share in it. Thus sexuality leads to a union of human beings, and in that union alone its exercise is possible. This condition of the use of sexuality, which is only fulfilled in marriage, is a moral condition. But let us pursue this aspect further and examine the case of a man who takes two wives. In such a case each wife would have but half a man, although she would be giving herself wholly and ought in consequence to be entitled to the whole man. To sum up: *vaga libido* is ruled out on moral grounds; the same applies to concubinage; there only remains matrimony, and in matrimony polygamy is ruled out also for moral reasons; we, therefore, reach the conclusion that the only feasible arrangement is that of monogamous marriage. Only under that condition can I indulge my *facultas sexualis.* We cannot here pursue the subject further.

But one other question arises, that of incest. Incest consists in intercourse between the sexes in a form which, by reason of consanguinity, must be ruled out; but are there moral grounds on which incest, in all forms of sexual intercourse, must be ruled out? They are grounds which apply conditionally, except in one case, in which they have absolute validity. The sole case in which the moral grounds against incest apply absolutely is that of intercourse between parents and children. Between parents and children there must be a respect which should continue throughout life, and this rules out of court any question of equality. Moreover, in sexual intercourse each person submits to the other in the highest degree, whereas between parents and children subjection is one-sided; the children must submit to the parents only; there can, therefore, be no equal union. This is the only case in which incest is absolutely forbidden by nature. In other cases incest forbids itself, but is not incest in the order of nature. The state prohibits incest, but at the beginning there must have been intermarriage between brothers and sisters. At the same time nature has implanted in our breasts a natural opposition to incest. She intended us to combine with other races and so to prevent too great a sameness in one society. Too close a connection, too intimate an acquaintance produces sexual indifference and repugnance. But this propensity must be restrained by modesty; otherwise it becomes commonplace, reduces the object of the desire to the commonplace and results in indifference. Sexual desire is very fastidious; nature has given it strength, but it must be restrained by modesty. It is on that account that savages, who go about stark-naked, are cold towards each other; for that reason, too, a person whom we have known from youth evokes no desire within us, but a strange person attracts us much more strongly. Thus nature has herself provided restraints upon any desire between brother and sister.

CRIMINA CARNIS

Crimina carnis are contrary to self-regarding duty because they are against the ends of humanity. They consist in abuse of one's sexuality. Every form of sexual indulgence, except in marriage, is a misuse of sexuality, and so a *crimen carnis*. All *crimina carnis* are either *secundum naturam* or *contra naturam*. *Crimina carnis secundum naturam* are contrary to sound reason; *crimina carnis contra naturam* are contrary to our animal nature. Among the former we reckon *vaga libido*, which is the opposite of matrimony and of which there are two kinds: *scortatio* and *concubinatus*. *Concubinatus* is indeed a *pactum*, but a *pactum inaequale*, in which the rights are not reciprocal. In this pact the woman surrenders her sex completely to the man, but the man does not completely surrender his sex to the woman. The second *crimen carnis secundum naturam* is *adulterium*. Adultery cannot take place except in marriage; it signifies a breach of mar-

riage. Just as the engagement to marry is the most serious and the most inviolable engagement between two persons and binds them for life, so also is adultery the greatest breach of faith that there can be, because it is disloyalty to an engagement than which there can be none more important. For this reason adultery is cause for divorce. Another cause is incompatibility and inability to be at one, whereby unity and concord of will between the two persons is impossible. Next comes the question whether incest is incest *per se,* or whether it is by the civil law that it is made a *crimen carnis,* natural or unnatural. The question might be answered either by natural instinct or by reason. From the point of view of natural instinct incest is a *crimen carnis secundum naturam,* for it is after all a union of the sexes; it is not *contra naturam animalium,* because animals do not differentiate in this respect in their practices. But on the judgment of the understanding incest is *contra naturam.*

Uses of sexuality which are contrary to natural instinct and to animal nature are *crimina carnis contra naturam*. First amongst them we have onanism. This is abuse of the sexual faculty without any object, the exercise of the faculty in the complete absence of any object of sexuality. The practice is contrary to the ends of humanity and even opposed to animal nature. By it man sets aside his person and degrades himself below the level of animals. A second *crimen carnis contra naturam* is intercourse between *sexus homogenii,* in which the object of sexual impulse is a human being but there is homogeneity instead of heterogeneity of sex, as when a woman satisfies her desire on a woman, or a man on a man. This practice too is contrary to the ends of humanity; for the end of humanity in respect of sexuality is to preserve the species without debasing the person; but in this instance the species is not being preserved (as it can be by a *crimen carnis secundum naturam*), but the person is set aside, the self is degraded below the level of the animals, and humanity is dishonoured. The third *crimen carnis contra naturam* occurs when the object of the desire is in fact of the opposite sex but is not human. Such is sodomy, or intercourse with animals. This, too, is contrary to the ends of humanity and against our natural instinct. It degrades mankind below the level of animals, for no animal turns in this way from its own species.

All *crimina carnis contra naturam* degrade human nature to a level below that of animal nature and make man unworthy of his humanity. He no longer deserves to be a person. From the point of view of duties towards himself such conduct is the most disgraceful and the most degrading of which man is capable. Suicide is the most dreadful, but it is not as dishonourable and base as the *crimina carnis contra naturam*. It is the most abominable conduct of which man can be guilty. So abominable are these *crimina carnis contra naturam* that they are unmentionable, for the very mention of them is nauseating, as is not the case with suicide. We all fight shy of mentioning these vices; teachers refrain from mentioning them, even when their intention is unobjectionable and they only wish to warn their charges against them. But as they are of frequent occurrence, we are in a dilemma: are we to name them in order that people should know and prevent their frequent occurrence, or are we to keep them dark in order that people should not learn of them and so not have the opportunity of transgressing? Frequent mention would familiarize people with them and the vices might as a result cease to disgust us and come to appear more tolerable. Hence our modesty in not referring to them. On the other hand, if we mention them only circumspectly and with disinclination, our aversion from them is still apparent. There is also another reason for our modesty. Each sex is ashamed of the vices of which its members are capable. Human beings feel, therefore, ashamed to mention those things of which it is shameful for humanity to be capable. These vices make us ashamed that we are human beings and, therefore, capable of them, for an animal is incapable of all such *crimina carnis contra naturam*.

15.   *IS ADULTERY IMMORAL?*

Richard Wasserstrom

Many discussions of the enforcement of morality by the law take as illustrative of the problem under consideration the regulation of various types of sexual behavior by the criminal law. It was, for example, the Wolfenden Report's recommendations concerning homosexuality and prostitution that led Lord Devlin to compose his now famous lecture, "The Enforcement of Morals." And that lecture in turn provoked important philosophical responses from H. L. A. Hart, Ronald Dworkin, and others.

Much, if not all, of the recent philosophical literature on the enforcement of morals appears to take for granted the immorality of the sexual behavior in question. The focus of discussion, at least, is whether such things as homosexuality, prostitution, and adultery ought to be made illegal even if they are immoral, and not whether they are immoral.

From Richard Wasserstrom, *Today's Moral Problems* (New York: Macmillan Publishing Co., Inc., 1975), pp. 240–252.

I propose in this paper to think about the latter, more neglected topic, that of sexual morality, and to do so in the following fashion. I shall consider just one kind of behavior that is often taken to be a case of sexual immorality—adultery. I am interested in pursuing at least two questions. First, I want to explore the question of in what respects adulterous behavior falls within the domain of morality at all: For this surely is one of the puzzles one encounters when considering the topic of sexual morality. It is often hard to see on what grounds much of the behavior is deemed to be either moral or immoral, for example, private homosexual behavior between consenting adults. I have purposely selected adultery because it seems a more plausible candidate for moral assessment than many other kinds of sexual behavior.

The second question I want to examine is that of what is to be said about adultery, without being especially concerned to stay within the area of morality. I shall endeavor, in other words, to identify and to assess a number of the major arguments that might be advanced against adultery. I believe that they are the chief arguments that would be given in support of the view that adultery is immoral, but I think they are worth considering even if some of them turn out to be nonmoral arguments and considerations.

A number of the issues involved seem to me to be complicated and difficult. In a number of places I have at best indicated where further philosophical exploration is required without having successfully conducted the exploration myself. The paper may very well be more useful as an illustration of how one might begin to think about the subject of sexual morality than as an elucidation of important truths about the topic.

Before I turn to the arguments themselves there are two preliminary points that require some clarification. Throughout the paper I shall refer to the immorality of such things as breaking a promise, deceiving someone, etc. In a very rough way, I mean by this that there is something morally wrong that is done in doing the action in question. I mean that the action is, in a strong sense, of *"prima facie"* prima facie wrong or unjustified. I do not mean that it may never be right or justifiable to do the action; just that the fact that it is an action of this description always does count against the rightness of the action. I leave entirely open the question of what it is that makes actions of this kind immoral in this sense of "immoral."

The second preliminary point concerns what is meant or implied by the concept of adultery. I mean by "adultery" any case of extramarital sex, and I want to explore the arguments for and against extramarital sex, undertaken in a variety of morally relevant situations. Someone might claim that the concept of adultery is conceptually connected with the concept of immorality, and that to characterize behavior as adulterous is already to characterize it as immoral or unjustified in the sense described above. There may be something to this. Hence the importance of making it clear that I want to talk about extramarital sexual relations. If they are always immoral, this is something that must be shown by argument. If the concept of adultery does in some sense entail or imply immorality, I want to ask whether that connection is a rationally based

one. If not all cases of extramarital sex are immoral (again, in the sense described above), then the concept of adultery should either be weakened accordingly or restricted to those classes of extramarital sex for which the predication of immorality is warranted.

One argument for the immorality of adultery might go something like this: what makes adultery immoral is that it involves the breaking of a promise, and what makes adultery seriously wrong is that it involves the breaking of an important promise. For, so the argument might continue, one of the things the two parties promise each other when they get married is that they will abstain from sexual relationships with third persons. Because of this promise both spouses quite reasonably entertain the expectation that the other will behave in conformity with it. Hence, when one of the parties has sexual intercourse with a third person he or she breaks that promise about sexual relationships which was made when the marriage was entered into, and defeats the reasonable expectations of exclusivity entertained by the spouse.

In many cases the immorality involved in breaching the promise relating to extramarital sex may be a good deal more serious than that involved in the breach of other promises. This is so because adherence to this promise may be of much greater importance to the parties than is adherence to many of the other promises given or received by them in their lifetime. The breaking of this promise may be much more hurtful and painful than is typically the case.

Why is this so? To begin with, it may have been difficult for the nonadulterous spouse to have kept the promise. Hence that spouse may feel the unfairness of having restrained himself or herself in the absence of reciprocal restraint having been exercised by the adulterous spouse. In addition, the spouse may perceive the breaking of the promise as an indication of a kind of indifference on the part of the adulterous spouse. If you really cared about me and my feelings—the spouse might say—you would not have done this to me. And third, and related to the above, the spouse may see the act of sexual intercourse with another as a sign of affection for the other person and as an additional rejection of the nonadulterous spouse as the one who is loved by the adulterous spouse. It is not just that the adulterous spouse does not take the feelings of the spouse sufficiently into account, the adulterous spouse also indicates through the act of adultery affection for someone other than the spouse. I will return to these points later. For the present, it is sufficient to note that a set of arguments can be developed in support of the proposition that certain kinds of adultery are wrong just because they involve the breach of a serious promise which, among other things, leads to the intentional infliction of substantial pain by one spouse upon the other.

Another argument for the immorality of adultery focuses not on the existence of a promise of sexual exclusivity but on the connection between adultery and deception. According to this argument, adultery involves deception. And because deception is wrong, so is adultery.

Although it is certainly not obviously so, I shall simply assume in this paper that deception is always immoral. Thus the crucial issue for my purposes is the asserted connection between extramarital sex and deception. Is it plausible to maintain, as this argument does, that adultery always does involve deception and is on that basis to be condemned?

The most obvious person on whom deceptions might be practiced is the non-participating spouse; and the most obvious thing about which the nonparticipating spouse can be deceived is the existence of the adulterous act. One clear case of deception is that of lying. Instead of saying that the afternoon was spent in bed with A, the adulterous spouse asserts that it was spent in the library with B, or on the golf course with C.

There can also be deception even when no lies are told. Suppose, for instance, that a person has sexual intercourse with someone other than his or her spouse and just does not tell the spouse about it. Is that deception? It may not be a case of lying if, for example, the spouse is never asked by the other about the situation. Still, we might say, it is surely deceptive because of the promises that were exchanged at marriage. As we saw earlier, these promises provide a foundation for the reasonable belief that neither spouse will engage in sexual relationships with any other persons. Hence the failure to bring the fact of extramarital sex to the attention of the

other spouse deceives that spouse about the present state of the marital relationship.

Adultery, in other words, can involve both active and passive deception. An adulterous spouse may just keep silent or, as is often the fact, the spouse may engage in an increasingly complex way of life devoted to the concealment of the facts from the nonparticipating spouse. Lies, halftruths, clandestine meetings, and the like may become a central feature of the adulterous spouse's existence. These are things that can and do happen, and when they do they make the case against adultery an easy one. Still, neither active nor passive deception is inevitably a feature of an extramarital relationship.

It is possible, though, that a more subtle but pervasive kind of deceptiveness is a feature of adultery. It comes about because of the connection in our culture between sexual intimacy and certain feelings of love and affection. The point can be made indirectly at first by seeing that one way in which we can, in our culture, mark off our close friends from our mere acquaintances is through the kinds of intimacies that we are prepared to share with them. I may, for instance, be willing to reveal my very private thoughts and emotions to my closest friends or to my wife, but to no one else. My sharing of these intimate facts about myself is from one perspective a way of making a gift to those who mean the most to me. Revealing these things and sharing them with those who mean the most to me is one means by which I create, maintain, and confirm those interpersonal relationships that are of most importance to me.

Now in our culture, it might be claimed, sexual intimacy is one of the chief currencies through which gifts of this sort are exchanged. One way to tell someone—particularly someone of the opposite sex—that you have feelings of affection and love for them is by allowing to them or sharing with them sexual behaviors that one doesn't share with the rest of the world. This way of measuring affection was certainly very much a part of the culture in which I matured. It worked something like this. If you were a girl, you showed how much you liked someone by the degree of sexual intimacy you would allow. If you liked a boy only a little, you never did more than kiss—and even the kiss was not very passionate. If you liked the boy a lot and if your feeling was reciprocated, necking, and possibly petting, was permissible. If the attachment was still stronger and you thought it might even become a permanent relationship, the sexual activity was correspondingly more intense and more intimate, although whether it would ever lead to sexual intercourse depended on whether the parties (and particularly the girl) accepted fully the prohibition on nonmarital sex. The situation for the boy was related, but not exactly the same. The assumption was that males did not naturally link sex with affection in the way in which females did. However, since women did, males had to take this into account. That is to say, because a woman would permit sexual intimacies only if she had feelings of affection for the male and only if those feelings were reciprocated, the male had to have and express those feelings, too, before sexual intimacies of any sort would occur.

The result was that the importance of a correlation between sexual intimacy and feelings of love and affection was taught by the culture and assimilated by those growing up in the culture. The scale of possible positive feelings toward persons of the other sex ran from casual liking at the one end to the love that was deemed essential to and characteristic of marriage at the other. The scale of possible sexual behavior ran from brief, passionless kissing or hand-holding at the one end to sexual intercourse at the other. And the correlation between the two scales was quite precise. As a result, any act of sexual intimacy carried substantial meaning with it, and no act of sexual intimacy was simply a pleasurable set of bodily sensations. Many such acts were, of course, more pleasurable to the participants because they were a way of saying what the participants feelings were. And sometimes they were less pleasurable for the same reason. The point is, however, that in any event sexual activity was much more than mere bodily enjoyment. It was not like eating a good meal, listening to good music, lying in the sun, or getting a pleasant back rub. It was behavior that meant a great deal concerning one's feelings for persons of the opposite sex in whom one was most interested and with whom one was most involved. It was among the most authoritative ways in which one could communicate to another the nature and degree of one's affection.

If this sketch is even roughly right, then several things become somewhat clearer. To begin with, a possible rationale for many of the rules of conventional sexual morality can be developed. If, for example, sexual intercourse is associated with the kind of affection and commitment to another that is regarded as characteristic of the marriage relationship, then it is natural that sexual intercourse should be thought properly to take place between persons who are married to each other. And if it is thought that this kind of affection and commitment is only to be found within the marriage relationship, then it is not surprising that sexual intercourse should only be thought to be proper within marriage.

Related to what has just been said is the idea that sexual intercourse ought to be restricted to those who are married to each other as a means by which to confirm the very special feelings that the spouses have for each other. Because the culture teaches that sexual intercourse means that the strongest of all feelings for each other are shared by the lovers, it is natural that persons who are married to each other should be able to say this to each other in this way. Revealing and confirming verbally that these feelings are present is one thing that helps to sustain the relationship; engaging in sexual intercourse is another.

In addition, this account would help to provide a framework within which to make sense of the notion that some sex is better than other sex. As I indicated earlier, the fact that sexual intimacy can be meaningful in the sense described tends to make it also the case that sexual intercourse can sometimes be more enjoyable than at other times. On this view, sexual intercourse will typically be more enjoyable where the strong feelings of affection are present than it will be where it is merely "mechanical." This is so in part because people enjoy being loved, especially by those whom they love. Just as we like to hear words of affection, so we like to receive affectionate behavior. And the meaning enhances the independently pleasureable behavior.

More to the point, moreover, an additional rationale for the prohibition on extramarital sex can now be developed. For given this way of viewing the sexual world, extramarital sex will almost always involve deception of a deeper sort. If the adulterous spouse does not in fact have the appropriate feelings of affection for the extramarital partner, then the adulterous spouse is deceiving that person about the presence of such feelings. If, on the other hand, the adulterous spouse does have the corresponding feelings for the extramarital partner but not toward the nonparticipating spouse, the adulterous spouse is very probably deceiving the nonparticipating spouse about the presence of such feelings toward that spouse. Indeed, it might be argued, whenever there is no longer love between the two persons who are married to each other, there is deception just because being married implies both to the participants and to the world that such a bond exists. Deception is inevitable, the argument might conclude, because the feelings of affection that ought to accompany any act of sexual intercourse can only be held toward one other person at any given time in one's life. And if this is so, then the adulterous spouse always deceives either the partner in adultery or the nonparticipating spouse about the existence of such feelings. Thus extramarital sex involves deception of this sort and is for this reason immoral even if no deception vis-à-vis the occurrence of the act of adultery takes place.

What might be said in response to the foregoing arguments? The first thing that might be said is that the account of the connection between sexual intimacy and feelings of affection is inaccurate. Not inaccurate in the sense that no one thinks of things that way, but in the sense that there is substantially more divergence of opinion than that account suggests. For example, the view I have delineated may describe reasonably accurately the concepts of the sexual world in which I grew up, but it does not capture the sexual *weltanschauung* of today's youth at all. Thus, whether or not adultery implies deception in respect to feelings depends very much on the persons who are involved and the way they look at the "meaning" of sexual intimacy.

Second, the argument leaves to be answered the question of whether it is desirable for sexual intimacy to carry the sorts of messages described above. For those persons for whom sex does have these implications, there are special feelings and sensibilities that must be taken into account. But it is another question entirely whether any valuable end—moral or otherwise —is served by investing sexual behavior with such significance. That is something that must be shown and not just assumed. It might, for instance, be the case that substantially more good than harm would come from a kind of demystification of sexual behavior: one that would encourage the enjoyment of sex more for its own sake and one that would reject the centrality both of the association of sex with love and of love with only one other person.

I regard these as two of the more difficult, unresolved issues that our culture faces today in respect to thinking sensibly about the attitudes toward sex and love that we should try to develop in ourselves and in our children. Much of the contemporary literature that advocates sexual liberation of one sort or another embraces one or the other of two different views about the relationship between sex and love.

One view holds that sex should be separated from love and affection. To be sure sex is probably better when the partners genuinely like and enjoy each other. But sex is basically an intensive, exciting sensuous activity that can be enjoyed in a variety of suitable settings with a variety of suitable partners. The situation in respect to sexual pleasure is no different from that of the person who knows and appreciates fine food and who can have a very satisfying meal in any number of good restaurants with any number of congenial companions. One question that must be settled here is whether sex can be so demystified; another, more important question is whether is would be desirable to do so. What would we gain and what might we lose if we all lived in a world in which an act of sexual intercourse was no more or less significant or enjoyable than having a delicious meal in a nice setting with a good friend? The answer to this question lies beyond the scope of this paper.

The second view seeks to drive the wedge in a different place. It is not the link between sex and love that needs to be broken; rather, on this view, it is the connection between love and exclusivity that ought to be severed. For a number of the reasons already given, it is desirable, so this argument goes, that sexual intimacy continue to be reserved to and shared with only those for whom one has very great affection. The mistake lies in thinking that any "normal" adult will only have those feelings toward one other adult during his or her lifetime—or even at any time in his or her life. It is the concept of adult love, not ideas about sex, that, on this view, needs demystification. What are thought to be both unrealistic and unfortunate are the notions of exclusivity and possessiveness that attach to the dominant conception of love between adults in our and other cultures. Parents of four, five, six, or even ten children can certainly claim and sometimes claim correctly that they love all of their children, that they love them all equally, and that it is simply untrue to their feelings to insist that the numbers involved diminish either the quantity or the quality of their love. If this is an idea that is readily understandable in the case of parents and children, there is no necessary reason why it is an impossible or undesirable ideal in the case of adults. To be sure, there is probably a limit to the number of intimate, "primary" relationships that any person can maintain at any given time without the quality of the relationship being affected. But one adult ought surely be able to love two, three, or even six other adults at any one time without that love being different in kind or degree from that of the traditional, monogomous, lifetime marriage. And as between the individuals in these relationships, whether within a marriage or without, sexual intimacy is fitting and good.

The issues raised by a position such as this one are also surely worth exploring in detail and with care. Is there something to be called "sexual love" which is different from parental love or the nonsexual love of close friends? Is there something about love in general that links it naturally and appropriately with feelings of exclusivity and possession? Or is there something about sexual love, whatever that may be, that makes these feelings especially fitting here? Once again the issues are conceptual, empirical, and normative all at once: What is love? How could it be different? Would it be a good thing or a bad thing if it were different?

Suppose, though, that having delineated these problems we were now to pass them by. Suppose, moreover, we were to be persuaded of the possibility and the desirability of weakening substantially either the links between sex and love or the links between sexual love and exclusivity. Would it not then be the case that adultery could be free from all of the morally

objectionable features described so far? To be more specific, let us imagine that a husband and wife have what is today sometimes characterized as an "open marriage." Suppose, that is, that they have agreed in advance that extramarital sex is—under certain circumstances—acceptable behavior for each to engage in. Suppose, that as a result there is no impulse to deceive each other about the occurrence or nature of any such relationships, and that no deception in fact occurs. Suppose, too, that there is no deception in respect to the feelings involved between the adulterous spouse and the extramarital partner. And suppose, finally, that one or the other or both of the spouses then has sexual intercourse in circumstances consistent with these understandings. Under this description, so the agreement might conclude, adultery is simply not immoral. At a minimum, adultery cannot very plausibly be condemned either on the ground that it involves deception or on the ground that it requires the breaking of a promise.

At least two responses are worth considering. One calls attention to the connection between marriage and adultery; the other looks to more instrumental arguments for the immorality of adultery. Both issues deserve further exploration.

One way to deal with the case of the "open marriage" is to question whether the two persons involved are still properly to be described as being married to each other. Part of the meaning of what it is for two persons to be married to each other, so this argument would go, is to have committed oneself to have sexual relationships only with one's spouse. Of course, it would be added, we know that that commitment is not always honored. We know that persons who are married to each other often do commit adultery. But there is a difference between being willing to make a commitment to marital fidelity, even though one may fail to honor that commitment, and not making the commitment at all. Whatever the relationship may be between the two individuals in the case described above, the absence of any commitment to sexual exclusivity requires the conclusion that their relationship is not a marital one. For a commitment to sexual exclusivity is a necessary although not a sufficient condition for the existence of a marriage.

Although there may be something to this suggestion, as it is stated it is too strong to be acceptable. To begin with, I think it is very doubtful that there are many, if any, *necessary* conditions for marriage; but even if there are, a commitment to sexual exclusivity is not such a condition.

To see that this is so, consider what might be taken to be some of the essential characteristics of a marriage. We might be tempted to propose that the concept of marriage requires the following: a formal ceremony of some sort in which mutual obligations are undertaken between two persons of the opposite sex; the capacity on the part of the persons involved to have sexual intercourse with each other; the willingness to have sexual intercourse only with each other; and the feelings of love and affection between the two persons. The problem is that we can imagine relationships that are clearly marital and yet lack one or more of these features. For example, in our own society, it is possible for two persons to be married without going through a formal ceremony, as in the common-law marriages recognized in some jurisdictions. It is also possible for two persons to get married even though one or both lacks the capacity to engage in sexual intercourse. Thus, two very elderly persons who have neither the desire nor the ability to have intercourse can, nonetheless, get married, as can persons whose sexual organs have been injured so that intercourse is not possible. And we certainly know of marriages in which love was not present at the time of the marriage, as, for instance, in marriages of state and marriages of convenience.

Counterexamples not satisfying the condition relating to the abstention from extramarital sex are even more easily produced. We certainly know of societies and cultures in which polygamy and polyandry are practiced, and we have no difficulty in recognizing these relationships as cases of marriages. It might be objected, though, that these are not counterexamples because they are plural marriages rather than marriages in which sex is permitted with someone other than with one of the persons to whom one is married. But we also know of societies in which it is permissible for married persons to have sexual relationships with persons to whom they were not married, for example, temple prostitutes, concubines, and homosexual lovers. And even if we knew of no such societies, the conceptual claim would still, I submit, not be well taken. For suppose all of the other indicia of marriage were present: suppose the two persons were of the opposite sex. Suppose they had the capacity and desire to have intercourse with each other, suppose they participated in a formal ceremony in which they understood themselves voluntarily to be entering into a relationship with each other in which substantial mutual commitments were assumed. If all these conditions were satisfied, we would not be in any doubt about whether or not the two persons were married even though they had not taken a commitment of sexual exclusivity and even though they had expressly agreed that extramarital sexual intercourse was a permissible behavior for each to engage in.

A commitment to sexual exclusivity is neither a necessary nor a sufficient condition for the existence of a marriage. It does, nonetheless, have this much to do with the nature of marriage: like the other indicia enumerated above, its presence tends to establish the existence of a marriage. Thus, in the absence of a formal ceremony of any sort, an explicit commitment to sexual exclusivity would count in favor of regarding the two persons as married. The conceptual role of the commitment to sexual exclusivity can, perhaps, be brought out through the following example. Suppose we found a tribe which had a practice in which all the other indicia of marriage were present but in which the two parties were *prohibited* ever from having sexual intercourse with each other. Moreover, suppose that sexual intercourse with others was clearly permitted. In such a case we would, I think, reject the idea that the two were married to each other and we would describe their relationship in other terms, for example, as some kind of formalized, special friendship relation—a kind of heterosexual "blood-brother" bond.

Compare that case with the following. Suppose again that the tribe had a practice in which all of the other indicia of marriage were present, but instead of a prohitibion on sexual intercourse between the persons in the relationship there was no rule at all. Sexual intercourse was permissible with the person with whom one had this ceremonial relationship, but it was no more or less permissible than with a number of other persons to whom one was not so related (for instance, all consenting adults of the opposite sex). Although we might be in doubt as to whether we ought to describe the persons as married to each other, we would probably conclude that they were married and that they simply were members of a tribe whose views about sex were quite different from our own.

What all of this shows is that *a prohibition* on sexual intercourse between the two persons involved in a relationship is conceptually incompatible with the claim that the two of them are married. The *permissibility* of intramarital sex is a necessary part of the idea of marriage. But no such incompatibility follows simply from the added permissibility of extramarital sex.

These arguments do not, of course, exhaust the arguments for the prohibition on extramarital sexual relations. The remaining argument that I wish to consider—as I indicated earlier—is a more instrumental one. It seeks to justify the prohibition by virtue of the role that it plays in the development and maintenance of nuclear families. The argument, or set of arguments, might, I believe, go something like this.

Consider first a farfetched nonsexual example. Suppose a society were organized so that after some suitable age—say, 18, 19, or 20—persons were forbidden to eat anything but bread and water with anyone but their spouse. Persons might still choose in such a society not to get married. Good food just might not be very important to them because they have underdeveloped taste buds. Or good food might be bad for them because there is something wrong with their digestive system. Or good food might be important to them, but they might decide that the enjoyment of good food would get in the way of the attainment of other things that were more important. But most persons would, I think, be led to favor marriage in part because they preferred a richer, more varied, diet to one of bread and water. And they might remain married because the family was the only legitimate setting within which good food was obtainable. If it is important to have society organized so that persons will both get married and stay married, such an arrangement would be well suited to the preservation of the family, and the prohibitions relating to food consumption could be understood as fulfilling that function.

It is obvious that one of the more powerful human desires is the desire for sexual gratification. The desire is a natural one, like hunger and thirst, in the sense that it need not be learned in order to be present within us and operative upon us. But there is in addition much that we do learn about what the act of sexual intercourse is like. Once we experience sexual intercourse ourselves—and in particular once we experience orgasm—we discover that it is among the most intensive, short-term pleasures of the body.

Because this is so, it is easy to see how the prohibition upon extramarital sex helps to hold marriage together. At least during that period of life when the enjoyment of sexual intercourse is one of the desirable bodily pleasures, persons will wish to enjoy those pleasures. If one consequence of being married is that one is prohibited from having sexual intercourse with anyone but one's spouse, then the spouses in a marriage are in a position to provide an important source of pleasure for each other that is unavailable to them elsewhere in the society.

The point emerges still more clearly if this rule of sexual morality is seen as of a piece with the other rules of sexual morality. When this prohibition is coupled, for example, with the prohibition on nonmarital sexual intercourse, we are presented with the inducement both to get married and to stay married. For if sexual intercourse in only legitimate within marriage, then persons seeking that gratification which is a feature of sexual intercourse are furnished explicit social directions for its attainment; namely marriage.

Nor, to continue the argument, is it necessary to focus exclusively on the bodily enjoyment that is involved. Orgasm may be a significant part of what there is to sexual intercourse, but it is not the whole of it. We need only recall the earlier discussion of the meaning that sexual intimacy has in our own culture to begin to see some of the more intricate ways in which sexual exclusivity may be connected with the establishment and maintenance of marriage as the primary heterosexual, love relationship. Adultery is wrong, in other words, because a prohibition on extramarital sex is a way to help maintain the institutions of marriage and the nuclear family.

Now I am frankly not sure what we are to say about an argument such as this one. What I am convinced of is that, like the arguments discussed earlier, this one also reveals something of the difficulty and complexity of the issues that are involved. So, what I want now to do—in the brief and final portion of this paper—is to try to delineate with reasonable precision what I take several of the fundamental, unresolved issues to be.

The first is whether this last argument is an argument for the *immorality* of extramarital sexual intercourse. What does seem clear is that there are differences between this argument and the ones considered earlier. The earlier arguments condemned adulterous behavior because it was behavior that involved breaking of a promise, taking unfair advantage, or deceiving another. To the degree to which the prohibition on extramarital sex can be supported by arguments which invoke considerations such as these, there is little question but that violations of the prohibition are properly regarded as immoral. And such a claim could be defended on one or both of two distinct grounds. The first is that things like promise-breaking and deception are just wrong. The second is that adultery involving promise-breaking or deception is wrong because it involves the straightforward infliction of harm on another human being—typically the nonadulterous spouse—who has a strong claim to have that harm so inflicted.

The argument that connects the prohibition on extramarital sex with the maintenance and preservation of the institution of marriage is an argument for the instrumental value of the prohibition. To some degree this counts, I think, against regarding all violations of the prohibition as obvious cases of immorality. This is so partly because hypothetical imperatives are less clearly within the domain of morality than are categorical ones, and even more because instrumental prohibitions are within the domain of morality only if the end they serve or the way they serve it is itself within the domain of morality.

What this should help us see, I think, is the fact that the argument that connects the prohibition on adultery with the preservation of marriage is at best seriously incomplete. Before we ought to be convinced by it, we ought to have reasons for believing that marriage is a morally desirable and just social institution. And this is not quite as easy or obvious a task as it may seem to be. For the concept of marriage is, as we have seen, both a loosely structured and a complicated one. There may be all sorts of intimate, interpersonal relationships which will resemble but not be identical with the typical marriage relationship presupposed by the traditional sexual morality. There may be a number of distinguishable sexual and loving arrangements which can all legitimately claim to be called *marriages*. The prohibitions of the traditional sexual morality may be effective ways to maintain some marriages and ineffective ways to promote and preserve others. The prohibitions of the traditional sexual morality may make good psychological sense if certain psychological theories are true, and they may be purveyors of immense psychological mischief if other psychological theories are true. The prohibitions of the traditional sexual morality may seem obviously correct if sexual intimacy carries the meaning that the dominant culture has often ascribed to it, and they may seem equally bizarre when sex is viewed through the perspective of the counter-culture. Irrespective of whether instrumental arguments of this sort are properly deemed moral arguments, they ought not to fully convince anyone until questions like these are answered.

16. *THE PRINCE*

Niccolò Machiavelli

OF THE QUALITIES IN RESPECT OF WHICH MEN, AND MOST OF ALL PRINCES, ARE PRAISED OR BLAMED

It now remains for us to consider what ought to be the conduct and bearing of a Prince in relation to his subjects and friends. And since I know that many have written on this subject, I fear it may be thought presumptuous in me to write of it also; the more so, because in my treatment of it I depart from the views that others have taken.

But since it is my object to write what shall be useful to whosoever understands it, it seems to me better to follow the real truth of things than an imaginary view of them. For many Republics and Princedoms have been imagined that were never seen or known to exist in reality. And the manner in which we live, and that in which we ought to live, are things so wide asunder, that he who quits the one to betake himself to the other is more likely to destroy than to save himself; since any one who would act up to a perfect standard of goodness in everything, must be ruined among so many who are not good. It is essential, therefore, for a Prince who desires to maintain his position, to have learned how to be other than good, and to use or not to use his goodness as necessity requires.

Laying aside, therefore, all fanciful notions concerning a Prince, and considering those only that are true, I say that all men when they are spoken of, and Princes more than others from their being set so high, are characterized by some one of those qualities which attach either praise or blame. Thus one is accounted liberal, another miserly (which word I use, rather than *avaricious,* to denote the man who is too sparing of what is his own, *avarice* being the disposition to take wrongfully what is another's); one is generous, another greedy; one cruel, another

tender-hearted; one is faithless, another true to his word; one effeminate and cowardly, another high-spirited and courageous; one is courteous, another haughty; one impure, another chaste; one simple, another crafty; one firm, another facile; one grave, another frivolous; one devout, another unbelieving; and the like. Every one, I know, will admit that it would be most laudable for a Prince to be endowed with all of the above qualities that are reckoned good; but since it is impossible for him to possess or constantly practise them all, the conditions of human nature not allowing it, he must be discreet enough to know how to avoid the infamy of those vices that would deprive him of his government, and, if possible, be on his guard also against those which might not deprive him of it; though if he cannot wholly restrain himself, he may with less scruple indulge in the latter. He need never hesitate, to incur the reproach of those vices without which his authority can hardly be preserved; for if he well consider the whole matter, he will find that there may be a line of conduct having the appearance of virtue, to follow which would be his ruin, and that there may be another course having the appearance of vice, by following which his safety and well-being are secured.

OF LIBERALITY AND MISERLINESS

Beginning, then, with the first of the qualities above noticed, I say that it may be a good thing to be reputed liberal, but, nevertheless, that liberality without the reputation of it is hurtful; because, though it be worthily and rightly used, still if it be not known, you escape not the reproach of its opposite vice. Hence, to have

From Niccolò Machiavelli, *The Prince,* translated by N. H. Thomson, Chapters 15–18.

credit for liberality with the world at large, you must neglect no circumstance of sumptuous display; the result being, that a Prince of a liberal disposition will consume his whole substance in things of this sort, and, after all, be obliged, if he would maintain his reputation for liberality, to burden his subjects with extraordinary taxes, and to resort to confiscations and all the other shifts whereby money is raised. But in this way he becomes hateful to his subjects, and growing impoverished is held in little esteem by any. So that in the end, having by his liberality offended many and obliged few, he is worse off than when he began, and is exposed to all his original dangers. Recognizing this, and endeavouring to retrace his steps, he at once incurs the infamy of miserliness.

A Prince, therefore, since he cannot without injury to himself practise the virtue of liberality so that it may be known, will not, if he be wise, greatly concern himself though he be called miserly. Because in time he will come to be regarded as more and more liberal, when it is seen that through his parsimony his revenues are sufficient; that he is able to defend himself against any who make war on him; that he can engage in enterprises against others without burdening his subjects; and thus exercise liberality towards all from whom he does not take, whose number is infinite, while he is miserly in respect of those only to whom he does not give, whose number is few.

In our own days we have seen no Princes accomplish great results save those who have been accounted miserly. All others have been ruined. Pope Julius II, after availing himself of his reputation for liberality to arrive at the Papacy, made no effort to preserve that reputation when making war on the King of France, but carried on all his numerous campaigns without levying from his subjects a single extraordinary tax, providing for the increased expenditure out of his long-continued savings. Had the present King of Spain been accounted liberal, he never could have engaged or succeeded in so many enterprises.

A Prince, therefore, if he is enabled thereby to forbear from plundering his subjects, to defend himself, to escape poverty and contempt, and the necessity of becoming rapacious, ought to care little though he incur the reproach of miserliness, for this is one of those vices which enable him to reign.

And should any object that Caesar by his liberality rose to power, and that many others have been advanced to the highest dignities from their having been liberal and so reputed, I reply, 'Either you are already a Prince or you seek to become one; in the former case liberality is hurtful, in the latter it is very necessary that you be thought liberal; Caesar was one of those who sought the sovereignty of Rome; but if after obtaining it he had lived on without retrenching his expenditure, he must have ruined the Empire.' And if it be further urged that many Princes reputed to have been most liberal have achieved great things with their armies, I answer that a Prince spends either what belongs to himself and his subjects, or what belongs to others; and that in the former case he ought to be sparing, but in the latter ought not to refrain from any kind of liberality. Because for a Prince who leads his armies in person and maintains them by plunder, pillage, and forced contributions, dealing as he does with the property of others this liberality is necessary, since otherwise he would not be followed by his soldiers. Of what does not belong to you or to your subjects you should, therefore, be a lavish giver, as were Cyrus, Caesar, and Alexander; for to be liberal with the property of others does not take from your reputation, but adds to it. What injures you is to give away what is your own. And there is no quality so self-destructive as liberality; for while you practise it you lose the means whereby it can be practised, and become poor and despised, or else, to avoid poverty, you become rapacious and hated. For liberality leads to one or other of these two results, against which, beyond all others, a Prince should guard.

Wherefore it is wiser to put up with the name of being miserly, which breeds ignominy, but without hate, than to be obliged, from the desire to be reckoned liberal, to incur the reproach of rapacity, which breeds hate as well as ignominy.

OF CRUELTY AND CLEMENCY, AND WHETHER IT IS BETTER TO BE LOVED OR FEARED

Passing to the other qualities above referred to, I say that every Prince should desire to be accounted merciful and not cruel. Nevertheless, he should be on his guard against the abuse of this quality of mercy. Cesare Borgia was reputed cruel, yet his cruelty restored Romagna, united it, and brought it to order and obedience; so that if we look at things in their true light, it will be seen that he was in reality far more merciful than the people of Florence, who, to avoid the imputation of cruelty, suffered Pistoja to be torn to pieces by factions.

A Prince should therefore disregard the reproach of being thought cruel where it enables him to keep his subjects united and obedient. For he who quells disorder by a very few signal examples will in the end be more merciful than he who from too great leniency permits things to take their course and so to result in rapine and bloodshed; for these hurt the whole State, whereas the severities of the Prince injure individuals only.

And for a new Prince, of all others, it is impossible to escape a name for cruelty, since new States are full of dangers. Wherefore Virgil, by the mouth of Dido, excuses the harshness of her reign on the plea that it was new, saying:—

'A fate unkind, and newness in my reign
Compel me thus to guard a wide domain.'

Nevertheless, the new Prince should not be too ready of belief, nor too easily set in motion; nor should he himself be the first to raise alarms; but should so temper prudence with kindliness that too great confidence in others shall not throw him off his guard, nor groundless distrust render him insupportable.

And here comes in the question whether it is better to be loved rather than feared, or feared rather than loved. It might perhaps be answered that we should wish to be both; but since love and fear can hardly exist together, if we must choose between them, it is far safer to be feared than loved. For of men it may generally be affirmed that they are thankless, fickle, false, studious to avoid danger, greedy of gain, devoted to you while you are able to confer benefits upon them, and ready, as I said before, while danger is distant, to shed their blood, and sacrifice their property, their lives, and their children for you; but in the hour of need they turn against you. The Prince, therefore, who

without otherwise securing himself builds wholly on their professions is undone. For the friendships which we buy with a price, and do not gain by greatness and nobility of character, though they be fairly earned are not made good, but fail us when we have occasion to use them.

Moreover, men are less careful how they offend him who makes himself loved than him who makes himself feared. For love is held by the tie of obligation, which, because men are a sorry breed, is broken on every whisper of private interest; but fear is bound by the apprehension of punishment which never relaxes its grasp.

Nevertheless a Prince should inspire fear in such a fashion that if he do not win love he may escape hate. For a man may very well be feared and yet not hated, and this will be the case so long as he does not meddle with the property or with the women of his citizens and subjects. And if constrained to put any to death, he should do so only when there is manifest cause or reasonable justification. But, above all, he must abstain from the property of others. For men will sooner forget the death of their father than the loss of their patrimony. Moreover, pretexts for confiscation are never to seek, and he who has once begun to live by rapine always finds reasons for taking what is not his; whereas reasons for shedding blood are fewer, and sooner exhausted.

But when a Prince is with his army, and has many soldiers under his command, he must needs disregard the reproach of cruelty, for without such a reputation in its Captain, no army can be held together or kept under any kind of control. Among other things remarkable in Hannibal this has been noted, that having a very great army, made up of men of many different nations and brought to fight in a foreign country, no dissension ever arose among the soldiers themselves, nor any mutiny against their leader, either in his good or in his evil fortunes. This we can only ascribe to the transcendent cruelty, which, joined with numberless great qualities, rendered him at once venerable and terrible in the eyes of his soldiers; for without this reputation for cruelty these other virtues would not have produced the like results.

Unreflecting writers, indeed, while they praise his achievements, have condemned the chief cause of them; but that his other merits would not by themselves have been so efficacious we may see from the case of Scipio, one of the greatest Captains, not of his own time only but of all times of which we have record, whose armies rose against him in Spain from no other cause than his too great leniency in allowing them a freedom inconsistent with military strictness. With which weakness Fabius Maximus taxed him in the Senate House, calling him the corrupter of the Roman soldiery. Again, when the Locrians were shamefully outraged by one of his lieutenants, he neither avenged them, nor punished the insolence of his officer; and this from the natural easiness of his disposition. So that it was said in the Senate by one who sought to excuse him, that there were many who knew better how to refrain from doing wrong themselves than how to correct the wrongdoings of others. This temper, however, must in time have marred the name and fame even of Scipio, had he continued in it, and retained his command. But living as he did under the control of the Senate, this hurtful quality was not merely disguised, but came to be regarded as a glory.

Returning to the question of being loved or feared, I sum up by saying, that since his being loved depends upon his subjects, while his being feared depends upon himself, a wise Prince should build on what is his own, and not on what rests with others. Only, as I have said, he must do his utmost to escape hatred.

HOW PRINCES SHOULD KEEP FAITH

Every one understands how praiseworthy it is in a Prince to keep faith, and to live uprightly and not craftily. Nevertheless, we see from what has taken place in our own days that Princes who have set little store by their word, but have known how to overreach men by their cunning, have accomplished great things, and in the end got the better of those who trusted to honest dealing.

Be it known, then, that there are two ways of contending, one in accordance with the laws, the other by force; the first of which is proper to men, the second to beasts. But since the first method is often ineffectual, it becomes necessary to resort to the second. A Prince should, therefore, understand how to use well both the man and the beast. And this lesson has been covertly taught by the ancient writers, who relate how Achilles and many others of these old Princes were given over to be brought up and trained by Chiron the Centaur; since the only meaning of their having for instructor one who was half man and half beast is, that it is necessary for a Prince to know how to use both natures, and that the one without the other has no stability.

But since a Prince should know how to use the beast's nature wisely, he ought of beasts to choose both the lion and the fox; for the lion cannot guard himself from the toils, nor the fox from wolves. He must therefore be a fox to discern toils, and a lion to drive off wolves.

To reply wholly on the lion is unwise; and for this reason a prudent Prince neither can nor ought to keep his word when to keep it is hurtful to him and the causes which led him to pledge it are removed. If all men were good, this would not be good advice, but since they are dishonest and do not keep faith with you, you, in return, need not keep faith with them; and no prince was ever at a loss for plausible reasons to cloak a breach of faith. Of this numberless recent instances could be given, and it might be shown how many solemn treaties and engagements have been rendered inoperative and idle through want of faith in Princes, and that he who was best known to play the fox has had the best success.

It is necessary, indeed, to put a good colour on this nature, and to be skilful in simulating and dissembling. But men are so simple, and governed so absolutely by their present needs, that he who wishes to deceive will never fail in finding willing dupes. One recent example I will not omit. Pope Alexander VI had no care or thought but how to deceive, and always found material to work on. No man ever had a more effective manner of asseverating, or made promises with more solemn protestations, or observed them less. And yet, because he understood this side of human nature, his frauds always succeeded.

It is not essential, then, that a Prince should have all the good qualities which I have enumerated above, but it is most essential that he should seem to have them; I will even venture to affirm that if he has and invariably practises them all, they are hurtful, whereas the appearance of having them is useful. Thus, it is well to seem merciful, faithful, humane, religious, and upright, and also to be so; but the mind should remain so balanced that were it needful not to be so, you should be able and know how to change to the contrary.

And you are to understand that a Prince, and most of all a new Prince, cannot observe all those rules of conduct in respect whereof men are accounted good, being often forced, in order to preserve his Princedom, to act in opposition to good faith, charity, humanity, and religion. He must therefore keep his mind ready to shift as the winds and tides of Fortune turn, and, as I have already said, he ought not to quit good courses if he can help it, but should know how to follow evil courses if he must.

A Prince should therefore be very careful that nothing ever escapes his lips which is not replete with the five qualities above named, so that to see and hear him, one would think him the embodiment of mercy, good faith, integrity, humanity, and religion. And there is no virtue which it is more necessary for him to seem to possess than this last; because men in general judge rather by the eye than by the hand, for every one can see but few can touch. Every one sees what you seem, but few know what you are, and these few dare not oppose themselves to the opinion of the many who have the majesty of the State to back them up.

Moreover, in the actions of all men, and most of all of Princes, where there is no tribunal to which we can appeal, we look to results. Wherefore if a Prince succeeds in establishing and maintaining his authority, the means will always be judged honourable and be approved by every one.

17. *ETHICAL AND POLITICAL THINKING*

E. F. Carritt

§ 12. When utilitarianism is not contaminated by the relics of egoism it has always seemed to me the most plausible and, if I may so speak, the most nearly true of false ethical theories. It recognizes an obligation; it recognizes that this is distinct from self-interest; and the obligation it recognizes is a very important one; its error is to recognize only one. A utilitarian, if he lived up to his theory by always doing his putative duty, would perhaps perform more of his subjective duties than most of us actually do who hold a truer theory; possibly more even than a man who *lived up to* a theory recognizing any *one* other type of obligation.

Suppose a utilitarian and myself both always to have complete knowledge of our situations, of our capacities, and the consequences of our possible actions. If he always did what, on his principle, he thought the situations demanded, namely to promote the maximum of general happiness, he might well come nearer to always doing what the situations really demanded than I do, though I also recognize other obligations; for I may both err in assessing their comparative strength and may fail to fulfil what I believe the strongest. And again supposing a utilitarian and one who recognized no obligation but that of justice both always to have complete knowledge of their situations, of their capacities, and of the consequences of their possible actions, then if both always fulfilled the obligations they recognized, I think the utilitarian might well fulfil

From E. F. Carritt, *Ethical and Political Thinking*, Chapter IV, pp. 60–69. © 1947 Oxford University Press. Reprinted by permission of The Clarendon Press, Oxford.

more of his objective duties. Both would be historically and scientifically omniscient and both mistaken in moral insight. Neither would ever admit conflicting obligations.

Utilitarianism, perhaps because of its initial identification of happiness with the only good, has seldom been given due credit for the insistence that what is good must be as good in one man *ceteris paribus* as in another, and that the preferential production of something good in oneself is not the promotion of *good* as such. Several objections, however, can be brought against the theory.

§ 13. (1) One criticism frequently brought against utilitarianism seems to me invalid. It is said that pleasures and pains cannot be measured or weighed like proteins or money and therefore cannot be compared, so that I can never tell whether I shall produce an overbalance of pleasure in this way or in that. I cannot weigh the pleasure of a starving man whom I feed on bread against my own in eating strawberries and say that his is twice as great as mine. Such an argument might seem hardly worth serious discussion had it not been used in defence of applying to conduct a theory of abstract economics: 'There is no scientific criterion which would enable us to compare or assess the relative importance of needs of different persons . . . illegitimate inter-personal comparison',[1] and 'There is no means of testing the magnitude of A's satisfaction as compared with B's'.[2]

§ 14. But this argument, though those who use it are not ready to admit so much, really should apply against any comparison of my own desires and needs. I cannot say that two glasses of beer will give me twice as much pleasure as one, and still less that hearing a concert will give me three times or half as much; yet I may know very well indeed which will give me *more,* and may act upon the knowledge, since the two things though not measurable are comparable. It is true that, not being measurable, they are less easy to discriminate precisely, where the difference is not great, than physical objects; I may be unable to say whether the smell of roasting coffee or of bacon fried gives me the greater pleasure (mixed with some pain of appetite) even at two successive moments. It is no doubt often easier to read off the luminosity of two very similar surfaces on a pointer than to say which looks brighter, though in the end I have to trust

my eyes for the pointer. As we have admitted, the mere existence of other minds is not demonstrable, still less is the intensity of their desires. But if in self-regarding acts I am sometimes prepared to spend my money in the belief that I shall desire to-morrow's bread more than to-morrow's jam, the utilitarian is justified, on his principles, in believing that it is his duty to provide bread for the starving sooner than jam for the well fed.

§ 15. In fact it would be no commendation of an ethical theory if, on its showing, moral or even beneficent choice were always clear, since in practice we know that it is not. We often wonder if we can do more for the happiness, even the immediate happiness, of our parents or of our children; the former seem more in need of enjoyments, the latter have a keener capacity but a quicker recovery from disappointment. Utilitarianism has no need to stake its case on the possibility of an accurate 'hedonistic (or agathistic[3]) calculus'. We have a well-founded belief that starvation hurts most people more than a shortage of grape-fuit, and no *knowledge how much* more it will hurt even ourselves to-morrow; and it is on such beliefs that we have to act; we can never know either our objective duty or our objective long-run interest.

§ 16. (2) The second objection to the utilitarians is serious and indeed fatal. They make no room for justice. Most of them really admitted this when they found it hard on their principle to allow for the admitted obligation to distribute happiness 'fairly', that is either equally or in proportion to desert. This led them to qualify their definition of duty as 'promoting the greatest amount of happiness', by adding 'of the greatest number',[4] and to emphasize this by the proviso 'every one to count for one and no more'. They can hardly have meant by this merely that it did not matter to whom I gave the happiness so long as I produced the most possible, for this they had already implied. They must at least have meant that if I could produce the same amount either in equal shares or in unequal I ought to prefer the former; and this means that I ought to be just as well as generous. The other demand of justice, that we should take account of past merit in our distribution, I think they would have denied, or rather explained away by the argument that to reward beneficence was to encourage such behaviour by example, and therefore a likely way to increase the total of happiness.[5]

§ 17. (3) A third criticism, incurred by some utilitarians[6] in the attempt to accommodate their theory to our moral judgements, was that of inconsistency in considering differences of quality or kind, as well as of amount, among pleasures when determining what we ought to do. It seems clear that people do not feel the same obligation to endow the art of cookery or potboiling as that of poetry or music, and this not because they are convinced that the one causes keener and more constant pleasure to a greater number than the other. Yet the recognition of a stronger obligation to promote 'higher' or 'better' pleasures implies that we think something good, say musical or poetic experience, not merely in proportion to its general pleasantness but by its own nature. The attempt to unite this 'qualification of pleasures' with hedonistic utilitarianism is like saying 'I care about nothing but money, but I would not come by it dishonestly'. The fundamental fact is that we do not think some pleasures, such as that of cruelty, good at all.[7]

§ 18. (4) Though the inconsistency of modifying their theory in these two ways seems to have escaped the notice of most utilitarians, they could not help seeing that they were bound to meet a fourth criticism by giving some account of the universal belief that we have obligations to keep our promises. It is obvious that the payment of money to a rich creditor may not immediately result in so much satisfaction as the keeping of it by a poor debtor or the giving of it to a useful charity,[8] and that yet it may, under most circumstances, be judged a duty and always an obligation. The argument of utilitarians to explain this has usually been as follows: It is true that a particular instance of justice may not directly increase the sum of human happiness but quite the contrary, and yet we often approve such an instance. This is because the *general* practice of such good faith, with the consequent possibility of credit and contract, is supremely conducive to happiness, and therefore so far as any violation of a bargain impairs this confidence, it is, indirectly and in the long run, pernicious.

Such an attempt to bring promise-keeping under the utilitarian formula breaks down because it only applies where the promise and its performance or neglect would be public and therefore serve as an example to others.[9]

Suppose that two explorers in the Arctic have only enough food to keep one alive till he can reach the base, and one offers to die if the other will promise to educate his children. No other person can know that such a promise was made, and the breaking or keeping of it cannot influence the future keeping of promises. On the utilitarian theory, then, it is the duty of the returned traveller to act precisely as he ought to have acted if no bargain had been made: to consider how he can spend his money most expediently for the happiness of mankind, and, if he thinks his own child is a genius, to spend it upon him.

§ 19. Or, to take a different kind of justice, the utilitarian must hold that we are justified in inflicting pain always and only in order to prevent worse pain or bring about greater happiness. This, then, is all we need consider in so-called punishment, which must be purely preventive.[10] But if some kind of very cruel crime becomes common, and none of the criminals can be caught, it might be highly expedient, as an example, to hang an innocent man, if a charge against him could be so framed that he were universally thought guilty; indeed this would only fail to be an ideal instance of utilitarian 'punishment' because the victim himself would not have been so likely as a real felon to commit such a crime in the future; in all other respects it would be perfectly deterrent and therefore felicific.[11]

In short, utilitarianism has forgotten rights; it allows no right to a man because he is innocent or because he has worked hard or has been promised or injured, or because he stands in any other special relation to us. It thinks only of duties or rather of a single duty, to dump happiness wherever we most conveniently can. If it speaks of rights at all it could only say all men have one and the same right, namely that all men should try to increase the total happiness. And this is a manifest misuse of language.

C. AGATHISTIC[12] UTILITARIANISM

§ 20. In the hope of escaping some of these difficulties, especially the fact that some pleasures are judged better than others as well as greater,[13] utilitarianism has been modified by the admission that there are other good states or activities besides pleasure and that our sole duty is to do the 'optimific' act, to produce the best results we can.[14] This, for brevity, I shall call the obligation of *improvement* as distinct from the hedonistic one of beneficence. This modification of hedonistic utilitarianism corresponds to that already criticized, of egoistic hedonism, into 'self-realization'.[15]

The usual list of good things offered, though it does not necessarily claim to be exhaustive, is: Happiness or Pleasure, Affection, Aesthetic experience, and Knowledge.[16] This version has not the same attractive simplicity as the hedonistic variety of utilitarianism, since it allows a diversity of goods between which we may have to choose, whether, for instance, on a given occasion we ought to aim at increasing knowledge or happiness. But this very lack of tidiness brings it nearer truth, since it is clear that we do have to make such decisions and sometimes remain doubtful of the right one. It was a wise caution of Bacon to philosophers, 'Many things in the world are heterogeneous on which the human mind tries to force uniformity.'[17]

§ 21. But by allowing good things other than the happiness which all men desire the theory has raised for itself a new problem. Among good things one, perhaps the best of all, is surely an act done by a man to his own hindrance because he believes it to be his duty. This has been expressed in arresting language by the sayings that 'the only unconditionally good thing is the good will',[18] that 'the moral law within and the starry heaven above give us the greatest sense of sublimity',[19] and that 'justice is more admirable than the morning or the evening star'.[20] But such goodness is not the *result* of an action, expectation of which *makes* us think it obligatory, it is in the nature itself of any action which is done because it is *already* thought a duty, whether on account of its expected results or for some other reason. Acts, then, which result in the best possible consequences have been called *optimific* or 'best-producing', and those whose intrinsic goodness combined with their good consequences together constitute the best possible whole have been called *optimizing* or 'best-rendering'. If, then, with the agathistic utilitarians we thought it always a man's objective duty to do

the really optimific act, we should have to admit, what they did not always recognize, that if such an act were done from bad or indifferent motives, it might not be so optimizing as the doing of a putative duty, though, owing to ignorance, this was the reverse of optimific. Indeed, if we could accept the view that a conscientious act is always *incomparably* better than any amount of other goods,[21] we should have to conclude that the doing of any putative duty is always optimizing and consequently that optimization cannot be the ground of obligation. For what has to be emphasized at the cost of repetition is that the goodness of doing an act because it is thought a duty cannot be the reason for its being thought a duty. It might be thought a duty because it was thought optimific, and whether this belief were true or false, the doing of it for that reason might be optimizing. But any form of utilitarianism is committed to finding the ground of obligation wholly subsequent to the action, in the preponderance of good *results*.

§ 22. The objection, then, which we found fatal to hedonistic utilitarianism is equally fatal to the agathistic emendation; neither gives any account of promise-keeping or of other justice. The accidental acquisition of £5 by a man who has been promised £5 is not necessarily good. Nobody except the promiser need be under any obligation to pay him £5; the payment by the promiser need not be optimific, and may not be optimizing if done from fear or favour; yet it may be thought a duty.

Some later agathistic utilitarians[22] have withdrawn from the position that the goodness which in their view is the ground of all obligation can always be found in the consequences of the act. They have also had to admit that what makes an act my duty cannot be the fact that if I do it because it *is* my duty it will be good. They have then entrenched themselves in the vaguer position that the goodness which is the alleged ground of obligation lies in some as yet unrealized rule or pattern of my own whole life or the life of some ideal community or of mankind, a rule to which my fulfilment of the obligation would conform. But surely there can only be an obligation to conform to a hypothetical rule, pattern, or ideal if it is a good one, and its goodness will partly depend upon its demanding for its realization the fulfilment of obligations; otherwise the position is that right action is mere self-consistency: *Pecca fortiter* or at least *Pecca constanter.* When 'drooling' during a committee meeting it has happened to me to make a blot in one corner of the pattern, and the pattern then demanded like blots elsewhere. But in conduct the blot may be an assault or a fib which fails to achieve my perhaps beneficent purpose unless it is followed by massacre or swindle on a systematic scale. An end that might conceivably justify one such action need not justify the systematic policy which would alone complete the pattern.

In patterns there are no rights to be infringed.

Neither form of utilitarianism is a satisfactory formula for all our duties. We believe we have various kinds of obligations, for which we can discover no common ground, arising out of the various situations in which we think ourselves. When these putative obligations conflict we have to judge which of them is the strongest so as to constitute our putative duty. It is only for the neglect of putative duty that remorse arises, blame can be incurred, or punishment deserved.

NOTES

1. Hayck, *Collectivist Economic Planning,* p. 25.
2. Robbins, *Nature and Significance of Economic Science,* pp. 122–4. Cf. Jay, *The Socialist Case,* ch. ii.
3. See § 19.
4. The *greatest Happiness* for the greatest Numbers', Hutcheson, *Enquiry into the Original of Our Ideas of Beauty and Virtue,* II. iii. 8.
5. See Ch. V.
6. e.g. J. S. Mill, Bentham more consistently held that 'the pleasure of push-pin is as good as the pleasure of poetry'.
7. See Ch. VIII.
8. Hume, *Treatise of Human Nature,* Bk. III, ii. I.
9. But see Ch. IX, § 13, and cf. the article by Mr. Mabbott in *Mind,* April 1939, pp. 155–7, where he shows that the reply to this 'indirect utilitarian' argument is 'keep it dark'.
10. Ch. V.
11. See next chapter.
12. $\dot{\alpha}\gamma\alpha\theta\dot{o}\nu$ = good.
13. See § 17 above.

14. e.g. Rashdall, *Theory of Good and Evil,* and Moore, *Principia Ethica* and *Ethics.*
15. Ch. IV, § 3.
16. See Chs. VII, VIII.
17. *Novum Organon,* xlv, and cf. my IV, § 14.
18. Kant, *Fundamental Principles of the Metaphysic of Morals,* trans. Abbot.
19. Kant, *Critique of Practical Reason* (conclusion).
20. Aristotle, *Nicomachean Ethics, 1129^{b}28, trans. Ross,* and cf. *Wordsworth, Ode to Duty.* For Aristotle justice covers all our obligations to others: $\dot{\alpha}\lambda\lambda\acute{o}\tau\rho\iota o\nu$ $\dot{\alpha}\gamma\alpha\theta\grave{o}\nu$ $\delta o\kappa\epsilon\hat{\iota}$ $\epsilon\iota\nu\alpha\iota$ $\dot{\eta}$ $\delta o\lambda\alpha o\pi\pi\theta\nu\eta$ $\mu\acute{o}\nu\eta$ $\tau\hat{\omega}\nu$ $\dot{\alpha}\rho\epsilon\tau\hat{\omega}\nu, o\tau\iota$ $\dot{\alpha}\rho\epsilon\tau\hat{\omega}\nu, o\tau\iota \pi\rho\grave{o}\sigma$ $\epsilon\tau\epsilon\pi\acute{o}\nu$ $\dot{\epsilon}o\tau\iota\nu$ (1030^a 3).
21. Ross, *The Right and the Good,* vi; but cf. Ch. VII, § I, below.
22. e.g. Joseph, *Problems in Ethics,* viii, and p. 48. I think Professor Paton held a similar theory in his *The Good Will.* In his recent *Can Reason be Practical?* (British Academy Hertz Lecture, 1946) I think he makes the possibility of universalizing an action coherently merely a criterion or perhaps a symptom of its rightness.

18. *TWO CONCEPTS OF RULES*

John Rawls

In this paper I want to show the importance of the distinction between justifying a practice[1] and justifying a particular action falling under it, and I want to explain the logical basis of this distinction and how it is possible to miss its significance. While the distinction has frequently been made,[2] and is now becoming commonplace, there remains the task of explaining the tendency either to overlook it altogether, or to fail to appreciate its importance.

To show the importance of the distinction I am going to defend utilitarianism against those objections which have traditionally been made against it in connection with punishment and the obligation to keep promises. I hope to show that if one uses the distinction in question then one can state utilitarianism in a way which makes it a much better explication of our considered moral judgments than these traditional objections would seem to admit.[3] Thus the importance of the distinction is shown by the way it strengthens the utilitarian view regardless of whether that view is completely defensible or not.

To explain how the significance of the distinction may be overlooked, I am going to discuss two conceptions of rules. One of these conceptions conceals the importance of distinguishing between the justification of a rule or practice and the justification of a particular action falling under it. The other conception makes it clear why this distinction must be made and what is its logical basis.

I

The subject of punishment, in the sense of attaching legal penalties to the violation of legal rules, has always been a troubling moral question.[4] The trouble about it has not been that

people disagree as to whether or not punishment is justifiable. Most people have held that, freed from certain abuses, it is an acceptable institution. Only a few have rejected punishment entirely, which is rather surprising when one considers all that can be said against it. The difficulty is with the justification of punishment: various arguments for it have been given by moral philosophers, but so far none of them has won any sort of general acceptance; no justification is without those who detest it. I hope to show that the use of the aforementioned distinction enables one to state the utilitarian view in a way which allows for the sound points of its critics.

For our purposes we may say that there are two justifications of punishment. What we may call the retributive view is that punishment is justified on the grounds that wrongdoing merits punishment. It is morally fitting that a person who does wrong should suffer in proportion to his wrongdoing. That a criminal should be punished follows from his guilt, and the severity of the appropriate punishment depends on the depravity of his act. The state of affairs where a wrongdoer suffers punishment is morally better than the state of affairs where he does not; and it is better irrespective of any of the consequences of punishing him.

What we may call the utilitarian view holds that on the principle that bygones are bygones and that only future consequences are material to present decisions, punishment is justifiable only by reference to the probable consequences of maintaining it as one of the devices of the social order. Wrongs committed in the past are, as such, not relevant considerations for deciding what to do. If punishment can be shown to promote effectively the interest of society it is justifiable, otherwise it is not.

I have stated these two competing views very roughly to make one feel the conflict between them: one feels the force of *both* arguments and one wonders how they can be reconciled. From

From John Rawls, "Two Concepts of Rules," *The Philosophical Review,* Vol. 64 (1955), pp. 3–32. Reprinted with the permission of the author and *The Philosophical Review.* This is a revision of a paper given at the Harvard Philosophy Club on April 30, 1954.

my introductory remarks it is obvious that the resolution which I am going to propose is that in this case one must distinguish between justifying a practice as a system of rules to be applied and enforced, and justifying a particular action which falls under these rules; utilitarian arguments are appropriate with regard to questions about practices, while retributive arguments fit the application of particular rules to particular cases.

We might try to get clear about this distinction by imagining how a father might answer the question of his son. Suppose the son asks, "Why was F put in jail yesterday?" The father answers, "Because he robbed the bank at B. He was duly tried and found guilty. That's why he was put in jail yesterday." But suppose the son had asked a different question, namely, "Why do people put other people in jail?" Then the father might answer, "To protect good people from bad people" or "To stop people from doing things that would make it uneasy for all of us; for otherwise we wouldn't be able to go to bed at night and sleep in peace." There are two very different questions here. One question emphasizes the proper name: it asks why F was punished rather than someone else, or it asks what he was punished for. The other question asks why we have the institution of punishment: why do people punish one another rather than, say, always forgiving one another?

Thus the father says in effect that a particular man is punished, rather than some other man, because he is guilty, and he is guilty because he broke the law (past tense). In his case the law looks back, the judge looks back, the jury looks back, and a penalty is visited upon him for something he did. That a man is to be punished, and what his punishment is to be, is settled by its being shown that he broke the law and that the law assigns that penalty for the violation of it.

On the other hand we have the institution of punishment itself, and recommend and accept various changes in it, because it is thought by the (ideal) legislator and by those to whom the law applies that, as a part of a system of law impartially applied from case to case arising under it, it will have the consequence, in the long run, of furthering the interests of society.

One can say, then, that the judge and the legislator stand in different positions and look in different directions: one to the past, the other to the future. The justification of what the judge does, *qua* judge, sounds like the retributive view; the justification of what the (ideal) legislator does, *qua* legislator, sounds like the utilitarian view. Thus both views have a point (this is as it should be since intelligent and sensitive persons have been on both sides of the argument); and one's initial confusion disappears once one sees that these views apply to persons holding different offices with different duties, and situated differently with respect to the system of rules that make up the criminal law.[5]

One might say, however, that the utilitarian view is more fundamental since it applies to a more fundamental office, for the judge carries out the legislator's will so far as he can determine it. Once the legislator decides to have laws and to assign penalties for their violation (as things are there must be both the law and the penalty) an institution is set up which involves a retributive conception of particular cases. It is part of the concept of the criminal law as a system of rules that the application and enforcement of these rules in particular cases should be justifiable by arguments of a retributive character. The decision whether or not to use law rather than some other mechanism of social control, and the decision as to what laws to have and what penalties to assign, may be settled by utilitarian arguments; but if one decides to have laws then one has decided on something whose working in particular cases is retributive in form.[6]

The answer, then, to the confusion engendered by the two views of punishment is quite simple: one distinguishes two offices, that of the judge and that of the legislator, and one distinguishes their different stations with respect to the system of rules which make up the law; and then one notes that the different sorts of considerations which would usually be offered as reasons for what is done under the cover of these offices can be paired off with the competing justifications of punishment. One reconciles the two views by the time-honored device of making them apply to different situations.

But can it really be this simple? Well, this answer allows for the apparent intent of each side. Does a person who advocates the retributive view necessarily advocate, as an *institution,* legal machinery whose essential purpose is to set up and preserve a correspondence between moral turpitude and suffering? Surely not.[7] What retributionists have rightly insisted upon is that no man can be punished unless he is guilty, that is, unless he has broken the law. Their fundamental criticism of the utilitarian account is that, as they interpret it, it sanctions an innocent person's being punished (if one may call it that) for the benefit of society.

On the other hand, utilitarians agree that punishment is to be inflicted only for the violation of law. They regard this much as understood from the concept of punishment itself.[8] The point of the utilitarian account concerns the institution as a system of rules: utilitarianism seeks to limit its use by declaring it justifiable only if it can be shown to foster effectively the good of society. Historically it is a protest against the indiscriminate and ineffective use of the criminal law.[9] It seeks to dissuade us from assigning to penal institutions the improper, if not sacrilegious, task of matching suffering with moral turpitude. Like others, utilitarians want penal institutions designed so that, as far as humanly possible, only those who break the law run afoul of it. They hold that no official should have discretionary power to inflict penalties whenever he thinks it for the benefit of society; for on utilitarian grounds an institution granting such power could not be justified.[10]

The suggested way of reconciling the retributive and the utilitarian justifications of punishment seems to account for what both sides have wanted to say. There are, however, two further questions which arise, and I shall devote the remainder of this section to them.

First, will not a difference of opinion as to the proper criterion of just law make the proposed reconciliation unacceptable to retributionists? Will they not question whether, if the utilitarian principle is used as the criterion, it follows that those who have broken the law are guilty in a way which satisfies their demand that those punished deserve to be punished? To answer this difficulty, suppose that the rules of the criminal law are justified on utilitarian grounds (it is only for laws that meet his criterion that the utilitarian can be held responsible). Then it follows that the actions which the criminal law specifies as offenses are such that, if they were tolerated,

terror and alarm would spread in society. Consequently, retributionists can only deny that those who are punished deserve to be punished if they deny that such actions are wrong. This they will not want to do.

The second question is whether utilitarianism doesn't justify too much. One pictures it as an engine of justification which, if consistently adopted, could be used to justify cruel and arbitrary institutions. Retributionists may be supposed to concede that utilitarians *intend* to reform the law and to make it more humane; that utilitarians do not *wish* to justify any such thing as punishment of the innocent; and that utilitarians may appeal to the fact that punishment presupposes guilt in the sense that by punishment one understands an institution attaching penalties to the infraction of legal rules, and therefore that it is logically absurd to suppose that utilitarians in justifying *punishment* might also have justified punishment (if we may call it that) of the innocent. The real question, however, is whether the utilitarian, in justifying punishment, hasn't used arguments which commit him to accepting the infliction of suffering on innocent persons if it is for the good of society (whether or not one calls this punishment). More generally, isn't the utilitarian committed in principle to accepting many practices which he, as a morally sensitive person, wouldn't want to accept? Retributionists are inclined to hold that there is no way to stop the utilitarian principle from justifying too much except by adding to it a principle which distributes certain rights to individuals. Then the amended criterion is not the greatest benefit of society *simpliciter,* but the greatest benefit of society subject to the constraint that no one's rights may be violated. Now while I think that the classical utilitarians proposed a criterion of this more complicated sort, I do not want to argue that point here.[11] What I want to show is that there is *another* way of preventing the utilitarian principle from justifying too much, or at least of making it much less likely to do so; namely, by stating utilitarianism in a way which accounts for the distinction between the justification of an institution and the justification of a particular action falling under it.

I begin by defining the institution of punishment as follows: a person is said to suffer punishment whenever he is legally deprived of some of the normal rights of a citizen on the ground that he has violated a rule of law, the violation having been established by trial according to the due process of law, provided that the deprivation is carried out by the recognized legal authorities of the state, that the rule of law clearly specifies both the offense and the attached penalty, that the courts construe statutes strictly, and that the statute was on the books prior to the time of the offense.[12] This definition specifies what I shall understand by punishment. The question is whether utilitarian arguments may be found to justify institutions widely different from this and such as one would find cruel and arbitrary.

This question is best answered, I think, by taking up a particular accusation. Consider the following from Carritt:

...the utilitarian must hold that we are justified in inflicting pain always and only to prevent worse pain or bring about greater happiness. This, then, is all we need to consider in so-called punishment, which must be purely preventive. But if some kind of very cruel crime becomes common, and none of the criminals can be caught, it might be highly expedient, as an example, to hang an innocent man, if a charge against him could be so framed that he were universally thought guilty; indeed this would only fail to be an ideal instance of utilitarian 'punishment' because the victim himself would not have been so likely as a real felon to commit such a crime in the future; in all other respects it would be perfectly deterrent and therefore felicific.[13]

Carritt is trying to show that there are occasions when a utilitarian argument would justify taking an action which would be generally condemned; and thus that utilitarianism justifies too much. But the failure of Carritt's argument lies in the fact that he makes no distinction between the justification of the general system of rules which constitutes penal institutions and the justification of particular applications of these rules to particular cases by the various officials whose job it is to administer them. This becomes perfectly clear when one asks who the "we" are of whom Carritt speaks. Who is this who has a sort of absolute authority on particular occasions to decide that an innocent man shall be "punished" if everyone can be convinced that he is guilty? Is this person the legislator, or the judge, or the body of private citizens, or what? It is

utterly crucial to know who is to decide such matters, and by what authority, for all of this must be written into the rules of the institution. Until one knows these things one doesn't know what the institution is whose justification is being challenged; and as the utilitarian principle applies to the institution one doesn't know whether it is justifiable or utilitarian grounds or not.

Once this is understood it is clear what the countermove to Carritt's argument is. One must describe more carefully what the *institution* is which his example suggests, and then ask oneself whether or not it is likely that having this institution would be for the benefit of society in the long run. One must not content oneself with the vague thought that, when it's a question of *this* case, it would be a good thing if *somebody* did something even if an innocent person were to suffer.

Try to imagine, then, an institution (which we may call "telishment") which is such that the officials set up by it have authority to arrange a trial for the condemnation of an innocent man whenever they are of the opinion that doing so would be in the best interests of society. The discretion of officials is limited, however, by the rule that they may not condemn an innocent man to undergo such an ordeal unless there is, at the time, a wave of offenses similar to that with which they charge him and telish him for. We may imagine that the officials having the discretionary authority are the judges of the higher courts in consultation with the chief of police, the minister of justice, and a committee of the legislature.

Once one realizes that one is involved in setting up an *institution,* one sees that the hazards are very great. For example, what check is there on the officials? How is one to tell whether or not their actions are authorized? How is one to limit the risks involved in allowing such systematic deception? How is one to avoid giving anything short of complete discretion to the authorities to telish anyone they like? In addition to these considerations, it is obvious that people will come to have a very different attitude towards their penal system when telishment is adjoined to it. They will be uncertain as to whether a convicted man has been punished or telished. They will wonder whether or not they should feel sorry for him. They will wonder whether the same fate won't at any time fall on them. If one pictures how such an institution would actually work, and the enormous risks involved in it, it seems clear that it would serve no useful purpose. A utilitarian justification for this institution is most unlikely.

It happens in general that as one drops off the defining features of punishment one ends up with an institution whose utilitarian justification is highly doubtful. One reason for this is that punishment works like a kind of price system: by altering the prices one has to pay for the performance of actions it supplies a motive for avoiding some actions and doing others. The defining features are essential if punishment is to work in this way; so that an institution which lacks these features, e.g., an institution which is set up to "punish" the innocent, is likely to have about as much point as a price system (if one may call it that) where the prices of things change at random from day to day and one learns the price of something after one has agreed to buy it.[14] If one is careful to apply the utilitarian principle to the institution which is to authorize particular actions, then there is *less* danger of its justifying too much. Carritt's example gains plausibility by its indefiniteness and by its concentration on the particular case. His argument will only hold if it can be shown that there are utilitarian arguments which justify an institution whose publicly ascertainable offices and powers are such as to permit officials to exercise that kind of discretion in particular cases. But the requirement of having to build the arbitrary features of the particular decision into the institutional practice makes the justification much less likely to go through.

II

I shall now consider the question of promises. The objection to utilitariansim in connection with promises seems to be this: it is believed that on the utilitarian view when a person makes a promise the only ground upon which he should keep it, if he should keep it, is that by keeping it he will realize the most good on the whole. So that if one asks the question "Why should I keep *my* promise?" the utilitarian answer is understood to be that doing so in this case will have the best consequences. And this answer is said,

quite rightly, to conflict with the way in which the obligation to keep promises is regarded.

Now of course critics of utilitarianism are not unaware that one defense sometimes attributed to utilitarians is the consideration involving the practice of promise-keeping.[15] In this connection they are supposed to argue something like this: it must be admitted that we feel strictly about keeping promises, more strictly than it might seem our view can account for. But when we consider the matter carefully it is always necessary to take into account the effect which our action will have on the practice of making promises. The promisor must weigh, not only the effects of breaking his promise on the particular case, but also the effect which his breaking his promise will have on the practice itself. Since the practice is of great utilitarian value, and since breaking one's promise always seriously damages it, one will seldom be justified in breaking one's promise. If we view our individual promises in the wider context of the practice of promising itself we can account for the strictness of the obligation to keep promises. There is always one very strong utilitarian consideration in favor of keeping them, and this will insure that when the question arises as to whether or not to keep a promise it will usually turn out that one should, even where the facts of the particular case taken by itself would seem to justify one's breaking it. In this way the strictness with which we view the obligation to keep promises is accounted for.

Ross has criticized this defense as follows:[16] however great the value or the practice of promising, on utilitarian grounds, there must be some value which is greater, and one can imagine it to be obtainable by breaking a promise. Therefore there might be a case where the promisor could argue that breaking his promise was justified as leading to a better state of affairs on the whole. And the promisor could argue in this way no matter how slight the advantage won by breaking the promise. If one were to challenge the promisor his defense would be that what he did was best on the whole in view of all the utilitarian considerations, which in this case *include* the importance of the practice. Ross feels that such a defense would be unacceptable. I think he is right insofar as he is protesting against the appeal to consequences in general and without further explanation. Yet it is extremely difficult to weigh the force of Ross's argument. The kind of case imagined seems unrealistic and one feels that it needs to be described. One is inclined to think that it would either turn out that such a case came under an exception defined by the practice itself, in which case there would not be an appeal to consequences in general on the particular case, or it would happen that the circumstances were so peculiar that the conditions which the practice presupposes no longer obtained. But certainly Ross is right in thinking that it strikes us as wrong for a person to defend breaking a promise by a general appeal to consequences. For a general utilitarian defense is not open to the promisor: it is not one of the defenses allowed by the practice of making promises.

Ross gives two further counterarguments:[17] First, he holds that it overestimates the damage done to the practice of promising by a failure to keep a promise. One who breaks a promise harms his own name certainly, but it isn't clear that a broken promise always damages the practice itself sufficiently to account for the strictness of the obligation. Second, and more important, I think, he raises the question of what one is to say of a promise which isn't known to have been made except to the promisor and the promisee, as in the case of a promise a son makes to his dying father concerning the handling of the estate.[18] In this sort of case the consideration relating to the practice doesn't weigh on the promisor at all, and yet one feels that this sort of promise is as binding as other promises. The question of the effect which breaking it has on the practice seems irrelevant. The only consequence seems to be that one can break the promise without running any risk of being censured; but the obligation itself seems not the least weakened. Hence it is doubtful whether the effect on the practice ever weighs in the particular case; certainly it cannot account for the strictness of the obligation where it fails to obtain. It seems to follow that a utilitarian account of the obligation to keep promises cannot be successfully carried out.

From what I have said in connection with punishment, one can foresee what I am going to say about these arguments and counterarguments. They fail to make the distinction between the justification of a practice and the justification of a particular action falling under it, and therefore they fall into the mistake of taking it for granted that the promisor, like Carritt's official, is entitled without restriction to bring utilitarian considerations to bear in deciding whether to keep *his* promise. But if one considers what the practice of promising is one will see, I think, that it is such as not to allow this sort of general discretion to the promisor. Indeed, the point of the practice is to abdicate one's title to act in accordance with utilitarian and prudential considerations in order that the future may be tied down and plans coordinated in advance. There are obvious utilitarian advantages in having a practice which denies to the promisor, as a defense, any general appeal to the utilitarian principle in accordance with which the practice itself may be justified. There is nothing contradictory, or surprising, in this: utilitarian (or aesthetic) reasons might properly be given in arguing that the game of chess, or baseball, is satisfactory just as it is, or in arguing that it should be changed in various respects, but a player in a game cannot properly appeal to such considerations as reasons for his making one move rather than another. It is a mistake to think that if the practice is justified on utilitarian grounds then the promisor must have complete liberty to use utilitarian arguments to decide whether or not to keep his promise. The practice forbids this general defense; and it is a purpose of the practice to do this. Therefore what the above arguments presuppose—the idea that if the utilitarian view is accepted then the promisor is bound if, and only if, the application of the utilitarian principle to his own case shows that keeping it is best on the whole—is false. The promisor is bound because he promised: weighing the case on its merits is not open to him.[19]

Is this to say that in particular cases one cannot deliberate whether or not to keep one's promise? Of course not. But to do so is to deliberate whether the various excuses, exceptions and defenses, which are understood by, and which constitute an important part of, the practice, apply to one's own case.[20] Various defenses for not keeping one's promise are allowed, but among them there isn't the one that, on general utilitarian grounds, the promisor (truly) thought his action best on the whole, even though there may be the defense that the consequences of keeping one's promise would have been *extremely* severe. While there are too many complexities here to consider all the necessary details, one can see that the general defense isn't allowed if one asks the following question: what would one say of someone who, when asked why he broke his promise, replied simply that breaking it was best on the whole? Assuming that his reply is sincere, and that his belief was reasonable (i.e., one need not consider the possibility that he was mistaken), I think that one would question whether or not he knows what it means to say "I promise" (in the appropriate circumstances). It would be said of someone who used this excuse without further explanation that he didn't understand what defenses the practice, which defines a promise, allows to him. If a child were to use this excuse one would correct him; for it is part of the way one is taught the concept of a promise to be corrected if one uses this excuse. The point of having the practice would be lost if the practice did allow this excuse.

It is no doubt part of the utilitarian view that every practice should admit the defense that the consequences of abiding by it would have been extremely severe; and utilitarians would be inclined to hold that some reliance on people's good sense and some concession to hard cases is necessary. They would hold that a practice is justified by serving the interests of those who take part in it; and as with any set of rules there is understood a background of circumstances under which it is expected to be applied and which need not—indeed which cannot—be fully stated. Should these circumstances change, then even if there is no rule which provides for the case, it may still be in accordance with the practice that one be released from one's obligation. But this sort of defense allowed by a practice must not be confused with the general option to weigh each particular case on utilitarian grounds which critics of utilitarianism have thought it necessarily to involve.

The concern which utilitarianism raises by its justification of punishment is that it may justify too much. The question in connection with promises is different: it is how utilitarianism can account for the obligation to keep promises at all. One feels that the recognized obligation to keep one's promise and utilitarianism are incompatible. And to be sure, they are incompatible if

one interprets the utilitarian view as necessarily holding that each person has complete liberty to weigh every particular action on general utilitarian grounds. But must one interpret utilitarianism in this way? I hope to show that, in the sorts of cases I have discussed, one cannot interpret it in this way.

III

So far I have tried to show the importance of the distinction between the justification of a practice and the justification of a particular action falling under it by indicating how this distinction might be used to defend utilitarianism against two long-standing objections. One might be tempted to close the discussion at this point by saying that utilitarian considerations should be understood as applying to practices in the first instance and not to particular actions falling under them except insofar as the practices admit of it. One might say that in this modified form it is a better account of our considered moral opinions and let it go at that. But to stop here would be to neglect the interesting question as to how one can fail to appreciate the significance of this rather obvious distinction and can take it for granted that utilitarianism has the consequence that particular cases may always be decided on general utilitarian grounds.[21] I want to argue that this mistake may be connected with misconceiving the logical status of the rules of practices; and to show this I am going to examine two conceptions of rules, two ways of placing them within the utilitarian theory.

The conception which conceals from us the significance of the distinction I am going to call the summary view. It regards rules in the following way: one supposes that each person decides what he shall do in particular cases by applying the utilitarian principle; one supposes further that different people will decide the same particular case in the same way and that there will be recurrences of cases similar to those previously decided. Thus it will happen that in cases of certain kinds the same decision will be made either by the same person at different times or by different persons at the same time. If a case occurs frequently enough one supposes that a rule is formulated to cover that sort of case. I have called this conception the summary view because rules are pictured as summaries of past decisions arrived at by the *direct* application of the utilitarian principle to particular cases. Rules are regarded as reports that cases of a certain sort have been found on *other* grounds to be properly decided in a certain way (although, of course, they do not *say* this).

There are several things to notice about this way of placing rules within the utilitarian theory.[22]

1. The point of having rules derives from the fact that similar cases tend to recur and that one can decide cases more quickly if one records past decisions in the form of rules. If similar cases didn't recur, one would be required to apply the utilitarian principle directly, case by case, and rules reporting past decisions would be of no use.

2. The decisions made on particular cases are logically prior to rules. Since rules gain their point from the need to apply the utilitarian principle to many similar cases, it follows that a particular case (or several cases similar to it) may exist whether or not there is a rule covering that case. We are pictured as recognizing particular cases prior to there being a rule which covers them, for it is only if we meet with a number of cases of a certain sort that we formulate a rule. Thus we are able to describe a particular case as a particular case of the requisite sort whether there is a rule regarding *that* sort of case or not. Put another way: what the *A*'s and the *B*'s refer to in rules of the form 'Whenever *A* do *B*' may be described as *A*'s and *B*'s whether or not there is the rule 'Whenever *A* do *B*', or whether or not there is any body of rules which make up a practice of which that rule is a part.

To illustrate this consider a rule, or maxim, which could arise in this way: suppose that a person is trying to decide whether to tell someone who is fatally ill what his illness is when he has been asked to do so. Suppose the person to reflect and then decide, on utilitarian grounds, that he should not answer truthfully; and suppose that on the basis of this and other like occasions he formulates a rule to the effect that when asked by someone fatally ill what his illness is, one should not tell him. The point to notice is that someone's being fatally ill and asking what his illness is, and someone's telling him, are things that can be described as such whether

or not there is this rule. The performance of the action to which the rule refers doesn't require the stage-setting of a practice of which this rule is a part. This is what is meant by saying that on the summary view particular cases are logically prior to rules.

3. Each person is in principle always entitled to reconsider the correctness of a rule and to question whether or not it is proper to follow it in a particular case. As rules are guides and aids, one may ask whether in past decisions there might not have been a mistake in applying the utilitarian principle to get the rule in question, and wonder whether or not it is best in this case. The reason for rules is that people are not able to apply the utilitarian principle effortlessly and flawlessly; there is need to save time and to post a guide. On this view a society of rational utilitarians would be a society without rules in which each person applied the utilitarian principle directly and smoothly, and without error, case by case. On the other hand, ours is a society in which rules are formulated to serve as aids in reaching these ideally rational decisions on particular cases, guides which have been built up and tested by the experience of generations. If one applies this view to rules, one is interpreting them as maxims, as "rules of thumb"; and it is doubtful that anything to which the summary conception did apply would be called a *rule*. Arguing as if one regarded rules in this way is a mistake one makes while doing philosophy.

4. The concept of a *general* rule takes the following form. One is pictured as estimating on what percentage of the cases likely to arise a given rule may be relied upon to express the correct decision, that is, the decision that would be arrived at if one were to correctly apply the utilitarian principle case by case. If one estimates that by and large the rule will give the correct decision, or if one estimates that the likelihood of making a mistake by applying the utilitarian principle directly on one's own is greater than the likelihood of making a mistake by following the rule, and if these considerations held of persons generally, then one would be justified in urging its adoption as a general rule. In this way *general* rules might be accounted for on the summary view. It will still make sense, however, to speak of applying the utilitarian principle case by case, for it was by trying to foresee the results of

doing this that one got the initial estimates upon which acceptance of the rule depends. That one is taking a rule in accordance with the summary conception will show itself in the naturalness with which one speaks of the rule as a guide, or as a maxim, or as a generalization from experience, and as something to be laid aside in extraordinary cases where there is no assurance that the generalization will hold and the case must therefore be treated on its merits. Thus there goes with this conception the notion of a particular exception which renders a rule suspect on a particular occasion.

The other conception of rules I will call the practice conception. On this view rules are pictured as defining a practice. Practices are set up for various reasons, but one of them is that in many areas of conduct each person's deciding what to do on utilitarian grounds case by case leads to confusion, and that the attempt to coordinate behavior by trying to foresee how others will act is bound to fail. As an alternative one realizes that what is required is the establishment of a practice, the specification of a new form of activity; and from this one sees that a practice necessarily involves the abdication of full liberty to act on utilitarian and prudential grounds. It is the mark of a practice that being taught how to engage in it involves being instructed in the rules which define it, and that appeal is made to those rules to correct the behavior of those engaged in it. Those engaged in a practice recognize the rules as defining it. The rules cannot be taken as simply describing how those engaged in the practice in fact behave: it is not simply that they act as if they were obeying the rules. Thus it is essential to the notion of a practice that the rules are publicly known and understood as definitive; and it is essential also that the rules of a practice can be taught and can be acted upon to yield a coherent practice. On this conception, then, rules are not generalizations from the decisions of individuals applying the utilitarian principle directly and independently to recurrent particular cases. On the contrary, rules define a practice and are themselves the subject of the utilitarian principle.

To show the important differences between this way of fitting rules into the utilitarian theory and the previous way, I shall consider the differences between the two conceptions on the points previously discussed.

1. In contrast with the summary view, the rules of practices are logically prior to particular cases. This is so because there cannot be a particular case of an action falling under a rule of a practice unless there is the practice. This can be made clearer as follows: in a practice there are rules setting up offices, specifying certain forms of action appropriate to various offices, establishing penalties for the breach of rules, and so on. We may think of the rules of a practice as defining offices, moves, and offenses. Now what is meant by saying that the practice is logically prior to particular cases is this: given any rule which specifies a form of action (a move), a particular action which would be taken as falling under this rule given that there is the practice would not be *described* as that sort of action unless there was the practice. In the case of actions specified by practices it is logically impossible to perform them outside the stage-setting provided by those practices, for unless there is the practice, and unless the requisite proprieties are fulfilled, whatever one does, whatever movements one makes, will fail to count as a form of action which the practice specifies. What one does will be described in some *other* way.

One may illustrate this point from the game of baseball. Many of the actions one performs in a game of baseball one can do by oneself or with others whether there is the game or not. For example, one can throw a ball, run, or swing a peculiarly shaped piece of wood. But one cannot steal base, or strike out, or draw a walk, or make an error, or balk; although one can do certain things which appear to resemble these actions such as sliding into a bag, missing a grounder and so on. Striking out, stealing a base, balking, etc., are all actions which can only happen in a game. No matter what a person did, what he did would not be described as stealing a base or striking out or drawing a walk unless he could also be described as playing baseball, and for him to be doing this presupposes the rule-like practice which constitutes the game. The practice is logically prior to particular cases: unless there is the practice the terms referring to actions specified by it lack a sense.[23]

2. The practice view leads to an entirely different conception of the authority which each per-

son has to decide on the propriety of following a rule in particular cases. To engage in a practice, to perform those actions specified by a practice, means to follow the appropriate rules. If one wants to do an action which a certain practice specifies then there is no way to do it except to follow the rules which define it. Therefore, it doesn't make sense for a person to raise the question whether or not a rule of a practice correctly applies to *his* case where the action he contemplates is a form of action defined by a practice. If someone were to raise such a question, he would simply show that he didn't understand the situation in which he was acting. If one wants to perform an action specified by a practice, the only legitimate question concerns the nature of the practice itself ("How do I go about making a will?").

This point is illustrated by the behavior expected of a player in games. If one wants to play a game, one doesn't treat the rules of the game as guides as to what is best in particular cases. In a game of baseball if a batter were to ask "Can I have four strikes?" it would be assumed that he was asking what the rule was; and if, when told what the rule was, he were to say that he meant that on this occasion he thought it would be best on the whole for him to have four strikes rather than three, this would be most kindly taken as a joke. One might contend that baseball would be a better game if four strikes were allowed instead of three; but one cannot picture the rules as guides to what is best on the whole in particular cases, and question their applicability to particular cases as particular cases.

3 and 4. To complete the four points of comparison with the summary conception, it is clear from what has been said that rules of practice are not guides to help one decide particular cases correctly as judged by some higher ethical principle. And neither the quasi-statistical notion of generality, nor the notion of a particular exception, can apply to the rules of practices. A more or less general rule of a practice must be a rule which according to the structure of the practice applies to more or fewer of the kinds of cases arising under it; or it must be a rule which is more or less basic to the understanding of the practice. Again, a particular case cannot be an exception to a rule of a practice. An exception is rather a qualification or a further specification of the rule.

It follows from what we have said about the practice conception of rules that if a person is engaged in a practice, and if he is asked why *he* does what *he* does, or if he is asked to defend what he does, then his explanation, or defense, lies in referring the questioner to the practice. He cannot say of *his* action, if it is an action specified by a practice, that he does it rather than some other because he thinks it is best on the whole.[24] When a man engaged in a practice is queried about his action he must assume that the questioner either doesn't know that he is engaged in it ("Why are you in a hurry to pay him?" "I promised to pay him today") or doesn't know what the practice is. One doesn't so much justify one's particular action as explain, or show, that it is in accordance with the practice. The reason for this is that it is only against the stage-setting of the practice that one's particular action is described as it is. Only by reference to the practice can one *say* what one is doing. To explain or to defend one's own action, as a particular action, one fits it into the practice which defines it. If this is not accepted it's a sign that a different question is being raised as to whether one is justified in accepting the practice, or in tolerating it. When the challenge is to the practice, citing the rules (saying what the practice is) is naturally to no avail. But when the challenge is to the particular action defined by the practice, there is nothing one can do but refer to the rules. Concerning particular actions there is only a question for one who isn't clear as to what the practice is, or who doesn't know that it is being engaged in. This is to be contrasted with the case of a maxim which may be taken as pointing to the correct decision on the case as decided on *other* grounds, and so giving a challenge on the case a sense by having it question whether these other grounds really support the decision on this case.

If one compares the two conceptions of rules I have discussed, one can see how the summary conception misses the significance of the distinction between justifying a practice and justifying actions falling under it. On this view rules are regarded as guides whose purpose it is to indicate the ideally rational decision on the given particular case which the flawless application of the utilitarian principle would yield. One has, in principle, full option to use the guides or to discard them as the situation warrants without one's moral office being altered in any way: whether one discards the rules or not, one always holds the office of a rational person seeking case by case to realize the best on the whole. But on the practice conception, if one holds an office defined by a practice then questions regarding one's actions in this office are settled by reference to the rules which define the practice. If one seeks to question these rules, then one's office undergoes a fundamental change: one then assumes the office of one empowered to change and criticize the rules, or the office of a reformer, and so on. The summary conception does away with the distinction of offices and the various forms of argument appropriate to each. On that conception there is one office and so no offices at all. It therefore obscures the fact that the utilitarian principle must, in the case of actions and offices defined by a practice, apply to the practice, so that general utilitarian arguments are not available to those who act in offices so defined.[25]

Some qualifications are necessary in what I have said. First, I may have talked of the summary and the practice conceptions of rules as if only one of them could be true of rules, and if true of any rules, then necessarily true of *all* rules. I do not, of course, mean this. (It is the critics of utilitarianism who make this mistake insofar as their arguments against utilitarianism presuppose a summary conception of the rules of practices.) Some rules will fit one conception, some rules the other; and so there are rules of practices (rules in the strict sense), and maxims and "rules of thumb."

Secondly, there are further distinctions that can be made in classifying rules, distinctions which should be made if one were considering other questions. The distinctions which I have drawn are those most relevant for the rather special matter I have discussed, and are not intended to be exhaustive.

Finally, there will be many border-line cases about which it will be difficult, if not impossible, to decide which conception of rules is applicable. One expects border-line cases with any concept, and they are especially likely in connection with such involved concepts as those of a practice, institution, game, rule, and so on. Wittgenstein has shown how fluid these notions are.[26] What I have done is to emphasize and sharpen two conceptions for the limited purpose of this paper.

IV

What I have tried to show by distinguishing between two conceptions of rules is that there is a way of regarding rules which allows the option to consider particular cases on general utilitarian grounds; whereas there is another conception which does not admit of such discretion except insofar as the rules themselves authorize it. I want to suggest that the tendency while doing philosophy to picture rules in accordance with the summary conception is what may have blinded moral philosophers to the significance of the distinction between justifying a practice and justifying a particular action falling under it; and it does so by misrepresenting the logical force of the reference to the rules in the case of a challenge to a particular action falling under a practice, and by obscuring the fact that where there is a practice, it is the practice itself that must be the subject of the utilitarian principle.

It is surely no accident that two of the traditional test cases of utilitarianism, punishment and promises, are clear cases of practices. Under the influence of the summary conception it is natural to suppose that the officials of a penal system, and one who has made a promise, may decide what to do in particular cases on utilitarian grounds. One fails to see that a general discretion to decide particular cases on utilitarian grounds is incompatible with the concept of a practice; and that what discretion one does have is itself defined by the practice (e.g., a judge may have discretion to determine the penalty within certain limits). The traditional objections to utilitarianism which I have discussed presuppose the attribution to judges, and to those who have made promises, of a plenitude of moral authority to decide particular cases on utilitarian grounds. But once one fits utilitarianism together with the notion of a practice, and notes that punishment and promising are practices, then one sees that this attribution is logically precluded.

That punishment and promising are practices is beyond question. In the case of promising this is shown by the fact that the form of words "I promise" is a performative utterance which presupposes the stage-setting of the practice and the properties defined by it. Saying the words "I promise" will only be promising given the existence of the practice. It would be absurd to interpret the rules about promising in accordance with the summary conception. It is absurd to say, for example, that the rule that promises should be kept could have arisen from its being found in past cases to be best on the whole to keep one's promise; for unless there were already the understanding that one keeps one's promises as part of the practice itself there couldn't have been any cases of promising.

It must, of course, be granted that the rules defining promising are not codified, and that one's conception of what they are necessarily depends on one's moral training. Therefore it is likely that there is considerable variation in the way people understand the practice, and room for argument as to how it is best set up. For example, differences as to how strictly various defenses are to be taken, or just what defenses are available, are likely to arise amongst persons with different backgrounds. But irrespective of these variations it belongs to the concept of the practice of promising that the general utilitarian defense is not available to the promisor. That this is so accounts for the force of the traditional objection which I have discussed. And the point I wish to make is that when one fits the utilitarian view together with the practice conception of rules, as one must in the appropriate cases, then there is nothing in that view which entails that there must be such a defense, either in the practice of promising, or in any other practice.

Punishment is also a clear case. There are many actions in the sequence of events which constitute someone's being punished which presuppose a practice. One can see this by considering the definition of punishment which I gave when discussing Carritt's criticism of utilitarianism. The definition there stated refers to such things as the normal rights of a citizen, rules of law, due process of law, trials and courts of law, statutes, etc., none of which can exist outside the elaborate stage-setting of a legal system. It is also the case that many of the actions for which people are punished presuppose practices. For example, one is punished for stealing, for trespassing, and the like, which presuppose the institution of property. It is impossible to say what punishment is, or to describe a particular instance of it, without referring to offices, actions, and offenses specified by practices. Punishment is a move in an elaborate legal game and

presupposes the complex of practices which make up the legal order. The same thing is true of the less formal sorts of punishment: a parent or guardian or someone in proper authority may punish a child, but no one else can.

There is one mistaken interpretation of what I have been saying which it is worthwhile to warn against. One might think that the use I am making of the distinction between justifying a practice and justifying the particular actions falling under it involves one in a definite social and political attitude in that it leads to a kind of conservatism. It might seem that I am saying that for each person the social practices of his society provide the standard of justification for his actions; therefore let each person abide by them and his conduct will be justified.

This interpretation is entirely wrong. The point I have been making is rather a logical point. To be sure, it has consequences in matters of ethical theory; but in itself it leads to no particular social or political attitude. It is simply that where a form of action is specified by a practice there is no justification possible of the particular action of a particular person save by reference to the practice. In such cases the action is what it is in virtue of the practice and to explain it is to refer to the practice. There is no inference whatsoever to be drawn with respect to whether or not one should accept the practices of one's society. One can be as radical as one likes but in the case of actions specified by practices the objects of one's radicalism must be the social practices and people's acceptance of them.

I have tried to show that when we fit the utilitarian view together with the practice conception of rules, where this conception is appropriate,[27] we can formulate it in a way which saves it from several traditional objections. I have further tried to show how the logical force of the distinction between justifying a practice and justifying an action falling under it is connected with the practice conception of rules and cannot be understood as long as one regards the rules of practices in accordance with the summary view. Why, when doing philosophy, one may be inclined to so regard them, I have not discussed. The reasons for this are evidently very deep and would require another paper.

NOTES

1. I use the word "practice" throughout as a sort of technical term meaning any form of activity specified by a system of rules which defines offices, roles, moves, penalties, defenses, and so on, and which gives the activity its structure. As examples one may think of games and rituals, trials and parliaments.

2. The distinction is central to Hume's discussion of justice in *A Treatise of Human Nature*, bk. III, pt. 11, esp. secs. 2–4. It is clearly stated by John Austin in the second lecture of *Lectures on Jurisprudence* (4th ed.; London, 1873), I, 116ff. (1st ed., 1832). Also it may be argued that J. S. Mill took it for granted in *Utilitarianism;* on this point cf. J. O. Urmson, "The Interpretation of the Moral Philosophy of J. S. Mill," *Philosophical Quarterly,* vol. III (1953). In addition to the arguments given by Urmson there are several clear statements of the distinction in *A System of Logic* (8th ed.; London, 1872), bk. VI, ch. xii pars. 2, 3, 7. The distinction is fundamental to J. D. Mabbott's important paper, "Punishment," *Mind,* n.s., vol. XLVIII (April, 1939). More recently the distinction has been stated with particular emphasis by S. E. Toulmin in *The Place of Reason in Ethics* (Cambridge, 1950), see esp. ch. xi, where it plays a major part in his account of moral reasoning. Toulmin doesn't explain the basis of the distinction, nor how one might overlook its importance, as I try to in this paper, as I in my review of his book (*Philosophical Review,* vol. LX [October, 1951]), as some of my criticisms show, I failed to understand the force of it. See also II D Aiken, "The Levels of Moral Discourse," *Ethics,* vol. LXII (1952), A. M. Quinton, "Punishment," *Analysis,* vol. XIV (June, 1954), and P. H. Nowell-Smith, *Ethics* (London, 1954), pp. 2, 6, 239, 271–273.

3. On the concept of explication see the author's paper *Philosophical Review,* vol. LX (April, 1951).

4. While this paper was being revised, Quinton's appeared; footnote 2 supra. There are several respects in which my remarks are similar to his. Yet as I consider some further questions and rely on somewhat different arguments, I have retained the discussion of punishment and promises together as two test cases for utilitarianism.

5. Note the fact that different sorts of arguments are suited to different offices. One way of taking the differences between ethical theories is to regard them as accounts of the reasons expected in different offices.

6. In this connection see Mabbott, *op. cit.,* pp. 163–164.

7. On this point see Sir David Ross, *The Right and the Good* (Oxford, 1930), pp. 57–60.

8. See Hobbes's definition of punishment in *Leviathan,* ch. xxviii; and Bentham's definition in *The Principle of Morals and Legislation,* ch. xii, par. 36, ch. xv, par. 28, and in *The Rationale of Punishment,* (London, 1830), bk. I, ch. i. They could agree with Bradley that: "Punishment is punishment only when it is deserved. We pay the penalty, because we owe it, and for no other reason; and if punishment is inflicted for any other reason whatever than because it is merited by wrong, it is a gross immorality, a crying injustice, an abominable crime, and not what it pretends to be." *Ethical Studies* (2nd ed.; Oxford, 1927), pp. 26–27. Certainly by definition it isn't what it pretends to be. The innocent can only be punished by mistake; deliberate "punishment" of the innocent necessarily involves fraud.

9. Cf. Leon Radzinowicz, *A History of English Criminal Law: The Movement for Reform 1750–1833* (London, 1948), esp. ch. xi on Bentham.

10. Bentham discusses how corresponding to a punitory provision of a criminal law there is another provision which stands to it as an antagonist and which needs a name as much as the punitory. He calls it, as one might expect, the *anaetiosostic,* and of it he says: "The punishment of guilt is the object of the former one: the preservation of innocence that of the latter." In the same connection he asserts that it is never thought fit to give the judge the option of deciding whether a thief (that is, a person whom he believes to be a thief, for the judge's belief is what the question must always turn upon) should hang or not, and so the law writes the provision: "The judge shall not cause a thief to be hanged unless he have been duly convicted and sentenced in course of law" (*The Limits of Jurisprudence Defined,* ed. C. W. Everett [New York, 1945], pp. 238–239).

11. By the classical utilitarians I understand Hobbes, Hume, Bentham, J. S. Mill, and Sidgwick.

12. All these features of punishment are mentioned by Hobbes; cf. *Leviathan,* ch. xxviii.

13. *Ethical and Political Thinking* (Oxford, 1947), p. 65.

14. The analogy with the price system suggests an answer to the question how utilitarian considerations insure that punishment is proportional to the offense. It is interesting to note that Sir David Ross, after making the distinction between justifying a penal law and justifying a particular application of it, and after stating that utilitarian considerations have a large place in determining the former, still holds back from accepting the utilitarian justification of punishment on the grounds that justice requires that punishment be proportional to the offense, and that utilitarianism is unable to account for this. Cf. *The Right and the Good,* pp. 61–62. I do not claim that utilitarianism can account for this requirement as Sir David might wish, but it happens, nevertheless, that if utilitarian considerations are followed penalties will be proportional to offenses in this sense: the order of offenses according to seriousness can be paired off with the order of penalties according to severity. Also the absolute level of penalties will be as low as possible. This follows from the assumption that people are rational (i.e., that they are able to take into account the "prices" the state puts on actions), the utilitarian rule that a penal system should provide a motive for preferring the less serious offense, and the principle that punishment as such is an evil. All this was carefully worked out by Bentham in *The Principles of Morals and Legislation,* chs. xiii–xv.

15. Ross, *The Right and the Good,* pp. 37–39. and *Foundations of Ethics* (Oxford, 1939), pp. 92–94. I know of no utilitarian who has used this argument except W. A. Pickard-Cambridge in "Two Problems about Duty," *Mind,* n.s., XLI (April, 1932), 153–157, although the argument goes with G. E. Moore's version of utilitarianism in *Principia Ethica* (Cambridge, 1903). To my knowledge it does not appear in the classical utilitarians; and if one interprets their view correctly this is no accident.

16. Ross, *The Right and the Good,* pp. 38–39.

17. Ross, *ibid.,* p. 39. The case of the nonpublic promise is discussed again in *Foundations of Ethics,* pp. 95–96, 104–105. It occurs also in Mabbott, "Punishment," *op. cit.,* pp. 155–157, and in A. I. Melden, "Two Comments on Utilitarianism," *Philosophical Review,* LX (October, 1951), 519–523, which discusses Carritt's example in *Ethical and Political Thinking,* p. 64.

18. Ross's example is described simply as that of two men dying alone where one makes a promise to the other. Carritt's example (cf. n. 17 supra) is that of two men at the North Pole. The example in the text is more realistic and is similar to Mabbott's. Another example is that of being told

something in confidence by one who subsequently dies. Such cases need not be "desert-island arguments" as Nowell-Smith seems to believe (cf. his *Ethics*, pp. 239–244).

19.   What I have said in this paragraph seems to me to coincide with Hume's important discussion in the *Treatise of Human Nature*, bk. III, pt. 11, sec. 5; and also sec. 6, par. 8.

20.   For a discussion of these, see H. Sidgwick, *The Methods of Ethics* (6th ed.; London, 1901), bk. III, ch. vi.

21.   So far as I can see it is not until Moore that the doctrine is expressly stated in this way. See, for example, *Principia Ethica*, p. 147, where it is said that the statement "I am morally bound to perform this action" is identical with the statement "*This* action will produce the greatest possible amount of good in the Universe" (my italics). It is important to remember that those whom I have called the classical utilitarians were largely interested in social institutions. They were among the leading economists and political theorists of their day, and they were not infrequently reformers interested in practical affairs. Utilitarianism historically goes together with a coherent view of society, and is not simply an ethical theory, much less an attempt at philosophical analysis in the modern sense. The utilitarian principle was quite naturally thought of, and used, as a criterion for judging social institutions (practices) and as a basis for urging reforms. It is not clear, therefore, how far it is necessary to amend utilitarianism in its classical form. For a discussion of utilitarianism as an integral part of a theory of society, see L. Robbins, *The Theory of Economic Policy in English Classical Political Economy* (London, 1952).

22.   This footnote should be read after sec. 3 and presupposes what I have said there. It provides a few references to statements by leading utilitarians of the summary conception. In general it appears that when they discussed the logical features of rules the summary conception prevailed and that it was typical of the way they talked about moral rules. I cite a rather lengthy group of passages from Austin as a full illustration.

John Austin in his *Lectures on Jurisprudence* meets the objection that deciding in accordance with the utilitarian principle case by case is impractical by saying that this is a misinterpretation of utilitarianism. According to the utilitarian view ". . . our conduct would conform to *rules* inferred from the tendencies of actions, but would not be determined by a direct resort to the principle of general utility. Utility would be the test of our conduct, ultimately, but not immediately: the immediate test of the rules to which our conduct would conform, but not the immediate test of specific or individual actions. Our rules would be fashioned on utility; our conduct, on our rules" (vol. I, p. 116). As to how one decides on the tendency of an action he says: "If we would try the tendency of a specific or individual act, we must not contemplate the act as if it were single and insulated, but must look at the class of acts to which it belongs. We must suppose that acts of the class were generally done or omitted, and consider the probable effect upon the general happiness or good. We must guess the consequences which would follow, if the class of acts were general; and also the consequences which would follow, if they were generally omitted. We must then compare the consequences on the positive and negative sides, and determine on which of the two the *balance* of advantage lies. . . . If we truly try the tendency of a specific or individual act, we try the tendency of the class to which that act belongs. The *particular* conclusion which we draw, with regard to the single act, implies a *general* conclusion embracing all similar acts. . . . To the rules thus inferred, and lodged in the memory, our conduct would conform *immediately* if it were truly adjusted to utility" (*ibid.*, p. 117). One might think that Austin meets the objection by

stating the practice conception of rules; and perhaps he did intend to. But it is not clear that he has stated this conception. Is the generality he refers to of the statistical sort? This is suggested by the notion of tendency. Or does he refer to the utility of setting up a practice? I don't know; but what suggests the summary view is his subsequent remarks. He says: "To consider the specific consequences of single or individual acts, would *seldom* [my italics] consist with that ultimate principle" (*ibid.*, p. 117). But would one ever do this? He continues: ". . . this being admitted, the necessity of pausing and calculating, which the objection in question supposes, is an imagined necessity. To preface each act or forbearance by a conjecture and comparison of consequences, were clearly *superfluous* [my italics] and mischievous. It were clearly superfluous, inasmuch as the *result of that process* [my italics] would be embodied in a known *rule*. It were clearly mischievous, inasmuch as the *true* result would be expressed by that rule, whilst the process would probably be faulty, if it were done on the spur of the occasion" (*ibid.*, pp. 117–118). He goes on: "If our experience and observation of particulars were not *generalized*, our experience and observation of particulars would seldom avail us in *practice*. . . . The inferences suggested to our minds by repeated experience and observation are, therefore, drawn into *principles*, or compressed into *maxims*. These we carry about us ready for use, and apply to individual cases promptly . . . without reverting to the process by which they were obtained; or without recalling, and arraying before our minds, the numerous and intricate considerations of which they are *handy abridgments* [my italics]. . . . True theory is a *compendium* of particular truths. . . . Speaking then, generally, human conduct is inevitably *guided* [my italics] by *rules*, or by *principles* or *maxims*" (*ibid.*, pp. 117–118). I need not trouble to show how all these remarks incline to the summary view. Further, when Austin comes to deal with cases "of comparatively rare occurrence" he holds that specific considerations may outweigh the general. "Looking at the reasons from which we had inferred the rule, it were absurd to think it inflexible. We should therefore dismiss the *rule*; resort directly to the *principle* upon which our rules were fashioned; and calculate *specific* consequences to the best of our knowledge and ability" (*ibid.*, pp. 120–121). Austin's view is interesting because it shows how one may come close to the practice conception and then slide away from it.

In *A System of Logic*, bk. VI, ch. xii, par. 2, Mill distinguishes clearly between the position of judge and legislator and in doing so suggests the distinction between the two concepts of rules. However, he distinguishes the two positions to illustrate the difference between cases where one is to apply a rule already established and cases where one must formulate a rule to govern subsequent conduct. It's the latter case that interests him and he takes the "maxim of policy" of a legislator as typical of rules. In par. 3 the summary conception is very clearly stated. For example, he says of rules of conduct that they should be taken provisionally, as they are made for the most numerous cases. He says that they "point out" the manner in which it is least perilous to act; they serve as an "admonition" that a certain mode of conduct has been found suited to the most common occurrences. In *Utilitarianism*, ch. ii, par. 24, the summary conception appears in Mill's answer to the same objection Austin considered. Here he speaks of rules as "corollaries" from the principle of utility; these "secondary" rules are compared to "landmarks" and "direction-posts." They are based on long experience and so make it unnecessary to apply the utilitarian principle to each case. In par. 25 Mill refers to the task of the utilitarian principle in adjudicating between competing moral rules. He talks here as if one then applies the utilitarian principle directly to the particular case. On the practice view one would rather use the principle to decide which of the ways that make the practice consistent is the best. It should be noted that while in par. 10 Mill's definition of utilitarianism makes the utilitarian principle apply to morality, i.e., to the rules and precepts of human conduct, the definition in par. 2 uses the phrase "actions are right in *proportion* as they *tend* to promote happiness" [my italics] and this inclines towards the summary view. In the last paragraph of the essay "On the Definition of Political Economy," *Westminster Review* (October, 1836), Mill says that it is only in art, as distinguished from science, that one can properly speak of exceptions. In a question of practice, if something is fit to be done "in the majority of cases" then it is made the rule. "We may . . . in talking of art *unobjectionably* speak of the *rule* and the *exception,* meaning by the rule the cases in which there exists a preponderance . . . of inducements for acting in a particular way; and by the exception, the cases in which the preponderance is on the contrary side." These remarks, too, suggest the summary view.

In Moore's *Principia Ethica,* ch. v, there is a complicated and difficult discussion of moral rules. I will not examine it here except to express my suspicion that the summary conception prevails. To be sure, Moore speaks frequently of the utility of rules as generally followed, and of actions as generally practiced, but it is possible that these passages fit the statistical notion of generality which the summary conception allows. This conception is suggested by Moore's taking the utilitarian principle as applying directly to particular actions (pp. 147–148) and by his notion of a rule as something indicating which of the few alternatives likely to occur to anyone will generally produce a greater total good in the immediate future (p. 154). He talks of an "ethical law" as a prediction, and as a generalization (pp. 146, 155). The summary conception is also suggested by his discussion of exceptions (pp. 162–163) and of the force of examples of breaching a rule (pp. 163–164).

23. One might feel that it is a mistake to say that a practice is logically prior to the forms of action it specifies on the grounds that if there were never any instances of actions falling under a practice then we should be strongly inclined to say that there wasn't the practice either. Blue-prints for a practice do not make a practice. That there is a practice entails that there are instances of people having been engaged and now being engaged in it (with suitable qualifications). This is correct, but it doesn't hurt the claim that any given particular instance of a form of action specified by a practice presupposes the practice. This isn't so on the summary picture, as each instance must be "there" prior to the rules, so to speak, as something from which one gets the rule by applying the utilitarian principle to it directly.

24. A philosophical joke (in the mouth of Jeremy Bentham): "When I run to the other wicket after my partner has struck a good ball I do so because it is best on the whole."

25. How do these remarks apply to the case of the promise known only to father and son? Well, at first sight the son certainly holds the office of promisor, and so he isn't allowed by the practice to weigh the particular case on general utilitarian grounds. Suppose instead that he wishes to consider himself in the office of one empowered to criticize and change the practice, leaving aside the question as to his right to move from his previously assumed office to another. Then he may consider utilitarian arguments as applied to the practice; but once he does this he will see that there are such arguments for not allowing a general utilitarian defense in the practice for this sort of case. For to do so would make it impossible to ask for and to give a kind of promise which one often wants to be able to ask for and to give. Therefore he will not want to change the practice, and so as a promisor he has no option but to keep his promise.

26. *Philosophical Investigations* (Oxford, 1953), I, pars. 65–71, for example.

27. As I have already stated, it is not always easy to say where the conception is appropriate. Nor do I care to discuss at this point the general sorts of cases to which it does apply except to say that one should not take it for granted that it applies to many so-called "moral rules." It is my feeling that relatively few actions of the moral life are defined by practices and that the practice conception is more relevant to understanding legal and legal-like arguments than it is to the more complex sort of moral arguments. Utilitarianism must be fitted to different conceptions of rules depending on the case, and no doubt the failure to do this has been one source of difficulty in interpreting it correctly.

19. *SOME MERITS OF ONE FORM OF RULE-UTILITARIANISM*

Richard B. Brandt

1. Utilitarianism is the thesis that the moral predicates of an act—at least its objective rightness or wrongness, and sometimes also its moral praiseworthiness or blameworthiness—are functions in some way, direct or indirect, of consequences for the welfare of sentient creatures, and of nothing else. Utilitarians differ about what precise function they are; and they differ about what constitutes welfare and how it is to be measured. But they agree that all one needs to know, in order to make moral appraisals correctly, is the consequences of certain things for welfare.

Utilitarianism is thus a normative ethical thesis and not, at least not necessarily, a metaethical position—that is, a position about the meaning and justification of ethical statements. It is true that some utilitarians have declared that the truth of the normative thesis follows, given the ordinary, or proper, meaning of moral terms such as "right." I shall ignore this further, metaethical claim. More recently some writers have suggested something very similar, to the effect that our concept of "morality" is such that we could not call a system of rules a "moral system" unless it were utilitarian in some sense.

This latter suggestion is of special interest to us, since the general topic of the present conference is "the concept of morality," and I wish to comment on it very briefly. It is true that there is a connection between utilitarianism and the concept of morality; at least I believe—and shall spell out the contention later—that utilitarianism cannot be explained, at least in its most plausible form, without making use of the concept of "morality" and, furthermore, without

From *University of Colorado Studies,* 1967, pp. 39–65. Reprinted by permission of the author and the University of Colorado Press. This is a revised version of a paper presented to a conference on moral philosophy held at the University of Colorado in October, 1965.

making use of an analysis of this concept. But the reverse relationship does not hold: it is not true that the concept "morality" is such that we cannot properly call a system of rules a morality unless it is a thoroughly utilitarian system, although possibly we would not call a system of rules a "morality" if it did not regulate at all the forms of conduct which may be expected to do good or harm to sentient persons. One reason why it is implausible to hold that any morality is necessarily utilitarian is that any plausible form of utilitarianism will be a rather complex thesis, and it seems that the concept of morality is hardly subtle enough to entail anything so complex—although, of course, such reasoning does not exclude the possibility of the concept of morality entailing some simple and unconvincing form of utilitarianism. A more decisive reason, however, is that we so use the term "morality" that we can say consistently that the morality of a society contains some prohibitions which considerations of utility do not support, or are not even thought to support: for example, some restrictions on sexual behavior. (Other examples are mentioned later.) Thus there is no reason to think that only a utilitarian code could properly be called a "moral code" or a "morality," as these are ordinarily used.

In any case, even if "nonutilitarian morality" (or "right, but harmful") were a contradiction in terms, utilitarianism as a normative thesis would not yet be established; for it would be open to a nonutilitarian to advocate changing the meaning of "morality" (or "right") in order to allow for his normative views. There is, of course, the other face of the coin: even if, as we actually use the term "morality" (or "right"), the above expressions are not contradictions in terms, it might be a good and justifiable thing for people to be taught to use words so that these expressions would become self-contradictory. But if there are good reasons for doing the last, presumably there are good and convincing reasons for adopting utilitarianism as a normative thesis, without undertaking such a roundabout route to the goal. I shall, therefore, discuss utilitarianism as a normative thesis, without supposing that it can be supported by arguing that a nonutilitarian morality is a contradiction in terms.

2. If an analysis of concepts like "morally wrong" and "morality" and "moral code" does not enable us to establish the truth of the utilitarian thesis, the question arises what standard a normative theory like utilitarianism has to meet in order for a reasonable presumption to be established in its favor. It is well known that the identity and justification of any such standard can be debated at length. In order to set bounds to the present discussion, I shall state briefly the standard I shall take for granted for purposes of the present discussion. Approximately this standard would be acceptable to a good many writers on normative ethics. However this may be, it would be agreed that it is worth knowing whether some form of utilitarianism meets this standard better than any other form of utilitarian theory, and it is this question which I shall discuss.

The standard which I suggest an acceptable normative moral theory has to meet is this: The theory must contain no unintelligible concepts or internal inconsistencies; it must not be inconsistent with known facts; it must be capable of precise formulation so that its implications for action can be determined; and—most important—its implications must be acceptable to thoughtful persons who have had reasonably wide experience, when taken in the light of supporting remarks that can be made, and when compared with the implications of other clearly statable normative theories. It is not required that the implications of a satisfactory theory be consonant with the uncriticized moral intuitions of intelligent and experienced people, but only with those intuitions which stand in the light of supporting remarks, etc. Furthermore, it is not required of an acceptable theory that the best consequences would be produced by people adopting that theory, in contrast to other theories by which they might be convinced. (The theory might be so complex that it would be a

good thing if most people did not try their hand at applying it to concrete situations!) It may be a moving *ad hominem* argument, if one can persuade an act-utilitarian that it would have bad consequences for people to try to determine the right act according to that theory, and to live by their conclusions; but such a showing would not be a reasonable ground for rejecting that normative theory.

3. Before turning to the details of various types of utilitarian theory, it may be helpful to offer some "supporting remarks" which will explain some reasons why some philosophers are favorably disposed toward a utilitarian type of normative theory.

(a) The utilitarian principle provides a clear and definite procedure for determining which acts are right or wrong (praiseworthy or blameworthy), by observation and the methods of science alone and without the use of any supplementary intuitions (assuming that empirical procedures can determine when something maximizes utility), for all cases, including the complex ones about which intuitions are apt to be mute, such as whether kleptomanic behavior is blameworthy or whether it is right to break a confidence in certain circumstances. The utilitarian presumably frames his thesis so as to conform with enlightened intuitions which are clear, but his thesis, being general, has implications for all cases, including those about which his intuitions are not clear. The utilitarian principle is like a general scientific theory, which checks with observations at many points, but can also be used as a guide to beliefs on matters inaccessible to observation (like the behavior of matter at absolute zero temperature).

Utilitarianism is not the only normative theory with this desirable property; egoism is another, and, with some qualifications, so is Kant's theory.

(b) Any reasonably plausible normative theory will give a large place to consequences for welfare in the moral assessment of actions, for this consideration enters continuously and substantially into ordinary moral thinking. Theories which ostensibly make no appeal of this sort either admit utilitarian considerations by the back door, or have counter-intuitive consequences. Therefore the ideal of simplicity leads us to hope for the possibility of a pure utilitarian theory. Moreover, utilitarianism avoids the necessity of weighing disparate things such as justice and utility.

(c) If a proposed course of action does not raise moral questions, it is generally regarded as rational, and its agent well advised to perform it, if and only if it will maximize expectable utility for the agent. In a similar vein, it can be argued that society's "choice" of an institution of morality is rational and well advised, if and only if having it will maximize expectable social utility —raise the expectable level of the average "utility curve" of the population. If morality is a system of traditional and arbitrary constraints on behavior, it cannot be viewed as a rational institution. But it can be, if the system of morality is utilitarian. In that case the institution of morality can be recommended to a person of broad human sympathies, as an institution which maximizes the expectation of general welfare; and to a selfish person, as an institution which, in the absence of particular evidence about his own case, may be expected to maximize his own expectation of welfare (his own welfare being viewed as a random sample from the population). To put it in other words, a utilitarian morality can be "vindicated" by appeal either to the humanity or to the selfishness of human beings.

To say this is not to deny that nonutilitarian moral principles may be capable of vindication in a rather similar way. For instance, to depict morality as an institution which fosters human equality is to recommend it by appeal to something which is perhaps as deep in man as his sympathy or humanity.[1]

4. The type of utilitarianism on which I wish to focus is a form of rule-utilitarianism, as contrasted with act-utilitarianism. According to the latter type of theory (espoused by Sidgwick and Moore), an act is objectively right if no other act the agent could perform would produce better consequences. (On this view, an act is blameworthy if and only if it is right to perform the act of blaming or condemning it; the principles of blameworthiness are a special case of the principle of objectively right actions.) Act-utilitarianism is hence a rather atomistic theory: the rightness of a single act is fixed by its effects on the world. Rule-utilitarianism, in contrast, is the view that the rightness of an act is fixed, not by its relative utility, but by the utility of having a relevant moral rule, or of most or all members of a certain class of acts being performed.

The implications of act-utilitarianism are seriously counter-intuitive, and I shall ignore it except to consider whether some ostensibly different theories really are different.

5. Rule-utilitarianisms may be divided into two main groups, according as the rightness of a particular act is made a function of ideal rules in some sense, or of the actual and recognized rules of a society. The variety of theory I shall explain more fully is of the former type.

According to the latter type of theory, a person's moral duties or obligations in a particular situation are determined, with some exceptions, solely by the moral rules, or institutions, or practices prevalent in the society, and not by what rules (etc.) it would ideally be best to have in the society. (It is sometimes held that actual moral rules, practices, etc., are only a necessary condition of an act's being morally obligatory or wrong.) Views roughly of this sort have been held in recent years by A. MacBeath, Stephen Toulmin, John Rawls, P. F. Strawson, J. O. Urmson, and B. J. Diggs. Indeed, Strawson says in effect that for there to be a moral obligation on one is just for there to be a socially sanctioned demand on him, in a situation where he has an interest in the system of demands which his society is wont to impose on its members, and where such demands are generally acknowledged and respected by members of his society.[2] And Toulmin asserts that when a person asks, "Is this the right thing to do?" what he is normally asking is whether a proposed action "conforms to the moral code" of his group, "whether the action in question belongs to a class of actions generally approved of in the agent's community." In deliberating about the question what is right to do, he says, "there is no more general 'reason' to be given beyond one which realted the action . . . to an accepted social practice."[3]

So far the proposal does not appear to be a form of utilitarianism at all. The theory is utilitarian, however, in the following way: it is thought that what is relevant for a decision whether to try to change moral codes, institutions, etc., or for a justification of them, is the relative utility of the code, practice, etc. The recognized code or practice determines the individual's moral obligations in a particular case; utility of the code or practice determines whether it is justified or ought to be changed. Furthermore, it is sometimes held that utilitarian considerations have some relevance to the rightness of a particular action. For instance, Toulmin thinks that in case the requirements of the recognized code or practice conflict in a particular case, the individual ought (although strictly, he is not morally obligated) to do what will maximize utility in the situation, and that in case an individual can relieve the distress of another, he ought (strictly, is not morally obligated) to do so, even if the recognized code does not require him to.[4]

This theory, at least in some of its forms or parts, has such conspicuously counter-intuitive implications that it fails to meet the standard for a satisfactory normative theory. In general, we do not believe that an act's being prohibited by the moral code of one's society is sufficient to make it morally wrong. Moral codes have prohibited such things as work on the Sabbath, marriage to a divorced person, medically necessary abortion, and suicide; but we do not believe it was really wrong for persons living in a society with such prohibitions, to do these things.[5]

Neither do we think it a necessary condition of an act's being wrong that it be prohibited by the code of the agent's society, or of an act's being obligatory that it be required by the code of his society. A society may permit a man to have his wife put to death for infidelity, or to have a child put to death for almost any reason; but we still think such actions wrong. Moreover, a society may permit a man absolute freedom in divorcing his wife, and recognize no obligations on his part toward her; but we think, I believe, that a man has some obligations for the welfare of a wife of thirty years' standing (with some qualifications), whatever his society may think.[6]

Some parts of the theory in some of its forms, however, appear to be correct. In particular, the theory in some forms implies that, if a person has a certain recognized obligation in an institution or practice (e.g., a child to support his aged parent, a citizen to pay his taxes), then he morally does have this obligation, with some exceptions, irrespective of whether in an ideal institution he would or would not have. This we do roughly believe, although we need not at the same time accept the reasoning which has been offered to explain how the fact of a practice or institution leads to the moral obligation. The fact that the theory seems right in this would be a strong point in its favor if charges were correct that "ideal" forms of rule-utilitarianism necessarily differ at this point. B. J. Diggs, for instance, has charged that the "ideal" theories imply that:

one may freely disregard a rule if ever he discovers that action on the rule is not maximally felicific, and in this respect makes moral rules like 'practical maxims.'. . . It deprives social and moral rules of their authority and naturally is in sharp conflict with practice. On this alternative rule-utilitarianism collapses into act-utilitarianism. Surely it is a mistake to maintain that a set of rules, thought to be ideally utilitarian or felicific, is the criterion of right action. . . . If we are presented with a list [of rules], but these are not rules in practice, the most one could reasonably do is to try to get them adopted.[7]

I believe, however, and shall explain in detail later that this charge is without foundation.

6. Let us turn now to "ideal" forms of rule-utilitarianism, which affirm that whether it is morally obligatory or morally right to do a certain thing in a particular situation is fixed, not by the actual code or practice of the society (these may be indirectly relevant, as forming part of the situation), but by some "ideal" rule—that is, by the utility of having a certain general moral rule, or by the utility of all or most actions being performed which are members of a relevant class of actions.

If the rightness of an act is fixed by the utility of a relevant rule (class), are we to say that the rule (class) which qualifies must be the optimific rule (class), the one which maximizes utility, or must the rule (class) meet only some less stringent requirement (e.g., be better than the absence of any rule regulating the type of conduct in question)? And, if it is to be of the optimific type, are all utilities to be counted, or perhaps only "negative" utilities, as is done when it is suggested that the rule (class) must be the one which minimizes suffering?[8]

The simplest proposal—that the rule (class which qualifies is the one that maximizes utility, with all utilities, whether "positive" or "negative," being counted—also seems to me to be the best, and it is the one I shall shortly explain more fully. Among the several possible theories different from this one I shall discuss briefly only one, which seems the most plausible of its kind, and is at least closely similar to the view defended by Professor Marcus Singer.

According to this theory, an action (or inaction) at time *t* in circumstances C is wrong if and only if, were everyone in circumstances C to perform a relevantly similar action, harm would be done—meaning by "doing harm" that affected persons would be made worse off by the action (or inaction) than they already were at time *t*. (I think it is not meant that the persons must be put in a state of "negative welfare" in some sense, but simply made worse off than they otherwise would have been.) Let us suppose a person is deciding whether to do A in circumstances C at *t*. The theory, then, implies the following: (1) If everyone doing A in circumstances C would make people worse off than they already were at *t* (A can be inaction, such as failing to pull a drowning man from the water) whereas some other act would not make them so, then it is wrong for anyone to do A. (2) If everyone doing A would not make people worse off, then even if everyone doing something else would make them better off, it is not wrong to do A. (3) If everyone doing A would make people worse off, but if there is no alternative act, the performance of which by everyone would avoid making people worse off, then it is right to do A, even though doing A would make people relatively much worse off then they would have been made by the performance of some other action instead. The "optimific rule" theory, roughly, would accept (1), but reject (2) and (3).

Implication (3) of the theory strikes me as clearly objectionable; I am unable to imagine circumstances in which we should think it not morally incumbent on one to avoid very bad avoidable consequences for others, even though a situation somewhat worse than the status quo could not be avoided. Implication (2) is less obviously dubious. But I should think we do have obligations to do things for others, when we are not merely avoiding being in the position of making them worse off. For instance, if one sees another person at a cocktail party, standing by himself and looking unhappy, I should sup-

pose one has some obligation to make an effort to put him at his ease, even though doing nothing would hardly make him worse off than he already is.

Why do proponents of this view, like Professor Singer, prefer his view to the simpler, "maximize utility" form of rule-utilitarianism? This is not clear. One objection sometimes raised is that an optimific theory implies that every act is morally weighty and none morally indifferent. And one may concede that this is a consequence of some forms of utilitarianism, even rule-utilitarianism of the optimific variety; but we shall see that it is by no means a consequence of the type of proposal described below. For the theory below will urge that an action is not morally indifferent only if it falls under some prescription of an optimific moral code, and, since there are disadvantages in a moral code regulating actions, optimific moral codes will prohibit or require actions of a certain type only when there are significant utilitarian reasons for it. As a consequence, a great many types of action are morally indifferent, according to the theory. Professor Singer also suggests that optimific-type theories have objectionable consequences for state-of-nature situations;[9] we may postpone judgment on this until we have examined these consequences of the theory here proposed, at a later stage. Other objections to the optimizing type of rule-utilitarianism with which I am familiar either confuse rule-utilitarianism with act-utilitarianism, or do not distinguish among the several possible forms of optimizing rule-utilitarianisms.

7. I propose, then, that we tentatively opt for an "ideal" rule-utilitarianism, of the "maximizing utility" variety. This decision, however, leaves various choices still to be made, between theories better or worse fitted to meet various problems. Rather than attempt to list alternatives, and explain why one choice rather than another between them would work out better, I propose to describe in some detail the type of theory which seems most plausible. I shall later show how this theory meets the one problem to which the "actual rule" type theories seemed to have a nice solution; and I shall discuss its merits, as compared with another quite similar type of theory which has been suggested by Jonathan Harrison and others.

The theory I wish to describe is rather similar to one proposed by J. D. Mabbott in his 1953 British Academy lecture, "Moral Rules." It is also very similar to the view defended by J. S. Mill in *Utilitarianism,* although Mill's formulation is ambiguous at some points, and he apparently did not draw some distinctions he should have drawn. (I shall revert to this historical point.)

For convenience I shall refer to the theory as the "ideal moral code" theory. The essence of it is as follows: Let us first say that a moral code is "ideal" if its currency in a particular society would produce at least as much good per person (the total divided by the number of persons) as the currency of any other moral code. (Two different codes might meet this condition, but, in order to avoid complicated formulations, the following discussion will ignore this possibility.) Given this stipulation for the meaning of "ideal," the Ideal Moral Code theory consists in the assertion of the following thesis: *An act is right if and only if it would not be prohibited by the moral code ideal for the society; and an agent is morally blameworthy (praiseworthy) for an act if, and to the degree that, the moral code ideal in that society would condemn (praise) him for it.* It is a virtue of this theory that it is a theory both about objective rightness and about moral blameworthiness (praiseworthiness) of actions, but the assertion about blameworthiness will be virtually ignored in what follows.

8. In order to have a clear proposal before us, however, the foregoing summary statement must be filled out in three ways: (1) by explaining what it is for a moral code to have currency; (2) by making clear what is the difference between the rules of a society's moral code and the rules of its institutions; and (3) by describing how the relative utility of a moral code is to be estimated.

First, then, the notion of a moral code having currency in a society.

For a moral code to have currency in a society, two things must be true. First, a high proportion of the adults in the society must subscribe to the moral principles, or have the moral opinions, constitutive of the code. Exactly how high the proportion should be, we can hardly decide on the basis of the ordinary meaning of "the moral code"; but probably it would not be wrong to require at least ninety per cent agreement. Thus, if at least ninety per cent of the adults subscribe to principle A, and ninety per cent to principle B, etc., we may say that a code consisting of A and B (etc.) has currency in the society, provided the second condition is met. Second, we want to say that certain principles A, B, etc. belong to the moral code of a society only if they are recognized as such. That is, it must be that a large proportion of the adults of the society would respond correctly if asked, with respect to A and B, whether most members of the society subscribed to them. (It need not be required that adults base their judgments on such good evidence as recollection of moral discussions; it is enough if for some reason the correct opinion about what is accepted is widespread.) It is of course possible for certain principles to constitute a moral code with currency in a society even if some persons in the society have no moral opinions at all, or if there is disagreement, e.g., if everyone in the society disagrees with every other person with respect to at least one principle.

The more difficult question is what it is for an individual to subscribe to a moral principle or to have a moral opinion. What is it, then, for someone to think sincerely that any action of the kind F is wrong? (1) He is to some extent motivated to avoid actions which he thinks are F, and often, if asked why he does not perform such an action when it appears to be to his advantage, offers, as one of his reasons, that it is F. In addition, the person's motivation to avoid F-actions does not derive entirely from his belief that F-actions on his part are likely to be harmful to him or to persons to whom he is somehow attached. (2) If he thinks he has just performed an F-action, he feels guilty or remorseful or uncomfortable about it, unless he thinks he has some excuse—unless, for instance, he knows that at the time of action he did not think his action would be an F-action. "Guilt" (etc.) is not to be understood as implying some special origin such as interiorization of parental prohibitions, or as being a vestige of anxiety about punishment. It is left open that it might be an unlearned emotional response to the thought of being the cause of the suffering of another person. Any feeling which must be viewed simply as anxiety about anticipated consequences, for one's self or person to whom one is attached, is not, however, to count as a "guilt" feeling. (3) If he believes that someone has performed an F-action, he will tend to admire him less as a person, unless he thinks that the individual has a good excuse. He thinks that action of this sort, without excuse, reflects on character—this being spelled out, in part, by reference to traits like honesty, respect for the rights of others, and so on. (4) He thinks that these attitudes of his are correct or well justified, in some sense, but with one restriction: it is not enough if he thinks that what justifies them is simply the fact that they are shared by all or most members of his society. This restriction corresponds with our distinction between a moral conviction and something else. For instance, we are inclined to think no moral attitude is involved if an Englishman disapproves of something but says that his disapproval is justified by the fact that it is shared by "well-bred Englishmen." In such cases we are inclined to say that the individual subscribes only to a custom, or to a rule of etiquette or manners. On the other hand, if the individual thinks that what justifies his attitude unfavorable to F-actions is that F-actions are contrary to the will of God (and the individual's attitude is not merely a prudential one), or inconsistent with the welfare of mankind, or contrary to human nature, we are disposed to say the attitude is a moral attitude and the opinion expressed a moral one. And the same if he thinks his attitude justified, but can give no reason. There are perhaps other restrictions we should make on acceptable justifications (perhaps to distinguish a moral code from a code of honor), and other types of justification we should wish to list as clearly acceptable (perhaps an appeal to human equality).

9. It is important to distinguish between the moral code of a society and its institutions, or the rules of its institutions. It is especially important for the Ideal Moral Code theory, for this theory involves the conception of a moral code ideal for a society in the context of its institutions, so that it is necessary to distinguish the moral code which a society does or might have from its institutions and their rules. The distinction is also one we actually do make in our thinking, although it is blurred in some cases. (For instance, is "Honor thy father and thy mother" a moral rule, or a rule of the family institution, in our society?)[10]

An institution is a set of positions or statuses, with which certain privileges and jobs are associated. (We can speak of these as "rights" and "duties" if we are careful to explain that we do not mean moral rights and duties.) That is, there are certain, usually nameable, positions which consist in the fact that anyone who is assigned to the position is expected to do certain things, and at the same time is expected to have certain things done for him. The individuals occupying these positions are a group of cooperating agents in a system which as a whole is thought to have the aim of serving certain ends. (E.g., a university is thought to serve the ends of education, research, etc.) The rules of the system concern jobs that must be done in order that the goals of the institution be achieved; they allocate the necessary jobs to different positions. Take, for instance, a university. There are various positions in it: the presidency, the professorial ranks, the registrars, librarians, etc. It is understood that one who occupies a certain post has certain duties, say teaching a specified number of classes or spending time working on research in the case of the instructing staff. Obviously the university cannot achieve its ends unless certain persons do the teaching, some tend to the administration, some do certain jobs in the library, and so on. Another such system is the family. We need not speculate on the "purpose" of the family, whether it is primarily a device for producing a new generation, etc. But it is clear that when a man enters marriage, he takes a position to which certain jobs are attached, such as providing support for the family to the best of his ability, and to which also certain rights are attached, such as exclusive sexual rights with his wife, and the right to be cared for should he become incapacitated.

If an "institution" is defined in this way, it is clear that the moral code of a society cannot itself be construed as an institution, nor its rules as rules of an institution. The moral code is society-wide, so if we were to identify its rules as institutional rules, we should presumably have to say that everyone belongs to this institution. But what is the "purpose" of society as a whole? Are there any distinctions of status, with rights and duties attached, which we could identify as the "positions" in the moral system? Can we say that moral rules consist in the assignment of jobs in such a way that the aims of the institution may be achieved? It is true that there is a certain analogy: society as a whole might be said to be aiming at the good life for all, and the moral rules of the society might be viewed as the rules with which all must conform in order to achieve this end. But the analogy is feeble. Society as a whole is obviously not an organization like a university, an educational system, the church, General Motors, etc.; there is no specific goal in the achievement of which each position has a designated role to play. Our answer to the above questions must be in the negative: morality is not an institution in the explained sense; nor are moral rules institutional expectations or rules.

The moral code of a society may, of course, have implications that bear on institutional rules. For one thing, the moral code may imply that an institutional system is morally wrong and ought to be changed. Moreover, the moral code may imply that a person has also a moral duty to do something which is his institutional job. For instance, it may be a moral rule that a person ought to do whatever he has undertaken to do, or that he ought not to accept the benefits of a position without performing its duties. Take for instance the rules, "A professor should meet his classes" or "Wives ought to make the beds." Since the professor has undertaken to do what pertains to his office, and the same for a wife, and since these tasks are known to pertain to the respective offices, the moral rule that a person is morally bound (with certain qualifications) to do what he has undertaken to do implies, in context, that the professor is morally bound to meet his classes and the wife to make the beds, other things being equal (viz., there being no contrary moral obligations in the situation). But these implications are not themselves part of the moral code. No one would say that a parent had neglected to teach his child the moral code of the society if he had neglected to teach him that professors must meet classes, and that wives must make the beds. A person becomes obligated to do these things only by participating in an institution, by taking on the status of professor or wife. Parents do not teach children to have guilt feelings about missing classes, or making beds. The moral code consists only of more

general rules, defining what is to be done in certain types of situations in which practically everyone will find himself. ("Do what you have promised!")

Admittedly some rules can be both moral and institutional: "Take care of your father in his old age" might be both an institutional rule of the family organization and also a part of the moral code of a society. (In this situation, one can still raise the question whether this moral rule is optimific in a society with that institutional rule; the answer could be negative.)

It is an interesting question whether "Keep your promises" is a moral rule, an institutional rule (a rule of an "institution" of promises), or both. Obviously it is a part of the moral code of western societies. But is it also a rule of an institution? There are difficulties in the way of affirming that it is. There is no structure of co-operating individuals with special functions, which serves to promote certain aims. Nor, when one steps into the "role" of a promisor, does one commit one's self to any specific duties; one fixes one's own duties by what one promises. Nor, in order to understand what one is committing one's self to by promising, need one have any knowledge of any system of expectations prevalent in the society. A three-year-old, who has never heard of any duties incumbent on promisors, can tell his friends, who wish to play baseball that afternoon, that he will bring the ball and bat, and that they need give no thought to the availability of these items. His invitation to rely on him for something needed for their common enjoyment, and his assurance that he will do something and his encouraging them thereby to set their minds at rest, *is* to make a promise. No one need suppose that the promisor is stepping into a socially recognized position, with all the rights and duties attendant on the same, although it is true he has placed himself in a position where he will properly be held responsible for the disappointment if he fails, and where inferences about his reliability as a person will properly be drawn if he forgets, or worse, if it turns out he was never in a position to perform. The bindingness of a promise is no more dependent on a set of expectations connected with an institution, than is the wrongness of striking another person without justifying reason.

Nevertheless, if one thinks it helpful to speak of a promise as an institution or a practice, in view of certain analogies (promisor and promisee may be said to have rights and duties like the occupants of roles in an institution, and there is the ritual word "promise" the utterance of which commits the speaker to certain performances), there is no harm in this. The similarities and dissimilarities are what they are, and as long as these are understood it seems to make little difference what we say. Nevertheless, even if making a promise is participating in a practice or institution, there is still the *moral* question whether one is morally bound to perform, and in what conditions and for what reasons. This question is left open, given the institution is whatever it is—as is the case with all rules of institutions.

10. It has been proposed above that an action is right if and only if it would not be prohibited by the moral code ideal for the society in which it occurs, where a moral code is taken to be "ideal" if and only if its currency would produce at least as much good per person as the currency of any other moral code.[11] We must now give more attention to the conception of an ideal moral code, and how it may be decided when a given moral code will produce as much good per person as any other. We may, however, reasonably bypass the familiar problems of judgments of comparative utilities, especially when different persons are involved, since these problems are faced by all moral theories that have any plausibility. We shall simply assume that rough judgments of this sort are made and can be justified.

(a) We should first notice that, as "currency" has been explained above, a moral code could not be current in a society if it were too complex to be learned or applied. We may therefore confine our consideration to codes simple enough to be absorbed by human beings, roughly in the way in which people learn actual moral codes.

(b) We have already distinguished the concept of an institution and its rules from the concept of a moral rule, or rule of the moral code. (We have, however, pointed out that in some cases a moral rule may prescribe the same thing that is also an institutional expectation. But this is not a necessary situation, and a moral code could condemn an institutional expectation.) Therefore, in deciding how much good the currency of a specific moral system would do, we consider the institutional setting as it is, as part of the situation. We are asking which moral code would produce the most good in the long run in this setting. One good to be reckoned, of course, might be that the currency of a given moral code would tend to change the institutional system.

(c) In deciding which moral code will produce the most per person good, we must take into account the probability that certain types of situation will arise in the society. For instance, we must take for granted that people will make promises and subsequently want to break them, that people will sometimes assault other persons in order to achieve their own ends, that people will be in distress and need the assistance of others, and so on. We may not suppose that, because an ideal moral code might have certain features, it need not have other features because they will not be required; for instance, we may not suppose, on the ground that an ideal moral system would forbid everyone to purchase a gun, that such a moral system needs no provisions about the possession and use of guns—just as our present moral and legal codes have provisions about self-defense, which would be unnecessary if everyone obeyed the provision never to assault anyone.

It is true that the currency of a moral code with certain provisions might bring about a reduction in certain types of situation, e.g., the number of assaults or cases of dishonesty. And the reduction might be substantial, if the moral code were current which prohibited these offenses very strongly. (We must remember that an ideal moral code might differ from the actual one not only in what it prohibits or enjoins, but also in how strongly it prohibits or enjoins.) But it is consistent to suppose that a moral code prohibits a certain form of behavior very severely, and yet that the behavior will occur, since the "currency" of a moral code requires only ninety per cent subscription to it, and a "strong" subscription, on the average, permits a great range from person to person. In any case there must be doubt whether the best moral code will prohibit many things very severely, since there are serious human costs in severe prohibitions: the burden of guilt feelings, the traumas caused by the severe criticism by others which is a part of having a strong injunction in a code, the risks of any training process which would succeed in interiorizing a severe prohibition, and so on.

(d) It would be a great oversimplification if, in assessing the comparative utility of various codes, we confined ourselves merely to counting the benefits of people doing (refraining from doing) certain things, as a result of subscribing to a certain code. To consider only this would be as absurd as estimating the utility of some feature of a legal system by attending only to the utility of people behaving in the way the law aims to make them behave—and overlooking the fact that the law only reduces and does not eliminate misbehavior, as well as the disutility of punishment to the convicted, and the cost of the administration of criminal law. In the case of morals, we must weigh the benefit of the improvement in behavior as a result of the restriction built into conscience, against the cost of the restriction—the burden of guilt feelings, the effects of the training process, etc. There is a further necessary refinement. In both law and morals we must adjust our estimates of utility by taking into account the envisaged system of excuses. That *mens rea* is required as a condition of guilt in the case of most legal offenses is most important; and it is highly important for the utility of a moral system whether accident, intent, and motives are taken into account in deciding a person's liability to moral criticism. A description of a moral code is incomplete until we have specified the severity of condemnation (by conscience or the criticism of others) to be attached to various actions, along with the excuses to be allowed as exculpating or mitigating.

11. Philosophers have taken considerable interest in the question what implications forms of rule-utilitarianism have for the moral relevance of the behavior of persons other than the agent. Such implications, it is thought, bring into focus the effective difference between any form of rule-utilitarianism, and act-utilitarianism. In particular, it has been thought that the implications of rule-utilitarianisms for two types of situation are especially significant: (a) for situations in which persons are generally violating the recognized moral code, or some feature of it: and (b) for situations in which, because the moral code is generally respected, maximum utility would be produced by violation of the code by the agent. An example of the former situation (sometimes called a "state of nature" situation) would be widespread perjury in making out income tax declarations. An example of the latter

situation would be widespread conformity to the rule forbidding walking on the grass in a park.

What are the implications of the suggested form of rule-utilitarianism for these types of situation? Will it prescribe conduct which is not utility maximizing in these situations? If it does, it will clearly have implications discrepant with those of act-utilitarianism—but perhaps unpalatable to some people.

It is easy to see how to go about determining what is right or wrong in such situations, on the above described form of rule-utilitarianism—it is a question of what an "ideal" moral code would prescribe. But it is by no means easy to see where a reasonable person would come out, after going through such an investigation. Our form of rule-utilitarianism does not rule out, as morally irrelevant, reference to the behavior of other persons; it implies that the behavior of others is morally relevant precisely to the extent to which an optimific moral code (the one the currency of which is optimific) would take it into account. How far, then, we might ask, would an optimific moral code take into account the behavior of other persons, and what would its specific prescriptions be for the two types of situations outlined?

It might be thought, and it has been suggested, that an ideal moral code could take no cognizance of the behavior of other persons, and in particular of the possibility that many persons are ignoring some prohibitions of the code, sometimes for the reason, apparently, that it is supposed that a code of behavior would be self-defeating if it prescribed for situations of its own breach, on a wide scale. It is a sufficient answer to this suggestion, to point out that our actual moral code appears to contain some such prescriptions. For instance, our present code seems to permit, for the case in which almost everyone is understating his income, that others do the same, on the ground that otherwise they will be paying more than their fair share. It is, of course, true that a code simple enough to be learned and applied cannot include prescriptions for all possible types of situation involving the behavior of other persons; but it can contain some prescriptions pertinent to some general features of the behavior of others.

Granted, then, that an ideal moral code may contain some special prescriptions which pay attention to the behavior of other persons, how in particular will it legislate for special situations such as the examples cited above? The proper answer to this question is that there would apparently be no blanket provision for all cases of these general types, and that a moral agent faced with such a concrete situation would have to think out what an ideal moral code would imply for his type of concrete situation. Some things do seem clear. An ideal moral code would not provide that a person is permitted to be cruel in a society where most other persons are cruel; there could only be loss of utility in any special provision permitting that. On the other hand, if there is some form of cooperative activity which enhances utility only if most persons cooperate, and nonparticipation in which does not reduce utility when most persons are not cooperating, utility would seem to be maximized if the moral code somehow permitted all to abstain—perhaps by an abstract formula stating this very condition. (This is on the assumption that the participation by some would not, by example, eventually bring about the participation of most or all.) Will there be any types of situation for which an ideal moral code would prescribe infringement of a generally respected moral code, by a few, when a few infringements (provided there are not many) would maximize utility? The possibility of this is not ruled out. Obviously there will be some regulations for emergencies; one may cut across park grass in order to rush a heartattack victim to a hospital. And there will be rules making special exceptions when considerable utility is involved: the boy with no other place to play may use the grass in the park. But, when an agent has no special claim which others could not make, it is certainly not clear that ideal moral rules will make him an exception on the ground that some benefit will come to him, and that restraint by him is unnecessary in view of the cooperation of others.

The implications of the above form of rule-utilitarianism, for these situations, are evidently different from those of act-utilitarianism.[12]

12. The Ideal Moral Code theory is very similar to the view put forward by J. S. Mill in *Utilitarianism.*

Mill wrote that his creed held that "actions are right in proportion as they tend to promote happiness; wrong as they tend to produce the reverse of happiness." Mill apparently did not intend by this any form of act-utilitarianism. He

was—doubtless with much less than full awareness—writing of act-*types,* and what he meant was that an act of a certain type is morally obligatory (wrong) if and only if acts of that type tend to promote happiness (the reverse). Mill supposed that it is known that certain kinds of acts, e.g., murder and theft, promote unhappiness, and that therefore we can say, with exceptions only for very special circumstances, that murder and theft are wrong. Mill recognized that there can be a discrepancy between the tendency of an act-type, and the probable effects, in context, of an individual act. He wrote: "In the case of abstinences, indeed—of things which people forbear to do from moral considerations, though the consequences in the particular case might be beneficial—, it would be unworthy of an intelligent agent not to be consciously aware that the action is of a class which, if practiced generally, would be generally injurious, and that this is the ground of the obligation to abstain from it."[13] Moreover, he specifically denied that one is morally obligated to perform (avoid) an act just on the ground that it can be expected to produce good consequences; he says that "there is no case of moral obligation in which some secondary principle is not involved." (op. cit., p. 33).

It appears, however, that Mill did not quite think that it is morally obligatory to perform (avoid) an act according as its general performance would promote (reduce) happiness in the world. For he said (p. 60) that "We do not call anything wrong unless we mean to imply that a person ought to be punished in some way or other for doing it—if not by law, by the opinion of his fellow creatures; if not by opinion, by the reproaches of his own conscience. This seems the real turning point of the distinction between morality and simple expediency." The suggestion here is that it is morally obligatory to perform (avoid) an act according as it is beneficial to have a system of sanctions (with what this promises in way of performance), whether formal, informal (criticism by others), or internal (one's own conscience), for enforcing the performance (avoidance) of the type of act in question. This is very substantially the Ideal Moral Code theory.

Not that there are no differences. Mill is not explicit about details, and the theory outlined above fills out what he actually said. Moreover,

Mill noticed that an act can fall under more than one secondary principle and that the relevant principles may give conflicting rulings about what is morally obligatory. In such a case, Mill thought, what one ought to do (but it is doubtful whether he believed there is a strict moral obligation in this situation) is what will maximize utility in the concrete situation. This proposal for conflicts of "ideal moral rules" is not a necessary part of the Ideal Moral Code theory as outlined above.

13. It is sometimes thought that a rule-utilitarianism rather like Mill's cannot differ in its implication about what is right or wrong from the act-utilitarian theory. This is a mistake.

The contention would be correct if two dubious assumptions happened to be true. The first is that one of the rules of an optimific moral code will be that a person ought always to do whatever will maximize utility. The second is that, when there is a conflict between the rules of an optimific code, what a person ought to do is to maximize utility. For then either the utilitarian rule is the only one that applies (and it always will be relevant), in which case the person ought to do what the act-utilitarian directs; or if there is a conflict among the relevant rules, the conflict resolving principle takes over, and this, of course, prescribes exactly what act-utilitarianism prescribes. Either way, we come out where the act-utilitarian comes out.

But there is no reason at all to suppose that there will be a utilitarian rule in an optimific moral code. In fact, obviously there will not be. It is true that there should be a directive to relieve the distress of others, when this can be done, say at relatively low personal cost; and there should be a directive not to injure other persons, except in special situations. And so on. But none of this amounts to a straight directive to do the most good possible. Life would be chaotic if people tried to observe any such moral requirement.

The second assumption was apparently acceptable to Mill. But a utilitarian principle is by no means the only possible conflict resolving principle. For if we say, with the Ideal Moral Code theory, that what is right is fixed by the content of the moral system with maximum utility, the possibility is open that the utility maximizing moral system will contain some rather different device for resolving conflicts between

lowest-level moral rules. The ideal system might contain several higher-level conflict resolving principles, all different from Mill's. Or, if there is a single one, it could be a directive to maximize utility; it could be a directive to do what an intelligent person who had fully interiorized the rest of the ideal moral system would feel best satisfied with doing; and so on. But the final court of appeal need not be an appeal to direct utilities. Hence the argument that Mill-like rule-utilitarianism must collapse into direct utilitarianism is doubly at fault.[14]

In fact, far from "collapsing" into act-utilitarianism, the Ideal Moral Code theory appears to avoid the serious objections which have been leveled at direct utilitarianism. One objection to the latter view is that it implies that various immoral actions (murdering one's elderly father, breaking solemn promises) are right or even obligatory if only they can be kept secret. The Ideal Moral Code theory has no such implication. For it obviously would not maximize utility to have a moral code which condoned secret murders or breaches of promise. W. D. Ross criticized act-utilitarianism on the ground that it ignored the personal relations important in ordinary morality, and he listed a half-dozen types of moral rule which he thought captured the main themes of thoughtful morality: obligations of fidelity, obligations of gratitude, obligations to make restitution for injuries, obligations to help other persons, to avoid injuring them, to improve one's self, and to bring about a just distribution of good things in life. An ideal moral code, however, would presumably contain substantially such rules in any society, doubtless not precisely as Ross stated them. So the rule-utilitarian need not fail to recognize the personal character of morality.

14. In contrast to the type of theory put forward by Toulmin and others, the Ideal Moral Code theory has the advantage of implying that the moral rules recognized in a given society are not necessarily morally binding. They are binding only in so far as they maximize welfare, as contrasted with other possible moral rules. Thus if, in a given society, it is thought wrong to work on the Sabbath, to perform socially desirable abortions, or to commit suicide, it does not follow, on the Ideal Moral Code theory, that these things are necessarily wrong. The question is whether a code containing such prohibitions

would maximize welfare. Similarly, according to this theory, a person may act wrongly in doing certain things which are condoned by his society.

A serious appeal of theories like Toulmin's is, however, their implications for institutional obligations. For instance, if in society A it is a recognized obligation to care for one's aged father, Toulmin's theory implies that it really is a moral obligation for a child in that society to care for his aged parent (with some qualifications); whereas if in society B it is one's recognized obligation not to care for one's aged father, but instead for one's aged maternal uncle, his theory implies that it really is the moral obligation of a person in that society to care for his aged maternal uncle—even if a better institutional system would put the responsibilities in different places. This seems approximately what we do believe.

The Ideal Moral Code theory, however, has much the same implications. According to it, an institutional system forms the setting within which the best (utility maximizing) moral code is to be applied, and one's obligation is to follow the best moral rules in that institutional setting —not to do what the best moral rules would require for some other, more ideal, setting.

Let us examine the implications of the Ideal Moral Code theory by considering a typical example. Among the Hopi Indians, a child is not expected to care for his father (he is always in a different clan), whereas he is expected to care for his mother, maternal aunt, and maternal uncle, and so on up the female line (all in the same clan). It would be agreed by observers that this system does not work very well. The trouble with it is that the lines of institutional obligation and the lines of natural affection do not coincide, and, as a result, an elderly male is apt not to be cared for by anyone.

Can we show that an "ideal moral code" would call on a young person to take care of his maternal uncle, in a system of this sort? (It might also imply he should try to change the system, but that is another point.) One important feature of the situation of the young man considering whether he should care for his maternal uncle is that, the situation including the expectations of others being what it is, if he does nothing to relieve the distress of his maternal uncle, it is probable that it will not be relieved. His sit-

uation is very like that of the sole observer of an automobile accident; he is a mere innocent bystander, but the fact is that if he does nothing, the injured persons will die. So the question for us is whether an ideal moral code will contain a rule that, if someone is in a position where he can relieve serious distress, and where it is known that in all probability it will not be relieved if he does not do so, he should relieve the distress. The answer seems to be that it will contain such a rule: we might call it an "obligation of humanity." But there is a second, and more important point. Failure of the young person to provide for his maternal uncle would be a case of unfairness or free riding. For the family system operates like a system of insurance; it provides one with various sorts of privileges or protections, in return for which one is expected to make certain payments, or accept the risk of making certain payments. Our young man has already benefited by the system, and stands to benefit further; he has received care and education as a child, and later on his own problems of illness and old age will be provided for. On the other hand, the old man, who has (we assume) paid such premiums as the system calls on him to pay in life, is now properly expecting, in accordance with the system, certain services from a particular person whom the system designates as the one to take care of him. Will the ideal moral code require such a person to pay the premium in such a system? I suggest that it will, and we can call the rule in question an "obligation of fairness."[15] So, we may infer that our young man will have a moral obligation to care for his maternal uncle, on grounds both of humanity and fairness.

We need not go so far as to say that such considerations mean that an ideal moral code will underwrite morally every institutional obligation. An institution may be grossly inequitable; or some part of it may serve no purpose at all but rather be injurious (as some legal prohibitions may be). But I believe we can be fairly sure that Professor Diggs went too far in saying that a system of this sort "deprives social and moral rules of their authority and naturally is in sharp conflict with practice" and that it "collapses into act-utilitarianism."

15. It may be helpful to contrast the Ideal Moral Code theory with a rather similar type of rule-utilitarianism, which in some ways is sim-

pler than the Ideal Moral Code theory, and which seems to be the only form of rule-utilitarianism recognized by some philosophers. This other type of theory is suggested in the writings of R. F. Harrod, Jonathan Harrison, perhaps John Hospers and Marcus Singer, although, as I shall describe it, it differs from the exact theory proposed by any of these individuals, in more or less important ways.

The theory is a combination of act-utilitarianism with a Kantian universalizability requirement for moral action. It denies that an act is necessarily right if it will produce consequences no worse than would any other action the agent might perform; rather, it affirms that an act is right if and only if universal action on the "maxim" of the act would not produce worse consequences than universal action on some other maxim on which the agent could act. Or, instead of talking of universal action on the "maxim" of the act in question, we can speak of all members of the class of relevantly similar actions being performed; then the proposal is that an action is right if and only if universal performance of the class of relevantly similar acts would not have worse consequences than universal performance of the class of acts relevantly similar to some alternative action the agent might perform. Evidently it is important how we identify the "maxim" of an act or the class of "relevantly similar" acts.

One proceeds as follows. One may begin with the class specified by the properties one thinks are the morally significant ones of the act in question. (One could as well start with the class defined by all properties of the act, if one practically could do this!) One then enlarges the class by omitting from its definition those properties which would not affect the average utility which would result from all the acts in the class being performed. (The total utility might be affected simply by enlarging the size of the class; merely enlarging the class does not affect the average utility.) Conversely, one must also narrow any proposed class of "relevantly similar" acts if it is found that properties have been omitted from the specification of it, the presence of which would affect the average utility which would result if all the acts in the class were performed. The relevant class must not be too large, because of omission of features which define subclasses with different utilities; or too small, because of the presence of features which make no difference to the utilities.

An obvious example of an irrelevant property is that of the agent having a certain name (in most situations), or being a certain person. On the other hand, the fact that the agent wants (does not want) to perform a certain act normally is relevant to the utility of the performance of that act.

So much by way of exposition of the theory.

For many cases this theory and the Ideal Moral Code theory have identical implications. For, when it is better for actions of type A to be performed in a certain situation than for actions of any other type to be performed, it will often be a good thing to have type A actions prescribed by the moral code, directly or indirectly.

The theory also appears more simple than the Ideal Moral Code theory. In order to decide whether a given act is right or wrong we are not asked to do anything as grand as decide what some part of an ideal moral code would be like, but merely whether it would be better, or worse, for all in a relevant class of acts to be performed, as compared with some other relevant class. Thus it offers simple answers to questions such as whether one should vote ("What if nobody did?"), pick wildflowers along the road ("What if everyone did?"), join the army in wartime, or walk on the grass in a park.[16] Furthermore, the theory has a simple way of dealing with conflicts of rules: one determines whether it would be better, or worse, for all members of the more complex class (about which the rules conflict) of actions to be performed (e.g., promises broken in the situation where the breach would save a life).

In one crucial respect, however, the two theories are totally different. For, in contrast with the Ideal Moral Code theory, this theory implies that exactly those acts are objectively right which are objectively right on the act-utilitarian theory. Hence the implications of this theory for action include the very counter-intuitive ones which led its proponents to seek an improvement over act-utilitarianism.

It must be conceded that this assessment of the implications of the theory is not yet a matter of general agreement,[17] and depends on a rather complex argument. In an earlier paper (loc. cit.) I argued that the theory does have these consequences, although my statement of the theory was rather misleading. More recently Professor David Lyons has come to the same conclusion, after an extensive discussion in which he urges that the illusion of a difference between the consequences of this theory and those of act-utilitarianism arises because of failure to notice certain important features of the context of actions, primarily the relative frequency of similar actions at about the same time, and "threshold effects" which an action may have on account of these features.[18]

It may be worthwhile to draw attention to the features of the Ideal Moral Code theory which avoid this particular result. In the first place, the Ideal Moral Code theory sets a limit to the number and complexity of the properties which define a class of morally similar actions. For, on this theory, properties of an act make a difference to its rightness, only if a moral principle referring to them (directly or indirectly) can be learned as part of the optimific moral code. Actual persons, with their emotional and intellectual limitations, are unable to learn a moral code which incorporates all the distinctions the other theory can recognize as morally relevant; and even if they could learn it, it would not be utility maximizing for them to try to apply it. In the second place, we noted that to be part of a moral code a proscription must be public, believed to be part of what is morally disapproved of by most adults. Thus whereas some actions (e.g., some performed in secret) would be utility maximizing, the Ideal Moral Code theory may imply that they are wrong, because it would be a bad thing for it to be generally recognized that a person is free to do that sort of thing.

16. I do not know of any reason to think that the Ideal Moral Code theory is a less plausible normative moral theory than any other form of utilitarianism. Other types of rule-utilitarianism are sufficiently like it, however, that it might be that relatively minor changes in formulation would make their implications for conduct indistinguishable from those of the Ideal Moral Code theory.

Two questions have not here been discussed. One is whether the Ideal Moral Code theory is open to the charge that it implies that some actions are right which are unjust in such an important way that they cannot be right. The second question is one a person would naturally wish to explore if he concluded that the right answer to the first question is affirmative: it is whether a rule-utilitarian view could be combined with some other principles like a principle of justice in a plausible way, without loss of all the features which make utilitarianism attractive. The foregoing discussion has not been intended to provide an answer to these questions.

NOTES

1. It would not be impossible to combine a restricted principle of utility with a morality of justice or equality. For instance, it might be said that an act is right only if it meets a certain condition of justice, and also if it is one which, among all the just actions open to the agent, meets a requirement of utility as well as any other.

2. P. F. Strawson, "Social Morality and Individual Ideal," *Philosophy*, XXXVI (1961), 1–17.

3. Stephen Toulmin, *An Examination of the Place of Reason in Ethics* (Cambridge University Press, 1950), pp. 144–45. See various acute criticisms, with which I mostly agree, in Rawls's review, *Philosophical Review*, LX (1951), 572–80.

4. Toulmin and Rawls sometimes go further, and suggest that a person is morally free to do something which the actual code or practice of his society prohibits, if he is convinced that the society would be better off if the code or practice were rewritten so as to permit that sort of thing, and he is prepared to live according to the ideally revised code. If their theory were developed in this direction, it need not be different from some "ideal" forms of rule-utilitarianism, although, as stated, the theory makes the recognized code the standard for moral obligations, with exceptions granted to individuals who hold certain moral opinions. See Toulmin,

op. cit., pp. 151–52, and Rawls, "Two Concepts of Rules," *Philosophical Review*, LXIV (1955), 28–29, especially ftnt. 25. It should be noticed that Rawls's proposal is different from Toulmin's in an important way. He is concerned with only a segment of the moral code, the part which can be viewed as the rules of practices. As he observes, this may be only a small part of the moral code.

5. Does a stranger living in a society have a moral obligation to conform to its moral code? I suggest we think that he does not, unless it is the right moral code or perhaps at least he thinks it is, although we think that offense he might give to the feelings of others should be taken into account, as well as the result his nonconformity might have in weakening regard for moral rules in general.

6. It is a different question whether we should hold offenders in such societies seriously morally blameworthy. People cannot be expected to rise much above the level of recognized morality, and we condemn them little when they do not.

7. "Rules and Utilitarianism," *American Philosophical Quarterly*, I (1964), 32–44.

8. In a footnote to Chapter 9 of *The Open Society*, Professor Popper suggested that utilitarianism would be more acceptable if its test were minimizing suffering rather than

maximizing welfare, to which J. J. C. Smart replied (*Mind*, 1958, pp. 542–43) that the proposal implies that we ought to destroy all living beings, as the surest way to eliminate suffering. It appears, however, that Professor Popper does not seriously advocate what seemed to be the position of the earlier footnote (Addendum to fourth edition, p. 386).

9.   M. G. Singer, *Generalization in Ethics,* (New York: Alfred A. Knopf, Inc., 1961), p. 192 [reprinted above, pp. 114–27].

10.   The confusion is compounded by the fact that terms like "obligation" and "duty" are used sometimes to speak about moral obligations and duties, and sometimes not. The fact that persons have a certain legal duty in certain situations is a rule of the legal institutions of the society; a person may not have a moral duty to do what is his legal duty. The fact that a person has an obligation to invite a certain individual to dinner is a matter of manners or etiquette, and at least may not be a matter of moral obligation. See R. B. Brandt, "The Concepts of Duty and Obligation," *Mind,* LXXIII (1964), especially 380–84.

11.   Some utilitarians have suggested that the right act is determined by the total net intrinsic good produced. This view can have embarrassing consequences for problems of population control. The view here advocated is that the right act is determined by the per person, average, net intrinsic good produced.

12.   The above proposal is different in various respects from that set forth in the writer's "Toward a Credible Form of Utilitarianism," in Castaneda and Nakhnikian, *Morality and the Language of Conduct,* 1963. The former paper did not make a distinction between institutional rules and moral rules. (The present paper, of course, allows that both may contain a common prescription.) A result of these differences is that the present theory is very much simpler, and avoids some counter-intuitive consequences which some writers have pointed out in criticism of the earlier proposal.

13.   *Utilitarianism,* (New York: Library of Liberal Arts, 1957), p. 25.

14.   Could some moral problems be so unique that they would not be provided for by the set of rules it is best for the society to have? If so, how should they be appraised morally? Must there be some appeal to rules covering cases most closely analogous, as seems to be the procedure in law? If so, should we say that an act is right if it is not prohibited, either explicitly or by close analogy, by an ideal moral code? I shall not attempt to answer these questions.

15.   See John Rawls, in "Justice as Fairness," *Philosophical Review,* LXVII (1958), 164–94, especially 179–84.

It seems to be held by some philosophers that an ideal moral code would contain no rule of fairness. The line of argument seems to be as follows: Assume we have an institution involving cooperative behavior for an end which will necessarily be of benefit to all in the institution. Assume further that the cooperative behavior required is burdensome. Assume finally that the good results will be produced even if fewer than all cooperate—perhaps ninety per cent is sufficient. It will then be to an individual's advantage to shirk making his contribution, since he will continue to enjoy the benefits. Shirking on the part of some actually maximizes utility, since the work is burdensome, and the burdensome effort of those who shirk (provided there are not too many) is useless.

I imagine that it would be agreed that, in this sort of system, there should be an agreed and known rule for exempting individuals from useless work. (E.g., someone who is ill would be excused.) In the absence of this, a person should feel free to excuse himself for good and special reason. Otherwise, I think we suppose everyone should do his share, and that it is not a sufficient reason for shirking, to know that enough are cooperating to produce the desired benefits. Let us call this requirement, of working except for special reason (etc.) a "rule of fairness."

Would an ideal moral code contain a rule of fairness? At least, there could hardly be a public rule permitting people to shirk while a sufficient number of others work. For what would the rule be? It would be all too easy for most people to believe that a sufficient number of others were working (like the well-known difficulty in farm planning, that if one plants what sold at a good price the preceding year, one is apt to find that prices for that product will drop, since most other farmers have the same idea). Would it even be a good idea to have a rule to the effect that if one absolutely knows that enough others are working, one may shirk? This seems highly doubtful.

Critics of rule-utilitarianism seem to have passed from the fact that the best system would combine the largest product with the least effort, to the conclusion that the best moral code would contain a rule advising not to work when there are enough workers already. This is a non sequitur.

16.   One should not, however, overemphasize the simplicity. Whether one should vote in these circumstances is not decided by determining that it would have bad consequences if no one voted at all. It is a question whether it would be the best thing for all those people to vote (or not vote) in the class of situations relevantly similar to this one. It should be added, however, that if I am correct in my (below) assessment of the identity of this theory with act-utilitarianism, in the end it is simple, on the theory, to answer these questions.

It hardly seems that an ideal moral code would contain prescriptions as specific as rules about these matters. But the implications for such matters would be fairly direct if, as suggested above, an ideal moral code would contain a principle enjoining fairness, i.e., commanding persons to do their share in common enterprises (or restraints), when everyone benefits if most persons do their share, when persons find doing their share a burden, and when it is not essential that everyone do his share although it is essential that most do so, for the common benefit to be realized.

17.   See, for instance, the interesting paper by Michael A. G. Stocker, "Consistency in Ethics," *Analysis* Supplement, XXV (January 1965), 116–22.

18.   David Lyons, *Forms and Limits of Utilitarianism* (Oxford: Clarendon Press, 1965).

20. *RIGHTNESS AND WRONGNESS OF ACTIONS and THE PLACE OF RULES IN ACT-UTILITARIANISM*

J. J. C. Smart

RIGHTNESS AND WRONGNESS OF ACTIONS

I shall now state the act-utilitarian doctrine. Purely for simplicity of exposition I shall put it forward in a broadly hedonistic form. If anyone values states of mind such as knowledge independently of their pleasurableness he can make appropriate verbal alterations to convert it from hedonistic to ideal utilitarianism. And I shall not here take sides on the issue between hedonistic and quasi-ideal utilitarianism. I shall concern myself with the evaluation signified by 'ought' in 'one ought to do that which will produce the best consequences,' and leave to one side the evaluation signified by the word 'best.'

Let us say, then, that the only reason for performing an action A rather than an alternative action B is that doing A will make mankind (or, perhaps, all sentient beings) happier than will doing B. (Here I put aside the consideration that in fact we can have only probable belief about the effects of our actions, and so our reason should be more precisely stated as that doing A will produce more probable benefit than will doing B. For convenience of exposition I shelve this question of probability for a page or two.) This is so simple and natural a doctrine that we can surely expect that many of my readers will have at least some propensity to agree. For I am talking, as I said earlier, to sympathetic and benevolent men, that is, to men who desire the happiness of mankind. Since they have a favourable attitude to the general happiness, surely they will have a tendency to submit to an ultimate moral principle which does no more than express this attitude. It is true that these men, being human, will also have purely selfish attitudes. Either these attitudes will be in harmony with the general happiness (in cases where everyone's looking after his own interests promotes the maximum general happiness) or they will not be in harmony with the general happiness, in which case they will largely cancel one another out, and so could not be made the basis of an interpersonal discussion anyway. It is possible, then, that many sympathetic and benevolent people depart from or fail to attain a utilitarian ethical principle only under the stress of tradition, of superstition, or of unsound philosophical reasoning. If this hypothesis should turn out to be correct, at least as far as these readers are concerned, then the utilitarian may contend that there is no need for him to defend his position directly, save by stating it in a consistent manner, and by showing that common objections to it are unsound. After all, it expresses an ultimate attitude, not a liking for something merely as a means to something else. Save for attempting to remove confusions and discredit superstitions which may get in the way of clear moral thinking, he cannot, of course, appeal to argument and must rest his hopes on the good feeling of his readers. If any reader is not a sympathetic and benevolent man, then of course it cannot be expected that he will have an

From J. J. C. Smart, "An Outline of a System of Utilitarian Ethics," in *Utilitarianism: For and Against,* by J. J. C. Smart and Bernard Williams (Cambridge: Cambridge University Press, 1973). Reprinted with permission of Cambridge University Press.

ultimate pro-attitude to human happiness in general. Also some good-hearted readers may reject the utilitarian position because of certain considerations relating to justice. I postpone discussion of these. . . .

The utilitarian's ultimate moral principle, let it be remembered, expresses the sentiment not of altruism but of benevolence, the agent counting himself neither more nor less than any other person. Pure altruism cannot be made the basis of a universal moral discussion in that it would lead different people to different and perhaps incompatible courses of action, even though the circumstances were identical. When two men each try to let the other through a door first a deadlock results. Altruism could hardly commend itself to those of a scientific, and hence universalistic, frame of mind. If you count in my calculations why should I not count in your calculations? And why should I pay more attention to my calculations than to yours? Of course we often tend to praise and honour altruism even more than generalized benevolence. This is because people too often err on the side of selfishness, and so altruism is a fault on the right side. If we can make a man try to be an altruist he may succeed as far as acquiring a generalized benevolence.

Suppose we could predict the future consequences of actions with certainty. Then it would be possible to say that the total future consequences of action A are such-and-such and that the total future consequences of action B are so-and-so. In order to help someone to decide whether to do A or to do B we could say to him: 'Envisage the total consequences of A, and think them over carefully and imaginatively. Now envisage the total consequences of B, and think them over carefully. As a benevolent and humane man, and thinking of yourself just as one man among others, would you prefer the consequences of A or those of B?' That is, we are asking for a comparison of one (present and future) *total* situation with another (present and future) *total* situation. So far we are not asking for a *summation* or *calculation* of pleasures or happiness. We are asking only for a comparison of total situations. And it seems clear that we can frequently make such a comparison and say that one total situation is better than another. For example few people would not prefer a total

situation in which a million people are well-fed, well-clothed, free of pain, doing interesting and enjoyable work, and enjoying the pleasures of conversation, study, business, art, humour, and so on, to a total situation where there are ten thousand such people only, or perhaps 999,999 such people plus one man with toothache, or neurotic, or shivering with cold. In general, we can sum things up by saying that if we are humane, kindly, benevolent people, we want as many people as possible now and in the future to be as happy as possible. Someone might object that we cannot envisage the total future situation, because this stretches into infinity. In reply to this we may say that it does not stretch into infinity, as all sentient life on earth will ultimately be extinguished, and furthermore we do not normally in practice need to consider very remote consequences, as these in the end approximate rapidly to zero like the furthermost ripples on a pond after a stone has been dropped into it.

But do the remote consequences of an action diminish to zero? Suppose that two people decide whether to have a child or remain childless. Let us suppose that they decide to have the child, and that they have a limitless succession of happy descendants. The remote consequences do not seem to get less. Not at any rate if these people are Adam and Eve. The difference would be between the end of the human race and a limitless accretion of human happiness, generation by generation. The Adam and Eve example shows that the 'ripples on the pond' postulate is not needed in every case for a rational utilitarian decision. If we had some reason for thinking that every generation would be more happy than not we would not (in the Adam and Eve sort of case) need to be worried that the remote consequences of our action would be in detail unknown. The necessity for the 'ripples in the pond' postulate comes from the fact that usually we do not know whether remote consequences will be good or bad. Therefore we cannot know what to do unless we can assume that remote consequences can be left out of account. This can often be done. Thus if we consider two actual parents, instead of Adam and Eve, then they need not worry about thousands of years hence. Not, at least, if we assume that there will be ecological forces determining the future population of the world. If these parents do not have remote descendants, then other people will presumably have more than they would otherwise. And there is no reason to suppose that my descendants would be more or less happy than yours. We must note, then, that unless we are dealing with 'all or nothing' situations (such as the Adam and Eve one, or that of someone in a position to end human life altogether) we need some sort of 'ripples in the pond' postulate to make utilitarianism workable in practice. I do not know how to prove such a postulate, though it seems plausible enough. If it is not accepted, not only utilitarianism, but also deontological systems like that of Sir David Ross, who at least admits beneficence as one *prima facie* duty among the others, will be fatally affected.

Sometimes, of course, more needs to be said. For example one course of action may make some people very happy and leave the rest as they are or perhaps slightly less happy. Another course of action may make all men rather more happy than before but no one very happy. Which course of action makes mankind happier on the whole? Again, one course of action may make it highly probable that everyone will be made a little happier whereas another course of action may give us a much smaller probability that everyone will be made very much happier. In the third place, one course of action may make everyone happy in a pig-like way, whereas another course of action may make a few people happy in a highly complex and intellectual way.

It seems therefore that we have to weigh the maximizing of happiness against equitable distribution, to weigh probabilities with happiness, and to weigh the intellectual and other qualities of states of mind with their pleasurableness. Are we not therefore driven back to the necessity of some calculus of happiness? Can we just say: "envisage two total situations and tell me which you prefer"? If this were possible, of course there would be no need to talk of summing happiness or of a calculus. All we should have to do would be to put total situations in an order of preference. Since this is not always possible there is a difficulty, to which I shall return shortly.

We have already considered the question of intellectual versus non-intellectual pleasures and activities. This is irrelevant to the present issue because there seems to be no reason why the ideal or quasi-ideal utilitarian cannot use the method of envisaging total situations just as much as the hedonistic utilitarian. It is just a matter of envisaging various alternative total situations, stretching out into the future, and saying which situation one prefers. The non-hedonistic utilitarian may evaluate the total situations differently from the hedonistic utilitarian, in which case there will be an ultimate ethical disagreement. This possibility of ultimate disagreement is always there, though we have given reasons for suspecting that it will not frequently lead to important disagreement in practice.

Let us now consider the question of equity. Suppose that we have the choice of sending four equally worthy and intelligent boys to a medium-grade public school or of leaving three in an adequate but uninspiring grammar school and sending one to Eton. (For sake of the example I am making the almost certainly incorrect assumption that Etonians are happier than other public-school boys and that these other public-school boys are happier than grammar-school boys.) Which course of action makes the most for the happiness of the four boys? Let us suppose that we can neglect complicating factors, such as that the superior Etonian education might lead one boy to develop his talents so much that he will have an extraordinary influence on the well-being of mankind, or that the unequal treatment of the boys might cause jealousy and rift in the family. Let us suppose that the Etonian will be as happy as (we may hope) Etonians usually are, and similarly for the other boys, and let us suppose that remote effects can be neglected. Should we prefer the greater happiness of one boy to the moderate happiness of all four? Clearly one parent may prefer one total situation (one boy at Eton and three at the grammar school) while another may prefer the other total situation (all four at the medium-grade public school). Surely both parents have an equal claim to being sympathetic and benevolent, and yet their difference of opinion here is not founded on an empirical disagreement about facts. I suggest, however, that there are not in fact many cases in which such a disagreement could arise. Probably the parent who wished to send one son to Eton would draw the line at sending one son to Eton plus giving him expensive private tuition during the holidays plus giving his other sons no secondary education at all. It is only within rather small limits that this sort of disagreement about equity can arise. Furthermore the cases in which we can make one person *very* much happier without increasing *general* happiness are rare ones. The law of diminishing returns comes in here. So, in most practical cases, a disagreement about what should be done will be an empirical disagreement about what total situation is likely to be brought about by an action, and will not be a disagreement about which total situation is preferable. For example the inequalitarian parent might get the other to agree with him if he could convince him that there was a much higher probability of an Etonian benefiting the human race, such as by inventing a valuable drug or opening up the mineral riches of Antarctica, than there is of a non-Etonian doing so. (Once more I should like to say that I do not myself take such a possibility very seriously!) I must again stress that since disagreement about what causes produce what effects is in practice so much the most important sort of disagreement, to have intelligent moral discussion with a person we do not in fact need complete agreement with him about ultimate ends: an approximate agreement is sufficient.

Rawls[1] has suggested that we must maximize the general happiness only if we do so in a *fair* way. An *unfair* way of maximizing the general happiness would be to do so by a method which involved making some people less happy than they might be otherwise.[2] As against this suggestion a utilitarian might make the following rhetorical objection: if it is rational for me to choose the pain of a visit to the dentist in order to prevent the pain of toothache, why is it not rational of me to choose a pain for Jones, similar to that of my visit to the dentist, if that is the only way in which I can prevent a pain, equal to that of my toothache, for Robinson? Such situations continually occur in war, in mining, and in the fight against disease, when we may often find ourselves in the position of having in the general interest to inflict suffering on good and happy men. However it must be conceded that these objections against fairness as an *ultimate* principle must be rhetorical only, and that Rawls's

principle could perhaps be incorporated in a restrained system of deontological ethics, which would avoid the artificiality of the usual forms of deontology. There are in any case plenty of good utilitarian reasons for adopting the principle of fairness as an important, but not inviolable, rule of thumb.

We must now deal with the difficulty about probability. We have so far avoided the common objection to utilitarianism that it involves the allegedly absurd notion of a summation or calculus of happiness or goodness. We have done this by using the method of comparing total situations. All we have to do is to envisage two or more total situations and say which we prefer. A purely ordinal, not a quantitative, judgment is all we require. However in taking this position we have oversimplified the matter. Unfortunately we cannot say with certainty what would be the various total situations which could result from our actions. Worse still, we cannot even assign rough probabilities to the total situations as a whole. All we can do is to assign various probabilities to the various possible effects of an action. For example, one course of action may almost certainly lead to a fairly good result next year together with a high probability of a slightly good result the year after, while another action may give a very small probability of a moderately good result the year after and a very small but not negligible probability of a rather bad result the year after that. (I am assuming that in both cases the still more remote results become negligible or such as to cancel one another out.) If we had to weight total situations with probabilities, this would give us enough conceptual difficulty, but it now appears that we have to go within total situations and weight different elements within them according to different probabilities. We seem to be driven back towards a calculus.

If it were possible to assign numerical probabilities to the various effects of our actions we could devise a way of applying the method of total situations. Suppose that we could say that an action X would either give Smith the pleasure of eating ice-cream with probability $4/5$ or the pain of toothache with probability $1/5$ and that it would give Jones the pleasure of sympathy with probability $3/5$ or the displeasure of envy with probability $2/5$ and that no other important results (direct or indirect) would accrue. Suppose that the only alternative action to X is Y and that this has no effect on Smith but causes Jones to go to sleep with probability $3/5$ or to go for a walk with probability $2/5$ and that no other important results (direct or indirect) would accrue. Then we could say that the total situations we have to imagine and to compare are (a) (for X): four people (just like Smith) eating ice-cream plus one (just like Smith) with toothache plus three sympathetic people (just like Jones) plus two envious people (just like Jones), and (b) (for Y): three people (just like Jones) who are asleep plus two (just like Jones) going for a walk. In the example I have, for convenience, taken all probabilities to be multiples of $1/5$. If they did not have common denominators we should have to make them such, by expressing them as multiples of a denominator which is the lowest common multiple of the original denominators.

However it is not usually possible to assign a numerical probability to a particular event. No doubt we could use actuarial tables to ascertain the probability that a friend of ours, who is of a certain age, a certain carefully specified medical history, and a certain occupation, will die within the next year. But can we give a numerical value to the probability that a new war will break out, that a proof of Fermat's last theorem will be found, or that our knowledge of genetical linkage in human chromosomes will be much improved in the next five years? Surely it is meaningless to talk of a numerical value for these probabilities, and it is probabilities of this sort with which we have to deal in our moral life.

When, however, we look at the way in which in fact we take some of our ordinary practical decisions we see that there is a sense in which most people think that we can weigh up probabilities and advantages. A man deciding whether to migrate to a tropical country may well say to himself, for example, that he can expect a pleasanter life for himself and his family in that country, unless there is a change in the system of government there, which is not very likely, or unless one of his children catches an epidemic disease, which is perhaps rather more likely, and so on, and thinking over all these advantages and disadvantages and probabilities and improbabilities he may come out with the statement that on the whole it seems preferable for him to go there or with the statement that on

the whole it seems preferable for him to stay at home.

If we are able to take account of probabilities in our ordinary prudential decisions it seems idle to say that in the field of ethics, the field of our universal and humane attitudes, we cannot do the same thing, but must rely on some dogmatic morality, in short on some set of rules or rigid criteria. Maybe sometimes we just will be unable to say whether we prefer for humanity an improbable great advantage or a probable small advantage, and in these cases perhaps we shall have to toss a penny to decide what to do. Maybe we have not any precise methods for deciding what to do, but then our imprecise methods must just serve their turn. We need not on that account be driven into authoritarianism, dogmatism or romanticism.

So, at any rate, it appears at first sight. But if I cannot say any more the utilitarian position as it is here presented has a serious weakness. The suggested method of developing normative ethics is to appeal to feelings, namely of benevolence, and to reason, in the sense of conceptual clarification and also of empirical enquiry, but not, as so many moralists do, to what the ordinary man says or thinks. The ordinary man is frequently irrational in his moral thinking. And if he can be irrational about morals why cannot he be irrational about probabilities? The fact that the ordinary man thinks that he can weigh up probabilities in making prudential decisions does not mean that there is really any sense in what he is doing. What utilitarianism badly needs, in order to make its theoretical foundations secure, is some method according to which numerical probabilities, even approximate ones, could in theory, though not necessarily always in practice, be assigned to any imagined future event.

D. Davidson and P. Suppes have proposed a method whereby, at any rate in simplified situations, *subjective* probabilities can be given a numerical value.[3] Their theory was to some extent anticipated in an essay by F. P. Ramsey,[4] in which he tries to show how numbers can be assigned to probabilities in the sense of degrees of belief. This allows us to give a theory of rational, in the sense of *self-consistent,* utilitarian choice, but to make utilitarianism thoroughly satisfactory we need something more. We need a method of assigning numbers to *objective,* not subjective, probabilities. Perhaps one method might be to accept the Davidson-Suppes method of assigning subjective probabilities, and define objective probabilities as the subjective probabilities of an unbiased and far-sighted man. This, however, would require independent criteria for lack of bias and for far-sightedness. I do not know how to do this, but I suspect, from the work that is at present being done on decision-making, that the situation may not be hopeless. But until we have an adequate theory of *objective* probability utilitarianism is not on a secure theoretical basis.[5] Nor, for that matter, is ordinary prudence; nor are deontological systems of ethics, like that of Sir David Ross, which assign some weight to beneficence. And any system of deontological ethics implies some method of weighing up the claims of conflicting *prima facie* duties, for it is impossible that deontological rules of conduct should *never* conflict, and the rationale of this is perhaps even more insecure than is the theory of objective probability.

THE PLACE OF RULES IN ACT-UTILITARIANISM

According to the act-utilitarian, then, the rational way to decide what to do is to decide to perform that one of those alternative actions open to us (including the null-action, the doing of nothing) which is likely to maximize the probable happiness or well-being of humanity as a whole, or more accurately, of all sentient beings.[6] The utilitarian position is here put forward as a criterion of rational choice. It is true that we may choose to habituate ourselves to behave in accordance with certain rules, such as to keep promises, in the belief that behaving in accordance with these rules is generally optimific, and in the knowledge that we most often just do not have time to work out individual pros and cons. When we act in such an habitual fashion we do not of course deliberate or make a choice. The act-utilitarian will, however, regard these rules as mere rules of thumb, and will use them only as rough guides. Normally he will act in accordance with them when he has no time for considering probable consequences or when the advantages of such a consideration of consequences are likely to be outweighed by the disadvantage of

the waste of time involved. He acts in accordance with rules, in short, when there is no time to think, and since he does not think, the actions which he does habitually are not the outcome of moral thinking. When he has to think what to do, then there is a question of deliberation or choice, and it is precisely for such situations that the utilitarian criterion is intended.

It is, moreover, important to realize that there is no inconsistency whatever in an act-utilitarian's schooling himself to act, in normal circumstances, habitually and in accordance with stereotyped rules. He knows that a man about to save a drowning person has no time to consider various possibilities, such as that the drowning person is a dangerous criminal who will cause death and destruction, or that he is suffering from a painful and incapacitating disease from which death would be a merciful release, or that various timid people, watching from the bank, will suffer a heart attack if they see anyone else in the water. No, he knows that it is almost always right to save a drowning man, and in he goes. Again, he knows that we would go mad if we went in detail into the probable consequences of keeping or not keeping every trivial promise: we will do most good and reserve our mental energies for more important matters if we simply habituate ourselves to keep promises in all normal situations. Moreover he may suspect that on some occasions personal bias may prevent him from reasoning in a correct utilitarian fashion. Suppose he is trying to decide between two jobs, one of which is more highly paid than the other, though he has given an informal promise that he will take the lesser paid one. He may well deceive himself by underestimating the effects of breaking the promise (in causing loss of confidence) and by overestimating the good he can do in the highly paid job. He may well feel that if he trusts to the accepted rules he is more likely to act in the way that an unbiased act-utilitarian would recommend than he would be if he tried to evaluate the consequences of his possible actions himself. Indeed Moore argued on act-utilitarian grounds that one should never in concrete cases think as an act-utilitarian.[7]

This, however, is surely to exaggerate both the usefulness of rules and the human mind's propensity to unconscious bias. Nevertheless, right or wrong, this attitude of Moore's has a rational basis and (though his argument from probability considerations is faulty in detail) is not the law worship of the rule-utilitarian, who would say that we ought to keep to a rule that is the most generally optimific, even though we *knew* that obeying it in this particular instance would have bad consequences.

Nor is this utilitarian doctrine incompatible, as M. A. Kaplan[8] has suggested it is, with a recognition of the importance of warm and spontaneous expressions of emotion. Consider a case in which a man sees that his wife is tired, and simply from a spontaneous feeling of affection for her he offers to wash the dishes. Does utilitarianism imply that he should have stopped to calculate the various consequences of his different possible courses of action? Certainly not. This would make married life a misery and the utilitarian knows very well as a rule of thumb that on occasions of this sort it is best to act spontaneously and without calculation. Moreover I have said that act-utilitarianism is meant to give a method of deciding what to do in those cases in which we do indeed decide what to do. On these occasions when we do not act as a result of deliberation and choice, that is, when we act spontaneously, no method of decision, whether utilitarian or non-utilitarian, comes into the matter. What does arise for the utilitarian is the question of whether or not he should consciously encourage in himself the tendency to certain types of spontaneous feeling. There are in fact very good utilitarian reasons why we should by all means cultivate in ourselves the tendency to certain types of warm and spontaneous feeling.

Though even the act-utilitarian may on occasion act habitually and in accordance with particular rules, his criterion is, as we have said, *applied* in cases in which he does not act habitually but in which he deliberates and chooses what to do. Now the right action for an agent in given circumstances is, we have said, that action which produces better results than any alternative action. If two or more actions produce equally good results, and if these results are better than the results of any other action open to the agent, then there is no such thing as *the* right action: there are two or more actions which are *a* right action. However this is a very exceptional state of affairs, which may well never in

fact occur, and so usually I will speak loosely of the action which is *the* right one. We are now able to specify more clearly what is meant by 'alternative action' here. The fact that the utilitarian criterion is meant to apply in situations of deliberation and choice enables us to say that the class of alternative actions which we have in mind when we talk about an action having the best possible results is the class of actions which the agent could have performed if he had tried. For example, it would be better to bring a man back to life than to offer financial assistance to his dependants, but because it is technologically impossible to bring a man back to life, bringing the man back to life is not something we could do if we tried. On the other hand it may well be possible for us to give financial assistance to the dependants, and this then may be the right action. The right action is the action among those which we could do, i.e. those which we *would* do if we chose to, which has the best possible results.

It is true that the general concept of action is wider than that of deliberate choice. Many actions are performed habitually and without deliberation. But the actions for whose rightness we as agents want a criterion are, in the nature of the case, those done thinkingly and deliberately. An action is at any rate that sort of human performance which it is appropriate to praise, blame, punish or reward, and since it is often appropriate to praise, blame, punish, or reward habitual performances, the concept of action cannot be identified with that of the outcome of deliberation and choice. With habitual actions the only question that arises for an agent is that of whether or not he should strengthen the habit or break himself of it. And individual acts of habit-strengthening or habit-breaking can themselves be deliberate.

The utilitarian criterion, then, is designed to help a person, who could do various things if he chose to do them, to decide which of these things he should do. His utilitarian deliberation is one of the causal antecedents of his action, and it would be pointless if it were not. The utilitarian view is therefore perfectly compatible with determinism. The only sense of 'he could have done otherwise' that we require is the sense 'he would have done otherwise if he had chosen.' Whether the utilitarian view necessitates complete metaphysical determinism is another matter. All that it requires is that deliberation should determine actions in the way that everyone knows it does anyway. If it is argued that any indeterminism in the universe entails that we can never know the outcome of our actions, we can reply that in normal cases these indeterminacies will be so numerous as approximately to cancel one another out, and anyway all that we require for rational action is that some consequences of our actions should be *more probable* than others, and this is something which no indeterminist is likely to deny.

The utilitarian may now conveniently make a terminological recommendation. Let us use the word 'rational' as a term of commendation for that action which is, on the evidence available to the agent, *likely* to produce the best results, and to reserve the word 'right' as a term of commendation for the action which does *in fact* produce the best results. That is, let us say that what is rational is to try to perform the right action, to try to produce the best results. Or at least this formulation will do where there is an equal probability of achieving each possible set of results. If there is a very low probability of producing very good results, then it is natural to say that the rational agent would perhaps go for other more probable though not quite so good results. For a more accurate formulation we should have to weight the goodness of the results with their probabilities. However, neglecting this complication, we can say, roughly, that it is rational to perform the action which is on the available evidence the one which will produce the best results. This allows us to say, for example, that the agent did the right thing but irrationally (he was trying to do something else, or was trying to do this very thing but went about it unscientifically) and that he acted rationally but by bad luck did the wrong thing, because the things that seemed probable to him, for the best reasons, just did not happen.

Roughly, then: we shall use 'right' and 'wrong' to appraise choices on account of their actual success in promoting the general happiness, and we shall use 'rational' and 'irrational' to appraise them on account of their likely success. As was noted above 'likely success' must be interpreted in terms of maximizing the probable benefit, not in terms of probably maximizing the benefit. In effect, it is rational to do what you reasonably think to be right, and what will be right is what will maximize the probable benefit. We need, however, to make one qualification to this. A person may unreasonably believe what it would in fact be reasonable to believe. We shall still call such a person's action irrational. If the agent has been unscientific in his calculation of means-ends relationships he may decide that a certain course of action is probably best for human happiness, and it may indeed be so. When he performs this action we may still call his action irrational, because it was pure luck, not sound reasoning, that brought him to his conclusion.

'Rational' and 'irrational' and 'right' and 'wrong' so far have been introduced as terms of appraisal for chosen or deliberate actions only. There is no reason why we should not use the pair of terms 'right' and 'wrong' more widely so as to appraise even habitual actions. Nevertheless we shall not have much occasion to appraise actions that are not the outcome of choice. What we do need is a pair of terms of appraisal for *agents* and *motives*. I suggest that we use the terms 'good' and 'bad' for these purposes. A good agent is one who acts more nearly in a generally optimific way than does the average one. A bad agent is one who acts in a less optimific way than the average. A good motive is one which generally results in beneficent actions, and a bad motive is one which generally ends in maleficent actions. Clearly there is no inconsistency in saying that on a particular occasion a good man did a wrong action, that a bad man did a right action, that a right action was done from a bad motive, or that a wrong action was done from a good motive. Many specious arguments against utilitarianism come from obscuring these distinctions. Thus one may be got to admit that an action is 'right,' meaning no more than that it is done from a good motive and is praiseworthy, and then it is pointed out that the action is not 'right' in the sense of being optimific. I do not wish to legislate as to how other people (particularly non-utilitarians) should use words like 'right' and 'wrong,' but in the interests of clarity it is important for me to state how I propose to use them myself, and to try to keep the various distinctions clear.

It should be noted that in making this terminological recommendation I am not trying to smuggle in valuations under the guise of definitions, as Ardon Lyon, in a review of the first edition of this monograph,[9] has suggested that I have done. It is merely a recommendation to pre-empt the already evaluative words 'rational' and 'irrational' for one lot of commendatory or discommendatory jobs, the already evaluative words 'right' and 'wrong' for another lot of commendatory or discommendatory jobs, and the already evaluative words 'good' and 'bad' for yet another lot of commendatory or discommendatory jobs.

We can also use 'good' and 'bad' as terms of commendation or discommendation of actions themselves. In this case to commend or discommend an action is to commend or discommend the motive from which it sprang. This allows us to say that a man performed a bad action but that it was the right one, or that he performed a good action but that it was wrong. For example, a man near Berchtesgaden in 1938 might have jumped into a river and rescued a drowning man, only to find that it was Hitler. He would have done the wrong thing, for he would have saved the world a lot of trouble if he had left Hitler below the surface. On the other hand his motive, the desire to save life, would have been one which we approve of people having: in general, though not in this case, the desire to save life leads to acting rightly. It is worth our while to strengthen such a desire. Not only should we praise the action (thus expressing our approval of it) but we should perhaps even give the man a medal, thus encouraging others to emulate it. Indeed praise itself comes to have some of the social functions of medal giving: we come to like praise for its own sake, and are thus influenced by the possibility of being given it. Praising a person is thus an important action in itself—it has significant effects. A utilitarian must therefore learn to control his acts of praise and dispraise, thus perhaps concealing his approval of an action when he thinks that the expression of such approval might have bad effects, and perhaps even praising actions of which he does not really approve. Consider, for example, the case of an act-utilitarian, fighting in a war, who succeeds in capturing the commander of an enemy submarine. Assuming that it is a just war and that the act-utilitarian is fighting on the right side, the very courage and ability of the submarine commander has a tendency which is the reverse of optimific. Everything that the submarine commander has been doing was (in my proposed sense of the word) wrong. (I do not of course

mean that he did anything wrong in the technological sense: presumably he knew how to manoeuvre his ship in the right way.) He has kept his boat cunningly concealed, when it would have been better for humanity if it had been a sitting duck, he has kept the morale of his crew high when it would have been better if they had been cowardly and inefficient, and has aimed his torpedoes with deadly effect so as to do the maximum harm. Nevertheless, once the enemy commander is captured, or even perhaps before he is captured, our act-utilitarian sailor does the right thing in praising the enemy commander, behaving chivalrously towards him, giving him honour and so on, for he is powerfully influencing his own men to aspire to similar professional courage and efficiency, to the ultimate benefit of mankind.

What I have said in the last paragraph about the occasional utility of praising harmful actions applies, I think, even when the utilitarian is speaking to other utilitarians. It applies even more when, as is more usually the case, the utilitarian is speaking to a predominantly non-utilitarian audience. To take an extreme case, suppose that the utilitarian is speaking to people who live in a society governed by a form of magical taboo ethics. He may consider that though on occasion keeping to the taboos does harm, on the whole the tendency of the taboo ethics is more beneficial than the sort of moral anarchy into which these people might fall if their reverence for their taboos was weakened. While, therefore, he would recognize that the system of taboos which governed these people's conduct was markedly inferior to a utilitarian ethic, nevertheless he might also recognize that these people's cultural background was such that they could not easily be persuaded to adopt a utilitarian ethic. He will, therefore, on act-utilitarian grounds, distribute his praise and blame in such a way as to strengthen, not to weaken, the system of taboo.

In an ordinary society we do not find such an extreme situation. Many people can be got to adopt a utilitarian, or almost utilitarian, way of thought, but many cannot. We may consider whether it may not be better to throw our weight on the side of the prevailing traditional morality, rather than on the side of trying to improve it with the risk of weakening respect for morality altogether. Sometimes the answer to this question will be 'yes,' and sometimes 'no.' As Sidgwick said:[10]

The doctrine that Universal Happiness is the ultimate *standard* must not be understood to imply that Universal Benevolence is . . . always the best *motive* of action. For . . . it is not necessary that the end which gives the criterion of rightness should always be the end at which we consciously aim: and if experience shows that the general happiness will be more satisfactorily attained if men frequently act from other motives than pure universal philanthropy, it is obvious that these other motives are to be preferred on Utilitarian principles.

In general, we may note, it is always dangerous to influence a person contrary to his conviction of what is right. More harm may be done in weakening his regard for duty than would be saved by preventing the particular action in question. Furthermore, to quote Sidgwick again, "any particular existing moral rule, though not the ideally best even for such beings, as existing men under the existing circumstances, may yet be the best that they can be got to obey."[11] We must also remember that some motives are likely to be present in excess rather than defect: in which case, however necessary they may be, it is not expedient to praise them. It is obviously useful to praise altruism, even though this is not pure generalized benevolence, the treating of oneself as neither more nor less important than anyone else, simply because most people err on the opposite side, from too much self-love and not enough altruism. It is, similarly, inexpedient to praise self-love, important though this is when it is kept in due proportion. In short, to quote Sidgwick once more, "in distributing our praise of human qualities, on utilitarian principles, we have to consider not primarily the usefulness of the quality, but the usefulness of the praise."[12]

Most men, we must never forget, are not act-utilitarians, and do not use the words 'good' and 'bad,' when applied to agents or to motives, quite in the way which has here been recommended. When a man says that another is wicked he may even be saying something of a partly metaphysical or superstitious connotation. He may be saying that there is something like a yellow stain on the other man's soul. Of course he would not think this quite literally. If you asked him whether souls could be coloured, or whether yellow was a particularly abhorrent colour, he would of course laugh at you. His views about sin and and wickedness may be left in comfortable obscurity. Nevertheless the things he *does* say may indeed entail something *like* the yellow stain view. 'Wicked' has thus come to have much more force than the utilitarian 'likely to be very harmful' or 'probably a menace.' To stigmatize a man as wicked is not, as things are, just to make men wary of him, but to make him the object of a peculiar and very powerful abhorrence, over and above the natural abhorrence one has from a dangerous natural object such as a typhoon or an octopus. And it may well be to the act-utilitarian's advantage, *qua* act-utilitarian, to acquiesce in this way of talking when he is in the company of non-utilitarians. He himself will not believe in yellow stains in souls, or anything like it. *Tout comprendre c'est tout pardonner;* a man is the result of heredity and environment. Nevertheless the utilitarian may influence behaviour in the way he desires by using 'wicked' in a quasi-superstitious way. Similarly a man about to be boiled alive by cannibals may usefully say that an imminent eclipse is a sign of the gods' displeasure at the proposed culinary activities. We have seen that in a completely utilitarian society the utility of praise of an agent's motives does not always go along with the utility of the action. Still more may this be so in a non-utilitarian society.

I cannot stress too often the importance of Sidgwick's distinction between the utility of an action and the utility of praise or blame of it, for many fallacious 'refutations' of utilitarianism depend for their plausibility on confusing the two things.

Thus A. N. Prior[13] quotes the nursery rhyme:

> For want of a nail
> The shoe was lost;
> For want of a shoe
> The horse was lost;
> For want of a horse
> The rider was lost;
> For want of a rider
> The battle was lost;
> For want of a battle
> The kingdom was lost;
> And all for the want
> Of a horse-shoe nail.

So it was all the blacksmith's fault! But, says Prior, it is surely hard to place on the smith's shoulders the responsibility for the loss of the kingdom. This is no objection, however, to act-utilitarianism. The utilitarian could quite consistently say that it would be useless to blame the blacksmith, or at any rate to blame him more than for any other more or less trivial case of 'bad maintenance.' The blacksmith had no reason to believe that the fate of the kingdom would depend on one nail. If you blame him you may make him neurotic and in future even more horses may be badly shod.

Moreover, says Prior, the loss of the kingdom was just as much the fault of someone whose negligence led to there being one fewer cannon in the field. If it had not been for this other piece of negligence the blacksmith's negligence would not have mattered. Whose was *the* responsibility? The act-utilitarian will quite consistently reply that the notion of *the* responsibility is a piece of metaphysical nonsense and should be replaced by 'Whom would it be useful to blame?' And in the case of such a close battle, no doubt it would be useful to blame quite a lot of people though no one very much. Unlike, for example, the case where a battle was lost on account of the general getting drunk, where considerable blame of one particular person would clearly be useful.

"But wouldn't a man go mad if he really tried to take the whole responsibility of everything upon himself in this way?" asks Prior. Clearly he would. The blacksmith must not mortify himself with morbid thoughts about his carelessness. He must remember that his carelessness was of the sort that is usually trivial, and that a lot of other people were equally careless. The battle was just a very close thing. But this refusal to blame himself, or blame himself very much, is surely consistent with the recognition that his action was *in fact* very wrong, that much harm would have been prevented if he had acted otherwise. Though if other people, e.g. the man whose fault it was that the extra cannon did not turn up, had acted differently, then the blacksmith's action would have in fact not been very wrong, though it would have been no more and no less blameworthy. A very wrong action is usually very blameworthy, but on some occasions, like the present one, a very wrong action can be hardly blameworthy at all. This seems paradoxical at first, but paradox disappears when we remember Sidgwick's distinction between the utility of an action and utility of praise of it.

The idea that a consistent utilitarian would go mad with worry about the various effects of his actions is perhaps closely connected with a curious argument against utilitarianism to be found in Baier's book *The Moral Point of View*.[14] Baier holds that (act-) utilitarianism must be rejected because it entails that we should never relax, that we should use up every available minute in good works, and we do not ordinarily think that this is so. The utilitarian has two effective replies. The first is that perhaps what we ordinarily think is false. Perhaps a rational investigation would lead us to the conclusion that we should relax much less than we do. The second reply is that act-utilitarianism premisses do not entail that we should never relax. Maybe relaxing and doing few good works today increases threefold our capacity to do good works tomorrow. So relaxation and play can be defended even if we ignore, as we should not, their intrinsic pleasures.

I beg the reader, therefore, if ever he is impressed by any alleged refutation of act-utilitarianism, to bear in mind the distinction between the rightness or wrongness of an action and the goodness or badness of the agent, and Sidgwick's correlative and most important distinction between the utility of an action and the utility of praise or blame of it. The neglect of this distinction is one of the commonest causes of fallacious refutations of act-utilitarianism.

It is also necessary to remember that we are here considering utilitarianism as a *normative* system. The fact that it has consequences which conflict with some of our particular moral judgments need not be decisive against it. In science general principles must be tested by reference to particular facts of observation. In ethics we may well take the opposite attitude, and test our particular moral attitudes by reference to more general ones. The utilitarian can contend that since his principles rests on something so simple and natural as generalized benevolence it is more securely founded than our particular feelings, which may be subtly distorted by analogies with similar looking (but in reality totally different) types of case, and by all sorts of hangovers from traditional and uncritical ethical thinking.

If, of course, act-utilitarianism were put forward as a descriptive systematization of how ordinary men, or even we ourselves in our unreflective and uncritical moments, actually think about ethics, then of course it is easy to refute and I have no wish to defend it. Similarly again if it is put forward not as a *descriptive* theory but as an *explanatory* one.

John Plamenatz, in his *English Utilitarians,* seems to hold that utilitarianism "is destroyed and no part of it left standing."[15] This is apparently on the ground that the utilitarian *explanation* of social institutions will not work: that we cannot *explain* various institutions as having come about because they lead to the maximum happiness. In this monograph I am not concerned with what our moral customs and institutions in fact are, and still less am I concerned with the question of *why* they are as they in fact are. I am concerned with a certain view about what they *ought* to be. The correctness of an ethical doctrine, when it is interpreted as recommendatory, is quite independent of its truth when it is interpreted as descriptive and of its truth when it is interpreted as explanatory. In fact it is precisely because a doctrine is false as description and as explanation that it becomes important as a possible recommendation.

NOTES

1. 'Justice as fairness,' *Philosophical Review* 67 (1958) 164–94.

2. See especially p. 168 of Rawls's article.

3. D. Davidson, P. Suppes, and S. Siegel, *Decision Making: An Experimental Approach* (Stanford University Press, Stanford, California, 1957).

4. F. P. Ramsey, *The Foundations of Mathematics* (Routledge and Kegan Paul, London, 1931), ch. 7, 'Truth and probability.'

5. R. McNaughton's interesting article 'A metrical concept of happiness,' *Philosophy and Phenomenological Research* 14 (1953–4) 171–83, does not enable us to propose a complete utilitarian calculus, because it neglects probability considerations.

6. In the first edition of this monograph I said 'which is likely to bring about the total situation now and in the future which is the best for the happiness or well-being of humanity as a whole, or more accurately, of all sentient beings.' This is inaccurate. To probably maximize the benefit is not the same as to maximize the probable benefit. This has been pointed out by David Braybrooke. See p. 35 of his article 'The choice between utilitarianisms,' *American Philosophical Quarterly* 4 (1967) 28–38.

7. *Principia Ethica,* p. 162.

8. Morton A. Kaplan, 'Some problems of the extreme utilitarian position,' *Ethics* 70 (1959–60) 228–32. This is a critique of my earlier article 'Extreme and restricted utilitarianism,' *Philosophical Quarterly* 6 (1956) 344–54. He also puts forward a game theoretic argument against me, but this seems cogent only against an egoistic utilitarian. Kaplan continued the discussion in his interesting note 'Restricted utilitarianism,' *Ethics* 71 (1960–1) 301–2.

9. *Durham University Journal* 55 (1963) 86–7.

10. *Methods of Ethics,* p. 413.

11. *Ibid.* p. 469.

12. *Ibid.* p. 428.

13. 'The consequences of actions,' *Aristotelian Society Supplementary Volume* 30 (1956) 91–9. See p. 95.

14. K. E. M. Baier, *The Moral Point of View* (Cornell University Press, Ithaca, New York, 1958), pp. 203–4.

15. *The English Utilitarians, 2nd edn* (Blackwell, Oxford, 1966), p. 145.

21. WHAT MAKES RIGHT ACTS RIGHT?

W. D. Ross

The real point at issue between hedonism and utilitarianism on the one hand and their opponents on the other is not whether 'right' means 'productive of so and so'; for it cannot with any plausibility be maintained that it does. The point at issue is that to which we now pass, viz. whether there is any general character which makes right acts right, and if so, what it is. Among the main historical attempts to state a single characteristic of all right actions which is the foundation of their rightness are those made by egoism and utilitarianism. But I do not propose to discuss these, not because the subject is unimportant, but because it has been dealt with so often and so well already, and because there has come to be so much agreement among moral philosophers that neither of these theories is satisfactory. A much more attractive theory has been put forward by Professor Moore: that what makes actions right is that they are productive of more *good* than could have been produced by any other action open to the agent.[1]

This theory is in fact the culmination of all the attempts to base rightness on productivity of some sort of result. The first form this attempt takes is the attempt to base rightness on conduciveness to the advantage or pleasure of the agent. This theory comes to grief over the fact, which stares us in the face, that a great part of duty consists in an observance of the rights and a furtherance of the interests of others, whatever the cost to ourselves may be. Plato and others may be right in holding that a regard for the rights of others never in the long run involves a loss of happiness for the agent, that 'the just life profits a man.' But this, even if true, is irrelevant to the rightness of the act. As soon as a man does an action *because* he thinks he will promote his own interests thereby, he is acting not from a sense of its rightness but from self-interest.

To the egoistic theory hedonistic utilitarianism supplies a much-needed amendment. It points out correctly that the fact that a certain pleasure will be enjoyed by the agent is no reason why he *ought* to bring it into being rather than an equal or greater pleasure to be enjoyed by another, though, human nature being what it is, it makes it not unlikely that he *will* try to bring it into being. But hedonistic utilitarianism in its turn needs a correction. On reflection it seems clear that pleasure is not the only thing in life that we think good in itself, that for instance we think the possession of a good character, or an intelligent understanding of the world, as good or better. A great advance is made by the substitution of 'productive of the greatest good' for 'productive of the greatest pleasure.'

Not only is this theory more attractive than hedonistic utilitarianism, but its logical relation to that theory is such that the latter could not be true unless *it* were true, while it might be true though hedonistic utilitarianism were not. It is in fact one of the logical bases of hedonistic utilitarianism. For the view that what produces the maximum pleasure is right has for its bases the views (1) that what produces the maximum good is right, and (2) that pleasure is the only thing good in itself. If they were not assuming that what produces the maximum *good* is right, the utilitarians' attempt to show that pleasure is the only thing good in itself, which is in fact the point they take most pains to establish, would have been quite irrelevant to their attempt to prove that only what produces the maximum *pleasure* is right. If, therefore, it can be shown that productivity of the maximum good is not what makes all right actions right, we shall *a fortiori* have refuted hedonistic utilitarianism.

From W. D. Ross, *The Right and the Good*, selections from Chapter II. © 1930 Oxford University Press. Reprinted by permission of The Clarendon Press, Oxford.

When a plain man fulfils a promise because he thinks he ought to do so, it seems clear that he does so with no thought of its total consequences, still less with any opinion that these are likely to be the best possible. He thinks in fact much more of the past than of the future. What makes him think it right to act in a certain way is the fact that he has promised to do so—that and, usually, nothing more. That his act will produce the best possible consequences is not his reason for calling it right. What lends colour to the theory we are examining, then, is not the actions (which form probably a great majority of our actions) in which some such reflection as 'I have promised' is the only reason we give ourselves for thinking a certain action right, but the exceptional cases in which the consequences of fulfilling a promise (for instance) would be so disastrous to others that we judge it right not to do so. It must of course be admitted that such cases exist. If I have promised to meet a friend at a particular time for some trivial purpose, I should certainly think myself justified in breaking my engagement if by doing so I could prevent a serious accident or bring relief to the victims of one. And the supporters of the view we are examining hold that my thinking so is due to my thinking that I shall bring more good into existence by the one action than by the other. A different account may, however, be given of the matter, an account which will, I believe, show itself to be the true one. It may be said that besides the duty of fulfilling promises I have and recognize a duty of relieving distress,[2] and that when I think it right to do the latter at the cost of not doing the former, it is not because I think I shall produce more good thereby but because I think it the duty which is in the circumstances more of a duty. This account surely corresponds much more closely with what we really think in such a situation. If, so far as I can see, I could bring equal amounts of good into being by fulfilling my promise and by helping some one to whom I had made no promise, I should not hesitate to regard the former as my duty. Yet on the view that what is right is right because it is productive of the most good I should not so regard it.

There are two theories, each in its way simple, that offer a solution of such cases of conscience. One is the view of Kant, that there are certain duties of perfect obligation, such as those of fulfilling promises, of paying debts, of telling the truth, which admit of no exception whatever in favour of duties of imperfect obligation, such as that of relieving distress. The other is the view of, for instance, Professor Moore and Dr. Rashdall, that there is only the duty of producing good, and that all 'conflicts of duties' should be resolved by asking 'by which action will most good be produced?' But it is more important that our theory fit the facts than that it be simple, and the account we have given above corresponds (it seems to me) better than either of the simpler theories with what we really think, viz. that normally promise-keeping, for example, should come before benevolence, but that when and only when the good to be produced by the benevolent act is very great and the promise comparatively trivial, the act of benevolence becomes our duty.

In fact the theory of 'ideal utilitarianism,' if I may for brevity refer so to the theory of Professor Moore, seems to simplify unduly our relations to our fellows. It says, in effect, that the only morally significant relation in which my neighbours stand to me is that of being possible beneficiaries by my action.[3] They do stand in this relation to me, and this relation is morally significant. But they may also stand to me in the relation of promisee to promiser, of creditor to debtor, of wife to husband, of child to parent, of friend to friend, of fellow countryman to fellow countryman, and the like; and each of these relations is the foundation of a *prima facie* duty, which is more or less incumbent on me according to the circumstances of the case. When I am in a situation, as perhaps I always am, in which more than one of these *prima facie* duties is incumbent on me, what I have to do is to study the situation as fully as I can until I form the considered opinion (it is never more) that in the circumstances one of them is more incumbent than any other; then I am bound to think that to do this *prima facie* duty is my duty *sans phrase* in the situation.

I suggest '*prima facie* duty' or 'conditional duty' as a brief way of referring to the characteristic (quite distinct from that of being a duty proper) which an act has, in virtue of being of a certain kind (e.g. the keeping of a promise), of being an act which would be a duty proper if it were not at the same time of another kind which is morally significant. Whether an act is a duty proper or actual duty depends on *all* the morally significant kinds it is an instance of. The phrase '*prima facie* duty' must be apologized for, since (1) it suggests that what we are speaking of is a certain kind of duty, whereas it is in fact not a duty, but something related in a special way to duty. Strictly speaking, we want not a phrase in which duty is qualified by an adjective, but a separate noun. (2) '*Prima*' facie suggests that one is speaking only of an appearance which a moral situation presents at first sight, and which may turn out to be illusory; whereas what I am speaking of is an objective fact involved in the nature of the situation, or more strictly in an element of its nature, though not, as duty proper does, arising from its *whole* nature. I can, however, think of no term which fully meets the case. 'Claim' has been suggested by Professor Prichard. The word 'claim' has the advantage of being quite a familiar one in this connexion, and it seems to cover much of the ground. It would be quite natural to say, 'a person to whom I have made a promise has a claim on me,' and also, 'a person whose distress I could relieve (at the cost of breaking the promise) has a claim on me.' But (1) while 'claim' is appropriate from *their* point of view, we want a word to express the corresponding fact from the agent's point of view—the fact of his being subject to claims that can be made against him; and ordinary language provides us with no such correlative to 'claim.' and (2) (what is more important) 'claim' seems inevitably to suggest two persons, one of whom might make a claim on the other; and while this covers the ground of social duty, it is inappropriate in the case of that important part of duty which is the duty of cultivating a certain kind of character in oneself. It would be artificial, I think, and at any rate metaphorical, to say that one's character has a claim on oneself.

There is nothing arbitrary about these *prima facie* duties. Each rests on a definite circumstance which cannot seriously be held to be without moral significance. Of *prima facie* duties I suggest, without claiming completeness or finality for it, the following division.[4]

(1) Some duties rest on previous acts of my own. These duties seem to include two kinds, (*a*) those resting on a promise or what may fairly be called an implicit promise, such as the implicit undertaking not to tell lies which seems to be implied in the act of entering into conversation (at any rate by civilized men), or of writing books that purport to be history and not fiction. These may be called the duties of fidelity. (*b*) Those resting on a previous wrongful act. These may be called the duties of reparation. (2) Some rest on previous acts of other men, i.e. services done by them to me. These may be loosely described as the duties of gratitude.[5] (3) Some rest on the fact or possibility of a distribution of pleasure or happiness (or of the means thereto) which is not in accordance with the merit of the persons concerned; in such cases there arises a duty to upset or prevent such a distribution. These are the duties of justice. (4) Some rest on the mere fact that there are other beings in the world whose condition we can make better in respect of virtue, or of intelligence, or of pleasure. These are the duties of beneficence. (5) Some rest on the fact that we can improve our own condition in respect of virtue or of intelligence. These are the duties of self-improvement. (6) I think that we should distinguish from (4) the duties that may be summed up under the title of 'not injuring others.' No doubt to injure others is incidentally to fail to do them good; but it seems to me clear that non-maleficence is apprehended as a duty distinct from that of beneficence, and as a duty of a more stringent character. It will be noticed that this alone among the types of duty has been stated in a negative way. An attempt might no doubt be made to state this duty, like the others, in a positive way. It might be said that it is really the duty to prevent ourselves from acting either from an inclination to harm others or from an inclination to seek our own pleasure, in doing which we should incidentally harm them. But on reflection it seems clear that the primary duty here is the duty not to harm others, this being a duty whether or not we have an inclination that if followed would lead to our harming them; and that when we have such an inclination the primary duty not to harm others gives rise to a consequential duty to resist the inclination. The recognition of this duty of non-maleficence is the first step on the way to the recognition of the duty of beneficence; and that accounts for the prominence of the commands 'thou shalt not kill,' 'thou shalt not commit adultery,' 'thou shalt

not steal,' 'thou shalt not bear false witness,' in so early a code as the Decalogue. But even when we have come to recognize the duty of beneficence, it appears to me that the duty of non-maleficence is recognized as a distinct one, and as *prima facie* more binding. We should not in general consider it justifiable to kill one person in order to keep another alive, or to steal from one in order to give alms to another.

The essential defect of the 'ideal utilitarian' theory is that it ignores, or at least does not do full justice to, the highly personal character of duty. If the only duty is to produce the maximum of good, the question who is to have the good—whether it is myself, or my benefactor, or a person to whom I have made a promise to confer that good on him, or a mere fellow man to whom I stand in no such special relation—should make no difference to my having a duty to produce that good. But we are all in fact sure that it makes a vast difference.

*   *   *

An attempt may be made to arrange in a more systematic way the main types of duty which we have indicated. In the first place it seems self-evident that if there are things that are intrinsically good, it is *prima facie* a duty to bring them into existence rather than not to do so, and to bring as much of them into existence as possible. It will be argued in our fifth chapter that there are three main things that are intrinsically good—virtue, knowledge, and, with certain limitations, pleasure. And since a given virtuous disposition, for instance, is equally good whether it is realized in myself or in another, it seems to be my duty to bring it into existence whether in myself or in another. So too with a given piece of knowledge.

*   *   *

In the fifth chapter I shall try to show that besides the three (comparatively) simple goods, virtue, knowledge, and pleasure, there is a more complex good, not reducible to these, consisting in the proportionment of happiness to virtue. The bringing of this about is a duty which we owe to all men alike, though it may be reinforced by special responsibilities that we have undertaken to particular men. This, therefore, with beneficence and self-improvement, comes under the general principle that we should produce as much good as possible, though the good here involved is different in kind from any other.

But besides this general obligation, there are special obligations. These may arise, in the first place, incidentally, from acts which were not essentially meant to create such an obligation, but which nevertheless create it. From the nature of the case such acts may be of two kinds—the infliction of injuries on others, and the acceptance of benefits from them. It seems clear that these put us under a special obligation to other men, and that only these acts can do so incidentally. From these arise the twin duties of reparation and gratitude.

And finally there are special obligations arising from acts the very intention of which, when they were done, was to put us under such an obligation. The name for such acts is 'promises'; the name is wide enough if we are willing to include under it implicit promises, i.e. modes of behaviour in which without explicit verbal promise we intentionally create an expectation that we can be counted on to behave in a certain way in the interest of another person.

These seem to be, in principle, all the ways in which *prima facie* duties arise. In actual experience they are compounded together in highly complex ways. Thus, for example, the duty of obeying laws of one's country arises partly (as Socrates contends in the *Crito*) from the duty of gratitude for the benefits one has received from it; partly from the implicit promise to obey which seems to be involved in permanent residence in a country whose laws we know we are *expected* to obey, and still more clearly involved when we ourselves invoke the protection of its laws (this is the truth underlying the doctrine of the social contract); and partly (if we are fortunate in our country) from the fact that its laws are potent instruments for the general good.

Or again, the sense of a general obligation to bring about (so far as we can) a just apportionment of happiness to merit is often greatly reinforced by the fact that many of the existing injustices are due to a social and economic system which we have, not indeed created, but taken part in and assented to; the duty of justice is then reinforced by the duty of reparation.

It is necessary to say something by way of clearing up the relation between *prima facie* duties and the actual or absolute duty to do one particular act in particular circumstances. If, as almost all moralists except Kant are agreed, and as most plain men think, it is sometimes right to tell a lie or to break a promise, it must be maintained that there is a difference between *prima facie* duty and actual or absolute duty. When we think ourselves justified in breaking, and indeed morally obliged to break, a promise in order to relieve some one's distress, we do not for a moment cease to recognize a *prima facie* duty to keep our promise, and this leads us to feel, not indeed shame or repentance, but certainly compunction, for behaving as we do; we recognize, further, that it is our duty to make up somehow to the promisee for the breaking of the promise. We have to distinguish from the characteristic of being our duty that of tending to be our duty. Any act that we do contains various elements in virtue of which it falls under various categories. In virtue of being the breaking of a promise, for instance, it tends to be wrong; in virtue of being an instance of relieving distress it tends to be right. Tendency to be one's duty may be called a parti-resultant attribute, i.e. one which belongs to an act in virtue of some one component in its nature. *Being* one's duty is a toti-resultant attribute, one which belongs to an act in virtue of its whole nature and of nothing less than this.

*   *   *

In what has preceded, a good deal of use has been made of 'what we really think' about moral questions; a certain theory has been rejected because it does not agree with what we really think. It might be said that this is in principle wrong; that we should not be content to expound what our present moral consciousness tells us but should aim at a criticism of our existing moral consciousness in the light of theory. Now I do not doubt that the moral consciousnes of men has in detail undergone a good deal of modification as regards the things we think right, at the hands of moral theory. But if we are told, for instance, that we should give up our view that there is a special obligatoriness attaching to the keeping of promises because it is self-evident that the only duty is to produce as much good as possible, we have to ask ourselves whether we really, when we reflect, *are* convinced that this is self-evident, and whether we really *can* get rid of

our view that promise-keeping has a bindingness independent of productiveness of maximum good. In my own experience I find that I cannot, in spite of a very genuine attempt to do so; and I venture to think that most people will find the same, and that just because they cannot lose the sense of special obligation, they cannot accept as self-evident, or even as true, the theory which would require them to do so. In fact it seems, on reflection, self-evident that a promise, simply as such, is something that *prima facie* ought to be kept, and it does *not,* on reflection, seem self-evident that production of maximum good is the only thing that makes an act obligatory. And to ask us to give up at the bidding of a theory our actual apprehension of what is right and what is wrong seems like asking people to repudiate their actual experience of beauty, at the bidding of a theory which says 'only that which satisfies such and such conditions can be beautiful.' If what I have called our actual apprehension is (as I would maintain that it is) truly an apprehension, i.e. an instance of knowledge, the request is nothing less than absurd.

I would maintain, in fact, that what we are apt to describe as 'what we think' about moral questions contains a considerable amount that we do not think but know, and that this forms the standard by reference to which the truth of any moral theory has to be tested, instead of having itself to be tested by reference to any theory. I hope that I have in what precedes indicated what in my view these elements of knowledge are that are involved in our ordinary moral consciousness.

It would be a mistake to found a natural science on 'what we really think,' i.e. on what reasonably thoughtful and well-educated people think about the subjects of the science before they have studied them scientifically. For such opinions are interpretations, and often misinterpretations, of sense-experience; and the man of science must appeal from these to sense-experience itself, which furnishes his real data. In ethics no such appeal is possible. We have no more direct way of access to the facts about rightness and goodness and about what things are right or good, than by thinking about them; the moral convictions of thoughtful and well-educated people are the data of ethics just as sense-perceptions are the data of a natural science. Just as some of the latter have to be rejected as illusory, so have some of the former; but as the latter are rejected only when they are in conflict with other more accurate sense-perceptions, the former are rejected only when they are in conflict with other convictions which stand better the test of reflection. The existing body of moral convictions of the best people is the cumulative product of the moral reflection of many generations, which has developed an extremely delicate power of appreciation of moral distinctions; and this the theorist cannot afford to treat with anything other than the greatest respect. The verdicts of the moral consciousness of the best people are the foundation on which he must build; though he must first compare them with one another and eliminate any contradictions they may contain.

NOTES

1.   I take the theory which, as I have tried to show, seems to be put forward in *Ethics* rather than the earlier and less plausible theory put forward in *Principia Ethica.* For the difference, cf. my pp. 8–11.

2.   These are not strictly speaking duties, but things that tend to be our duty, or *prima facie* duties. Cf. pp. 19–20.

3.   Some will think it, apart from other considerations, a sufficient refutation of this view to point out that I also stand in that relation to myself, so that for this view the distinction of oneself from others is morally insignificant.

4.   I should make it plain at this stage that I am *assuming* the correctness of some of our main convictions as to *prima facie* duties, or, more strictly, am claiming that we *know* them to be true. To me it seems as self-evident as anything could be, that to make a promise, for instance, is to create a moral claim on us in someone else. Many readers will perhaps say that they do *not* know this to be true. If so, I certainly cannot prove it to them; I can only ask them to reflect again, in the hope that they will ultimately agree that they also know it to be true. The main moral convictions of the plain man seem to me to be, not opinions which it is for philosophy to prove or disprove, but knowledge from the start; and in my own case I seem to find little difficulty in distinguishing these essential convictions from other moral convictions which I also have, which are merely fallible opinions based on an imperfect study of the working for good or evil of certain institutions or types of action.

5.   For a needed correction of this statement, cf. pp. 22–3.

SUGGESTIONS FOR FURTHER READING

A. THE MORALITY OF KILLING

Bennett, Jonathan, "Whatever the Consequences," *Analysis,* Vol. 26 (1966).

Broad, C. D. *Ethics and the History of Philosophy* (London: Routledge and Kegan Paul Ltd., 1952), essay entitled, "Ought We to Fight for Our Country?"

Feinberg, Joel (ed.), *The Problem of Abortion* (Belmont, Calif.: Wadsworth Publishing Co., Inc., 1969).

Fletcher, Joseph, *Morals and Medicine* (Boston: Beacon Press, 1960).

Foot, Philippa, "The Problem of Abortion and the Doctrine of the Double Effect," *Oxford Review,* No. 5 (1967). Reprinted in *Moral Problems,* ed. by James Rachels (New York: Harper & Row, 1971).

Fried, Charles, *An Anatomy of Values* (Cambridge, Mass.: Harvard University Press, 1970), Part Three.

Goodrich, T., "The Morality of Killing," *Philosophy,* Vol. 44 (1969).

Hume, David, "Of Suicide," in *Essays: Moral, Political, and Literary* (Oxford: Oxford University Press, 1963).

Kant, Immanuel, "Suicide," in *Lectures on Ethics* (New York: Harper Torchbooks, 1963).

Labby, Daniel H. (ed.), *Life or Death: Ethics and Options* (Seattle: University of Washington Press, 1968).

Nagel, Thomas, "Death," *Nous,* Vol. 4 (1971).

Ramsey, Paul, *The Just War* (New York: Scribner's, 1968).

Stein, Walter (ed.), *Nuclear Weapons: A Catholic Response* (New York: Sheed & Ward, 1961).

Who Shall Live? Man's Control Over Birth and Death. A Report Prepared for the American Friends Service Committee (New York: Hill & Wang, 1970).

Wasserstrom, R. A. (ed.), *War and Morality* (Belmont, Calif.: Wadsworth Publishing Company, Inc., 1970).

Wells, Donald A., *The War Myth* (New York: Pegasus, 1967).

Williams, Glanville, *The Sanctity of Life and the Criminal Law* (New York: Knopf, 1968).

Zinn, Howard, "Vietnam: Setting the Moral Equation," *The Nation,* Vol. 202 (1966).

B. SEXUAL ETHICS

Anscombe, G. E. M., "Contraception and Chastity," *The Human World,* No. 7 (1972).

Atkinson, Ronald, *Sexual Morality* (New York: Harcourt, Brace, Jovanovich, 1966).

Fletcher, Joseph, *Moral Responsibility* (Philadelphia: Westminster Press, 1967) Chapters 5–8.

Heron, Alastair (ed.), *Towards a Quaker View of Sex* (London: Friends Home Service Committee, 1964).

Kardiner, Abram, *Sex and Morality* (Indianapolis: Bobbs-Merrill, 1954).

Nagel, Thomas, "Sexual Perversion," *Journal of Philosophy,* Vol. 66 (1969).

Ramsey, Paul, "On Taking Sexual Responsibility Seriously Enough," *Christianity and Crisis,* Vol. 23 (1964).

Ruddick, Sara, "On Sexual Morality," in *Moral Problems,* ed. by James Rachels (New York: Harper & Row, 1971).

Sex and Morality: A Report to the British Council of Churches (Philadelphia: Fortress Press, 1966).

Storr, Anthony, *Sexual Deviation* (Harmondsworth, Middlesex: Penguin Books, 1965).

Whiteley, C. H. and W. M., *Sex and Morals* (London: B. T. Batsford, 1967).

Williams, Bernard, and Tanner, Michael, "Reply to Professor Anscombe" (printed with a brief rejoinder from Professor Anscombe), *The Human World,* No. 9 (1972).

C. UTILITARIANISM PRO AND CON

Bayles, Michael D., (ed.), *Contemporary Utilitarianism* (New York: Doubleday, 1968).

Hare, R. M., *Freedom and Reason* (Oxford: Clarendon Press, 1963), Chap. 7.

Harrod, R. F., "Utilitarianism Revised," *Mind,* Vol. 45 (1936).

Hearn, Thomas K., Jr. (ed.), *Studies in Utilitarianism* (New York: Appleton-Century-Crofts, 1971).

Hodgson, D. H., *Consequences of Utilitarianism* (London: Oxford University Press, 1967).

Lyons, David, *The Forms and Limits of Utilitarianism* (London: Oxford University Press, 1965).

Narveson, Jan, *Morality and Utility* (Baltimore: Johns-Hopkins Press, 1967).

Quinton, Anthony, *Utilitarianism* (London: Macmillan, 1972).

Rawls, John, *A Theory of Justice* (Cambridge, Mass.: Harvard University Press, 1971), pp. 22–33, 183–192.

Sartorius, Rolf, *Individual Conduct and Social Norms* (Encino, Calif.: Dickenson Publishing Company, Inc., 1975).

Sidgwick, Henry, *Methods of Ethics* (London: Macmillan, 1962).

Singer, M. G., *Generalization in Ethics* (New York: Knopf, 1961).

Smart, J. J. C., "An Outline of a System of Utilitarian Ethics," in *Utilitarianism For and Against* (Cambridge: Cambridge University Press, 1973).

———, "Utilitarianism," *The Encyclopedia of Philosophy* vol. 8, pp. 206–212.

Sobel, Howard, "Utilitarianisms, Simple and General," *Inquiry,* Vol. 13 (1970).

———, "The Need for Coercion," in *Coercion,* ed. by J. R. Pennock and J. W. Chapman (Chicago: Aldine, Atherton, 1972).

West, Henry R., "Utilitarianism," *Encyclopedia Britannica,* fifteenth edition (Chicago, 1974).

Williams, Bernard, "A Critique of Utilitarianism" in *Utilitarianism For and Against* (Cambridge: Cambridge University Press, 1973).

D. ALTERNATIVES TO CONSEQUENTIALISM

Anscombe, G. E. M., "Modern Moral Philosophy," *Philosophy,* Vol. 33 (1958).

McCloskey, H. J., *Meta-Ethics and Normative Ethics* (The Hague: Martinus Nijhoff, 1969).

Rawls, John, *A Theory of Justice* (Cambridge, Mass.: Harvard University Press, 1971).

Ross, W. D., *Foundations of Ethics* (Oxford: Clarendon Press, 1939).

(Note that Stoicism and Kantianism are leading alternatives to consequentialism.)

Part IV   Rights, Justice and Punishment

One of the less controversial features of John Stuart Mill's account of justice in Chapter Five of *Utilitarianism*[1] (though one which is by no means unanimously accepted by current writers) is his explanation of the distinction between justice and "other branches of morality." Injustice, he writes, "implies two things—a wrong done, and some assignable person who is wronged." When a moral duty or obligation is a matter of justice, on Mill's view, there must be some definite person or persons who can claim performances of that duty as his or their *due*. When I am generally unfriendly, or dour, or ungenerous, I may fall below acceptable moral standards and be subject to blame, but I have not been *unjust* unless I have been unjust *to* someone, and have violated someone's *rights*.

Justice would seem therefore not to be the whole of morality, but rather only one part, albeit a most important subdivision of the whole. Justice, moreover, is the most legalistic branch of morality: arguments over justice and fairness characteristically involve references to rights, claims and counterclaims, commitments and obligations. Mill was hardly the first writer in the history of ethics to note the legalistic character of the realm of justice, and to insist that it does not include the whole of morality. Kant was of one mind with him in those respects, and so were the leading writers in the Aristotelian tradition, especially the scholastic philosophers of the middle ages, notably St. Thomas Aquinas.[2] Josef Pieper has recently composed a kind of gloss on St. Thomas's theory designed to "bring it face to face with the modern world."[3] The underlying notion in all talk of justice, Pieper writes, is the ancient saying *"suum cuique"*—"that each person is to be given his due." What in fact is a given person's "due" is determined by her or his rights. Some rights result

---

[1]Included in Part I of this volume, pp. 128–40.
[2]St. Thomas Aquinas, *Summer Theologica,* Second Part of the Second Part, Questions 57–122; and Commentary on the Nicomachean Ethics of Aristotle, Book Five, Numbers 885–1108.
[3]Josef Pieper, *Justice* (London: Faber and Faber, 1957), p. 13.

from a person's prior doings, some do not. But in any case, "justice is something that comes second: right comes before justice."[4]

Aristotle, St. Thomas, Kant, and Mill agree that acting from a sense of justice is not one and the same as acting from love. There is no gainsaying the poets who celebrate the beauty and moral preciousness of love, but it is quite impossible for all but saints to love everybody. It is impossible for most of us even to like, or to have sympathy, for everybody. But whether we like a person or not, we *can* recognize and respect his or her rights and act accordingly, even if we must do so while hating, or resenting, or holding our noses. Love if you can, but do justice whether you love or not. In obedience to this maxim there is a kind of moral beauty to rival that of love and benevolence themselves. Perhaps, as Kant maintained, it is the distinctive and essential *moral* beauty.[5]

Nevertheless justice, while an essential component of morally admirable conduct and character, is not by itself sufficient. Pieper argues persuasively that even though justice deserves to be called, as Aristotle called it, "the supreme moral virtue," it is not sufficient for overall personal merit, and "the world cannot be kept in order through justice alone."[6] Devotion, piety, respect, gratitude, mercy, and the virtues of friendship (liberality, affability, kindness) are also required, even though most of these are not strictly "due" to other persons nor rightfully claimed, demanded, or compelled. Without friendship, for example, it is impossible, as St. Thomas puts it, "for men to live together joyfully (*delectabiliter*)."[7] The point about gratitude is especially well taken:

---

[4]*Ibid.*, p. 15.
[5]In his discussions of the nature of morally worthy motives in the *Grundlegung* included in Part I of this volume, pp. 83–90.
[6]Pieper, *op. cit.*, p. 97.
[7]*Ibid.*, p. 108.

"Being grateful" and "returning thanks" are not of the same order as "paying" and "making restitution." That is why Thomas says, quoting Seneca, that a person who wants to repay a gift too quickly with a gift in return is an unwilling debtor and an ungrateful person.[8]

Yet an ungrateful person who pays all debts and gives all people their due is a just person, for all that.

What then is a "right?" A great tangle of subtle issues underlies this simple question, as the reader of the contrasting articles, "Rights," by H. J. McCloskey and "The Nature and Value of Rights," by Joel Feinberg, will quickly note. Jurisprudential writers, following the famous analysis of Wesley Hohfeld,[9] commonly distinguish four basic kinds of legal relations: claim-rights, liberties, powers, and immunities. Hohfeld himself claimed that the phrase "a right," as it is used in the law, can mean any of these four kinds of thing. McCloskey and Feinberg both propose analyses of the generic idea of a right, of which moral and legal rights are two prominent species. McCloskey rejects the idea that a right, in any familiar sense that would interest a moralist, is a kind of *power,* and Feinberg presumably agrees. Neither considers the possibility that a right (in the generic sense) could be a kind of *immunity.* Feinberg does not deny that there is an everyday sense of "right" in which to have a right to *x* is simply to be *at liberty* to do or have *x* if one pleases, that is, to have no duty to refrain from doing or having *x,* but the morally interesting and "valuable" kind of right, he insists, is that which corresponds in the moral realm to the legal concept of a *claim-right.* To have a claim-right to do *x* is not merely to be at liberty to do *x* (though it is at least that); it is also to have a claim against others to performance or to noninterference, as the case may be. A right, according to Feinberg, is always held *against* someone or other; it is necessarily correlated with another party's duties.

McCloskey, on the contrary, insists that it is foreign to the essential character of a right that it be *against* someone (though he doesn't deny that it sometimes is correlated with other people's duties). The essential point about a right, he argues, is that it is an *entitlement to* something or other, not that it is a claim against someone. The latter, when present, is an added, rather than an essential feature. A claim against someone, of course, requires the existence of the person against whom it is held. An entitlement, on the other hand, might be held by the last person on earth. His example is telling:

Imagine that the last person is a woman [who alone survived a nuclear war] capable of reproducing by artificial insemination, a large sperm bank having also survived. I suggest that talk about rights would have real application in such a situation. Suppose the woman had good reason to believe that if she reproduced, her offspring would be monsters. . . . In such a case she would have to conclude that she did not possess the right to reproduce. If she had every reason to believe that her offspring would be healthy, she would conclude that she had the right to reproduce unless of course she regarded artificial insemination as wrong. This suggests that the actual existence of other human beings is irrelevant to whether rights may or may not be possessed . . .[10]

It is probably not open to Feinberg to deny that talk of the hypothetical last woman's "rights" is intelligible and coherent. The one move open to him, in

---

[8]*Ibid.,* p. 107.
[9]Wesley Hohfeld, *Fundamental Legal Conceptions* (New Haven: Yale University Press, 1923).
[10]H. J. McCloskey, "Rights," this volume, p. 321.

reply to McCloskey, is to claim that the only sense of "right" that makes sense in this context is that corresponding to the jurisprudential "liberty." To say that the woman has a right to inseminate herself is simply to deny that she has a duty to refrain from doing so; to deny that she has such a right is simply to assert that she has a duty to refrain. The "actual existence of other human beings," he could admit, *is* irrelevant to whether a given person has *duties*. The concept of "a right" to which Feinberg attributes special moral importance, however, is that of a claim-right, and that concept, he could insist, requires other persons if it is to have real application.

Problems about justice and fairness arise in almost every department of social life. We apply the epithets "just" and "unjust" (in some instances "fair" and "unfair" sound better) to persons and traits of character, actions, rules, and judgments. We condemn as unfair or unjust instances of partiality, favoritism, arbitrary inequality, exploitation, cheating, freeloading, and un-merited derogatory judgment. The particular targets of our wrath can be players in games, umpires, literary critics, prosecutors, and judges; or laws, verdicts, contracts, wages, and prices. In this section of the book attention is focused on only two areas of controversy, but these are surely of fundamental importance. One is the problem of "distributive justice": what is the criterion for the fair distribution of wealth among the members of a political commu-nity? The other is the problem of "retributive justice": under what conditions, if any, is the infliction of criminal punishment just, and what factors determine how much punishment is deserved by particular crimes?

The first important discussion of distributive justice, and one which has remained influential to this day, is that in Book Five of Aristotle's *Nicomachean Ethics*.[11] The student would be well advised to consult (or reread) it before proceeding to the articles by Henry West and John Rawls. To understand Aristotle, it is important to have at least an approximate grasp of the Greek concept of justice that he was applying and analyzing. From the earliest period, there was a linkage between the ideas of justice, and of law and property. The earliest poets and cosmologists spoke of a cosmic law (more on the juridical than the modern scientific model) assigning everything in the universe its own proper place, and of a cosmic justice that consists of every *thing* staying in its assigned orbit. Against this background it was natural to think of human justice as consisting of every *person* getting and keeping his "due"—not only his own proper job or social function, but his own property and the keeping of promises made to him.

The evolving Greek concept of justice, however, was not only linked in this partial way with the idea of property; it was also connected analytically with the idea of equality. Democratic politicians in most city-states made justice their rallying cry in support of their demands for equality of wealth and political power. In fact, the Greek word for "just" at one time virtually *meant* "equal." Aristotle shared Plato's scorn for the "absolute equality" demanded by Greek democrats, convinced as he was that there are many just inequalities (even though that conviction when voiced must have had the ring of paradox, even strict contradiction). Aristotle ingeniously purged the antiequalitarian conception of justice of paradox by analyzing distributive justice as pro-portionate rather than absolute equality, that is, an *equality of ratios:* one

[11]Included in this volume, pp. 52–65.

person's share must be to his relevant characteristics (or "merits" in a broad sense) as another person's share is to *his* relevant characteristics. Aristotle himself must have realized what many subsequent misguided commentators put forward as a charge against him, that his analysis is a purely formal one, providing those who must distribute shares of benefits and burdens little practical guidance until it is supplemented by an account of *which* characteristics are "relevant" for the purposes of justice.

A full-bodied practical criterion of distributive justice that could in principle support specific judgments would not be purely formal, then, in the way Aristotle's account is formal, but it would possess the form that Aristotle prescribes, while filling in the variables. It would identify distributive justice with an equality of ratios, so that justice is accomplished between A and B when:

$$\frac{\text{A's share of certain benefits or burdens}}{\text{B's share of those benefits or burdens}} = \frac{\text{A's possession of X}}{\text{B's possession of X}}$$

The full criterion (or "material principle") of distributive justice, then, would fill in the variable X. Strict "meritarians" would substitute for X "moral or intellectual virtue" or "skill"; others would substitute hereditary class, degree of effort or labor, or amount of actual past contributions to the public wealth; equalitarians would substitute simply "need." Others would defend different answers in different contexts, depending on the nature of the benefit or burden to be distributed.

The following are the main possible views about the relation between distributive justice and net social utility:[12]

1. Justice and social utility, properly conceived, can *never* conflict. That is because "justice is a name for certain moral requirements which, regarded collectively, stand higher in the scale of social utility, and are therefore of more paramount obligation, than any others . . ."

2. Justice and social utility do sometimes conflict, and when they do, so much the worse for justice.

3. Justice and social utility do sometimes conflict, and when they do, so much the worse for social utility.

4. Justice and social utility do sometimes conflict, but it is impossible to say in advance that one must always have a stronger claim than the other. These opposing irreconcilable claims can only be "balanced" against one another in the concrete circumstances of their conflict.

Views 1 and 2 are both utilitarian, but they are answers to different questions. The first *analyzes* justice in terms of utility and thus logically implies that the two can never conflict. The second is quite consistent with a nonutilitarian analysis of justice, that is, an analysis that makes no reference to "social utility," but holds nevertheless that in those rare and tragic instances where individual justice is not in the public interest, it is individual justice that must yield.

[12]The following distinctions are drawn from Joel Feinberg, "Justice, Fairness, and Rationality," *The Yale Law Journal*, Vol. 81 (1972), p. 1006.

In either case, a utilitarian theory of what ought to be done in distributive contexts would require that mode of distribution that itself produces a greater net total of good, or a smaller net total of harm, than any alternative mode of distribution. To take a very abstract and artificial example, suppose that a given political community has a choice between two ways of distributing its benefits (economic incomes, liberties, privileges) and its burdens (taxation, conscription, public duties). Method A would be more or less equalitarian with the state manipulating taxation rates, incentives, penalties, and other devices in such a way as to keep the differences between the wealthiest and poorest citizens within a very narrow range. Method B however, in the interests of greater efficiency and greater productivity, permits very great differences in wealth, privilege, and power between the best- and worst-off citizens. Suppose that method A produces a grand total of 1,000,000 units of happiness (if sense can be made of that way of speaking) and 500,000 units of unhappiness, leaving a positive net balance of 500,000 units distributed quite evenly through the population. Method B, let us suppose, produces a society with large class differences, but with an overall positive balance of 600,000 units of happiness. Under method B, let us imagine, greater efficiency produces a greater total amount of good, but those who enjoy that good do so at the expense of a substantial minority who suffer severe deprivation. If our only criterion of justice (or alternatively, of what ought to be done, all things considered) is the utilitarian one, then it would seem that we must choose method B. If happiness is the only thing good in itself, then it matters not how it is produced or how it is distributed: the more of it the better. Critics of utilitarianism argue that this consequence runs directly counter to our spontaneous moral feelings or "intuitions" in the matter, and is not only an embarrassment for utilitarianism, but a virtual reductio ad absurdam. Utilitarians, as might be expected, have been quick with their rejoinders to this attack, some of them denying the possibility of the facts in the hypothetical example used against them, others denying the antiutilitarian account of our "moral intuitions." The standard arguments on both sides are presented and appraised in "Justice and Utility" by Henry West.

Views 3 and 4 on the foregoing list are the two major nonutilitarian theories of the relation of distributive justice to social utility. The fourth view is sometimes called "pluralism" because it denies that a plurality of moral principles can be reduced to one ultimate and superior one, and sometimes called "intuitionism" because of its insistence on the need for "weighing" and "balancing" conflicting principles when they yield different results. The most common form of this view[13] holds that there are two distinct valid principles governing distributions of burdens and benefits, one of which is utilitarian and the other equalitarian. We can know with confidence, according to this theory, that likely amounts of social utility being equal, the method that distributes more equally is right, and where both alternatives distribute with the same degree of equality, the one likely to produce the greater net total of social utility is right. (The "equality" in question is usually some version of Aristotelian "proportionate equality.") But when circumstances bring the principles of utility and equality into opposition, there is no higher-order criterion to settle the conflict.

[13]Cf. Nicholas Rescher, *Distributive Justice* (New York: Bobbs-Merrill Company, 1966), and Brian Barry, *Political Argument* (London: Routledge & Kegan Paul, and New York: Humanities Press, 1965).

John Rawls represents the third listed approach to the question of the relation between distributive justice and social utility. He is one opponent of utilitarianism who finds the fourth or "pluralistic" alternative untidy and unsatisfying. He is not content with a theory that merely places limits or amendments on utilitarianism in an ad hoc way; rather he seeks to develop an equally thorough and systematic theory which is a genuine alternative to utilitarianism, equally capable of giving decisive guidance to our decisions and choices in hard cases, but more in accord with our precritical "intuitions." His article included here, "Distributive Justice," is a precursor of his large and influential book, *A Theory of Justice,* published in 1971. In both, he is concerned primarily with the justice of basic political and economic *institutions,* as opposed to the justice of individual actions, persons, or policies. "The primary subject of justice," he writes, "is the basic structure of society."[14] In his article on distributive justice, then, Rawls seeks a basic criterion of justice to apply to economic systems rather than to individual economic transactions. The criterion he formulates and defends is a further articulation of the traditional doctrine (compare Aristotle again) that equals are to be treated equally unless there is sufficient reason to treat them differently. His fundamental thesis is that the only sufficient reason for departing from equality in the distribution of economic goods is that an unequal distribution would be to everybody's advantage; not the "general advantage," not the "average person's advantage," but *everybody's* advantage, including that of the worst-off persons. The mode of distribution itself can have effects on the amount of goods produced, and in some cases, a particular sort of unequal distribution might be an essential component of a system that vastly increases the amount of goods subsequently available for distribution. Surely any reasonable person, Rawls argues, would prefer a system that gives him a larger amount of goods, though a smaller portion than his neighbor's, to a system that gives him a smaller absolute amount, though one which is an equal share. It would be contrary to reason, Rawls insists, to prefer a lesser to a greater good for oneself on the sole ground that the greater good would be part of a scheme in which others get greater goods still.

Perhaps the most novel and influential feature of Rawls's view is the way he *derives* his substantive principles of justice. Far from being utilitarian, the method comes ultimately from the theory of the social contract, a tradition of moral and political thought in which Immanuel Kant has a prominent place. In his article here Rawls refers briefly to his earlier article "Justice as Fairness" in which the derivation is worked out in greater detail. Like Kant, Rawls takes the theory of justice, "and indeed ethics itself" to be "part of the general theory of rational choice." A proposed principle of justice (for example, the utilitarian's, the intuitionist's, Rawls's own) is correct, according to the contractarian method of derivation, providing it would be chosen over any alternative principle that could be proposed to a group of normally self-interested, rational persons. All these persons can be imagined to have gathered together voluntarily in an "original position" of equal power, for the purpose of designing the institutions that will regulate their future lives. We

---

[14]John Rawls, *A Theory of Justice* (Cambridge, Mass.: Harvard University Press, 1971), p. 7.

are also to suppose that all wear a kind of "veil of ignorance" which prevents them from knowing facts about their own future condition that could tempt them ("rationally" self-interested beings that they are) to base their choice on the desire to promote their own interest to the disadvantage of others. If these hypothetical choosers are neither rich nor poor, white nor black, male nor female, old nor young—so far as they know—then they cannot be lobbyists for any particular class interests, and must choose their principles from a more disinterested vantage point. Formulating the correct principles of justice, then, (including the principles of economic justice) is simply determining which principles such hypothetical, rational persons, in such hypothetical circumstances, would choose to govern the design of their political and economic institutions.

The problem of punishment has always played a prominent part in the controversies between utilitarians and their opponents. The reader of this book may already have encountered the subject in Part III, where E. F. Carritt strongly criticizes the criteria of justification to which he thinks all utilitarians are committed, and where John Rawls in his "Two Concepts of Rules" summarizes the controversy between utilitarians and retributivist critics like Carritt and suggests a way of reconciling what is sound in these rival theories. Rawls's article represents a new and important twist in an ancient controversy, and should definitely be read (or reread) in this section following the selection from Edmund L. Pincoff's *The Rationale of Legal Punishment*.

Pincoff's summary of "The Classical Debate" between the two great rival theories of punishment is remarkably clear and penetrating. The classic source of the retributive theory is the *Rechtslehre* (Philosophy of Law) of Immanuel Kant. That great work is notoriously difficult, and obscure to the point of opacity in some of its English translations. The other great German retributivist, Georg Wilhelm Friedrich von Hegel (1770–1831), is perhaps even harder to understand. Yet Pincoffs has found clear and plausible doctrines in their theories of punishment, and presents them in an easily comprehensible form. Pincoffs then does the same kind of job for the classical utilitarians, William Paley (1743–1805) and Jeremy Bentham (1748–1832). The utilitarian account of the conditions which must be satisfied by just punishment, especially as qualified by Bentham, also has a certain plausibility about it, so that serious students of the classic debate are bound to find themselves in something of a quandry. At this point they must attempt to follow Aristotle who once recommended to philosophers that when faced with contradictions they should try to make distinctions. Perhaps then it will turn out that the plausible variants of the utilitarian and retributivist theories, rather than being contradictory answers to the same question, are complementary answers to quite different questions about the justification of punishment. Pincoffs suggests how that might be so at the end of his chapter included here, and Rawls, in "Two Concepts of Rules," works out a similar suggestion in considerable detail.

"The Expressive Function of Punishment," by Joel Feinberg, is not directly concerned with the "classical debate" over the justification of legal punishment, but rather with the analytic question it presupposes about the nature and meaning of punishment itself. How does punishment in the strict and narrow sense that interests the moralist differ from such other authoritative deprivations as sackings, disqualifications, football penalties, parking fines, taxes, withdrawals of privileges, and compulsory therapeutic confinement? Feinberg proposes an answer to this question and argues that the question itself has a direct strategic bearing on the classical debate over the justification of punishment.

J. F.

22. *RIGHTS*

H. J. McCloskey

In this article, I propose to consider two of three closely inter-related, questions, namely: 'What is a right?' 'Who or what may possess rights?' The third question, 'What are the grounds and nature of the rights beings actually possess?', although vitally relevant to the former two questions raises issues too extensive in scope to be treated of in a single paper.

A. CONCEPTUAL ISSUES: RIGHTS AS ENTITLEMENTS

A moral right is commonly explained as being some sort of *claim* or *power* which ought to be recognized. D. G. Ritchie, for instance, observes that a moral right may be defined as *"the claim of an individual upon others recognized by society, irrespective of its recognition by the State."*[1] Ryan and Boland, explaining the Catholic (Thomist) view of rights, state: "A right in the moral sense of the term may be defined as an inviolable moral *claim* to some personal good. When this claim is created as it sometimes is, by civil authority, it is a positive or legal right; when it is derived from man's rational nature it is a natural right."[2] T. H. Green, on the other hand, argues: "A right is *a power* of acting for his own ends,—for what he conceives to be his good,—secured to an individual by the community on the supposition that its exercise contributes to the good of the community."[3] Plamenatz follows Green in explaining rights in terms of powers, but in other respects his definition differs substantially from that of Green. Plamenatz states: "A right is *a power* which a creature ought to possess because its exercise by him is itself good, or else because it is a means to what is good, and in the exercise of which all rational beings ought to protect him."[4] There are obvious grounds for rejecting such accounts of the concept of a right, whether it be a legal, moral, social, or institutional right. To consider first rights other than moral rights.

To have *a legal right* is not to have a power conferred or recognized by law, nor is it a power which ought to be recognized by law or by officials administering the law. I may have a legal right to drive a car but lack the power to do so because temporarily paralysed or because too poor to buy or rent a car. A lot of laws which confer rights are called "private power-conferring laws" but, as Cohen has argued against Hart, they are not really power-conferring laws at all.[5] The laws giving me the right to marry, divorce, or to make a will, are not conferring powers on me; yet they are clearly conferring legal rights. Similarly, criminal laws deny me legal rights but they do not interfere with my powers. Nor are legal rights powers recognized by the state, for legal rights may exist where there is no power to exercise the right. Similarly, a legal right does not amount to a claim upon others recognized by the state, although a right may provide a ground for such a claim. My legal right to marry consists primarily in the recognition of my entitlement to marry and to have my act recognized. It indirectly gives rise to claims on others not to prevent me so acting, but it does not primarily consist in these claims. I am legally entitled under our legal system to do whatever is not forbidden by the law. Thus I have a legal right to grow roses in my garden. This legal right is not simply a claim I can make under the law that others not interfere with me when selecting plants for my garden. It is essentially an entitlement to act as I please. It may give rise to derivative entitlements, and claims on others and the state.

With *institutional rights,* e.g. rights as a member of a religious organization or a social club, the possession of a right does not consist in some sort of power or claim. A right to vote in the election of the elders of the Church is an entitlement to take part in the election; and an

From H. J. McCloskey, "Rights," *Philosophical Quarterly,* Vol. 15 (1965), pp. 115–127. Reprinted by permission of the author and of *The Philosophical Quarterly.*

entitlement is very different from a power, whether it be a power conferred, recognized, or which ought to be recognized. To have the right to vote is not simply or necessarily to have the power to vote, nor is it a power to act which has been conferred or recognized or which ought to be recognized. In a laxly policed election non-members may have the power but not the right to vote. Similarly, the right does not consist primarily in claims on others. Consider the right of the Church member to partake of Holy Communion. The right and the power are clearly distinct, and the right is related to claims only in that, besides entitling the member to partake of Holy Communion, it also entitles him to resist any official or member of the Church who seeks to prevent him partaking. So too with rights as a member of a social club. My right to use the club —its writing room, library, bar—is an entitlement. I may lack the power to exercise this right, and still possess it; and I may enjoy it without making claims on others—e.g. if it were a small, self-service club with no staff. The right equally exists for the member who is unable to get to the club, i.e. who cannot make claims on others, and for the member who admits himself to the club building and who makes no claims on others.

Rights also figure in *games,* although of course they are rights of a conceptually different kind from moral rights such as the right to liberty. However, the essence of rights in games as elsewhere consists in their being entitlements. In Australian Rules football players have the right to place-kick after a mark or free kick; and it is clearly meaningful and correct to assert that the player who doesn't know how to place-kick, and the player who never marks the ball nor receives a free kick, enjoy the right as fully as the skilful place-kick who receives many free kicks. The right consists in an entitlement, which, if denied, would provide the player with grounds for making demands and claims on others, viz., the umpire, which may or may not succeed. It is to misconstrue rights in games to construe them as the claims to which they may or may not give rise. It is a mistake comparable with that against which Hart argues, of construing rules of games as directions to scorers.[6]

If we look at *moral rights,* in particular at what we intend to claim when we claim a right, we find

here too that a right is an entitlement. It may be an entitlement to do, to demand, to enjoy, to be, to have done for us. Rights may be rights to act, to exist, to enjoy, to demand. We speak of rights as being *possessed, exercised,* and *enjoyed.* In these respects there is an affinity between our talk about rights and our talk about capacities, powers, and the like, and a distinct contrast with talk about claims, for we *make* claims but do not possess, exercise, or enjoy them. But, since a right may exist and be possessed in the absence of the relevant power or capacity, rights are distinct from powers. I possess the rights to life, liberty and happiness; my possession of these rights means that I am entitled to live, to act freely without interference, and be unimpeded in my search for happiness.

It is often argued that rights are conceptually linked with *rules.* Benn and Peters, for instance, state: "To say that X has a right to £5 is to imply that there is a rule which, when applied to the case of X and some other person Y, imposes on Y a duty to pay X £5 if X so chooses. Without the possibility of the correlative duty resting somewhere, the attribution of the right to X would be meaningless."[7] Our foregoing consideration of legal rights suggests that this is not the case. We have legal rights in the absence of legal rules, and the way in which rules are relevant to legal rights varies. Sometimes the rule explicitly denies a right, other rules confer rights, other rules sustain rights which are rule-grounded only in the very weakened sense that 'what is not forbidden in our legal system is permitted' may be said to be itself a rule of sorts. However, it is not a rule in the same sense or senses of 'rule' as that in which criminal and power-conferring laws are rules. With rights as members of organizations, rules figure prominently, but rights may nonetheless exist which are not grounded on rules. There may be no rule concerning private worship in the church building on weekdays, but in the absence of a rule forbidding it, and even in the absence of a general rule stating that what is not forbidden is permitted, the member may reasonably claim the right to worship privately in the church each day. He could offer good reasons, not in terms of some rule, but in terms of the purpose of the building and the character of the religious organization. The same is true of moral rights. We do not always have to point to a rule of some sort to show that we have a moral right. A claim to a right such as the right to life may be supported by a large variety of kinds of reasons. Indeed, the characteristic reasons appropriate as reasons in support of moral rights seem not to be reasons in terms of rules.

We speak of our rights as being *rights to*—as in the rights to life, liberty and happiness—not as *rights against,* as has so often mistakenly been claimed. Special rights are sometimes against specific individuals or institutions—e.g. rights created by promises, contracts, etc. The wife has rights against the husband, the creditor against the debtor, but these are special, nongeneral rights which differ from the characteristic cases of general rights, where the right is simply a right to (i.e. an entitlement to)—e.g. of the man to marry the woman of his choice. It is strangely artificial to suggest that this is a right against someone or some thing. Against whom or what is it a right? My right to life is not a right against anyone. It is *my* right and by virtue of it, it is normally permissible for me to sustain my life in the face of obstacles. It does give rise to rights against others *in the sense* that others have or may come to have duties to refrain from killing me, but it is essentially a right of mine, not an infinite list of claims, hypothetical and actual, against an infinite number of actual, potential, and as yet nonexistent human beings. Even non-moral rights such as legal rights, rights as a member of a club, rights in games, are not typically rights against but rights to have, to do, to be, to have done for us. My legal right to drive a car, having passed a test for a licence and paid the appropriate fee, is a right to do certain things, not a right against the police, magistrates, and other officials. Similarly, the right of the tennis club member to play on the club courts is a right to play, not a right against some vague group of potential or possible obstructors. Similarly, the right of the football player to place-kick if he so chooses is a right to do just that. It is not a right against his opponent or against the umpire. And if it is a right by virtue of his having taken a mark it is especially hard to see against whom it might be said to be.

Rights are entitlements to do, have, enjoy or have done. That it is a serious error to construe general rights as rights against rather than rights to or as entitlements, is confirmed by considera-

tion of people who live in isolation. It is meaningful to speak of the hermit on an isolated island as having rights to do or have certain things, but it would be strange to speak of him as having rights against others. His rights may give rise to rights against others, but the right—e.g. to live—is not primarily against others. The infliction of avoidable suffering on animals is obviously *prima facie* wrong, but the fact that a person possesses the right to life, whether he be a hermit or not, justifies him in killing animals—and in the process causing them to suffer—in order to sustain himself. His right to life is inaptly described in such a situation as a right against the animals he kills. Many, although not myself, would wish to argue that there is no right to suicide. Clearly it is not *prima facie* absurd so to argue. Yet if there is no such right, the hermit would not be entitled to take his own life, although he would have rights to do other things.

The difficulties of "rights against" talk, and of any attempt to write into the concept of a right, that it must be against someone, are evident if we consider the extreme case of the last person in the universe, who alone survives the nuclear war. Imagine that the last person is a woman capable of reproducing by artificial insemination, a large sperm bank having also survived. I suggest that talk about rights would have real application in such a situation. Suppose the woman had good reason to believe that if she reproduced, her off-spring would be monsters, defectives, imbeciles, doomed to life-long suffering. In such a case she would have to conclude that she did not possess the right to reproduce. If she had every reason to believe that her off-spring would be healthy, she would conclude that she had the right to reproduce, unless of course she regarded artificial insemination as wrong. This suggests that the actual existence of other human beings is irrelevant to whether rights may or may not be possessed. Clearly *the possible existence* of other human beings is more than adequate as a basis for talk about rights to have point. And, as I argued earlier, even this seems not to be necessary.

Other difficulties of "rights against" talk could be noted—e.g. the accounts it involves of what it is to lack a right, the difficulty of *possessing* rights against, where possession by us of the right depends on the existence of others. But enough has already been said to permit us to dismiss this sort of account, which seems to be adopted, where it is adopted, to fit in with a predetermined ethical theory.

So far I have spoken of rights, whether they be legal, moral, social, institutional, or in games, as essentially entitlements of some sort; yet obviously they are different sorts of entitlements, such that we should describe them as being conceptually different from one another. The concept of a legal right is a different concept from that of a right in a game, and both are different from rights which are created by membership of a club. Similarly, although all moral rights are entitlements, there are conceptual differences between various of the rights which may be characterized as moral rights, which makes it desirable to distinguish different *concepts* of moral rights, and to speak of legal, moral, social, etc. rights as rights of different *kinds*.

It is a commonplace for political philosophers to offer *the* definition of a moral right. Some such definitions were indicated at the outset. Elsewhere, in a brief discussion of the nature and grounds of rights, I have similarly assumed that there is only one concept and only one definition of a right.[8] In fact, if we look at the sorts of rights that are claimed as moral rights, at actual theories about rights, and at ordinary discourse, we find that there are at least four distinct concepts of moral rights, all of which are to be explained as entitlements.

(a) There is *the negative concept* of a right apparent in some of Locke's arguments for rights, particularly for the rights to life and liberty.[9] To have a negative right to X is for it not to be wrong for us to do or have X and for other people to lack the right or have a duty not to interfere; and here the duty is obviously not a duty against us. For example, to have a right to life of this kind, would be for it to be right (or not wrong) for us to sustain ourselves, and for others to be obliged not to take our lives or at least not to be entitled to deprive us of our lives. This concept of a right lends itself most easily to modification to permit talk about animal rights, but it will be argued later that such modification is not in order as animals cannot be possessors of rights. Negative rights are not simply rights by analogy, nor are negative rights, rights in a sense parasitic on some other concept of a right. It is

logically possible that all rights be of this negative character. A community which conceived of all rights as being of this kind would obviously be said to have grasped the concept of a right, although it would not have grasped the richest and fullest concept of a right. (It is still possible to speak of such negative rights as being possessed, but the sense of 'possessed' is weaker than in the other cases.)

(b) There is also *the positive concept* of a right such that to have a right is to have a moral authority or entitlement to act in a certain way. This concept is often elucidated in terms of legitimate claims on others, but such accounts obviously will not do, for we explain and justify our claim on others in terms of having a right, i.e. in terms of our having a positive moral entitlement, to act in a certain way. It is this that entitles us to demand freedom from interference. The rights for which Thomists argue on the basis of the natural law are of this kind. e.g. rights to seek the truth, to rear one's offspring, to preserve oneself.

(c) There is a more positive, fuller concept which we may characterize as *the welfare concept* of a right such that a right is not merely a moral entitlement to do or to have, but also an entitlement to the efforts of others or to make demands on others to aid and promote our seeking after or enjoyment of some good. Thus, in terms of this welfare concept of a right, it is written into the concept that the conditions for its enjoyment be promoted. Such a concept underlies many arguments for welfare legislation, for many such arguments proceed by maintaining that respect for human rights involves removing not simply *man-made* obstacles but also *natural* hindrances and impediments to the enjoyment of some power or good. For example, many demands for conditions to promote the enjoyment of the rights to health, life, etc., proceed from such a welfare concept of a right. Indeed, if such a concept is denied significance, a great deal of controversy about rights in this century becomes meaningless.

(d) There are also *special rights* noted above as admitting of being described as rights against, and which spring from duties to particular individuals. The right of the creditor to repayment of his loan on the due date is a right or entitlement of this kind.

The above distinctions between different concepts of rights are obviously relevant to the vexed question of the relation between *rights and duties*. And, of course, the question of the relation between rights and duties raises many important issues, not the least that concerning who or what may be the possessor of rights. It is commonly argued that there is a close conceptual connexion between rights and duties. To consider in what respects this is so. (i) Where the right is of type (*a*), its existence depends in part on there being a duty on others not to interfere *or* on others lacking a right of type (*b*) to interfere. Where the right is of type (*b*) A's right creates actual and potential duties for others and for potential and hypothetical others. To explain: My right to liberty creates no duty for the Hottentot or the Eskimo, for they cannot interfere with me and do not know of my existence. If they could come to interfere, my right would constitute a ground for the duty not to interfere. Similarly with infants. My rights do not create duties for them unless and until they become full moral agents and have some relationship or connexion with me, when my right causes them to have duties not to interfere. Similarly with those as yet unborn. (ii) Rights of type (*c*) obviously give rise to duties and to potential duties. If the blind man whose sight can be restored has a right to sight (as part of the right to health) he has a right to our efforts on his behalf; and we have a duty to make the relevant effort. Such rights seem also to be possessed by those who are not full moral agents, for instances, by infants, curable lunatics, idiots, etc. If a minimal I.Q. idiot could be cured by a pill as cheap as an aspirin, it would be reasonable to claim that he has a right to the necessary treatment and that we have a duty to see that it is made available to him. (iii) Where the right is of type (*d*), i.e. a special right against another, the right implies a duty in the person against whom it is held. The husband of the wife who has promised to obey him has a right to her obedience, and she the duty to obey. In this case the duty is primary. It springs from the wife's promise and the right is created by the promise and the duty to keep the promise. (iv) Duties and rights. To have a duty is to have a right. One has the right to do what is necessary for the fulfilment of one's duty. But to have a duty is not necessarily for another to have a right. Ross notes the case of duties to animals, and other duties could be cited.[10] For example, the duty to perfect one's talents is not a duty against oneself, nor is it a duty to one's self. It is simply a duty and creates no rights in others. Similarly with the duty to maximize good. The last person in the universe would have the duty to maximize good and to produce other human beings if this were a means to or part of maximizing good; but there would be no one with a right resulting from the duty. The duty of the artist to produce good and not slovenly paintings does not give to others the right to demand of the artist that he produce the best paintings of which he is capable. Again, I may have a duty to the state, e.g. to pay my income tax; but the sense in which the state might be said to have a right to my tax is distinct from the sense of 'right' in which we speak of moral rights as possessed by individuals. The state cannot be the possessor of the sorts of rights human beings may possess. Yet it may be the object of duties. Further, not all duties to the state or to other institutions create these rights in the institutions. It does not follow that, because the Church member has a duty to give generously to his Church, the Church has a right to his gifts.[11] In brief: When a right is attributed, we cannot always significantly ask 'Who has the corresponding duties?' And, when a duty is postulated, we cannot always find someone who possesses a corresponding right.

B. WHO OR WHAT ARE LOGICALLY POSSIBLE POSSESSORS OF RIGHTS?

The issue as to who or what may be a possessor of rights is not simply a matter of academic, conceptual interest. Obviously, important conclusions follow from any answer. If, for instance, it is determined that gravely mentally defective human beings and monsters born of human parents are not the kinds of beings who may possess rights, this bears on how we may treat them. It does not settle such questions as to whether it is right to kill them if they are a burden or if they are enduring pointless suffering, but it does bear in an important way on such questions. Even if such beings cannot be possessors of rights it might still be wrong to kill them, but the case against killing those who endure pain is obviously easier to set out if they can be shown to be capable of possessing rights and in fact possess rights. Similarly, important conclusions follow from the question as to whether animals have rights. If they do, as Salt argued, it would seem an illegitimate invasion of animal rights to kill and eat them, if, as seems to be the case, we can sustain ourselves without killing animals.[12] If animals have rights, the case for vegetarianism is *prima facie* very strong, and is comparable with the case against cannibalism.

These issues, then, are not without importance, but they present very considerable difficulties. If we follow our unreflective moral consciousness we find ourselves drawn strongly to conclusions which seem radically inconsistent with one another; yet if we attempt to reason to a conclusion it is extremely difficult even to begin to set out an argument, let alone develop a carefully worked out, convincing argument in favour of one conclusion rather than another. And, whilst our analysis of the concept of a right takes us some way—it excludes some possibilities and some arguments—it seems on the face of it to leave open a very large number of possibilities.

Although an important and difficult problem, this is one to which few theorists have applied themselves with the attention and critical scrutiny which might be expected in such an important issue. Ross, Plamenatz and Green are typical of thinkers in this area. Ross notes difficulties in respect of idiots, infants and animals, but seems quietly to forget to deal with them, and offers his conclusions without the support of reasons. Plamenatz seems simply to legislate. He asserts that animals do have rights, and hence states that any definition of rights must be such as to admit that animals do have rights. However, no argument is offered to support the view. T. H. Green does address himself to the problem to the extent of claiming that we have rights only as members of a community, that rights involve mutual recognition, and that they can therefore only be possessed by moral persons, i.e. rational beings. However, he offers only very general, sketchy arguments for these contentions, and seems to fail to realize that besides excluding animals as possible possessors of rights, they exclude infants, imbeciles, and other mentally defective human beings. Ritchie perhaps comes closest to offering an argument

when he notes the difficultes which arise if animals are attributed rights. If animals have rights, the cat invades the right of the mouse, the tiger of the cow, etc. Should we restrict the liberty of the cat and of the tiger out of respect for the rights of the mouse and the cow? And should we, out of respect for the rights of animals, allow parasites to continue to inhabit us if they do not have seriously deleterious effects on our health? Plamenatz seeks a way out of such difficulties, whilst at the same time allowing that animals have rights, by claiming that rights are *rights against rational beings,* hence the cow has no rights against the tiger but only against human beings. This obviously will not do, for the reasons noted above, namely, that rights are not primarily rights against but rights to. They may rationally be demanded only of rational beings, for the obvious reason that only rational beings are capable of complying with the demands, but this does not mean that the tiger is not invading the rights of the cow when he kills it. The absurdity of the conclusions which follow from the admission of animal rights may, as Ritchie claims, *suggest* that animals cannot be possessors of rights, but it does not *establish* that this is so.

The general tendency has been to maintain that free agents and potential free agents have rights, with idiots, and all born of human parents being treated as potentially free agents, although many are obviously not such. Those who have claimed that animals have rights have rarely explained whether they mean all animals; equally seriously, they seem not to explain why they think some or all sentient beings have rights, and why not all animate objects and even perhaps things. The unspoken premiss seems to be either that where there is a possibility of "action" of some sort there is the possibility of rights, or that where there is a possibility of pain, there is the possibility of possession of rights. But the reasons underlying the assumption are not evident. Clearly, if lower animals, especially parasitic animals such as the flea, are allowed to be capable of possessing rights, argument is needed to show why such animals, and not all animate objects, e.g. a beautiful oak or mountain ash, can possess rights. If it were allowed that all sentient beings and all animate objects possess some rights—e.g. to life—why, it might be asked, should rights be denied of inanimate things?

Might not beautiful works of art, paintings of Raphael and Leonardo da Vinci also have a right to continued existence? Argument is needed here, yet argument is notably lacking. Where it is to be found, it is of the very unconvincing kind offered by Thomists, that rational beings, being subject to the natural law, have rights, since rights are grounded on the natural law; that infants, lunatics, idiots have rights and are subject to natural law since they are rational beings. Obviously, even if the theory of natural law could be established—and this I should wish to deny—infants, lunatics and idiots are not subject to it as rational agents any more than is an intelligent dog or ape. The natural law is law, and is binding on men because and in so far as it is promulgated through reason. It is not promulgated to infants, idiots and certain lunatics. And, whilst it might be argued that it is promulgated potentially to infants, and hypothetically to idiots, potential and hypothetical promulgation are not promulgation, and to be a potential or a hypothetical possessor of rights is not to be a possessor of potential or hypothetical rights, nor of actual rights.

To consider what can be done towards reaching an answer, I have argued that rights are entitlements to do, have, enjoy, or have done for us, and not claims or powers. An obvious answer to the question 'Who may possess entitlements?' is 'Free moral agents'. They obviously may and do possess and claim entitlements of the sorts claimed in rights to life, liberty and health. However, it is unduly and arbitrarily to narrow and limit the field of possible possessors of rights to limit it to free moral agents. Consider the lunatic who has completely lost his grip on the world, who is devoid of all free choice, and who thinks (in so far as he can be said to think) that he is a cabbage. If he could be treated and made sane by being given a drug costing 1/-, would it not be meaningful to claim that he has a right to the drug, that others ought to exert themselves to respect his rights to secure his enjoyment of his rights? Here the difficulty lies in distinguishing an attribution of a duty and an attribution of a right or entitlement. Clearly others would have a duty towards the lunatic, hence, on that account, he might in some sort of analogous sense be said to have a right. However, I suggest that we should be inclined to assert that he can have and

has rights in a fuller, more literal sense. Compare him with the blind, rational, free agent who can equally be cured of his blindness, but not by his own efforts. Each would be said to have a right to the necessary treatment; and when we attribute the right to the one, we seem to be using language in the same meaningful way as when attributing a right to the other. We are saying that each is entitled or has an entitlement to the efforts of others for their own good. This suggests that, although free agents may possess rights, the test of who or what can be a possessor of a right or an entitlement is not that of freedom or rationality. A lunatic can be a possessor of an entitlement, of kinds (a) and (c). Further, the lunatic does not have to be one capable of attaining free will, i.e. to be a potential or hypothetical free agent. It is not *prima facie* absurd to claim that an incurable lunatic is entitled to decent treatment. His relatives can reasonably claim that his rights be respected, and if he is regularly being beaten up by a sadistic attendant, they can properly claim that his rights are being denied. So too with infants. There seems to be no logical paradox in asserting that the infant is entitled to care and nurture from his parents. This is because an entitlement does not have to admit of being demanded by its possessor any more than does a legitimate claim. Entitlements may be demanded (and claims made) by proxies on behalf of the holder of the entitlement. Logically we do not have to be able to say that we are entitled, to be entitled. The cases of the infant and lunatic suggest this, but obviously there are limits to those who/which may logically be possessors of entitlements.

Here it is useful to consider legal rights and entitlements in respect of animals. Legal claims may be made on behalf of animals, e.g. against trustees who embezzle money left for the care of a cat. In such cases we should be disinclined to speak of the courts upholding the legal rights of the cat. Our uneasiness, and the grounds for our uneasiness, can be brought out by the following examples. Suppose that, as a result of deliberate legal enactment, the kangaroo came to be accorded something like the privileged position of the cow in India, the kangaroo having full rights of movement, on the roads, on private property, etc. I suggest that we should be reluctant to speak of the legal rights of kangaroos. This is clear from our manner of speaking of native birds and animals in sanctuaries today. We speak of our being obliged to leave them alone, not of them as having legal rights, nor of them as being legally entitled to be left alone. The law confers duties on us, not rights in the animals. This is confirmed by another possible group of cases, of legal systems in which animals which kill men are tried, and if found guilty, executed. If an animal is given an unfair trial under such a system and its legal representative demands a new trial, he could perhaps say that the animal had not received its legal rights (lawyers seem inclined to speak in this way) but it seems more accurate and less misleading simply to say that the law has not been properly observed in the original trial. Compare with a trial of a man.

Why we are reluctant to speak of the legal rights of animals, even under such legal systems, becomes clearer if we consider *things,* and why things cannot have legal rights. Things do not have legal rights in our legal system, but not because this is a peculiarity of our legal system. It is because anything which might seem to come close to a thing having legal rights is not so described. A man can leave his money to preserve a building, a park, etc., and appoint trustees, but we do not say of the trustees who embezzle the money that they have failed to respect the legal rights of the building or gardens they were appointed to care for. (Similarly with legal systems where things such as cars or locomotives are given trials before being destroyed when guilty of killing men.) The reasons for this seem to be two. First, things such as parks, buildings, paintings, etc., do not have *interests* in the strict sense of interests, such that we could literally speak of the trustees caring for their interests. The trustees care for the thing, not for the interests of the thing. Secondly, and partly for this reason, the trustees could hardly be said to be the representatives of the thing. Here we might speak of them as custodians, etc.

What holds in respect of legal rights seems also to hold of moral rights. Moral rights can be possessed by beings who can claim them, and by those who can have them claimed on their behalf by others and whose interests are violated or disregarded if the rights are not respected. The concept of interests which is so important here is an obscure and elusive one. Interests are distinct from welfare, and are more inclusive in certain respects—usually what is dictated by concern for a man's welfare is in his interests. However, interests suggest much more than that which is indicated by the person's welfare. They suggest that which is or ought to be or which would be of *concern* to the person/being. It is partly for this reason—because the concept of interests has this evaluative-prescriptive overtone—that we decline to speak of the interests of animals, and speak rather of their welfare.

That the possibility of possessing rights is limited in this way is confirmed by the very fact that we speak of rights as being *possessed and enjoyed.* A right cannot not be possessed by someone; hence, only beings which can possess things can possess rights. My right to life is mine; I possess it. It is as much mine as any of my possessions—indeed more so—for I possess them by virtue of my rights. It is true that I may possess rights and not know or enjoy my possession of them. Thus, whilst rights must be possessed by a possessor, they need not be enjoyed. All we can say is that they may admit of enjoyment by their possessors.

All these considerations seem to exclude the lower animals in a decisive way, and the higher animals in a less decisive but still fairly conclusive way as possible possessors of rights. (Consider 'possess' in its literal use. Can a horse possess anything, e.g. its stable, its rug, in a literal sense of 'possess'?) It might, however, be argued that animals can possess special rights, e.g. rights arising out of relations such as the owner's "debt of gratitude" to the animal for special services. Consider the blind man and his guide dog who repeatedly saves his life. The difficulty that rights are possessed and that animals cannot possess things remains; and, in any case, the animal's special services are more naturally described as creating special duties rather than as giving rise to entitlements in the animal.

It would seem to follow from all this that monsters born of human parents whose level of existence falls far short of that of the highest animals would also seem not to be possible possessors of rights. However, two qualifications may usefully be made here. Animals, or at least the higher animals, may usefully be said to have *rights by analogy.* We have duties involving them, and these duties might be said to create rights by analogy. (The latter are not the same as rights in sense (*a*), for a right by analogy is not an entitlement, whereas a negative right is such; and the difference leads to important implications.) With those born of human parents, even the most inferior beings, it may be *a useful lie* to attribute rights where they are not and cannot be possessed, since to deny the very inferior beings born of human parents rights, opens the way to a dangerous slide. But whether useful or not, it is a lie or a mistake to attribute rights or the possibility of rights to such beings. More difficult are the cases of the infant, lunatic, etc. As indicated earlier, we do attribute rights and interests to infants, lunatics, and even to incurable lunatics. Part of the reason for this is the thought that such beings, unlike the congenital idiot, etc., are possibly potential possessors of interests. Hence, until it is clear that they can never really be said to have interests, we treat them as if they do. Also relevant is the fact that even a mentally defective human being —e.g. an imbecile, or a lunatic with periods of sanity—may literally demand some rights and possess others and generally be attributed interests in a literal sense.

I have not considered theories to the effect that possessors of immortal souls, and only such, are logically possible possessors of rights. This is because those who argue that possessors of immortal souls possess rights—and that animals do not—usually make their claim a factual and not a logical one. They argue that this is in fact the case, and do not concern themselves with the issue as to whether it is logically possible for a being without an immortal soul to possess rights. In any case, there is a quick answer to any such contention, namely, that it is possible to deny that man has an immortal soul, without being logically impelled to deny that he may possess rights.

NOTES

1. D. G. Ritchie, *Natural Rights,* London, 1894, pp. 78–9. The emphasis on the key word in this and subsequent definitions is mine.

2. J. A. Ryan and F. J. Boland, *Catholic Principles of Politics,* New York, 1940, p. 13.

3. T. H. Green, *Lectures on the Principles of Political Obligation,* London, 1941. p. 207.

4. J. P. Plamenatz, *Consent, Freedom and Political Obligation,* Oxford, 1938, p. 82. Plamenatz has since rejected this definition in favour of the definition, "A man (or an animal) has a right whenever other men ought not to prevent him doing what he wants or refuse some service he asks for or needs" (Ar. Soc. Suppl. Vol. XXIV (1950), p. 75).

5. L. J. Cohen, "H. L. A. Hart, *The Concept of Law,*" *Mind,* LXXI (1962), pp. 345–412, esp. pp. 396–7.

6. H. L. A. Hart, *The Concept of Law,* Oxford, 1961. See, e.g., p. 40.

7. S. I. Benn and R. S. Peters, *Social Principles and the Democratic State,* London, 1959, p. 83.

8. "The State and Evil," *Ethics,* LXIX, 3 (April 1959), p. 182.

9. *Civil Government,* Bk. 2, ch. 2.

10. W. D. Ross, *The Right and The Good,* Oxford, 1930, ch. 2, appendix 1.

11. The notion of *a duty to* needs examination. We often speak of duties to when we really mean duties concerning, involving, etc., as in talk about duties to oneself. However, we do have duties which are properly described as duties to —e.g. a duty of gratitude to our benefactor, a duty to our creditor, a duty of fidelity to one's spouse, a duty of loyalty to one's country. However, it is difficult to see what the principle is that leads us to speak of such duties as "duties to." With things, and even with animals, we seem to speak of duties as involving them, rather than as being to them. If institutions such as the State and the Church may be objects of duties to, why not things and animals? Yet the duty to preserve a great painting (even if the duty of the last person in the universe) is not a duty *to* the painting. Similarly with animals. If I don't feed my cat, I can be reproached as not having done what I ought and as having no right to treat it as I did, but we should be disinclined to speak of my duty to my cat, or to justify such remarks by talk about its right to a square meal a day. Rather, we should speak of duties not to be cruel, etc.; by contrast, if parents neglected their offspring, allusions to their duties *to* their children would be made quickly and naturally.

12. H. S. Salt, *Animal Rights,* London, 1892.

23. THE NATURE AND VALUE OF RIGHTS

Joel Feinberg

1

I would like to begin by conducting a thought experiment. Try to imagine Nowheresville—a world very much like our own except that no one, or hardly any one (the qualification is not important), has *rights*. If this flaw makes Nowheresville too ugly to hold very long in contemplation, we can make it as pretty as we wish in other moral respects. We can, for example, make the human beings in it as attractive and virtuous as possible without taxing our conceptions of the limits of human nature. In particular, let the virtues of moral sensibility flourish. Fill this imagined world with as much benevolence, compassion, sympathy, and pity as it will conveniently hold without strain. Now we can imagine people helping one another from compassionate motives merely, quite as much or even more than they do in our actual world from a variety of more complicated motives.

This picture, pleasant as it is in some respects, would hardly have satisfied Immanuel Kant. Benevolently motivated actions do good, Kant admitted, and therefore are better, *ceteris paribus,* than malevolently motivated actions; but no action can have supreme kind of worth—what Kant called "moral worth"—unless its whole motivating power derives from the thought that it is *required by duty.* Accordingly, let us try to make Nowheresville more appealing to Kant by introducing the idea of duty into it, and letting the sense of duty be a sufficient motive for many beneficent and honorable actions. But doesn't this bring our original thought experiment to an abortive conclusion? If duties are permitted entry into Nowheresville, are not rights necessarily smuggled in along with them?

The question is well-asked, and requires here a brief digression so that we might consider the so-called "doctrine of the logical correlativity of rights and duties." This is the doctrine that (i) all duties entail other people's rights and (ii) all rights entail other people's duties. Only the first part of the doctrine, the alleged entailment from duties to rights, need concern us here. Is this part of the doctrine correct? It should not be surprising that my answer is: "In a sense yes and in a sense no." Etymologically, the word "duty" is associated with actions that are *due* someone else, the payments of debts *to* creditors, the keeping of agreements with promises, the payment of club dues, or legal fees, or tariff levies to appropriate authorities or their representatives. In this original sense of "duty," all duties are correlated with the rights of those *to* whom the duty is owed. On the other hand, there seem to be numerous classes of duties, both of a legal and non-legal kind, that are *not* logically correlated with the rights of other persons. This seems to be a consequence of the fact that the word "duty" has come to be used for *any* action understood to be *required,* whether by the rights of others, or by law, or by higher authority, or by conscience, or whatever. When the notion of requirement is in clear focus it is likely to seem the only element in the idea of duty that is essential, and the other component notion—that a duty is something *due* someone else—drops off. Thus, in this widespread but derivative usage, "duty" tends to be used for any action we feel we *must* (for whatever reason) do. It comes, in short, to be a term of moral modality merely; and it is no wonder that the first thesis of the logical correlativity doctrine often fails.

From Joel Feinberg, "The Nature and Value of Rights," *Journal of Value Inquiry,* Vol. IV, No. 4, Winter, 1970, pp. 243–57. Reprinted by permission of the author and the *Journal of Value Inquiry.*

Let us then introduce duties into No-wheresville, but only in the sense of actions that are, or are believed to be, morally mandatory, but not in the older sense of actions that are due others and can be claimed by others as their right. Nowheresville now can have duties of the sort imposed by positive law. A legal duty is not something we are implored or advised to do merely; it is something the law, or an authority under the law, *requires* us to do whether we want to or not, under pain of penalty. When traffic lights turn red, however, there is no determinate person who can plausibly be said to claim our stopping as his due, so that the motorist owes it to *him* to stop, in the way a debtor owes it to his creditor to pay. In our own actual world, of course, we sometimes owe it to our *fellow motorists* to stop; but that kind of right-correlated duty does not exist in Nowheresville. There, motorists "owe" obedience to the Law, but they owe nothing to one another. When they collide, no matter who is at fault, no one is morally accountable to anyone else, and no one has any sound grievance or "right to complain."

When we leave legal contexts to consider moral obligations and other extra-legal duties, a greater variety of duties-without-correlative-rights present themselves. Duties of charity, for example, require us to contribute to one or another of a large number of eligible recipients, no one of whom can claim our contribution from us as his due. Charitable contributions are more like gratuitous services, favors, and gifts than like repayments of debts or reparations; and yet we do have duties to be charitable. Many persons, moreover, in our actual world believe that they are required by their own consciences to do more than that "duty" that *can* be demanded of them by their prospective beneficiaries. I have quoted elsewhere the citation from H. B. Acton of a character in a Malraux novel who "gave all his supply of poison to his fellow prisoners to enable them by suicide to escape the burning alive which was to be their fate and his." This man, Acton adds, "probably did not think that [the others] had more of a right to the poison than he had, though he thought it his duty to give it to them."[1] I am sure that there are many actual examples, less dramatically heroic than this fictional one, of persons who believe, rightly or wrongly, that they *must do* something (hence the word "duty") for another person in excess of what that person can appropriately demand of him (hence the absence of "right").

Now the digression is over and we can return to Nowheresville and summarize what we have put in it thus far. We now find spontaneous benevolence in somewhat larger degree than in our actual world, and also the acknowledged existence of duties of obedience, duties of charity, and duties imposed by exacting private consciences, and also, let us suppose, a degree of conscientiousness in respect to those duties somewhat in excess of what is to be found in our actual world. I doubt that Kant would be fully satisfied with Nowheresville even now that duty and respect for law and authority have been added to it; but I feel certain that he would regard their addition at least as an improvement. I will now introduce two further moral practices into Nowheresville that will make that world very little more appealing to Kant, but will make it appear more familiar to us. These are the practices connected with the notions of *personal desert* and what I call a *sovereign monopoly of rights*.

When a person is said to deserve something good from us what is meant in part is that there would be a certain propriety in our giving that good thing to him in virtue of the kind of person he is, perhaps, or more likely, in virtue of some specific thing he has done. The propriety involved here is a much weaker kind than that which derives from our having promised him the good thing or from his having qualified for it by satisfying the well-advertised conditions of some public rule. In the latter case he could be said not merely to deserve the good thing but also to have a *right* to it, that is to be in a position to demand it as his due; and of course we will not have that sort of thing in Nowheresville. That weaker kind of propriety which is mere desert is simply a kind of *fittingness* between one party's character or action and another party's favorable response, much like that between humor and laughter, or good performance and applause.

The following seems to be the origin of the idea of deserving good or bad treatment from others: A master or lord was under no obligation to reward his servant for especially good service; still a master might naturally feel that there would be a special fittingness in giving a gratuitous reward as a grateful response to the good service (or conversely imposing a penalty for bad service). Such an act while surely fitting and proper was entirely supererogatory. The fitting response in turn from the rewarded servant should be gratitude. If the deserved reward had not been given him he should have had no complaint, since he only *deserved* the reward, as opposed to having a *right* to it, or a ground for claiming it as his due.

The idea of desert has evolved a good bit away from its beginnings by now, but nevertheless, it seems clearly to be one of those words J. L. Austin said "never entirely forget their pasts."[2] Today servants qualify for their wages by doing their agreed upon chores, no more and no less. If their wages are not forthcoming, their contractual rights have been violated and they can make legal claim to the money that is their due. If they do less than they agreed to do, however, their employers may "dock" them, by paying them proportionately less than the agreed upon fee. This is all a matter of right. But if the servant does a splendid job, above and beyond his minimal contractual duties, the employer is under no further obligation to reward him, for this was not agreed upon, even tacitly, in advance. The additional service was all the servant's idea and done entirely on his own. Nevertheless, the morally sensitive employer may feel that it would be exceptionally appropriate for him to respond, freely on *his* own, to the servant's meritorious service, with a reward. The employee cannot demand it as his due, but he will happily accept it, with gratitude, as a fitting response to his desert.

In our age of organized labor, even this picture is now archaic; for almost every kind of exchange of service is governed by hard bargained contracts so that even bonuses can sometimes be demanded as a matter of right, and nothing is given for nothing on either side of the bargaining table. And perhaps that is a good thing; for consider an anachoronistic instance of the earlier kind of practice that survives, at least as a matter of form, in the quaint old practice of "tipping." The tip was originally conceived as a reward that has to be earned by "zealous service." It is not something to be taken for granted as a standard response to *any* service. That is to say that its payment is a *"gratuity,"* not a discharge of obligation, but something given apart from, or in addition to, anything the recipient

can expect as a matter of right. That is what tipping originally meant at any rate, and tips are still referred to as "gratuities" in the tax forms. But try to explain all that to a New York cab driver! If he has *earned* his gratuity, by God, he has it coming, and there had better be sufficient acknowledgement of his desert or he'll give you a piece of his mind! I'm not generally prone to defend New York cab drivers, but they do have a point here. There is the making of a paradox in the queerly unstable concept of an "earned gratuity." One can understand how "desert" in the weak sense of "propriety" or "mere fittingness" tends to generate a stronger sense in which desert is itself the ground for a claim of right.

In Nowheresville, nevertheless, we will have only the original weak kind of desert. Indeed, it will be impossible to keep this idea out if we allow such practices as teachers grading students, judges awarding prizes, and servants serving benevolent but class-conscious masters. Nowheresville is a reasonably good world in many ways, and its teachers, judges, and masters will generally try to give students, contestants, and servants the grades, prizes, and rewards they deserve. For this the recipients will be grateful; but they will never think to complain, or even feel aggrieved, when expected responses to desert fail. The masters, judges, and teachers don't *have* to do good things, after all, for *anyone.* One should be happy that they *ever* treat us well, and not grumble over their occasional lapses. Their hoped for responses, after all, are *gratuities,* and there is no wrong in the omission of what is merely gratuitous. Such is the response of persons who have no concept of *rights,* even persons who are proud of their own deserts.[3]

Surely, one might ask, rights have to come in somewhere, if we are to have even moderately complex forms of social organization. Without rules that confer rights and impose obligations, how can we have ownership of property, bargains and deals, promises and contracts, appointments and loans, marriages and partnerships? Very well, let us introduce all of these social and economic practices into Nowheresville, but *with one big twist.* With them I should like to introduce the curious notion of a "sovereign right-monopoly." You will recall that the subjects in Hobbes's *Leviathan* had no rights whatever against their sovereign. He could do as he liked with them, even gratuitously harm them, but this gave them no valid grievance against him. The sovereign, to be sure, had a certain duty to treat his subjects well, but this duty was owed not to the subjects directly, but to God, just as we might have a duty to a person to treat his property well, but of course no duty to the property itself but only to its owner. Thus, while the sovereign was quite capable of *harming* his subjects, he could commit no wrong against them that they could complain about, since they had no prior claims against his conduct. The only party *wronged* by the sovereign's mistreatment of his subjects was God, the supreme lawmaker. Thus, in repenting cruelty to his subjects, the sovereign might say to God, as David did after killing Uriah, "to Thee only have I sinned."[4]

Even in the *Leviathan,* however, ordinary people had ordinary rights *against one another.* They played roles, occupied offices, made agreements, and signed contracts. In a genuine "sovereign right-monopoly," as I shall be using that phrase, they will do all those things too, and thus incur genuine obligations toward one another; but the obligations (here is the twist) will not be owed directly *to* promisees, creditors, parents, and the like, but rather to God alone, or to the members of some elite, or to a single sovereign under God. Hence, the rights correlative to the obligations that derive from these transactions are all owned by some "outside" authority.

As far as I know, no philosopher has ever suggested that even our role and contract obligations (in this, our actual world) are all owed directly to a divine intermediary; but some theologians have approached such extreme moral occasionalism. I have in mind the familiar phrase in certain widely distributed religious tracts that "it takes three to marry," which suggests that marital vows are not made between bride and groom directly but between each spouse and God, so that if one breaks his vow, the other cannot rightly complain of being wronged, since only God could have claimed performance of the marital duties as his *own* due; and hence God alone had a claim-right violated by non-performance. If John breaks his vow to God, he might then properly repent in the words of David: "To Thee only have I sinned."

In our actual world, very few spouses conceive of their mutual obligations in this way; but their small children, at a certain stage in their moral upbringing, are likely to feel precisely this way toward *their* mutual obligations. If Billy kicks Bobby and is punished by Daddy, he may come to feel contrition for his naughtiness induced by his painful estrangement from the loved parent. He may then be happy to make amends and sincere apology *to Daddy;* but when Daddy insists that he apologize to his wronged brother, that is another story. A direct apology to Billy would be a tacit recognition of Billy's status as a right-holder against him, some one he can wrong as well as harm, and someone to whom he is directly accountable for his wrongs. This is a status Bobby will happily accord Daddy; but it would imply a respect for Billy that he does not presently feel, so he bitterly resents according it to him. On the "three-to-marry" model, the relations between each spouse and God would be like those between Bobby and Daddy; respect for the other spouse as an independent claimant would not even be necessary; and where present, of course, never sufficient.

The advocates of the "three to marry" model who conceive it either as a description of our actual institution of marriage or a recommendation of what marriage ought to be, may wish to escape this embarrassment by granting rights to spouses in capacities other than as promisees. They may wish to say, for example, that when John promises God that he will be faithful to Mary, a right is thus conferred not only on God as promisee but also on Mary herself as third-party beneficiary, just as when John contracts with an insurance company and names Mary as his intended beneficiary, she has a right to the accumulated funds after John's death, even though the insurance company made no promise to her. But this seems to be an unnecessarily cumbersome complication contributing nothing to our understanding of the marriage bond. The life insurance transaction is necessarily a three party relation, involving occupants of three distinct offices, no two of whom alone could do the whole job. The transaction, after all, is defined as the purchase by the customer (first office) from the vendor (second office) of protection for a beneficiary (third office) against the customer's untimely death. Marriage, on the other hand, in this our actual world, appears to be a binary relation between a husband and wife, and even though third parties such as children, neighbors, psychiatrists, and priests may sometimes be helpful and even causally necessary for the sur-

vival of the relation, they are not logically necessary to our *conception* of the relation, and indeed
many married couples do quite well without
them. Still, I am not now purporting to describe
our actual world, but rather trying to contrast it
with a counterpart world of the imagination. In
that world, it takes three to make almost *any*
moral relation and all rights are owned by God
or some sovereign under God.

There will, of course, be delegated authorities
in the imaginary world, empowered to give commands to their underlings and to punish them
for their disobedience. But the commands are all
given in the name of the right-monopoly who in
turn are the only persons to whom obligations
are owed. Hence, even intermediate superiors
do not have claim-rights against their subordinates but only legal *powers* to create obligations in the subordinates *to* the monopolistic
right-holders, and also the legal *privilege* to impose penalties in the name of that monopoly.

2

So much for the imaginary "world without
rights." If some of the moral concepts and practices I have allowed into that world do not sit
well with one another, no matter. Imagine Nowheresville with all of these practices if you can,
or with any harmonious subset of them, if you
prefer. The important thing is not what I've let
into it, but what I have kept out. The remainder
of this paper will be devoted to an analysis of
what precisely a world is missing when it does
not contain rights and why that absence is morally important.

The most conspicuous difference, I think, between the Nowheresvillians and ourselves has
something to do with the activity of *claiming*.
Nowheresvillians, even when they are dis-
criminated against invidiously, or left without
the things they need, or otherwise badly treated,
do not think to leap to their feet and make
righteous demands against one another, though
they may not hesitate to resort to force and
trickery to get what they want. They have no
notion of rights, so they do not have a notion of
what is their due; hence they do not claim before
they take. The conceptual linkage between personal rights and claiming has long been noticed
by legal writers and is reflected in the standard

usage in which "claim-rights" are distinguished
from the mere liberties, immunities, and powers, also sometimes called "rights," with which
they are easily confused. When a person has a
legal claim-right to X, it must be the case (i) that
he is at liberty in respect to X, i.e., that he has no
duty to refrain from or relinquish X, and also
(ii) that his liberty is the ground of other people's *duties* to grant him X or not to interfere
with him in respect to X. Thus, in the sense of
claim-rights, it is true by definition that rights
logically entail other people's duties. The paradigmatic examples of such rights are the creditor's right to be paid a debt by his debtor, and
the landowner's right not to be interfered with
by anyone in the exclusive occupancy of his land.
The creditor's right against his debtor, for example, and the debtor's duty to his creditor, are
precisely the same relation seen from two different vantage points, as inextricably linked as the
two sides of the same coin.

And yet, this is not quite an accurate account
of the matter, for it fails to do justice to the way
claim-rights are somehow prior to, or more basic
than, the duties with which they are necessarily
correlated. If Nip has a claim-right against Tuck,
it is because of this fact that Tuck has a duty to
Nip. It is only because something from Tuck is
due Nip (directional element) that there is something Tuck *must do* (modal element). This is a
relation, moreover, in which Tuck is bound and
Nip is free. Nip not only *has* a right, but he can
choose whether or not to exercise it, whether to
claim it, whether to register complaints upon its
infringement, even whether to release Tuck
from his duty, and forget the whole thing. If the
personal claim-right is also backed up by criminal sanctions, however, Tuck may yet have a
duty of obedience to the law from which no one,
not even Nip, may release him. He would even
have such duties if he lived in Nowheresville;
but duties subject to acts of claiming, duties
derivative from and contingent upon the personal rights of others, are unknown and un-
dreamed of in Nowheresville.

Many philosophical writers have simply
identified rights with claims. The dictionaries
tend to define "claims," in turn, as "assertions of
right," a dizzying piece of circularity that led one
philosopher to complain—"We go in search of
rights and are directed to claims, and then back

again to rights in bureaucratic futility."[5] What then is the relation between a claim and a right?

As we shall see, a right *is* a kind of claim, and a claim is "an assertion of right," so that a formal definition of either notion in terms of the other will not get us very far. Thus if a "formal definition" of the usual philosophical sort is what we are after, the game is over before it has begun, and we can say that the concept of a right is a "simple, undefinable, unanalysable primitive." Here as elsewhere in philosophy this will have the effect of making the commonplace seem unnecessarily mysterious. We would be better advised, I think, not to attempt a formal definition of either "right" or "claim," but rather to use the idea of a claim in informal elucidation of the idea of a right. This is made possible by the fact that *claiming* is an elaborate sort of rule-governed *activity*. A claim is that which is claimed, the object of the act of claiming. There is, after all, a verb "to claim," but no verb "to right." If we concentrate on the whole activity of claiming, which is public, familiar, and open to our observation, rather than on its upshot alone, we may learn more about the generic nature of rights than we could ever hope to learn from a formal definition, even if one were possible. Moreover, certain facts about rights more easily, if not solely, expressible in the language of claims and claiming are essential to a full understanding not only of what rights are, but also why they are so vitally important.

Let us begin then by distinguishing between: (i) making claim to . . ., (ii) claiming that . . ., and (iii) having a claim. One sort of thing we may be doing when we claim is to *make claim to something*. This is "to petition or seek by virtue of supposed right; to demand as due." Sometimes this is done by an acknowledged right-holder when he serves notice that he now wants turned over to him that which has already been acknowledged to be his, something borrowed, say, or improperly taken from him. This is often done by turning in a chit, a receipt, an I.O.U., a check, an insurance policy, or a deed, that is, a *title* to something currently in the possession of someone else. On other occasions, making claim is making application for titles or rights themselves, as when a mining prospector stakes a claim to mineral rights, or a householder to a tract of land in the public domain, or an inventor

to his patent rights. In the one kind of case, to make claim is to exercise rights one already has by presenting title; in the other kind of case it is to apply for the title itself, by showing that one has satisfied the conditions specified by a rule for the ownership of title and therefore that one can demand it as one's due.

Generally speaking, only the person who has a title or who has qualified for it, or someone speaking in his name, can make claim to something as a matter of right. It is an important fact about rights (or claims), then, that they can be claimed only by those who have them. Anyone can claim, of course, *that* this umbrella is yours, but only you or your representative can actually claim the umbrella. If Smith owes Jones five dollars, only Jones can claim the five dollars as his own, though any bystander can *claim that* it belongs to Jones. One important difference then between *making legal claim to* and *claiming that* is that the former is a legal performance with direct legal consequences whereas the latter is often a mere piece of descriptive commentary with no legal force. Legally speaking, *making claim to* can itself make things happen. This sense of "claiming," then, might well be called "the performative sense." The legal power to claim (performatively) one's right or the things to which one has a right seems to be essential to the very notion of a right. A right to which one could not make claim (i.e. not even for recognition) would be a very "imperfect" right indeed!

Claiming that one has a right (what we can call "propositional claiming" as opposed to "performative claiming") is another sort of thing one can do with language, but it is not the sort of doing that characteristically has legal consequences. To claim that one has rights is to make an assertion that one has them, and to make it in such a manner as to demand or insist that they be recognized. In this sense of "claim" many things in addition to rights can be claimed, that is, many other kinds of proposition can be asserted in the claiming way. I can claim, for example, that you, he, or she has certain rights, or that Julius Caesar once had certain rights; or I can claim that certain statements are true, or that I have certain skills, or accomplishments, or virtually anything at all. I can claim that the earth is flat. What is essential to *claiming that* is the manner of assertion. One can assert without even caring very much whether any one is listening, but part of the point of propositional claiming is to *make sure* people listen. When I claim to others that I know something, for example, I am not merely asserting it, but rather "obtruding my putative knowledge upon their attention, demanding that it be recognized, that appropriate notice be taken of it by those concerned . . ."[6] Not every truth is properly assertable, much less claimable, in every context. To claim that something is the case in circumstances that justify no more than calm assertion is to behave like a boor. (This kind of boorishness, I might add, is probably less common in Nowheresville.) But not to claim in the appropriate circumstances that one has a right is to be spiritless or foolish. A list of "appropriate circumstances" would include occasions when one is challenged, when one's possession is denied, or seems insufficiently acknowledged or appreciated; and of course even in these circumstances, the claiming should be done only with an appropriate degree of vehemence.

Even if there are conceivable circumstances in which one would admit rights diffidently, there is no doubt that their characteristic use and that for which they are distinctively well suited, is to be claimed, demanded, affirmed, insisted upon. They are especially sturdy objects to "stand upon," a most useful sort of moral furniture. Having rights, of course, makes claiming possible; but it is claiming that gives rights their special moral significance. This feature of rights is connected in a way with the customary rhetoric about what it is to be a human being. Having rights enables us to "stand up like men," to look others in the eye, and to feel in some fundamental way the equal of anyone. To think of oneself as the holder of rights is not to be unduly but properly proud, to have that minimal self-respect that is necessary to be worthy of the love and esteem of others. Indeed, respect for persons (this is an intriguing idea) may simply be respect for their rights, so that there cannot be the one without the other; and what is called "human dignity" may simply be the recognizable capacity to assert claims. To respect a person then, or to think of him as possessed of human dignity, simply *is* to think of him as a potential maker of claims. Not all of this can be packed

into a definition of "rights;" but these are *facts* about the possession of rights that argue well their supreme moral importance. More than anything else I am going to say, these facts explain what is wrong with Nowheresville.

We come now to the third interesting employment of the claiming vocabulary, that involving not the verb "to claim" but the substantive "a claim." What is it to *have a claim* and how is this related to rights? I would like to suggest that *having a claim consists in being in a position to claim, that is, to make claim to or claim that.* If this suggestion is correct it shows the primacy of the verbal over the nominative forms. It links claims to a kind of activity and obviates the temptation to think of claims as *things,* on the model of coins, pencils, and other material possessions which we can carry in our hip pockets. To be sure, we often make or establish our claims by presenting titles, and these typically have the form of receipts, tickets, certificates, and other pieces of paper or parchment. The title, however, is not the same thing as the claim; rather it is the evidence that establishes the claim as valid. On this analysis, one might have a claim without ever claiming that to which one is entitled, or without even knowing that one has the claim; for one might simply be ignorant of the fact that one is in a position to claim; or one might be unwilling to exploit that position for one reason or another, including fear that the legal machinery is broken down or corrupt and will not enforce one's claim despite its validity.

Nearly all writers maintain that there is some intimate connection between having a claim and having a right. Some identify right and claim without qualification; some define "right" as justified or justifiable claim, others as recognized claim, still others as valid claim. My own preference is for the latter definition. Some writers, however, reject the identification of rights with valid claims on the ground that all claims as such are valid, so that the expression "valid claim" is redundant. These writers, therefore, would identify rights with claims *simpliciter.* But this is a very simple confusion. All claims, to be sure, are *put forward* as justified, whether they are justified in fact or not. A claim conceded even by its maker to have no validity is not a claim at all, but a mere demand. The highwayman, for example, *demands* his victim's money; but he hardly makes claim to it as rightfully his own.

But it does not follow from this sound point that it is redundant to qualify claims as justified (or as I prefer, valid) in the definition of a right; for it remains true that not all claims put forward as valid really are valid; and only the valid ones can be acknowledged as rights.

If having a valid claim is not redundant, i.e., if it is not redundant to pronounce *another's* claim valid, there must be such a thing as having a claim that is not valid. What would this be like? One might accumulate just enough evidence to argue with relevance and cogency that one has a right (or ought to be granted a right), although one's case might not be overwhelmingly conclusive. In such a case, one might have strong enough argument to be entitled to a hearing and given fair consideration. When one is in this position, it might be said that one "has a claim" that deserves to be weighed carefully. Nevertheless, the balance of reasons may turn out to militate against recognition of the claim, so that the claim, which one admittedly had, and perhaps still does, is not a valid claim or right. "Having a claim" in this sense is an expression very much like the legal phrase "having a *prima facie* case." A plaintiff establishes a *prima facie* case for the defendant's liability when he establishes grounds that will be sufficient for liability unless outweighed by reasons of a different sort that may be offered by the defendant. Similarly, in the criminal law, a grand jury returns an indictment when it thinks that the prosecution has sufficient evidence to be taken seriously and given a fair hearing, whatever countervailing reasons may eventually be offered on the other side. That initial evidence, serious but not conclusive, is also sometimes called a *prima facie* case. In a parallel "*prima facie* sense" of "claim," having a claim to X is not (yet) the same as having a right to X, but is rather having a case of at least minimal plausibility that one has a right to X, a case that does establish a right, not to X, but to a fair hearing and consideration. Claims, so conceived, differ in degree: some are stronger than others. Rights, on the other hand, do not differ in degree: no one right is more of a right than another.[7]

Another reason for not identifying rights with claims *simply* is that there is a well-established usage in international law that makes a theoretically interesting distinction between claims and rights. Statesmen are sometimes led to speak of "claims" when they are concerned with the natural needs of deprived human beings in conditions of scarcity. Young orphans *need* good upbringings, balanced diets, education, and technical training everywhere in the world: but unfortunately there are many places where these goods are in such short supply that it is impossible to provision all who need them. If we persist, nevertheless, in speaking of these needs as constituting rights and not merely claims, we are committed to the conception of a right which is an entitlement *to* some good, but not a valid claim *against* any particular individual; for in conditions of scarcity there may be no determinate individuals who can plausibly be said to have a duty to provide the missing goods to those in need. J. E. S. Fawcett therefore prefers to keep the distinction between claims and rights firmly in mind. "Claims," he writes, "are needs and demands in movement, and there is a continuous transformation, as a society advances [toward greater abundance] of economic and social claims into civil and political rights . . . and not all countries or all claims are by any means at the same stage in the process."[8] The manifesto writers on the other side who seem to identify needs, or at least basic needs, with what they call "human rights," are more properly described, I think, as urging upon the world community the moral principle that *all* basic human needs ought to be recognized as *claims* (in the customary *prima facie* sense) worthy of sympathy and serious consideration right now, even though, in many cases, they cannot yet plausibly be treated as *valid* claims, that is, as grounds of any other people's duties. This way of talking avoids the anomaly of ascribing to all human beings now, even those in pre-industrial societies, such "economic and social rights" as "periodic holidays with pay."[9]

Still, for all of that, I have a certain sympathy with the manifesto writers, and I am even willing to speak of a special "manifesto sense" of "right," in which a right need not be correlated with another's duty. Natural needs are real claims if only upon hypothetical future beings not yet in existence. I accept the moral principle that to have an unfulfilled need is to have a kind of claim against the world, even if against no one in particular. A natural need for some good as such, like a natural desert, is always a reason in support of a claim to that good. A person in need, then, is always "in a position" to make a claim, even where there is no one in the corresponding position to do anything about it. Such claims, based on need alone, are "permanent possibilities of rights," the natural seed from which rights grow. When manifesto writers speak of them as if already actual rights, they are easily forgiven, for this is but a powerful way of expressing the conviction that they ought to be recognized by states here and now as potential rights and consequently as determinants of *present* aspirations and guides to *present* policies. That usage, I think, is a valid exercise of rhetorical licence.

I prefer to characterize rights as valid claims rather than justified ones, because I suspect that justification is rather too broad a qualification. "Validity," as I understand it, is justification of a peculiar and narrow kind, namely justification within a system of rules. A man has a legal right when the official recognition of his claim (as valid) is called for by the governing rules. This definition, of course, hardly applies to moral rights, but that is not because the genus of which moral rights are a species is something other than *claims*. A man has a moral right when he has a claim the recognition of which is called for— not (necessarily) by legal rules—but by moral principles, or the principles of an enlightened conscience.

There is one final kind of attack on the generic identification of rights with claims, and it has been launched with great spirit in a recent article by H. J. McCloskey, who holds that rights are not essentially claims at all, but rather entitlements. The springboard of his argument is his insistence that rights in their essential character are always *rights to*, not *rights against:*

My right to life is not a right against anyone. It is my right and by virtue of it, it is normally permissible for me to sustain my life in the face of obstacles. It does give rise to rights against others *in the sense* that others have or may come to have duties to refrain from

killing me, but it is essentially a right of mine, not an infinite list of claims, hypothetical and actual, against an infinite number of actual, potential, and as yet nonexistent human beings. . . . Similarly, the right of the tennis club member to play on the club courts is a right to play, not a right against some vague group of potential or possible obstructors.[10]

The argument seems to be that since rights are essentially rights *to*, whereas claims are essentially claims *against*, rights cannot be claims, though they can be grounds for claims. The argument is doubly defective though. First of all, contrary to McCloskey, rights (at least legal claim-rights) *are* held *against* others. McCloskey admits this in the case of *in personam* rights (what he calls "special rights") but denies it in the case of *in rem* rights (which he calls "general rights"):

Special rights are sometimes against specific individuals or institutions—e.g. rights created by promises, contracts, etc. . . . but these differ from . . . characteristic . . . general rights where the right is simply a right to. . . .[11]

As far as I can tell, the only reason McCloskey gives for denying that *in rem* rights are against others is that those against whom they would have to hold make up an enormously multitudinous and "vague" group, including hypothetical people not yet even in existence. Many others have found this a paradoxical consequence of the notion of *in rem* rights, but I see nothing troublesome in it. If a general rule gives me a right of noninterference in a certain respect against everybody, then there are literally hundreds of millions of people who have a duty toward me in that respect; and if the same general rule gives the same right to everyone else, then it imposes on me literally hundreds of millions of duties—or duties towards hundreds of millions of people. I see nothing paradoxical about this, however. The duties, after all, are negative; and I can discharge all of them at a stroke simply by minding my own business. And if all human beings make up one moral community and there are hundreds of millions of human beings, we should expect there to be hundreds of millions of moral relations holding between them.

McCloskey's other premise is even more obviously defective. There is no good reason to think that all *claims* are "essentially" *against,* rather than *to.* Indeed most of the discussion of claims above has been of claims *to,* and as we have seen, the law finds it useful to recognize claims *to* (or "mere claims") that are not yet qualified to be claims *against,* or rights (except in a "manifesto sense" of "rights").

Whether we are speaking of claims or rights, however, we must notice that they seem to have two dimensions, as indicated by the prepositions "to" and "against," and it is quite natural to wonder whether either of these dimensions is somehow more fundamental or essential than the other. All rights seem to merge *entitlements to* do, have, omit, or be something with *claims against* others to act or refrain from acting in certain ways. In some statements of rights the entitlement is perfectly determinate (e.g. *to* play tennis) and the claim vague (e.g. *against* "some vague group of potential or possible obstructors"); but in other cases the object of the claim is clear and determinate (e.g. *against* one's parents), and the entitlement general and indeterminate (e.g. to be given a proper upbringing). If we mean by "entitlement" that *to* which one has a right and by "claim" something directed at those *against* whom the right holds (as McCloskey apparently does), then we can say that all claim-rights necessarily involve both, though in individual cases the one element or the other may be in sharper focus.

In brief conclusion: To have a right is to have a claim against someone whose recognition as valid is called for by some set of governing rules or moral principles. To have a *claim* in turn, is to have a case meriting consideration, that is, to have reasons or grounds that put one in a position to engage in performative and propositional claiming. The activity of claiming, finally, as much as any other thing, makes for self-respect and respect for others, gives a sense to the notion of personal dignity, and distinguishes this otherwise morally flawed world from the even worse world of Nowheresville.

NOTES

1. H. B. Acton, "Symposium on 'Rights'," *Proceedings of the Aristotelian Society,* Supplementary Volume 24 (1950), pp. 107–8.

2. J. L. Austin, "A Plea for Excuses," *Proceedings of the Aristotelian Society,* Vol. 57 (1956–57).

3. For a fuller discussion of the concept of personal desert see my "Justice and Personal Desert," *Nomos VI, Justice,* ed. by C. J. Friedrich and J. Chapman (New York: Atherton Press, 1963), pp. 69–97.

4. II Sam. 11. Cited with approval by Thomas Hobbes in *The Leviathan,* Part II, Chap. 21.

5. H. B. Acton, *Op. cit.*

6. G. J. Warnock, "Claims to Knowledge," *Proceedings of the Aristotelian Society,* Supplementary Volume 36 (1962), p. 21.

7. This is the important difference between rights and mere claims. It is analogous to the difference between *evidence* of guilt (subject to degrees of cogency) and conviction of guilt (which is all or nothing). One can "have evidence" that is not conclusive just as one can "have a claim" that is not valid. "Prima-facieness" is built into the sense of "claim," but the notion of a "prima-facie right" makes little sense. On the latter point see A. I. Melden, *Rights and Right Conduct* (Oxford: Basil Blackwell, 1959), pp. 18–20, and Herbert Morris, "Persons and Punishment," *The Monist,* Vol. 52 (1968), pp. 498–9.

8. J. E. S. Fawcett, "The International Protection of Human Rights," in *Political Theory and the Rights of Man,* ed. by D. D. Raphael (Bloomington: Indiana University Press, 1967), pp. 125 and 128.

9. As declared in Article 24 of *The Universal Declaration of Human Rights* adopted on December 10, 1948, by the General Assembly of the United Nations.

10. H. J. McCloskey, "Rights," *Philosophical Quarterly,* Vol. 15 (1965), p. 118.

11. *Loc. cit.*

24. *JUSTICE AND UTILITY*

Henry R. West

In this essay I am interested in the degree to which principles of distributive justice are subordinate to the principle of utility, which is the foundation of utilitarian ethics. There are good things in life and there are undesirable things in life, and in any society these are distributed according to laws and mores such as property rights, job opportunities, the power and prestige of family, class, race, and educational background. A conception of distributive justice is a set of principles for choosing or criticizing social arrangements which determine the distribution of welfare and hardships.

Illustrations of competing conceptions of distributive justice are found in John Stuart Mill's *Utilitarianism* where he raises the question as to whether the produce of the labor of the community should be shared on any basis other than that of exact equality, or whether those should receive more whose wants are greatest, or whether those who work harder, or produce more, or whose services are more valuable to the community may justly claim a larger quota in the division of the produce. Again, when he presents alternative standards for the imposition of taxation, in numerical proportion to pecuniary means, or graduated taxation—taking a higher percentage from those who have more to spare, or taking the same absolute sum (whenever it could be got) from everyone—he is dealing with the just distribution of one of the burdens of society, and thus a question of distributive justice.[1]

Economic institutions are not the only ones included within the subject matter. Objections to discrimination on the basis of sex or race would be instances of claims of distributive injustice, whether it be job discrimination or in other areas, such as the right to vote or hold public office, or simply in public esteem, symbolized by separate facilities and seating arrangements. Conscription into the armed forces, if just at all, may be debated as fairer if by lottery rather than by selective criteria. A conception of distributive justice is thus a set of principles for choosing or criticizing social arrangements in order that the benefits and burdens, rights and responsibilities, opportunities and necessary tasks, should be apportioned as fairly as possible.

In Chapter V of *Utilitarianism,* entitled "On the Connection between Justice and Utility," Mill acknowledges that one of the strongest objections to utilitarianism as a complete account of ethics is the apparent independence of the idea of justice from the idea of what produces the greatest happiness, even if adherence to principles of justice does, in the long run, have that effect. If considerations of justice are independent of considerations of utility, it is possible that the two should come into conflict, that an unjust social arrangement could produce more happiness than a just one. In that case even someone sympathetic to utilitarianism on other grounds may feel that justice should take precedence in some or all such cases and that utilitarianism is not a complete ethical system. I shall return to Mill's analysis of justice later in this essay. At this point I want to show intuitively how the conflict might arise.

Suppose for the sake of argument that it is possible to make interpersonal comparisons between quantities of utility. This is a controversial assumption and need not be precise in order for utilitarian judgments to be made, but suppose that some three particular persons, A, B, and C, who are equally deserving or equally undeserving, can be given the utility shares (a), (b), and (c), respectively, in accordance with either Scheme I or Scheme II:[2]

Share	Scheme I	Scheme II
(a)	3 units	2 units
(b)	3 units	2 units
(c)	3 units	6 units

This essay was written for this volume.

Scheme I seems intuitively more just, yet Scheme II produces the greatest total welfare. If it is the doctrine of Utilitarianism that Scheme II is more just simply because it has the greatest total welfare, this seems outrageously contrary to our common sense idea of justice. If it is the doctrine of Utilitarianism that Scheme II should be adopted, even though it is unjust, this makes utilitarianism a questionable moral doctrine. There are a number of assumptions in the example, however, which must be made explicit. That Scheme II is less just may not be so obvious upon examination of these assumptions.

A first assumption is that it is appropriate to raise the question which scheme is just, but there are many contexts in which this seems inappropriate. In some contexts questions of justice and injustice simply do not arise, either because the difference in utility is not great enough to warrant use of the powerful normative terms "just" and "unjust," or because the basic requirements for anyone to complain of the injustice of the situation are not present, so it would be presumptuous to raise the question.

Suppose, for example, that A, B, and C are at a party and there is a choice between singing, which all like equally well (Scheme I), and dancing, which C likes twice as much as singing and three times as much as the others like dancing (Scheme II). We may be inclined to say that it isn't worth dignifying the issue with the word "injustice" if the host insists on dancing. Or, we may want to say that since A and B are there as guests, they have no right to complain. A similar kind of phenomenon can make some inequalities irrelevant in situations where questions of justice do arise. If two equally qualified applicants seek a position, we may not consider it a matter of justice or of injustice which one is employed, even if one would be happier in the job than the other or one would suffer greater disappointment in not getting it. To take into consideration such matters may be regarded as a praiseworthy sign of sensitivity to human feelings, but not a question of justice. It may also be possible to call a decision just without calling a contrary decision unjust. If one of the two equally qualified candidates has overcome some handicap in becoming qualified for the position, we may wish to praise as just a decision to appoint that person, without calling a contrary decision unjust. So long as the most important criteria are observed, we may want to say that there has been no injustice, even if there are other criteria which could also be considered.

In some other contexts the question of justice or injustice arises only regarding procedure, not regarding the relative size of distributive shares. For example, if A, B, and C are playing roulette, they would not regard Scheme II as less just than Scheme I simply because of the inequality of shares and the fact that A, B, and C are all equally "deserving." They are neither deserving nor undeserving of any size distributive share, only deserving of a fair chance at winning. Assuming that there is an equal chance of getting the larger share, they would presumably opt for Scheme II as a pay-off schedule.

Now, to return to the illustration with the assumption that the context is one in which questions of justice and injustice are appropriate, it is still not obvious that Scheme II is less just. Three features of the example must be kept in mind in examining it.

A first point to observe is that the units are units of intrinsic value, such as happiness, not units of the means of happiness. If they were units of the means of happiness such as, for example, income, it would not be obvious that Scheme II would result in greater happiness: suppose that each unit were $10,000 of annual income. Three persons with annual income of $30,000 each might have a sum total of happiness greater than two with $20,000 and one with $60,000. This is due to the common applicability of what is known in economics as the Principle of Diminishing Marginal Utility. The marginal utility of something in classical economic theory is the ability of an additional unit to satisfy human wants. The Principle of Diminishing Marginal Utility reflects the phenomenon that as larger quantities of something are possessed, an additional unit has less ability to satisfy wants, because there are fewer wants left to be satisfied. In our example the last $30,000 in annual income for person C in Scheme II may satisfy fewer wants than an additional $10,000 for each of persons A and B. Thus, in interpreting the example, we must keep in mind that there really is more happiness as a result of Scheme II.

A second point to keep in mind is that if A and B feel any resentment or envy or frustration over being relatively less well off, or any sense of injustice in unequal shares, it is already reflected in the numbers. If, for example, A and B each feel ½ unit of unhappiness over their inferior lives in Scheme II, the Scheme would be 2½, 2½, and 6 (a total of 11) without that unhappiness. Otherwise, if the unhappiness has not already been subtracted, Scheme II should be 1½, 1½, 6 (a total of 9), and it would have no greater total than Scheme I.

A third, and most important point, is that any instrumental value of the distribution is already reflected in the numbers. If A, B, and C work equally hard and do not receive equal happiness as a result, there may be a loss of incentive for further work with a loss in total utility in the long run. We shall see that this is the chief utilitarian argument for principles of justice which appear to be independent of the principle of utility. Principles requiring a certain pattern of distribution may be justified by the principle of utility and thus subordinate to it, if in fact they produce the greatest total utility in the long run, even if they appear to be independent because in a particular case they directly require only certain patterns of distribution, regardless of total to be distributed.

These three characteristics of the illustration are difficult to discount in our intuitive reaction to it. Part of our feeling of the "injustice" of Scheme II may be the feeling that if C has twice as much money as A or B, that money *could be put to better use* by distributing it more equitably. But such a reaction is one based on diminishing marginal utility. The supposed injustice is subordinate to the maximization of intrinsic value, not independent of it. Part of the feeling of the injustice of Scheme II may be the sympathetic reaction that if I were A or B, I couldn't help resenting C's being better off, even if I ought to be benevolent and have only love for my neighbor, and that a society in which there are such feelings can't be as good as one where all are equals in welfare, and resentment and envy do not arise. Again, there are hidden utilities, those of social harmony and resentment, entering the intuition of injustice, and these must be discounted. And, finally, as mentioned, there is the problem of instrumental utilities creeping in. Supposing, now, that we have shorn the example of extraneous considerations, would Scheme II be less just? I shall argue that under certain

conditions it would not be; then I shall argue that under others, although it would be *justified* from an impartial point of view, it would be contrary to the standard concept of *justice*. This will lead to a discussion of the utility of the standard concept of justice.

Suppose that two parents have three children, A, B, and C, and are faced with the choice (on their limited income) of giving all an equal education with an outcome according to Scheme I or of concentrating their resources upon the education of one with an outcome according to Scheme II. If they choose Scheme II, are they doing an injustice? To be sure that they don't play favorites, suppose that they choose which child is to benefit by some random method. It may seem unjust, in that C, who is no more deserving, is benefiting at the expense of A and B without their consent. But wouldn't they give their consent to enter the lottery if they were able? Assuming that we have the figures for utility correct, we can multiply the benefit times its probability to give an "expected" utility. Each child would have $\frac{1}{3}$ chance of 6 units and $\frac{2}{3}$ of 2, which gives an expected utility of $3\frac{1}{3}$ for Scheme II, compared with 3 on Scheme I. The rational choice would be Scheme II, so the parents are acting in the interests of each child—the way a rational person would choose for himself —in making the decision. Thus, Scheme II under these conditions is a just system.

Suppose, however, that the children have individual differences which make only one capable of benefiting from the concentration of resources. In that case the roulette analogy does not apply. The parents cannot use a random method of selection and choose as the child himself would have rationally chosen. But is it clear that Scheme II would be unjust? Suppose that Scheme II is adopted. In that case A and B are worse off, by one unit, than they would be otherwise, in order that C should benefit. That seems unjust. But suppose that Scheme I is adopted. In that case C is worse off, by three units, than he would be otherwise. Isn't it a greater injustice to deprive C of three units of his potential happiness for the total benefit to his siblings of only two units than to deprive A and B of only one unit each for the benefit to C to the extent of three units? Why shouldn't the parents look at this as they would a decision within their own lives? If A, B, and C are not different individuals but different stages in my own life and I have a choice of three days (or three years) of enjoying myself according to Scheme I or Scheme II, the sensible thing to do, assuming the numbers are correct measures of happiness, is to opt for Scheme II. I would feel I had done no injustice to myself on the other two days (or years) if the enjoyment on all three added up to greater total enjoyment. This very analogy, however, seems to lead to the fundamental objection to utilitarianism as a foundation for justice. Utilitarianism doesn't seem to recognize the different self-interests of different individuals. It treats different individuals as if they were different stages in the life of a single individual such that a greater benefit to one compensates for a lesser loss to another. This goes against our common sense intuitions concerning justice, that different people have a right not to be treated this way, and, at the same time, it challenges this right with the argument that if greater happiness results, why shouldn't they? Couldn't parents *justify* their decision to favor C over A and B on grounds that he would gain more than they would lose? As long as the welfare of all three individuals as a totality is kept in mind, this seems an adequate justification. It is inadequate only from a partial point of view; only when there is no genuine identity of interest. If A and B have an interest in C equal to their own, that is, if they are impartial, they will accept the justification that greater good results, but if A and B do not have an interest in C equal to their own, the "justification" which deprives them of a good for the greater good of another will be unacceptable. It is based upon a principle of justice which does not assure them even minimal security in their own welfare. By this principle a scheme of shares in which A and B suffer negative welfare for C's greater welfare (for example, a Scheme III in which A, B, and C receive -1, -1, and 12, respectively) would be justified. This seems rational when A, B, and C are stages of one's life, but to accept this distribution seems heroic or saintly rather than the recognition of justice when A, B, and C are different persons. Thus, the preceding model of justification, which is appropriate for an impartial decision among competing claims when there is unifying identity of interest, does not

appear to be an adequate analysis of the standard conception of justice where there is not a unifying identity of interest.

We have not yet developed an analysis of the standard conception of justice, but it has at least been shown to be capable of coming into conflict with principles of distribution which simply justify the distribution which maximizes total welfare. There are at least three ways to view this potential conflict. One is to see the standard principles of justice, to the extent that they conflict with total welfare, as claims based on self-interest and hence such that they should be overridden from a moral point of view. A second is to see the standard conception of justice as an independent set of moral considerations which at least sometimes, if not always, take precedence over or place restrictions upon considerations of total welfare in case of conflict. A third is to view the standard conception of justice as a set of principles which can take precedence over the criterion of total welfare in particular cases but which ultimately derive their moral authority from their contribution to the production of greatest total welfare in the long run. According to this third position, if there were to be only one distribution of welfare ever, the criterion of total welfare would be adequate. But since the principles of distributive justice are a set of principles for criticizing social arrangements which determine distribution on a recurring basis, they must require not just the best result on one occasion but a structure which will produce the best result on a recurring basis. The structure which has this effect may be one which adjudicates self-interested claims on principles other than simply greatest total welfare case by case. To return to an earlier model, if life were a one-shot lottery, the greatest total welfare (taking into account diminishing marginal utility, envy, etc.) might be acceptable as a just pay-off scheme. But since life is a competitive struggle in which some have more talent than others, some have more wealth and power than others, et cetera, it is not a fair lottery with equal opportunity to win, and there is no relevantly informed impartial judge to make and enforce decisions which maximize total welfare even if that were the acceptable criterion. In real life, considerations of justice function to allow claims to be made by self-interested parties, especially for the weaker party to envoke moral standards of justice as a counter to the greater non-moral power of the adversary, and to impose moral standards of justice as a counter to the greater nonmoral power of the adversary, and to impose moral restrictions upon the exercise of that greater power. In a world in which there are self-interested parties competing for the benefits and to avoid the burdens of society, a social structure which recognizes a set of principles giving parties legitimate claims to benefits and to avoidance of burdens offers the participants, especially weaker competitors, a system of security which in the long run has good consequences. In a particular case a decision in accordance with the recognition of such rights may have consequences which are not as good as an impartial decision in the absence of such rights, but in the long run the best consequences are obtained by recognition and respect for such rights, and this requires that they be recognized and respected even in some cases where an alternative decision would produce greater total welfare.

The position at which we have now arrived is, I believe, the position of Mill in Chapter V of *Utilitarianism*. Justice, according to his analysis of the concept, coincides with those duties in virtue of which a correlative right resides in some person or persons. If injustice consists in treating a person worse than he deserves, there is some assignable person who can claim the violation of his moral right; if the injustice consists in treating a person better than others, the wrong in this case is to his competitors, who are also assignable persons, and are entitled to complain. In this respect justice is distinguishable from generosity and beneficence, in that although we ought to practice those virtues, no one can claim them from us as his moral right; or, if the moralist attempts, as some have done, to claim that mankind have a *right* to all the good that we can do them, he thereby includes generosity and beneficence within the category of justice, merging all morality into justice.[3] As to an analysis of what is meant by the possession of a "right," Mill says that when we call anything a person's right, "we mean that he has a valid claim on society to protect him in the possession of it, either by the force of law or by that of education and opinion. If he has what we consider a sufficient claim, on whatever account, to have

something guaranteed to him by society, we say that he has a right to it."[4] Such valid claims, Mill believes, rest ultimately on general utility—on the general obligation to promote greatest good —but Mill claims that rights involve the most important and impressive kind of utility, namely, security. All other earthly benefits, he says, are needed by one person, not needed by another, but security no human being can possibly do without. Nothing but the gratification of the instant could be of any worth to us if we could be deprived of everything the next instant by whoever was momentarily stronger than ourselves. Thus it is appropriate on utilitarian grounds that claims to justice should take on "that character of absoluteness, that apparent infinity and incommensurability with all other considerations" which also constitute the distinction between the feeling of right and wrong and that of ordinary expedience and inexpediency.[5] But Mill reminds us that particular cases may occur, such as to save a life, in which some other social duty is so important as to overrule any one of the general maxims of justice. Thus, the priority of respect for rights at the expense of certain other utilities is defended on utilitarian grounds, but the possibility of overriding such rights on utilitarian grounds is also recognized. Furthermore, the substance of legitimate rights is decided, and the conflicts between these rights resolved, by appeal to what has best consequences.

The principles which determine what is one's due should be such that their recognition generally has good consequences. It turns out that there are many of these, and they may come into conflict with one another. Mill gives two illustrations in the area of distributive justice, as mentioned above, in which there can be conflicting claims which appeal to conflicting principles of justice. A review of Mill's discussion of these will illustrate the role of utilitarian considerations in constructing and criticizing principles of distributive justice.

(1) Should those with superior skill and talent receive more remuneration than others in a co-operative industrial enterprise? On the one hand, society receives more from the skilled and efficient laborer; his services being more beneficial, it may be argued that society owes him a larger return for them. Furthermore, a greater share of the product being actually his

work, not to reward him proportionately may be regarded as a kind of robbery. Here Mill is appealing to still more fundamental principles of justice, such as the obligation to return good for good, or the obligation to respect as property that with which one has mixed his labor. These in turn could be given a justification as having good consequences. In this particular case, one could also appeal to the utility of having those with skills and talents develop their skills and talents and utilize them for productive use, which is stimulated by a system of pecuniary incentives. On the other hand, Mill points out, it is argued that whoever does the best he can deserves equally well, and ought not in justice to be put in a position of inferiority for no fault of his own; that superior abilities have already advantage more than enough, in the admiration they excite, the personal influence they command, and the self-satisfaction of exercising them, without adding to these a superior share of the world's goods; and that society is bound in justice rather to make compensation to the less favored for this unmerited inequality of advantage than to aggravate it. Here Mill is appealing to equalitarian tendencies in the concept of justice which can be based in turn on the principle of diminishing marginal utility and on the envy which arises from invidious differences. These are grounds for equality or even compensatory justice to make up for natural or educational inequalities. Mill thinks that justice in this case has two sides to it, which it is impossible to bring into harmony on grounds of justice alone. Social utility alone can decide the preference. The question then becomes, which will have better consequences—to reward pay in accordance with product or effort (or need, which is a third criterion)? Traditional and capitalist pay schemes are almost all based on the first. Here I think the utilitarian should be driven to a demand for radical change.

(2) Should taxes be assessed equally or according to pecuniary means, and if the latter, in simple proportion to wealth and income or graduated so that those with more pay at a higher rate

as well? Mill points out that an argument can be made that it is just to take the same absolute sum from all, since the protection of law and government is (supposedly) afforded to and is equally required by all. Against this it is claimed that the state does more for the rich than the poor, protecting more property, but Mill denies this, pointing out that the rich would be far better able to protect themselves, in the absence of law or government, than the poor. (Mill obviously does not have a Marxist conception of the bourgeois state.) Mill thinks the only resolution of the dispute is the utilitarian—what scheme would have best consequences—and it is implicitly on this basis that higher taxes have been exacted from the rich.

These examples show that on utilitarian grounds some traditional principles of justice can be generated. For one to have a right to the product of his labor provides security in possession of the means of happiness, gives meaning to one's work, and is an incentive for productive labor. For one to have a right to equality of distribution usually produces greater welfare because of the principle of diminishing marginal utility, because it reduces envy, and it prevents abuse of power which comes from concentrations of power. These are empirical claims, but they are generally recognized as having some validity. They are the grounds for specific principles of justice, and if they are mistaken, or if their significance is exaggerated, the traditional claims of justice should be revised. Questions as to which form of society is most just cannot be settled *a priori* by an analysis of the concept of justice nor by intuition as to which is most just. An empirical analysis of which has best consequences is required, and the result of such an inquiry may dictate revisions in the substantive content of traditional rights or traditional principles of justice. Justice is conceptually tied to rights, which in turn are legitimate claims, but which claims should be recognized as legitimate is not a conceptual matter. It is a question of the greatest utility in the long run.

NOTES

1. John Stuart Mill, *Utilitarianism,* Chapter V. Included in this volume, p. 128.
2. Example found in Nicholas Rescher, *Distributive Justice* (Indianapolis: The Bobbs-Merrill Company, Inc., 1966), p. 25.
3. Mill, *Utilitarianism,* Chapter V.
4. *Ibid.*
5. *Ibid.*

25. *DISTRIBUTIVE JUSTICE*[1]

John Rawls

I

We may think of a human society as a more or less self-sufficient association regulated by a common conception of justice and aimed at advancing the good of its members. As a co-operative venture for mutual advantage, it is characterized by a conflict as well as an identity of interests. There is an identity of interests since social co-operation makes possible a better life for all than any would have if everyone were to try to live by his own efforts; yet at the same time men are not indifferent as to how the greater benefits produced by their joint labours are distributed, for in order to further their own aims each prefers a larger to a lesser share. A conception of justice is a set of principles for choosing between the social arrangements which determine this division and for underwriting a consensus as to the proper distributive shares.

Now at first sight the most rational conception of justice would seem to be utilitarian. For consider: each man in realizing his own good can certainly balance his own losses against his own gains. We can impose a sacrifice on ourselves now for the sake of a greater advantage later. A man quite properly acts, as long as others are not affected, to achieve his own greatest good, to advance his ends as far as possible. Now, why should not a society act on precisely the same principle? Why is not that which is rational in the case of one man right in the case of a group of men? Surely the simplest and most direct conception of the right, and so of justice, is that of maximizing the good. This assumes a prior understanding of what is good, but we can think of the good as already given by the interests of rational individuals. Thus just as the principle of individual choice is to achieve one's greatest good, to advance so far as possible one's own

system of rational desires, so the principle of social choice is to realize the greatest good (similarly defined) summed over all the members of society. We arrive at the principle of utility in a natural way: by this principle a society is rightly ordered, and hence just, when its institutions are arranged so as to realize the greatest sum of satisfactions.

The striking feature of the principle of utility is that it does not matter, except indirectly, how this sum of satisfactions is distributed among individuals, any more than it matters, except indirectly, how one man distributes his satisfactions over time. Since certain ways of distributing things affect the total sum of satisfactions, this fact must be taken into account in arranging social institutions; but according to this principle the explanation of common-sense precepts of justice and their seemingly stringent character is that they are those rules which experience shows must be strictly respected and departed from only under exceptional circumstances if the sum of advantages is to be maximized. The precepts of justice are derivative from the one end of attaining the greatest net balance of satisfactions. There is no reason in principle why the greater gains of some should not compensate for the lesser losses of others; or why the violation of the liberty of a few might not be made right by a greater good shared by many. It simply happens, at least under most conditions, that the greatest sum of advantages is not generally achieved in this way. From the standpoint of utility the strictness of common-sense notions of justice has a certain usefulness, but as a philosophical doctrine it is irrational.

If, then, we believe that as a matter of principle each member of society has an inviolability founded on justice which even the welfare of everyone else cannot over-ride, and that a loss of freedom for some is not made right by a greater sum of satisfactions enjoyed by many, we shall

From John Rawls, "Distributive Justice," *Philosophy, Politics and Society,* Third Series, edited by Peter Laslett and W. G. Runciman (Oxford: 1967), pp. 58–82. Reprinted by permission of the author.

have to look for another account of the principles of justice. The principle of utility is incapable of explaining the fact that in a just society the liberties of equal citizenship are taken for granted, and the rights secured by justice are not subject to political bargaining nor to the calculus of social interests. Now, the most natural alternative to the principle of utility is its traditional rival, the theory of the social contract. The aim of the contract doctrine is precisely to account for the strictness of justice by supposing that its principles arise from an agreement among free and independent persons in an original position of equality and hence reflect the integrity and equal sovereignty of the rational persons who are the contractees. Instead of supposing that a conception of right, and so a conception of justice, is simply an extension of the principle of choice for one man to society as a whole, the contract doctrine assumes that the rational individuals who belong to society must choose together, in one joint act, what is to count among them as just and unjust. They are to decide among themselves once and for all what is to be their conception of justice. This decision is thought of as being made in a suitably defined initial situation one of the significant features of which is that no one knows his position in society, nor even his place in the distribution of natural talents and abilities. The principles of justice to which all are forever bound are chosen in the absence of this sort of specific information. A veil of ignorance prevents anyone from being advantaged or disadvantaged by the contingencies of social class and fortune; and hence the bargaining problems which arise in everyday life from the possession of this knowledge do not affect the choice of principles. On the contract doctrine, then, the theory of justice, and indeed ethics itself, is part of the general theory of rational choice, a fact perfectly clear in its Kantian formulation.

Once justice is thought of as arising from an original agreement of this kind, it is evident that the principle of utility is problematical. For why should rational individuals who have a system of ends they wish to advance agree to a violation of their liberty for the sake of a greater balance of satisfactions enjoyed by others? It seems more plausible to suppose that, when situated in an original position of equal right, they would insist upon institutions which returned compensating advantages for any sacrifices required. A rational man would not accept an institution merely because it maximized the sum of advantages irrespective of its effect on his own interests. It appears, then, that the principle of utility would be rejected as a principle of justice, although we shall not try to argue this important question here. Rather, our aim is to give a brief sketch of the conception of distributive shares implicit in the principles of justice which, it seems, would be chosen in the original position. The philosophical appeal of utilitarianism is that it seems to offer a single principle on the basis of which a consistent and complete conception of right can be developed. The problem is to work out a contractarian alternative in such a way that it has comparable if not all the same virtues.

II

In our discussion we shall make no attempt to derive the two principles of justice which we shall examine; that is, we shall not try to show that they would be chosen in the original position.[2] It must suffice that it is plausible that they would be, at least in preference to the standard forms of traditional theories. Instead we shall be mainly concerned with three questions: first, how to interpret these principles so that they define a consistent and complete conception of justice; second, whether it is possible to arrange the institutions of a constitutional democracy so that these principles are satisfied, at least approximately; and third, whether the conception of distributive shares which they define is compatible with common-sense notions of justice. The significance of these principles is that they allow for the strictness of the claims of justice; and if they can be understood so as to yield a consistent and complete conception, the contractarian alternative would seem all the more attractive.

The two principles of justice which we shall discuss may be formulated as follows: first, each person engaged in an institution or affected by it has an equal right to the most extensive liberty compatible with a like liberty for all; and second, inequalities as defined by the institutional structure or fostered by it are arbitrary unless it is reasonable to expect that they will work out to everyone's advantage and provided that the positions and offices to which they attach or from which they may be gained are open to all. These principles regulate the distributive aspects of institutions by controlling the assignment of rights and duties throughout the whole social structure, beginning with the adoption of a political constitution in accordance with which they are then to be applied to legislation. It is upon a correct choice of a basic structure of society, its fundamental system of rights and duties, that the justice of distributive shares depends.

The two principles of justice apply in the first instance to this basic structure, that is, to the main institutions of the social system and their arrangement, how they are combined together. Thus this structure includes the political constitution and the principal economic and social institutions which together define a person's liberties and rights and affect his life-prospects, what he may expect to be and how well he may expect to fare. The intuitive idea here is that those born into the social system at different positions, say in different social classes, have varying life-prospects determined, in part, by the system of political liberties and personal rights, and by the economic and social opportunities which are made available to these positions. In this way the basic structure of society favours certain men over others, and these are the basic inequalities, the ones which affect their whole life-prospects. It is inequalities of this kind, presumably inevitable in any society, with which the two principles of justice are primarily designed to deal.

Now the second principle holds that an inequality is allowed only if there is reason to believe that the institution with the inequality, or permitting it, will work out for the advantage of every person engaged in it. In the case of the basic structure this means that all inequalities which affect life-prospects, say the inequalities of income and wealth which exist between social classes, must be to the advantage of everyone. Since the principle applies to institutions, we interpret this to mean that inequalities must be to the advantage of the representative man for each relevant social position; they should improve each such man's expectation. Here we assume that it is possible to attach to each position an expectation, and that this expectation is a function of the whole institutional structure: it can be raised and lowered by reassigning rights and duties throughout the system. Thus the expectation of any position depends upon the expectations of the others, and these in turn depend upon the pattern of rights and duties established by the basic structure. But it is not clear what is meant by saying that inequalities must be to the advantage of every representative man, and hence our first question.

III

One possibility is to say that everyone is made better off in comparison with some historically relevant benchmark. An interpretation of this kind is suggested by Hume.[3] He sometimes says that the institutions of justice, that is, the rules regulating property and contracts, and so on, are to everyone's advantage, since each man can count himself the gainer on balance when he considers his permanent interests. Even though the application of the rules is sometimes to his disadvantage, and he loses in the particular case, each man gains in the long-run by the steady administration of the whole system of justice. But all Hume seems to mean by this is that everyone is better off in comparison with the situation of men in the state of nature, understood either as some primitive condition or as the circumstances which would obtain at any time if the existing institutions of justice were to break down. While this sense of everyone's being made better off is perhaps clear enough, Hume's interpretation is surely unsatisfactory. For even if all men including slaves are made better off by a system of slavery than they would be in the state of nature, it is not true that slavery makes everyone (even a slave) better off, at least not in a sense which makes the arrangement just. The benefits and burdens of social co-operation are unjustly distributed even if everyone does gain in comparison with the state of nature; this historical or hypothetical benchmark is simply irrelevant to the question of justice. In fact, any past state of society other than a recent one seems irrelevant offhand, and this suggests that we should look for an interpretation independent of historical comparisons altogether. Our problem is to identify the correct hypothetical comparisons defined by currently feasible changes.

Now the well-known criterion of Pareto[4] offers a possibility along these lines once it is formulated so as to apply to institutions. Indeed, this is the most natural way of taking the second principle (or rather the first part of it, leaving aside the requirement about open positions). This criterion says that group welfare is at an optimum when it is impossible to make any one man better off without at the same time making at least one other man worse off. Applying this criterion to allocating a given bundle of goods among given individuals, a particular allocation yields an optimum if there is no redistribution which would improve one individual's position without worsening that of another. Thus a distribution is optimal when there is no further exchange which is to the advantage of the other. But there are many such distributions, since there are many ways of allocating commodities so that no further mutually beneficial exchange is possible. Hence the Pareto criterion, as important as it is, admittedly does not identify the best distribution, but rather a class of optimal, or efficient, distributions. Moreover, we cannot say that a given optimal distribution is better than any nonoptimal one; it is only superior to those which it dominates. The criterion is at best an incomplete principle for ordering distributions.

Pareto's idea can be applied to institutions. We assume, as remarked above, that it is possible to associate with each social position an expectation which depends upon the assignment of rights and duties in the basic structure. Given this assumption, we get a principle which says that the pattern of expectations (inequalities in life-prospects) is optimal if and only if it is impossible to change the rules, to redefine the scheme of rights and duties, so as to raise the expectations of any representative man without at the same time lowering the expectations of some other representative man. Hence the basic structure satisfies this principle when it is impossible to change the assignment of fundamental rights and duties and to alter the availability of economic and social opportunities so as to make some representative man better off without making another worse off. Thus, in comparing different arrangements of the social system, we can say that one is better than another if in one arrangement all expectations are at least as high, and some higher, than in the other. The

principle gives grounds for reform, for if there is an arrangement which is optimal in comparison with the existing state of things, then, other things equal, it is a better situation all around and should be adopted.

The satisfaction of this principle, then, defines a second sense in which the basic structure makes everyone better off; namely, that from the standpoint of its representative men in the relevant positions, there exists no change which would improve anyone's condition without worsening that of another. Now we shall assume that this principle would be chosen in the original position, for surely it is a desirable feature of a social system that it is optimal in this sense. In fact, we shall suppose that this principle defines the concept of efficiency for institutions, as can be seen from the fact that if the social system does not satisfy it, this implies that there is some change which can be made which will lead people to act more effectively so that the expectations of some at least can be raised. Perhaps an economic reform will lead to an increase in production with given resources and techniques, and with greater output someone's expectations are raised.

It is not difficult to see, however, that while this principle provides another sense for an institution's making everyone better off, it is an inadequate conception of justice. For one thing, there is the same incompleteness as before. There are presumably many arrangements of an institution and of the basic structure which are optimal in this sense. There may also be many arrangements which are optimal with respect to existing conditions, and so many reforms which would be improvements by this principle. If so, how is one to choose between them? It is impossible to say that the many optimal arrangements are equally just, and the choice between them a matter of indifference, since efficient institutions allow extremely wide variations in the pattern of distributive shares.

Thus it may be that under certain conditions serfdom cannot be significantly reformed without lowering the expectations of some representative man, say that of landowners, in which case serfdom is optimal. But equally it may happen under the same conditions that a system of free labour could not be changed without lowering the expectations of some representative man, say that of free labourers, so that this arrangement likewise is optimal. More generally, whenever a society is relevantly divided into a number of classes, it is possible, let's suppose, to maximize with respect to any one of its representative men at a time. These maxima give at least this many optimal positions, for none of them can be departed from to raise the expectations of any man without lowering those of another, namely, the man with respect to whom the maximum is defined. Hence each of these extremes is optimal. All this corresponds to the obvious fact that, in distributing particular goods to given individuals, those distributions are also optimal which give the whole stock to any one person; for once a single person has everything, there is no change which will not make him worse off.

We see, then, that social systems which we should judge very differently from the standpoint of justice may be optimal by this criterion. This conclusion is not surprising. There is no reason to think that, even when applied to social systems, justice and efficiency come to the same thing. These reflections only show what we knew all along, which is that we must find another way of interpreting the second principle, or rather the first part of it. For while the two principles taken together incorporate strong requirements of equal liberty and equality of opportunity, we cannot be sure that even these constraints are sufficient to make the social structure acceptable from the standpoint of justice. As they stand the two principles would appear to place the burden of ensuring justice entirely upon these prior constraints and to leave indeterminate the preferred distributive shares.

IV

There is, however, a third interpretation which is immediately suggested by the previous remarks, and this is to choose some social position by reference to which the pattern of expectations as a whole is to be judged, and then to maximize with respect to the expectations of this representative man consistent with the demands of equal liberty and equality of opportunity. Now, the one obvious candidate is the representative man of those who are least favoured by the system of institutional inequalities. Thus we arrive at the following idea: the basic structure of

the social system affects the life-prospects of typical individuals according to their initial places in society, say the various income classes into which they are born, or depending upon certain natural attributes, as when institutions make discriminations between men and women or allow certain advantages to be gained by those with greater natural abilities. The fundamental problem of distributive justice concerns the differences in life-prospects which come about in this way. We interpret the second principle to hold that these differences are just if and only if the greater expectations of the more advantaged, when playing a part in the working of the whole social system, improve the expectations of the least advantaged. The basic structure is just throughout when the advantages of the more fortunate promote the well-being of the least fortunate, that is, when a decrease in their advantages would make the least fortunate even worse off than they are. The basic structure is perfectly just when the prospects of the least fortunate are as great as they can be.

In interpreting the second principle (or rather the first part of it which we may, for obvious reasons, refer to as the difference principle), we assume that the first principle requires a basic equal liberty for all, and that the resulting political system, when circumstances permit, is that of a constitutional democracy in some form. There must be liberty of the person and political equality as well as liberty of conscience and freedom of thought. There is one class of equal citizens which defines a common status for all. We also assume that there is equality of opportunity and a fair competition for the available positions on the basis of reasonable qualifications. Now, given this background, the differences to be justified are the various economic and social inequalities in the basic structure which must inevitably arise in such a scheme. These are the inequalities in the distribution of income and wealth and the distinctions in social prestige and status which attach to the various positions and classes. The difference principle says that these inequalities are just if and only if they are part of a larger system in which they work out to the advantage of the most unfortunate representative man. The just distributive shares determined by the basic structure are those specified by this constrained maximum principle.

Thus, consider the chief problem of distributive justice, that concerning the distribution of wealth as it affects the life-prospects of those starting out in the various income groups. These income classes define the relevant representative men from which the social system is to be judged. Now, a son of a member of the entrepreneurial class (in a capitalist society) has a better prospect than that of the son of an unskilled labourer. This will be true, it seems, even when the social injustices which presently exist are removed and the two men are of equal talent and ability; the inequality cannot be done away with as long as something like the family is maintained. What, then, can justify this inequality in life-prospects? According to the second principle it is justified only if it is to the advantage of the representative man who is worst off, in this case the representative unskilled labourer. The inequality is permissible because lowering it would, let's suppose, make the working man even worse off than he is. Presumably, given the principle of open offices (the second part of the second principle), the greater expectations allowed to entrepreneurs has the effect in the longer run of raising the life-prospects of the labouring class. The inequality in expectation provides an incentive so that the economy is more efficient, industrial advance proceeds at a quicker pace, and so on, the end result of which is that greater material and other benefits are distributed throughout the system. Of course, all of this is familiar, and whether true or not in particular cases, it is the sort of thing which must be argued if the inequality in income and wealth is to be acceptable by the difference principle.

We should now verify that this interpretation of the second principle gives a natural sense in which everyone may be said to be made better off. Let us suppose that inequalities are chain-connected: that is, if an inequality raises the expectations of the lowest position, it raises the expectations of all positions in between. For example, if the greater expectations of the representative entrepreneur raises that of the unskilled labourer, it also raises that of the semi-skilled. Let us further assume that inequalities are close-knit: that is, it is impossible to raise (or lower) the expectation of any representative man without raising (or lowering) the expectations of every other representative man,

and in particular, without affecting one way or the other that of the least fortunate. There is no loose-jointedness, so to speak, in the way in which expectations depend upon one another. Now, with these assumptions, everyone does benefit from an inequality which satisfies the difference principle, and the second principle as we have formulated it reads correctly. For the representative man who is better off in any pairwise comparison gains by being allowed to have his advantage, and the man who is worse off benefits from the contribution which all inequalities make to each position below. Of course, chain-connection and close-knitness may not obtain; but in this case those who are better off should not have a veto over the advantages available for the least advantaged. The stricter interpretation of the difference principle should be followed, and all inequalities should be arranged for the advantage of the most unfortunate even if some inequalities are not to the advantage of those in middle positions. Should these conditions fail, then, the second principle would have to be stated in another way.

It may be observed that the difference principle represents, in effect, an original agreement to share in the benefits of the distribution of natural talents and abilities, whatever this distribution turns out to be, in order to alleviate as far as possible the arbitrary handicaps resulting from our initial starting places in society. Those who have been favoured by nature, whoever they are, may gain from their good fortune only on terms that improve the well-being of those who have lost out. The naturally advantaged are not to gain simply because they are more gifted, but only to cover the costs of training and cultivating their endowments and for putting them to use in a way which improves the position of the less fortunate. We are led to the difference principle if we wish to arrange the basic social structure so that no one gains (or loses) from his luck in the natural lottery of talent and ability, or from his initial place in society, without giving (or receiving) compensating advantages in return. (The parties in the original position are not said to be attracted by this idea and so agree to it; rather, given the symmetries of their situation, and particularly their lack of knowledge, and so on, they will find it to their interest to agree to a principle which can be understood in this way.)

And we should note also that when the difference principle is perfectly satisfied, the basic structure is optimal by the efficiency principle. There is no way to make anyone better off without making someone worse off, namely, the least fortunate representative man. Thus the two principles of justice define distributive shares in a way compatible with efficiency, at least as long as we move on this highly abstract level. If we want to say (as we do, although it cannot be argued here) that the demands of justice have an absolute weight with respect to efficiency, this claim may seem less paradoxical when it is kept in mind that perfectly just institutions are also efficient.

V

Our second question is whether it is possible to arrange the institutions of a constitutional democracy so that the two principles of justice are satisfied, at least approximately. We shall try to show that this can be done provided the government regulates a free economy in a certain way. More fully, if law and government act effectively to keep markets competitive, resources fully employed, property and wealth widely distributed over time, and to maintain the appropriate social minimum, then if there is equality of opportunity underwritten by education for all, the resulting distribution will be just. Of course, all of these arrangements and policies are familiar. The only novelty in the following remarks, if there is any novelty at all, is that this framework of institutions can be made to satisfy the difference principle. To argue this, we must sketch the relations of these institutions and how they work together.

First of all, we assume that the basic social structure is controlled by a just constitution which secures the various liberties of equal citizenship. Thus the legal order is administered in accordance with the principle of legality, and liberty of conscience and freedom of thought are taken for granted. The political process is conducted, so far as possible, as a just procedure for choosing between governments and for enacting just legislation. From the standpoint of distributive justice, it is also essential that there be equality of opportunity in several senses. Thus, we suppose that, in addition to maintaining the usual social overhead capital, government provides for equal educational opportunities for all either by subsidizing private schools or by operating a public school system. It also enforces and underwrites equality of opportunity in commercial ventures and in the free choice of occupation. This result is achieved by policing business behaviour and by preventing the establishment of barriers and restriction to the desirable positions and markets. Lastly, there is a guarantee of a social minimum which the government meets by family allowances and special payments in times of unemployment, or by a negative income tax.

In maintaining this system of institutions the government may be thought of as divided into four branches. Each branch is represented by various agencies (or activities thereof) charged with preserving certain social and economic conditions. These branches do not necessarily overlap with the usual organization of government, but should be understood as purely conceptual. Thus the allocation branch is to keep the economy feasibly competitive, that is, to prevent the formation of unreasonable market power. Markets are competitive in this sense when they cannot be made more so consistent with the requirements of efficiency and the acceptance of the facts of consumer preferences and geography. The allocation branch is also charged with identifying and correcting, say by suitable taxes and subsidies wherever possible, the more obvious departures from efficiency caused by the failure of prices to measure accurately social benefits and costs. The stabilization branch strives to maintain reasonably full employment so that there is no waste through failure to use resources and the free choice of occupation and the deployment of finance is supported by strong effective demand. These two branches together are to preserve the efficiency of the market economy generally.

The social minimum is established through the operations of the transfer branch. Later on we shall consider at what level this minimum should be set, since this is a crucial matter; but for the moment, a few general remarks will suffice. The main idea is that the workings of the transfer branch take into account the precept of need and assign it an appropriate weight with respect to the other common-sense precepts of justice. A market economy ignores the claims of need altogether. Hence there is a division of labour between the parts of the social system as different institutions answer to different common-sense precepts. Competitive markets (properly supplemented by government operations) handle the problem of the efficient allocation of labour and resources and set a weight to the conventional precepts associated with wages and earnings (the precepts of each according to his work and experience, or responsibility and the hazards of the job, and so on), whereas the transfer branch guarantees a certain level of well-being and meets the claims of need. Thus it is obvious that the justice of distributive shares depends upon the whole social system and how it distributes total income, wages plus transfers. There is with reason strong objection to the competitive determination of total income, since this would leave out of account the claims of need and of a decent standard of life. From the standpoint of the original position it is clearly rational to insure oneself against these contingencies. But now, if the appropriate minimum is provided by transfers, it may be perfectly fair that the other part of total income is competitively determined. Moreover, this way of dealing with the claims of need is doubtless more efficient, at least from a theoretical point of view, than trying to regulate prices by minimum wage standards and so on. It is preferable to handle these claims by a separate branch which supports a social minimum. Henceforth, in considering whether the second principle of justice is satisfied, the answer turns on whether the total income of the least advantaged, that is, wages plus transfers, is such as to maximize their long-term expectations consistent with the demands of liberty.

Finally, the distribution branch is to preserve an approximately just distribution of income and wealth over time by affecting the background conditions of the market from period to period. Two aspects of this branch may be distinguished. First of all, it operates a system of inheritance and gift taxes. The aim of these levies is not to raise revenue, but gradually and continually to correct the distribution of wealth and to prevent the concentrations of power to the detriment of liberty and equality of opportunity. It is perfectly true, as some have said,[5]

that unequal inheritance of wealth is no more inherently unjust than unequal inheritance of intelligence; as far as possible the inequalities founded on either should satisfy the difference principle. Thus, the inheritance of greater wealth is just as long as it is to the advantage of the worst off and consistent with liberty, including equality of opportunity. Now by the latter we do not mean, of course, the equality of expectations between classes, since differences in life-prospects arising from the basic structure are inevitable, and it is precisely the aim of the second principle to say when these differences are just. Instead, equality of opportunity is a certain set of institutions which assures equally good education and chances of culture for all and which keeps open the competition for positions on the basis of qualities reasonably related to performance, and so on. It is these institutions which are put in jeopardy when inequalities and concentrations of wealth reach a certain limit; and the taxes imposed by the distribution branch are to prevent this limit from being exceeded. Naturally enough where this limit lies is a matter for political judgment guided by theory, practical experience, and plain hunch; on this question the theory of justice has nothing to say.

The second part of the distribution branch is a scheme of taxation for raising revenue to cover the costs of public goods, to make transfer payments, and the like. This scheme belongs to the distribution branch since the burden of taxation must be justly shared. Although we cannot examine the legal and economic complications involved, there are several points in favour of proportional expenditure taxes as part of an ideally just arrangement. For one thing, they are preferable to income taxes at the level of common-sense precepts of justice, since they impose a levy according to how much a man takes out of the common store of goods and not according to how much he contributes (assuming that income is fairly earned in return for productive efforts). On the other hand, proportional taxes treat everyone in a clearly defined uniform way (again assuming that income is fairly earned) and hence it is preferable to use progressive rates only when they are necessary to preserve the justice of the system as a whole, that is, to prevent large fortunes hazardous to liberty and equality of opportunity, and the like. If proportional expenditure taxes should also prove more efficient, say because they interfere less with incentives, or whatever, this would make the case for them decisive provided a feasible scheme could be worked out.[6] Yet these are questions of political judgment which are not our concern; and, in any case, a proportional expenditure tax is part of an idealized scheme which we are describing. It does not follow that even steeply progressive income taxes, given the injustice of existing systems, do not improve justice and efficiency all things considered. In practice we must usually choose between unjust arrangements and then it is a matter of finding the lesser injustice.

Whatever form the distribution branch assumes, the argument for it is to be based on justice: we must hold that once it is accepted the social system as a whole—the competitive economy surrounded by a just constitutional and legal framework—can be made to satisfy the principles of justice with the smallest loss in efficiency. The long-term expectations of the least advantaged are raised to the highest level consistent with the demands of equal liberty. In discussing the choice of a distribution scheme we have made no reference to the traditional criteria of taxation according to ability to pay or benefits received; nor have we mentioned any of the variants of the sacrifice principle. These standards are subordinate to the two principles of justice; once the problem is seen as that of designing a whole social system, they assume the status of secondary precepts with no more independent force than the precepts of common sense in regard to wages. To suppose otherwise is not to take a sufficiently comprehensive point of view. In setting up a just distribution branch these precepts may or may not have a place depending upon the demands of the two principles of justice when applied to the entire system.

VI

Our problem now is whether the whole system of institutions which we have described, the competitive economy surrounded by the four branches of government, can be made to satisfy the two principles of justice. It seems intuitively plausible that this can be done, but we must try to make sure. We assume that the social system as a whole meets the demands of liberty; it secures the rights required by the first principle and the principle of open offices. Thus the question is whether, consistent with these liberties, there is any way of operating the four branches of government so as to bring the inequalities of the basic structure in line with the difference principle.

Now, quite clearly the thing to do is to set the social minimum at the appropriate level. So far we have said nothing about how high this minimum should be. Common sense might be content to say that the right level depends on the average wealth of the country, and that, other things equal, the minimum should be higher if this average is higher; or it might hold that the proper level depends on customary expectations. Both of these ideas are unsatisfactory. The first is not precise enough since it does not state how the minimum should depend on wealth and it overlooks other relevant considerations such as distribution; and the second provides no criterion for when customary expectations are themselves reasonable. Once the difference principle is accepted, however, it follows that the minimum should be set at the level which, taking wages into account, maximizes the expectations of the lowest income class. By adjusting the amount of transfers, and the benefits from public goods which improve their circumstances, it is possible to increase or decrease the total income of the least advantaged (wages plus transfers plus benefits from public goods). Controlling the sum of transfers and benefits, thereby raising or lowering the social minimum, gives sufficient leeway in the whole scheme to satisfy the difference principle.

Now, offhand it might appear that this arrangement requires a very high minimum. It is easy to imagine the greater wealth of those better off being scaled down until eventually all stand on nearly the same level. But this is a misconception. The relevant expectation of the least advantaged is their long-term expectation extending over all generations; and hence over any period of time the economy must put aside the appropriate amount of real capital accumulation. Assuming for the moment that this amount is given, the social minimum is determined in the following way. Suppose, for simplicity, that transfer payments and the benefits from public goods are supported by expenditure (or income) taxes. Then raising the minimum entails raising the constant proportion at which consumption (or income) is taxed. Now presumably as this proportion is increased there comes a point beyond which one of two things happens: either the savings required cannot be made or the increased taxes interfere so much with the efficiency of the economy that the expectations of the lowest class for that period no longer improve but begin to decline. In either case the appropriate level for the minimum has been reached and no further increase should be made.

In order to make the whole system of institutions satisfy the two principles of justice, a just savings principle is presupposed. Hence we must try to say something about this difficult question. Unfortunately there are no very precise limits on what the rate of saving should be; how the burden of real saving should be shared between generations seems to admit of no definite answer. It does not follow, however, that certain general bounds cannot be prescribed which are ethically significant. For example, it seems clear that the classical principle of utility, which requires us to maximize total well-being over all generations, results in much too high a rate of saving, at least for the earlier generations. On the contract doctrine the question is approached from the standpoint of the parties in the original position who do not know to which generation they belong, or what comes to the same thing, they do not know the stage of economic advance of their society. The veil of ignorance is complete in this respect. Hence the parties ask themselves how much they would be willing to save at each stage on the assumption that other generations save at the same rates. That is, a person is to consider his willingness to save at every phase of development with the understanding that the rates he proposes will regulate the whole span of accumulation. Since no one knows to which generation he belongs, the problem is looked at from the standpoint of each. Now it is immediately obvious that all generations, except possibly the first, gain from a reasonable rate of accumulation being maintained. Once the saving process is begun, it is to the advantage of all later generations. Each generation passes on to the next a fair equivalent in real capital as defined by a just savings principle,

this equivalent being in return for what is received from previous generations and enabling the later ones to have a higher standard of life than would otherwise be possible. Only those in the first generation do not benefit, let's suppose; while they begin the whole process, they do not share in the fruits of their provision. At this initial stage, then, in order to obtain unanimity from the point of view of generations, we must assume that fathers, say, are willing to save for the sake of their sons, and hence that, in this case at least, one generation cares for its immediate descendants. With these suppositions, it seems that some just savings principle would be agreed to.

Now a just savings principle will presumably require a lower rate of saving in the earlier stages of development when a society is poor, and a greater rate as it becomes wealthier and more industrialized. As their circumstances become easier men would find it reasonable to agree to save more since the real burden is less. Eventually, perhaps, there will come a point beyond which the rate of saving may decline or stop altogether, at least if we suppose that there is a state of affluence when a society may concentrate on other things and it is sufficient that improvements in productive techniques be introduced only to the extent covered by depreciation. Here we are referring to what a society must save as a matter of justice; if it wishes to save for various grand projects, this is another matter.

We should note a special feature of the reciprocity principle in the case of just savings. Normally this principle applies when there is an exchange of advantages, that is, when each party gives something to the other. But in the accumulation process no one gives to those from whom he has received. Each gives to subsequent generations and receives from his predecessors. The first generation obtains no benefits at all, whereas the last generations, those living when no further saving is required, gain the most and give the least. Now this may appear unjust; and contrary to the formulation of the difference principle, the worst off save for those better off. But although this relation is unusual, it does not give rise to any difficulty. It simply expresses the fact that generations are spread out in time and exchanges between them can take place in only one direction. Therefore, from the standpoint of the original position, if all are to gain, they must agree to receive from their predecessors and to pass along a fair equivalent to those who come after them. The criterion of justice is the principle which would be chosen in the original position; and since a just savings principle would, let's suppose, be agreed to, the accumulation process is just. The savings principle may be reconciled with the difference principle by assuming that the representative man in any generation required to save belongs to the lowest income class. Of course, this saving is not done so much, if at all, by taking an active part in the investment process; rather it takes the form of approving of the economic arrangements which promote accumulation. The saving of those worse off is undertaken by accepting, as a matter of political judgment, those policies designed to improve the standard of life, thereby abstaining from the immediate advantages which are available to them. By supporting these arrangements and policies the appropriate savings can be made, and no representative man regardless of generation can complain of another for not doing his part.

Of the nature of the society at which the saving process aims we can give only the most general description. It is a society of persons with the greatest equal talent enjoying the benefits of the greatest equal liberty under economic conditions reached immediately after the highest average income *per capita* at which any saving at all is required. There is no longer a lowest income class in the traditional sense; such differences in wealth as exist are freely chosen and accepted as a price of doing things less in demand. All of this is, unfortunately, terribly vague. But, in any case, this general conception specifies a horizon of sorts at which the savings process aims so that the just savings principle is not completely indeterminate. That is, we suppose that the intention is to reach a certain social state, and the problem of the proper rate of accumulation is how to share fairly in the burdens of achieving it. The contractarian idea is that if we look at this question from the perspective of those in the original position, then, even though the savings principle which results is inevitably imprecise, it does impose ethically significant bounds. What is of first importance is that the problem of just savings be

approached in the right way; the initial conception of what we are to do determines everything else. Thus, from the standpoint of the original position, representatives of all generations, so to speak, must agree on how to distribute the hardships of building and preserving a just society. They all gain from adopting a savings principle, but also they have their own interests which they cannot sacrifice for another.

VII

The sketch of the system of institutions satisfying the two principles of justice is now complete. For once the just rate of savings is determined, at least within broad limits, we have a criterion for setting the level of the social minimum. The sum of transfers should be that which maximizes the expectations of the lowest income class consistent with the appropriate saving being undertaken and the system of equal liberties maintained. This arrangement of institutions working over time results in a definite pattern of distributive shares, and each man receives a total income (wages plus transfers) to which he is entitled under the rules upon which his legitimate expectations are founded. Now an essential feature of this whole scheme is that it contains an element of pure procedural justice. That is, no attempt is made to specify the just distribution of particular goods and services to particular persons, as if there were only one way in which, independently of the choices of economic agents, these things should be shared. Rather, the idea is to design a scheme such that the resulting distribution, whatever it is, which is brought about by the efforts of those engaged in co-operation and elicited by their legitimate expectations, is just.

The notion of pure procedural justice may be explained by a comparison with perfect and imperfect procedural justice. Consider the simplest problem of fair division. A number of men are to divide a cake: assuming that a fair division is an equal one, which procedure will give this outcome? The obvious solution is to have the man who divides the cake take the last piece. He will divide it equally, since in this way he assures for himself as large a share as he can. Now in this case there is an independent criterion for which is the fair division. The problem is to devise a procedure, a set of rules for dividing the cake, which will yield this outcome. The problem of fair division exemplifies the features of perfect procedural justice. There is an independent criterion for which the outcome is just;—and we can design a procedure guaranteed to lead to it.

The case of imperfect procedural justice is found in a criminal trial. The desired outcome is that the defendant should be declared guilty if and only if he has committed the offence as charged. The trial procedure is framed to search for and to establish this result, but we cannot design rules guaranteed to reach it. The theory of trial procedures examines which rules of evidence, and the like, are best calculated to advance this purpose. Different procedures may reasonably be expected in different circumstances to yield the right result, not always, but at least most of the time, Hence a trial is a case of imperfect procedural justice. Even though the law may be carefully followed, and the trial fairly and properly conducted, it may reach the wrong outcome. An innocent man may be found guilty, a guilty man may be set free. In such cases we speak of a miscarriage of justice: the injustice springs from no human fault but from a combination of circumstances which defeats the purpose of the rules.

The notion of pure procedural justice is illustrated by gambling. If a number of persons engage in a series of fair bets, the distribution of cash after the last bet is fair, or at least not unfair, whatever this distribution is. (We are assuming, of course, that fair bets are those which define a zero expectation, that the bets are made voluntarily, that no one cheats, and so on.) Any distribution summing to the initial stock of cash held by everyone could result from a series of fair bets; hence all of these distributions are, in this sense, equally fair. The distribution which results is fair simply because it is the outcome. Now when there is pure procedural justice, the procedure for determining the just result must actually be carried out; for in this case there is no independent criterion by reference to which an outcome can be known to be just. Obviously we cannot say that a particular state of affairs is just because it could have been reached by following a just procedure. This would permit far too much and lead to absurdly unjust consequences. In the case of gambling, for example, it would

entail that any distribution whatever could be imposed. What makes the final outcome of the betting fair, or not unfair, is that it is the one which has arisen after a series of fair gambles.

In order, therefore, to establish just distributive shares a just total system of institutions must be set up and impartially administered. Given a just constitution and the smooth working of the four branches of government, and so on, there exists a procedure such that the actual distribution of wealth, whatever it turns out to be, is just. It will have come about as a consequence of a just system of institutions satisfying the principles to which everyone would agree and against which no one can complain. The situation is one of pure procedural justice, since there is no independent criterion by which the outcome can be judged. Nor can we say that a particular distribution of wealth is just because it is one which could have resulted from just institutions although it has not, as this would be to allow too much. Clearly there are many distributions which may be reached by just institutions, and this is true whether we count patterns of distributions among social classes or whether we count distributions of particular goods and services among particular individuals. There are indefinitely many outcomes and what makes one of these just is that it has been achieved by actually carrying out a just scheme of co-operation as it is publicly understood. It is the result which has arisen when everyone receives that to which he is entitled given his and others' actions guided by their legitimate expectations and their obligations to one another. We can no more arrive at a just distribution of wealth except by working together within the framework of a just system of institutions than we can win or lose fairly without actually betting.

This account of distributive shares is simply an elaboration of the familiar idea that economic rewards will be just once a perfectly competitive price system is organized as a fair game. But in order to do this we have to begin with the choice of a social system as a whole, for the basic structure of the entire arrangement must be just. The economy must be surrounded with the appropriate framework of institutions, since even a perfectly efficient price system has no tendency to determine just distributive shares when left to itself. Not only must economic activity be regulated by a just constitution and controlled by the four branches of government, but a just saving-function must be adopted to estimate the provision to be made for future generations. Thus, we cannot, in general, consider only piecewise reforms, for unless all of these fundamental questions are properly handled, there is no assurance that the resulting distributive shares will be just; while if the correct initial choices of institutions are made, the matter of distributive justice may be left to take care of itself. Within the framework of a just system men may be permitted to form associations and groupings as they please so long as they respect the like liberty of others. With social ingenuity it should be possible to invent many different kinds of economic and social activities appealing to a wide variety of tastes and talents; and as long as the justice of the basic structure of the whole is not affected, men may be allowed, in accordance with the principle of free association, to enter into and to take part in whatever activities they wish. The resulting distribution will be just whatever it happens to be. The system of institutions which we have described is, let's suppose, the basic structure of a well-ordered society. This system exhibits the content of the two principles of justice by showing how they may be perfectly satisfied; and it defines a social ideal by reference to which political judgment among second-bests, and the long range direction of reform, may be guided.

VIII

We may conclude by considering the third question: whether this conception of distributive shares is compatible with common-sense notions of justice. In elaborating the contract doctrine we have been led to what seems to be a rather special, even eccentric, conception the peculiarities of which centre in the difference principle. Clear statements of it seem to be rare, and it differs rather widely from traditional utilitarian and intuitionist notions.[7] But this question is not an easy one to answer, for philosophical conceptions of justice, including the one we have just put forward, and our common-sense convictions, are not very precise. Moreover, a comparison is made difficult by our tendency in

practice to adopt combinations of principles and precepts the consequences of which depend essentially upon how they are weighted; but the weighting may be undefined and allowed to vary with circumstances, and thus relies on the intuitive judgments which we are trying to systematize.

Consider the following conception of right: social justice depends positively on two things, on the equality of distribution (understood as equality in levels of well-being) and total welfare (understood as the sum of utilities taken over all individuals). On this view one social system is better than another without ambiguity if it is better on both counts, that is, if the expectations it defines are both less unequal and sum to a larger total. Another conception of right can be obtained by substituting the principle of a social minimum for the principle of equality; and thus an arrangement of institutions is preferable to another without ambiguity if the expectations sum to a larger total and it provides for a higher minimum. The idea here is to maximize the sum of expectations subject to the constraint that no one be allowed to fall below some recognized standard of life. In these conceptions the principles of equality and of a social minimum represent the demands of justice, and the principle of total welfare that of efficiency. The principle of utility assumes the role of the principle of efficiency the force of which is limited by a principle of justice.

Now in practice combinations of principles of this kind are not without value. There is no question but that they identify plausible standards by reference to which policies may be appraised, and given the appropriate background of institutions, they may give correct conclusions. Consider the first conception: a person guided by it may frequently decide rightly. For example, he would be in favour of equality of opportunity, for it seems evident that having more equal chances for all both improves efficiency and decreases inequality. The real question arises, however, when an institution is approved by one principle but not by the other. In this case everything depends on how the principles are weighted, but how is this to be done? The combination of principles yields no answer to this question, and the judgment must be left to intuition. For every arrangement combining a particular total welfare with a particular degree of inequality one simply has to decide, without the guidance from principle, how much of an increase (or decrease) in total welfare, say, compensates for a given decrease (or increase) in equality.

Anyone using the two principles of justice, however, would also appear to be striking a balance between equality and total welfare. How do we know, then, that a person who claims to adopt a combination of principles does not, in fact, rely on the two principles of justice in weighing them, not consciously certainly, but in the sense that the weights he gives to equality and total welfare are those which he would give to them if he applied the two principles of justice? We need not say, of course, that those who in practice refer to a combination of principles, or whatever, rely on the contract doctrine, but only that until their conception of right is completely specified the question is still open. The leeway provided by the determination of weights leaves the matter unsettled.

Moreover, the same sort of situation arises with other practical standards. It is widely agreed, for example, that the distribution of income should depend upon the claims of entitlement, such as training and experience, responsibility and contribution, and so on, weighed against the claims of need and security. But how are these commonsense precepts to be balanced? Again, it is generally accepted that the ends of economic policy are competitive efficiency, full employment, an appropriate rate of growth, a decent social minimum, and a more equal distribution of income. In a modern democratic state these aims are to be advanced in ways consistent with equal liberty and equality of opportunity. There is no argument with these objectives; they would be recognized by anyone who accepted the two principles of justice. But different political views balance these ends differently, and how are we to choose between them? The fact is that we agree to little when we acknowledge precepts and ends of this kind; it must be recognized that a fairly detailed weighting is implicit in any complete conception of justice. Often we content ourselves with enumerating, sense precepts and objectives of policy, adding that on particular questions we must strike a balance between them having studied the relevant facts. While this is sound practical advice, it does not express a conception of justice. Whereas on the contract doctrine all combinations of principle, precepts, and objectives of policy are given a weight in maximizing the expectations of the lowest income class consistent with making the required saving and maintaining the system of equal liberty and equality of opportunity.

Thus despite the fact that the contract doctrine seems at first to be a somewhat special conception, particularly in its treatment of inequalities, it may still express the principles of justice which stand in the background and control the weights expressed in our everyday judgments. Whether this is indeed the case can by decided only by developing the consequences of the two principles in more detail and noting if any discrepancies turn up. Possibly there will be no conflicts; certainly we hope there are none with the fixed points of our considered judgments. The main question perhaps is whether one is prepared to accept the further definition of one's conception of right which the two principles represent. For, as we have seen, common sense presumably leaves the matter of weights undecided. The two principles may not so much oppose ordinary ideas as provide a relatively precise principle where common sense has little to say.

Finally, it is a political convention in a democratic society to appeal to the common good. No political party would admit to pressing for legislation to the disadvantage of any recognized social interest. But how, from a philosophical point of view, is this convention to be understood? Surely it is something more than the principle of efficiency (in its Paretian form) and we cannot assume that government always affects everyone's interests equally. Yet since we cannot maximize with respect to more than one point of view, it is natural, given the ethos of a democratic society, to single out that of the least advantaged and maximize their long-term prospects consistent with the liberties of equal citizenship. Moreover, it does seem that the policies which we most confidently think to be just do at least contribute positively to the well-being of this class, and hence that these policies are just throughout. Thus the difference principle is a reasonable extension of the political convention of a democracy once we face up to the necessity of choosing a complete conception of justice.

NOTES

1.   In this essay I try to work out some of the implications of the two principles of justice discussed in 'Justice as Fairness' which first appeared in the *Philosophical Review*, 1958, and which is reprinted in *Philosophy, Politics and Society*, Series II, pp. 132–57.

2.   This question is discussed very briefly in 'Justice as Fairness,' see pp. 138–41. The intuitive idea is as follows. Given the circumstances of the original position, it is rational for a man to choose as if he were designing a society in which his enemy is to assign him his place. Thus, in particular, given the complete lack of knowledge (which makes the choice one under uncertainty), the fact that the decision involves one's life-prospects as a whole and is constrained by obligations to third parties (e.g. one's descendants) and duties to certain values (e.g. to religious truth), it is rational to be conservative and so to choose in accordance with an analogue of the maximin principle. Viewing the situation in this way, the interpretation given to the principles of justice in Section IV is perhaps natural enough. Moreover, it seems clear how the principle of utility can be interpreted: it is the analogue of the Laplacean principle for choice uncertainty. (For a discussion of these choice criteria, see R. D. Luce and H. Raiffa, *Games and Decisions* (1957), pp. 275–98).

3.   For this observation I am indebted to Brian Barry.

4.   Introduced by him in his *Manuel d'économie politique* (1909) and long since a basic principle of welfare economics.

5.   See for example F. von Hayek, *The Constitution of Liberty* (1960), p. 90.

6.   See N. Kaldor, *An Expenditure Tax* (1955).

7.   The nearest statement known to me is by Santayana. See the last part of ch. IV in *Reason and Society* (1906) on the aristocratic ideal. He says, for example, '. . . an aristocratic regimen can only be justified by radiating benefit and by proving that were less given to those above, less would be attained by those beneath them.' But see also Christian Bay, *The Structure of Freedom* (1958), who adopts the principle of maximizing freedom, giving special attention to the freedom of the marginal, least privileged man. Cf. pp. 59, 374f.

26.   *THE RATIONALE OF LEGAL PUNISHMENT*

Edmund L. Pincoffs

I. THE CLASSICAL DEBATE

If it were done when 'tis done, then 'twere well
It were done quickly. If the assassination
Could trammel up the consequence, and catch
With his surcease, success; that but this blow
Might be the be-all and the end-all here,
But here, upon this bank and shoal of time,
We'd jump the life to come. But in these cases
We still have judgment here; that we but teach
Bloody instructions, which being taught return
To plague th' inventor. This even-handed justice
Commends th' ingredients of our poisoned chalice
To our own lips.

SHAKESPEARE, *Macbeth*

Punishment has in it the notion of a remedy, and
has the place of a mean, not of an end.

BENJAMIN WHICHCOTE, *Moral and Religious Aphorisms*

From Edmund L. Pincoffs, *The Rationale of Legal Punishment*, (New York: Humanities Press, 1966), Chapter 1. Reprinted by permission of Humanities Press, Inc.

Legal punishment is viewed by some of the most sensitive and well-educated people of our time as a survival of barbarism, bereft of rational foundation, supported only by inertia and the wish to have vengeance on criminals. In this book, I shall be concerned solely with the rational foundations of punishment; not with its history, sociology, or psychology. I shall argue that though the question concerning the grounds of punishment is indeed vexed and confused, there are grounds; and that he who would substitute some other practice for punishment should be aware of them.

If the confusion concerning the foundations, or grounds, or rationale (I use the terms synonymously) of punishment is to be removed, a famous theoretical impasse must be examined in detail: the impasse between the retributivistic and the utilitarian positions. This will be the first order of business. What the critics of legal punishment have suspected, I hope to show more precisely: that the traditional theories are contraries. More seriously, neither theory is alone adequate to provide a satisfactory rationale for punishment. And, more seriously yet, modern attempts to show that the contrariety is merely apparent, arising out of failure to distinguish different levels of punishment-justification, fail. The second order of business consists in an attempted reconstruction of the rationale of punishment.

I hope that it will be apparent that my intention is not to carry on a polemic against retributivists, utilitarians, skeptics who despair of finding rational grounds, or humanitarians who rejoice in finding none. It is, rather, understanding and a carefully reasoned stance. It should be apparent that the human stakes are too high to wager on the outcome of professorial jousting matches.

In this chapter, I attempt to reconstruct the traditional retributivist position held by Kant, Hegel, and Bradley; and the traditional utilitarian position, as expounded by Paley and Bentham. Modern readers have much more difficulty understanding (not merely agreeing with) the retributive view than the utilitarian one.[1] Thus, I devote far more space to it. This explanation of the opposing views is examined in Chapter II, where the chief arguments in the age-old debate are examined; and in Chapters IV and V, where the implications for judicial procedure and legislation are traced out. Chapter III is an attempt to sort out some of the main issues in the arguments over the rationale of punishment, Chapter VI takes up the proposed substitution of treatment for punishment, and VII offers a qualified defense of the practice of legal punishment. Those readers who are familiar with the historical debate would do well to proceed directly to the second Chapter.

I

The classification of Kant as a retributivist is usually accompanied by a reference to some part of the following passage from the *Rechtslehre,* which is worth quoting at length.

Juridical punishment can never be administered merely as a means for promoting another good either with regard to the criminal himself or to civil society, but must in all cases be imposed only because the individual on whom it is inflicted *has committed a crime.* For one man ought never to be dealt with merely as a means subservient to the purpose of another, nor be mixed up with the subjects of real right. Against such treatment his inborn personality has a right to protect him, even although he may be condemned to lose his civil personality. He must first be found guilty and *punishable* before there can be any thought of drawing from his punishment any benefit for himself or his fellow-citizens. The penal law is a categorical imperative; and woe to him who creeps through the serpent-windings of utilitarianism to discover some advantage that may discharge him from the justice of punishment, or even from the due measure of it, according to the Pharisaic maxim: "It is better that *one* man should die than the whole people should perish." For if justice and righteousness perish, human life would no longer have any value in the world. . . .

But what is the mode and measure of punishment which public justice takes as its principle and standard? It is just the principle of equality, by which the pointer of the scale of justice is made to incline no more to the one side than the other. It may be rendered by saying that the undeserved evil which any one commits on another, is to be regarded as perpetrated on himself. Hence it may be said: "If you slander another, you slander yourself; if you steal from another, you steal from yourself; if you strike another, you strike yourself; if you kill another, you kill yourself." This is the Right of RETALIATION (*jus talionis*); and properly understood, it is the only principle which in regulating a public court, as distinguished from mere private judgment, can definitely assign both the quality and the quantity of a just penalty. All other standards are wavering and uncertain; and on account of other considerations involved in them, they contain no principle conformable to the sentence of pure and strict justice.[2]

Obviously we could mull over this passage for a long time. What, exactly, is the distinction between the Inborn and the Civil Personality? How is the Penal Law a Categorical Imperative: by derivation from one of the five formulations in the *Grundlegung,* or as a separate formulation? But we are on the trail of the traditional retributive theory of punishment and do not want to lose ourselves in niceties. There are two main points in this passage to which we should give particular attention:

i. The only acceptable reason for punishing a man is that he has committed a crime.

ii. The only acceptable reason for punishing a man in a given manner and degree is that the punishment is "equal" to the crime for which he is punished.

These propositions, I think it will be agreed, express the main points of the first and second paragraphs respectively. Before stopping over these points, let us go on to a third. It is brought out in the following passage from the *Rechtslehre,* which is also often referred to by writers on retributivism.

Even if a civil society resolved to dissolve itself with the consent of all its members—as might be supposed in the case of a people inhabiting an island resolving to separate and scatter themselves throughout the whole world—the last murderer lying in prison ought to be executed before the resolution was carried out. This ought to be done in order that every one may realize the desert of his deeds, and that bloodguiltiness may not remain upon the people; for otherwise they will all be regarded as participators in the murder as a public violation of justice.[3]

It is apparent from this passage that, so far anyway as the punishment of death for murder is concerned, the punishment awarded not only may but must be carried out. If it must be carried out "so that everyone may realize the desert of his deeds," then punishment for deeds other than murder must be carried out too. We will take it, then, that Kant holds that:

iii. Whoever commits a crime must be punished in accordance with his desert.

Whereas (i) tells us what kind of reason we must have *if* we punish, (iii) now tells us that we must punish *whenever* there is desert of punishment. Punishment, Kant tells us elsewhere, is "The *juridical* effect or consequence of a culpable act of Demerit."[4] Any crime is a culpable act of demerit, in that it is an "*intentional* transgression —that is, an act accompanied with the consciousness that it is a transgression."[5] This is an unusually narrow definition of crime, since crime is not ordinarily limited to intentional acts of transgression, but may also include unintentional ones, such as acts done in ignorance of the law, and criminally negligent acts. However, Kant apparently leaves room for "culpable acts of demerit" outside of the category of crime.

These he calls "faults," which are unintentional transgressions of duty, but "are nevertheless imputable to a person."[6] I can only suppose, though it is a difficulty in the interpretation of the *Rechtslehre,* that when Kant says that punishment must be inflicted "only because he has committed a crime," he is not including in "crime" what he would call a fault. Crime would, then, refer to any *intentional* imputable transgressions of duty; and these are what must be punished as involving ill desert. The difficulties involved in the definition of crime as the transgression of duty, as opposed to the mere violation of a legal prohibition, will be taken up later.

Taking the three propositions we have isolated as expressing the essence of the Kantian retributivistic position, we must now ask a direct and obvious question. What makes Kant hold this position? Why does he think it apparent that consequences should have *nothing to do* with the decision whether, and how, and how much to punish? There are two directions an answer to this question might follow. One would lead us into an extensive excursus on the philosophical position of Kant, the relation of this to his ethical theory, and the relation of his general theory of ethics to his philosophy of law. It would, in short, take our question as one about the consistency of Kant's position concerning the justification of punishment with the whole of the Kantian philosophy. This would involve discussion of Kant's reasons for believing that moral laws must be universal and categorical in virtue of their form alone, and divorced from any empirical content; of his attempt to make out a moral decision-procedure based upon an "empty" categorical imperative; and, above all, of the concept of freedom as a postulate of practical reason, and as the central concept of the philosophy of law. This kind of answer, however, we must forego here; for while it would have considerable interest in its own right, it would lead us astray from our purpose, which is to understand as well as we can the retributivist position, not as a part of this or that philosophical system but for its own sake. It is a position taken by philosophers with diverse philosophical systems; we want to take another direction, then, in our answer. Is there any *general* (nonspecial, nonsystematic) reason why Kant rejects consequences in the justification of punishment?

Kant believes that consequences have nothing to do with the justification of punishment partly because of his assumptions about the *direction* of justification; and these assumptions are, I believe, also to be found underlying the thought of Hegel and Bradley. Justification is not only *of* something, it is also *to* someone: it has an addressee. Now there are important confusions in Kant's and other traditional justifications of punishment turning on the question what the "punishment" *is* which is being justified. In Chapter IV, we will examine some of these. But if we are to feel the force of the retributivist position, we can no longer put off the question of the addressee of justification.

To whom is the Kantian justification of punishment directed? The question may seem a difficult one to answer, since Kant does not consider it himself as a separate issue. Indeed, it is not the kind of question likely to occur to a philosopher of Kant's formalistic leanings. A Kantian justification or rationale stands, so to speak, on its own. It is a structure which can be examined, tested, probed by any rational being. Even to speak of the addressee of justification has an uncomfortably relativistic sound, as if only persuasion of A or B or C is possible, and proof impossible. Yet, in practice, Kant does not address his proffered justification of punishment so much to any rational being (which, to put it otherwise, is to address it not at all), as to the being most affected: the criminal himself.

It is the criminal who is cautioned not to creep through the serpent-windings of utilitarianism. It is the criminal's rights which are in question in the debate with Beccaria over capital punishment. It is the criminal we are warned not to mix up with property or things: the "subjects of Real Right." In the *Kritik der Praktischen Vernunst,* the intended direction of justification becomes especially clear.

Now the notion of punishment, as such, cannot be united with that of becoming a partaker of happiness; for although he who inflicts the punishment may at the same time have the benevolent purpose of directing this punishment to this end, yet it must be justified in itself as punishment, i.e., as mere harm, so that if it stopped there, and the person punished could get no glimpse of kindness hidden behind this harsh-

ness, he must yet admit that justice was done him, and that his reward was perfectly suitable to his conduct. In every punishment, as such, there must first be justice, and this constitutes the essence of the notion. Benevolence may, indeed, be united with it, but the man who has deserved punishment has not the least reason to reckon upon this.[7]

Since this matter of the direction of justification is central in our understanding of traditional retributivism, and not generally appreciated, it will be worth our while to pause over this paragraph. Kant holds here, as he later holds in the *Rechtslehre,* that once it has been decided that a given "mode and measure" of punishment is justified, then "he who inflicts punishment" may do so in such a way as to increase the long-term happiness of the criminal. This could be accomplished, e.g., by using a prison term as an opportunity for reforming the criminal. But Kant's point is that reforming the criminal has nothing to do with justifying the infliction of punishment. It is not inflicted because it will give an opportunity for reform, but because it is merited. The passage does not need my gloss; it is transparently clear. Kant wants the justification of punishment to be such that the criminal "who could get no glimpse of kindness behind this harshness" would have to admit that punishment is warranted.

Suppose we tell the criminal, "We are punishing you for your own good." This is wrong, because it is then open to him to raise the question whether he deserves punishment, and what you consider good to be. If he does not deserve punishment, we have no right to inflict it, especially in the name of some good of which the criminal may not approve. So long as we are to treat him as rational—a being with dignity—we cannot force our judgments of good upon him. This is what makes the appeal to supposedly good consequences "wavering and uncertain." They waver because the criminal has as much right as anyone to question them. They concern ends which he may reject, and means which he might rightly regard as unsuited to the ends.

In the "Supplementary Explanations of the Principles of Right" of the *Rechtslehre,* Kant distinguishes between "punitive justice (*justitia punitiva*), in which the ground of the penalty is moral (*quia peccatum est*)," and "punitive *expediency,* the foundation of which is merely pragmatic (*ne peccetur*) as being grounded upon the experience of what operates most effectively to prevent crime." Punitive justice, says Kant, has an "entirely distinct place (*locus justi*) in the topical arrangement of the juridical conceptions." It does not seem reasonable to suppose that Kant makes this distinction merely to discard punitive expediency entirely, that he has no concern at all for the *ne peccetur*. But he does hold that there is no place for it in the justification of punishment proper: for this can only be to show the criminal that the punishment is just.

How is this to be done? The difficulty is that on the one hand the criminal must be treated as a rational being, an end in himself; but on the other hand the justification we offer him cannot be allowed to appear as the opening move in a rational discussion. It cannot turn on the criminal's acceptance of some premise which, as rational being, he has a perfect right to question. If the end in question is the well-being of society, we are assuming that the criminal will not have a different view of what that well-being consists in, and we are telling him that he should sacrifice himself *to* that end. As a rational being, he can question whether any end we propose is a good end. And we have no right to demand that he sacrifice himself to the public well-being, even supposing he agrees with us on what that consists in. No man has a duty, on Kant's view, to be benevolent.[8]

The way out of the quandary is to show the criminal that we are not inflicting the punishment on him for some questionable purpose of our own choice, but that he, as a free agent, has exercised *his* choice in such a way as to make the punishment a necessary consequence. "His own evil deed draws the punishment upon himself."[9] "The undeserved evil which anyone commits on another, is to be regarded as perpetuated on himself."[10] But may not the criminal rationally question this asserted connection between crime and punishment? Suppose he wishes to regard the punishment *not* as "drawn upon himself" by his own "evil deed?" Suppose he argues that no good purpose will be served by punishing him? But this line of thought leads into the "serpent-windings of utilitarianism," for if it is good consequences that govern, then justice goes by the board. What may not be done to him in the name of good consequences? What pro-

portion would remain between what he has done and what he suffers?[11]

But punishment is *inflicted*. To tell the criminal that he "draws it upon himself" is all very well, only how do we justify *to ourselves* the infliction of it? Kant's answer is found early in the *Rechtslehre*.[12] There he relates punishment to crime *via* freedom. Crime consists in compulsion or constraint of some kind: a hindrance of freedom.[13] If it is wrong that freedom should be hindered, it is right to block this hindrance. But to block the constraint of freedom it is necessary to apply constraint. Punishment is a "hindering of a hindrance of freedom." Compulsion of the criminal is, then, justified only to the extent that it hinders his compulsion of another.

But how are we to understand Kant here? Punishment comes after the crime. How can it hinder the crime? The reference cannot be to the hindrance of future crime, or Kant's doctrine reduces to a variety of utilitarianism. The picture of compulsion *vs.* compulsion is clear enough, but how are we to apply it? Our answer must be somewhat speculative, since there is no direct answer to be found in the *Rechtslehre*. The answer must begin from yet another extension of the concept of a crime. For the crime cannot consist merely in an act. What is criminal is acting in accordance with a wrong maxim: a maxim which would, if made universal, destroy freedom. The adoption of the maxim is criminal. Should we regard punishment, then, as the hindrance of a wrong maxim? But how do we hinder a maxim? We show, exhibit, its wrongness by taking it at face value. If the criminal has adopted it, he is claiming that it can be universalized. But if it is universalized it warrants the same treatment of the criminal as he has accorded to his victim. So if he murders he must be executed; if he steals we must "steal from" him.[14] What we do to him he willed, in willing to adopt his maxim as universalizable. To justify the punishment to the criminal is to show him that the compulsion we use on him proceeds according to the same rule by which he acts. This is how he "draws the punishment upon himself." In punishing, we are not adopting his maxim but demonstrating its logical consequences if universalized: we show the criminal *what* he has willed. This is the positive side of the Kantian rationale of punishment.

II

Hegel's version of this rationale has attracted more attention, and disagreement, in recent literature. It is the Hegelian metaphysical terminology which is in part responsible for the disagreement, and which has stood in the way of an understanding of the retributivist position. The difficulty turns around the notions of "annulment of crime," and of punishment as the "right" of the criminal. Let us consider "annulment" first.

In the *Philosophie des Rechts*[15] Hegel tells us that

Abstract right is a right to coerce, because the wrong which transgresses it is an exercise of force against the existence of my freedom in an external thing. The maintenance of this existent against the exercise of force therefore itself takes the form of an external act and an exercise of force annulling the force originally brought against it.[16]

Holmes complains that by the use of his logical apparatus, involving the negation of negations (or annulment), Hegel professes to establish what is only a mystic (though generally felt) bond between wrong and punishment.[17] Hastings Rashdall asks how any rational connection can be shown between the evil of the pain of punishment, and the twin evils of the suffering of the victim and the moral evil which "pollutes the offender's soul," unless appeal is made to the probable good consequences of punishment. The notion that the "guilt" of the offense must be, in some mysterious way, wiped out by the suffering of the offender does not seem to provide it.[18] Crime, which is an evil, is apparently to be "annulled" by the addition to it of punishment, which is another evil. How can two evils yield a good?[19]

But in fact Hegel is following the *Rechtslehre* quite closely here, and his doctrine is very near to Kant's. In the notes taken at Hegel's lectures,[20] we find Hegel quoted as follows:

If crime and its annulment . . . are treated as if they were unqualified evils, it must, of course, seem quite unreasonable to will an evil merely because "another evil is there already." . . . But it is not merely a question of an evil or of this, that, or the other good; the precise point at issue is wrong, and the righting of

it. . . . The various considerations which are relevant to punishment as a phenomenon and to the bearing it has on the particular consciousness, and which concern its effects (deterrent, reformative, etc.) on the imagination, are an essential topic for examination in their place, especially in connection with modes of punishment, but all these considerations presuppose as their foundation the fact that punishment is inherently and actually just. In discussing this matter the only important things are, first, that crime is to be annulled, not because it is the producing of an evil, but because it is the infringing of the right as right, and secondly, the question of what that positive existence is which crime possesses and which must be annulled; it is this existence which is the real evil to be removed, and the essential point is the question of where it lies. So long as the concepts here at issue are not clearly apprehended, confusion must continue to reign in the theory of punishment.[21]

While this passage is not likely to dethrone confusion, it does bring us closer to the basically Kantian heart of Hegel's theory. To "annul crime" should be read "right wrong." Crime is a wrong which consists in an "infringement of the right as right."[22] It would be unjust, says Hegel, to allow crime, which is the invasion of a right, to go unrequited. For to allow this is to admit that the crime is "valid": that is, that it is not in conflict with justice. But this is what we do want to admit, and the only way of showing this is to pay back the deed to the agent: coerce the coercer. For by intentionally violating his victim's rights, the criminal in effect claims that the rights of others are not binding on him; and this is to attack *das Recht* itself: the system of justice in which there are rights which must be respected. Punishment not only keeps the system in balance, it vindicates the system itself.

Besides talking about punishment's "annulment" of crime, Hegel has argued that it is the "right of the criminal." The obvious reaction to this is that it is a strange justification of punishment which makes it someone's right, for it is at best a strange kind of right which no one would ever want to claim! McTaggart's explanation of this facet of Hegel's theory is epitomized in the following quotation:

What, then, is Hegel's theory? It is, I think, briefly this: In sin, man rejects and defies the moral law. Punishment is pain inflicted on him because he has done this, and in order that he may, by the fact of his punishment, be forced into recognizing as valid the law which he rejected in sinning, and so repent of his sin—really repent, and not merely be frightened out of doing it again.[23]

If McTaggart is right, then we are obviously not going to find in Hegel anything relevant to the justification of legal punishment, where the notions of sin and repentance are out of place. And this is the conclusion McTaggart of course reaches. "Hegel's view of punishment," he insists, "cannot properly be applied in jurisprudence, and . . . his chief mistake regarding it lay in supposing that it could."[24]

But though McTaggart may be right in emphasizing the theological aspect of Hegel's doctrine of punishment, he is wrong in denying it a jurisprudential aspect. In fact, Hegel is only saying what Kant emphasized: that to justify punishment to the criminal is to show him that *he* has chosen to be treated as he is being treated.

The injury (the penalty) which falls on the criminal is not merely *implicitly* just—as just, it is *eo ipso* his implicit will, an embodiment of his freedom, his right; on the contrary, it is also a right *established* within the criminal himself, i.e. in his objectively embodied will, in his action. The reason for this is that his action is the action of a rational being and this implies that it is something universal and that by doing it the criminal has laid down a law which he has explicitly recognized in his action and under which in consequence he should be brought as under his right.[25]

To accept the retributivist position, then, is to accept a thesis about the burden of proof in the justification of punishment. Provided we make the punishment "equal" to the crime it is not up to us to justify it to the criminal, beyond pointing out to him that it is what he willed. It is not that he initiated a chain of events likely to result in his punishment, but that in willing the crime he willed that he himself should suffer in the same degree as his victim. But what if the criminal simply wanted to commit his crime and get away with it (break the window and run, take the funds and retire to Brazil, kill but live?) Suppose we explain to the criminal that *really* in willing to kill he willed to lose his life; and, unimpressed, he replies that *really* he wished to kill and save his skin. The retributivist answer is that to the extent that the criminal understands freedom

and justice he will understand that his punishment was made inevitable by his own choice. No moral theory can hope to provide a justification of punishment which will seem such to the criminal merely as a nexus of passions and desires. The retributivist addresses him as a rational being, aware of the significance of his action. The burden of proof, the retributivist would argue, is on the theorist who would not start from this assumption. For to assume from the beginning that the criminal is not rational is to treat him, from the beginning, as merely a "harmful animal."

What is involved in the action of the criminal is not only the concept of crime, the rational aspect present in crime as such whether the individual wills it or not, the aspect which the state has to vindicate, but also the abstract rationality of the individual's *volition*. Since that is so, punishment is regarded as containing the criminal's right and hence by being punished he is honored as a rational being. He does not receive this due of honor unless the concept and measure of his punishment are derived from his own act. Still less does he receive it if he is treated as a harmful animal who has to be made harmless, or with a view to deterring and reforming him.[26]

To address the criminal as a rational being aware of the significance of his action is to address him as a person who knows that he has not committed a "bare" act; to commit an act is to commit oneself to the universalization of the rule by which one acted. For a man to complain about the death sentence for murder is as absurd as for a man to complain that when he pushes down one tray of the scales, the other tray goes up; whereas the action, rightly considered, is of pushing down *and* up. "The criminal gives his consent already by his very act."[27] "The Eumenides sleep, but crime awakens them, and hence it is the very act of crime which vindicates itself."[28]

F. H. Bradley's contribution to the retributive theory of punishment adds heat but not much light. The central, and best-known, passage is the following:

If there is any opinion to which the man of uncultivated morals is attached, it is the belief in the necessary connection of Punishment and guilt. Punishment is punishment, only where it is deserved. We pay the penalty because we owe it, and for no other reason; and if punishment is inflicted for any other reason whatever than because it is merited by wrong, it is a gross immorality, a crying injustice, an abominable crime, and not what it pretends to be. We may have regard for whatever considerations we please—our own convenience, the good of society, the benefit of the offender; we are fools, and worse, if we fail to do so. Having once the right to punish, we may modify the punishment according to the useful and the pleasant; but these are external to the matter, they cannot give us a right to punish, and nothing can do that but criminal desert. This is not a subject to waste words over; if the fact of the vulgar view is not palpable to the reader, we have no hope, and no wish, to make it so.[29]

Bradley's sympathy with the "vulgar view" should be apparent.[30] And there is at least a seeming variation between the position he expresses here and that we have attributed to Kant and Hegel. For Bradley can be read here as leaving an open field for utilitarian reasoning, when the question is how and how much to punish. Ewing interprets Bradley this way, and argues at some length that Bradley is involved in an inconsistency.[31] However, it is quite possible that Bradley did not mean to allow kind and quantity of punishment to be determined by utilitarian considerations. He could mean, as Kant meant, that once punishment is awarded, then "it" (what the criminal must suffer: time in jail, e.g.) may be made use of for utilitarian purposes. But, it should by this time go without saying, the retributivist would then wish to insist that we not argue backward from the likelihood of attaining these good purposes to the rightness of inflicting the punishment.

Bradley's language is beyond question loose when he speaks, in the passage quoted, of our "modifying" the punishment, "having once the right to punish." But when he says that "we pay the penalty because we owe it, and for no other reason," Bradley must surely be credited with the insight that we may owe more or less according to the gravity of the crime. The popular view, he says, is "that punishment is justice; that justice implies the giving what is due."[32] And, "punishment is the complement of criminal desert; is justifiable only so far as deserved."[33] If Bradley accepts this popular view, then Ewing must be wrong in attributing to him the position

that kind and degree of punishment may be determined by utilitarian considerations.[34]

III

Let us sum up traditional retributivism, as we have found it expressed in the paradigmatic passage we have examined. We have found no reason, in Hegel or Bradley, to take back or qualify importantly the *three propositions* we found central in Kant's retributivism:

i. The only acceptable reason for punishing a man is that he has committed a crime.
ii. The only acceptable reason for punishing a man in a given manner and degree is that the punishment is "equal" to the crime.
iii. Whoever commits a crime must be punished in accordance with his desert.

To these propositions should be added *two underlying assumptions:*

i. An assumption about the direction of justification: to the criminal.
ii. An assumption about the nature of justification: to show the criminal that it is he who has willed what he now suffers.

Though it may have been stated in forbidding metaphysical terms, traditional retributivism cannot be dismissed as unintelligible, or absurd, or implausible.[35] There is no obvious contradiction in it; and there are no important disagreements between the philosophers we have studied over what it contends. Yet in spite of the importance of the theory, no one has yet done much more than sketch it in broad strokes. If, as I have surmised, it turns mainly on an assumption concerning the direction of justification, then this assumption should be explained and defended.

And the key concept of "desert" is intolerably vague. What does it mean to say that punishment must be proportionate to what a man *deserves?* This seems to imply, in the theory of the traditional retributivists, that there is some way of measuring desert, or at least of balancing punishment against it. How this measuring or balancing is supposed to be done, we will discuss later. What we must recognize here is that there are alternative criteria of "desert," and that it is not always clear which of these the traditional retributivist means to imply.

When we say of a man that he "deserves severe punishment" how, if at all, may we support our position by arguments? What kinds of considerations tend to show what a man does or does not deserve? There are at least two general sorts: those which tend to show that what he has done is a member of a class of actions which is especially heinous; and those which tend to show that his doing of this action was, in (or because of) the circumstances, particularly wicked. The argument that a man deserves punishment may rest on the first kind of appeal alone, or on both kinds. Retributivists who rely on the first sort of consideration alone would say that anyone who would do a certain sort of thing, no matter what the circumstances may have been, deserves punishment. Whether there are any such retributivists I do not know. Kant, because of his insistence on *intention* as a necessary condition of committing a crime, clearly wishes to bring in considerations of the second sort as well. It is not, on his view, merely *what* was done, but the intention of the agent which must be taken into account. No matter what the intention, a man cannot commit a crime deserving punishment if his deed is not a transgression. But if he does commit a transgression, he must do so intentionally to commit a crime; and all crime is deserving of punishment. The desert of the crime is a factor both of the seriousness of the transgression, considered by itself, and the degree to which the intention to transgress was present. If, for Kant, the essence of morality consists in knowingly acting from duty, the essence of immorality consists in knowingly acting against duty.

The retributivist can perhaps avoid the question of how we decide that one crime is morally more heinous than another by hewing to his position that no such decision is necessary so long as we make the punishment "equal" to the crime. To accomplish this, he might argue, it is not necessary to argue to the *relative* wickedness of crimes. But at best this leaves us with the problem how we *do* make punishments equal to crimes, a problem which will not stop plaguing retributivists. And there is the problem *which* transgressions, intentionally committed, the ret-

ributivist is to regard as crimes. Surely not every morally wrong action![36]

And how is the retributivist to fit in appeals to punitive expediency? None of our authors deny that such appeals may be made, but where and how do they tie into punitive justice? It will not do simply to say that justifying punishment to the criminal is one thing, and justifying it to society is another. Suppose we must justify in both directions at once? And who are "we" anyway—the players of which roles, at what stage of the game?[37] And has the retributivist cleared himself of the charge, sure to arise, that the theory is but a cover for a much less commendable motive than respect for justice: elegant draping for naked revenge?[38]

IV

The utilitarian theory of punishment can be regarded as but a subheading of a highly developed general theory of ethics which has had numerous advocates in the history of philosophy, and remains popular today. It is therefore tempting to begin our analysis with some very general formulation of utilitarianism (e.g. "An act, policy, course of action, or practice is right if and only if the set of consequences it initiates would be better on the whole than the consequences initiated by any alternative act, policy, course of action, or practice.") and to show how, if this general position be accepted, the special utilitarian theory of punishment follows. But this approach would be mistaken. It would lead us to settle by fiat a vigorous debate among utilitarians over the way in which the general position should be formulated and defended. (Should acts be justified by reference to rules, rules by reference to practices, and practices by reference to their tendency to maximize good consequences; or should we reserve the right to short-cut the rules and practices, and calculate the consequences of the act? And what are the consequences which should be maximized?) It would also lead us to ignore the real possibility that a philosopher might without inconsistency adopt a utilitarian position with respect to punishment, but reject it as a general theory of ethics.

Our concern must be, rather, at this stage of our analysis, to delineate as sharply as possible the general outlines of the traditional utilitarian theory of punishment: to set it out, if we can, in propositions which can be contrasted with those we have taken as expressing the retributive position. To accomplish this we turn again to the history of philosophy, to philosophers generally accepted as promulgating a utilitarian view of punishment. Here, as in the previous section, we will make no attempt to survey the whole field, but will discuss positions which would be universally accepted as paradigmatic: those of William Paley and Jeremy Bentham.

There are advantages in beginning with William Paley beyond that of mere chronological appropriateness. Paley's formulation of the utilitarian theory of punishment was enormously influential, since it was expressed in a book which was a text at Cambridge, and a standard reference on philosophy, running through fifteen editions in Paley's own lifetime.[39] So highly regarded was this book, and so conservative in tendency, that Sir Samuel Romilly, the great reformer of the English criminal law, was obliged to devote a large proportion of his major address of 1810 to a critical analysis of it.[40] More importantly for our purposes, it provides us with a bold and uncomplicated first statement of the position we wish to understand.

"The proper end of human punishment is not," Paley tells us, "the satisfaction of justice, but the prevention of crimes." And since the prevention of crimes is the "sole consideration which authorizes the infliction of punishment by human laws," punishment must be proportioned to prevention, not to guilt. "The crime must be prevented by some means or other; and consequently, whatever means appear necessary to this end, whether they be proportionable to the guilt of the criminal or not, are adopted rightly, because they are adopted upon the principle which alone justifies the infliction of punishment at all." Since punishment is itself an evil, it should be resorted to only when a greater evil can be prevented. "The sanguinary laws which have been made against counterfeiting or diminishing the gold coin of the kingdom might be just, until the method of detecting the fraud by weighing the money, was introduced into general usage." The facility with which a crime can be committed constitutes a ground for more severe punishment. The stealing of cloth from bleaching grounds must be punished more severely than most other simple felonies not because this crime is in its "own nature more heinous" but because the property is more exposed.[41]

"From the justice of God," says Paley, "we are taught to look for a graduation of punishment, exactly proportioned to the guilt of the offender." But, not finding this proportion in human law, we question its wisdom. However, we must recognize that

when the care of the public safety is entrusted to men, whose authority over their fellow creatures is limited by defects of power and knowledge; from whose utmost vigilance and sagacity the greatest offenders often lie hid; whose wisest precautions and speediest pursuit may be eluded by artifice or concealment; a different necessity, a new rule of proceeding results from the very imperfection of their faculties. In their hands the uncertainty of punishment must be compensated by the severity. The ease with which crimes are committed or concealed, must be counteracted by additional penalities and increased terrors. The very end for which human government is established, requires that its regulations be adapted to the suppression of crimes. This end, whatever it may do in the plans of infinite wisdom, does not in the designation of temporal penalties, always coincide with the proportionate punishment of guilt.[42]

This is flat opposition to retributivism. To Kant's thesis that the only reason for which we may punish is that a crime has been committed, Paley replies that the only reason for punishment is the prevention of crime. To Kant's thesis that the only ground for choosing a given "mode and measure" of punishment is that it equals the crime, Paley counters that mode and measure must be determined by the utility of the proposed punishment in preventing crime. Paley could not agree that the last prisoner, in Kant's example of the dispersing community, should be executed; since he holds that if crime can be prevented by means short of punishment it should be, but it is a truism that if the community is dispersed the opportunity for crime will not arise again in the community. To each of the propositions to which we reduced Kantian retributivism, Paley would oppose a contrary proposition.

i. The only acceptable reason for punishing a man is that punishing him will serve the end of the prevention of crimes.

ii. The only acceptable reason for punishing a man in a given manner and degree is that this is the manner and degree of punishment most likely to prevent the crime.

iii. Whether or not a man should be punished depends upon the possibility of preventing the crime in question by nonpunitive means.

V

Paley's theory of punishment is but a sketch, so cryptic that we do not know what directions he might have taken in developing it. Bentham's is the most comprehensive theory in the history of philosophy.[43] He extends Paley's theory by: (1) Providing a general theoretical foundation for the justification of punishment; (2) Distinguishing carefully between punishment and other "remedies" for crime; (3) Drawing the limits beyond which punishment should not be applied; and (4) Offering rules for the determination of manner and degree of punishing.

In the wealth of important material to be found in Bentham's published work on the subject of punishment, any selection is bound to seem arbitrary; yet select we must. Our object will be merely to give some indication of what traditional utilitarianism with respect to punishment is like in its most highly developed form.

(1) *Theoretical foundation.* Bentham is not content to begin with the purpose of punishment, but, thinking of punishment as but one tool in the hands of the legislator, asks what the end is which this and other legislative tools should be made to serve. This end is "to augment the total happiness of the community; and therefore, in the first place, to exclude, as far as may be, every thing that tends to subtract from happiness: in other words to exclude mischief."[44]

This broader foundation will allow Bentham to include more under punishment than prevention of crimes as they arise, and to take a wider view of prevention than Paley did. Bentham agrees with Paley that punishment is itself an evil and should, if used, be used as sparingly as possible: "Upon the principle of utility, if it ought at

all to be admitted, it ought only to be admitted in as far as it promises to exclude some greater evil." But here again he takes a wider view, by setting for himself the task of discriminating between those situations in which punishment should be used and those in which it should not.

(2) *Distinction between punishment and other possible remedies for crime.* The mischief of crime obstructs happiness, but the mischief of punishment does too; so we must be chary in our use of punishment and look about for other means of dealing with the mischief of crime. All such means, including punishment, Bentham terms "remedies," and there are four sorts: (a) Preventive, (b) Suppressive, (c) Satisfactory, and (d) Penal remedies or Punishment.

(a) The first of these remedies has an unfortunate title, since on Bentham's view, punishment is preventive also. What he has in mind are, first, direct moves which can be made by the police or private citizens, like admonitions, threats, or seizure of arms, to prevent the occurrences of a particular crime which is thought likely to occur: as when we see a man apparently preparing to commit armed robbery and warn him away.[45] Secondly, there is the whole vast class of indirect moves which can be made to prevent crime: indirect in that they refer not to this or that particular crime, but to a class of crimes which might be committed—preventive medicine as opposed to treating the cholera of crime when it breaks out. Under this important heading, Bentham discusses[46] at length such topics as removal of temptations to crime, like easily concealed arms and tools for the counterfeiting of money; substituting innocuous for dangerous desires and inclinations; and putting people on guard against certain types of offenses.

(b) Suppressive remedies "tend to put a stop to an offense in progress, but not completed, and so prevent the evil, or at least a part of it."[47] Bentham gives no examples, but mentions that suppressive means are the same as preventive ones. The difference apparently lies in the stage of the game at which they are applied: the crime of murder is suppressed if we wrest away the would-be killer's gun, prevented if we warn his victim to leave town or pass and enforce a law prohibiting the sale of weapons which can easily be concealed.

(c) Satisfactory remedies "consist of reparations or indemnities, secured to those who have suffered from offenses."[48] They assume the crime done and try to remove all or part of the mischief it caused. Thus the money taken from the bank must be returned, the damage to a house repaired, the public calumny publicly admitted to be false. The object is to make it as if the crime had never occurred. The object is not, as with Kant's Principle of Equality, that the criminal must suffer in the way and to the degree that his victim suffered; but that the suffering of the victim must somehow be compensated to him.[49]

(d) Punishment is distinguished from the other remedies for the mischief of crime in that, like satisfactory remedies, it occurs only after the crime, but, unlike satisfactory remedies, its purpose is preventive: "to prevent like offenses, whether on the part of the offender or of others."[50]

What is past is but one act; the future is infinite. The offense already committed concerns only a single individual; similar offenses may affect all. In many cases it is impossible to redress the evil that is done; but it is always possible to take away the will to repeat it; for however great may be the advantage of the offense, the evil of the punishment may be always made out to outweigh it.[51]

The punishment which serves to deter the criminal from repeating his crime is called by Bentham "particular prevention." This may be achieved in three ways: by taking away from the criminal the physical power of repeating his offense (incapacitation), by taking away the desire of offending (reformation), or by making him afraid of offending (intimidation). It is general prevention, however, the prevention of crime by example of the punishment suffered by the offender, which "ought to be the chief end of punishment, as it is its real justification."[52]

That punishment which, considered in itself, appeared base and repugnant to all generous sentiments, is elevated to the first rank of benefits, when it is regarded not as an act of wrath or of vengeance against a guilty or unfortunate individual who has given way to mischievous inclinations, but as an indispensable sacrifice to the common safety.[53]

(3) *The limits of punishment.* When we understand that punishment is but one of the remedies which may be used against crime, and the conditions under which and the purpose for which it should be used, we are ready to approach the topic of the limits of punishment: "cases unmeet for punishment." Given the general preventive end of punishment, it ought not to be inflicted where it is (a) groundless, (b) inefficacious, (c) unprofitable, or (d) needless. Since punishment is itself an evil, the burden of proof is on him who would inflict it, and this is so even though a crime has been committed. This contrasts with traditional retributivism, where the burden is on the criminal to show why he should not be punished equally with his crime, but does not rest (provided the proper proportion is observed) on the person inflicting punishment.

(a) Punishment is groundless when there is no mischief for it to prevent. For example, though it seemed mischievous (breaking into a man's house, burning his fields), yet the "victim" gave his (free and fairly obtained) consent; or though it is mischievous it was necessary as a means to an over-all good (tearing down a man's house to get material for plugging the dike).

(b) Punishment is inefficacious when it cannot act preventively. Examples are *ex-post facto* laws; laws not sufficiently promulgated; punishment of infants or insane persons, or persons under physical compulsion.

(c) Punishment is unprofitable when the punishment would produce more evil than the offense it is meant to prevent (capital punishment for picking pockets).

(d) Punishment is needless when the mischief can be prevented at a "cheaper rate." This limitation (recognized by Paley in the coinage example mentioned above) comes about when there is some means short of punishment which will accomplish the same thing. (Instructing misguided people concerning the moral principles by which they should be guided.)[54]

(4) *Rules for the determination of manner and degree of punishment.* It is here that the subtlety and caution of Bentham are especially apparent. He could not be satisfied with Paley's rough dictum that the crime must be prevented by some means or other and that proportion between guilt and punishment must therefore be ignored. Among the factors (to be examined in

more detail later) which Bentham considers, are the need to set penalties in such a way that where a person is tempted to commit one of two crimes he will commit the lesser, that the evil consequences (mischief) of the crime will be minimized even if the crime is committed, that the least amount possible of punishment be used for the prevention of a given crime.

VI

That Bentham moves well beyond Paley in intelligibility and careful analysis there can be no question. Does the Benthamite analysis conflict with the Paleian position: force us to alter the formulation of the utilitarian theory of punishment which we understood Paley to express? It does not so much require alteration as careful qualification of the bare and bold Paleian pronouncements:

i. The only acceptable reason for punishing a man is that punishing him will serve the end of the prevention of crimes.

Yes, Bentham would say, but we must not forget that there are some deeds it will not be worthwhile to denominate crimes and try to prevent; nor that prevention is itself a very complex notion, the analysis of which bears importantly on the means we use.

ii. The only acceptable reason for punishing a man in a given manner and degree is that this manner and degree of punishment is most likely to prevent the crime.

Bentham would add: Consistently with the reduction of mischief in general! We cannot look at the prevention of each crime as a separate problem. We want to reduce the mischief of *all* crime at the least possible expense. Otherwise, we will fall into feckless severity, as did Madan, and Paley himself.

iii. Whether or not a man should be punished depends upon the possibility of preventing the crime in question by nonpunitive means.

Yes, Bentham would agree, since punishment is but one of four possible remedies for crime, and should be reserved until remedies involving less mischief have been tried.

Paley looks only to the prevention of the crime in question, or (at best) of crimes in general. For Bentham, prevention of crime is but a subheading under prevention of mischief, and that a subheading under the promotion of happiness. But since there is no question but what mischief must be prevented if happiness is to be promoted, and that crime is mischief, the justification of punishment turns inevitably only on the prevention of crime at the least cost, in mischief, of the means used.

It is, of course, the word "only" which gives rise to the trouble, for the retributivist creed has an "only" in it, too: it is only by reference to desert that punishment may be justified. Both of these positions cannot be true, so much is obvious. And both could be false.

If we were to follow out the lead developed in the first section, we would look for the addressee, if there is just one, of the Benthamite justification of punishment. And we would find that Bentham does not appear to have so much in mind justification to the criminal (or to any of us who might have to play that role) as justification to the noninvolved citizen whose interest is simply in the best ordering of society. But to make this out in detail would be tedious. It might also be misleading, for it might suggest that the whole controversy could be resolved by showing that the retributivist is talking to one addressee and is concerned with one set of problems, and the utilitarian to another and another set of problems.

This is indeed a promising approach, for it looks as if it might be a way out of the ancient quandary. And it is not far from the road we shall now follow, which will lead us to distinguish a number of disparate undertakings which have traditionally been lumped together as "the justification of punishment." Whether these distinctions, once made, will resolve the quandary remains to be seen.

NOTES

1. What is the cause of this difficulty? Perhaps it is mainly that, since in our own time there are few defenders of retributivism, the position is most often referred to by writers who are opposed to it. This does not make for clarity. In the past few years, however, there has been an upsurge of interest, and some good articles have been written. Cf. esp. J. D. Mabbott, "Punishment," *Mind*, XLVIII (1939), pp. 152–67; C. S. Lewis, "The Humanitarian Theory of Punishment," *20th Century* (Australian), March, 1949; C. W. K. Mundle, "Punishment and Desert," *The Philosophical Quarterly*, IV (1954), pp. 216–228; A. S. Kaufman, "Anthony Quinton on Punishment," *Analysis*, October, 1959; and K. G. Armstrong, "The Retributivist Hits Back," LXX (1961), pp. 471–90.

2. *Rechtslehre*, Part Second, 49, E. Hastie translation, Edinburgh, 1887, pp. 195–7.

3. *Ibid.*, p. 198. Cf. also the passage on p. 196 beginning "What, then, is to be said of such a proposal as to keep a Criminal alive who has been condemned to death . . ."

4. *Ibid.*, Prolegomena, General Divisions of the Metaphysic of Morals, IV. (Hastie, p. 38).

5. *Ibid.*, p. 32.

6. *Ibid.*, p. 32.

7. Book I, Ch. I, Sect. VIII, Theorem IV, Remark II (T. K. Abbott translation, 5th ed., revised, London, 1898, p. 127).

8. *Rechtslehre*.

9. "Supplementary Explanation of The Principles of Right," V.

10. Cf. long quote from the *Rechtslehre*, above.

11. How can the retributivist allow utilitarian considerations even in the administration of the sentence? Are we not then opportunistically imposing our conception of good on the convicted man? How did we come by this right, which we did not have when he stood before the bar awaiting sentence? Kant would refer to the loss of his "Civil Personality;" but what rights remain with the "Inborn Personality," which is not lost? How is human dignity modified by conviction of crime?

12. Introduction to The Science of Right, General Definitions and Divisions, D. Right is Joined with the Title to Compel. (Hastie, p. 47).

13. This extends the definition of crime Kant has given earlier by specifying the nature of an imputable transgression of duty.

14. There are serious difficulties in the application of the "Principle of Equality" to the "mode and measure" of punishment. This will be considered in Chapter V.

15. I shall use this short title for the work with the formidable double title of *Naturrecht und Staatswissenchaft in Grundrisse; Grundlinien der Philosophie des Rechts (Natural Law and Political Science in Outline; Elements of The Philosophy of Right.)* References will be to the T. M. Knox translation (*Hegel's Philosophy of Right*, Oxford, 1942).

16. *Philosophie des Rechts*, Sect. 93 (Knox, p. 67).

17. O. W. Holmes, Jr., *The Common Law*, Boston, 1881, p. 42.

18. Hastings Rashdall, *The Theory of Good and Evil*, 2nd. Edn., Oxford, 1924, vol. 1, pp. 285–6.

19. G. E. Moore holds that, consistently with his doctrine of organic wholes, they might; or at least they might yield that which is less evil than the sum of the constituent evils. This indicates for him a possible vindication of the Retributive theory of punishment. (*Principia Ethica*, Cambridge, 1903, pp. 213–214).

20. Included in the Knox translation.

21. Knox translation, pp. 69–70.

22. There is an unfortunate ambiguity in the German word *Recht*, here translated as "right." The word can mean either that which is a right or that which is in accordance with the law. So when Hegel speaks of "infringing the right as right" it is not certain whether he means a right as such or the law as such, or whether, in fact, he is aware of the ambiguity. But to say that the crime infringes the law is analytic, so we will take it that Hegel uses *Recht* here to refer to that which is right. But what the criminal does is not merely to infringe a right, but "the right (*das Recht*) as right," that is, to challenge by his action the whole system of rights. (On "*Recht*," Cf. J. Austin, *The Province of Jurisprudence Determined*, London, Library of Ideas end., 1954), Note 26, pp. 285–288 esp. pp. 287–8).

23. J. M. E. McTaggart, *Studies in the Hegelian Cosmology*, Cambridge, 1901, Ch. V, p. 133.

24. *Ibid.*, p. 145.

25. *Op. Cit.*, Sect. 100 (Hastie, p. 70.)

26. *Ibid.*, Lecture-notes on Sect. 100, Hastie, p. 71.

27. *Ibid.*, Addition to Sect. 100, Hastie, p. 246.

28. *Ibid.*, Addition to Sect. 101, Hastie, p. 247. There is something ineradicably *curious* about retributivism. We keep coming back to the metaphor of the balance scale. Why is the metaphor powerful and at the same time strange? Why do we agree so readily that "the assassination" cannot "trammel up the consequence," that "even-handed justice commends the ingredients of our poisoned chalice to our own lips?"

29. F. H. Bradley, *Ethical Studies*, Oxford, 1952, pp. 26–7. Bradley's later article, "Some Remarks on Punishment" is considered in Chapter V.

30. Yet it may not be amiss to note the part played by the "vulgar view" in Bradley's essay. In "The Vulgar Notion of Responsibility in Connection with the Theories of Free Will and Necessity," from which this passage is quoted, Bradley is concerned to show that neither the "Libertarian" nor the "Necessitarian" position can be accepted. Both of these "two great schools" which "divide our philosophy" "stand out of relation to vulgar morality." Bradley suggests that perhaps the truth is to be found not in either of these "two undying and opposite one-sidednesses but in a philosophy which "thinks what the vulgar believe." Cf. also the contrasting of the "ordinary consciousness" with the "philosophical" or "debauched" morality (p. 4). On p. 3 he says that by going to "vulgar morality" we "gain in integrity" what we "lose in refinement." Nevertheless, he does say (p. 4) "seeing the vulgar are after all the vulgar, we should not be at pains to agree with their superstitions."

31. A. C. Ewing, *The Morality of Punishment*, London, 1929, pp. 41–42.

32. *Op. Cit.*, p. 29.

33. *Ibid.*, p. 30.

34. *Op. Cit.*, p. 41.

35. Or, more ingeniously, "merely logical," the "elucidation of the use of a word;" answering the question, "When (logically) *can* we punish?" as opposed to the question answered by the utilitarians, "When (morally) *may* or *ought* we to punish?" (Cf. A. M. Quinton, "On Punishment," *Analysis*, June, 1954, pp. 133–142).

36. Cf. Ch. V.

37. Distinctions to be made in Chapter III.

38. To be discussed in the next chapter.

39. *The Principles of Moral and Political Philosophy.* References are to the 6th edition, corrected, London, 1788.

40. L. Radzinowiez, *A History of English Criminal Law and its Administration from 1750.* London, 1948, pp. 257–259.

41. *Op. Cit.,* Vol. II, Book VI, Ch. IX, pp. 268–70.

42. *Ibid.,* pp. 273–4.

43. The sources used here are *Introduction to the Principles of Morals and Legislation,* Wilfrid Harrison, ed., Oxford, 1948: *The Theory of Legislation,* originally edited and published in French by Etienne Dumont re-translated, and re-edited by C. K. Ogden, London, 1931; and *The Rationale of Punishment,* also re-translated from Dumont's edition, London, 1830. There is much overlap in these books, which were all mined from the same lode of manuscripts. Where there is overlap, reference will be made to the *Principles* or

the *Theory,* since the *Rationale* is out of print and not generally available.

44. *Principles,* p. 281.

45. Examples are mainly mine, here and in the following paragraphs, since Bentham gives few.

46. *Theory,* "Principles of The Penal Code," IV (pp. 358–472).

47. *Ibid.,* p. 271.

48. *Ibid.,* p. 271.

49. A connecting link could be the vindictive satisfaction felt by the victim on seeing the criminal punished, considered as compensation to the victim. But the victim may not want this kind of "compensation." (Cf. *Theory,* Principles of the Penal Code, II, XVI).

50. *Ibid.,* p. 272.

51. *Ibid.,* p. 272.

52. *Rationale,* I, III, p. 20.

53. *Ibid.,* p. 21.

54. *Principles,* pp. 281–288.

27. *THE EXPRESSIVE FUNCTION OF PUNISHMENT*

Joel Feinberg

It might well appear to a moral philosopher absorbed in the classical literature of his discipline, or to a moralist sensitive to injustice and suffering, that recent philosophical discussions of the problem of punishment have somehow missed the point of his interest. Recent influential articles[1] have quite sensibly distinguished between questions of definition and justification, between justifying general rules and particular decisions, between moral and legal guilt. So much is all to the good. When these articles go on to *define* 'punishment', however, it seems to many that they leave out of their ken altogether the very element that makes punishment theoretically puzzling and morally disquieting. Punishment is defined, in effect, as the infliction of hard treatment by an authority on a person for his prior failing in some respect (usually an infraction of a rule or command).[2] There

may be a very general sense of the word 'punishment' which is well expressed by this definition; but even if that is so, we can distinguish a narrower, more emphatic sense that slips through its meshes. Imprisonment at hard labor for committing a felony is a clear case of punishment in the emphatic sense; but I think we would be less willing to apply that term to parking tickets, offside penalties, sackings, flunkings, and disqualifications. Examples of the latter sort I propose to call *penalties* (merely), so that I may inquire further what distinguishes punishment, in the strict and narrow sense that interests the moralist, from other kinds of penalties.[3]

One method of answering this question is to focus one's attention on the class of nonpunitive penalties in an effort to discover some clearly identifiable characteristic common to them all, and absent from all punishments, on which the distinction between the two might be grounded. The hypotheses yielded by this approach, however, are not likely to survive close scrutiny. One might conclude, for example, that mere

From Joel Feinberg, "The Expressive Function of Punishment," *The Monist,* Vol. 49, No. 3 (July, 1965), pp. 397–423. Reprinted with permission of the publisher and the author.

penalties are less severe than punishments, but although this is generally true, it is not necessarily and universally so. Again we might be tempted to interpret penalties as mere 'price-tags' attached to certain types of behavior that are generally undesirable, so that only those with especially strong motivation will be willing to pay the price.[4] So, for example, deliberate efforts on the part of some western states to keep roads from urban centers to wilderness areas few in number and poor in quality are essentially no different from various parking fines and football penalties. In each case a certain kind of conduct is discouraged without being absolutely prohibited: Anyone who desires strongly enough to get to the wilderness (or park overtime, or interfere with a pass) may do so provided he is willing to pay the penalty (price). On this view penalties are, in effect, licensing fees, different from other purchased permits in that the price is often paid afterward rather than in advance. Since a similar interpretation of punishments seem implausible, it might be alleged that this is the basis of the distinction between penalties and punishments. However, while a great number of penalties can, no doubt, plausibly be treated as retroactive license fees, this is hardly true of all of them. It is certainly not true, for example, of most demotions, firings, and flunkings, that they are 'prices' paid for some already consumed benefit; and even parking fines are sanctions for rules "meant to be taken seriously as . . . standard[s] of behavior,"[5] and thus are more than mere public parking fees.

Rather than look for a characteristic common and peculiar to the penalties on which to ground the distinction between penalties and punishments, we would be better advised, I think, to cast our attention to the examples of punishments. Both penalties and punishments are authoritative deprivations for failures; but apart from these common features, penalties have a miscellaneous character, whereas punishments have an important additional characteristic in common. That characteristic, or specific difference, I shall argue, is a certain expressive function: Punishment is a conventional device for the expression of attitudes of resentment and indignation, and of judgments of disapproval and reprobation, either on the part of the punishing authority himself or of those "in whose

name" the punishment is inflicted. Punishment, in short, has a *symbolic significance* largely missing from other kinds of penalties.

The reprobative symbolism of punishment and its character as 'hard treatment', while never separate in reality, must be carefully distinguished for purposes of analysis. Reprobation is itself painful, whether or not it is accompanied by further 'hard treatment'; and hard treatment, such as fine or imprisonment, because of its conventional symbolism, can itself be reprobatory; but still we can conceive of ritualistic condemnation unaccompanied by any *further* hard treatment, and of inflictions and deprivations which, because of different symbolic conventions, have no reprobative force. It will be my thesis in this essay that (1) both the hard treatment aspect of punishment and its reprobative function must be part of the *definition* of legal punishment; and (2) each of these aspects raises its own kind of question about the *justification* of legal punishment as a general practice. I shall argue that some of the jobs punishment does, and some of the conceptual problems it raises, cannot be intelligibly described unless (1) is true; and that the incoherence of a familiar form of the retributive theory results from failure to appreciate the force of (2).

I. PUNISHMENT AS CONDEMNATION

That the expression of the community's condemnation is an essential ingredient in legal punishment is widely acknowledged by legal writers. Henry M. Hart, for example, gives eloquent emphasis to the point:

> What distinguishes a criminal from a civil sanction and all that distinguishes it, it is ventured, is the judgment of community condemnation which accompanies . . . its imposition. As Professor Gardner wrote not long ago, in a distinct but cognate connection:
> 'The essence of punishment for moral delinquency lies in the criminal conviction itself. One may lose more money on the stock market than in a courtroom; a prisoner of war camp may well provide a harsher environment than a state prison; death on the field of battle has the same physical characteristics as death by sentence of law. It is the expression of the community's hatred, fear, or contempt for the convict which alone characterizes physical hardship as punishment.'

Professor Hart's compendious definition needs qualification in one respect. The moral condemnation and the 'unpleasant consequences' that he rightly identifies as essential elements of punishment are not as distinct and separate as he suggests. It is not always the case that the convicted prisoner is first solemnly condemned and then subjected to unpleasant physical treatment. It would be more accurate in many cases to say that the unpleasant treatment itself expresses the condemnation, and that this expressive aspect of his incarceration is precisely the element by reason of which it is properly characterized as punishment and not mere penalty. The administrator who regretfully suspends the license of a conscientious but accident-prone driver can inflict a deprivation without any scolding, express or implied; but the reckless motorist who is sent to prison for six months is thereby inevitably subject to shame and ignominy—the very walls of his cell condemn him and his record becomes a stigma.

To say that the very physical treatment itself expresses condemnation is to say simply that certain forms of hard treatment have become the conventional symbols of public reprobation. This is neither more nor less paradoxical than to say that certain words have become conventional vehicles in our language for the expression of certain attitudes, or that champagne is the alcoholic beverage traditionally used in celebration of great events, or that black is the color of mourning. Moreover, particular kinds of punishment are often used to express quite specific attitudes (loosely speaking, this is part of their 'meaning'); note the differences, for example, between beheading a nobleman and hanging a yeoman, burning a heretic and hanging a traitor, hanging an enemy soldier and executing him by firing squad.

It is much easier to show that punishment has a symbolic significance than to say exactly what it is that punishment expresses. At its best, in civilized and democratic countries, punishment surely expresses the community's strong *disapproval* of what the criminal did. Indeed it can be said that punishment expresses the *judgment* (as distinct from any emotion) of the community that what the criminal did was wrong. I think it is fair to say of our community, however, that punishment generally expresses more than judg-

ments of disapproval; it is also a symbolic way of getting back at the criminal, of expressing a kind of vindictive resentment. To any reader who has in fact spent time in a prison, I venture to say, even Professor Gardner's strong terms—'hatred, fear, or contempt for the convict'—will not seem too strong an account of what imprisonment is universally taken to express. Not only does the criminal feel the naked hostility of his guards and the outside world—that would be fierce enough—but that hostility is self-righteous as well. His punishment bears the aspect of legitimized vengefulness; hence there is much truth in J. F. Stephen's celebrated remark that "The criminal law stands to the passion of revenge in much the same relation as marriage to the sexual appetite."[7]

If we reserve the less dramatic term 'resentment' for the various vengeful attitudes, and the term 'reprobation' for the stern judgment of disapproval, then perhaps we can characterize *condemnation* (or denunciation) as a kind of fusing of resentment and reprobation. That these two elements are generally to be found in legal punishment was well understood by the authors of the Report of the Royal Commission on Capital Punishment:

Discussion of the principle of *retribution* is apt to be confused because the word is not always used in the same sense. Sometimes it is intended to mean vengeance, sometimes reprobation. In the first sense the idea is that of satisfaction by the State of a wronged individual's desire to be avenged; in the second it is that of the State's *marking its disapproval* of the breaking of its laws by a punishment proportionate to the gravity of the offense [my italics].[8]

II. SOME DERIVATIVE SYMBOLIC FUNCTIONS OF PUNISHMENT

The relation of the expressive function of punishment to its various central purposes is not always easy to trace. Symbolic public condemnation added to deprivation may help or hinder deterrence, reform, and rehabilitation—the evidence is not clear. On the other hand, there are other functions of punishment, often lost sight of in the preoccupation with deterrence and reform, that presuppose the expressive function and would be impossible without it.

1. *Authoritative Disavowal.* Consider the standard international practice of demanding that a nation whose agent has unlawfully violated the complaining nation's rights should punish the offending agent. For example, suppose that an airplane of nation *A* fires on an airplane of nation *B* while the latter is flying over international waters. Very likely high authorities in nation *B* will send a note of protest to their counterparts in nation *A* demanding, among other things, that the transgressive pilot be punished. Punishing the pilot is an emphatic, dramatic, and well understood way of *condemning* and thereby *disavowing* his act. It tells the world that the pilot had no right to do what he did, that he was on his own in doing it, that his government does not condone that sort of thing. It testifies thereby to government *A*'s recognition of the violated rights of government *B* in the affected area, and therefore to the wrongfulness of the pilot's act. Failure to punish the pilot tells the world that government *A* does not consider him to have been personally at fault. That in turn is to claim responsibility for the act, which in effect labels that act as an 'instrument of deliberate national policy', and therefore an act of war. In that case either formal hostilities or humiliating loss of face by one side or the other almost certainly follows. None of this makes any sense without the well understood reprobative symbolism of punishment. In quite parallel ways punishment enables employers to disavow the acts of their employees (though not civil liability for those acts), and fathers the destructive acts of their sons.

2. *Symbolic Non-Acquiescence: 'Speaking in the Name of the People'.* The symbolic function of punishment also explains why even those sophisticated persons who abjure resentment of criminals and look with small favor generally on the penal law are likely to demand that certain kinds of conduct be punished when or if the law lets them go by. In the state of Texas, so-called 'paramour killings' are regarded by the law as not merely mitigated, but completely justifiable.[9] Many humanitarians, I believe, will feel quite spontaneously that a great injustice is done when such killings are left unpunished. The sense of violated justice, moreover, might be distinct and unaccompanied by any frustrated *schaden-freude* toward the killer, lust for blood or

vengeance, or metaphysical concern lest the universe stay 'out of joint'. The demand for punishment in cases of this sort may instead represent the feeling that paramour killings deserve to be *condemned,* that the law in condoning, even approving of them, speaks for all citizens in expressing a wholly inappropriate attitude toward them. For, in effect, the law expresses the judgment of the 'people of Texas', in whose name it speaks, that the vindictive satisfaction in the mind of a cuckolded husband is a thing of greater value than the very life of his wife's lover. The demand that paramour killings be punished may simply be the demand that this lopsided value judgment be withdrawn and that the state *go on record* against paramour killings, and the law *testify to the recognition* that such killings are wrongful. Punishment no doubt would also help deter killers. This too is a desideratum and a closely related one, but it is not to be identified with reprobation; for deterrence might be achieved by a dozen other techniques, from simple penalties and forfeitures to exhortation and propaganda; but effective public denunciation and, through it, symbolic non-acquiescence in the crime, seem virtually to require punishment.

This symbolic function of punishment was given great emphasis by Kant, who, characteristically, proceeded to exaggerate its importance. Even if a desert island community were to disband, Kant argued, its members should first execute the last murderer left in its jails, "for otherwise they might all be regarded as participators in the [unpunished] murder. . . ."[10] This Kantian idea that in failing to punish wicked acts society endorses them and thus becomes *particeps criminis* does seem to reflect, however dimly, something embedded in common sense. A similar notion underlies whatever is intelligible in the widespread notion that all citizens share the responsibility for political atrocities. Insofar as there is a coherent argument behind the extravagant distributions of guilt made by existentialists and other literary figures, it can be reconstructed in some way as this: To whatever extent a political act is done 'in one's name', to that extent one is responsible for it. A citizen can avoid responsibility in advance by explicitly disowning the government as his spokesman, or after the fact through open protest, resistance, and so on. Otherwise, by 'acquiescing' in what is done in one's name, one incurs the responsibility for it. The root notion here is a kind of 'power of attorney' a government has for its citizens.

3. *Vindication of the Law.* Sometimes the state goes on record through its statutes, in a way that might well please a conscientious citizen in whose name it speaks, but then through official evasion and unreliable enforcement, gives rise to doubts that the law really means what it says. It is murder in Mississippi, as elsewhere, for a white man intentionally to kill a Negro; but if grand juries refuse to issue indictments or if trial juries refuse to convict, and this is well understood by most citizens, then it is in a purely formal and empty sense indeed that killings of Negroes by whites are illegal in Mississippi. Yet the law stays on the books, to give ever-less-convincing lip service to a noble moral judgment. A statute honored mainly in the breach begins to lose its character as law, unless, as we say, it is *vindicated* (emphatically reaffirmed); and clearly the way to do this (indeed the only way) is to punish those who violate it.

Similarly, *punitive damages,* so-called, are sometimes awarded the plaintiff in a civil action, as a supplement to compensation for his injuries. What more dramatic way of vindicating his violated right can be imagined than to have a court thus forcibly condemn its violation through the symbolic machinery of punishment?

4. *Absolution of Others.* When something scandalous has occurred and it is clear that the wrongdoer must be one of a small number of suspects, then the state, by punishing one of these parties, thereby relieves the others of suspicion, and informally absolves them of blame. Moreover, quite often the absolution of an accuser hangs as much in the balance at a criminal trial as the inculpation of the accused. A good example of this can be found in James Gould Cozzens's novel, *By Love Possessed.* A young girl, after an evening of illicit sexual activity with her boy friend, is found out by her bullying mother, who then insists that she clear her name by bringing criminal charges against the boy. He used physical force, the girl charges; she freely consented, he replies. If the jury finds him guilty of rape, it will by the same token absolve her from (moral) guilt; and her reputation as well as

his rides on the outcome. Could not the state do this job without punishment? Perhaps, but when it speaks by punishing, its message is loud, and sure of getting across.

III. THE CONSTITUTIONAL PROBLEM OF DEFINING LEGAL PUNISHMENT

A philosophical theory of punishment that, through inadequate definition, leaves out the condemnatory function, not only will disappoint the moralist and the traditional moral philosopher; it will seem offensively irrelevant as well to the constitutional lawyer, whose vital concern with punishment is both conceptual, and therefore genuinely philosophical, and practically urgent. The distinction between punishment and mere penalties is a familiar one in the criminal law, where theorists have long engaged in what Jerome Hall calls "dubious dogmatics distinguishing 'civil penalties' from punitive sanctions, and 'public wrongs' from crimes."[11] Our courts now regard it as true (by definition) that all criminal statutes are punitive (merely labeling an act a crime does not make it one unless sanctions are specified); but to the converse question whether all statutes specifying sanctions are *criminal* statutes, the courts are reluctant to give an affirmative reply. There are now a great number of statutes that permit 'unpleasant consequences' to be inflicted on persons and yet are surely not criminal statutes—tax bills, for example, are aimed at regulating, not forbidding, certain types of activity. How to classify borderline cases as either 'regulative' or 'punitive' is not merely an idle conceptual riddle; it very quickly draws the courts into questions of great constitutional import. There are elaborate constitutional safeguards for persons faced with the prospect of punishment; but these do not, or need not, apply when the threatened hard treatment merely 'regulates an activity'.

The 1960 Supreme Court case of Flemming *v.* Nestor[12] is a dramatic (and shocking) example of how a man's fate can depend on whether a government-inflicted deprivation is interpreted as a 'regulative' or 'punitive' sanction. Nestor had immigrated to the United States from Bulgaria in 1913, and in 1955 became eligible for old-age benefits under the Social Security Act. In 1956, however, he was deported in accordance with the Immigration and Nationality Act, for having been a member of the Communist Party from 1933 to 1939. This was a hard fate for a man who had been in America for forty-three years and who was no longer a Communist; but at least he would have his social security benefits to support him in his exiled old age. Or so he thought. Section 202 of the amended Social Security Act, however,

provides for the termination of old-age, survivor, and disability insurance benefits payable to . . . an alien individual who, after September 1, 1954 (the date of enactment of the section) is deported under the Immigration and Nationality Act on any one of certain specified grounds, including past membership in the Communist Party.[13]

Accordingly, Nestor was informed that his benefits would cease.

Nestor then brought suit in a District Court for a reversal of the administrative decision. The court found in his favor and held §202 of the Social Security Act unconstitutional, on the grounds that

termination of [Nestor's] benefits amounts to punishing him without a judicial trial, that [it] constitutes the imposition of punishment by legislative act rendering §202 a bill of attainder; and that the punishment exacted is imposed for past conduct not unlawful when engaged in, thereby violating the constitutional prohibition on *ex post facto* laws.[14]

The Secretary of Health, Education, and Welfare, Mr. Flemming, then appealed this decision to the Supreme Court.

It was essential to the argument of the District Court that the termination of old-age benefits under §202 was in fact punishment, for if it were properly classified as nonpunitive deprivation, then none of the cited constitutional guarantees was relevant. The constitution, for example, does not forbid all retroactive laws, but only those providing punishment. (Retroactive tax laws may also be hard and unfair, but they are not unconstitutional.) The question before the Supreme Court then was whether the hardship imposed by §202 was punishment. Did this not bring the Court face to face with the properly philosophical question 'What is punishment?'

and is it not clear that under the usual definition that fails to distinguish punishment from mere penalties, this particular judicial problem could not even arise?

The fate of the appellee Nestor can be recounted briefly. The five man majority of the court held that he had not been punished—this despite Mr. Justice Brennan's eloquent characterization of him in a dissenting opinion as "an aging man deprived of the means with which to live after being separated from his family and exiled to live among strangers in a land he quit forty-seven years ago."[15] Mr. Justice Harlan, writing for the majority, argued that the termination of benefits, like the deportation itself, was the exercise of the plenary power of Congress incident to the regulation of an activity.

Similarly, the setting by a State of qualifications for the practice of medicine, and their modification from time to time, is an incident of the State's power to protect the health and safety of its citizens, and its decision to bar from practice persons who commit or have committed a felony is taken as evidencing an intent to exercise that regulatory power, and not a purpose to add to the punishment of ex-felons.[16]

Mr. Justice Brennan, on the other hand, argued that it is impossible to think of any purpose the provision in question could possibly serve except to "strike" at "aliens deported for conduct displeasing to the lawmakers."[17]

Surely Justice Brennan seems right in finding in the sanction the expression of Congressional reprobation, and therefore 'punitive intent'; but the sanction itself (in Justice Harlan's words, "the mere denial of a noncontractual governmental benefit"[18]) was not a conventional vehicle for the expression of censure, being wholly outside the apparatus of the criminal law. It therefore lacked the reprobative symbolism essential to punishment generally, and was thus, in its hybrid character, able to generate confusion and judicial disagreement. It was as if Congress had 'condemned' a certain class of persons privately in stage whispers, rather than by pinning the infamous label of criminal on them and letting that symbol do the condemning in an open and public way. Congress without question "intended" to punish a certain class of aliens and did indeed select sanctions of appropriate severity for that use; but the deprivation they selected was not of an appropriate kind to perform the function of public condemnation. A father who 'punishes' his son for a displeasing act the father had not thought to forbid in advance, by sneaking up on him from behind and then throwing him bodily across the room against the wall, would be in much the same position as the legislators of the amended Social Security Act, especially if he then denied to the son that his physical assault on him had had any 'punitive intent', asserting that it was a mere exercise of his paternal prerogative to rearrange the household furnishings and other objects in his own living room. This would be to tarnish the paternal authority and infect all later genuine punishments with hollow hypocrisy. This also happens when legislators go outside the criminal law to do the criminal law's job.

In 1961 the New York State Legislature passed the so-called "Subversive Drivers Act" requiring "suspension and revocation of the driver's license of anyone who has been convicted, under the Smith Act, of advocating the overthrow of the Federal government." *The Reporter* magazine[19] quoted the sponsor of the bill as admitting that it was aimed primarily at one person, Communist Benjamin Davis, who had only recently won a court fight to regain his driver's license after his five year term in prison. *The Reporter* estimated that at most a "few dozen" people would be kept from driving by the new legislation. Was this punishment? Not at all, said the bill's sponsor, Assemblyman Paul Taylor. The legislature was simply exercising its right to regulate automobile traffic in the interest of public safety:

Driving licenses, Assemblyman Taylor explained . . . are not a 'right' but a 'valuable privilege.' The Smith Act Communists, after all, were convicted of advocating the overthrow of the government by force, violence, or assassination. ('They always leave out the assassination,' he remarked. 'I like to put it in.') Anyone who was convicted under such an act had to be 'a person pretty well dedicated to a certain point of view,' the assemblyman continued, and anyone with that particular point of view 'can't be concerned about the rights of others.' Being concerned about the rights of others, he concluded, 'is a prerequisite of being a good driver.'[20]

This shows how transparent can be the effort to mask punitive intent. The Smith Act ex-convicts

were treated with such severity and in such circumstances that no nonpunitive legislative purpose could *plausibly* be maintained; yet that *kind* of treatment (quite apart from its severity) lacks the reprobative symbolism essential to clear public denunciation. After all, aged, crippled, and blind persons are also deprived of their licenses, so it is not *necessarily* the case that reprobation attaches to that kind of sanction. And so victims of a cruel law understandably claim that they have been punished, and retroactively at that. Yet strictly speaking they have not been *punished*; they have been treated much worse.

IV. THE PROBLEM OF STRICT CRIMINAL LIABILITY

The distinction between punishments and mere penalties, and the essentially reprobative function of the former, can also help clarify the controversy among writers on the criminal law about the propriety of so-called 'strict liability offenses'—offenses for the conviction of which there need be no showing of 'fault' or 'culpability' on the part of the accused. If it can be shown that he committed an act proscribed by statute then he is guilty irrespective of whether he had justification or excuse for what he did. Perhaps the most familiar examples come from the traffic laws: Leaving a car parked beyond the permitted time in a restricted zone is automatically to violate the law, and penalties will be imposed however good the excuse. Many strict liability statutes do not even require an overt act; these proscribe not certain conduct but certain *results*. Some make mere unconscious possession of contraband, firearms, or narcotics a crime, others the sale of misbranded articles or impure foods. The liability for so-called 'public welfare offenses' may seem especially severe:

. . . with rare exceptions, it became definitely established that *mens rea* is not essential in the public welfare offenses, indeed that even a very high degree of care is irrelevant. Thus a seller of cattle feed was convicted of violating a statute forbidding misrepresentation of the percentage of oil in the product, despite the fact that he had employed a reputable chemist to make the analysis and had even understated the chemist's findings.[21]

The rationale of strict liability in public welfare statutes is that violation est is more likely to be prevented by unconditional liability than by liability that can be defeated by some kind of excuse; that even though liability without 'fault' is severe, it is one of the known risks incurred by businessmen; and that besides, the sanctions are *only fines,* hence not really 'punitive' in character. On the other hand, strict liability to *imprisonment* (or 'punishment proper') "has been held by many to be incompatible with the basic requirements of our Anglo-American, and indeed, any civilized jurisprudence."[22] Why should this be? In both kinds of case, defendants may have sanctions inflicted upon them even though they are acknowledged to be without fault; and the difference cannot be simply that imprisonment is always and necessarily a greater hurt than fine, for this is not always so. Rather, the reason why strict liability to imprisonment (punishment) is so much more repugnant to our sense of justice than is strict liability to fine (penalty) is simply that imprisonment in modern times has taken on the symbolism of public reprobation. In the words of Justice Brandeis, "It is . . . imprisonment in a penitentiary, which now renders a crime infamous."[23] We are familiar with the practice of penalizing persons for 'offenses' they could not help. It happens every day in football games, business firms, traffic courts, and the like. But there is something very odd and offensive in *punishing* people for admittedly faultless conduct; for not only is it arbitrary and cruel to *condemn* someone for something he did (admittedly) without fault, it is also self-defeating and irrational.

Though their abundant proliferation[24] is a relatively recent phenomenon, statutory offenses with nonpunitive sanctions have long been familiar to legal commentators, and long a source of uneasiness to them. This is "indicated by the persistent search for an appropriate label, such as 'public torts,' 'public welfare offenses,' 'prohibitory laws,' 'prohibited acts,' 'regulatory offenses,' 'police regulations,' 'administrative misdemeanors,' 'quasi-crimes,' or 'civil offenses.' "[25] These represent alternatives to the unacceptable categorization of traffic infractions, inadvertent violations of commercial regulations, and the like, as *crimes,* their perpetrators as *criminals,* and their penalties as *punishments.* The drafters of the new Model Penal Code have defined a class of infractions of penal law forming no part of the substantive criminal law. These they call 'violations', and their sanctions 'civil penalties'.

Section 1.04. Classes of Crimes: Violations
(1) An offense defined by this code or by any other statute of this State, for which a sentence of [death or of] imprisonment is authorized, constitutes a crime. Crimes are classified as felonies, misdemeanors, or petty misdemeanors.
[(2), (3), (4) define felonies, misdemeanors, and petty misdemeanors.]
(5) An offense defined by this Code or by any other statute of this State constitutes a violation if it is so designated in this Code or in the law defining the offense or if no other sentence than a fine, or fine and forfeiture or other civil penalty is authorized upon conviction or if it is defined by a statute other than this Code which now provides that the offense shall not constitute a crime. A violation does not constitute a crime and conviction of a violation shall not give rise to any disability or legal disadvantage based on conviction of a criminal offense.[26]

Since violations, unlike crimes, carry no social stigma, it is often argued that there is no serious injustice if, in the interest of quick and effective law enforcement, violators are held unconditionally liable. This line of argument is persuasive when we consider only parking and minor traffic violations, illegal sales of various kinds, and violations of health and safety codes, where the penalties serve as warnings and the fines are light. But the argument loses all cogency when the 'civil penalties' are severe—heavy fines, forfeitures of property, removal from office, suspension of a license, withholding of an important 'benefit', and the like. The condemnation of the faultless may be the most flagrant injustice, but the good natured, noncondemnatory infliction of severe hardship on the innocent is little better. It is useful to distinguish violations and civil penalties from crimes and punishments; but it does not follow that the safeguards of culpability requirements and due process which justice demands for the latter are always irrelevant encumbrances to the former. Two things are morally wrong: (1) to condemn a faultless man while inflicting pain or deprivation on him however slight (unjust punishment); and (2) to inflict unnecessary and severe suffering on a faultless man even in the absence of condemnation (unjust civil penalty). To exact a two dollar fine from a hapless violator for overtime parking, however, even though he could not possibly have helped it, is to do neither of these things.

V. JUSTIFYING LEGAL PUNISHMENT: LETTING THE PUNISHMENT FIT THE CRIME

Public condemnation, whether avowed through the stigmatizing symbolism of punishment or unavowed but clearly discernible (mere 'punitive intent'), can greatly magnify the suffering caused by its attendant mode of hard treatment. Samuel Butler keenly appreciated the difference between reprobative hard treatment (punishment) and the same treatment sans reprobation:

. . . we should hate a single flogging given in the way of mere punishment more than the amputation of a limb, if it were kindly and courteously performed from a wish to help us out of our difficulty, and with the full consciousness on the part of the doctor that it was only by an accident of constitution that he was not in the like plight himself. So the Erewhonians take a flogging once a week, and a diet of bread and water for two or three months together, whenever their straightener recommends it.[27]

Even floggings and imposed fastings do not constitute punishments, then, where social conventions are such that they do not express public censure (what Butler called 'scouting'); and as therapeutic treatments simply, rather than punishments, they are easier to take.

Yet floggings and fastings do hurt, and far more than is justified by their Erewhonian (therapeutic) objectives. The same is true of our own State Mental Hospitals where criminal psychopaths are often sent for 'rehabilitation': Solitary confinement may not hurt *quite* so much when called 'the quiet room', or the forced support of heavy fire extinguishers when called 'hydrotherapy';[28] but their infliction on patients can be so cruel (whether or not their quasi-medical names mask punitive intent) as to demand justification.

Hard treatment and symbolic condemnation, then, are not only both necessary to an adequate definition of 'punishment'; each also poses a special problem for the justification of punishment.

The reprobative symbolism of punishment is subject to attack not only as an independent source of suffering but as the vehicle of undeserved responsive attitudes and unfair judgments of blame. One kind of skeptic, granting that penalties are needed if legal rules are to be enforced, and also that society would be impossible without general and predictable obedience to such rules, might nevertheless question the need to add condemnation to the penalizing of violators. Hard treatment of violators, he might grant, is an unhappy necessity, but reprobation of the offender is offensively self-righteous and cruel; adding gratuitous insult to necessary injury can serve no useful purpose. A partial answer to this kind of skeptic has already been given. The condemnatory aspect of punishment does serve a socially useful purpose: It is precisely the element in punishment that makes possible the performance of such symbolic functions as disavowal, non-acquiescence, vindication, and absolution.

Another kind of skeptic might readily grant that the reprobative symbolism of punishment is necessary to and justified by these various derivative functions. Indeed, he may even add deterrence to the list, for condemnation is likely to make it clear where it would not otherwise be so that a penalty is not a mere price-tag. Granting that point, however, this kind of skeptic would have us consider whether the ends that justify public condemnation of criminal conduct might not be achieved equally well by means of less painful symbolic machinery. There was a time, after all, when the gallows and the rack were the leading clear symbols of shame and ignominy. Now we condemn felons to penal servitude as the way of rendering their crimes infamous. Could not the job be done still more economically? Isn't there a way to stigmatize without inflicting any further (pointless) pain to the body, to family, to creative capacity?

One can imagine an elaborate public ritual, exploiting the trustiest devices of religion and mystery, music and drama, to express in the most solemn way the community's condemnation of a criminal for his dastardly deed. Such a ritual might condemn so very emphatically that there could be no doubt of its genuineness, thus rendering symbolically superfluous any further hard physical treatment. Such a device would preserve the condemnatory function of punishment while dispensing with its usual physical forms—incarceration and corporal mistreatment. Perhaps this is only idle fantasy; perhaps there is more to it. The question is surely open. The only point I wish to make here is one about the nature of the question. The problem of justifying punishment, when it takes this form, may really be that of justifying our particular symbols of infamy.

Whatever the form of skeptical challenge to the institution of punishment, however, there is one traditional answer to it that seems to me to be incoherent. I refer to that form of the Retributive Theory which mentions neither condemnation nor vengeance, but insists instead that the ultimate justifying purpose of punishment is to match off moral gravity and pain, to give each offender exactly that amount of pain the evil of his offense calls for, on the alleged principle of justice that the wicked should suffer pain in exact proportion to their turpitude.

I will only mention in passing the familiar and potent objections to this view.[29] The innocent presumably deserve *not* to suffer just as the guilty are supposed to deserve to suffer; yet it is impossible to hurt an evil man without imposing suffering on those who love or depend on him. Deciding the right amount of suffering to inflict in a given case would require an assessment of the character of the offender as manifested through his whole life, and also his total lifelong balance of pleasure and pain, an obvious impossibility. Moreover, justice would probably demand the abandonment of general rules in the interest of individuation of punishment since there will inevitably be inequalities of moral guilt in the commission of the same crime, and inequalities of suffering from the same punishment. If not dispensed with, however, general rules must list all crimes in the order of their moral gravity, all punishments in the order of their severity, and the matchings between the two scales. But the moral gravity scale would have to list motives and purposes, not simply types of overt acts, for a given crime can be committed from any kind of 'mental state', and its 'moral gravity' in a given case surely must depend in part on its accompanying motive. Condign punishment then would have to match suffering to motive (desire, belief, etc.), not to dangerousness or to amount of harm done. Hence some petty larcenies would be punished more severely than some murders. It is not likely we should wish to give power to judges and juries to make such difficult moral judgments. Worse than this, the judgments required are not merely 'difficult', they are in principle impossible. It may seem 'self-evident' to some moralists that the passionate impulsive killer, for example, deserves less suffering for his wickedness than the scheming deliberate killer; but if the question of comparative *dangerousness* is left out of mind, reasonable men not only can but will disagree in their appraisals of comparative blameworthiness, and there appears no rational way of resolving the issue.[30] Certainly, there is no rational way of demonstrating that one deserves exactly twice or three-eighths or twelve-ninths as much suffering as the other; yet on some forms, at least, of this theory, the amount of suffering inflicted for any two crimes should stand in exact proportion to the 'amounts' of wickedness in the criminals.

For all that, however, the pain-fitting-wickedness version of the retributive theory does erect its edifice of moral superstition on a foundation in moral common sense, for justice *does* require that in some (other) sense "the punishment fit the crime." What justice requires is that the *condemnatory aspect* of the punishment suit the crime, that the crime be of a kind that is truly worthy of reprobation. Further, the degree of disapproval expressed by the punishment should 'fit' the crime only in the unproblematic sense that the more serious crimes should receive stronger disapproval than the less serious ones, the seriousness of the crime being determined by the amount of harm it generally causes and the degree to which people are disposed to commit it. That is quite another thing than requiring that the hard treatment component, considered apart from its symbolic function, should 'fit' the moral quality of a specific criminal act, assessed quite independently of its relation to social harm. Given our conventions, of course, condemnation is expressed by hard treatment, and the degree of harshness of the latter expresses the degree of reprobation of the former; still this should not blind us to the fact that it is social disapproval and its appropriate expression that should fit the crime, and not hard treatment (pain) as such. Pain should match guilt only insofar as its infliction is the symbolic vehicle of public condemnation.

NOTES

1. See especially the following: A. Flew, "The Justification of Punishment," *Philosophy*, 29 (1954), 291–307; S. I. Benn, "An Approach to the Problems of Punishment," *Philosophy*, 33 (1958), 325–341; and H. L. A. Hart, "Prolegomenon to the Principles of Punishment," *Proceedings of the Aristotelian Society*, 60 (1959–60), 1–26.

2. Hart and Benn both borrow Flew's definition. In Hart's paraphrase, punishment "(i) . . . must involve pain or other consequences normally considered unplesant. (ii) It must be for an offense against legal rules. (iii) It must be of an actual or supposed offender for his offense. (iv) It must be intentionally administered by human beings other than the offender. (v) It must be imposed and administered by an authority constituted by a legal system against which the offense is committed." (*op. cit.*, p. 4.)

3. The distinction between punishments and penalties was first called to my attention by Dr. Anita Fritz of the University of Connecticut. Similar distinctions in different terminologies have been made by many. Pollock and Maitland speak of 'true afflictive punishments' as opposed to outlawry, private vengeance, fine, and emendation. (*History of English Law*, 2d ed., II, pp. 451 ff.) The phrase 'afflictive punishment' was invented by Bentham (*Rationale of Punishment*, London, 1830): "These [corporal] punishments are almost always attended with a portion of ignomiry, and this does not always increase with the organic pain, but principally depends upon the condition [social class] of the offender." (p. 83). James Stephen says of legal punishment that it "should always connote . . . moral infamy." (*History of the Criminal Law*, II, p. 171.) Lasswell and Donnelly distinguish 'condemnation sanctions' and 'other deprivations.' ("The Continuing Debate over Responsibility: An Introduction to Isolating the Condemnation Sanction," *Yale Law Journal*, 68, 1959.) The traditional common law distinction is between 'infamous' and 'noninfamous' crimes and punishments. Conviction of an 'infamous crime' rendered a person liable to such postpunitive civil disabilities as incompetence to be a witness.

4. That even punishments proper are to be interpreted as taxes on certain kinds of conduct is a view often associated with O. W. Holmes, Jr. For an excellent discussion of Holmes's fluctuations of this question see Mark De Wolfe Howe, *Justice Holmes, The Proving Years* (Cambridge, Mass., 1963), pp. 74–80. See also Lon Fuller, *The Morality of Law* (New Haven, 1964), Chap. II, part 7, and H. L. A. Hart, *The Concept of Law* (Oxford, 1961), p. 39, for illuminating comparisons and contrasts of punishment and taxation.

5. H. L. A. Hart, *loc. cit.*

6. Henry M. Hart, "The Aims of the Criminal Law," *Law and Contemporary Problems*, 23 (1958), II, A, 4.

7. *General View of the Criminal Law of England*, First ed. (London, 1863), p. 99.

8. (London, 1953), pp. 17–18.

9. The Texas Penal Code (Art. 1220) states: "Homicide is justifiable when committed by the husband upon one taken in the act of adultery with the wife, provided the killing takes place before the parties to the act have separated. Such circumstances cannot justify a homicide when it appears that there has been on the part of the husband, any connivance in or assent to the adulterous connection." New Mexico and Utah have similar statutes. For some striking descriptions of perfectly legal paramour killings in Texas, see John Bainbridge, *The Super-Americans* (Garden City, 1961), pp. 238 ff.

10. *The Philosophy of Law*, trans. W. Hastie (Edinburgh, 1887), p. 198.

11. *General Principles of Criminal Law*, 2d ed. (Indianapolis, 1960), p. 328, hereafter cited as GPCL.

12. Flemming *v.* Nestor 80 S. Ct. 1367 (1960). 56

13. *Ibid.*, p. 1370.

14. *Ibid.*, p. 1374 (Interspersed citations omitted).

15. *Ibid.*, p. 1385.

16. *Ibid.*, pp. 1375–6.

17. *Ibid.*, p. 1387.

18. *Ibid.*, p. 1376.

19. *The Reporter* (May 11, 1961), p. 14.

20. *Loc. cit.*

21. Jerome Hall, GPCL, p. 329.

22. Richard A. Wasserstrom, "Strict Liability in the Criminal Law," *Stanford Law Review*, 12 (1960), p. 730.

23. United States v. Moreland, 258 U.S. 433, 447–48. Quoted in Hall, GPCL, p. 327.

24. "A depth study of Wisconsin statutes in 1956 revealed that of 1113 statutes creating criminal offenses [punishable by fine, imprisonment, or both] which were in force in 1953, no less than 660 used language in the definitions of the offenses which omitted all reference to a mental element, and which therefore, under the canons of construction which have come to govern these matters, left it open to the courts to impose strict liability if they saw fit." Colin Howard, "Not Proven," *Adelaide Law Review*, 1 (1962), 274. The study cited is: Remington, Robinson and Zick, "Liability Without Fault Criminal Statutes," *Wisconsin Law Review* (1956), 625, 636.

25. Rollin M. Perkins, *Criminal Law* (Brooklyn, 1957), pp. 701–2.

26. American Law Institute, *Model Penal Code, Proposed Official Draft* (Philadelphia, 1962).

27. *Erewhon*. (London, 1901), Chapter 10.

28. These two examples are cited by Francis A. Allen in "Criminal Justice, Legal Values and the Rehabilitative Ideal," *Journal of Criminal Law, Criminology and Police Science*, 50 (1959), 229.

29. For more convincing statements of these arguments, see *iter alia*: W. D. Ross, *The Right and the Good* (Oxford, 1930), pp. 56–65; J. D. Mabbott, "Punishment," *Mind*, 49 (1939); A. C. Ewing, *The Morality of Punishment* (London, 1929), Chap. 1; and F. Dostoevsky, *The House of the Dead*.

30. Cf. Jerome Michael and Herbert Wechsler, *Criminal Law and its Administration* (Chicago, 1940), "Note on Deliberation and Character," pp. 170–2.

SUGGESTIONS FOR FURTHER READING

A. RIGHTS

Acton, H. B., "Rights," *Proceedings of the Aristotelian Society,* suppl. Vol. 24 (1950).

Benn, S. I. and Peters, R. S., *Social Principles and the Democratic State* (London: Allen & Unwin, 1959).

Brandt, Richard, *Ethical Theory* (Englewood Cliffs, N.J.: Prentice-Hall, 1957), Chapter 17.

Corbin, Arthur L., "Legal Analysis and Terminology," *Yale Law Journal,* Vol. 29 (1919).

Feinberg, Joel, "Duties, Rights, and Claims," *American Philosophical Quarterly,* Vol. 3 (1966).

_____ , *Social Philosophy* (Englewood Cliffs, N.J.: Prentice-Hall, 1973), Chapters 4–6.

_____ , "The Rights of Animals and Future Generations," in *Philosophy and Environmental Crisis,* ed. by W. T. Blackstone (Athens, Ga.: University of Georgia Press, 1974).

Hart, H. L. A., "Definition and Theory in Jurisprudence," *Law Quarterly Review,* Vol. 70 (1954).

Hohfeld, Wesley, *Fundamental Legal Conceptions* (New Haven: Yale University Press, 1923).

Lyons, David, "Rights, Claimants, and Beneficiaries," *American Philosophical Quarterly,* Vol. 6 (1969), pp. 173–185.

Melden, A. I., *Rights and Right Conduct* (Oxford: Basil Blackwell, 1959).

Raphael, D. D. (ed.), *Political Theory and the Rights of Man* (Bloomington: Indiana University Press, 1967).

Salmond, John, *Jurisprudence* (11th edit.) ed. by Glanville Williams (London: Sweet & Maxwell, 1967), Chapters 10, 11.

Wasserstrom, R. A., "Rights, Human Rights, and Racial Discrimination," *Journal of Philosophy,* Vol. 61 (1964).

B. DISTRIBUTIVE JUSTICE

Barry, Brian, *Political Argument* (London: Routledge & Kegan Paul, 1965), Chapters 5, 6.

_____ , *The Liberal Theory of Justice* (Oxford: Oxford University Press, 1973).

Brandt, Richard B. (editor), *Social Justice* (Englewood Cliffs, N.J.: Prentice Hall, Inc., 1962), especially the essay by Gregory Vlastos, pp. 31–72.

Daniels, Norman (ed.), *Rawls's Theory of Justice* (New York: Basic Books, 1975).

Feinberg, Joel, *Social Philosophy* (Englewood Cliffs, N.J.: Prentice-Hall, 1973), Chapter 7.

Frankena, W. K., "Some Beliefs About Justice," *The Lindley Lecture,* Dept. of Philosophy Pamphlet. (Lawrence: University of Kansas, 1966).

Hobhouse, L. T., *Elements of Social Justice* (London: Allen & Unwin, Ltd., 1922), Chapter 9.

Kamenka, Eugene, *The Ethical Foundations of Marxism* (London: Routledge & Kegan Paul, 1962).

Katzner, Louis I., *Man, Government, and the State* (Encino, Calif.: Dickenson, 1975), Chapter 5.

Narveson, Jan, *Morality and Utility* (Baltimore: Johns-Hopkins University Press, 1967), Chapter VII.

Nozick, Robert, *Anarchy, State, and Utopia* (New York: Basic Books, 1974).

Pieper, Josef *Justice,* translated by Lawrence E. Lynch (London: Faber and Faber, 1957).

Rawls, John, *A Theory of Justice* (Cambridge, Mass.: Harvard University Press, 1971).

Rescher, Nicholas, *Distributive Justice* (New York: Bobbs-Merrill Company, 1966).

C. PUNISHMENT

Benn, S. I. and Peters, R. S., *Social Principles and the Democratic State* (London: Allen & Unwin, 1959), Chapter 8.

Ewing, A. C., *The Morality of Punishment* (London: Kegan Paul, Trench, Trubner & Co., 1929).

Flew, Antony, "The Justification of Punishment," *Philosophy,* Vol. 29 (1954).

Ezorsky, Gertrude (ed.), *Philosophical Perspectives on Punishment* Albany: State University of New York Press, 1972).

Feinberg, Joel, *Doing and Deserving* (Princeton: Princeton University Press, 1970).

Friedrich, Carl, (ed.) *Nomos III, Responsibility* (New York: Liberal Arts Press, 1960).

Hart, H. L. A., *Punishment and Responsibility* (Oxford: Clarendon Press, 1969).

Kleinig, John, *Punishment and Desert* (The Hague, Netherlands: Martinus Nijhoff, 1974). This book contains an exhaustive bibliography.

Mabbott, J. D., "Punishment," *Mind,* Vol. 49 (1939).

Morris, Herbert, "Persons and Punishment," *The Monist,* October, 1968.

Ross, W. D., *The Right and the Good* (Oxford: Clarendon Press, 1930), pp. 56–65.

Part V   The Role of Reason in Ethics

The readings in Part V represent three closely related issues. They are ethical relativism, a very ambiguous concept; the analysis of ethical language, which has come to be called "Metaethics"; and the nature of moral argument. The theme which unifies these three topics is the role of reason in ethics. If ethics is merely a matter of social convention, or if ethical "judgments" are merely the expression of emotion, reason may have a very limited role to play. For that matter, however, if ethics is based upon the perception of some distinctly ethical properties of actions or things which can be known only by intuition, reason may also have a very limited role to play. On the other hand, moral arguments do occur, and there seem to be some rules of reason which these arguments follow, even if there is no assurance of ultimate agreement. If there is a disagreement in ethics, how is it to be resolved?

The first reading in this section, from "Validation and Vindication," by Herbert Feigl, dramatizes the problems in resolving such a dispute. There may be agreement in all factual matters yet disagreement in moral judgment or attitude. In that case, the disagreement cannot be resolved simply by more factual information, although many ethical disputes—those which do rely upon divergence in factual judgments—can be. In Feigl's dialogue, one person holds the view that attitudes are the result of conditioning from one's culture or subculture and have no objective validity. The other holds that his attitudes do have objective and universal validity. This dispute raises the problem of ethical relativism.

Ethical relativism is an ambiguous concept. It may be a factual claim that there is diversity in moral standards among different cultures or different individuals and that types of behavior have a different significance according to cultural context. As such, this is not an ethical position but a finding of social science. This thesis is one aspect of what in anthropology is called *cultural relativism.* A different meaning of ethical relativism is the normative position that one ought to follow the moral code which is accepted in one's own culture or society, a view which we can label *ethical conventionalism.* In a different form the view holds that it is not social standards which are ultimate but each individual's own standards, that what an individual sincerely believes is right is right, a position which is usually called *ethical subjectivism.* It is important to notice that conventionalism and subjectivism, as here described, are normative ethical positions, competing with the sort of positions represented in Parts I, II, and III of this volume. Instead of holding that acts are right or wrong according to whether they promote or fail to promote the greatest happiness, or because they are such that the maxim of the action can or can't be willed to become a universal law, the ethical conventionalist or subjectivist is saying that an act is right or wrong according to whether it is approved or disapproved by one's society or by one's own sincere judgment. This is quite different from holding merely that different things are approved in different societies or that sincere people differ in their moral attitudes. The implications of conventionalism would seem to be that within a slave-holding culture slavery is not just thought to be morally permissible, but is morally permissible. (How, then, should one interpret the moral "reformer," for example the abolitionist who claims that slavery is morally wrong?) The implications of subjectivism would seem to be that if Hitler was sincere in his belief that exterminating Jews was the right thing to do, that made it right for him to do it.

Still another interpretation of ethical relativism is the position that one is conditioned to hold the moral attitudes one holds by the teachings of parents, teachers, friends, and, in general, one's culture, and that therefore these moral attitudes have no validity. Nothing is right or wrong; things are merely held to be right or wrong according to one's conditioning. This type of relativism is *ethical nihilism.*

In the article entitled "The Issue of Relativity," John Ladd discusses critically some of the ethical implications which cultural relativism has been thought to have, and he analyzes two ways in which ethical relativism can play an important role in normative ethics. Ladd finds that what is common to the normative and the nihilistic varieties is the thesis that popular opinion or custom in some way or other constitutes what is right or wrong, that it legislates for morals analogous to the way that a legislature legislates laws. He then distinguishes what he calls "constructive relativism," the view that different cultures have different "experiments in living," alternative ways of solving the problems of the good life, from "destructive relativism." The latter, instead of raising moral opinion or custom to the level of justified morality, reduces moral opinion or custom to the level of mere opinion or custom, depriving it of its normative moral character altogether. But he suggests that this is never to destroy ethics as such, only to destroy traditional values so that a new system of values can be erected in their stead.

"Metaethics" is that part of ethics which seeks to analyze the nature of normative ethical judgments, not to make such judgments. When someone seriously makes a normative ethical assertion, such as, "The highest value in life is the use of reason" or "Euthanasia is morally wrong," what kind of linguistic behavior is he or she engaged in? Are these statements of fact, claims to knowledge which are either true or false? Or are they merely expressions of emotion or attitude which only appear to be statements of fact from the form of the sentences in which they are expressed? If they are factual assertions, are the facts "ordinary" facts which can be confirmed or disconfirmed by empirical evidence, or are they special moral or valuational facts which cannot be ascertained by ordinary empirical means?

One possibility is that moral and valuational words can always be defined in terms of nonmoral and nonvaluational words so that the ethical assertions can be translated into ordinary descriptive statements. For example, "Euthanasia is morally wrong" means "Euthanasia is contrary to the moral code of my culture" or "It would maximize pleasure or minimize pain if euthanasia were contrary to the moral code of my culture" or something of the sort. These translations are factual assertions which can presumably be confirmed or disconfirmed by the sciences of sociology and psychology. The problems of identifying what is my culture and what is its moral code, or of predicting the maximization of pleasure or minimization of pain which would be caused by a particular element being part of the moral code of my culture are by no means simple problems, but they are empirical questions whose solution depends upon empirical research as the appropriate method, although the judgment of a native participant in the culture may be a good guess as to what the answer would be.

The twentieth-century British philosopher G. E. Moore, in *Principia Ethica,* excerpted here, attacked the effort to define ethical words in terms of concepts amenable to empirical investigation. He called any such definitional analysis a form of "Naturalism" and charged that it committed the "naturalistic fallacy." Moore believed that some ethical words could be defined by other ethical words, for example, perhaps "right" could be defined using the word "good," but he thought statements with ethical terms could never be translated into statements with no ethical terms. Moore claimed that a value term such as "good" refers to a simple "nonnatural" property of good things, and what "natural" properties a thing has to have in order to have the unique property of goodness cannot be settled by definition.

Some historians of philosophy have questioned whether anyone has ever committed the naturalistic fallacy as described by Moore. Other philosophers have disputed whether the "naturalistic fallacy" is a fallacy. A position approximating Naturalism is represented by the selection from *Good Will and Ill Will* by F. C. Sharp. Sharp defines "right" in terms of impersonal approval of an action with complete acquaintance with all relevant consequences. From this it follows that moral judgments are susceptible to revision if they can be shown to be partial, not impersonal, or if they can be shown to rely upon false or incomplete information concerning relevant consequences. This view has sometimes been called the "ideal observer" theory ("ideal approver" would be more accurate), since ethical judgments are true or false according to whether they measure up to the standards of an ideal observer with complete relevant information and pure impartiality.

Although Moore rejected the definition of ethical terms by nonethical terms, he still analyzed ethical judgments as being factual assertions which are true or false. According to Moore they state unique ethical facts, but he as well as Sharp can be classified as a "Descriptivist," the difference being that for Moore they are descriptive of a world of values, not merely the natural universe. A more radical possibility is that ethical assertions do not state facts at all, but are essentially expressive of emotion and dynamic in causing others to have similar emotions, like the cheers and boos of a football game. This position is articulated by C. L. Stevenson in his article "The Emotive Meaning of Ethical Terms," and subsequent developments are described in the selection from R. M. Hare's essay entitled "Ethics." Hare agrees with Stevenson that ethical assertions are not fact-stating, that they are "noncognitive" in that they are not primarily knowledge-claims, but Hare emphasizes the role which ethical statements play in guiding choices. He regards them as primarily *prescriptive,* like commands, rather than expressive of emotion or a stimulation to similar emotion. At the same time, according to Hare, an act is prescribed in virtue of some characteristic which makes it prescriptive on any similar occasion. Thus, Hare calls his position *universal prescriptivism.*

It should be pointed out that noncognitivist theories of the nature of ethical judgments still admit of the use of reason in settling ethical disputes. An emotion may be appropriate or inappropriate in a given situation or toward a specific kind of object, and reasons may be given concerning appropriateness. A prescription which guides a choice may be justified or unjustified, according to whether the choice is wise or unwise, or, according to Hare, according to whether the prescription can be universalized. This leaves room for practical reasoning concerning its wisdom or universalization as well as for theoretical reasoning concerning any factual presuppositions. Thus the analysis of ethical language as emotive or prescriptive does not eliminate the relevance of moral reasoning, but it does, to some extent, determine the character of reasoning which is appropriate.

The final two selections in this section are discussions of moral reasoning, which is, as indicated, closely related to the analysis of moral language. Reflection upon some of the metaethical theories already reviewed reveals this relation. A naturalist would believe that moral reasoning consists in the correct analysis of the meaning of ethical terms into nonethical terms and the identification of these natural properties. The nonnaturalistic cognitivist, such as G. E. Moore, believes that ethics is a body of knowledge, but known by a special faculty of cognition which intuits what is good. Stevenson analyzes ethical disputes as based on a disagreement in interest. Sometimes this disagreement is in turn based on disagreement in belief and can be resolved by reasons which may be empirically established, because our knowledge of the world is a determining factor to our interests, but it is possible for disagreement in interest to be rooted simply in disagreement in ultimate attitude. In that case, according to Stevenson, there is no empirical or rational method for settling the difference, but there may still be persuasive rhetoric which will change the attitude of one or both parties.

In the selection by R. M. Hare entitled "Moral Reasoning" we find Hare arguing that the rules of moral reasoning correspond to the two features of moral judgments which he considers essential, namely, prescriptivity and universalizability. According to Hare, when we are trying in a concrete case to decide what ought to be done, we are looking for an act which we can commit ourselves to being done (prescriptivity) but which we are at the same time prepared to accept as exemplifying a principle of action to be prescribed for anyone in like circumstances (universalizability). If, when we consider some proposed action, we find that when universalized it yields prescriptions which we cannot accept, we reject this action as a solution to our moral problem. According to Hare's analysis, one of the essential features of moral reasoning is that one imagine oneself to be each of the affected parties of any proposed prescription. If being in any of these roles is inconsistent with one's desires and aversions, then the prescription is unacceptable. It follows from this that people with very eccentric tastes could accept moral principles that would be rejected by someone with ordinary tastes. The fanatic Nazi who desires that he be sent to the gas chamber if it should turn out that he really is a Jew can consistently accept the moral principle that Jews ought to be exterminated, but most people could not. In this respect, according to Hare, all moral arguments are *ad hominem,* that is, they are addressed to a person's particular preferences, and an argument can be effective addressed to one person and ineffective addressed to another.

Both Hare and Stevenson hold that at a certain point ethical disagreements and disputes may be irreconcilable by reason. After all factual disagreements are resolved, there may be an impasse because of a basic disagreement in attitude or interest or inclination. Philippa Foot, in her article "Moral Arguments," challenges this conclusion. She argues that there may be the strictest rules of evidence, even when an evaluative conclusion is concerned, and that anyone who uses moral terms at all must abide by the rules for their use, including the rules about what shall count as evidence for or against the moral judgment concerned. In contrast to Hare and Stevenson, she holds that the content of moral principles is one of their identifying features, not simply the elements of feeling or attitude with which they are held or the universal and prescriptive character of the principles.

H. W.

28. *VALIDATION AND VINDICATION: AN ANALYSIS OF THE NATURE AND THE LIMITS OF ETHICAL ARGUMENTS*[1]

Herbert Feigl

The following schematic dialogue was constructed with the intention of illustrating some of the typical turns and twists which occur almost invariably when argument in moral issues is pursued through successive levels of critical reflection. A more systematic formulation of the philosophical conclusions that may be derived from a study of such justificatory arguments will be presented in the second part of this essay.

I. A DIALOGUE

A.: Under what conditions can war be morally justified?

B.: Under no conditions. I am a convinced pacifist and conscientious objector. There is no greater evil than war and deliberate killing.

A.: Would you rather be killed or enslaved than do any killing? Are there no circumstances, such as a need for self-defense that would justify killing?

B.: There are none.

A.: If you were saying that wanton killing and cruelty are to be condemned, I should heartily agree with you. But there are occasions in which killing is the only choice: a necessary evil, surely, but justifiable because it may be the lesser evil in the given circumstances.

The point of view of the radical pacifist is unreasonable. More lives might ultimately be saved, and greater happiness for a larger number

of people might result if the innocent victims of aggression were to wage a victorious war upon the aggressor. This is essentially the same reasoning that I would apply to the situation in which, for example, a robber threatened my own life or that of a friend.

B.: I admit that all these are very unfortunate situations. My sincerest efforts would be devoted to prevent their very occurrence (by whatever suitable means: education, reform, arbitration, compromise, reconciliation, etc.). But once such a situation arises I still believe that one should not kill.

A.: How do you justify this position?

B.: How does one justify *any* moral judgment? Obviously by deriving it from the basic moral laws. Respect for the life, the rights, the happiness of others is surely such a basic norm, is it not?

A.: I shall be curious to find out how such basic moral laws are proved or established. But before we enter into this deep question, tell me how you defend such a rigid adherence to non-violence, even if you yourself may easily become the victim of aggression or war.

B.: I shall not invoke religious principles here. Perhaps I can convince you if I make you aware of the consequences of the pacifist attitude. Once practiced by many it would tend to spread by way of emulation and thus sooner or later eradicate the evil of killing altogether.

A.: This is an optimistic assertion concerning the probability of certain consequences. In any case it is a question of fact which is not easily decided. However, your disagreement with me seems to go beyond whatever we may think about the facts, namely the conditions and consequences of attitudes. True enough, in your last remark you have tried to establish a common basis of evaluation. You appealed to a humanitarian principle which I do share with you. Still, I think that to kill is morally better than to be enslaved. Since you disagree with me on this, it is obvious that we diverge in *some* of our basic norms. This divergence in attitude can apparently not be removed by considerations of fact.

B.: Are ethical principles then a matter of personal whim and caprice?

A.: I did not mean to imply this at all. As our own cases show, we tend to have very strong and serious convictions in these matters. Far from being chosen arbitrarily, our moral attitudes are a result of the culture and the subculture in which our personalities are formed.

B.: We are not necessarily conforming to the prevailing patterns. I for one, am certainly not. I arrived at my views by independent and serious reflection.

A.: I don't wish to dispute it. And yet your attitudes are a causal consequence of many factors: heredity, environment (physical, and especially social; the influence of parents, friends, teachers, attractive and abhorrent examples, crucial experiences, etc.) and, yes, your (more or less) intelligent reflection upon the facts as they impress *you-as-you-are*.

B.: If you are right, there are limits beyond which rational (i.e. logical and/or factual) argument cannot be extended. Intelligent reflection concerning means and ends, conditions and consequences operates within the frame of basic evaluations. Beyond those limits there could be only conversion by persuasion (rhetoric, propaganda, suggestion, promises, threats, re-education, psycho-therapy, etc.). There are also techniques of settlement of disagreements by way of compromise, segregation (separation, divorce) or higher synthesis. By "higher synthesis" I mean, for example, the abandonment or severe restriction of the sovereignty of individual nations and a transfer of all sentiments of loyalty to a world government. Only if none of these techniques succeeds, then indeed coercion by violence, alas, seems inevitable.—(Universal pacifism is the only solution! But that's not my point at the moment.)

A.: You have expressed my point of view very well. But you are obviously unwilling to agree to it.

B.: Indeed not. Everything in me cries out for a belief in objectively and universally valid standards of moral evaluation.

A.: You will not get very far if you assume some theological or metaphysical absolutes. Any reference to the revealed commands of a divine authority is futile. For you would have to tell how you can know those imperatives as divine; and even if you were to know them as such you would have to state a reason as to why anybody should obey them. The same criticisms apply to any alleged metaphysical insight into what man ought to be. And if you dismiss theological and metaphysical foundations for morality you will find it difficult to argue for standards that are independent of human needs and interests.

B.: It's precisely human needs and interests that provide a solid foundation for moral standards. In all cultures that we call 'civilized' there are essentially the same ideals of cooperation (as opposed to conflict), of helpfulness (as opposed to harmfulness), of love (as opposed to hatred), of justice (as opposed to inequity), and of perfection and growth (as opposed to stagnation and decay). Cultural relativity and the variability of human nature have been exaggerated. There is a significant core of essential features shared by all human beings. Human nature as it is constituted biologically and psychologically, and as it finds its existence in a context of interdependence with other human beings, could scarcely fail to develop just those ideals of morality. I admit that these ideals are only rarely fulfilled or even approximated in actual conduct. But they are *the* standards of ethical evaluation. It is with reference to this frame that we make our judgments of "good" and "bad," "right" and "wrong."

A.: Much as I share your ideals, I can't refrain from calling your attention to the fact that there are notable exceptions that restrict severely not only the universality of certain types of conduct (this is what you admitted), but also the universality of the very standards or ideals of morality. To many an ancient or oriental culture the idea of perfection or progress remained completely strange. The prevailing ideologies of capitalism and nationalism basically extol the ideals of competition over those of cooperation. Only superficially and often hypocritically do they pay lip service to humanitarian or Christian ideals. And the very principle of justice (in the sense of equal rights for all) has been flouted not only by tyrants, aristocrats and fascists but also by such eminent philosophers as Plato and Nietzsche. Our own divergence on the issue of radical pacificism is equally a case in point. There are countless further, possibly secondary and yet radical divergencies as regards attitudes toward civil liberties, sex and marriage, birth control, euthanasia, the role of religion (church and state), animals (vegetarianism, vivisection), etc., etc.

B.: Disregarding the secondary divergencies, I must say that the deviations from the more fundamental and true moral ideals are simply perversions and corruptions. Whoever denies the principles of justice and neighborliness is immoral. Kant was essentially right and convincingly logical in defining moral conduct by his categorical imperative. Only a principle that is binding for all and excludes any sort of arbitrary privilege and partiality can justifiably be called ethical. The ideals that I enumerated are the very essence of what is meant by "morality." To be moral consists precisely in placing oneself in the service of interests and ideals that transcend purely selfish purposes.

A.: That is what *you* mean by 'morality.' (And, of course, it is in keeping with traditional morality). But Nietzsche, for example, explicitly proposed a revolution in all traditional morality. Clearly, he considered his own value-system as the "true ethics." Are you not aware that you are begging the very question at issue? You speak of "true moral ideals"; you call certain views "immoral," "perverse," "corrupt"; you say that only certain types of principles can "justifiably be called ethical." You are using persuasive definitions[2] here. You call "moral" or "ethical" only such doctrines or principles as agree with your own convictions about what is *right*. The fascination with the "*logicality*" of Kant's categorical imperative may in part lie in its implicit appeal to some version of the principle of sufficient reason: If there is no reason to discriminate (as regards rights and obligations) between two persons then such discrimination is willful, arbitrary, unjust. But far from involving strictly logical contradictions

such "unjustifiable" discriminations would merely violate *one* (not as you would say "*the*") definition of justice. A reason for discrimination could always be found. That it may not be accepted as a "good," "relevant" or "sufficient" reason is but a consequence of the ethical principles or fundamental evaluations of some alternative system. Let me assure you again that I share your moral attitudes. But strongly as I feel about them, I see no need for, and no profit in defending them with bad logic. You cannot by some verbal magic establish justifications for ideals which obviously are neither logically nor empirically unique. These ideals compete with genuine alternatives.

B.: I can't believe this. The ideals that I have listed are the ones that will benefit humanity in the long run. Not just a particular group, but all of mankind.

Moreover these ideals are comprised by the essence of *rationality*. Man, the rational animal, is by his very nature not only characterized by his capacity for adequate deductive and inductive thinking, but also by his sense of justice and his abhorrence of violence as a method for the settlement of disputes.

A.: You are still begging the question. Those who do not accept the principle of equality are not interested in *all* of mankind. Furthermore, your time-honored conception of human nature is clearly not an account of actual fact, but of an ideal (by no means universally shared) which you utilize for a persuasive definition of MAN. You won't convince any serious opponents by mere *definitions*. But you might try to entice, persuade, educate or reform them in other ways. You may also hope that the increasing interdependence of all of mankind on this planet will eventually generate a fundamental uniformity in the principles of moral evaluation.

B.: You underestimate the rôle of experience in the settlement of moral conflicts and disputes. Those who have had an opportunity to experience different ways of life soon learn to discriminate between the better and the worse. Experience in the context of needs and interests, of claims and counter-claims, of existing and emerging rights and obligations in the social milieu soon enough mould the moral conscience of man. We do not live in a vacuum. The constant encouragements and discouragements of our actions and their underlying attitudes form the very atmosphere of the life in the family, the workshop, the market place, the tribunal, etc. Add to that the basic sympathy human beings feel for each other and you will have to admit that there is a large mass of empirical factors that operate in the direction of a common standard of social morality.

A.: If I may use a parallel drawn from the field of aesthetics, there are a great many people who prefer pulp-magazine stories to "good" literature; or swing (jazz, jive or whatever is the fashion) to "great" music. Similarly, there are plenty of people who have had an opportunity to experience both the ruthless and the kindly way of life and yet subscribe to the principles of the former. Kropotkin rightly, though somewhat sentimentally, pointed out that despite the cruel struggle for existence in the animal kingdom there is also a good deal of mutual help and self-sacrifice. If human sympathy were as fundamental as (he and) you claim it is, there could hardly be such views as those of Nietzsche, Hitler, and

Mussolini on the "greatness" of war. Only by endorsing one norm against other possible alternatives can you avail yourself of the premises by which to validate the special moral precepts which are dear to your heart.

B.: You still have failed to give me a single good reason why I or you or anyone should adhere to even those moral principles which we happen to share. Your position is a skepticism that could easily lead to moral indifference and cynicism.

A.: And what sort of a reason do you expect me to give you? If I provided you with premises from which you could *deduce* our moral standards, you would ask me for a justification of those premises. And you surely don't want a reason in the sense of a motive. You are motivated already. You do not seriously entertain doubt as long as this motivation prevails. And nothing that I've said was intended to undermine it. The aim of my remarks was clarification; not education, fortification or edification. Too many philosophers have sold their birthright for a pot of message.

NOTES

1.   This essay is a revision of an earlier (hitherto unpublished and altogether different) version of my essay "De Principiis Non Disputandum . . .?" included in *Philosophical Analysis,* edited by Max Black, Cornell University Press, Ithaca, N.Y., 1950. In "De Principiis. . . ." the problem of justification is discussed not only with reference to ethical principles but also in regard to the more fundamental principles of deduction, induction and the criterion of factual meaningfulness.—For an important analysis of closely related issues see also the essay by Wilfrid Sellars: "Language, Rules and Behavior," contained in the volume *John Dewey, Philosopher of Science and Freedom,* ed. S. Hook, The Dial Press, New York, 1950.

2.   This useful phrase was coined by C. L. Stevenson. In his book *Ethics and Language* (Yale University Press, 1944), p. 210 he explains it as follows:

"In any 'persuasive definition' the term defined is a familiar one, whose meaning is both descriptive and strongly emotive. The purport of the definition is to alter the descriptive meaning of the term, usually by giving it greater precision within the boundaries of its customary vagueness; but the definition does *not* make any substantial change in the term's emotive meaning. And the definition is used, consciously or unconsciously, in an effort to secure, by this interplay between emotive and descriptive meaning, a redirection of people's attitudes."

29. THE ISSUE OF RELATIVITY

John Ladd

Any discussion of the relations between anthropology and ethics leads inevitably to the ticklish issue of relativism. Even when not explicitly recognized as such, this issue has been the skeleton in the closet for every philosophical moralist since the time of Plato and the Sophists; for the critical implications of the fact of the diversity and discordance between moral precepts and moral codes in different societies are inescapable. Yet it is difficult to pin down the precise relevance of these differences for morals. To the layman it seems obvious that the lack of universal agreement concerning morals derogates somehow from their validity; in particular he is ready to think twice about a moral precept if it appears to him as a purely local or provincial custom. And yet, on the other hand, he is willing to acknowledge some truth in the ancient maxim: "When in Rome do as the Romans do"! Thus already for the layman there is a kind of ambiguous message conveyed by the facts of cultural relativism. Quite significantly, however, this same kind of ambiguity is incorporated into the leading ideology of our times, namely Marxism, which, as 'scientific socialism', is based on the relativity of ideologies and social relations.

Despite the natural perplexities and practical challenges that appear to arise from the facts of cultural diversity and relativity, discussions by moral philosophers of their relevance to ethics are curiously vapid and, it seems to me, beside the point. If, as is maintained by some, cultural relativism somehow undermines ethics, it is necessary to show how and why it does so, and this has not been done. On the other hand, if, as others maintain, cultural relativism is totally irrelevant to ethics, as irrelevant, perhaps, as is the fact of diversity of human beliefs concerning the causes of tuberculosis to the latest expert opinion or medical science, then why does this fact create so much uneasiness among philosophers and laymen alike? Finally, there are some who try to cope with cultural relativity by denying it, that is, by maintaining that basically there is no real disagreement between people of different cultures concerning morals. Why, we may ask, are they so anxious to refute cultural relativism? These three attitudes appear to comprehend all of the prevalent conceptions of the relevance of cultural relativity to ethics, yet none of them is very satisfactory. The reason for this is that the issue of relativism has never been stated clearly.

It is the purpose of this paper to set forth what I conceive to be some of the issues that are involved in this complicated problem. The position that I wish to defend is that the relevance of cultural relativism to ethics has constantly been misconstrued by relativists and non-relativists alike because they have taken for granted a mistaken view of the nature of ethics itself, namely, that it is a kind of knowledge differing only in subject-matter from, say, science. Recent developments in ethical theory have revived and revivified the classical Aristotelian notion of practical reason and have, in my opinion, conclusively shown that ethics is not basically susceptible of a purely epistemic analysis. Concerning this repudiation of the epistemic point of view. Frankena has recently written: "But today, on both sides of the Channel, . . . except in Thomistic circles, the main effort toward understanding morality is based on the conviction that it is not a body of knowledge, natural or non-natural, empirical or *a priori*."[1]

It seems clear to me that philosophically unsophisticated relativists are guilty of an *ignoratio elenchi,* since they train their guns on an oversimple and now out-dated conception of ethics, and that their philosophical refuters, by assuming the same conception have shamefully dodged the issue. Elsewhere I have tried to show how new philosophical conceptions of the nature and logic of ethics can be profitably employed in anthropological researches. Here I

From John Ladd, "The Issue of Relativity," *The Monist,* Vol. 47, No. 4 (1963), pp. 585–609. Reprinted with the permission of the author and publisher.

should like to show that they can also be used to illuminate the issue of relativism. I shall contend that once we understand the true nature of ethics as a practical rational discipline rather than as a mode of theoretical knowledge, we will be able to see more clearly how and why the facts of cultural relativity are relevant to ethics but yet not destructive of it.

Contrary to what is generally thought, the relevance of the facts of cultural relativity does not consist in their being used to establish a rather strange kind of conclusion that goes by the name of 'ethical relativism'; rather it consists in their being used in various kinds of ethical arguments that have largely been ignored because of epistemic preconceptions about ethics. It follows, I contend, that coping with cultural relativity is a task for normative ethics, that is, for the moralist, rather than for meta-ethics, the 'epistemology of ethics'. In other words, the challenge of relativism is an ethical challenge that must be met head-on and cannot be avoided through purported metaphysical, epistemological, or linguistic refutations.

Let us begin by defining 'cultural relativism'. I shall assume that this is an anthropological doctrine which is scientific and empirical in nature and which rests on actual observations of other cultures and on related psychological and sociological theories. Consequently, I regard cultural relativism as itself a descriptive theory and in this sense neutral as far as evaluations are concerned. (This is, of course, not to deny that it may be relevant to ethics and evaluations in general. If 'cultural relativism' is defined as an ethical doctrine, as it is by some anthropologists, then the issues I want to discuss are lost in verbal quibbles.)

Cultural relativism, I shall assume, consists of two different theses, which may respectively be called the *diversity thesis* and the *relativity thesis*. The first of these, the diversity thesis, asserts that there is a diversity of moral opinions from one society to another and hence that there is no *consensus gentium* concerning morals: what is regarded as right in one society is regarded as wrong in another. Furthermore, it asserts that these ethical differences relate not only to the evaluations of particular acts, but also to rules, principles, ideals, goals and character evaluations.

The second thesis, the relativity thesis, maintains that the character of people's moral opinions is to be explained by cultural and social factors of some sort, such as linguistic structure, economic determinants, psychological conditioning, psychoanalytic mechanisms, historical factors, or the unique pattern of culture of the society in question. In other words, moral opinions are relative to cultural determinants of some kind in the sense that they are causally dependent upon them. Although most contemporary cultural relativists combine these two theses, it is possible to accept one without the other. Hume, for example, would subscribe to the relativity thesis inasmuch as he presents a psychological theory of the origin of moral sentiments (opinions), although more than likely he would have denied the diversity thesis.

The question with which we shall be concerned is simply this: supposing that cultural relativism in some form or other is true, what follows with regard to ethics? A survey of the conclusions of those who stress the significance of cultural relativism for ethics reveals nothing but confusion. If I am right, then it is easy to see why this should be so, for cultural relativism is not really used to establish any simple ethical conclusion at all. Instead, it is used as a form of argument, or rather, as several forms of argument that are quite peculiar to ethics. In order to show the absurdity of supposing that cultural relativism directly establishes a conclusion of some sort, let us briefly survey some of the conclusions that it is supposed to entail.

First, cultural relativism is supposed to show that what is right for one person in one social and cultural situation is wrong for another person in another social and cultural situation. There is, however, nothing especially novel about the contention that the rightness or wrongness of acts is dependent upon the agent's situation, including his social and cultural situation. It is generally agreed by moral philosophers of every school that circumstances require us to apply moral principles differently to different cases. Elsewhere I have called this phenomenon *applicational relativity*. (The accusation by social scientists that the Western ethical tradition has paid no attention to the applicational relativity of morals merely reflects their ignorance of the history of ethics.)

① rightness & wrongness depend on society

② tolerance

③ scepticism

Now it is quite clear that the facts of cultural relativism, and cultural anthropology in general, do not prove the principle of applicational relativity, nor do they need to do so, although they may help us to use this principle more intelligently by calling our attention to the differentials that require our principles to be applied differently. The question of which situational factors are ultimately to be taken as morally relevant is, of course, a question for ethics rather than anthropology. One cannot, for example, persuasively justify the institution of polygamy in a certain society on the grounds of its effectiveness in promoting social stability if such considerations are rejected as morally irrelevant to the proper or just conception of marriage. At any rate, what is and what is not a morally relevant factor in the evaluation of institutions like marriage is an *open question* and one that I believe it is the role of moral philosophers to discuss.

Let us assume, therefore, that the issue of relativism is not related to questions involving the principle of applicational relativity as such. Indeed, the principle of applicational relativity itself presupposes the validity of some sort of moral principle to be applied, which cannot be established by anthropology. We must therefore search elsewhere in our effort to pin down the conclusions that are supposed to follow from cultural relativism.

Sometimes it is insinuated or implied that the facts of cultural relativity lead us in a new way to recognize the importance of tolerance and mutual understanding. Through the recognition of cultural relativity "we shall arrive then at a more realistic social faith, accepting as grounds of hope and as new bases for tolerance the co-existing and equally valid patterns of life which mankind has created for itself from the raw materials of existence.² "The very core of cultural relativism is the social discipline that comes of respect for differences—of mutual respect."³ The principle of tolerance and of mutual respect is itself, however, an ethical principle, not an anthropological truth, and if I am not mistaken, no one supposes that it is a principle which is established by cultural relativism. Rather, cultural relativism merely provides ammunition for the 'attack' on certain accepted ethical dogmas, namely, those that are incompatible with tolerance.⁴

Let us try once more to find an ethically relevant conclusion from the facts of cultural relativity. It might be held that a recognition of these facts leads to ethical skepticism, the denial of any difference between right and wrong. In contrast to the views already discussed, this one maintains, or appears to maintain, that there are no ethical positions at all. At first glance it would appear that we have a proposition somewhat like this: since there is disagreement about the rightness and wrongness of acts, there can be no objective rightness or wrongness. ". . . nothing is good by nature."⁵ Rightness and wrongness, goodness and badness, are subjective qualities analogous to secondary qualities like color and smell, which have traditionally been regarded as subjective and relative. Nevertheless, this view still conceives them as qualities, albeit subjective ones. Consequently this kind of skepticism turns into subjectivism, a view which is quite compatible with the assertion of truth-claims regarding, e.g., what is good. (This is the view that was refuted by Moore.)

This is how Sextus Empiricus presents the case against ethics, and, of course, it is a case that goes back to the pre-Socratics. It is, however, in my opinion, a completely mistaken interpretation of relativism and quite beside the point made by cultural relativism. Sextus, the Sophists, and modern philosophers like Brentano mistakenly want to assimilate the arguments for ethical skepticism to those for epistemological skepticism. The two kinds of skepticism are, however, *toto coelo* different. Epistemological skepticism typically argues that the immediate data (e.g. of sense) are inadequate to prove certain further propositions, e.g. about the external world, about the future, or about other minds. It asserts that we cannot know these propositions to be true because we are not justified in making the inferences.⁶ In ethics, in contrast, there are no such data to begin with! The question of justifying transitional inferences analogous to those mentioned is not the issue at all. Skepticism in ethics arises in quite a different way from skepticism in epistemology. In ethics the fact that not all societies accept the same moral standards as we do, i.e., the fact of ethical differences, is taken to prove something akin to skepticism: the crucial point in the argument is the fact of differences of opinion. The fact of differences of opinion, is not, however, any part of the epistemologist's armory; this is not the kind of argument that is made use of by Descartes or Hume to establish their type of skepticism. Not only are the kinds of argument used by the two types of skepticism entirely different, but the basic conclusions are also different in kind: in epistemology the conclusion is that we cannot *know;* no fact beside the fact of knowledge is brought into question. In ethics, on the other hand, the skeptical conclusion relates to morals themselves, for it asserts that nothing is either right or wrong. Perhaps, therefore, it would be more apt to call this kind of ethical conclusion 'nihilism' rather than 'skepticism'. (I shall return to a further consideration of nihilism later on in this paper.)

It is obvious by now that the decisive and distinctive import for ethics of the facts of cultural relativity hinges on the assumption of an intimate, perhaps even logical connection between people's moral opinions and the rightness and wrongness of their actions; for it is clear that cultural relativism, insofar as it relates to what is thought to be right or wrong in different societies, will be relevant to ethics only if it is assumed that moral opinion reflects, constitutes, validates or in some other way determines moral principle. Science and other standard types of knowledge do not admit this kind of assumption; it would be highly irregular indeed to try to prove or disprove a scientific hypothesis by reference to popular opinion! (This statement will require slight modification later.) The kind of assumed relationship between moral opinion and moral principle that we are concerned with here is much more like the relationship holding between opinion and rule, say, in etiquette. In matters of etiquette the opinion of the upper social classes is authoritative and determines what is socially proper or improper: what is considered to be proper or improper is no different from what actually is proper or improper. (To quote Hamlet: "There is nothing either good or bad but thinking makes it so.")

*   *   *

There are good reasons for maintaining that popular opinion, or custom, in some way or other constitutes what is morally right and wrong, and that, in a way, it legislates for morals.

Since morality is concerned with aspects of conduct and evaluation that are bound up with social institutions and practices, it is natural to suppose that the latter in some way or other define what is right or wrong. Institutions like marriage and property, which certainly have a basic moral import, are, of course, culturally defined, that is, the conditions under which a social relationship is to be considered a marriage or a relationship to things is to be considered that of ownership are determined culturally; social opinion concerning these conditions is both necessary and sufficient to determine what these conditions are. (I include under 'social opinion' the dictates of social authorities such as the legislature or the courts.)

Here the analogy with law is useful. The positive law, insofar as it is created (by legislature or courts), lays down the conditions of being married or of owning property as well as a host of conditions of other types of social transactions. Without such definition of these concepts, which, of course, entails legal consequences involving mutual rights and duties, the concepts themselves would be vacuous and have no application. (How, for instance, can one be married in a state of nature?) Furthermore, it is the *ipse dixit* of the law-making authority itself that constitutes the content and range of these concepts (or institutions); in other words, the opinion itself (of the right body under the right conditions) makes law. We need not, of course, assume that power to make positive law has no limits or general directions which it must follow.

The point that I wish to make can be illustrated by Thomas Aquinas's natural law doctrine, for, as he points out, the human law may be derived from the natural law by way of "particular determination"—so that human laws may vary from place to place and yet be determinations of the natural law.[7] The human laws, then, have a conventional component.

Hobbes makes a somewhat similar point when he writes.

Theft, murder, adultery and all injuries are forbid by the laws of nature; but what is to be called theft, what murder, what adultery, what injury in a citizen, this is not to be determined by the natural, but by the civil law. . . . What therefore theft, what murder, what adultery and in general what injury is, must be known by the civil laws. . . .[8]

The theory I am considering maintains that within any particular society it is culture, popular opinion or custom, rather than the civil law, that defines these concepts for morals. (In some cases, obviously, the civil law is required to do so.) Accordingly, what is right (e.g. as far as marriage is concerned) in one society will be wrong in another society, somewhat as divorce is legally possible in Nevada but not in South Carolina. Inasmuch as opinion, in some cases at least, determines what is right or wrong, and opinion varies from one society to another, what is right or wrong will likewise vary from society to society. So we have a theory that makes sense out of the contention that cultural relativism is relevant to ethics; for, indeed, if and to the extent that opinion constitutes morals, what is right or wrong will be relative to one's society in a non-pernicious sense. Furthermore, this view enables us to say with Ruth Benedict that different moral conceptions, e.g. of property, in different societies are "equally valid," for, indeed, they are valid and binding within the society that prescribes them, and the fact that they are not valid in other societies does not derogate from their validity within the society in question.

Although I have stated this quasi-legislative position in terms of one version of the natural law theory, it is, of course, much broader. This is, for example, the view that I believe is held by MacBeath, when he states that:

... all these moralities, past and present, and all the moral judgments in which they find expression, or at least all the considered moral judgments among them, are equally data of ethics; and that ethical theorists neglect any of them at their peril.[9]

They are data of ethics because, in a sense, they constitute the morals of the group in question; they are "experiments in living." And, one can say that the different moral systems are alternative experiments, alternative ways of solving the problem of the good life. As such we can say that different moral codes in other societies, as representing different experiments, should not be regarded as ethically inferior to our own, or vice versa.

Now the view that we have just been considering has certain affinities with the general ethical position known as voluntarism, for, by analogy, we can conceive of popular opinion as embodying the will of the people which determines what is right and wrong. There is, and must be, in my opinion, a voluntaristic element in any legal or moral system. However, there must also be a non-voluntaristic element, that is, some part of the system must be independent of a constitutive, legislative will. In the natural law theory it is, of course, the natural law itself, which is over and above the human law. In MacBeath's system, it is the "inner or subjective or purely personal aspect consisting of the motives, spirit or attitude of mind of the agent. . . . Moreover, this inner aspect of conduct does not vary from people to people."[10] There must be, for theoretical reasons, a principle, however formal and general, that confers authority and legitimacy on the quasi-legislative cultural definitions of what is right or wrong. This principle might be regarded as providing, as it were, a schema for morals, which is to be filled in by the culture itself as it "experiments in living." We still have relativism, of course, but it might be described as a restricted relativism, restricted, that is, by the schema. Incidentally, by recognizing some limits, however vague and general, we have answered the rather obvious objection to Ruth Benedict's position that it would require our recognizing Nazism and its idealization of atrocities as "equally valid." The position I have only vaguely outlined would allow for a variety of differing moral institutions while excluding from our tolerance rules and codes that are absolutely intolerable.

The position that I have just considered uses differences in morals constructively, that is, to determine what we ought to do. Hence I call it *constructive relativism*. We shall now turn to a consideration of the destructive use of cultural relativism.

In contrast to the constructive relativism just considered, which, as it were, raises popular opinion to the moral level, we now come to the opposite view, namely, one that reduces morality to the level of popular opinion thus depriving it of its moral character altogether. The position is a familiar one: moral principles are nothing but opinions, conventions or customs; and the conclusion is that therefore they are not binding.

The form of argument involved here is one that is used every day. I say: "So and so does such and such," and your rejoinder is: "That's what you think"! or "That's just your opinion." It is a familiar and sometimes devastating device in argumentation to transform a proposition into an opinion. The effect is to emasculate the original statement by changing it from a statement about a fact to a statement about the speaker. In the language of values we have a similar ploy: "That was a good book" Reply: "You just mean that you liked it." "That is the right thing to do" Reply: "You mean that is what people in your society approve." In ethics, what happens in this kind of reduction is that a normative ethical statement is converted into a descriptive statement about a person's opinions. The effect of this conversion is to neutralize the normative component.

It is surprising that moral philosophers have paid so little attention to this process of ethical neutralizing. It is precisely the opposite of Stevenson's persuasive definition, which seeks to redirect people's attitudes by altering the descriptive meaning of a word while retaining its emotive meaning. Naturalistic definitions of words like 'good', and 'right', illustrate this method of persuasive definition. On the other hand, it is possible to proceed in a direction opposite to this by eliminating the emotive meaning, to use Stevenson's terms, thus neutralizing the concept emotively through the use of a definition. Such definitions could be called *dissuasive definitions.*

In his own discussion of relativism, Stevenson provides an admirable illustration of what might be called the method of dissuasive definition, that is, the use of definition to neutralize an ethical claim. A relativistic theory of value, he says:

is simply one that expands 'X is good,' for example, into 'X is approved by _____.' . . . And for varying utterances of 'good', relativism maintains, we must fill in the blank now with reference to the speaker, now with a reference to some group to which the speaker belongs, now with a reference merely to most or to many people at many or most times, etc. . . . The only restriction is that the people must be specified by factual terms. . . .[11]

Obviously the effect of this type of naturalistic definition of 'good' is exactly the opposite of that of a persuasive definition. In effect, what such a reduction does is to eliminate the ethical significance of the statement 'X is good', by reducing it to a statement that has no ethical significance of its own, i.e., an ethically neutral statement about someone's approval. In particular, by 'relativizing' the statement, it is rendered innocuous ethically and its objective validity as a moral principle is destroyed.

This mode of argument in ethics has many illustrations in the history of thought. It is clearly exemplified in Thrasymachus's position in the *Republic* when he gives a dissuasive, neutralizing definition of "justice" as the "interest of the stronger." By means of this definition he has turned the concept of justice into a neutral, descriptive concept. Having done so, he can then go on to ask: "Why should we be just? i.e. do what is in the interest of the stronger?" Having already robbed 'justice' of its normative, ethical meaning and given it a descriptive relative meaning, he is now in a position to say that one ought not to be just, viz. one ought not to do what is in the interest of the stronger, since this interest must inevitably be incompatible with one's own personal interest. The effect of the relativistic definition has been to undermine the concept of justice as an ethical concept.[12]

When used destructively, as it is when moral principles are reduced by definition to moral opinions, cultural relativism acquires a stronger force if emphasis is put on what I have called the relativity thesis; for example, when moral principles (moral opinions) are described as the products of some environmental factor or other. A very good illustration of this is to be found in the Marxist theory of morality, which maintains that Western morality is nothing but an ideological superstructure which is determined by the social relations, which, in turn, are determined by the modes of production. Thus Engels writes:

. . . we can only draw the conclusion, that men, consciously or unconsciously, derive their moral ideas in the last resort from the practical relations on which their class position is based—from the economic relations in which they carry on production and exchange. . . . We therefore reject every attempt to impose on us any moral dogma whatsoever as an eternal, ultimate and forever immutable moral law. . . . We maintain on the contrary that all former moral theories are the product, in the last analysis, of the economic stage which society had reached at that particular epoch. And as society has hitherto moved in class antagonisms, morality was always a class morality.[13]

Having, in his opinion, undermined Western morality by showing it to be a class morality, thus depriving it of its objective validity by a relativistic definition, Engels can go on to speak of "a truly human morality which transcends class antagonisms, etc.," just as Thrasymachus, having destroyed the ordinary Greek concept of justice, can proceed to recommend another morality that requires what Adkins calls the "Homeric competitive virtues." Thus, in a sense, Engels, Thrasymachus, and anyone else who uses relativistic arguments negatively may be called nihilists; but basically they are not nihilists, for they are destroying an old morality only in order to erect a new one; their purpose is ultimately a positive one. (There are many schools of thought which make use of a relativistic analysis to destroy traditional values so that a new system of values can be erected in their stead. I need only mention Nietzsche, Freud, the Existentialists, etc. All of these could be described as nihilists, but, as Camus says, "within the limits of nihilism, it is possible to find the means to proceed beyond nihilism.")

I hope that it will now be clear that, as I suggested earlier, relativism is not used to establish a position but is used instead as a mode of argument with which to refute other ethical positions by undermining them through neutralizing definitions. Furthermore, it will be clear how and why the destructive use of relativism is a preliminary to the construction of a new system. In other words, relativism is never used to destroy ethics as such, but only to destroy a particular moral code that is in the way and must first be cleared out.

NOTES

1. William K. Frankena, "Recent Conceptions of Morality," in Castaneda and Nakhnikian, *Morality and the Language of Conduct* (Detroit, 1963), p. 2.

2. Ruth Benedict, *Patterns of Culture* (New York, 1934), p. 257.

3. Herskovits, *Cultural Anthropology* (New York, 1955), p. 365.

4. I shall refrain from the unkind interpretation of the exaggerations of anthropologists that relativism proves that we are never justified in criticizing the moral codes of others, however evil they may be. It does not call for the sympathetic valuation of, say, Nazism. In this connection, there is a useful discussion by Robert Redfield, *The Primitive World and its Transformations* (Cornell, 1953), pp. 144ff.

5. Sextus Empiricus, *Against the Ethicists,* p. 75. Loeb edition, p. 423.

6. A. J. Ayer, *The Problem of Knowledge* (London, 1956), chap. 2. "What is respectively put in question is our right to make the transition from sense-experiences to physical objects, from the world of common sense to the entities of science, from the overt behavior of other people to their inner thoughts and feelings, from present to past. These are distinct problems, but the pattern of the sceptic's argument is the same in every case." P. 72.

7. See Thomas Aquinas, *Summa Theologica*, IaIIae, questions 95–96. Also, Aristotle, *Nicomachean Ethics,* Book V, chapter 7.

8. Thomas Hobbes, *De Cive,* chap. VI, para. 16.

9. A. MacBeath, *Experiments in Living* (London, 1952), p. 7.

10. *Ibid.,* p. 26.

11. C. L. Stevenson, "Relativism and Non-Relativism in Theory of Value," pp. 29–30.

12. For an illuminating discussion of Thrasymachus's view, see A. W. H. Adkins, *Merit and Responsibility* (Oxford, 1960).

13. Friedrich Engels, *Anti-Dühring* (London, 1934), pp. 107–108.

30. *PRINCIPIA ETHICA*

G. E. Moore

... What, then, is good? How is good to be defined? Now, it may be thought that this is a verbal question. A definition does indeed often mean the expressing of one word's meaning in other words. But this is not the sort of definition I am asking for. Such a definition can never be of ultimate importance in any study except lexicography. If I wanted that kind of definition I should have to consider in the first place how people generally used the word 'good'; but my business is not with its proper usage, as established by custom. I should, indeed, be foolish, if I tried to use it for something which it did not usually denote: if, for instance, I were to announce that, whenever I used the word 'good,' I must be understood to be thinking of that object which is usually denoted by the word 'table.' I shall, therefore, use the word in the sense in which I think it is ordinarily used; but at the same time I am not anxious to discuss whether I am right in thinking that it is so used. My business is solely with that object or idea, which I hold, rightly or wrongly, that the word is generally used to stand for. What I want to discover is the nature of that object or idea, and about this I am extremely anxious to arrive at an agreement.

But, if we understand the question in this sense, my answer to it may seem a very disappointing one. If I am asked 'What is good?' my answer is that good is good, and that is the end of the matter. Or if I am asked 'How is good to be defined?' my answer is that it cannot be defined, and that is all I have to say about it. But disappointing as these answers may appear, they are of the very last importance. To readers who are familiar with philosophic terminology, I can express their importance by saying that they amount to this: That propositions about the good are all of them synthetic and never analytic; and that is plainly no trivial matter. And the

same thing may be expressed more popularly, by saying that, if I am right, then nobody can foist upon us such an axiom as that 'Pleasure is the only good' or that 'The good is the desired' on the pretence that this is 'the very meaning of the word.'

Let us, then, consider this position. My point is that 'good' is a simple notion, just as 'yellow' is a simple notion; that, just as you cannot, by any manner of means, explain to any one who does not already know it, what yellow is, so you cannot explain what good is. Definitions of the kind that I was asking for, definitions which describe the real nature of the object or notion denoted by a word, and which do not merely tell us what the word is used to mean, are only possible when the object or notion in question is something complex. You can give a definition of a horse, because a horse has many different properties and qualities, all of which you can enumerate. But when you have enumerated them all, when you have reduced a horse to his simplest terms, then you can no longer define those terms. They are simply something which you think of or perceive, and to any one who cannot think of or perceive them, you can never, by any definition, make their nature known. It may perhaps be objected to this that we are able to describe to others, objects which they have never seen or thought of. We can, for instance, make a man understand what a chimaera is, although he has never heard of one or seen one. You can tell him that it is an animal with a lioness's head and body, with a goat's head growing from the middle of its back, and with a snake in place of a tail. But here the object which you are describing is a complex object; it is entirely composed of parts, with which we are all perfectly familiar—a snake, a goat, a lioness; and we know, too, the manner in which those parts are to be put together, because we know what is meant by the middle of a lioness's back, and where her tail is wont to grow. And so it is with all objects, not previously known, which we are able to define: they are all

From George Edward Moore, *Principia Ethica* (Cambridge: Cambridge University Press. First edition 1903), selections from Chapter I. Reprinted by permission of Cambridge University Press.

complex; all composed of parts, which may themselves, in the first instance, be capable of similar definition, but which must in the end be reducible to simplest parts, which can no longer be defined. But yellow and good, we say, are not complex: they are notions of that simple kind, out of which definitions are composed and with which the power of further defining ceases.

When we say, as Webster says, 'The definition of horse is "A hoofed quadruped of the genus Equus,"' we may, in fact, mean three different things. (1) We may mean merely: 'When I say "horse," you are to understand that I am talking about a hoofed quadruped of the genus Equus.' This might be called the arbitrary verbal definition: and I do not mean that good is indefinable in that sense. (2) We may mean, as Webster ought to mean: 'When most English people say "horse," they mean a hoofed quadruped of the genus Equus.' This may be called the verbal definition proper, and I do not say that good is indefinable in this sense either; for it is certainly possible to discover how people use a word: otherwise, we could never have known that 'good' may be translated by 'gut' in German and by 'bon' in French. But (3) we may, when we define horse, mean something much more important. We may mean that a certain object, which we all of us know, is composed in a certain manner: that it has four legs, a head, a heart, a liver, etc., etc., all of them arranged in definite relations to one another. It is in this sense that I deny good to be definable. I say that it is not composed of any parts, which we can substitute for it in our minds when we are thinking of it. We might think just as clearly and correctly about a horse, if we thought of all its parts and their arrangement instead of thinking of the whole: we could, I say, think how a horse differed from a donkey just as well, just as truly, in this way, as now we do, only not so easily; but there is nothing whatsoever which we could so substitute for good; and that is what I mean, when I say that good is indefinable.

But I am afraid I have still not removed the chief difficulty which may prevent acceptance of the proposition that good is indefinable. I do not mean to say that *the* good, that which is good, is thus indefinable; if I did think so, I should not be writing on Ethics, for my main object is to help towards discovering that definition. It is just because I think there will be less risk of error in our search for a definition of 'the good,' that I am now insisting that *good* is indefinable. I must try to explain the difference between these two. I suppose it may be granted that 'good' is an adjective. Well 'the good, 'that which is good,' must therefore be the substantive to which the adjective 'good' will apply: it must be the whole of that to which the adjective will apply, and the adjective must *always* truly apply to it. But if it is that to which the adjective will apply, it must be something different from that adjective itself; and the whole of that something different, whatever it is, will be our definition of *the* good. Now it may be that this something will have other adjectives, beside 'good,' that will apply to it. It may be full of pleasure, for example; it may be intelligent: and if these two adjectives are really part of its definition, then it will certainly be true, that pleasure and intelligence are good. And many people appear to think that, if we say 'Pleasure and intelligence are good,' or if we say 'Only pleasure and intelligence are good,' we are defining 'good.' Well, I cannot deny that propositions of this nature may sometimes be called definitions; I do not know well enough how the word is generally used to decide upon this point. I only wish it to be understood that that is not what I mean when I say there is no possible definition of good, and that I shall not mean this if I use the word again. I do most fully believe that some true proposition of the form 'Intelligence is good and intelligence alone is good' can be found; if none could be found, our definition of *the* good would be impossible. As it is, I believe *the* good to be definable; and yet I still say that good itself is indefinable.

'Good,' then, if we mean by it that quality which we assert to belong to a thing, when we say that the thing is good, is incapable of any definition, in the most important sense of that word. The most important sense of 'definition' is that in which a definition states what are the parts which invariably compose a certain whole; and in this sense 'good' has no definition because it is simple and has no parts. It is one of those innumerable objects of thought which are themselves incapable of definition, because they are the ultimate terms by reference to which whatever *is* capable of definition must be defined. That there must be an indefinite number of such terms is obvious, on reflection; since we cannot define anything except by an analysis, which, when carried as far as it will go, refers us to something, which is simply different from anything else, and which by that ultimate difference explains the peculiarity of the whole which we are defining: for every whole contains some parts which are common to other wholes also. There is, therefore, no intrinsic difficulty in the contention that 'good' denotes a simple and indefinable quality. There are many other instances of such qualities.

Consider yellow, for example. We may try to define it, by describing its physical equivalent; we may state what kind of light-vibrations must stimulate the normal eye, in order that we may perceive it. But a moment's reflection is sufficient to shew that those light-vibrations are not themselves what we mean by yellow. *They* are not what we perceive. Indeed we should never have been able to discover their existence, unless we had first been struck by the patent difference of quality between the different colours. The most we can be entitled to say of those vibrations is that they are what corresponds in space to the yellow which we actually perceive.

Yet a mistake of this simple kind has commonly been made about 'good.' It may be true that all things which are good are *also* something else, just as it is true that all things which are yellow produce a certain kind of vibration in the light. And it is a fact, that Ethics aims at discovering what are those other properties belonging to all things which are good. But far too many philosophers have thought that when they named those other properties they were actually defining good; that these properties, in fact, were simply not 'other,' but absolutely and entirely the same with goodness. This view I propose to call the 'naturalistic fallacy' and of it I shall now endeavour to dispose.

Let us consider what it is such philosophers say. And first it is to be noticed that they do not agree among themselves. They not only say that they are right as to what good is, but they endeavour to prove that other people who say that it is something else, are wrong. One, for instance, will affirm that good is pleasure, another, perhaps, that good is that which is desired; and each of these will argue eagerly to prove that the other is wrong. But how is that possible? One of them says that good is nothing but the object of desire, and at the same time tries to prove that it is not pleasure. But from his first assertion, that good just means the object of desire, one of two things must follow as regards his proof:

(1) He may be trying to prove that the object of desire is not pleasure. But, if this be all, where is his Ethics? The position he is maintaining is merely a psychological one. Desire is something which occurs in our minds, and pleasure is something else which so occurs; and our would-be ethical philosopher is merely holding that the latter is not the object of the former. But what has that to do with the question in dispute? His opponent held the ethical proposition that pleasure was the good, and although he should prove a million times over the psychological proposition that pleasure is not the object of desire, he is no nearer proving his opponent to be wrong. The position is like this. One man says a triangle is a circle: another replies 'A triangle is a straight line, and I will prove to you that I am right: *for*' (this is the only argument) 'a straight line is not a circle.' 'That is quite true,' the other may reply, 'but nevertheless a triangle is a circle, and you have said nothing whatever to prove the contrary. What is proved is that one of us is wrong, for we agree that a triangle cannot be both a straight line and a circle: but which is wrong, there can be no earthly means of proving, since you define triangle as straight line and I define it as circle.'—Well, that is one alternative which any naturalistic Ethics has to face; if good is *defined* as something else, it is then impossible either to prove that any other definition is wrong or even to deny such definition.

(2) The other alternative will scarcely be more welcome. It is that the discussion is after all a verbal one. When A says 'Good means pleasant' and B says 'Good means desired,' they may merely wish to assert that most people have used the word for what is pleasant and for what is desired respectively. And this is quite an interesting subject for discussion: only it is not a whit more an ethical discussion than the last was. Nor do I think that any exponent of naturalistic Ethics would be willing to allow that this was all he meant. They are all so anxious to persuade us that what they call the good is what we really ought to do. 'Do, pray, act so, because the word "good" is generally used to denote actions of this

nature': such, on this view, would be the substance of their teaching. And in so far as they tell us how we ought to act, their teaching is truly ethical, as they mean it to be. But how perfectly absurd is the reason they would give for it! 'You are to do this, because most people use a certain word to denote conduct such as this.' 'You are to say the thing which is not, because most people call it lying.' That is an argument just as good!— My dear sirs, what we want to know from you as ethical teachers, is not how people use a word; it is not even, what kind of actions they approve, which the use of this word 'good' may certainly imply: what we want to know is simply what *is* good. We may indeed agree that what most people do think good, is actually so; we shall at all events be glad to know their opinions: but when we say their opinions about what *is* good, we do mean what we say; we do not care whether they call that thing which they mean 'horse' or 'table' or 'chair', 'gut' or 'bon' or '$\dot{\alpha}\gamma\alpha\theta\acute{o}\varsigma$'; we want to know what it is that they so call. When they say 'Pleasure is good,' we cannot believe that they merely mean 'Pleasure is pleasure' and nothing more than that.

Suppose a man says 'I am pleased'; and suppose that is not a lie or a mistake but the truth. Well, if it is true, what does that mean? It means that his mind, a certain definite mind, distinguished by certain definite marks from all others, has at this moment a certain definite feeling called pleasure. 'Pleased' *means* nothing but having pleasure, and though we may be more pleased or less pleased, and even, we may admit for the present, have one or another kind of pleasure; yet in so far as it is pleasure we have, whether there be more or less of it, and whether it be of one kind or another, what we have is one definite thing, absolutely indefinable, some one thing that is the same in all the various degrees and in all the various kinds of it that there may be. We may be able to say how it is related to other things: that, for example, it is in the mind, that it causes desire, that we are conscious of it, etc., etc. We can, I say, describe its relations to other things, but define it we can *not*. And if anybody tried to define pleasure for us as being any other natural object; if anybody were to say, for instance, that pleasure *means* the sensation of red, and were to proceed to deduce from that that pleasure is a colour, we should be entitled to

laugh at him and to distrust his future statements about pleasure. Well, that would be the same fallacy which I have called the naturalistic fallacy. That 'pleased' does not mean 'having the sensation of red,' or anything else whatever, does not prevent us from understanding what it does mean. It is enough for us to know that 'pleased' does mean 'having the sensation of pleasure,' and though pleasure is absolutely indefinable, though pleasure is pleasure and nothing else whatever, yet we feel no difficulty in saying that we are pleased. The reason is, of course, that when I say 'I am pleased.' I do *not* mean that 'I' am the same thing as 'having pleasure.' And similarly no difficulty need be found in my saying that 'pleasure is good' and yet not meaning that 'pleasure' is the same thing as 'good,' that pleasure *means* good, and that good *means* pleasure. If I were to imagine that when I said 'I am pleased,' I meant that I was exactly the same thing as pleased,' I should not indeed call that a naturalistic fallacy, although it would be the same fallacy as I have called naturalistic with reference to Ethics. The reason of this is obvious enough. When a man confuses two natural objects with one another, defining the one by the other, if for instance, he confuses himself, who is one natural object, with 'pleased' or with 'pleasure' which are others, then there is no reason to call the fallacy naturalistic. But if he confuses 'good,' which is not in the same sense a natural object, with any natural object whatever, then there is a reason for calling that a naturalistic fallacy; its being made with regard to 'good' marks it as something quite specific, and this specific mistake deserves a name because it is so common. As for the reasons why good is not to be considered a natural object, they may be reserved for discussion in another place. But, for the present, it is sufficient to notice this: Even if it were a natural object, that would not alter the nature of the fallacy nor diminish its importance one whit. All that I have said about it would remain quite equally true: only the name which I have called it would not be so appropriate as I think it is. And I do not care about the name: what I do care about is the fallacy. It does not matter what we call it, provided we recognise it when we meet with it. It is to be met with in almost every book on Ethics; and yet it is not recognised: and that is why it is necessary to multiply illustrations of it, and convenient to give it a name. It is a very simple fallacy indeed. When we say that an orange is yellow, we do not think our statement binds us to hold that 'orange' means nothing else that 'yellow,' or that nothing can be yellow but an orange. Supposing the orange is also sweet! Does that bind us to say that 'sweet' is exactly the same thing as 'yellow,' that 'sweet' must be defined as 'yellow'? And supposing it be recognised that 'yellow' just means 'yellow' and nothing else whatever, does that make it any more difficult to hold that oranges are yellow? Most certainly it does not: on the contrary, it would be absolutely meaningless to say that oranges were yellow, unless yellow did in the end mean just 'yellow' and nothing else whatever—unless it was absolutely indefinable. We should not get any very clear notion about things, which are yellow—we should not get very far with our science, if we were bound to hold that everything which was yellow, *meant* exactly the same thing as yellow. We should find we had to hold that an orange was exactly the same thing as a stool, a piece of paper, a lemon, anything you like. We could prove any number of absurdities; but should we be the nearer to the truth? Why, then, should it be different with 'good'? Why, if good is good and indefinable, should I be held to deny that pleasure is good? Is there any difficulty in holding both to be true at once? On the contrary, there is no meaning in saying that pleasure is good, unless good is something different from pleasure. It is absolutely useless, so far as Ethics is concerned, to prove, as Mr. Spencer tries to do, that increase of pleasure coincides with increase of life, unless good *means* something different from either life or pleasure. He might just as well try to prove that an orange is yellow by shewing that it always is wrapped up in paper.

In fact, if it is not the case that 'good' denotes something simple and indefinable, only two alternatives are possible: either it is a complex, a given whole, about the correct analysis of which there may be disagreement; or else it means nothing at all, and there is no such subject as Ethics. In general, however, ethical philosophers have attempted to define good, without recognising what such an attempt must mean. They actually use arguments which involve one or both of the absurdities considered in § 11. We

are, therefore, justified in concluding that the attempt to define good is chiefly due to want of clearness as to the possible nature of definition. There are, in fact, only two serious alternatives to be considered, in order to establish the conclusion that 'good' does denote a simple and indefinable notion. It might possibly denote a complex, as 'horse' does; or it might have no meaning at all. Neither of these possibilities has, however, been clearly conceived and seriously maintained, as such, by those who presume to define good; and both may be dismissed by a simple appeal to facts.

(1) The hypothesis that disagreement about the meaning of good is disagreement with regard to the correct analysis of a given whole, may be most plainly seen to be incorrect by consideration of the fact that, whatever definition be offered, it may be always asked, with significance, of the complex so defined, whether it is itself good. To take, for instance, one of the more plausible, because one of the more complicated, of such proposed definitions, it may easily be thought, at first sight, that to be good may mean to be that which we desire to desire. Thus if we apply this definition to a particular instance and say 'When we think that A is good, we are thinking that A is one of the things which we desire to desire,' our proposition may seem quite plausible. But, if we carry the investigation further, and ask ourselves 'Is it good to desire to desire A?' it is apparent, on a little reflection, that this question is itself as intelligible, as the original question 'Is A good?'—that we are, in fact, now asking for exactly the same information about the desire to desire A, for which we formerly asked with regard to A itself. But it is also apparent that the meaning of this second question cannot be correctly analysed into 'Is the desire to desire A one of the things which we desire to desire?': we have not before our minds anything so complicated as the question 'Do we desire to desire to desire to desire A?' Moreover any one can easily convince himself by inspection that the predicate of this proposition—'good'—is positively different from the notion of 'desiring to desire' which enters into its subject: 'That we should desire to desire A is good' is *not* merely equivalent to 'That A should be good is good.' It may indeed be true that what we desire to desire is always also good; perhaps, even the converse

may be true: but it is very doubtful whether this is the case, and the mere fact that we understand very well what is meant by doubting it, shews clearly that we have two different notions before our minds.

(2) And the same consideration is sufficient to dismiss the hypothesis that 'good' has no meaning whatsoever. It is very natural to make the mistake of supposing that what is universally true is of such a nature that its negation would be self-contradictory: the importance which has been assigned to analytic propositions in the history of philosophy shews how easy such a mistake is. And thus it is very easy to conclude that what seems to be a universal ethical principle is in fact an identical proposition; that, if, for example, whatever is called 'good' seems to be pleasant, the proposition 'Pleasure is the good' does not assert a connection between two different notions, but involves only one, that of pleasure, which is easily recognised as a distinct entity. But whoever will attentively consider with himself what is actually before his mind when he asks the question 'Is pleasure (or whatever it may be) after all good?' can easily satisfy himself that he is not merely wondering whether pleasure is pleasant. And if he will try this experiment with each suggested definition in succession, he may become expert enough to recognise that in every case he has before his mind a unique object, with regard to the connection of which with any other object, a distinct question may be asked. Every one does in fact understand the question 'Is this good?' When he thinks of it, his state of mind is different from what it would be, were he asked 'Is this pleasant, or desired, or approved?' It has a distinct meaning for him, even though he may not recognise in what respect it is distinct. Whenever he thinks of 'intrinsic value,' or 'intrinsic worth,' or says that a thing 'ought to exist,' he has before his mind the unique object—the unique property of things—which I mean by 'good.' Everybody is constantly aware of this notion, although he may never become aware at all that it is different from other notions of which he is also aware. But, for correct ethical reasoning, it is extremely important that he should become aware of this fact; and, as soon as the nature of the problem is clearly understood, there should be little difficulty in advancing so far in analysis.

'Good,' then, is indefinable; and yet, so far as I know, there is only one ethical writer, Prof. Henry Sidgwick, who has clearly recognised and stated this fact. We shall see, indeed, how far many of the most reputed ethical systems fall short of drawing the conclusions which follow from such a recognition. At present I will only quote one instance, which will serve to illustrate the meaning and importance of this principle that 'good' is indefinable, or, as Prof. Sidgwick says, an 'unanalysable notion.' It is an instance to which Prof. Sidgwick himself refers in a note on the passage, in which he argues that 'ought' is unanalysable[1].

'Bentham,' says Sidgwick, 'explains that his fundamental principle "states the greatest happiness of all those whose interest is in question as being the right and proper end of human action" '; and yet 'his language in other passages of the same chapter would seem to imply' that he *means* by the word "right" "conducive to the general happiness." Prof. Sidgwick sees that, if you take these two statements together, you get the absurd result that 'greatest happiness is the end of human action, which is conducive to the general happiness'; and so absurd does it seem to him to call this result, as Bentham calls it, 'the fundamental principle of a moral system' that he suggests that Bentham cannot have meant it. Yet Prof. Sidgwick himself states elsewhere[2] that Psychological Hedonism is 'not seldom confounded with Egoistic Hedonism'; and that confusion, as we shall see, rests chiefly on that same fallacy, the naturalistic fallacy, which is implied in Bentham's statements. Prof. Sidgwick admits therefore that this fallacy is sometimes committed, absurd as it is; and I am inclined to think that Bentham may really have been one of those who committed it. Mill, as we shall see, certainly did commit it. In any case, whether Bentham committed it or not, his doctrine, as above quoted, will serve as a very good illustration of this fallacy, and of the importance of the contrary proposition that good is indefinable.

Let us consider this doctrine. Bentham seems to imply, so Prof. Sidgwick says, that the word 'right' *means* 'conducive to general happiness.' Now this, by itself, need not necessarily involve the naturalistic fallacy. For the word 'right' is very commonly appropriated to actions which lead to the attainment of what is good; which are regarded as *means* to the ideal and not as ends-in-themselves. This use of 'right,' as denoting what is good as a means, whether or not it be also good as an end, is indeed the use to which I shall confine the word. Had Bentham been using 'right' in this sense, it might be perfectly consistent for him to *define* right as 'conducive to the general happiness,' *provided only* (and notice this proviso) he had already proved, or laid down as an axiom, that general happiness was *the* good, or (what is equivalent to this) that general happiness alone was good. For in that case he would have already defined *the* good as general happiness (a position perfectly consistent, as we have seen, with the contention that 'good' is indefinable), and, since right was to be defined as 'conducive to *the* good,' it would actually *mean* 'conducive to general happiness.' But this method of escape from the charge of having committed the naturalistic fallacy has been closed by Bentham himself. For his fundamental principle is, we see, that the greatest happiness of all concerned is the *right* and proper *end* of human action. He applies the word 'right,' therefore, to the end, as such, not only to the means which are conducive to it; and, that being so, right can no longer be defined as 'conducive to the general happiness,' without involving the fallacy in question. For now it is obvious that the definition of right as conducive to general happiness can be used by him in support of the fundamental principle that general happiness is the right end; instead of being itself derived from that principle. If right, by definition, means conducive to general happiness, then it is obvious that general happiness is the right end. It is not necessary now first to prove or assert that general happiness is the right end, before right is defined as conducive to general happiness—a perfectly valid procedure; but on the contrary the definition of right as conducive to general happiness proves general happiness to be the right end—a perfectly invalid procedure, since in this case the statement that 'general happiness is the right end of human action' is not an ethical principle at all, but either, as we have seen, a proposition about the meaning of words, or else a proposition about the *nature* of general happiness, not about its rightness or goodness.

Now, I do not wish the importance I assign to this fallacy to be misunderstood. The discovery of it does not at all refute Bentham's contention that greatest happiness is the proper end of human action, if that be understood as an ethical proposition, as he undoubtedly intended it. That principle may be true all the same; we shall consider whether it is so in succeeding chapters. Bentham might have maintained it, as Prof. Sidgwick does, even if the fallacy had been pointed out to him. What I am maintaining is that the *reasons* which he actually gives for his ethical proposition are fallacious ones so far as they consist in a definition of right. What I suggest is that he did not perceive them to be fallacious; that, if he had done so, he would have been led to seek for other reasons in support of his Utilitarianism; and that, had he sought for other reasons, he *might* have found none which he thought to be sufficient. In that case he would have changed his whole system—a most important consequence. It is undoubtedly also possible that he would have thought other reasons to be sufficient, and in that case his ethical system, in its main results, would still have stood. But, even in this latter case, his use of the fallacy would be a serious objection to him as an ethical philosopher. For it is the business of Ethics, I must insist, not only to obtain true results, but also to find valid reasons for them. The direct object of Ethics is knowledge and not practice; and any one who uses the naturalistic fallacy has certainly not fulfilled this first object, however correct his practical principles may be.

My objections to Naturalism are then, in the first place, that it offers no reason at all, far less any valid reason, for any ethical principle whatever; and in this it already fails to satisfy the requirements of Ethics, as a scientific study. But in the second place I contend that, though it gives a reason for no ethical principle, it is a *cause* of the acceptance of false principles—it deludes the mind into accepting ethical principles, which are false; and in this it is contrary to every aim of Ethics. It is easy to see that if we start with a definition of right conduct as conduct conducive to general happiness; then, knowing that right conduct is universally conduct conducive to the good, we very easily arrive at the result that the good is general happiness. If, on the other hand, we once recognise that we must start our Ethics without a definition, we shall be much more apt to look about us, before we adopt any ethical principle whatever; and the more we look about us, the less likely are we to adopt a false one. It may be replied to this: Yes, but we shall look about us just as much, before we settle on our definition, and are therefore just as likely to be right. But I will try to shew that this is not the case. If we start with the conviction that a definition of good can be found, we start with the conviction that good *can mean* nothing else than some one property of things; and our only business will then be to discover what that property is. But if we recognise that, so far as the meaning of good goes, anything whatever may be good, we start with a much more open mind. Moreover, apart from the fact that, when we think we have a definition, we cannot logically defend our ethical principles in any way whatever, we shall also be much less apt to defend them well, even if illogically. For we shall start with the conviction that good must mean so and so, and shall therefore be inclined either to misunderstand our opponent's arguments or to cut them short with the reply, 'This is not an open question: the very meaning of the word decides it; no one can think otherwise except through confusion.'

Our first conclusion as to the subject-matter of Ethics is, then, that there is a simple, indefinable, unanalysable object of thought by reference to which it must be defined. By what name we call this unique object is a matter of indifference, so long as we clearly recognise what it is and that it does differ from other objects. The words which are commonly taken as the signs of ethical judgments all do refer to it; and they are expressions of ethical judgments solely because they do so refer.

NOTES

1. *Methods of Ethics,* Bk. 1, Chap. iii, § 1 (6th edition).
2. *Ibid.,* Bk. 1, Chap. iv, § 1.

31. *GOOD WILL AND ILL WILL*

Frank Chapman Sharp

The moral judgment takes the form: Action S is right—or wrong. It thus consists in the application of the predicate "right" to conduct. We have now to inquire into the meaning of this predicate.

The subject matter of our studies is still the man on the street. It is what *he* means by "right" that interests us. And the difficulty we face is that he cannot tell us. Ask him to define the term, and he will not even understand what you are driving at. This difficulty, however, is not one peculiar to the vocabulary of ethics. John Smith cannot tell you what he means by "cause," "probable," or "now"; he cannot give a really satisfactory answer to so apparently simple a question as "What is 'money'?"

This difficulty we can meet today as we met it again and again when we were three years old. We heard the people about us using such terms as "very" or "if"; and we wanted to know what they meant. Undoubtedly we were very far from persistent or systematic in our search for enlightenment; indeed, perhaps we did not *search* at all. But, at any rate, when we had been told that this milk was very hot, this stool very heavy, this glass very easily broken, and that we had been very naughty, the meaning of "very" dawned upon our minds, not in the sense that we could define it but that we could use it intelligently. It is in precisely this same way that we can discover what the layman means by the fundamental terms in the moral vocabulary. We

From Frank Chapman Sharp, *Good Will and Ill Will* (Chicago: The University of Chicago Press, 1950), pp. 156–162. Copyright 1950 by The University. Reprinted by permission of The University of Chicago Press.

watch his use of them. Thereupon, proceeding one step farther than the child, we generalize our observations and in doing so form a definition.

It is indeed a curious fact that men can go through life using words with a fair degree of definiteness and consistency with no formulated definition before the mind. But it is fact, nonetheless. "I cannot define poetry," says A. E. Housman in effect, "but I know it when I see it. In the same way a terrier cannot define rat, but he knows one when he sees it."

If the analysis of this chapter is correct, "right" must be definable in terms of desire, or approbation, that is to say, in terms of "feeling." When John Smith calls an action "right" or "wrong," however, he means something other than that he happens to feel about it in a certain way at that particular moment. This was clearly pointed out by Hume two hundred years ago and should have become commonplace among moralists by this time. A successful swindle may arouse feelings of very different intensity according to who happens to be the victim—myself, my son, my intimate friend, an acquaintance, a stranger, a foreigner, a man who died a hundred years ago. Indeed, in some of the latter cases the feeling component may drop out entirely. Again, an incident I myself have witnessed, such as an act of malicious cruelty or the bullying of the weak by the strong, makes me feel very different from that about which I have only read or heard. And my feelings in the latter case are likely to depend on the vividness and completeness with which the narrator brings the situation home to my imagination. An incident which I can realize because I have been through just such an experience myself appeals to me far otherwise than one which I know only through having viewed it from the outside. The robbery or oppression of those whom I see from day to day or am personally acquainted with arouses in me far more indignation than if they are merely unknown people living for all practical purposes in a world other than my own. With all these variations in my feelings, I recognize upon reflection that what is really right or wrong in the premises remains unchanged. Wrong does not become innocent or right merely because the act took place a hundred years ago instead of this morning, because I did not happen to see it myself, because I myself have never happened

to be in that position, or because one of the persons involved happens to be an acquaintance, a member of my family, or myself.

In view of these facts, we must define "right," if we are to use the term in the sense in which the ordinary man uses it, as *that which arouses approbation under certain conditions.* Accordingly the question arises: What are these conditions?

We shall not expect to discover them by asking John Smith to enumerate and describe them. The man in the street does not carry about with him in his mental kit a set of formulas covering these conditions, any more than when he cuts a corner he says to himself, "A straight line is the shortest distance between two points." That the conditions in question represent real forces may be shown empirically by what John Smith does when in doubt or when he changes his mind or when the correctness of his predication is challenged by others.

In the first place, then, John Smith does not apply the predicates right and wrong to conduct unless he supposes himself to be viewing it from an impersonal standpoint. This means that he supposes, negatively, that his attitude is not determined by his egoistic interests or by any purely personal relations to the parties concerned; positively, that the act is one that he would approve of anyone's performing under the same conditions. This attitude is expressed in the familiar maxim: What is right for one is right for everyone else under the same conditions. This maxim is an analytic, not a synthetic, proposition. It is no discovery of moralists, least of all of Kant, to whom it is often attributed, for its governing role in the moral world was noted in effect by Cumberland and quite explicitly by Clarke before Kant was born. As a matter of fact, the "discovery" has been made countless millions of times, for it is a dull-witted seven-year-old who does not remind his parents on occasions that what they require him to do they are bound to do themselves.

Here, again, enters the all-important distinction between correct and incorrect moral judgments, or, as I should prefer to say, between valid and invalid; for, as we have seen in this chapter, John Smith frequently regards an action as innocent or even obligatory when he profits by it and wrong when he happens to be the sufferer. In calling it "wrong" instead of "harmful," he implies that it is an act which, performed under the conditions, he would condemn in any-one, including himself. His supposition being false, his judgment expresses an opinion which can only be called "incorrect."

As soon as John Smith realizes this lack of impersonality, he recognizes at once the incorrectness of the judgment and therewith the necessity of modifying or abandoning it. In a certain city, the university YMCA, having included a barber shop among the attractions of its new building, engaged as its manager the popular head-barber of the city's leading "tonsorial parlor"; whereupon the proprietor complained loudly of the action of the association in attracting his most valuable employee away from him as being "unfair." When he was reminded that he himself had obtained this same employee in precisely the same way, by attracting him from another shop by a better financial offer, nothing more was heard from him on this subject.

Common sense thus recognizes the existence of such a thing as a mistaken moral judgment. Those moralists who ignore this fact thereby show that their picture of the workings of the moral consciousness is an arbitrary construction, out of touch with the realities of life.

Impersonality, however, is not the only condition which John Smith recognizes the moral judgment must meet if it is to conform to the implications involved in this conception of right. The second condition is a consequence of the essential character of the evaluating judgment as such. When we pass judgment upon anything whatever, whether it be a candidate for public office or Titian's "Assumption of the Virgin," we suppose that we know what it is. Really to know what anything is, is to have an apprehension of its nature, which is at once accurate and complete. In practice, of course, this ideal is ordinarily incapable of attainment. But, in proportion as we approach certainty of conviction, our confidence increases that our view possesses an amount of accuracy and completeness such that any correction of or addition to the data in our possession would make no difference in the conclusion reached. And our task is lightened by growing insight into what kinds of data are relevant and what are not. A datum is relevant when its introduction would tend to make any difference in the resulting judgment.

The application of these observations to the moral judgment is obvious. The subject of the moral judgment is voluntary action. A voluntary act is an attempt to produce certain effects. The moral judgment, accordingly, is supposed, with varying degrees of confidence, by the judger to be based upon an accurate and complete knowledge of these effects or upon as much knowledge as would involve no change of opinion if the rest of the effects were displayed accurately and in order before the mind's eye. If this supposition is true, the judgment is in so far forth correct or valid. On the other hand, if the judgment turns on an incomplete or otherwise inaccurate view of these effects, including, of course, a view of the situation in which they operate, it may properly be termed incorrect or invalid, because it is not what the judger supposes it to be.

Observation verifies this analysis. Our study of the causes that lead to the diversities in moral judgments has shown that a leading cause is difference of opinion as to what the consequences of the act will be. And in the majority of instances when John Smith begins to doubt the correctness of one of his past judgments, it is upon the consequences believed to be involved that his decision turns. Under such and such circumstances is a man justified in lying? in breaking a promise or a contract? in helping himself to someone else's property? in giving a dose of poison to a hopeless invalid? in making a true statement injurious to the reputation of a neighbor? in giving money to a street beggar? Whatever decision is reached turns fundamentally upon what are believed to be the good or evil consequences involved.

If, then, we are to conform to the implications of everyday usage in applying the predicates right and wrong to the effects of volitions, we must know what these effects are. Now, knowledge is of two kinds; or, if you prefer, it has two levels. Using Professor James's terminology, one is acquaintance with; the other, knowledge about. The former is given in immediate experience, whether in the world of sense or in the inner world of pleasure, pain, emotion, or desire. It may be re-created, when past, in those persons who are fortunate enough to possess the capacity for full and vivid imagery. We may call this "realization." The second kind, or level, reveals reality through the instrumentality of concepts. Now, the concept is an abstract idea, such as "length" or "walking" or "very." It represents one or a group of aspects torn from the concrete objects that make up the real world and held before the mind in more or less complete isolation from such objects.

The ability to form and use concepts is the most powerful instrument in the possession of the human mind. Among other things, as a constituent of desire it determines the direction of every voluntary action we perform. But, like everything else in the world, the concept has its limitations. In its very nature as an abstraction, it reveals only a part, usually only a very small part, of the object at which it points. It may report truth but never the whole truth. In this respect it is like a map. Show a map of Switzerland to a person who has never been away from a North Dakota prairie or even seen a picture of a mountain. Compare the knowledge thus gained with that of a Swiss who has spent his vacations for many years exploring his native country. Or, again, let some one of us who has never come in contact with death and has never had to carry crushing financial burdens read in the newspaper that some stranger, formerly a clerk in a certain grocery store, died yesterday after a painful and lingering illness; he was thirty-five years old; a widow and three children survive him. How small a fraction of the grim realities at which these words hint would enter our consciousness!

Quite apart from poverty of detail, conceptual thought, again like a map, has another limitation. It reveals relations but can never reveal the things related. In other words, thought at its best, conceptual thought, merely performs the functions of a mathematical formula. It is a commonplace that a person born blind may know all the laws of light and yet have no acquaintance with color.

Thus, notwithstanding its marvelous range, conceptual thought is a very inadequate substitute for "acquaintance with" as a revelation of reality. There is only one road to genuine acquaintance with the world outside the consciousness of the moment, and it is through imagery, the power to realize. If, then, a moral judgment is to be valid, it must be either a judgment based upon a complete acquaintance with the whole situation in all its relevant details or, since this is rarely or perhaps never attainable, such a judgment as would result from an acquaintance with the whole situation.[1]

The influence of realization upon the processes of moral judgment exhibits itself frequently in those pseudo-moral judgments in which the predicates right and wrong follow the judger's personal interests, and a vivid sense of his own gain or loss eclipses the vague concept of the loss or gain of the other part. Let the other side of the case come home to him and the victim's plight be fully realized, he "changes his mind," thereby bringing his judgment into conformity with his new insight. This phenomenon has been abundantly illustrated in this chapter.

The definition emerging from the preceding analysis is the following: When John Smith calls an action "right," he means that complete acquaintance with its results would evoke impersonal approval. Exchanging the negative term "impersonal" for a positive one, "right" characterizes the kind of action he would want all human beings to perform under the given conditions if he had a complete acquaintance with all the relevant consequences. The evidence for the correctness of this analysis is that when John Smith discovers that he has failed to meet some one of these conditions, he recognizes that his judgment calls for reconsideration.

NOTE

1. Cf. Sir Leslie Stephen, *The Science of Ethics* (New York: G. P. Putnam's Sons, 1882), chap. ii, Sec. 26: "The sentiment excited by any general name should represent that which is actually excited in each particular case."

32. THE EMOTIVE MEANING OF ETHICAL TERMS

Charles L. Stevenson

1

Ethical questions first arise in the form "is so and so good?" or "is this alternative better than that?" These questions are difficult partly because we don't quite know what we are seeking. We are asking, "is there a needle in the haystack?" without even knowing just what a needle is. So the first thing to do is to examine the questions themselves. We must try to make them clearer, either by defining the terms in which they are expressed or by any other method that is available.

The present essay is concerned wholly with this preliminary step of making ethical questions clear. In order to help answer the question "is X good?" we must *substitute* for it a question that is free from ambiguity and confusion.

It is obvious that in substituting a clearer question we must not introduce some utterly different kind of question. It won't do (to take an extreme instance of a prevalent fallacy) to substitute for "is X good?" the question "is X pink with yellow trimmings?" and then point out how easy the question really is. This would beg the original question, not help answer it. On the other hand, we must not expect the substituted question to be strictly "identical" with the original one. The original question may embody hypostatization, anthropomorphism, vagueness, and all the other ills to which our ordinary discourse is subject. If our substituted question is to be clearer it must remove these ills. The questions will be identical only in the sense that a child is identical with the man he later becomes. Hence we must not demand that the substi-

From C. L. Stevenson, "The Emotive Meaning of Ethical Terms," *Mind*, Vol. 46 (1937) as reprinted in *Facts and Values* (New Haven, Yale University Press, 1963). Reprinted by permission of the author and Basil Blackwell, publisher.

tution strike us, on immediate introspection, as making no change in meaning.

Just how, then, must the substituted question be related to the original? Let us assume (inaccurately) that it must result from replacing "good" by some set of terms that define it. The question then resolves itself to this: How must the defined meaning of "good" be related to its original meaning?

I answer that it must be *relevant*. A defined meaning will be called "relevant" to the original meaning under these circumstances: Those who have understood the definition must be able to say all that they then want to say by using the term in the defined way. They must never have occasion to use the term in the old, unclear sense. (If a person did have to go on using the word in the old sense, then to this extent his meaning would not be clarified and the philosophical task would not be completed.) It frequently happens that a word is used so confusedly and ambiguously that we must give it *several* defined meanings, rather than one. In this case only the whole set of defined meanings will be called "relevant," and any one of them will be called "partially relevant." This is not a rigorous treatment of *relevance*, by any means, but it will serve for the present purposes.

Let us now turn to our particular task—that of giving a relevant definition of "good." Let us first examine some of the ways in which others have attempted to do this.

The word "good" has often been defined in terms of *approval*, or similar psychological attitudes. We may take as typical examples: "good" means *desired by me* (Hobbes); and "good" means *approved by most people* (Hume, in effect).[1] It will be convenient to refer to definitions of this sort as "interest theories," following R. B. Perry, although neither "interest" nor "theory" is used in the most usual way.[2]

Are definitions of this sort relevant?

It is idle to deny their *partial relevance.* The most superficial inquiry will reveal that "good" is exceedingly ambiguous. To maintain that "good" is *never* used in Hobbes' sense, and never in Hume's, is only to manifest an insensitivity to the complexities of language. We must recognize, perhaps, not only these senses, but a variety of similar ones, differing both with regard to the kind of interest in question and with regard to the people who are said to have the interest.

But that is a minor matter. The essential question is not whether interest theories are *partially* relevant, but whether they are *wholly* relevant. This is the only point for intelligent dispute. Briefly: Granted that some senses of "good" may relevantly be defined in terms of interest, is there some *other* sense which is *not* relevantly so defined? We must give this question careful attention. For it is quite possible that when philosophers (and many others) have found the question "is X good?" so difficult, they have been grasping for this *other* sense of "good" and not any sense relevantly defined in terms of interest. If we insist on defining "good" in terms of interest, and answer the question when thus interpreted, we may be begging *their* question entirely. Of course this *other* sense of "good" may not exist, or it may be a complete confusion; but that is what we must discover.

Now many have maintained that interest theories are *far* from being completely relevant. They have argued that such theories neglect the very sense of "good" that is most typical of ethics. And certainly, their arguments are not without plausibility.

Only—what *is* this typical sense of "good"? The answers have been so vague and so beset with difficulties that one can scarcely determine.

There are certain requirements, however, with which the typical sense has been expected to comply—requirements which appeal strongly to our common sense. It will be helpful to summarize these, showing how they exclude the interest theories:

In the first place, we must be able sensibly to *disagree* about whether something is "good." This condition rules out Hobbes' definition. For consider the following argument: "This is good." "That isn't so; it's not good." As translated by Hobbes, this becomes: "I desire this." "That isn't so, for *I* don't." The speakers are not contradicting one another, and think they are only because of an elementary confusion in the use of pronouns. The definition, "good" means *desired by my community,* is also excluded, for how could people from different communities disagree?[3]

In the second place, "goodness" must have, so to speak, a magnetism. A person who recognizes X to be "good" must ipso facto acquire a stronger tendency to act in its favor than he otherwise would have had. This rules out the Humian type of definition. For according to Hume, to recognize that something is "good" is simply to recognize that the majority approve of it. Clearly, a man may see that the majority approve of X without having, himself, a stronger tendency to favor it. This requirement excludes any attempt to define "good" in terms of the interest of people *other* than the speaker.[4]

In the third place, the "goodness" of anything must not be verifiable solely by use of the scientific method. "Ethics must not be psychology." This restriction rules out all of the traditional interest theories without exception. It is so sweeping a restriction that we must examine its plausibility. What are the methodological implications of interest theories which are here rejected?

According to Hobbes' definition a person can prove his ethical judgments with finality by showing that he is not making an introspective error about his desires. According to Hume's definition one may prove ethical judgments (roughly speaking) by taking a vote. *This* use of the empirical method, at any rate, seems highly remote from what we usually accept as proof and reflects on the complete relevance of the definitions that imply it.

But are there not more complicated interest theories that are immune from such methodological implications? No, for the same factors appear; they are only put off for a while. Consider, for example, the definition: "X is good" means *most people would approve of X if they knew its nature and consequences.* How, according to this definition, could we prove that a certain X was good? We should first have to find out, empirically, just what X was like and what its consequences would be. To this extent the empirical method as required by the definition seems beyond intelligent objection. But what remains? We should next have to discover whether most people would approve of the sort of thing we had discovered X to be. This could not be determined by popular vote—but only because it would be too difficult to explain to the voters, beforehand, what the nature and consequences of X really were. Apart from this, voting would be a pertinent method. We are again reduced to counting noses as a *perfectly final* appeal.

Now we need not scorn voting entirely. A man who rejected interest theories as irrelevant might readily make the following statement: "If I believed that X would be approved by the majority, when they knew all about it, I should be strongly *led* to say that X was good." But he would continue: "*Need* I say that X was good, under the circumstances? Wouldn't my acceptance of the alleged 'final proof' result simply from my being democratic? What about the more aristocratic people? They would simply say that the approval of most people, even when they knew all about the object of their approval, simply had nothing to do with the goodness of anything, and they would probably add a few remarks about the low state of people's interests." It would indeed seem, from these considerations, that the definition we have been considering has presupposed democratic ideals from the start; it has dressed up democratic propaganda in the guise of a definition.

The omnipotence of the empirical method, as implied by interest theories and others, may be shown unacceptable in a somewhat different way. G. E. Moore's familiar objection about the open question is chiefly pertinent in this regard. No matter what set of scientifically knowable properties a thing may have (says Moore, in effect), you will find, on careful introspection, that it is an open question to ask whether anything having these properties is *good*. It is difficult to believe that this recurrent question is a totally confused one, or that it seems open only because of the ambiguity of "good." Rather, we must be using some sense of "good" which is not definable, relevantly, in terms of anything scientifically knowable. That is, the scientific method is not sufficient for ethics.[5]

These, then, are the requirements with which the "typical" sense of "good" is expected to comply: (1) goodness must be a topic for intelligent disagreement; (2) it must be "magnetic"; and

(3) it must not be discoverable solely through the scientific method.

2

I can now turn to my proposed analysis of ethical judgments. First let me present my position dogmatically, showing to what extent I vary from tradition.

I believe that the three requirements given above are perfectly sensible, that there is some *one* sense of "good" which satisfies all three requirements, and that no traditional interest theory satisfies them all. But this does not imply that "good" must be explained in terms of a Platonic Idea, or of a categorical imperative, or of a unique, unanalyzable property. On the contrary, the three requirements can be met by a *kind* of interest theory. *But we must give up a presupposition that all the traditional interest theories have made.*

Traditional interest theories hold that ethical statements are *descriptive* of the existing state of interests—that they simply *give information* about interests. (More accurately, ethical judgments are said to describe what the state of interests is, was, or will be, or to indicate what the state of interests *would* be under specified circumstances.) It is this emphasis on description, on information, which leads to their incomplete relevance. Doubtless there is always *some* element of description in ethical judgments, but this is by no means all. Their major use is not to indicate facts but to *create an influence*. Instead of merely describing people's interests they *change* or *intensify* them. They *recommend* an interest in an object, rather than state that the interest already exists.

For instance: When you tell a man that he ought not to steal, your object is not merely to let him know that people disapprove of stealing. You are attempting, rather, to get *him* to disapprove of it. Your ethical judgment has a quasi-imperative force which, operating through suggestion and intensified by your tone of voice, readily permits you to begin to *influence*, to *modify*, his interests. If in the end you do not succeed in getting *him* to disapprove of stealing, you will feel that you have failed to convince him that stealing is wrong. You will continue to feel this, even though he fully acknowledges that you disapprove of it and that almost everyone else does. When you point out to him the consequences of his actions—consequences which you suspect he already disapproves of—these *reasons* which support your ethical judgment are simply a means of facilitating your influence. If you think you can change his interests by making vivid to him how others will disapprove of him, you will do so, otherwise not. So the consideration about other people's interest is just an additional means you may employ in order to move him and is not a part of the ethical judgment itself. Your ethical judgment does not merely describe interests to him, it directs his very interests. The difference between the traditional interest theories and my view is like the difference between describing a desert and irrigating it.

Another example: A munitions maker declares that war is a good thing. If he merely meant that he approved of it, he would not have to insist so strongly nor grow so excited in his argument. People would be quite easily convinced that he approved of it. If he merely meant that most people approved of war, or that most people would approve of it if they knew the consequences, he would have to yield his point if it were proved that his was not so. But he would not do this, nor does consistency require it. He is not *describing* the state of people's approval; he is trying to *change* it by his influence. If he found that few people approved of war, he might insist all the more strongly that it was good, for there would be more changing to be done.

This example illustrates how "good" may be used for what most of us would call bad purposes. Such cases are as pertinent as any others. I am not indicating the *good* way of using "good." I am not influencing people but am describing the way this influence sometimes goes on. If the reader wishes to say that the munitions maker's influence is bad—that is, if the reader wishes to awaken people's disapproval of the man, and to make him disapprove of his own actions—I should at another time be willing to join in this undertaking. But this is not the present concern. I am not using ethical terms but an indicating how they *are* used. The munitions maker, in his use of "good," illustrates the persuasive character of the word just as well as does the unselfish man who, eager to encourage in each of us a desire for the happiness of all, contends that the supreme good is peace.

Thus ethical terms are *instruments* used in the complicated interplay and readjustment of human interests. This can be seen plainly from more general observations. People from widely separated communities have different moral attitudes. Why? To a great extent because they have been subject to different social influences. Now clearly this influence does not operate through sticks and stones alone; words play a great part. People praise one another to encourage certain inclinations and blame one another to discourage others. Those of forceful personalities issue commands which weaker people, for complicated instinctive reasons, find it difficult to disobey, quite apart from fears of consequences. Further influence is brought to bear by writers and orators. Thus social influence is exerted, to an enormous extent, by means that have nothing to do with physical force or material reward. The ethical terms facilitate such influence. Being suited for use in *suggestion,* they are a means by which men's attitudes may be led this way or that. The reason, then, that we find a greater similarity in the moral attitudes of one community than in those of different communities is largely this: ethical judgments propagate themselves. One man says "this is good"; this may influence the approval of another person, who then makes the same ethical judgment, which in turn influences another person, and so on. In the end, by a process of mutual influence, people take up more or less the same attitudes. Between people of widely separated communities, of course, the influence is less strong; hence different communities have different attitudes.

These remarks will serve to give a general idea of my point of view. We must now go into more detail. There are several questions which must be answered: How does an ethical sentence acquire its power of influencing people—why is it suited to suggestion? Again, what has this influence to do with the *meaning* of ethical terms? And finally, do these considerations really lead us to a sense of "good" which meets the requirements mentioned in the preceding section?

Let us deal first with the question about *meaning.* This is far from an easy question, so we must enter into a preliminary inquiry about meaning in general. Although a seeming digression this will prove indispensable.

3

Broadly speaking, there are two different *purposes* which lead us to use language. On the one hand we use words (as in science) to record, clarify, and communicate *beliefs*. On the other hand we use words to give vent to our feelings (interjections), or to create moods (poetry), or to incite people to actions or attitudes (oratory).

The first use of words I shall call "descriptive," the second, "dynamic." Note that the distinction depends solely upon the *purpose* of the *speaker*.

When a person says "hydrogen is the lightest known gas," his purpose *may* be simply to lead the hearer to believe this, or to believe that the speaker believes it. In that case the words are used descriptively. When a person cuts himself and says "damn," his purpose is not ordinarily to record, clarify, or communicate any belief. The word is used dynamically. The two ways of using words, however, are by no means mutually exclusive. This is obvious from the fact that our purposes are often complex. Thus when one says "I want you to close the door," part of his purpose, ordinarily, is to lead the hearer to believe that he has this want. To that extent the words are used descriptively. But the major part of one's purpose is to lead the hearer to *satisfy* the want. To that extent the words are used dynamically.

It very frequently happens that the same sentence may have a dynamic use on one occasion and not on another, and that it may have different dynamic uses on different occasions. For instance: A man says to a visiting neighbor, "I am loaded down with work." His purpose may be to let the neighbor know how life is going with him. This would *not* be a dynamic use of words. He may make the remark, however, in order to drop a hint. This *would* be dynamic usage (as well as descriptive). Again, he may make the remark to arouse the neighbor's sympathy. This would be a *different* dynamic usage from that of hinting.

Or again, when we say to a man, "of course you won't make those mistakes any more," we *may* simply be making a prediction. But we are more likely to be using "suggestion," in order to encourage him and hence *keep* him from making mistakes. The first use would be descriptive, the second, mainly dynamic.

From these examples it will be clear that we can not determine whether words are used dynamically or not merely by reading the dictionary—even assuming that everyone is faithful to dictionary meanings. Indeed, to know whether a person is using a word dynamically we must note his tone of voice, his gestures, the general circumstances under which he is speaking, and so on.

We must now proceed to an important question: What has the dynamic use of words to do with their *meaning?* One thing is clear—we must not define "meaning" in a way that would make meaning vary with dynamic usage. If we did, we should have no use for the term. All that we could say about such "meaning" would be that it is very complicated and subject to constant change. So we must certainly distinguish between the dynamic use of words and their meaning.

It does not follow, however, that we must define "meaning" in some nonpsychological fashion. We must simply restrict the psychological field. Instead of identifying meaning with *all* the psychological causes and effects that attend a word's utterance, we must identify it with those that it has a *tendency* (causal property, dispositional property) to be connected with. The tendency must be of a particular kind, moreover. It must exist for all who speak the language; it must be persistent and must be realizable more or less independently of determinate circumstances attending the word's utterance. There will be further restrictions dealing with the interrelations of word in different contexts. Moreover, we must include, under the psychological responses which the words tend to produce, not only immediately introspectable experiences but *dispositions* to react in a given way with appropriate stimuli. I hope to go into these matters in a subsequent essay.[6] Suffice it now to say that I think "meaning" may be thus defined in a way to include "propositional" meaning as an important kind.

The definition will readily permit a distinction between meaning and dynamic use. For when words are accompanied by dynamic purposes, it does not follow that they *tend* to be accompanied by them in the way mentioned above. E.g. there need be no tendency realizable more or less independently of the determinate circumstances under which the words are uttered.

There will be a kind of meaning, however, in the sense above defined, which has an intimate relation to dynamic usage. I refer to "emotive" meaning (in a sense roughly like that employed by Ogden and Richards).[7] The emotive meaning of a word is a tendency of a word, arising through the history of its usage, to produce (result from) *affective* responses in people. It is the immediate aura of feeling which hovers about a word.[8] Such tendencies to produce affective responses cling to words very tenaciously. It would be difficult, for instance, to express merriment by using the interjection "alas." Because of the persistence of such affective tendencies (among other reasons) it becomes feasible to classify them as "meanings."

Just *what* is the relation between emotive meaning and the dynamic use of words? Let us take an example. Suppose that a man tells his hostess, at the end of a party, that he thoroughly enjoyed himself, and suppose that he was in fact bored. If we consider his remark an innocent one, are we likely to remind him, later, that he "lied" to his hostess? Obviously not, or at least, not without a broad smile; for although he told her something that he believed to be false, and with the intent of making her believe that it was true—those being the ordinary earmarks of a lie —the expression, "you lied to her," would be emotively too strong for our purposes. It would seem to be a reproach, even if we intended it not to be a reproach. So it will be evident that such words as "lied" (and many parallel examples could be cited) become suited, on account of their emotive meaning, to a certain kind of dynamic use—so well suited, in fact, that the hearer is likely to be misled when we use them in any other way. The more pronounced a word's emotive meaning is, the less likely people are to use it purely descriptively. Some words are suited to encourage people, some to discourage them, some to quiet them, and so on.

Even in these cases, of course, the dynamic purposes are not to be identified with any sort of meaning; for the emotive meaning accompanies a word much more persistently than do the dynamic purposes. But there is an important contingent relation between emotive meaning and dynamic purpose: the former assists the latter. Hence if we define emotively laden terms in a way that neglects their emotive meaning, we become seriously confused. *We lead people to think that the terms defined are used dynamically less often than they are.*

Let us now apply these remarks in defining "good." This word may be used morally or non-morally. I shall deal with the nonmoral usage almost entirely, but only because it is simpler. The main points of the analysis will apply equally well to either usage.

As a preliminary definition let us take an inaccurate approximation. It may be more misleading than helpful but will do to begin with. Roughly, then, the sentence "X is good" means *we like X.* ("We" includes the hearer or hearers.)

At first glance this definition sounds absurd. If used, we should expect to find the following sort of conversation: A. "This is good." B. "But I *don't* like it. What led you to believe that I did?" The unnaturalness of B's reply, judged by ordinary word usage, would seem to cast doubt on the relevance of my definition.

B's unnaturalness, however, lies simply in this: he is assuming that "we like it" (as would occur implicitly in the use of "good") is being used descriptively. This will not do. When "we like it" is to take the place of "this is good," the former sentence must be used not purely descriptively, but dynamically. More specifically, it must be used to promote a very subtle (and for the nonmoral sense in question, a very easily resisted) kind of *suggestion.* To the extent that "we" refers to the hearer it must have the dynamic use, essential to suggestion, of leading the hearer to *make* true what is said, rather than merely to believe it. And to the extent that "we" refers to the speaker, the sentence must have not only the descriptive use of indicating belief about the speaker's interest, but the quasi-interjectory, dynamic function of giving direct expression to the interest. (This immediate expression of feelings assists in the process of suggestion. It is difficult to disapprove in the face of another's enthusiasm.)

For an example of a case where "we like this" is used in the dynamic way that "this is good" is used, consider the case of a mother who says to her several children, "one thing is certain, *we all like to be neat.*" If she really believed this, she would not bother to say so. But she is not using the words descriptively. She is *encouraging* the children to like neatness. By telling them that they like neatness, she will lead them to *make* her statement true, so to speak. If, instead of saying "we all like to be neat" in this way, she had said "it's a good thing to be neat," the effect would have been approximately the same.

But these remarks are still misleading. Even when "we like it" is used for suggestion, it is not quite like "this is good." The latter is more subtle. With such a sentence as "this is a good book," for example, it would be practically impossible to use instead "we like this book." When the latter is used it must be accompanied by so exaggerated an intonation, to prevent its becoming confused with a descriptive statement, that the force of suggestion becomes stronger and ludicrously more overt than when "good" is used.

The definition is inadequate, further, in that the definiens has been restricted to dynamic usage. Having said that dynamic usage was different from meaning, I should not have to mention it in giving the *meaning* of "good."

It is in connection with this last point that we must return to emotive meaning. The word "good" has a laudatory emotive meaning that fits it for the dynamic use of suggesting favorable interest. But the sentence "we like it" has no such emotive meaning. Hence my definition has neglected emotive meaning entirely. Now to neglect emotive meaning serves to foster serious confusions, as I have previously intimated; so I have sought to make up for the inadequacy of the definition by letting the restriction about dynamic usage take the place of emotive meaning. What I should do, of course, is to find a definiens whose emotive meaning, like that of "good," simply does *lead* to dynamic usage.

Why did I not do this? I answer that it is not possible if the definition is to afford us increased clarity. No two words, in the first place, have quite the same emotive meaning. The most we can hope for is a rough approximation. But if we seek for such an approximation for "good," we shall find nothing more than synonyms, such as "desirable" or "valuable"; and these are profitless because they do not clear up the connection between "good" and favorable interest. If we reject such synonyms, in favor of nonethical terms, we shall be highly misleading. For instance "this is good" has something like the meaning of "I *do* like this; do so as well." But this is certainly not accurate. For the imperative makes an appeal to the conscious efforts of the hearer. Of course he cannot like something just by trying. He must be led to like it through

suggestion. Hence an ethical sentence differs from an imperative in that it enables one to make changes in a much more subtle, less fully conscious way. Note that the ethical sentence centers the hearer's attention not on his interests but on the object of interest, and thereby facilitates suggestion. Because of its subtlety, moreover, an ethical sentence readily permits counter-suggestion and leads to the give and take situation that is so characteristic of arguments about values.

Strictly speaking, then, it is impossible to define "good" in terms of favorable interest if emotive meaning is not to be distorted. Yet it is possible to say that "this is good" is *about* the favorable interest of the speaker and the hearer or hearers, and that it has a laudatory emotive meaning which fits the words for use in suggestion. This is a rough description of meaning, not a definition. But it serves the same clarifying function that a definition ordinarily does, and that, after all, is enough.

A word must be added about the moral use of "good." This differs from the above in that it is about a different kind of interest. Instead of being about what the hearer and speaker *like,* it is about a stronger sort of approval. When a person *likes* something, he is pleased when it prospers and disappointed when it does not. When a person *morally approves* of something he experiences a rich feeling of security when it prospers and is indignant or "shocked" when it does not. These are rough and inaccurate examples of the many factors which one would have to mention in distinguishing the two kinds of interest. In the moral usage, as well as in the nonmoral, "good" has an emotive meaning which adapts it to suggestion.

And now, are these considerations of any importance? Why do I stress emotive meanings in this fashion? Does the omission of them really lead people into errors? I think, indeed, that the errors resulting from such omissions are enormous. In order to see this, however, we must return to the restrictions, mentioned in Section 1, with which the typical sense of "good" has been expected to comply.

5

The first restriction, it will be remembered, had to do with disagreement. Now there is clearly some sense in which people disagree on ethical points, but we must not rashly assume that all disagreement is modeled after the sort that occurs in the natural sciences. We must distinguish between "disagreement in belief" (typical of the sciences) and "disagreement in interest." Disagreement in belief occurs when A believes *p* and B disbelieves it. Disagreement in interest occurs when A has a favorable interest in X and when B has an unfavorable one in it. (For a full-bodied disagreement, neither party is content with the discrepancy.)

Let me give an example of disagreement in interest. A. "Let's go to a cinema tonight." B. "I don't want to do that. Let's go to the symphony." A continues to insist on the cinema, B on the symphony. This is disagreement in a perfectly conventional sense. They cannot agree on where they want to go, and each is trying to redirect the other's interest. (Note that imperatives are used in the example.)

It is disagreement in *interest* which takes places in ethics. When C says "this is good," and D says "no, it's bad," we have a case of suggestion and counter-suggestion. Each man is trying to redirect the other's interest. There obviously need be no domineering, since each may be willing to give ear to the other's influence; but each is trying to move the other none the less. It is in this sense that they disagree. Those who argue that certain interest theories make no provision for disagreement have been misled, I believe, simply because the traditional theories, in leaving out emotive meaning, give the impression that ethical judgments are used descriptively only; and of course when judgments are used purely descriptively, the only disagreement that can arise is disagreement *in belief*. Such disagreement may be disagreement in belief *about* interests, but this is not the same as disagreement *in* interest. My definition does not provide for disagreement in belief about interests any more than does Hobbes'; but that is no matter, for there is no reason to believe, at least on common sense grounds, that this kind of disagreement exists. There is only disagreement *in* interest. (We shall see in a moment that disagreement in interest does not remove ethics from sober argument—that this kind of disagreement may often be resolved through empirical means.)

The second restriction, about "magnetism," or the connection between goodness and actions, requires only a word. This rules out only those interest theories that do *not* include the interest of the speaker in defining "good." My account does include the speaker's interest, hence is immune.

The third restriction, about the empirical method, may be met in a way that springs naturally from the above account of disagreement. Let us put the question in this way: When two people disagree over an ethical matter, can they completely resolve the disagreement through empirical considerations, assuming that each applies the empirical method exhaustively, consistently, and without error?

I answer that sometimes they can and sometimes they cannot, and that at any rate, even when they can, the relation between empirical knowledge and ethical judgments is quite different from the one that traditional interest theories seem to imply.

This can best be seen from an analogy. Let us return to the example where A and B could not agree on a cinema or a symphony. The example differed from an ethical argument in that imperatives were used, rather than ethical judgments, but was analogous to the extent that each person was endeavoring to modify the other's interest. Now how would these people argue the case, assuming that they were too intelligent just to shout at one another?

Clearly, they would give "reasons" to support their imperatives. A might say, "but you know, Garbo is at the Bijou." His hope is that B, who admires Garbo, will acquire a desire to go to the cinema when he knows what film will be there. B may counter, "but Toscanini is guest conductor tonight, in an all-Beethoven program." And so on. Each supports his imperative ("*let's* do so and so") by reasons which may be empirically established.

To generalize from this: disagreement in interest may be rooted in disagreement in belief. That is to say, people who disagree in interest would often cease to do so if they knew the precise nature and consequences of the object of their interest. To this extent disagreement in interest may be resolved by securing agreement in belief, which in turn may be secured empirically.

This generalization holds for ethics. If A and B, instead of using imperatives, had said, respectively, "it would be *better* to go to the cinema," and "it would be better to go to the symphony," the reasons which they would advance would be roughly the same. They would each give a more thorough account of the object of interest, with the purpose of completing the redirection of interest which was begun by the suggestive force of the ethical sentence. On the whole, of course, the suggestive force of the ethical statement merely exerts enough pressure to start such trains of reasons, since the reasons are much more essential in resolving disagreement in interest than the persuasive effect of the ethical judgment itself.

Thus the empirical method is relevant to ethics simply because our knowledge of the world is a determining factor to our interests. But note that empirical facts are not inductive grounds from which the ethical judgment problematically follows. (This is what traditional interest theories imply.) If someone said "close the door," and added the reason "we'll catch cold," the latter would scarcely be called an inductive ground of the former. Now imperatives are related to the reasons which support them in the same way that ethical judgments are related to reasons.

Is the empirical method *sufficient* for attaining ethical agreement? Clearly not. For empirical knowledge resolves disagreement in interest only to the extent that such disagreement is rooted in disagreement in belief. Not all disagreement in interest is of this sort. For instance: A is of a sympathetic nature and B is not. They are arguing about whether a public dole would be good. Suppose that they discovered all the consequences of the dole. Is it not possible, even so, that A will say that it is good and B that it is bad? The disagreement in interest may arise not from limited factual knowledge but simply from A's sympathy and B's coldness. Or again, suppose in the above argument that A was poor and unemployed and that B was rich. Here again the disagreement might not be due to different factual knowledge. It would be due to the different social positions of the men, together with their predominant self-interest.

When ethical disagreement is not rooted in disagreement in belief, is there *any* method by which it may be settled? If one means by "method" a *rational* method, then there is no method. But in any case there is a "way." Let us consider the above example again, where disagreement was due to A's sympathy and B's coldness. Must they end by saying, "well, it's just a matter of our having different temperaments"? Not necessarily. A, for instance, may try to *change* the temperament of his opponent. He may pour out his enthusiasms in such a moving way—present the sufferings of the poor with such appeal—that he will lead his opponent to see life through different eyes. He may build up by the contagion of his feelings an influence which will modify B's temperament and create in him a sympathy for the poor which did not previously exist. This is often the only way to obtain ethical agreement, if there is any way at all. It is persuasive, not empirical or rational; but that is no reason for neglecting it. There is no reason to scorn it, either, for it is only by such means that our personalities are able to grow, through our contact with others.

The point I wish to stress, however, is simply that the empirical method is instrumental to ethical agreement only to the extent that disagreement in interest is rooted in disagreement in belief. There is little reason to believe that all disagreements is of this sort. Hence the empirical method is not sufficient for ethics. In any case, ethics is not psychology, since psychology does not endeavour to *direct* our interests; it discovers facts about the ways in which interests are or can be directed, but that is quite another matter.

To summarize this section: my analysis of ethical judgments meets the three requirements for the typical sense of "good" that were mentioned in Section 1. The traditional interest theories fail to meet these requirements simply because they neglect emotive meaning. This neglect leads them to neglect dynamic usage, and the sort of disagreement that results from such usage, together with the method of resolving the disagreement. I may add that my analysis answers Moore's objection about the open question. Whatever scientifically knowable properties a thing may have, it *is* always open to question whether a thing having these (enumerated) qualities is good. For to ask whether it is good is to ask for *influence*. And whatever I may know about an object, I can still ask, quite pertinently, to be influenced with regard to my interest in it.

6

And now, have I really pointed out the "typical" sense of "good"?

I suppose that many will still say "no," claiming that I have simply failed to set down *enough* requirements that this sense must meet, and that my analysis, like all others given in terms of interest, is a way of begging the issue. They will say: "When we ask 'is X good?' we don't want mere influence, mere advice. We decidedly don't want to be influenced through persuasion, nor are we fully content when the influence is supported by a wide scientific knowledge of X. The answer to our question will, of course, modify our interests. But this is only because a unique sort of truth will be revealed to us—a truth that must be apprehended a priori. We want our interests to be guided by this truth and by nothing else. To substitute for this special truth mere emotive meaning and mere factual truth is to conceal from us the very object of our search."

I can only answer that I do not understand. What is this truth to be *about?* For I recollect no Platonic Idea, nor do I know what to *try* to recollect. I find no indefinable property nor do I know what to look for. And the "self-evident" deliverances of reason, which so many philoso-phers have mentioned, seem on examination to be deliverances of their respective reasons only (if of anyone's) and not of mine.

I strongly suspect, indeed, that any sense of "good" which is expected both to unite itself in synthetic a priori fashion with other concepts and to influence interests as well, is really a great confusion. I extract from this meaning the power of influence alone, which I find the only intelligible part. If the rest is confusion, however, then it certainly deserves more than the shrug of one's shoulders. What I should like to do is to *account* for the confusion—to examine the psychological needs which have given rise to it and show how these needs may be satisfied in another way. This is *the* problem, if confusion is to be stopped at its source. But it is an enormous problem and my reflections on it, which are at present worked out only roughly, must be reserved until some later time.

I may add that if "X is good" has the meaning that I ascribe to it, then it is not a judgment that professional philosophers and only professional philosophers are qualified to make. To the extent that ethics predicates the ethical terms of anything, rather that explains their meaning, it becomes more than a purely intellectual study. Ethical judgments are social instruments. They are used in a cooperative enterprise that leads to a mutual readjustment of human interests. Philosophers have a part in this; but so too do all men.

NOTES

1. The definition ascribed to Hume is oversimplified, but not, I think, in a way that weakens the force of the observations that I am about to make. Perhaps the same should be said of Hobbes.

A more accurate account of Hume's Ethics is given in *Ethics and Language* (New Haven, 1944), pp. 273–76.

2. In *General Theory of Value* (New York, 1926) Perry used "interest" to refer to any sort of favoring or disfavoring, or any sort of disposition to be for or against something. And he used "theory" where he might, alternatively, have used "proposed definition," or "proposed analysis of a common sense meaning."

In most of the (chronologically) later essays in the present volume the term "interest" systematically gives place to the term "attitude." The purpose of the change was solely to provide a more transparent terminology: it was not intended to repudiate Perry's *conception* of interest.

3. See G. E. Moore, *Philosophical Studies* (New York, 1922), pp. 332–34.

4. See G. C. Field, *Moral Theory* (London, 1921) pp. 52, 56–57.

5. See G. E. Moore, *Principia Ethica* (Cambridge, 1903), ch 1. I am simply trying to preserve the spirit of Moore's objection and not the exact form of it.

6. The "subsequent essay" became instead, Chapter 3 of *Ethics and Language,* which among other points defends those that follow:

(1) When used in a generic sense that emphasizes what C. W. Morris calls the *pragmatic* aspects of language, the term "meaning" designates a tendency of words to express or evoke states of mind in the people who use the words. The tendency is of a special kind, however, and many qualifications are needed (including some that bear on syntax) to specify its nature.

(2) When the states of mind in question are cognitive, the meaning can conveniently be called *descriptive;* and when they are feelings, emotions, or attitudes, the meanings can conveniently be called *emotive.*

(3) The states of mind (in a rough and tentative sense of that term) are normally quite complicated. They are not necessarily images or feelings but may in their turn be further tendencies—tendencies to respond to various stimuli

that may subsequently arise. A word may have a constant meaning, accordingly, even though it is accompanied, at various times that it is used, by different images or feelings.

(4) Emotive meaning is sometimes more than a by-product of descriptive meaning. When a term has both sorts of meaning, for example, a change in its descriptive meaning may not be attended by a change in emotive meaning.

(5) When a speaker's use of emotive terms evokes an attitude in a hearer (as it sometimes may not, since it has only a *tendency* to do so), it must not be conceived as merely adding to the hearer's attitude in the way that a spark might add its heat to the atmosphere. For a more appropriate analogy, in many cases, we must think rather of a spark that ignites tinder.

7.   See C. K. Ogden and I. A. Richards, *The Meaning of Meaning* (2nd ed. London, 1927). On p. 125 there is a passage on ethics which is the source of the ideas embodied in this essay.

8.   In *Ethics and Language* the phrase "aura of feeling" was expressly repudiated. If the present essay had been more successful in anticipating the analysis given in that later work, it would have introduced the notion of emotive meaning in some such way as this:

The emotive meaning of a word or phrase is a strong and persistent tendency, built up in the course of linguistic history, to give direct expression (quasi-interjectionally) to certain of the speaker's feelings or emotions or attitudes; and it is also a tendency to evoke (quasi-imperatively) corresponding feelings, emotions, or attitudes in those to whom the speaker's remarks are addressed. It is the emotive meaning of a word, accordingly, that leads us to characterize it as *laudatory* or *derogatory*—that rather generic characterization being of particular importance when we are dealing with terms like "good" and "bad" or "right and wrong." But emotive meanings are of great variety: they may yield terms that express or evoke horror, amazement, sadness, sympathy, and so on.

33.   *ETHICS: EMOTIVISM AND*

OUTSTANDING PROBLEMS

R. M. Hare

EMOTIVISM

Though emotivism was, historically, the first kind of non-descriptivism to be canvassed, it is a mistake to think of it as the only kind, or even as commanding general support among non-descriptivists at the present time. It is common even now for non-descriptivists of all kinds to be misleadingly called 'emotivists', even though their theories do not depend on any reference to the emotions. Emotivism proper embraces a variety of views, which may be held concurrently. According to the best-known, moral judgements have it as their function to 'express' or 'evince' the moral emotions (for example, approval) of the speaker. According to another version, their use is to arouse or evoke similar emotions in the person to whom they are addressed, and so stimulate him to actions of the

From R. M. Hare, "Ethics," Sections 6 and 7, in *The Concise Encyclopedia of Western Philosophy and Philosophers,* edited by J. O. Urmson. Reprinted by permission of Hawthorn Books, Inc., from *The Concise Encyclopedia of Western Philosophy and Philosophers,* edited by J. O. Urmson. Copyright © 1960 by James Opie Urmson. All rights reserved.

kind approved. A. J. Ayer when he wrote *Language, Truth and Logic* (1936), which contains the most famous exposition of emotivism, attributed both these functions to moral judgements; but he has since abandoned emotivism, though remaining a non-descriptivist. C. L. Stevenson put forward a kindred view, with the difference that, instead of the word 'emotion', he most commonly used the word 'attitude'. An attitude was usually thought of by him as a disposition to be in certain mental states or to do certain kinds of actions. Stevenson's 'attitudes' are much closer to the 'moral principles' of the older philosophers (especially Aristotle) than is usually noticed by those who use the misleading 'objectivist-subjectivist' classification. Stevenson made the important qualification to his view that, besides their 'emotive meaning', moral judgements may also have a 'descriptive meaning'. In one of his several 'patterns of analysis' the meaning of a moral judgment is analysed into two components: (1) a non-moral assertion about, for example, an act (explicable naturalistically in terms of empirical properties of the act); and (2) a specifically moral component (the emotive meaning) whose presence prevents a naturalistic account being given of the meaning of the whole judgement. This specifically moral element in the meaning is the function which these judgements have of *expressing* attitudes and *persuading* or *influencing* people to adopt them, towards the act described. Stevenson's views did not, of course, find favour with descriptivists; and even non-descriptivists who have written after him, while recognising the seminal importance of his work, have for the most part rejected the implied irrationalism of the view that the only specifically moral element in the meaning of moral terms is their emotive force. This, it has been felt, makes moral judgements too like rhetoric or propaganda, and does insufficient justice to the possibility of reasoned argument about moral questions. If moral argument is possible, there must be *some* logical relations between a moral judgement and other moral judgements, even if Hume was right to hold that a moral judgement is not derivable from statements of non-moral fact. Stevenson has some important things to say about moral arguments, but his account of them has been generally held to be inadequate.

OUTSTANDING PROBLEMS

Most of the main problems which occupy ethical thinkers at the present time arise from the complexity of the meaning of moral terms, which combines two very different elements.

(1) *The evaluative or prescriptive meaning* (these more non-committal terms are now often preferred to Stevenson's 'emotive meaning'). It is not necessary, and probably false, to attribute to moral judgements, as such, any impulsive or causative force or power to *make* or *induce us to* do what they enjoin; but even descriptivists sometimes admit that moral judgements have the function of *guiding* conduct. It is indeed fairly evident that in many typical cases we ask, for example, 'What ought I to do?' because we have to decide what to do, and think that the answer to the 'ought' question has a bearing on our decision greater and more intimate than that possessed by answers to questions of non-moral fact. To take another example, it is fairly evident

that there is an intimate connexion between thinking A better than B, and preferring A to B, and between the latter and being disposed to choose A rather than B. This intimate connexion is emphasised in the old tag (whose substance goes back to Socrates): 'Whatever is sought, is sought under the appearance of its being good'. It would follow from this that to call a thing good is thereby to offer guidance about choices; and the same might be said of the other moral terms. Descriptivists, however, refuse to admit that this feature is part of the *meaning* of moral terms.

Their principal opponents, who may be called 'prescriptivists', hold that it *is* part of the meaning. Moral judgements, on this view, share with imperatives the characteristic that to utter one is to commit oneself, directly or indirectly, to some sort of precept or prescription about actual or conceivable decisions or choices. In typical cases, disagreement with a moral judgement is displayed by failure to act on it—as when someone has told me that the right thing to do is such and such, and I immediately do the opposite. Such a view does not, like the emotive theory, make moral argument impossible; for according to some prescriptivists logical relations may hold between prescriptions as well as between ordinary statements.

Prescriptivists have to face, like Socrates, the difficulty that in cases of so-called 'weakness of will' we may choose to do something which we think bad or wrong. The most promising line for prescriptivists to take in answer to this objection is to point out that in such cases either the chooser is *unable* to resist the temptation (as is indicated by the expression '*weakness* of will'; cf. also St Paul, Romans 7: 23); or else he thinks the thing bad or wrong only in some weaker, conventional sense, having the descriptive meaning of 'bad' or 'wrong' but lacking their prescriptive force.

(2) *The descriptive meaning.* The second main feature of moral judgements is that which distinguishes them from imperatives: whenever we make a moral judgement about, for example, an act, we must make it because of *something about* the act, and it always makes sense to ask what this something is (though it may be hard to put a reply into words). This (although it has been denied by some recent thinkers) follows from the 'consequential' character of moral 'proper-

ties' (see above, section 4). To every particular moral judgement, then, there corresponds a universal judgement to the effect that a certain feature of the thing judged is, so far as it goes, a reason for making a certain moral judgement about it. For instance, if I say that a particular act is good because it is the act of helping a blind man across a road, I seem to be adhering thereby to the universal judgement that it is good to help blind people across roads (and not merely this particular blind man across this particular road). Those who accept this argument may be called 'universalists'; and their opponents, who do not, may be called 'particularists'. A universalist is not committed to the view that, if it is a good act to help a blind man across a road on this occasion, it would be a good act on all occasions (for example, it would not be a good act if the blind man was known to be hopelessly lost and his destination lay on this side of the road); he is committed only to the view that it would be a good act in the absence of something to make a difference between the two acts—something more than the mere numerical difference between the acts.

The universalist thesis is closely connected with the thesis that moral judgements, besides their function as prescriptions, have also a descriptive meaning (see above, section 6). On this view, in calling an act, for example, good, we are commending it (the prescriptive element in the meaning), but commending it because of something about it. These two elements are well summarised by the *Oxford English Dictionary*'s first definition of 'good': 'The most general adjective of commendation, implying the existence in a high, or at least satisfactory, degree of characteristic qualities which are either admirable in themselves or useful for some purpose'. The word 'characteristic' is important; it draws attention to the fact that the word which follows 'good' makes a difference to the qualities which a

thing has to have in order to be called good (for example, a good strawberry does not have to have the same qualities as a good man). In the case of some words (for example, 'knife'), if we know what they mean, we know some of the conditions that have to be fulfilled before we can call a thing of that kind good. Some philosophers (for example Plato and Aristotle) have held that the same is true of all words—that, for example, if we could determine 'the nature of man' we should therefore be able to say what makes a man a good man. But this type of argument may be based on a false analogy between words like 'man' and words like 'knife'.

A more promising way of bringing the universalist thesis to bear on moral arguments (and thus to some extent satisfying those who insist that ethical studies should be relevant to moral questions) is that exemplified by the 'Golden Rule' and worked out in some detail (though obscurely) by Kant and his followers. In certain cases it may be a powerful argument, if a man is contemplating some act, to ask what it is about the act which makes him call it right, and whether, if some other act possessed the same features, but his own role in it were different, he would judge it in the same way. This type of argument occurs in two famous passages of Scripture (2 Samuel 12:7 and Matthew 18:32). It has been held that a judgement is not a *moral* judgement unless the speaker is prepared to 'universalise his maxim'. But this raises the vexed question of the criteria for calling judgements 'moral judgements'—a question which is beyond the scope of this article.

This question, and the whole problem of the relation between the prescriptive and the descriptive elements in the meaning of moral judgements, continues to tax ethical thinkers. It has been impossible in this article to do more than sketch the principal issues and give some account of their origin.

34. FREEDOM AND REASON

R. M. Hare

MORAL REASONING

*And as ye would that men should do to you, do ye also
to them likewise.*

ST. LUKE, VI, 31

A MORAL ARGUMENT

Historically, one of the chief incentives to the
study of ethics has been the hope that its findings
might be of help to those faced with difficult
moral problems. That this is still a principal incentive for many people is shown by the fact that
modern philosophers are often reproached for
failing to make ethics relevant to morals.[1] This is
because one of the main tenets of many recent
moral philosophers has been that the most popular method by which it was sought to bring
ethics to bear on moral problems was not feasible—namely the method followed by the
group of theories loosely known as 'naturalist'.

The method of naturalism is so to characterize
the *meanings* of the key moral terms that, given
certain factual premises, not themselves moral
judgements, moral conclusions can be deduced
from them. If this could be done, it was thought
that it would be of great assistance to us in making moral decisions; we should only have to find
out the non-moral facts, and the moral conclusion as to what we ought to do would follow.
Those who say that it cannot be done leave
themselves the task of giving an alternative account of moral reasoning.

Naturalism seeks to make the findings of ethics *relevant* to moral decisions by making the
former not morally *neutral*. It is a very natural
assumption that if a statement of ethics is relevant to morals, then it cannot be neutral as between different moral judgements; and naturalism is a tempting view for those who make this

From R. M. Hare, *Freedom and Reason* (Oxford: at the Clarendon Press, 1963), sections 6.1–6.4 and 6.9. © 1963,
Oxford University Press. Reprinted with permission of the
author and The Clarendon Press, Oxford. Notes edited.

assumption. Naturalistic definitions are not
morally neutral, because with their aid we could
show that statements of non-moral facts *entailed*
moral conclusions. And some have thought that
unless such an entailment can be shown to hold,
the moral philosopher has not made moral reasoning possible.

One way of escaping this conclusion is to say
that the relation linking a set of non-moral premisses with a moral conclusion is not one of
entailment, but that some other logical relation,
peculiar to morals, justifies the inference. This is
the view put forward, for example, by Mr. Toulmin.[2] Since I have argued elsewhere against this
approach, I shall not discuss it here. Its advocates have, however, hit upon an important insight: that moral reasoning does not necessarily
proceed by way of *deduction* of moral conclusions from non-moral premisses. Their further
suggestion, that therefore it makes this transition by means of some other, peculiar, non-
deductive kind of inference, is not the only possibility. It may be that moral reasoning is not,
typically, any kind of 'straightline' or 'linear' reasoning from premisses to conclusion.

A parallel from the philosophy of science will
perhaps make this point clear. It is natural to
suppose that what the scientist does is to reason
from premisses, which are the data of observation, to conclusions, which are his 'scientific laws', by means of a special sort of inference called 'inductive'. Against this view,
Professor Popper has forcibly argued that in
science there are no inferences other than deductive; the typical procedure of scientists is to
propound hypotheses, and then look for ways of
testing them—i.e. experiments which, if they
are false, will show them to be so. A hypothesis
which, try as we may, we fail to falsify, we accept
provisionally, though ready to abandon it if, after all, further experiment refutes it; and of
those that are so accepted we rate highest the
ones which say most, and which would, therefore, be most likely to have been falsified if they

were false. The only inferences which occur in this process are deductive ones, from the truth of certain observations to the falsity of a hypothesis. There is no reasoning which proceeds from the data of observation to the *truth* of a hypothesis. Scientific inquiry is rather a kind of *exploration,* or looking for hypotheses which will stand up to the test of experiment.[3]

We must ask whether moral reasoning exhibits any similar features. I want to suggest that it too is a kind of exploration, and not a kind of linear inference, and that the only inferences which take place in it are deductive. What we are doing in moral reasoning is to look for moral judgements and moral principles which, when we have considered their logical consequences and the facts of the case, we can still accept. As we shall see, this approach to the problem enables us to reject the assumption, which seemed so natural, that ethics cannot be relevant to moral decisions without ceasing to be neutral. This is because we are not going to demand any inferences in our reasoning other than deductive ones, and because none of these deductive inferences rely for their validity upon naturalistic definitions of moral terms.

Two further parallels may help to make clear the sense in which ethics is morally neutral. In the kind of scientific reasoning just described, mathematics plays a major part, for many of the deductive inferences that occur are mathematical in character. So we are bound to admit that mathematics is relevant to scientific inquiry. Nevertheless, it is also neutral, in the sense that no discoveries about matters of physical fact can be made with the aid of mathematics alone, and that no mathematical inference can have a conclusion which says more, in the way of prediction of observations, than its premisses implicitly do.

An even simpler parallel is provided by the rules of games. The rules of a game are neutral as between the players, in the sense that they do not, by themselves, determine which player is going to win. In order to decide who wins, the players have to play the game in accordance with the rules, which involves their making, themselves, a great many individual decisions. On the other hand, the 'neutrality' of the rules of a game does not turn it into a game of chance, in which the bad player is as likely to win as the good.

Ethical theory, which determines the meanings and functions of the moral words, and thus the 'rules' of the moral 'game', provides only a clarification of the conceptual framework within which moral reasoning takes place; it is therefore, in the required sense, neutral as between different moral opinions. But it is highly relevant to moral reasoning because, as with the rules of a game, there could be no such thing as moral reasoning without this framework, and the framework dictates the form of the reasoning. It follows that naturalism is not the only way of providing for the possibility of moral reasoning; and this may, perhaps, induce those who have espoused naturalism as a way of making moral thought a rational activity to consider other possibilities.

The rules of moral reasoning are, basically, two, corresponding to the two features of moral judgements which I argued for in the first half of this book, prescriptivity and universalizability. When we are trying, in a concrete case, to decide what we ought to do, what we are looking for (as I have already said) is an action to which we can commit ourselves (prescriptivity) but which we are at the same time prepared to accept as exemplifying a principle of action to be prescribed for others in like circumstances (universalizability). If, when we consider some proposed action, we find that, when universalized, it yields prescriptions which we cannot accept, we reject this action as a solution to our moral problem—if we cannot universalize the prescription, it cannot become an 'ought'.

It is to be noticed that, troublesome as was the problem of moral weakness when we were dealing theoretically with the logical character of the moral concepts, it cannot trouble us here. For if a person is going to reason seriously at all about a moral question, he has to presuppose that the moral concepts are going, in his reasoning, to be used prescriptively. One cannot start a moral argument about a certain proposal on the basis that, whatever the conclusion of it, it makes no difference to what anybody is to do. When one has arrived at a conclusion, one may then be too weak to put it into practice. But *in arguing* one has to discount this possibility; for, as we shall see, to abandon the prescriptivity of one's moral judgements is to unscrew an essential part of the logical mechanism on which such arguments rely. This is why, if a person were to say 'Let's have an argument about this grave moral question which faces us, but let's not think of any conclusion we may come to as requiring anybody to *do* one thing rather than another', we should be likely to accuse him of flippancy, or worse.

I will now try to exhibit the bare bones of the theory of moral reasoning that I wish to advocate by considering a very simple (indeed over-simplified) example. As we shall see, even this very simple case generates the most baffling complexities; and so we may be pardoned for not attempting anything more difficult to start with.

The example is adapted from a well-known parable.[4] *A* owes money to *B,* and *B* owes money to *C,* and it is the law that creditors may exact their debts by putting their debtors into prison. *B* asks himself, 'Can I say that I ought to take this measure against *A* in order to make him pay?' He is no doubt *inclined* to do this, or *wants* to do it. Therefore, if there were no question of universalizing his prescriptions, he would assent readily to the *singular* prescription 'Let me put *A* into prison'. But when he seeks to turn this prescription into a moral judgement, and say, 'I *ought* to put *A* into prison because he will not pay me what he owes', he reflects that this would involve accepting the principle 'Anyone who is in my position ought to put his debtor into prison if he does not pay'. But then he reflects that *C* is in the same position of unpaid creditor with regard to himself (*B*), and that the cases are otherwise identical; and that if anyone in this position ought to put his debtors into prison, then so ought *C* to put him (*B*) into prison. And to accept the moral prescription '*C* ought to put me into prison' would commit him (since, as we have seen, he must be using the word 'ought' prescriptively) to accepting the singular prescription 'Let *C* put me into prison'; and this he is not ready to accept. But if he is not, then neither can he accept the original judgement that he (*B*) ought to put *A* into prison for debt. Notice that the whole of this argument would break down if 'ought' were not being used both universalizably *and prescriptively;* for if it were not being used prescriptively, the step from '*C* ought to put me into prison' to 'Let *C* put me into prison' would not be valid.

The structure and ingredients of this argument must now be examined. We must first notice an analogy between it and the Popperian theory of scientific method. What has happened is that a provisional or suggested moral principle has been rejected because one of its particular consequences proved unacceptable. But an important difference between the two kinds of reasoning must also be noted; it is what we should expect, given that the data of scientific observation are recorded in descriptive statements, whereas we are here dealing with prescriptions. What knocks out a suggested hypothesis, on Popper's theory, is a singular statement of fact: the hypothesis has the consequence that *p;* but not-*p.* Here the logic is just the same, except that in place of the observation-statements '*p*' and 'not-*p*' we have the singular *prescriptions* 'Let *C* put *B* into prison for debt' and its contradictory. Nevertheless, given that *B* is disposed to reject the first of these prescriptions, the argument against him is just as cogent as in the scientific case.

We may carry the parallel further. Just as science, seriously pursued, is the search for hypotheses and the testing of them by the attempt to falsify their particular consequences, so morals, as a serious endeavour, consists in the search for principles and the testing of them against particular cases. Any rational activity has its discipline, and this is the discipline of moral thought: to test the moral principles that suggest themselves to us by following out their consequences and seeing whether we can accept *them.*

No argument, however, starts from nothing. We must therefore ask what we have to have before moral arguments of the sort of which I have given a simple example can proceed. The first requisite is that the facts of the case should be given; for all moral discussion is about some particular set of facts, whether actual or supposed. Secondly we have the logical framework provided by the meaning of the word 'ought' (i.e. prescriptivity and universalizability, both of which we saw to be necessary). Because moral judgements have to be universalizable, *B* cannot say that he ought to put *A* into prison for debt without committing himself to the view that *C,* who is *ex hypothesi* in the same position *vis-à-vis* himself, ought to put *him* into prison; and because moral judgements are prescriptive, this would be, in effect, prescribing to C to put him into prison; and this he is unwilling to do, since he has a strong inclination not to go to prison. This inclination gives us the third necessary ingredient in the argument: if B were a completely apathetic person, who literally did not mind what happened to himself or to anybody else, the argument would not touch him. The three necessary ingredients which we have noticed, then, are (1) facts; (2) logic; (3) inclinations. These ingredients enable us, not indeed to arrive at an evaluative conclusion, but to *reject* an evaluative proposition. We shall see later that these are not, in all cases, the only necessary ingredients.

In the example which we have been using, the position was deliberately made simpler by supposing that B actually stood to some other person in exactly the same relation as A does to him. Such cases are unlikely to arise in practice. But it is not necessary for the force of the argument that B should *in fact* stand in this relation to anyone; it is sufficient that he should consider hypothetically such a case, and see what would be the consequences in it of those moral principles between whose acceptance and rejection he has to decide. Here we have an important point of difference from the parallel scientific argument, in that the crucial case which leads to rejection of the principle can itself be a supposed, not an observed, one. That hypothetical cases will do as well as actual ones is important, since it enables us to guard against a possible misinterpretation of the argument which I have outlined. It might be thought that what moves B is the *fear* that C will actually do to him as he does to A—as happens in the gospel parable. But this fear is not only irrelevant to the moral argument; it does not even provide a particularly strong non-moral motive unless the circumstances are somewhat exceptional. C may, after all, not find out what B has done to A; or C's moral principles may be different from B's, and independent of them, so that what moral principle B accepts makes no difference to the moral principles on which C acts.

Even, therefore, if C did not exist, it would be no answer to the argument for B to say 'But in my case there is no fear that anybody will ever be in a position to do to me what I am proposing to do to A'. For the argument does not rest on any such fear. All that is essential to it is that B should disregard the fact that he plays the particular role in the situation which he does, without disregarding the inclinations which people have in situations of this sort. In other words, he must be prepared to give weight to A's inclinations and interests as if they were his own. This is what turns selfish prudential reasoning into moral reasoning. It is much easier, psychologically, for B to do this if he is actually placed in a situation like A's *vis-à-vis* somebody else; but this is not necessary, provided that he has sufficient imagination to envisage what it is like to be A. For our first example, a case was deliberately chosen in which little imagination was necessary; but in most normal cases a certain power of imagination and readiness to use it is a fourth necessary ingredient in moral arguments, alongside those already mentioned, viz. logic (in the shape of universalizability and prescriptivity), the facts, and the inclinations or interests of the people concerned.

It must be pointed out that the absence of even one of these ingredients may render the rest ineffective. For example, impartiality by itself is not enough. If, in becoming impartial, B became also completely dispassionate and apathetic, and moved as little by other people's interests as by his own, then, as we have seen, there would be nothing to make him accept or reject one moral principle rather than another. That is why those who, like Adam Smith and Professor Kneale, advocate what have been called 'Ideal Observer Theories' of ethics, sometimes postulate as their imaginary ideal observer not merely an impartial spectator, but an impartially *sympathetic* spectator.[5] To take another example, if the person who faces the moral decision has no imagination, then even the fact that someone can do the very same thing to him may pass him by. If, again, he lacks the readiness to universalize, then the vivid imagination of the sufferings which he is inflicting on others may only spur him on to intensify them, to increase his own vindictive enjoyment. And if he is ignorant of the material facts (for example about what is likely to happen to a person if one takes out a writ against him), then there is nothing to tie the moral argument to particular choices.

*   *   *

It is necessary, in order to avoid misunderstanding, to add two notes to the foregoing discussion. The misunderstanding arises through a too literal interpretation of the common forms of expression—which constantly recur in arguments of this type—'How would you like it if . . .?' and 'Do as you would be done by'. Though I shall later, for convenience, refer to the type of arguments here discussed as 'golden-rule' arguments, we must not be misled by these forms of expression.

First of all, we shall make the nature of the argument clearer if, when we are asking B to imagine himself in the position of his victim, we phrase our question, never in the form 'What *would* you say, or feel, or think, or how *would* you like it, if you were he?', but always in the form 'What *do* you say (*in propria persona*) about a hypothetical case in which you are in your victim's position?' The importance of this way of phrasing the question is that, if the question were put in the first way, B might reply 'Well, of course, if anybody did this to me I should resent it very much and make all sorts of adverse moral judgements about the act; but this has absolutely no bearing on the validity of the moral opinion which I am *now* expressing'. To involve him in contradiction, we have to show that he *now* holds an opinion about the hypothetical case which is inconsistent with his opinion about the actual case.

The second thing which has to be noticed is that the argument, as set out, does not involve any sort of deduction of a moral judgement, or even of the negation of a moral judgement, from a factual statement about people's inclinations, interests, etc. We are not saying to B 'You are as a matter of fact averse to this being done to you in a hypothetical case; and from this it follows logically that you ought not to do it to another'. Such a deduction would be a breach of Hume's Law ('No "ought" from an "is" '), to which I have repeatedly declared my adherence. The point is, rather, that because of his aversion to its being done to him in the hypothetical case, he cannot accept the singular *prescription* that in the hypothetical case it should be done to him; and this,

because of the logic of 'ought', precludes him from accepting the moral judgement that he ought to do likewise to another in the actual case. It is not a question of a factual statement about a person's inclinations being inconsistent with a moral judgement; rather, his inclinations being what they are, he cannot assent sincerely to a certain singular prescription, and if he cannot do this, he cannot assent to a certain universal prescription which entails it, when conjoined with factual statements about the circumstances whose truth he admits. Because of this entailment, if he assented to the factual statements and to the universal prescription, but refused (as he must, his inclinations being what they are) to assent to the singular prescription, he would be guilty of a logical inconsistency.

If it be asked what the relation is between his aversion to being put in prison in the hypothetical case, and his inability to accept the hypothetical singular prescription that if he were in such a situation he should be put into prison, it would seem that the relation is not unlike that between a belief that the cat is on the mat, and an inability to accept the proposition that the cat is not on the mat. Further attention to this parallel will perhaps make the position clearer. Suppose that somebody advances the hypothesis that cats never sit on mats, and that we refute him by pointing to a cat on a mat. The logic of our refutation proceeds in two stages. Of these, the second is: 'Here is a cat sitting on a mat, so it is not the case that cats never sit on mats'. This is a piece of logical deduction; and to it, in the moral case, corresponds the step from 'Let this not be done to me' to 'It is not the case that I ought to do it to another in similar circumstances'. But in both cases there is a first stage whose nature is more obscure, and different in the two cases, though there is an analogy between them.

In the 'cat' case, it is logically possible for a man to look straight at the cat on the mat, and yet believe that there is no cat on the mat. But if a person with normal eyesight and no psychological aberrations does this, we say that he does not understand the meaning of the words, 'The cat is on the mat'. And even if he does not have normal eyesight, or suffers from some psychological aberration (such a phobia of cats, say, that he just *cannot* admit to himself that he is face to face with one), yet, if we can convince him that everyone else can see a cat there, he will have to admit that there *is* a cat there, or be accused of misusing the language.

If, on the other hand, a man says 'But I *want* to be put in prison, if ever I am in that situation', we can, indeed, get as far as accusing him of having eccentric desires; but we cannot, when we have proved to him that nobody else has such a desire, face him with the choice of either saying, with the rest, 'Let this not be done to me', or else being open to the accusation of not understanding what he is saying. For it is not an incorrect use of words to want eccentric things. Logic does not prevent me wanting to be put in a gas chamber if a Jew. It is perhaps true that I logically cannot want for its own sake an experience which I think of as *unpleasant;* for to say that I think of it as unpleasant may be logically inconsistent with saying that I want it for its own sake. If this is so, it is because 'unpleasant' is a prescriptive expression. But 'to be put in prison' and 'to be put in a gas chamber if a Jew', are not prescriptive expressions; and therefore these things can be wanted without offence to logic. It is, indeed, in the logical possibility of wanting *anything* (neutrally described) that the 'freedom' which is alluded to in my title essentially consists. And it is this, as we shall see, that lets by the person whom I shall call the 'fanatic'.

There is not, then, a complete analogy between the man who says 'There is no cat on the mat' when there is, and the man who wants things which others do not. But there is a partial analogy, which, having noticed this difference, we may be able to isolate. The analogy is between two relations: the relations between, in both cases, the 'mental state' of these men and

what they say. If I believe that there is a cat on the mat I cannot sincerely say that there is not; and, if I want not to be put into prison more than I want anything else, I cannot sincerely say 'Let me be put into prison'. When, therefore, I said above 'His inclinations being what they are, he cannot assent sincerely to a certain singular prescription', I was making an analytic statement (although the 'cannot' is not a logical 'cannot'); for if he were to assent sincerely to the prescription, that would entail *ex vi terminorum* that his inclinations had changed—in the very same way that it is analytically true that, if the other man were to say sincerely that there was a cat on the mat, when before he had sincerely denied this, he must have changed his belief.

If, however, instead of writing 'His inclinations being what they are, he cannot . . .', we leave out the first clause and write simply 'He cannot . . .', the statement is no longer analytic; we are making a statement about his psychology which might be false. For it is logically possible for inclinations to change; hence it is possible for a man to come sincerely to hold an ideal which requires that he himself should be sent to a gas chamber if a Jew. That is the price we have to pay for our freedom. But, as we shall see, in order for reason to have a place in morals it is not necessary for us to close this way of escape by means of a logical barrier; it is sufficient that, men and the world being what they are, we can be very sure that hardly anybody is going to take it with his eyes open. And when we are arguing with one of the vast majority who are not going to take it, the reply that somebody else *might* take it does not help his case against us. In this respect, all moral arguments are *ad hominem*.

NOTES

1.   I have tried to fill in some of the historical background of these reproaches, and to assess the justification for them, in my article in *The Philosophy of C. D. Broad,* ed. P. Schilpp.

2.   S. E. Toulmin, *The Place of Reason in Ethics,* esp. pp. 38–60. See my review in *Philosophical Quarterly,* i (1950/1), 372, and *LM* 3.4.

3.   K. R. Popper, *The Logic of Scientific Discovery* (esp. pp. 32 f.). See also his article in C. A. Mace (ed.), *British Philosophy in the Mid-Century,* p. 155.

4.   Matthew xviii, 23.

5.   It will be plain that there are affinities, though there are also differences, between this type of theory and my own. For such theories see W. C. Kneale, *Philosophy,* xxv (1950), 162: R. Firth and R. B. Brandt, *Philosophy and Phenomenological Research,* xii (1951/2), 317, and xv (1954/5), 407, 414, 422; and J. Harrison, *Aristotelian Society,* supp. vol. xxviii (1954), 132. Firth, unlike Kneale, says that the observer must be 'dispassionate', but see Brandt, op. cit., p. 411 n.

35. MORAL ARGUMENTS

Philippa Foot

Those who are influenced by the emotivist theory of ethics, and yet wish to defend what Hare has called "the rationality of moral discourse", generally talk a lot about "giving reasons" for saying that one thing is right, and another wrong. The fact that moral judgements need defence seems to distinguish the impact of one man's moral views upon others from mere persuasion or coercion, and the judgements themselves from mere expressions of likes and dislikes. Yet the version of argument in morals currently accepted seems to say that, while reasons must be given, no one need accept them unless he happens to hold particular moral views. It follows that disputes about what is right and wrong can be resolved only if certain contingent conditions are fulfilled; if they are not fulfilled, the argument breaks down, and the disputants are left face to face in an opposition which is merely an expression of attitude and will. Much energy is expended in trying to show that no sceptical conclusion can be drawn. It is suggested, for instance, that anyone who has considered all the facts which could bear on his moral position has *ipso facto* produced a 'well founded' moral judgement; in spite of the fact that anyone else who has considered the same facts may well come to the opposite conclusion. How 'x is good' can be a well founded moral judgement when 'x is bad' can be equally well founded it is not easy to see.

The statement that moral arguments 'may always break down' is often thought of as something that has to be accepted, and it is thought that those who deny it fail to take account of what was proved once for all by Hume, and elaborated by Stevenson, by Ayer, and by Hare. This article is an attempt to expose the assumptions which give the 'breakdown' theory so tenacious a hold, and to suggest an alternative view.

Looked at in one way, the assertion that moral arguments "may always break down" appears to make a large claim. What is meant is that they may break down in a way in which other arguments may not. We are therefore working on a model on which such factors as shortage of time or temper are not shown; the suggestion is not that A's argument with B may break down because B refuses for one reason or another to go on with it, but that their positions as such are irreconcilable. Now the question is: how can we assert that any disagreement about what is right and wrong may end like this? How do we know, without consulting the details of each argument, that there is always an impregnable position both for the man who says that X is right, or good, or what he ought to do, and for the man who denies it? How do we know that each is able to deal with every argument the other may bring?

Thus, when Hare describes someone who listens to all his adversary has to say and then at the end simply rejects his conclusion, we want to ask "How can he?" Hare clearly supposes that he can, for he says that at this point the objector can only be asked to make up his mind for himself.[1] No one would ever paint such a picture of other kinds of argument—suggesting, for instance, that a man might listen to all that could be said about the shape of the earth, and then ask why he should believe that it was round. We should want, in such a case, to know how he met the case put to him; and it is remarkable that in ethics this question is thought not to be in place.

If a man making a moral judgement is to be invulnerable to criticism, he must be free from reproach on two scores: (*a*) he must have brought forward evidence, where evidence is needed; and (*b*) he must have disposed of any contrary evidence offered. It is worth showing why writers who insist that moral arguments may always break down assume, for both sides in a moral dispute, invulnerability on both counts. The critical assumption appears in different forms because different descriptions of moral arguments are given; and I shall consider briefly what has been said by Stevenson and by Hare.

From Philippa Foot, "Moral Arguments," *Mind*, Vol. 67 (1958), pp. 502–513. Reprinted with permission of the author and Basil Blackwell, Publisher.

I. Stevenson sees the process of giving reasons for ethical conclusions as a special process of non-deductive inference, in which statements expressing beliefs (R) form the premises and emotive (evaluative) utterances (E) the conclusion. There are no rules validating particular inferences, but only causal connections between the beliefs and attitudes concerned. "Suppose", he writes, "that a theorist should *tabulate* the 'valid' inferences from R's to E's. It is difficult to see how he could be doing anything more than specify what R's he thereby resolves to *accept* as supporting the various E's. . . . Under the name of 'validity' he will be selecting those inferences to which he is psychologically disposed to give assent, and perhaps inducing others to give a similar assent to them."[2] It follows that disputes in which each man backs up his moral judgement with "reasons" may always break down, and this is an implication on which Stevenson insists. So long as he does not contradict himself and gets his facts right, a man may argue as he chooses, or as he finds himself psychologically disposed. He alone says which facts are relevant to ethical conclusions, so that he is invulnerable on counts (*a*) and (*b*): he can simply assert that what he brings forward is evidence, and can simply deny the relevance of any other. His argument may be ineffective, but it cannot be said to be wrong. Stevenson speaks of ethical "inference' and of giving "reasons", but the process which he describes is rather that of trying to produce a result, an attitude, by means of a special kind of adjustment, an alteration in belief. All that is needed for a breakdown is for different attitudes in different people to be causally connected to the same beliefs. Then even complete agreement in belief will not settle a moral dispute.

II. Hare gives a picture of moral reasoning which escapes the difficulties of a special form of inference without rules of validity. He regards an argument to a moral conclusion as a syllogistic inference, with the ordinary rules. The facts, such as "this is stealing", which are to back up a moral judgement are to be stated in a "descriptive" minor premise, and their relevance is to be guaranteed by an "evaluative" major premise in which that kind of thing is said to be good or bad. There is thus no difficulty about the validity of the argument; but one does arise about the status of the major premise. We are supposed to say that a particular action is bad

because it is a case of stealing, and because stealing is wrong; but if we ask why stealing is wrong, we can only be presented with another argument of the same form, with another exposed moral principle as its major premise. In the end everyone is forced back to some moral principle which he simply asserts—and which someone else may simply deny. It can therefore be no reproach to anyone that he gives no reasons for a statement of moral principle, since any moral argument must contain some undefended premise of this kind. Nor can he be accused of failing to meet arguments put forward by opponents arguing from different principles; for by denying their ultimate major premises he can successfully deny the relevance of anything they say.

Both these accounts of moral argument are governed by the thought that there is no logical connection between statements of fact and statements of value, so that each man makes his own decision as to the facts about an action which are relevant to its evaluation. To oppose this view we should need to show that, on the contrary, it is laid down that some things do, and some things do not, count in favour of a moral conclusion, and that a man can no more decide for himself what is evidence for rightness and wrongness than he can decide what is evidence for monetary inflation or a tumour on the brain. If such objective relations between facts and values existed, they could be of two kinds: descriptive, or factual premises might *entail* evaluative conclusions, or they might count as *evidence* for them. It is the second possibility which chiefly concerns me, but I shall nevertheless consider the arguments which are supposed to show that the stronger relationship cannot exist. For I want to show that the arguments usually brought forward do not *even* prove this. I want to say that it has not even been proved that moral conclusions cannot be entailed by factual or descriptive premises.

It is often thought that Hume showed the impossibility of deducing "ought", from "is", but the form in which this view is now defended is, of course, that in which it was rediscovered by G. E. Moore at the beginning of the present century, and developed by such other critics of "naturalistic" ethics as Stevenson, Ayer and Hare. We need therefore to look into the case against naturalism to see exactly what was proved.

Moore tried to show that goodness was a non-natural property, and thus not to be defined in terms of natural properties; the problem was to explain the concept of a "natural property", and to prove that no ethical definition in terms of natural properties could be correct. As Frankena[3] and Prior[4] pointed out, the argument against naturalism was always in danger of degenerating into a truism. A natural property tended to become one not identical with goodness, and the naturalistic fallacy that of identifying goodness with "some other thing".

What was needed to give the attack on naturalism new life was the identification of some deficiency common to the whole range of definitions rejected by Moore, a reason why they all failed. This was provided by the theory that value terms in general, and moral terms in particular, were used for a special function—variously identified as expressing feelings, expressing and inducing attitudes, or commending. Now it was said that words with emotive or commendatory force, such as "good", were not to be defined by the use of words whose meaning was merely "descriptive". This discovery tended to appear greater than it was, because it looked as if the two categories of fact and value had been identified separately and found never to coincide, whereas actually the factual or descriptive was defined by exclusion from the realm of value. In the ordinary sense of "descriptive" the word "good" is a descriptive word and in the ordinary sense of "fact" we say that it is a fact about so and so that he is a good man, so that the words must be used in a special sense in moral philosophy. But a special philosopher's sense of these words has never, so far as I know, been explained except by contrasting value and fact. A word or sentence seems to be called "descriptive" on account of the fact that it is *not* emotive, does *not* commend, does *not* entail an imperative, and so on according to the theory involved. This might seem to reduce the case against naturalism once more to an uninteresting tautology, but it does not do so. For if the non-naturalist has discovered a special feature found in all value judgements, he can no longer be accused of saying merely that nothing is a definition of "good" unless it is a definition of "good" and not "some other thing". His part is now to insist that any definition which fails to allow for the special feature of value judgements

must be rejected, and to label as "naturalistic" all the definitions which fail to pass this test.

I shall suppose, for the sake of argument, that the non-naturalist really has identified some characteristic (let us call it f) essential to evaluative words; that he is right in saying that evaluations involve emotions, attitudes, the acceptance of imperatives, or something of the kind. He is therefore justified in insisting that no word or statement which does not have the property f can be taken as equivalent to any evaluation, and that no account of the use of an evaluative term can leave out f and yet be complete. What, if anything, follows about the relation between premises and conclusion in an argument designed to support an evaluation?

It is often said that what follows is that evaluative conclusion cannot be deduced from descriptive premises, but how is this to be shown? Of course if a descriptive premise is redefined, as one which does not entail an evaluative conclusion, the non-naturalist will once more have bought security at the price of becoming a bore. He can once more improve his position by pointing to the characteristic f belonging to all evaluations, and asserting that no set of premises which do not entail an f proposition can entail an evaluation. If he takes this course he will be more like the man who says that a proposition which entails a proposition about a dog must be one which entails a proposition about an animal; he is telling us what to look out for in checking the entailment. What he is not so far telling us is that we can test for the entailment by looking to see whether the premise itself has the characteristic f. For all that has yet been shown it might be possible for a premise which is not f to entail a conclusion which is f, and it is obviously this proposition which the non-naturalist wants to deny.

Now it may seem obvious that a non-evaluative premise could not entail an evaluative conclusion, but it remains unclear how it is supposed to be proved.

In one form, the theory that an evaluative conclusion of a deductive argument needs evaluative premises is clearly unwarrantable; I mention it only to get it out of the way. We cannot possibly say that at least one of the premises must be evaluative if the conclusion is to be so; for there is nothing to tell us that whatever can truly be said of the conclusion of a deductive argument can truly be said of any one of the premises. It is not necessary that the evaluative element should "come in whole", so to speak. If f has to belong to the premises it can only be necessary that it should belong to the premises *together,* and it may be no easy matter to see whether a set of propositions has the property f.

How in any case is it to be proved that if the conclusion is to have the characteristic f the premises taken together must also have it? Can it be said that unless this is so it will always be possible to assert the premises and yet deny the conclusion? I shall try to show that this at least is false, and in order to do so I shall consider the case of arguments designed to show that a certain piece of behaviour is or is not rude.

I think it will be agreed that in the wide sense in which philosophers speak of evaluation, "rude" is an evaluative word. At any rate it has the kind of characteristics upon which non-naturalists fasten: it expresses disapproval, is meant to be used when action is to be discouraged, implies that other things being equal the behaviour to which it is applied will be avoided by the speaker, and so on. For the purpose of this argument I shall ignore the cases in which it is admitted that there are reasons why something should be done in spite of, or even because of, the fact that it is rude. Clearly there are occasions when a little rudeness is in place, but this does not alter the fact that "rude" is a condemnatory word.

It is obvious that there is something else to be said about the word "rude" besides the fact that it expresses, fairly mild, condemnation: it can only be used where certain descriptions apply. The right account of the situation in which it is correct to say that a piece of behaviour is rude, is, I think, that this kind of behaviour causes offence by indicating lack of respect. Sometimes it is merely conventional that such behaviour does indicate lack of respect (*e.g.* when a man keeps his hat on in someone else's house); sometimes the behaviour is naturally disrespectful, as when one man pushes another out of the way. (It should be mentioned that rudeness and the absence of rudeness do not exhaust the subject of etiquette; some things are not rude, and yet are "not done." It is rude to wear flannels at a formal dinner party, but merely not done to wear a dinner jacket for tennis.)

Given that this reference to offence is to be included in any account of the concept of rude-ness, we may ask what the relation is between the assertion that these conditions of offence are fulfilled—let us call it O—and the statement that a piece of behaviour is rude—let us call it R. Can someone who accepts the proposition O (that this kind of offence is caused) deny the proposition R (that the behaviour is rude)? I should have thought that this was just what he could not do, for if he says that it is not rude, we shall stare, and ask him what sort of behaviour would be rude; and what is he to say? Suppose that he were to answer "a man is rude when he behaves conventionally", or "a man is rude when he walks slowly up to a front door", and this not because he believes that such behaviour causes offence, but with the intention of leaving behind entirely the usual criteria of rudeness. It is evident that with the usual criteria of rudeness he leaves behind the concept itself; he may say the words "I think this rude", but it will not on that account be right to describe him as "thinking it rude". If I *say* "I am sitting on a pile of hay" and bring as evidence the fact that the object I am sitting on has four wooden legs and a hard wooden back, I shall hardly be described as thinking, even mistakenly, that I am sitting on a pile of hay; all I am doing is to use the *words* "pile of hay".

It might be thought that the two cases were not parallel, for while the meaning of "pile of hay" is given by the characteristics which piles of hay must possess, the meaning of "rude" is given by the attitude it expresses. The answer is that if "thinking a thing rude" is to be described as having a particular attitude to it, then having an attitude presupposes, in this case, believing that certain conditions are fulfilled. If "attitudes" were solely a matter of reactions such as wrinkling the nose, and tendencies to such things as making resolutions and scolding, then thinking something rude would not be describable solely in terms of attitudes. Either thinking something rude is not to be described in terms of attitudes, or attitudes are not to be described in terms of such things. Even if we could suppose that a particular individual could react towards conventional behaviour, or to walking slowly up to an English front door, *exactly* as most people react to behaviour which gives offence, this would not mean that he was to be described as thinking these things rude. And in any case the supposition is nonsense. Although he could behave in some ways as if he thought them rude, e.g. by scolding conventional or slow-walking children, but not turning daughters with these proclivities out of doors, his behaviour could not be just as if he thought them rude. For as the social reaction to conventional behaviour is not the same as the social reaction to offensive behaviour, he could not act in just the same way. He could not for instance apologise for what he would call his "rudeness", for he would have to admit that it had caused no offence.

I conclude that whether a man is speaking of behaviour as rude or not rude, he must use the same criteria as anyone else, and that since the criteria are satisfied if O is true, it is impossible for him to assert O while denying R. It follows that if it is a sufficient condition of P's entailing Q that the assertion of P is inconsistent with the denial of Q, we have here an example of a non-evaluative premise from which an evaluative conclusion can be deduced.

It is of course possible to admit O while refusing to assert R, and this will not be like the refusal to say about prunes what one has already admitted about dried plums. Calling an action 'rude' is using a concept which a man might want to reject, rejecting the whole practice of praising and blaming embodied in terms such as 'polite' and 'rude'. Such a man would refuse to discuss points of etiquette, and arguments with him about what is rude would not so much break down as never begin. But once he did accept the question "Is this rude?", he would have to abide by the rules of this kind of argument; he could not bring forward any evidence he liked, and he could not deny the relevance of any piece of evidence brought forward by his opponent. Nor could he say that he was unable to move from O to R on this occasion because the belief in O had not induced in him feelings or attitudes warranting the assertion of R. If he had agreed to discuss rudeness he had committed himself to accepting O as evidence for R, and evidence is not a sort of medicine which is taken in the hope that it will work. To suggest that he could refuse to admit that certain behaviour was rude because the right psychological state had not been induced, is as odd as to suppose that one might refuse to speak of the world as round because in spite of the good evidence of roundness a feeling of confidence in the proposition had not been produced. When given good evidence it is one's

business to act on it, not to hang around waiting for the right state of mind. It follows that if a man is prepared to discuss questions of rudeness, and hence to accept as evidence the fact that behaviour causes a certain kind of offence, he cannot refuse to admit R when O has been proved.

The point of considering this example was to show that there may be the strictest rules of evidence even where an evaluative conclusion is concerned. Applying this principle to the case of moral judgements, we see that—for all that the non-naturalist has proved to the contrary—Bentham, for instance, may be right in saying that when used in conjunction with the principle of utility "the words *ought* and *right* and *wrong,* and others of that stamp, have a meaning: when otherwise they have none".[5] Anyone who uses moral terms at all, whether to assert or deny a moral proposition, must abide by the rules for their use, including the rules about what shall count as evidence for or against the moral judgement concerned. For anything that has yet been shown to the contrary these rules could be entailment rules, forbidding the assertion of factual propositions in conjunction with the denial of moral propositions. The only recourse of the man who refused to accept the things which counted in favour of a moral proposition as giving him a reason to do certain things or to take up a particular attitude, would be to leave the moral discussion and abjure altogether the use of moral terms.

To say what Bentham said is not, then, to commit any sort of "naturalistic fallacy". It is open to us to enquire whether moral terms do lose their meaning when divorced from the pleasure principle, or from some other set of criteria, as the word "rude" loses its meaning when the criterion of offensiveness is dropped. To me it seems that this is clearly the case; I do not know what could be meant by saying that it was someone's duty to do something unless there was an attempt to show why it mattered if this sort of thing was not done. How can questions such as "what does it matter?", "what harm does it do?", "what advantage is there in . . .?", "why is it important?", be set aside here? Is it even to be suggested that the harm done by a certain trait of character could be taken, by some extreme moral eccentric, to be just what made it a virtue? I suggest that such a man would not even be a moral eccentric, any more than the man who used the word "rude" of conventional behaviour was putting forward strange views about what was rude. Both descriptions have their proper application, but it is not here. How exactly the concepts of harm, advantage, benefit, importance, etc., are related to the different moral concepts, such as rightness, obligation, goodness, duty and virtue, is something that needs the most patient investigation, but that they are so related seems undeniable, and it follows that a man cannot make his own personal decision about the considerations which are to count as evidence in morals.

Perhaps it will be argued that this kind of freedom of choice is not ruled out after all, because a man has to decide for himself what is to count as advantage, benefit, or harm. But is this really plausible? Consider the man described by Hare as thinking that torturing is morally permissible.[6] Apparently he is not supposed to be arguing that in spite of everything torture is justifiable as a means of extracting confessions from enemies of the state, for the argument is supposed to be at an end when he has said that torturing people is permissible, and his opponent has said that it is not. How is he supposed to have answered the objection that to inflict torture is to do harm? If he is supposed to have said that pain is good for a man in the long run, rather than bad, he will have to show the benefits involved, and he can no more choose what shall count as a benefit than he could have chosen what counted as harm. Is he supposed perhaps to count as harm only harm to himself? In this case he is guilty of *ignoratio elenchi*. By refusing to count as harm anything except harm to himself, he puts himself outside the pale of moral discussion, and should have explained that this was his position. One might compare his case to that of a man who in some discussion of common policy says "this will be the best thing to do", and announces afterwards that *he* meant best for himself. This is not what the word "best" does mean in the context of such a discussion.

It may be objected that these considerations about the evidence which must be brought for saying that one thing is good and another bad, could not in any case be of the least importance; such rules of evidence, even if they exist, only reflecting the connection between our existing moral code and our existing moral terms; if there are no "free" moral terms in our language, it can always be supposed that some have been invented—as indeed they will have to be invented if we are to be able to argue with people who subscribe to a moral code entirely different from our own. This objection rests on a doubtful assumption about the concept of *morality*. It assumes that even if there are rules about the grounds on which actions can be called good, right, or obligatory, there are no rules about the grounds on which a principle which is to be called a moral principle may be asserted. Those who believe this must think it possible to identify an element of feeling or attitude which carries the meaning of the word "moral". It must be supposed, for instance, that if we describe a man as being for or against certain actions, bringing them under universal rules, adopting these rules for himself, and thinking himself bound to urge them on others, we shall be able to identify him as holding moral principles, whatever the content of the principle at which he stops. But why should it be supposed that the concept of morality is to be caught in this particular kind of net? The consequences of such an assumption are very hard to stomach; for it follows that a rule which was admitted by those who obeyed it to be completely pointless could yet be recognised as a moral rule. If people happened to insist that no one should run round trees left handed, or look at hedgehogs in the light of the moon, this might count as a basic moral principle about which nothing more need be said.

I think that the main reason why this view is so often held in spite of these difficulties, is that we fear the charge of making a verbal decision in favour of our own moral code. But those who bring that charge are merely begging the question against arguments such as those given above. Of course if the rules we are refusing to call moral rules can really be given this name, then we are merely legislating against alien *moral codes*. But the suggestion which has been put forward is that this could not be the right description for rules of behaviour for which an entirely different defence is offered from that which we offer for our moral beliefs. If this suggestion is right, the difference between ourselves and the people who have these rules is not to be described as a difference of moral outlook, but rather as a difference between a moral and a non-moral point of view. The example of etiquette is again useful here. No one is tempted to say that the ruling out, *a priori,* of rules of etiquette which each man decides on for himself when he feels so inclined, represents a mere verbal decision in favour of our kind of socially determined standards of etiquette. On what grounds could one call a rule which someone was allowed to invent for himself a rule of *etiquette?* It is not just a fact about the use of our words "rude", "not done", etc., that they could not be applied in such a case; it is also a fact about etiquette that if terms in another language did appear in such situations they would not be terms of etiquette. We can make a similar point about the terms "legal" and "illegal" and the concept of law. If any individual was allowed to apply a certain pair of terms expressing approval and disapproval off his own bat, without taking notice of any recognised authority, such terms could not be legal terms. Similarly it is a fact about etiquette and law that they are both conventional as morality is not.

It may be that in attempting to state the rules which govern the assertion of moral propositions we shall legislate against a moral system radically opposed to our own. But this is only to say that we may make a mistake. The remedy is to look more carefully at the rules of evidence, not to assume that there cannot be any at all. If a moral system such as Nietzsche's has been refused recognition as a moral system, then we have got the criteria wrong. The fact that Nietzsche was a moralist cannot, however, be quoted in favour of the private enterprise theory of moral criteria. Admittedly Nietzsche said "You want to decrease suffering; I want precisely to increase it" but he did not *just* say this. Nor did he offer as a justification the fact that suffering causes a tendency to absent-mindedness, or lines on the human face. We recognise Nietzsche as a moralist because he tries to justify an increase in suffering by connecting it with strength as opposed to weakness, and individuality as opposed to conformity. That strength is a good thing can only be denied by someone who can show that the strong man overreaches himself, or in some other way brings harm to himself or other people. That individuality is a good thing is something that has to be shown, but in a vague way we connect it with originality, and with courage, and hence there is no difficulty in conceiving Nietzsche as a moralist when he appeals to such a thing.

In conclusion it is worth remarking that moral arguments break down more often than philosophers tend to think, but that the breakdown is of a different kind. When people argue about what is right, good, or obligatory, or whether a certain character trait is or is not a virtue, they do not confine their remarks to the adducing of facts which can be established by simple observation, or by some clear-cut technique. What is said may well be subtle or profound, and in this sort of discussion as in others, in the field of literary criticism for instance, or the discussion of character, much depends on experience and imagination. It is quite common for one man to be unable to see what the other is getting at, and this sort of misunderstanding will not always be resolvable by anything which could be called argument in the ordinary sense.

NOTES

1. *The Language of Morals*, p. 69.
2. *Ethics and Language*, pp. 170–171.
3. W. K. Frankena, "The Naturalistic Fallacy", *Mind* (1939).
4. A. N. Prior, *Logic and the Basis of Ethics,* Chap. 1.
5. *Principles of Morals in Legislation*, Chap. 1, x.
6. *Universalisbility, P.A.S.* 1954–1955, p. 304.

SUGGESTIONS FOR FURTHER READING

A. ETHICAL RELATIVISM

Benedict, Ruth, *Patterns of Culture* (Boston: Houghton Mifflin, 1934), Chapters 1–3.

Brandt, R. B., "Ethical Relativism," *The Encyclopedia of Philosophy,* Vol. 3, pp. 75–78.

———, *Ethical Theory* (Englewood Cliffs, N.J.: Prentice-Hall, Inc., 1959), Chapter 11.

Howard, V. A., "Do Anthropologists Become Moral Relativists by Mistake?" *Inquiry,* Vol. 11 (1968), pp. 175–189.

Kneale, William, "Objectivity in Morals," *Philosophy,* Vol. 25 (1950), pp. 146–166, reprinted in Sellars, Wilfrid, and Hospers, John (editors), *Readings in Ethical Theory* (New York: Appleton-Century-Crofts, Inc., 1952).

Kupperman, J. J., *Ethical Knowledge.* (London: Allen & Unwin, 1970).

Ladd, John (editor), *Ethical Relativism.* (Belmont, Calif.: Wadsworth Publishing Company, Inc., 1973).

McClintock, Thomas, "The Definition of Ethical Relativism," *Personalist,* Vol. 50 (1969), pp. 435–447.

Moser, S. *Absolutism and Relativism in Ethics* (Springfield, Ill.: Charles C. Thomas, 1968).

———, "Some Remarks about Relativism and Pseudo-Relativism in Ethics," *Inquiry,* Vol. 5 (1962), pp. 295–304.

Plato, *Protagoras.*

Stace, W. T., *The Concept of Morals* (New York: Macmillan, 1937), Chapters 1, 2, 4, and 10.

Stevenson, Charles L., *Facts and Values* (New Haven, Conn.: Yale University Press, 1963), Chapter 5.

Sumner, W. G., *Folkways* (Boston: Ginn & Company, 1907).

Wellman, Carl, "The Ethical Implications of Cultural Relativity," *Journal of Philosophy,* Vol. LX (1963), pp. 169–184.

Westermarck, Edvard, *The Origin and Development of the Moral Ideas* (New York: Macmillan, 1906), Vol. 1, Chapters 1–5.

———, *Ethical Relativity* (New York: Harcourt, 1932), Chapters 1 and 2.

B. ETHICS AND LANGUAGE

Ayer, A. J., *Language, Truth and Logic* (London: Victor Gollancz, Ltd., 1936), Chapter VI.

Broad, C. D., "Is 'Goodness' a Name of a Simple Non-Natural Quality?" *Proceedings of the Aristotelian Society,* Vol. 34 (1933–34), pp. 249–268.

Carnap, R., *Philosophy and Logical Syntax* (London: Kegan Paul, Trench, Trubner, 1935), Sections 1, 2, and 4.

Dewey, John, "Ethical Subject-Matter and Language," *The Journal of Philosophy,* Vol. 42 (1945), pp. 701–711.

———, "The Meaning of Value," *The Journal of Philosophy,* Vol. 23 (1924), pp. 126–133.

Edwards, Paul, *The Logic of Moral Discourse* (Glencoe, Ill.: The Free Press, 1955).

Ewing, A. C., *The Definition of Good* (New York: Macmillan, 1947).

———, *Ethics* (London: English Universities Press, 1953).

———, *Second Thoughts in Moral Philosophy* (London: Routledge, 1959).

Frankena, W. K., "The Naturalistic Fallacy," *Mind,* Vol. 48 (1939), pp. 103–114. Reprinted in Feigl and Sellars.

Hare, R. M., *The Language of Morals* (Oxford: Clarendon Press, 1952).

Nowell-Smith, P. H., *Ethics* (Baltimore, Md.: Penguin Books, 1954).

Ogden, C. K., and Richards, I. A., *The Meaning of Meaning* (London: Kegan Paul, 1923).

Perry, R. B., "Value as an Objective Predicate," *The Journal of Philosophy,* Vol. 28 (1931).

Russell, Bertrand, "The Elements of Ethics," *Philosophical Essays* (London: George Allen & Unwin Ltd., 1910). Reprinted in Feigl and Sellars.

Schilpp, P. A. (editor), *The Philosophy of G. E. Moore* (Evanston, Ill.: Northwestern University Press, 1942; second edition, New York: Tudor Publishing Company, 1952), especially Stevenson, C. L., "Moore's Arguments against Certain Forms of Ethical Naturalism" and Moore's "A Reply to My Critics."

Sellars, Wilfrid, and Hospers, John (editors), *Readings in Ethical Theory* (New York: Appleton-Century-Crofts, Inc., 1952), Chapters II–V.

Stevenson, Charles L., *Ethics and Language* (New Haven: Yale University Press, 1943).

Strawson, P. F., "Ethical Intuitionism," *Philosophy,* Vol. 24 (1949), pp. 23–33. Reprinted in Sellars and Hospers.

Urmson, J. O., *The Emotive Theory of Ethics* (London: Hutchinson University Library, 1968).

———, "Grading," *Mind,* Vol. 59 (1950), pp. 145–169.

Warnock, G. J., *Contemporary Moral Philosophy* (London: Macmillan and Company Ltd., 1967).

Wellman, Carl, *The Language of Ethics* (Cambridge, Mass.: Harvard University Press, 1961).

C. MORAL REASONING

Baier, K., "Good Reasons," *Philosophical Studies*, Vol. 4 (1953), pp. 1–15.

———, *The Moral Point of View: A Rational Basis of Ethics* (Ithaca, N.Y.: Cornell University Press, 1958; abridged edition, New York: Random House, Inc., 1965).

Falk, W. D., "Goading and Guiding," *Mind*, Vol. 62 (1953), pp. 145–171.

Foot, Philippa, "Moral Beliefs," *Proceedings of the Aristotelian Society*, Vol. 59 (1958–59), pp. 83–104.

Kovesi, Julius, *Moral Notions* (London: Routledge & Kegan Paul, 1967).

Pritchard, H. A., "Does Moral Philosophy Rest on a Mistake?" *Mind*, Vol. 21 (1912), pp. 487–499.

Rawls, John, "Outline of a Decision Proceedure for Ethics," *The Philosophical Review*, Vol. 66 (1957), pp. 177–197.

———, *A Theory of Justice* (Cambridge, Mass.: The Belknap Press of Harvard University Press, 1971), Chapter 1, especially pp. 46–53.

Scarrow, David S., "Hare's Account of Moral Reasoning," *Ethics*, Vol. 76 (1965–66), pp. 137–141.

Singer, Marcus, *Generalization in Ethics* (New York: Alfred A. Knopf, Inc., 1961).

Taylor, C. C. W., "Critical Notice of *Freedom and Reason*," *Mind*, Vol. 74 (1965), pp. 280–298.

Toulmin, S., *An Examination of the Place of Reason in Ethics* (Cambridge: Cambridge University Press, 1950).

Part VI   *Egoism and the Ethics of Character*

When a person asks "Why should I be moral anyway?" he may be raising any one of at least three distinct challenges. He may be challenging a moralist to demonstrate that what passes as morality in his community really is morality, that the content of conventional morality really does correspond with the content of true morality. The word "moral" when used in this way should be understood to have quotation marks around it, so that it means (roughly) "what people around here call 'moral.'" "Why be moral?" then, in its first interpretation, may be a demand for reasons to support the strictures of a prevailing code of (say) business or sexual ethics. As such, it is a straightforward question of normative ethics of a kind already encountered in Part III of this volume.

The questioner, however, may be raising a quite different kind of inquiry. In its second interpretation, "Why Be Moral?" might ask (roughly): "What's in it for me in doing what I concede true morality requires?" This of course is a motivational question rather than a normative one, but it is closely related in a subtle way to normative questions of great difficulty. Sometimes, at least, there appear to be sharp divergences between the requirements of morality and self-interest. There have been persons, for example, who have found themselves "torn twixt love and duty," so that their own moral convictions seem to require them to renounce fulfillment and to break their own hearts. Less dramatically but more commonly, morality requires us to return the lost wallets or purses of strangers when we find them by chance, instead of accepting a windfall profit at their expense, as the motive of self-interest would have us do. In the most extreme cases, morality might even require the sacrifice, as in war, of one's very life. Now, these facts (or apparent facts) have troubled moralists from the ancient Greeks on. Many have held that it is profoundly contrary to reason voluntarily to choose a loss rather than a gain for oneself, as morality sometimes seems to require. If that is so, then true morality would seem to be infected with a degree of irrationality that weakens its binding force. Others (called "psychological egoists") have held that rationality aside, it is contrary to the actual constitution of human nature freely to choose a loss rather than a gain for oneself. Human nature being what it is, it is psychologically impossible (on this view) to act voluntarily against what one takes to be one's own best interest. In either case, troubled moralists have concluded that "morality needs a sanction," that there must be a way of showing that ultimately only the moral life pays off, and that there is a perfect correspondence, after all, between duty and self-interest, superficial appearances to the contrary notwithstanding.

A. I. Melden, in the opening selection in this section, considers still a third interpretation of the question "Why be moral?" The questioner, in this interpretation, is raising no doubts about the actual content of (true) morality, as in interpretation 1; nor is he requesting mere motivating reasons, as in interpretation 2. Rather, he is asking for *rational justification* for living as he concedes true morality requires, rather than adopting a totally "amoral" outlook of utter indifference to the claims of others except when they affect his own interests. In a sense, as Melden points out, the amoralist is unabashedly inconsistent in his evaluations (though he commits no *logical* contradictions). He values his own welfare and attaches no value whatever to the welfare of other human beings who are (as he will admit) equally human and essentially similar to himself. "Very well," the amoralist might reply, "I am in a sense 'inconsistent,' but there is nothing particularly irrational about that. Perhaps such 'inconsistency' is ultimately (though of course not *morally*) justifiable. Can you show me otherwise?"

Early in his article Melden mentions the famous legend of "the ring of Gyges," which is told in graphic detail by Glaucon, a character in Plato's philosophical dialogue, *The Republic,* a work composed in Athens in the fourth century B.C. The legendary Gyges was a shepherd in Lydia. One day after a great storm and earthquake, he entered a newly opened chasm and discovered in a hollow bronze horse an enormous corpse. He took a gold ring from its finger and then made his way out.

> He was wearing this ring when he attended the usual meeting of shepherds which reported monthly to the king on the state of his flocks; and as he was sitting there with the others he happened to twist the bezel of the ring towards the inside of his hand. Thereupon he became invisible to his companions, and they began to refer to him as if he had left them. He was astonished, and began fingering the ring again, and turned the bezel outwards; whereupon he became visible again. When he saw this he started experimenting with the ring to see if it really had this power, and found that every time he turned the bezel inwards he became invisible, and when he turned it outwards he became visible. Having made this discovery he managed to get himself included in the party that was to report to the king, and when he arrived seduced the queen, and with her help attacked and murdered the king and seized the throne.[1]

Perhaps not many "amoralists" would be interested in seizing political power if they had the impunity conferred by Gyges's ring, but there would be no bar to the acquisition of great wealth and through it a life of luxury, if the ring were used shrewdly and sparingly. Both Plato and Melden think of Gyges as their "hypothetical amoralist." Melden thinks of him as the person who asks the question "Why be moral?" in its third interpretation. No reason at all can be given him, Melden concludes, but he argues ingeniously that the reasonableness of morality remains untarnished for all that.

C. D. Broad, in "Egoism as a Theory of Humam Motives," discusses critically the theory called "psychological egoism" which holds that ultimately there is only one possible human motive: the desire to promote one's own good. It would seem, at first sight, that psychological egoism has very grave consequences for morality as we normally conceive it. For if no one is capable of voluntarily sacrificing his or her own interests, as morality sometimes seems to require, then no one can be under a duty ever to sacrifice his or her own interests, since one cannot have a duty to do what one is incapable of doing. If one is capable only of selfishness then it cannot be true that one *ought* to be unselfish or altruistic.

Broad's thorough and painstaking analysis of human motivation aims at removing the threat to altruistic morality posed by egoism as a theory of human motives. By distinguishing types of motives and senses of "egoistic," Broad is able to formulate extreme egoistic theories which he quickly dismisses as "empirically false," and also a more subtle and complex egoistic theory which is at least plausible on first appearance. He concludes an admittedly indecisive discussion of psychological egoism "in its more modest form" by admitting that it is very close to the truth but claiming that it is probably false if "taken as a universal proposition." Among the hypothetical cases that no form of egoistic psychology can accommodate, Broad claims, are apparent instances of genuinely disinterested benevolence, as when a person subscribes anonymously to a charity, or "deliberately chooses to devote his life to working among lepers in the full knowledge that he will almost certainly contract leprosy and die in a particularly loathsome way." Perhaps the most interesting and important feature of Broad's discussion of these hard cases is his rejection of a famous argument put forward by the great English philosopher John Locke (1632–1704), an argument which remains popular among students. Locke suggested that the primary motive in cases of apparently

---

[1]Plato, *The Republic,* translated by H. D. P. Lee (Harmondsworth, Middlesex: Penguin Books, Ltd., 1955) Book II, 359–60, pp. 90–91.

disinterested benevolence is always egoistic, namely the desire to rid *oneself* of the unpleasant experience that comes from imagining the sufferings of others. This cannot be the primary and sole motive, Broad maintains, but at best a derivative or "parasitic" motive, for if a person cared nothing about the sufferings of others to begin with, there could be no explanation of why his imaginings of those sufferings should be "unpleasant."

The theory called "ethical egoism," as interpreted by Brian Medlin and W. D. Glasgow, is to be distinguished both from psychological egoism (which purports to describe actual human motives but to make no moral judgments) and from the "amoralism" which is the target of A. I. Melden's essay. Melden's amoralist, modeled on the legendary Gyges, is self-righteously indifferent to the acknowledged requirements of morality. The Medlin-Glasgow ethical egoist takes morality very seriously, but has a radically different conception from the prevailing one of the content of (true) morality, a conception, incidentally, which is consistent with the tenets of psychological egoism, a strong point in its favor should psychological egoism happen to be true. Ethical egoism holds that the fundamental moral principle is that "everyone *should* look after his own interests regardless of the interests of others." One paradoxical (though probably not fatal) consequence of this view is that the ethical egoist himself cannot defend his or her doctrine or attempt to persuade others of its truth without violating his own principles, for the more convinced ethical egoists there are in circulation, the more dangerous they are to his own interests!

In "Ultimate Principles and Ethical Egoism," Medlin argues against ethical egoism from a noncognitive metaethical position quite similar to that of Charles L. Stevenson (see above, pp. 411–421). "We assert our ultimate principles not only to express our own attitudes, but also to induce similar attitudes in others, to dispose them to conduct themselves as we wish." The attitude expressed by the ethical egoist's ultimate principle, however, is an *inconsistent attitude,* according to Medlin, for it expresses the desire (put very crudely) that every one come out ahead of every one else. The expression of such an incoherent attitude "cannot serve as an ultimate principle of conduct."

W. D. Glasgow is no more friendly to ethical egoism than is Medlin, and he too finds some sort of incoherence in the egoistic doctrine. But he is not satisfied with Medlin's arguments against their common opponent. Part of the difference between Medlin and Glasgow stems from their quite divergent metaethical views. In "The Contradiction in Ethical Egoism," Glasgow, who is certainly not a noncognitivist, states that moral convictions are not primarily expressions of wants, desires, or attitudes. Thus one can acknowledge, for example, that a certain act is one's duty, and then even "rise to duty," without really wanting to do one's duty. Thus, "it is logically possible for a person to believe that he ought to do what is in his own interest without in any way wanting to do what is in his own interest." My attitudes towards the interest of others, my desires for their well- or ill-being, my "carings" toward them, are logically independent of my moral beliefs and principles. That being the case, Glasgow concludes, there is no necessarily inconsistent *attitude* expressed by the egoistic ethic. An egoist conceivably could adopt the strict Kantian attitude towards his or her duty (see above, pages 85–89), while differing sharply with Kant, of course, about what that duty is in fact.

Nevertheless, Glasgow does share Medlin's view that there is *something* inconsistent in the ethical egoist's position. He locates that inconsistency, however, not in the egoist's attitudes, but rather in the clash between his own principle and his recognition (implied in the universal formulation of his principle) of the autonomy of other persons. Another interesting feature of Glasgow's article is his exemption from the force of his arguments of the view he calls "metaphysical egoism," the doctrine that ethical egoism is true but that God, on pain of eternal punishment, commands that we respect the autonomy of others. If metaphysical egoism is true, we all ought to behave honorably and benevolently toward one another, but only as a necessary means to our own good (our only proper ultimate aim).

Moral philosophy, as Aristotle well understood, is concerned not only with what we ought to do, and the appraisal of actions as right or wrong, but also with the evaluation of *persons* as good or bad, admirable or reprehensible, virtuous or vicious. Most moralists agree with Mill that we need know nothing of a person's *motives* in order to determine whether his action was right or wrong:

... utilitarian moralists have gone beyond almost all others in affirming that the motive has nothing to do with the morality of the action, though much with the worth of the agent [actor]. He who saves a fellow creature from drowning does what is morally right, whether his motive be duty, or the hope of being paid for his trouble; he who betrays the friend that trusts him is guilty of a [moral] crime, even if his object be to serve another friend ...[2]

Knowledge of the actor's motives might be quite essential, however, to a determination of whether he is worthy of praise or blame (or neither) for what he did.

Even morally good persons may act from blameworthy motives from time to time, and upon certain occasions even evil persons may act from praise-worthy motives. Hardly anyone is perfectly and unfailingly good or bad, and even those who come closest to ideal virtue or depravity may act (or feel, or desire) "out of character" from time to time. A person's general character, then, is determined by more than his or her particular motives at specific occasions for action. Richard Brandt, in "Character and Conscientiousness," follows Aristotle's lead in defining a trait of character (in part) as a *disposition* to be motivated in certain desirable or undesirable ways in one's conduct. A person's character, then, can be defined as the sum total of his or her character traits, and may be good in some respects (for example, conscientiousness, honesty) and poor in other respects (for example, generosity, benevolence). Brandt's account of moral praiseworthiness and blameworthiness is much more complicated than that of various writers in the Kantian tradition who think that devotion to duty (conscientiousness) is "just all that there is to good character" or else all that is relevant to a "distinctively moral" appraisal of a person. Conscientiousness, for Brandt, is one desirable character trait among others, "highly important but not the whole of good [or even morally good] character."

Elizabeth L. Beardsley's account of moral praiseworthiness and blame-worthiness, "Moral Worth and Moral Credit," is more complicated still. She argues that our ordinary judgments of praise and blame imply two irreducibly distinct standards which she chooses to call the standards of *moral worth* (positive and negative) and *moral credit* (positive and negative). Beardsley's

[2]John Stuart Mill, *Utilitarianism,* Chapter II. paragraph 19. See this volume, p. 117.

account of moral worth seems to incorporate and clarify much of Brandt's analysis. Considering only negative moral worth (blameworthiness) for the moment, we can say that a person is blameworthy for her or his act just so far as the act was a breach of a moral rule (that is, was morally wrong), was voluntary, was not done in ignorance of relevant facts, and was motivated by a bad desire, for example, the desire to hurt others, or to gain at their expense. Comparative judgments of moral worth constitute something of a problem for this analysis. We do say, for example, of equally wrong acts done by different persons that one is more blameworthy than the other. If the two acts under comparison are alike in all respects relevant to negative moral worth but one, then there is no problem, for we can say that the act that is worse in that one respect is more blameworthy. But what if John's wrong act violated a more serious moral rule than Richard's, but Richard's was closer to being *fully* voluntary (say there was a stronger element of neurotic compulsiveness in John's motivation), and further that Richard's act was done in partial ignorance of relevant facts but John's was not, whereas Richard's actuating desire was somewhat worse than John's; for example, he acted out of petty vindictiveness while John acted out of pure greed. John's action then was more blameworthy in respect to the stringency of the rule violated and his degree of awareness of the facts, whereas Richard's action was more blameworthy in respect to degree of voluntariness and the badness of the motivating desire. Which act then was the more blameworthy all told (that is, the more deficient in "moral worth")? Unless there is some way of weighing the various positive and negative worth-determining factors against one another, there would seem to be no way of answering the question, and Beardsley's single standard of moral worth would seem really to be four distinct and mutually incommensurable standards. Beardsley anticipates this theoretical difficulty, however, and argues in response to it, that in actual cases of comparative judgments there is widespread agreement which of two quite different acts is the more deficient in moral worth, so that in actual moral discourse, this kind of potential incommensurability rarely poses any problem for our judgments. Despite the ever present possibility of incommensurability, therefore, the worth-determining factors constitute a "unitary and coherent standard."

Again taking only blameworthiness for our example (putting aside praiseworthiness) we can say that persons are blameworthy by Beardsley's second standard (negative moral credit) if their actions had negative moral worth *and* to the extent that the circumstances were "unfavorable" to the performance of their acts. Just as we give persons more (positive) credit for doing worthy things that were not easy for them to do in the circumstances, so we assign persons more negative credit for doing unworthy things in circumstances that made it easy for them to refrain from doing what they did. If the circumstances made it difficult to refrain from doing the unworthy thing, we take that fact to be a "mitigating consideration" reducing the degree of discredit ("blame" in Beardsley's second sense) but not affecting the degree of negative worth ("blame" in Beardsley's first sense).

Beardsley insists that her two standards of praise-and-blameworthiness *are* genuinely independent and unavoidably incommensurable. We do often say that equally wrong, equally informed and voluntary, equally badly motivated acts are nevertheless not equally blameworthy, for the person who did the first (say) came from a broken home or was under an emotional strain. But in some cases, one person's act is somewhat more unworthy but also somewhat more mitigated by unfavorable circumstances than another person's equally wrong act. In those cases, there is no one single standard for determining comparative blameworthiness. Rather we must say simply that one action is more blameworthy by one standard and the other action is more blameworthy by another standard.

Beardsley defends her distinction between worth and credit on grounds of clarity, flexibility, and justice. But her discussion of practical applications in the final section of the article should suggest to the thoughtful reader how her distinction can also throw light on such other topics as Kant's moral psychology, ethical relativism, and the retributive theory of punishment.

One final problem of moral philosophy is suggested by the other topics of this section—egoism, the ethics of character, and the moral evaluation of persons—and serves, to some degree, to tie them together. What is the proper character and degree of self-regard? Christianity holds humility (interpreted in a special way) to be a virtue, and pride, a sin. Aristotle, in contrast, finds a place for "proper pride" in his catalogue of moral virtues. (See above, pp. 45–48.) Ethical egoism and extreme altruism, which agree about nothing else, join in maintaining that one's attitudes and duties toward oneself should be strikingly different from one's attitude and duties toward others; egoism, of course claiming priority for the self, altruism claiming priority for others. Utilitarians and Kantians, in contrast, though they agree on little else, unite in proclaiming an equality between one's own moral status and that of others. Jeremy Bentham is often quoted as stating that in the utilitarian calculation of duty, "each is to count as one, and no one as more than one," so that an actor should consider his own interests to be neither more nor less important than those of any other person likely to be affected by his action. Similarly, Kant, in the second formulation of his Categorical Imperative urges each person "to treat humanity, *whether in thine own person or in that of any other,* in every case as an end withal, never as means only." (Emphasis added. See above, pp. 99–101.) The Kantian formulation of the supreme moral law, then, also requires a respect for every person as such, oneself neither more nor less than others.

The final essay in this section, "Servility and Self-Respect," by Thomas Hill Jr., is written in the Kantian spirit. Hill takes it as given (and few readers will gainsay him in this) that excessive servility is a morally repulsive trait, and a genuine character flaw. If there is any doubt, Hill's vivid examples of "the Uncle Tom," "the Self-Deprecator," and "the Deferential Wife" should remove it. The reader should note, however, how carefully Hill defines the defect of servility, and especially how his definition excludes (as it should) self-sacrificing saints and heroes such as Broad's devoted worker in a leper colony. The servile person is not described as such because he sacrifices his own welfare; rather he is called servile because he is deficient in a very special kind of self-regard. His servility is perfectly consistent with his having an accurate (low) self-assessment of his merits and skills, and even perhaps with normal self-love. What is missing in the servile person is adequate *self-respect,* which Hill, following Kant, interprets as respect for his own *rights* as a person.

Hill's account of servility seems plausible enough up to this point, but as he himself realizes, there is something puzzling and disturbing about it. To be sure, servility, as Hill defines and analyzes it, is a character flaw, but—"The questions remains: why should anyone regard this as a moral defect? After all, the rights which [the servile person] denies are his own. He may be unfortunate, foolish, or even distasteful; but why *morally* deficient?" Hill proceeds to reconstruct, from suggestions in Kant's moral theory, a reasoned answer to this question. The duty to avoid servility, he suggests, is a *duty to oneself,* imposed upon everyone by moral principles. While different in important ways from some of the duties we have to other persons, it is similar to them in important ways too. Disrespect, indifference, or contempt for human rights is thus a dereliction of duty and a serious moral failing, whether those rights be "in thine own person" or that of another.

36. WHY BE MORAL?[1]

A. I. Melden

Our question is notoriously ambiguous and sometimes rather disturbing. It poses what appears to be a reasonable demand for a reason. But the mere demand for a reason provides no assurance that one is possible in principle, and, if it is not, any difficulty which the question occasions is best dispelled by removing the confusions that prompt the question itself. So it is, I shall argue, with that sense of the question that is apt to be most disturbing to the moral theorist because it suggests a skepticism with respect to the foundations of moral theory. To remove any possible misapprehensions concerning my thesis, however, I shall begin by stating those senses of the question with respect to which this thesis is *not* being argued. I shall then attempt to state the precise sense of the question with which I am concerned, and I shall argue that in this sense the question is, appearances to the contrary notwithstanding, impossible.

(1) I am not concerned with the silly question of why I ought to promote the good. That question answers itself. (2) The question I shall discuss is not the empirical question of what the causes are of the occurrence of the moral attitude. (3) The question is not the pragmatic question whether it is prudent or useful to be moral or to act in those ways commonly described with approval as moral. (4) I shall not discuss the familiar question of whether certain commonly accepted moral principles are morally justified. Such a question is not in general a skeptical attack against the foundations of morality; at the worst, it is a demand for a moral justification of a particular moral code. (5) The question could be construed as a theoretical question that may arise when ordinary attempts to provide moral justifications fail or when intellectual curiosity arises.[2] For what might be intended is a question having to do with the analysis of ethical terms in the light of which assured moral justifications of commonly accepted moral principles can be given. Such a question may be disturbing, for it is not easy to answer; but it poses a reasonable demand which any moral theorist, as theorist, sets out to satisfy.

There is, however, a quite different sense of the question with which I am concerned. It is commonly assumed that there are values and ideals with respect to which there are moral obligations. Now there is a sense of "moral" in which one would be described as a moral being even though the particular values and ideals he selected, and with respect to which he assumed his obligations, were defective. In this sense of the term, the moral is opposed to the non-moral or amoral, and one would be described as an amoralist if he refused to accept any moral obligations at all, however these might be specified or defined. Within this wider meaning of the term "moral" we should then distinguish between the moral in the narrower sense of right or praiseworthy and the immoral. And within the immoral we distinguish between those cases in which a person recognizes what in fact are his duties but acts in a contrary manner because of the superior strength of his inclinations and those cases in which a person acts in accordance with what, erroneously, he takes to be his duties. It follows that being moral in this wider sense is a necessary but not sufficient condition of being moral in the praiseworthy sense. What further conditions are necessary is a matter that has to do with the nature of the values and ideals selected. And whether or not agreement about these further matters is possible it will be well to agree upon a usage of "morality" (and hence of the cognate term "moral") in which we may speak of a morality of which we disapprove, because of the values selected in the determining ideal, e.g., the morality of the Nietzschean superman. For we shall want to be able to contrast an attitude of devotion to ideals of which we do not approve with what in principle at least

From A. I. Melden, "Why Be Moral?," *Journal of Philosophy,* Vol. XLV, No. 17 (August 12, 1948), pp. 449–456. Reprinted with permission of the author and the *Journal of Philosophy.*

is possible, namely, an amoral attitude in which, to consider one illustration, the only concern felt is a concern with personal satisfactions and the only attitude felt toward others is that of indifference except when they serve to promote or inhibit personal gratification. We can, therefore, put the question I propose to consider as follows: Is there any reason that can be offered that would suffice to persuade one, who was not initially disposed to do so, to be consistent in his valuations by treating as values and dis-values without regard to the locus of their occurrence those things which in his own experience he values and dis-values respectively. For to be moral in the wider sense of the term is to be consistent in one's valuations by assuming or accepting *some* obligations and by taking something to be good or bad; it is to avoid the attitude that is expressed by saying "What of it?" with respect to those matters in the experience of others about which we are concerned when they occur in our own.[3]

Unless a commitment to this principle of consistency in valuation is given, the story of the costs and consequences of dishonesty, to take one case, serves only to demonstrate that dishonesty is possible if it is not the general rule and painful if found out. Unless it is given, the argument of *The Republic* is gratuitous. For it is contended there that a man can not get away with injustice—he may escape the punishments usually imposed by his society, but he can not escape the costs which his soul must assume—but unless men are concerned with each other's wants and satisfactions, the alleged torments of the soul do not follow. Why not an amoral Gyges who is wholly indifferent to the welfare of others except when it affects his own, smugly cheerful in the harmony of soul obtained by virtue of a clever imposition of constraints upon his desires and appetites—concerned with *his* future but satisfied in his indifference to the fortunes of others? Such a conception is, at any rate, logically possible. If we protest that such a being can not be happy, do we mean anything other than either (a) we morally disapprove, (b) no man is clever enough so to conceal his total amoralism, or (c) men, by nature, can not be cheerful in their injustice because of their essential morality—because they have some propensity to be consistent in their valuations?

That we be consistent with respect to what are in fact the proper values and ideals in our valuations is assumed on any moral theory. Whether goodness be a natural or a non-natural property, it is repeatable and is to be prized for its own sake in whosesoever's experience it may occur. No ethicist has, as far as I can see, ever maintained, in any analysis or description of ethical terms or in any statement of the criteria for their proper application, that the names of particular persons are relevant. If there is any reference to persons, it is to all persons or almost all persons (as in Hume's case) or all persons of a certain type. Despite the enormous difference between a Kantian universalism and a Nietzschean ethics of the superman, it would be a mistake to deny that Nietzsche was a moralist and that between you and me, provided that we are both heroic and aggressive members of the knightly community or both weak and submissive members of the supporting class of helots, there is nothing to favor the one or the other with respect to the Nietzschean table of values and disvalues. And if a captious critic will protest that he will be consistent in his valuations, notwithstanding a total indifference to the misfortunes of others, provided that he defines values as those things which *he* prizes, we shall describe his view as an amoralism, since values, whatever else they may be, are repeatable in a way in which values, as construed by our critic, are not.

For the moralist the question, as I have stated it, is disturbing. The moralist assumes that ethical terms have meaning and application; his task is to explain something given for explanation. What is given is the datum of morality, that there are moral obligations—that, if anything is good, we ought to be consistent in prizing the kind of thing it is simply because it is good. To ask, now, for a reason for being consistent in one's valuations is to ask for something with which the moral theorist as theorist is not concerned; for it is to ask in effect why I should treat anything as good or bad and why I should accept any obligation whatsoever. And yet the question is disturbing, for in the absence of a satisfactory answer the moral theorist's program would seem to be otiose and the moral claims which we make upon one another unreasonable.

Clearly, a reason for our being consistent in our valuations can not be given in terms of logical consistency. Moral consistency is that consistency in action and attitude every breach of which attests to the *logical* possibility and consistency of a perverse *moral* inconsistency or amoralism. The principles of logic are doubly neutral toward ethics: they serve no more as criteria of moral validity than they do of truth, and in themselves they provide no more reason for adopting a moral consistency than for rejecting all consistency of action in a totally perverse, because totally indifferent, attitude to the fortunes and misfortunes of ourselves and others.

The question of the relation between the logical and the moral has been revived by C. I. Lewis in his recent Paul Carus Lectures. Lewis is concerned to repudiate the familiar view, according to which the rational is defined in terms of the principles of logical validity. On the contrary it is, according to Lewis, the converse relation that holds, and this is true where the rationality in question is that rationality that characterizes the moral attitude.

To be rational, instead of foolish or perverse, means to be capable of constraint by prevision of some future good or ill; to be amenable to the consideration, "you will be sorry if you don't," or "if you do."

Rationality, in this sense, is not derivative from the logical: rather it is the other way about. The validity of reasoning turns upon, and can be summarized in terms of consistency. And consistency is, at bottom, nothing more than the adherence throughout to what we have accepted. . . . Thinking and discoursing are important and peculiarly human ways of acting. Insofar as our actions of this sort are affected with concern for what we may later think or wish to affirm, we attempt to be consistent or rational: and when we achieve this kind of self-accord, then we are logical.[4]

Whether we are concerned with the consistency of thinking or of acting—the former logical and the latter moral consistency—in each case we have that rationality that consists in "this same attempt to avoid any attitude . . . which later must be recanted or regretted."[5] Hence,

The final and universal imperative, "Be consistent in valuation and in thought and action" . . . is one which is categorical. It requires no reason; being itself the expression of that which is the source of all reason; that in the absence of which there could be no reason of any sort or for anything.[6]

Now I should agree that there is a use of the term "rational" in which a person who is indifferent to his future in his demands on the present is said to be irrational; and there is a use of "reasonable" in which a person who is morally inconsistent by disregarding completely these very things in the lives of others which he values in his own would be said to be unreasonable. "Being reasonable" does often mean being morally consistent. But it would be well to note that the imperative "Be morally consistent" is categorical only on the proviso that the values and ideals selected are adequate, whatever the criteria and analysis of moral adequacy or validity may be; for we should be morally justified in refusing to say to a Nietzschean "Be morally consistent," knowing the values he prizes and the ideal to which he subscribes. "Be moral!" is categorical only where "moral" is used in the common praiseworthy sense. But it is very doubtful that the rationality that consists in being morally principled can be assimilated with that rationality in whose absence, as Lewis puts it, "there could be no reason of any sort or for anything."

(1) The contention that consistency of thought and of action are "at bottom" the same, namely, "the adherence throughout to what we have accepted" rests upon a confusion of two senses of "consistency of thought." In one sense consistency of thought is a *practical* consistency or consistency of thought—the maintenance, throughout a period of time, of the same attitude of assertion towards a given proposition.[7] In another sense, it consists in a logical relation between the propositions asserted, the absence of which is logical contradiction. In the logical sense it is just false to say that consistency is "at bottom nothing more than the adherence throughout to what we have accepted"; one can be practically inconsistent or inconstant when, for example, one changes one's mind, and in this case there need be no logical inconsistency in any assertion actually made. It is this confusion that leads Lewis to assert that "if it were not that present valuing and doing may later be a matter of regret, then there would be no point and no imperative to consistency of any kind." For supposing our concern with the future provided the only reason for being constant in our willing and doing, it would not follow that without that con-

cern there would be no point to logical consistency. For the imperative "Be logically consistent," all that is necessary is that a person be willing to say anything at all and this could be satisfied by one who is indifferent to the future or by one who is not rational in that sense in which "to be rational means to be capable of constraint by prevision of some future good or ill." (2) But it is misleading, surely, to suggest that our concern for the future does provide us with a sufficient reason for being consistent in any sense. It might well be that in our concern for the future we will be inconstant in our willing and doing by abandoning just those courses of action that jeopardize our future. Indeed, consistency in the sense of constancy is not moral consistency at all. For even if in my concern for my future I avoid any attitude which I shall later recant, by a practical consistency or constancy of willing and doing, I could do this in the manner of an amoral Gyges who orders his appetites by circumspect application of constraints designed with a view to the future. What is required for moral consistency is that we be concerned with what will happen and is now happening to others, as we are with what affects us, whether in the present or in the future. In short, nothing less than a moral concern—a concern consistently applied to all loci of values—will support the moral attitude; and if, as Lewis rightly urges that we do, we look within ourselves for the reasons that impel us to adopt the moral attitude, the only reason that can suffice is that which can not serve as a reason because it is the datum of the commitment to morality itself.

There are those who would appeal to metaphysics at this point. But the mere appeal to an intelligence to see goodness and duty writ large in the nature of the real will not suffice. Indeed, nothing in this respect can be gained that has not already been conceded in the recognition of the truism that we ought to promote the good. A Gyges, however persuaded he may be to accept these demonstrations, will pay his intellectual respects but ignore his moral responsibilities unless he can be shown that the kind of life which he desires is impossible. But the metaphysical arguments designed to demonstrate such impossibility are highly precarious, and the empirical generalization, upon which the arguments for the pragmatic values of the adoption of the moral attitude must rest, presupposes conditions contrary to those given in the case of our hypothetical amoralist and hence are irrelevant to his special case. For if such a person were not concerned with others and hence with the ideal of a community of persons, it would not follow that he would suffer any slights and discomforts by viewing the misfortunes of others. For us, the inducement is genuine; we do want to participate in a community, and given such a concern, happiness, or well-being is not genuinely possible unless we take account of others in our evaluations. But this is not to say that being moral is useful; it serves, rather, as a reminder of our basic morality and of the fact that we will not be able to ignore or expunge it in any attempt to realize any end.

For a thoroughly amoral intelligence, nothing in principle can serve as a reason for *inducing* him to accept any moral responsibilities. Metaphysical elaborations, logical arguments, empirical generalization and data and, finally, all moral discourse with its lavish, complex, and ingenious devices of persuasion are wholly inadequate. No reasons are possible. To conclude, however, that the moral attitude, since it can not be supported by any reason, is unreasonable is to confuse the present case in which no reason in principle is possible with the familiar situation in which reasons, while possible, are not forthcoming. Indeed, the moral attitude requires no reason since it *defines*, implicitly, what it means to be reasonable in our attitude toward others.[8] To be reasonable in one's valuations entails being morally consistent, and it is simply to confuse the meanings of "reason" to suppose that the sense in which people are reasonable when they adopt the moral attitude is reducible to or analyzable in terms of those other senses of "reason" in which logical arguments, causes, purposes, etc., are commonly said to provide reasons. Nothing short of the moral commitment can provide a "reason" for the commitment in question; no reason can be offered for being morally reasonable and none may reasonably be requested.

How then shall we argue with one who challenges us to persuade him to adopt the moral attitude? We have, here, no theoretical issue, but a practical problem. He will not incur logical contradiction by resisting the effects of our discourse in the way in which this would occur in the case of one who disputed the principle of logic. And if his discourse is more than a clever intellectual game we shall take all the steps necessary to ensure us from harm. For this we have a reason that is sufficient, namely, a moral justification.

But if a consistent amoralism is to be maintained, no moral attitude must be evidenced by the use of hortative language. As Lewis has rightly observed,[9] the amoralist can not solicit us to share his amoral attitude, for this will betray the so-called amoralist's concern for us; once he does this he has committed himself in practice to what he denies in theory. He must not moralize or apologize. Just as we need only provoke one who denies the principle of logic to an assertion in order to affect his persuasion, so we need only provoke the professing amoralist to express his concern for others in his concern to persuade us. And the fact is that we are social beings. We may fail in our duties and forget our moral commitments, but we will betray our persistent, even though interrupted, moralism in every attempt to rationalize to others our indifference to our obligations. Why then be moral? This is, appearances to the contrary notwithstanding, no theoretical question. For the *practical* problem it poses, we can offer no theoretical compulsion, but only the datum of morality itself, a practical necessity, in the absence of which nothing else will or can do.

NOTES

1. Read at the meeting of the American Philosophical Association, Pacific Division, University of California at Los Angeles, Dec. 30, 1947.

2. This is the question with which Plato is concerned in *The Republic.* Cf. A. E. Taylor's discussion of this point in "The Right and the Good," *Mind,* N.S., No. 48.

3. I do not intend the identification of the selfish with the amoral. The unprincipled emotionalism of the chief character in Chekhov's short story *The Darling* serves to remind us that sympathy as a particular feeling or sentiment is not the sentiment of morality, for it may occur capriciously, or, as we sometimes say, without rhyme or reason. What is intended by "amoral" in this context is an attitude in which valuation is capricious or oriented by some capriciously accepted rule or principle. This may be the selfish rule that the values in question count only when they occur in my own experience; it may be the sentimental rule that the values in question must occur in the experience of one to whom I am emotionally attached, or it may be a rule as capricious as any you please. In any case, what will be evidenced in all such cases is an attitude of indifference to values and dis-values except when they occur in arbitrarily or capriciously selected circumstances. For an amoralist will recognize that what he prizes in some special context occurs also outside this context; he will not moralize by arguing that the difference in context makes a moral difference since he will, as I have defined the term, dismiss all moral responsibility with a contemptuous "What of it?"

4. C. I. Lewis, *An Analysis of Knowledge and Valuation,* Open Court, p. 480.

5. *Ibid.*

6. *Ibid.,* p. 481.

7. The term "constancy" was suggested to me by Professor D. S. Mackay.

8. This, indeed, is the contention of Lewis, but it requires no dubious identification of the morally rational with the logically rational to secure its acceptance.

9. *Op. cit.,* p. 482.

37. EGOISM AS A THEORY OF HUMAN MOTIVES

C. D. Broad

There seem *prima facie* to be a number of different kinds of ultimate desire which all or most men have. Plausible examples would be the desire to get pleasant experiences and to avoid unpleasant ones, the desire to get and exercise power over others, and the desire to do what is right and to avoid doing what is wrong. Very naturally philosophers have tried to reduce this plurality. They have tried to show that there is one and only one kind of ultimate desire, and that all other desires which seem at first sight to be ultimate are really subordinate to this. I shall call the view that there really are several different kinds of ultimate desire *Pluralism of Ultimate Desires,* and I shall call the view that there is really only one kind of ultimate desire *Monism of Ultimate Desires.* Even if a person were a pluralist about ultimate desires, he might hold that there are certain important features common to all the different kinds of ultimate desire.

Now much the most important theory on this subject is that all kinds of ultimate desire are *egoistic.* This is not in itself necessarily a monistic theory. For there might be several irreducibly different kinds of ultimate desire, even if they were all egoistic. Moreover, there might be several irreducibly different, though not necessarily unrelated, senses of the word 'egoistic'; and some desires might be egoistic in one sense and some in another, even if all were egoistic in some sense. But the theory often takes the special form that the only kind of ultimate desire is the desire to get or to prolong pleasant experiences, and to avoid or to cut short unpleasant experiences, for oneself. That *is* a monistic theory. I shall call the wider theory *Psychological Egoism,* and this special form of it *Psychological Hedonism.*

From *Ethics and the History of Philosophy* (London: Routledge & Kegan Paul Ltd., 1952), pp. 218–231. Reprinted with permission of the publisher.

Psychological Egoism might be true, even though psychological hedonism were false; but, if psychological egoism be false, psychological hedonism cannot be true.

I shall now discuss Psychological Egoism. I think it is best to begin by enumerating all the kinds of desire that I can think of which might reasonably be called 'egoistic' in one sense or another.

(1) Everyone has a special desire for the continued existence of himself in his present bodily life, and a special dread of his own death. This may be called *Desire for Self-preservation.* (2) Everyone desires to get and to prolong experiences of certain kinds, and to avoid and to cut short experiences of certain other kinds, because the former are pleasant to him and the latter unpleasant. This may be called *Desire for one's own Happiness.* (3) Everyone desires to acquire, keep, and develop certain mental and bodily powers and dispositions, and to avoid, get rid of, or check certain others. In general he wants to be or to become a person of a certain kind, and wants not to be or to become a person of certain other kinds. This may be called *Desire to be a Self of a certain kind.* (4) Everyone desires to feel certain kinds of emotion towards himself and his own powers and dispositions, and not to feel certain other kinds of reflexive emotion. This may be called *Desire for Self-respect.* (5) Everyone desires to get and to keep for himself the exclusive possession of certain material objects or the means of buying and keeping such objects. This may be called *Desire to get and to keep Property.* (6) Everyone desires to get and to exercise power over certain other persons, so as to make them do what he wishes, regardless of whether they wish it or not. This may be called *Desire for Self-assertion.* (7) Everyone desires that other persons shall believe certain things about him and feel certain kinds of emotion towards him.

He wants to be noticed, to be respected by some, to be loved by some, to be feared by some, and so on. Under this head come the *Desire for Self-display,* for *Affection,* and so on.

Lastly, it must be noted that some desires, which are concerned primarily with other things or persons, either would not exist at all or would be very much weaker or would take a different form if it were not for the fact that those things or persons already stand in certain relations to oneself. I shall call such relations *egoistic motive-stimulants.* The following are among the most important of these. (i) The relation of ownership. If a person owns a house or a wife, e.g. he feels a much stronger desire to improve the house or to make the woman happy than if the house belongs to another or the woman is married to someone else. (ii) Blood-relationship. A person desires, e.g. the well-being of his own children much more strongly than that of other children. (iii) Relations of love and friendship. A person desires strongly, e.g. to be loved and respected by those whom he loves. He may desire only to be feared by those whom he hates. And he may desire only very mildly, if at all, to be loved and respected by those to whom he feels indifferent. (iv) The relationship of being fellow-members of an institution to which one feels loyalty and affection. Thus, e.g. an Englishman will be inclined to do services to another Englishman which he would not do for a foreigner, and an Old Etonian will be inclined to do services to another Old Etonian which he would not do for an Old Harrovian.

I think that I have now given a reasonably adequate list of motives and motive-stimulants which could fairly be called 'egoistic' in some sense or other. Our next business is to try to classify them and to consider their inter-relations.

(1) Let us begin by asking ourselves the following question. Which of these motives could act on a person if he had been the only person or thing that had ever existed? The answer is that he could still have had desires for *self-preservation,* for *his own happiness,* to be a *self of a certain kind,* and for *self-respect.* But he could not, unless he were under the delusion that there were other persons or things, have desires for *property,* for *self-assertion,* or for *self-display.* Nor could he have any of those desires which are stimulated by family or other alio-relative re-

lationships. I shall call those desires, and only those, which could be felt by a person who knew or believed himself to be the only existent in the universe, *Self-confined.*

(2) Any desire which is not self-confined may be described as *extra-verted;* for the person who has such a desire is necessarily considering, not only himself and his own qualities, dispositions, and states, but also some other thing or person. If the desire is egoistic, it will also be *intro-verted;* for the person who has such a desire will also be considering himself and his relations to that other person or thing, and this will be an essential factor conditioning his experience. Thus a self-confined desire is purely intro-verted, whilst a desire which is egoistic but not self-confined is both intro-verted and extra-verted. Now we may subdivide desires of the latter kind into two classes, according as the primary emphasis is on the former or the latter aspect. Suppose that the person is concerned primarily with himself and his own acts and experiences, and that he is concerned with the other thing or person only or mainly as an object of these acts or experiences or as the other term in a relationship to himself. Then I shall call the desire *Self-centred.* I shall use the term *Self-regarding* to include both desires which are self-centred and those which are self-confined. Under the head of self-centred desires come the desire for *property,* for self-assertion, for *self-display,* and for *affection.*

(3) Lastly, we come to desires which are both intro-verted and extra-verted, but where the primary emphasis is on the other person or thing and its states. Here the relationship of the other person or thing to oneself acts as a strong egoistic motive-stimulant, but one's primary desire is that the other person or thing shall be in a certain state. I will call such desires *Other-regarding.* A desire which is other-regarding, but involves an egoistic motive-stimulant, may be described as *Self-referential.* The desire of a mother to render services to her own children which she would not be willing to render to other children is an instance of a desire which is other-regarding but self-referential. So, too, is the desire of a man to inflict suffering on one who has injured him or one whom he envies.

Having thus classified the various kinds of egoistic desire, I will now say something about their inter-relations.

(1) It is obvious that self-preservation may be desired as a necessary condition of one's own happiness; since one cannot acquire or prolong pleasant experiences unless one continues to exist. So the desire for self-preservation *may* be subordinate to the desire for one's own happiness. But it seems pretty clear that a person often desires to go on living even when there is no prospect that the remainder of his life will contain a balance of pleasant over unpleasant experiences. This attitude is expressed very strongly in the loathsome lines of Maecenas which Seneca has handed down to posterity:

Debilem facito manu, debilem pede coxo
tuber adstrue gibberum, lubricos quate dentes;
vita dum superest, bene est; hanc mihi, vel acuta
si sedeam cruce, sustine.

(2) It is also obvious that property and power over others may be desired as a means to self-preservation or to happiness. So the desire to get and keep property, and the desire to get and exert power over others, *may* be subordinate to the desire for self-preservation or for one's own happiness. But it seems fairly certain that the former desires are sometimes independent of the latter. Even if a person begins by desiring property or power only as a means—and it is very doubtful whether we always do begin in that way—it seems plain that he often comes to desire them for themselves, and to sacrifice happiness, security, and even life for them. Any miser, and almost any keen politician, provides an instance of this.

It is no answer to this to say that a person who desires power or property enjoys the experiences of getting and exercising power or of amassing and owning property, and then to argue that therefore his ultimate desire is to give himself those pleasant experiences. The premiss here is true, but the argument is self-stultifying. The experiences in question are pleasant to a person only in so far as he desires power or property. This kind of pleasant experience presupposes desires for something other than pleasant experiences, and therefore the latter desires cannot be derived from desire for that kind of pleasant experience.

Similar remarks apply to the desire for self-respect and the desire for self-display. If one already desires to feel certain emotions towards oneself, or to be the object of certain emotions in others, the experience of feeling those emotions or of knowing that others feel them towards one will be pleasant, because it will be the fulfilment of a pre-existing desire. But this kind of pleasure presupposes the existence of these desires, and therefore they cannot be derived from the desire for that kind of pleasure.

(3) Although the various kinds of egoistic desire cannot be reduced to a single ultimate egoistic desire, e.g. the desire for one's own happiness, they are often very much mixed up with each other. Take, e.g. the special desire which a mother feels for the health, happiness, and prosperity of her children. This is predominantly other-regarding, though it is self-referential. The mother is directly attracted by the thought of her child as surviving, as having good dispositions and pleasant experiences, and as being the object of love and respect to other persons. She is directly repelled by the thought of his dying, or having bad dispositions or unpleasant experiences, or being the object of hatred or contempt to other persons. The desire is therefore other-regarding. It is self-referential, because the fact that it is *her* child and not another's acts as a powerful motive-stimulant. She would not be prepared to make the same sacrifices for the survival or the welfare of a child which was not her own. But this self-referential other-regarding motive is almost always mingled with other motives which are self-regarding. One motive which a woman has for wanting her child to be happy, healthy and popular is the desire that other women shall envy her as the mother of a happy, healthy and popular child. This motive is subordinate to the self-centred desire for self-display. Another motive, which may be present, is the desire not to be burdened with an ailing, unhappy, and unpopular child. This motive is subordinate to the self-contained desire for one's own happiness. But, although the self-referential other-regarding motive is nearly always mixed with motives which are self-centred or self-confined, we cannot plausibly explain the behaviour of many mothers on many occasions towards their children without postulating the other-regarding motive.

We can now consider the various forms which Psychological Egoism might take. The most rigid form is that all human motives are ultimately egoistic, and that all egoistic motives are ultimately of one kind. That one kind has generally been supposed to be the desire for one's own happiness, and so this form of Psychological Egoism may in practice be identified with Psychological Hedonism. This theory amounts to saying that the only ultimate motives are *self-confined,* and that the only ultimate self-confined motive is *desire for one's own happiness.*

I have already tried to show by examples that this is false. Among self-confined motives, e.g. is the desire for self-preservation, and this cannot be reduced to desire for one's own happiness. Then, again, there are self-regarding motives which are self-centred but not self-confined, such as the desire for affection, for gratitude, for power over others, and so on. And, finally, there are motives which are self-referential but predominantly other-regarding, such as a mother's desire for her children's welfare or a man's desire to injure one whom he hates.

It follows that the only form of Psychological Egoism that is worth discussing is the following. It might be alleged that all ultimate motives are *either* self-confined *or* self-centred *or* other-regarding but self-referential, some being of one kind and some of another. This is a much more modest theory than, e.g. Psychological Hedonism. I think that it covers satisfactorily an immensely wide field of human motivation, but I am not sure that it is true without exception. I shall now discuss it in the light of some examples.

Case A. Take first the case of a man who does not expect to survive the death of his present body, and who makes a will, the contents of which will be known to no one during his lifetime.

(1) The motive of such a testator cannot possibly be the expectation of any experiences which he will enjoy after death through the provisions of his will being carried out; for he believes that he will have no more experiences after the death of his body. The only way in which this motive could be ascribed to such a man is by supposing that, although he is intellectually convinced of his future extinction, yet in practice he cannot help imagining himself as surviving and witnessing events which will happen after his death. I think that this kind of mental confusion is possible, and perhaps not uncommon; but I

should doubt whether it is a plausible account of such a man's motives to say that they all involve this mistake.

(2) Can we say that his motive is the desire to enjoy during his life the pleasant experience of imagining the gratitude which the beneficiaries will feel towards him after his death? The answer is that this may well be *one* of his motives, but it cannot be primary, and therefore cannot be the only one. Unless he desired to be thought about in one way rather than another after his death, the present experience of imagining himself as becoming the object of certain retrospective thoughts and emotions on the part of the beneficiaries would be neither attractive nor repulsive to him.

(3) I think it is plain, then, that the ultimate motive of such a man cannot be desire for his own happiness. But it might be desire for power over others. For he may be said to be exercising this power when he makes his will, even though the effects will not begin until after his death.

(4) Can we say that his motive in making the will is simply to ensure that certain persons will think about him and feel towards him in certain ways after his death? In that case his motive would come under the head of self-display. (This must, of course, be distinguished from the question, already discussed, whether his motive might be to give himself the pleasant experience of imagining their future feelings of gratitude towards him.) The answer is that self-display, in a wide sense, may be a motive, and a very strong one, in making a will; but it could hardly be the sole motive. A testator generally considers the relative needs of various possible beneficiaries, the question whether a certain person would appreciate and take care of a certain picture or house or book, the question whether a certain institution is doing work which he thinks important, and so on. In so far as he is influenced by these considerations, his motives are other-regarding. But they may all be self-referential. In making his will he may desire to benefit persons only in so far as they are *his* relatives or friends. He may desire to benefit institutions only in so far as *he* is or has been a member of them. And so on. I think that it would be quite plausible to hold that the motives of such a testator are all either self-regarding or self-referential, but that it would not be in the least plausible to say that

they are all self-confined or that none of them are other-regarding.

Case B. Let us next consider the case of a man who subscribes anonymously to a certain charity. His motive cannot possibly be that of self-display. Can we say that his motive is to enjoy the pleasant experience of self-approval and of seeing an institution in which he is interested flourishing? The answer is, again, that these motives may exist and may be strong, but they cannot be primary and therefore cannot be his only motives. Unless he wants the institution to flourish, there will be nothing to attract him in the experience of seeing it flourish. And, unless he subscribes from some other motive than the desire to enjoy a feeling of self-approval, he will not obtain a feeling of self-approval. So here, again, it seems to me that some of his motives must be other-regarding. But it is quite possible that his other-regarding motives may all be self-referential. An essential factor in making him want to benefit this institution may be that it is *his* old college or that a great friend of *his* is at the head of it.

The question, then, that remains is this. Are there any cases in which it is reasonable to think that a person's motive is not egoistic in any of the senses mentioned? In practice, as we now see, this comes down to the question whether there are any cases in which an other-regarding motive is not stimulated by an egoistic motive-stimulus, i.e. whether there is any other-regarding motive which is not also and essentially self-referential.

Case C. Let us consider the case of a person who deliberately chooses to devote his life to working among lepers, in the full knowledge that he will almost certainly contract leprosy and die in a particularly loathsome way. This is not an imaginary case. To give the Psychological Egoist the longest possible run for his money I will suppose that the person is a Roman Catholic priest, who believes that his action may secure for him a place in heaven in the next world and a reputation for sanctity and heroism in this, that it may be rewarded posthumously with canonization, and that it will redound to the credit of the church of which he is an ordained member.

It is difficult to see what self-regarding or self-referential motives there could be *for* the action beside desire for happiness in heaven, desire to

gain a reputation for sanctity and heroism and perhaps to be canonized after death, and desire to glorify the church of which one is a priest. Obviously there are extremely strong self-confined and self-centred motives *against* choosing this kind of life. And in many cases there must have been very strong self-referential other-regarding motives *against* it. For the person who made such a choice must sometimes have been a young man of good family and brilliant prospects, whose parents were heart-broken at his decision, and whose friends thought him an obstinate fool for making it.

Now there is no doubt at all that there was an other-regarding motive, viz. a direct desire to alleviate the sufferings of the lepers. No one who was not dying in the last ditch for an over-simple theory of human nature would deny this. The only questions that are worth raising about it are these. (1) Is this other-regarding motive stimulated by an egoistic motive-stimulus and thus rendered self-referential? (2) Suppose that this motive had not been supported by the various self-regarding and self-referential motives *for* deciding to go and work among the lepers, would it have sufficed, in presence of the motives *against* doing so, to ensure the choice that was actually made?

As regards the first question, I cannot see that there was any special pre-existing relationship between a young priest in Europe and a number of unknown lepers in Asia which might plausibly be held to act as an egoistic motive-stimulus. The lepers are neither his relatives nor his friends nor his benefactors nor members of any community or institution to which he belongs.

As regards the sufficiency of the other-regarding motive, whether stimulated egoistically or not, in the absence of all self-regarding motives tending in the same direction, no conclusive answer can be given. I cannot prove that a single person in the whole course of history *would* have decided to work among lepers, if all the motives against doing so had been present, whilst the hope of heaven, the desire to gain a reputation for sanctity and heroism, and the desire to glorify and extend one's church had been wholly absent. Nor can the Psychological Egoist prove that *no* single person would have so decided under these hypothetical conditions. Factors which cannot be eliminated cannot be shown to be necessary and cannot be shown to be superfluous; and there we must leave the matter.

I suspect that a Psychological Egoist might be tempted to say that the intending medical missionary found the experience of imagining the sufferings of the lepers intensely unpleasant, and that his primary motive for deciding to spend his life working among them was to get rid of this unpleasant experience. This, I think, is what Locke, e.g. would have had to say in accordance with his theory of motivation. About this suggestion there are two remarks to be made.

(1) This motive cannot have been primary, and therefore cannot have been the only motive. Unless this person desired that the lepers should have their sufferings alleviated, there is no reason why the thought of their sufferings should be an unpleasant experience to him. A malicious man, e.g. finds the thought of the sufferings of an enemy a very pleasant experience. This kind of pleasure presupposes a desire for the well-being or the ill-being of others.

(2) If his primary motive were to rid himself of the unpleasant experience of imagining the sufferings of the lepers, he could hardly choose a less effective means than to go and work among them. For the imagination would then be replaced by actual sense-perception; whilst, if he stayed at home and devoted himself to other activities, he would have a reasonably good chance of diverting his attention from the sufferings of the lepers. In point of fact one knows that such a person would reproach himself in so far as he managed to forget about the lepers. He would *wish* to keep them and their sufferings constantly in mind, as an additional stimulus to doing what he believes he ought to do, viz. to take active steps to help and relieve them.

In this connexion it is important to notice the following facts. For most people the best way to realize the sufferings of strangers is to imagine oneself or one's parents or children or some intimate and beloved friend in the situation in which the stranger is placed. This, as we say, 'brings home to one' his sufferings. A large proportion of the cruelty which decent people applaud or tolerate is applauded or tolerated by them only because they are either too stupid to put themselves imaginatively into the position of the victims or because they deliberately re-

frain from doing so. One important cause of their deliberately refraining is the notion of retributive justice, i.e. the belief that these persons, or a group taken as a collective whole to which they belong, have *deserved* suffering by wrongdoing, and the desire that they shall get their deserts. Another important cause of this deliberate refrainment is the knowledge that one is utterly powerless to help the victims. However this may be, the fact that imagining oneself in their position is often a necessary condition of desiring to relieve the sufferings of strangers does not make that desire self-referential. Imagining oneself in their place is merely a condition for becoming vividly *aware of* their sufferings. Whether one will then desire to relieve them or to prolong them or will remain indifferent to them, depends on motives which are not primarily self-regarding or self-referential.

I will now summarize the results of this discussion.

(1) If Psychological Egoism asserts that all ultimate motives are self-confined; or that they are all either self-confined or self-centred, some being of one kind and some of the other; or that all self-confined motives can be reduced to the desire for one's own happiness, it is certainly false. It is not even a close approximation to the truth.

(2) If it asserts that all ultimate motives are either self-regarding or self-referential, some being of one kind and some of the other; and that all other-regarding motives require a self-referential stimulus, it is a close approximation to the truth. It is true, I think, that in most people and at most times other-regarding motives are very weak unless stimulated by a self-referential stimulus. As England's wisest and wittiest statesman put it in his inimitable way: 'Temporal things will have their weight in the world, and, though zeal may prevail for a time and get the better in a skirmish, yet the war endeth generally on the side of flesh and blood, and will do so until mankind is another thing than it is at present.'[1]

(3) Nevertheless, Psychological Egoism, even in its most diluted form, is very doubtful if taken as a universal proposition. Some persons at some times are strongly influenced by other-regarding motives which cannot plausibly be held to be stimulated by a self-referential stim-

ulus. It seems reasonable to hold that the presence of these other-regarding motives is *necessary* to account for their choice of alternatives which they do choose, and for their persistence in the course which they have adopted, though this can never be conclusively established in any particular case. Whether it is also *sufficient* cannot be decided with certainty, for self-regarding and self-referential components are always present in one's total motive for choosing such an action.

I think that the summary which I have just given fairly represents the results of introspection and reflection on one's own and other men's voluntary action. Yet Psychological Egoism in general and Psychological Hedonism in particular have seemed almost self-evident to many highly intelligent thinkers, and they do still seem highly plausible to nearly everyone when he first begins to speculate on human motivation. I believe that this depends, not on empirical facts, but on certain verbal ambiguities and misunderstandings. As so often happens in philosophy, clever people accept a false general principle on *a priori* grounds and then devote endless labour and ingenuity to explaining away plain facts which obviously conflict with it. A full discussion of the subject would require an analysis of the confusions which have made these theories seem so plausible; but this must be omitted here.

I must content myself with the following remarks in conclusion. I have tried to show that Psychological Egoism, in the only form in which it could possibly fit the facts of human life, is not a monistic theory of motives. On this extended interpretation of the theory the only feature common to all motives is that every motive which can *act on* a person has one or another of a large number of different kinds of special *reference to* that person. I have tried to show that this certainly covers a very wide field, but that it is by no means certain that there is even this amount of unity among *all* human motives. I think that Psychological Egoism is much the most plausible attempt to reduce the *prima facie* plurality of ultimate kinds of desire to a unity. If it fails, I think it is most unlikely that any alternative attempt on a different basis will succeed.

For my part I am inclined to accept an irreducibly pluralistic view of human motives. This does not, of course, entail that the present irreducible plurality of ultimate motives may not have evolved, in some sense of that highly ambiguous word, out of fewer, either in the history of each individual or in that of the human race. About that I express no opinion here and now.

Now, if Psychological Hedonism had been true, all conflict of motives would have been between motives of the *same kind*. It would always be of the form 'Shall I go to the dentist and certainly be hurt now but probably avoid thereby frequent and prolonged toothache in future? Or shall I take the risk in order to avoid the certainty of being hurt by the dentist now?' On any pluralistic view there is also conflict between motives of irreducibly *different kinds,* e.g. between aversion to painful experience and desire to be thought manly, or between a desire to shine in conversation and aversion to hurting a sensitive person's feelings by a witty but wounding remark.

It seems to me plain that, in our ordinary moral judgments about ourselves and about others, we always unhesitatingly assume that there can be and often is conflict between motives of radically different kinds. Now I do not myself share that superstitious reverence for the beliefs of common sense which many contemporary philosophers profess. But I think that we must start from them, and that we ought to depart from them only when we find good reason to do so. If Psychological Hedonism, or any other monistic theory of motives had been true, we should have had to begin the study of Ethics by recognizing that most moral judgments which we pass on ourselves or on others are made under a profound misapprehension of the psychological facts and are largely vitiated thereby. If Psychological Hedonism, e.g. had been true, the only ethical theory worth discussing would have been an egoistic form of Ethical Hedonism. For one cannot be under an obligation to attempt to do what is psychologically impossible. And, on the hypothesis of Psychological Hedonism, it is psychologically impossible for anyone ultimately to desire anything except to prolong or acquire experiences which he knows or expects to be pleasant and to cut short or avoid experiences which he knows or expects to be unpleasant. If it were still possible to talk of having duties at all, each person's duties would be confined within the limits which that psychological impossibility marks out. And it would clearly be impossible to suppose that any part of anyone's ultimate motive for doing any act is his belief that it would be right in the circumstances together with his desire to do what is right as such. For, if Psychological Hedonism were true, a desire to do what is right could not be ultimate, it must be subordinate to the desire to get or prolong pleasant experiences and to avoid or cut short unpleasant ones.

NOTE

1. Halifax: *The Character of a Trimmer.*

38. *ULTIMATE PRINCIPLES AND ETHICAL EGOISM*

Brian Medlin

I believe that it is now pretty generally accepted by professional philosophers that ultimate ethical principles must be arbitrary. One cannot derive conclusions about what should be merely from accounts of what is the case; one cannot decide how people ought to behave merely from one's knowledge of how they do behave. To arrive at a conclusion in ethics one must have at least one ethical premiss. The premiss, if it be in turn a conclusion, must be the conclusion of an argument containing at least one ethical premiss. And so we can go back, indefinitely but not for ever. Sooner or later, we must come to at least one ethical premiss which is not deduced but baldly asserted. Here we must be a-rational; neither rational nor irrational, for here there is no room for reason even to go wrong.

But the triumph of Hume in ethics has been a

From Brian Medlin, "Ultimate Principles and Ethical Egoism," *Australasian Journal of Philosophy,* Vol. 35 (1957), pp. 111–118. Reprinted with permission of the author and the *Australasian Journal of Philosophy.*

Now it is plain that such consequences as these conflict sharply with common-sense notions of morality. If we had been obliged to accept Psychological Egoism, in any of its narrower forms, on its merits, we should have had to say: 'So much the worse for the common-sense notions of morality!' But, if I am right, the morality of common sense, with all its difficulties and incoherences, is immune at least to attacks from the basis of Psychological Egoism.

limited one. What appears quite natural to a handful of specialists appears quite monstrous to the majority of decent intelligent men. At any rate, it has been my experience that people who are normally rational resist the above account of the logic of moral language, not by argument—for that can't be done—but by tooth and nail. And they resist from the best motives. They see the philosopher wantonly unravelling the whole fabric of morality. If our ultimate principles are arbitrary, they say, if those principles came out of thin air, then anyone can hold any principle he pleases. Unless moral assertions are statements of fact about the world and either true or false, we can't claim that any man is wrong, whatever his principles may be, whatever his behaviour. We have to surrender the luxury of calling one another scoundrels. That this anxiety flourishes because its roots are in confusion is evident when we consider that we don't call people scoundrels, anyhow, for being mistaken about their facts. Fools, perhaps, but that's another matter. Nevertheless, it doesn't become us to be high-up. The layman's uneasiness, however irrational it may be, is very natural and he must be reassured.

People cling to objectivist theories of morality from moral motives. It's a very queer thing that by doing so they often thwart their own purposes. There are evil opinions abroad, as anyone who walks abroad knows. The one we meet with most often, whether in pub or parlour, is the doctrine that everyone should look after himself. However refreshing he may find it after the high-minded pomposities of this morning's editorial, the good fellow knows this doctrine is wrong and he wants to knock it down. But while he believes that moral language is used to make statements either true or false, the best he can do is to claim that what the egoist says is false. Unfortunately, the egoist can claim that it's true. And since the supposed fact in question between them is not a publicly ascertainable one, their disagreement can never be resolved. And it is here that even good fellows waver, when they find they have no refutation available. The egoist's word seems as reliable as their own. Some begin half to believe that perhaps it is possible to supply an egoistic basis for conventional morality, some that it may be impossible to supply any other basis. I'm not going to try to prop up our conventional morality, which I fear to be a task beyond my strength, but in what follows I do want to refute the doctrine of ethical egoism. I want to resolve this disagreement by showing that what the egoist says is inconsistent. It is true that there are moral disagreements which can never be resolved, but this isn't one of them. The proper objection to the man who says 'Everyone should look after his own interests regardless of the interests of others' is not that he isn't speaking the truth, but simply that he isn't speaking.

We should first make two distinctions. This done, ethical egoism will lose much of its plausibility.

1. UNIVERSAL AND INDIVIDUAL EGOISM

Universal egoism maintains that everyone (including the speaker) ought to look after his own interests and to disregard those of other people except in so far as their interests contribute towards his own.

Individual egoism is the attitude that the egoist is going to look after himself and no one else. The egoist cannot promulgate that he is going to look after himself. He can't even preach that he *should* look after himself and preach this alone. When he tries to convince me that he should look after himself, he is attempting so to dispose me that I shall approve when he drinks my beer and steals Tom's wife. I cannot approve of his looking after himself and himself alone without so far approving of his achieving his happiness, regardless of the happiness of myself and others. So that when he sets out to persuade me that he should look after himself regardless of others, he must also set out to persuade me that I should look after him regardless of myself and others. Very small chance he has! And if the individual egoist cannot promulgate his doctrine without enlarging it, what he has is no doctrine at all.

A person enjoying such an attitude may believe that other people are fools not to look after themselves. Yet he himself would be a fool to tell them so. If he did tell them, though, he wouldn't consider that he was giving them *moral* advice. Persuasion to the effect that one should ignore the claims of morality because morality doesn't pay, to the effect that one has insufficient selfish motive and, therefore, insufficient motive for moral behaviour is not moral persuasion. For this reason I doubt that we should call the individual egoist's attitude an ethical one. And I don't doubt this in the way someone may doubt whether to call the ethical standards of Satan "ethical" standards. A malign morality is none the less a morality for being malign. But the attitude we're considering is one of mere contempt for all moral considerations whatsoever. An indifference to morals may be wicked, but it is not a perverse morality. So far as I am aware, most egoists imagine that they are putting forward a doctrine in ethics, though there may be a few who are prepared to proclaim themselves individual egoists. If the good fellow wants to know how he should justify conventional morality to an individual egoist, the answer is that he shouldn't and can't. Buy your car elsewhere, blackguard him whenever you meet, and let it go at that.

2. CATEGORICAL AND HYPOTHETICAL EGOISM

Categorical egoism is the doctrine that we all ought to observe our own interests, *because that is what we ought to do.* For the categorical egoist the egoistic dogma is the ultimate principle in ethics.

The hypothetical egoist, on the other hand, maintains that we all ought to observe our own interests, because. . . . If we want such and such an end, we must do so and so (look after ourselves). The hypothetical egoist is not a real egoist at all. He is very likely an unwitting utilitarian who believes mistakenly that the general happiness will be increased if each man looks wisely to his own. Of course, a man may believe that egoism is enjoined on us by God and he may therefore promulgate the doctrine and observe it in his conduct, not in the hope of achieving thereby a remote end, but simply in order to obey God. But neither is *he* a real egoist. He believes, ultimately, that we should obey God, even should God command us to altruism.

An ethical egoist will have to maintain the doctrine in both its universal and categorical forms. Should he retreat to hypothetical egoism he is no longer an egoist. Should he retreat to individual egoism his doctrine, while logically impregnable, is no longer ethical, no longer even a doctrine. He may wish to quarrel with this and if so, I submit peacefully. Let him call himself what he will, it makes no difference. I'm a philosopher, not a rat-catcher, and I don't see it as my job to dig vermin out of such burrows as individual egoism.

Obviously something strange goes on as soon as the ethical egoist tries to promulgate his doctrine. What is he doing when he urges upon his audience that they should each observe his own interests and those interests alone? Is he not acting contrary to the egoistic principle? It cannot be to his advantage to convince them, for seizing always their own advantage they will impair his. Surely if he does believe what he says, he should try to persuade them otherwise. Not perhaps that they should devote themselves to his interests, for they'd hardly swallow that; but that everyone should devote himself to the service of others. But is not to believe that someone should act in a certain way to try to persuade him

to do so? Of course, we don't always try to persuade people to act as we think they should act. We may be lazy, for instance. But in so far as we believe that Tom should do so and so, we have a tendency to induce him to do so and so. Does it make sense to say: "Of course you should do this, but for goodness' sake don't"? Only where we mean: "You should do this for certain reasons, but here are even more persuasive reasons for not doing it." If the egoist believes ultimately that others should mind themselves alone, then, he must persuade them accordingly. If he doesn't persuade them, he is no universal egoist. It certainly makes sense to say: "I know very well that Tom should act in such and such a way. But I know also that it's not to my advantage that he should so act. So I'd better dissuade him from it." And this is just what the egoist must say, if he is to consider his own advantage and disregard everyone else's. That is, he must behave as an individual egoist, if he is to be an egoist at all.

He may want to make two kinds of objection here:

1. That it will not be to his disadvantage to promulgate the doctrine, provided that his audience fully understand what is to their ultimate advantage. This objection can be developed in a number of ways, but I think that it will always be possible to push the egoist into either individual or hypothetical egoism.

2. That it is to the egoist's advantage to preach the doctrine if the pleasure he gets out of doing this more than pays for the injuries he must endure at the hands of his converts. It is hard to believe that many people would be satisfied with a doctrine which they could only consistently promulgate in very special circumstances. Besides, this looks suspiciously like individual egoism in disguise.

I shall say no more on these two points because I want to advance a further criticism which seems to me at once fatal and irrefutable.

Now it is time to show the anxious layman that we have means of dealing with ethical egoism which are denied him; and denied him by just that objectivism which he thinks essential to morality. For the very fact that our ultimate principles must be arbitrary means they can't be anything we please. Just because they come out of thin air they can't come out of hot air. Because these principles are not propositions about matters of fact and cannot be deduced from propositions about matters of fact, they must be the fruit of our own attitudes. We assert them largely to modify the attitudes of our fellows but by asserting them we express our own desires and purposes. This means that we cannot use moral language cavalierly. Evidently, we cannot say something like 'All human desires and purposes are bad'. This would be to express our own desires and purposes, thereby committing a kind of absurdity. Nor, I shall argue, can we say 'Everyone should observe his own interests regardless of the interests of others'.

Remembering that the principle is meant to be both universal and categorical, let us ask what kind of attitude the egoist is expressing. Wouldn't that attitude be equally well expressed by the conjunction of an infinite number of avowals thus?—

I want myself to come out on top	and	I don't care about Tom, Dick, Harry. . .
and		and
I want Tom to come out on top	and	I don't care about myself, Dick, Harry. . .
and		and
I want Dick to come out on top	and	I don't care about myself, Tom, Harry. . .
and		and
I want Harry to come out on top	and	I don't care about myself, Dick, Tom . . .
etc.		etc.

From this analysis it is obvious that the principle expressing such an attitude must be inconsistent.

But now the egoist may claim that he hasn't been properly understood. When he says 'Everyone should look after himself and himself alone', he means 'Let each man do what he wants regardless of what anyone else wants'. The egoist may claim that what he values is merely that he and Tom and Dick and Harry should each do what he wants and not care about what anyone else may want and that this doesn't involve his principle in any inconsistency. Nor need it. But even if it doesn't, he's no better off. Just what does he value? Is it the well-being of himself,

Tom, Dick and Harry or merely their going on in a certain way regardless of whether or not this is going to promote their well-being? When he urges Tom, say, to do what he wants, is he appealing to Tom's self-interest? If so, his attitude can be expressed thus:

I want myself to be happy		I want myself not to care
and	and	about Tom, Dick,
I want Tom to be happy		Harry . . .

We need go no further to see that the principle expressing such an attitude must be inconsistent. I have made this kind of move already. What concerns me now is the alternative position the egoist must take up to be safe from it. If the egoist values merely that people should go on in a certain way, regardless of whether or not this is going to promote their well-being, then he is not appealing to the self-interest of his audience when he urges them to regard their own interests. If Tom has any regard for himself at all, the egoist's blandishments will leave him cold. Further, the egoist doesn't even have his own interest in mind when he says that, like everyone else, he should look after himself. A funny kind of egoism this turns out to be.

Perhaps now, claiming that he is indeed appealing to the self-interest of his audience, the egoist may attempt to counter the objection of the previous paragraph. He may move into "Let each man do what he wants and let each man disregard what others want when their desires clash with his own". Now his attitude may be expressed thus:

I want everyone to be happy	and	I want everyone to disregard the happiness of others when their happiness clashes with his own.

The egoist may claim justly that a man can have such an attitude and also that in a certain kind of world such a man could get what he wanted. Our objection to the egoist has been that his desires are incompatible. And this is still so. If he and Tom and Dick and Harry did go on as he recommends by saying 'Let each man disregard the happiness of others, when their happiness conflicts with his own', then assuredly they'd all be completely miserable. Yet he wants them to be happy. He is attempting to counter this by saying that it is merely a fact about the world that they'd make one another miserable by going on as he recommends. The world could conceivably have been different. For this reason, he says, this principle is not inconsistent. This argument may not seem very compelling, but I advance it on the egoist's behalf because I'm interested in the reply to it. For now we don't even need to tell him that the world isn't in fact like that. (What it's like makes no difference.) Now we can point out to him that he is arguing not as an egoist but as a utilitarian. He has slipped into hypothetical egoism to save his principle from inconsistency. If the world were such that we always made ourselves and others happy by doing one another down, then we could find good utilitarian reasons for urging that we should do one another down.

If, then, he is to save his principle, the egoist must do one of two things. He must give up the claim that he is appealing to the self-interest of his audience, that he has even his own interest in mind. Or he must admit that, in the preceding conjunction, although 'I want everyone to be happy' refers to ends, nevertheless 'I want everyone to disregard the happiness of others when their happiness conflicts with his own' can refer only to means. That is, his so-called ultimate principle is really compounded of a principle and a moral rule subordinate to that principle. That is, he is really a utilitarian who is urging everyone to go on in a certain way so that everyone may be happy. A utilitarian, what's more, who is ludicrously mistaken about the nature of the world. Things being as they are, his moral rule is a very bad one. Things being as they are, it can only be deduced from his principle by means of an empirical premiss which is man-

ifestly false. Good fellows don't need to fear him. They may rest easy that the world is and must be on their side and the best thing they can do is be good.

It may be worth pointing out that objections similar to those I have brought against the egoist can be made to the altruist. The man who holds that the principle 'Let everyone observe the interests of others' is both universal and categorical can be compelled to choose between two alternatives, equally repugnant. He must give up the claim that he is concerned for the well-being of himself and others. Or he must admit that, though 'I want everyone to be happy' refers to ends, nevertheless 'I want everyone to disregard his own happiness when it conflicts with the happiness of others' can refer only to means.

I have said from time to time that the egoistic principle is inconsistent. I have not said it is contradictory. This for the reason that we can, without contradiction, express inconsistent desires and purposes. To do so is not to say anything like 'Goliath was ten feet tall and not ten feet tall'. Don't we all want to eat our cake and have it too? And when we say we do we aren't asserting a contradiction. We are not asserting a contradiction whether we be making an avowal of our attitudes or stating a fact about them. We all have conflicting motives. As a utilitarian exuding benevolence I want the man who mows my landlord's grass to be happy, but as a slug-a-bed I should like to see him scourged. None of this, however, can do the egoist any good. For we assert our ultimate principles not only to express our own attitudes but also to induce similar attitudes in others, to dispose them to conduct themselves as we wish. In so far as their desires conflict, people don't know what to do. And, therefore, no expression of incompatible desires can ever serve for an ultimate principle of human conduct.

39. THE CONTRADICTION IN ETHICAL EGOISM

W. D. Glasgow

Ethical egoism is the doctrine that the agent has but one duty, viz., to produce for himself the greatest balance of good over evil. Such a theory is quite compatible with what is ordinarily regarded as the highest standards of human conduct. It is possible, that is, for the egoist to be considerate and benevolent to others, especially if he considers it to be in his own best interest to be so. In this paper I wish to point out what I consider to be the basic defect of this theory.

Brian Medlin, in an influential paper, suggests that the principle of ethical egoism itself involves inconsistency.[1] He argues in the following way: Any such principle expresses an attitude, and in asserting the principle we are trying to modify the attitudes of our fellows. At the same time, we are also expressing our own desires and purposes. But what kind of attitude is the egoist expressing? Medlin contends that his attitude can be expressed "by the conjunction of any infinite number of avowals" thus

A		B
I want myself to come out on top	*and*	I don't care about Tom, Dick, Harry . . .
and		*and*
I want Tom to come out on top	*and*	I don't care about myself, Dick, Harry. . .
and		*and*
I want Dick to come out on top	*and*	I don't care about myself, Tom, Harry . . .
and		*and*
I want Harry to come out on top	*and*	I don't care about myself, Dick, Tom . . .
etc.		*etc.*

From W. D. Glasgow, "The Contradiction in Ethical Egoism," *Philosophical Studies*, Vol. 19 (1968), pp. 81–85. Reprinted with permission of the editor of *Philosophical Studies*.

From this analysis it is obvious that the principle expressing such an attitude must be inconsistent.

This seems to me to be a rather old explication of the ethical egoist's position. In the first place, the egoist may well believe that "coming out on top" does not represent what is in his own best interest. After all, the Thrasymachean conception of self-interest is not the only possible one. Again, the second column does not necessarily follow from the principle of ethical egoism. As I have suggested in my first paragraph, the egoist may consider it to be in his own best interest to care for Tom, Dick, and Harry. Thirdly, it is logically possible for a person to believe that he *ought* to do what is in his own interest, without in any way *wanting* to do what is in his own interest. Medlin does not in these avowals bring out the important point that ethical egoism is a normative theory. To do so he would have to rewrite his series of avowals thus:

A		B
I ought to do what is in my own interest (coming out on top?)	*and*	I may or may not care about Tom, Dick, Harry . . .
and		*and*
Tom ought to do what is in his own interest	*and*	Tom may or may not care about myself, Dick, Harry . . .
and		*and*
Dick ought to do what is in his own interest	*and*	Dick may or may not care about myself, Tom, Harry
etc.		*etc.*

Now this revision does help to bring out the inconsistency that there is in ethical egoism. The egoist argues that Tom, Dick, Harry, in fact everyone, *ought* to look after his own interest. To say this is to grant at least that there are other human beings who are autonomous. By an autonomous individual is meant an individual who has the ability to consider the possibilities of action that are open to him in a particular situation, who can deliberate upon each of these possibilities, in the sense that he can weigh up the reasons for and against actualizing any given possibility, and who can come to a decision which he has the ability to carry out. But it is quite possible for the individual to be autonomous in this sense, and yet deliberate, decide, and act within the confines of his own wants. Such would be the characterization of the prudent man. He would accept others, whom he could regard as autonomous in the sense outlined above, only insofar as they promote or impede his own interest. Their value to him would be instrumental not intrinsic. Such an attitude would be consistent with that implied in Column B.

Yet the ethical egoist, as portrayed in Column A, does not seem to accept this position. He agrees that there are other autonomous individuals, in the sense that there are individuals who can deliberate, decide, and act as the prudent man deliberates, decides, and acts. But he wants to say more than this. In stressing the normative character of his principle 'everyone *ought* to . . .' he is recognizing that the judgments and actions of other individuals can be rationally justified, just as he himself can justify his own judgments and actions. In emphasizing that everyone must look after 'his own interest' he is acknowledging that the wants of others can provide reasons for action for them, just as his own wants can provide reasons for action for him. So in believing that *every* rational agent ought to behave in a certain way, viz., look after his own interest, he implies that he, as a rational agent, is willing to consider seriously, and sometimes accept, the judgments, and the resultant actions, of other rational individuals. That is, he accepts the view that the possession of rationality confers upon him the ability to regard acceptable reasons for others as being also acceptable reasons for him.

There is, however, a problem here that is peculiar to the ethical egoist. In what way are such reasons 'acceptable' to the egoist if they support a judgment and resultant action that is against the egoist's own best interest? In such a case he may 'accept' the reasonableness of the

judgment: he may be willing to say, for example, that Tom ought to do X, even though to do X is against his own best interest. He cannot, however, advise Tom to do X, since to do so would be to encourage Tom to do something which from the egoist's point of view would be immoral. In fact, it is his duty to encourage Tom *not* to do X. So he finds himself in the position of recognizing that Tom ought to do X, but *advising* Tom that he ought not to do X. But if the egoist recognizes that Tom ought to do X, then he implies that he would approve of Tom's doing X. This, however, he cannot do, since he would be approving of something not in his own best interest—a position logically intolerable for the ethical egoist. The egoist, therefore, cannot really accept in any full-blooded sense that in a case of conflict of interests, Tom ought to do X. He seems, in fact, driven to use the word 'ought' in his own highly individual and emasculated sense. If, however, he insists that he is using ordinary language in Column A, then in recognizing that Tom ought to do X, he must concede that in so doing he is *respecting* the autonomy of Tom. But respect for the autonomy of Tom is not consistent with ethical egoism. There is, after all, for the egoist but one autonomous individual (himself) who is also an end in himself. To respect the autonomy of other individuals is to give up this position. Therefore, a study of Column A alone, which surely makes explicit the essence of the doctrine of ethical egoism reveals inconsistency.

It now becomes apparent where the inconsistency of which Medlin speaks lies. To the nonegoist, who interprets ethical egoism in terms of ordinary moral concepts, it seems that in the statement of his doctrine, the ethical egoist implies that all autonomous (or potentially autonomous) individuals are ends in themselves. But it is also basic to his position to deny this, in making out that, apart from himself, there are no autonomous individuals who are also ends in themselves. The inconsistency, mentioned above, is indeed a contradiction.

It might, of course, be possible for the egoist to make his position consistent. He can do so only by changing the logic of the language of morals. For example, he might stipulate that first-person 'ought' statements have prescriptive force, in contrast to second-person and third-person 'ought' statements which for him would have none. By making such a distinction, the egoist, as I have hinted above, could recognize the autonomy of another person, without respecting it. The contradiction would disappear, but what else would disappear with it? The doctrine of ethical egosim itself?

There is, however, one type of ethical egoism which remains unscathed by my strictures. This I shall call metaphysical egoism. In it the egoist believes in a personal God, who has ultimate power and will to grant him eternal life, or to punish him everlastingly, according to whether or not he carries out His will. He believes that it is part of God's will that we humans should love one another. Now the egoist who has these beliefs, allied with his basic normative principle, will see before him two logically possible alternatives—salvation or damnation. He must, of course, aim at the salvation of his own soul, just because his principle, translated into Christian terms, is that everyone ought to aim at his own salvation. This aim can be achieved by carrying out God's will. Now an important part of God's will is, apparently, that each of us should respect the autonomy of other individuals, that is, treat them as ends in themselves. The metaphysical egoist, therefore, unlike the other type of ethical egoist I have considered, can be consistent in his treatment of other individuals: he need not at any time deny the respect due to others. By behaving in this way to other individuals, he is at the same time achieving what is in his own best interest—his own salvation. He is the only type of ethical egoist who will acknowledge the existence of a Kingdom of Ends.

NOTES

1. Brian Medlin, "Ultimate Principles and Ethical Egoism," *Australasian Journal of Philosophy,* 35:111–18 (August 1957). [Reprinted here, p. 460.]

40. *CHARACTER AND CONSCIENTIOUSNESS*

Richard B. Brandt

Two further notions play an important role in our moral assessments: character and conscientiousness. The first is of particular interest if we are right in our suggestion that it is involved in the concept of the reprehensible or the morally admirable. The second, again, is of great interest because various philosophers have thought that actions are reprehensible if and only if they show deficiency in conscientiousness (interest in doing one's duty), and that

From Richard B. Brandt, *Ethical Theory: The Problems of Normative and Critical Ethics* © 1959. Reprinted by permission of Prentice-Hall, Inc., Englewood Cliffs, N.J.

they are morally admirable only if they show conscientiousness of a high degree.

CHARACTER

A person's "character" may be defined as "all his traits of character." Therefore the central job is to explain the phrase "trait of character," or "character trait."

In speaking of a "trait of character" we have in mind the usage by which we say that either honesty or dishonesty is a trait of character, whereas intelligence or energy is not. Thus, we are using "trait of character" in such a way that bad traits (dishonesty) as well as good ones can be traits of character.[1] At the same time, we are using it in a sufficiently narrow sense that intelligence does not count as a trait of character. Our usage, probably, is by far the most natural one. If someone asks us to write him about the "character" of a prospective employee, he is not asking us to write about his intelligence or his energy level; and he is asking us to tell about both good and bad traits of character.

What, then, can we say about the meaning of "trait of character"? The first thing is that a trait of character is a special kind of *trait of personality,* in the sense in which "trait of personality" is used by psychologists. But what is a "trait of personality"? First of all, it is a response-tendency of a person in the broad sense in which being soluble in water may be said to be a response-tendency of a piece of sugar. It is a response-tendency of a person in such a sense that to say that something has a certain response-tendency is to say that, if it is in certain specified circumstances, it will or will probably or very frequently behave in a certain way. For instance, being irritable is a response-tendency of a person: To say of a man that he is irritable is to say that if he is placed in a certain typical situation (the description of which may be complex), then, at least very often, he will get angry. Or again, being energetic is a response-tendency of a person: To say of a person that he is energetic is to say that in some conditions, for example, after hours of work of a kind to tire out most people, he is still active and ready to do more things. To say that something is a "trait of personality," then, is in part to say that it is a response-tendency of a person in this sense. But what specific kinds of response-tendencies of a person will count as traits of personality? Psychologists do not regard the disposition to have knee-reflexes as a "trait of personality." A trait of personality is concerned somehow with the person *as a whole.* Being energetic, then, even though to be so may be a purely physical characteristic, is counted as a trait of personality; a specific skill like capacity to play the piano is not counted as a trait. Nor is a specific affection for a particular person counted as such. A trait is, at least normally, something we can describe by a sentence beginning with "He is" followed by an adjective such as "humble" or "cruel" or "absent-minded" or "affable." A trait of personality must also be a *relatively enduring* response-tendency of the whole per-

son; thus, homesickness does not count as a trait of personality, although the lack of independence from which perhaps it springs is so classified.

A trait of character, we have said, is a special kind of trait of personality. But what kind? The first thing to notice is that people do identify certain traits, and not others, as traits of character. Among examples of traits of character are virtues such as courage, self-control, generosity, and fairness. In contrast, there are other traits of personality that would be universally denied to be traits of character: intelligence, energy, and a sense of humor. Most people are probably uncertain how to classify certain other traits of personality: for example, caution, excitability, orderliness, self-confidence, shyness, tact, and so on.

Are there any properties that distinguish the traits of personality generally agreed to be traits of character, from those generally agreed not to be? Yes, there are two properties that all character traits have. Many or most noncharacter traits of personality have neither of them, at least to any marked degree; and no noncharacter trait appears to have them both.

The first is that traits of character are either social assets or social liabilities, usually important ones. That a man is reliable and responsible —that he can be counted on to fulfill his commitments or role, irrespective of impulses or inconveniences or distractions—is an important and favorable fact about him, from the point of view of society and interpersonal relations. That he is generous, in the broad sense—interested in others and glad of their welfare and success, not perpetually concerned about putting himself forward—is an important and favorable fact about him, one that helps make life with him tolerable and pleasant. That he is courageous will mean that support can be expected of him when large issues are at stake and the personal risks considerable. And so on for the other qualities that we ordinarily count as good traits of character; the "virtues" are assets for living, usually important ones. The "vices," on the other hand—such as dishonesty, selfishness, cowardice—are always liabilities for living, usually serious ones.[2]

There is a second feature that traits we classify as traits of character have in common. The having of them, or at least behavior as if we had any one of them, is within our voluntary control at least in the sense that we could have behaved as if we had them if our desires or interests had been what they really should be.[3] Can we act honestly if we wish? Of course: all we need do is pay our debts, refrain from deceit, and so on. Can we act generously if we wish? We can pay regard to the welfare of others; we can make gifts. Most noncharacter traits are different. We cannot act intelligently on order. We cannot become gay or effervescent just because we want to; we can try, and to some extent we can succeed, but if we are not naturally gay, we shall need histrionic skill in order to act as if we were.

It is this feature of traits of character that makes it possible for us to feel strong indignation, contempt, and disgust toward a person on account of behavior that shows a defect of character. It is true that there are traits of personality (not character) that makes us dislike people; perhaps we dislike a person who is always glum and cheerless. But attitudes like indignation and contempt are at least less sharp and stinging when we think a person could not have acted differently no matter how hard he tried, no matter how different his interests.

Noncharacter traits never have both these features. Energy, for instance, is an important feature of personality; but it may be expended in useless activities or antisocial channels, and it is not within our control. A sense of humor is, to be sure, an asset for living; but it is hardly an important one, and whether we have it is not a matter we can control.

Can we say, then, that what we *mean* by "trait of character" is "trait of personality that is either an asset or a liability for social living, and is within our control to a high degree"? Certainly not in the sense of *overt* meaning . . ., in the sense of "same meaning" . . ., perhaps we do. What we can be most sure of, however, is that the things we *call* traits of character have these properties; and that traits of personality that we do not ordinarily call traits of character do not have them both.

Is a person's *motivation* in any way related to his traits of character? This is an important question, for we suggested, a few pages back, that whether an action is reprehensible or morally admirable depends largely if not entirely on its motivation. The connection is close. We cannot say that every kind of motivation is an ex-

pression of character (desire for food or drink, for instance, is not), but many kinds of motivation are. In fact, *any* kind of motivation on account of which an action can be accounted reprehensible or morally admirable is of this kind. For instance, suppose a deed is reprehensible because it failed to be motivated by regard for the welfare of other persons—say, some selfish act that injured others. But the disposition to ignore the welfare of others—a readiness not to be motivated by thought of injury to them—is precisely a trait of character: one we call "selfishness." Or consider, again, the case of the widow's mite. We praise her act because she was motivated to give, by the thought of the plight of others, money that she needed badly herself. Her doing so showed something about her—concern for others—which again is precisely a trait of character: generosity or sympathy. In general, if we pick out that defect in a person's motivation that we regard as the reason why his action is properly called reprehensible, we shall find that the disposition to be so motivated is something we recognize as a trait of character.

It is for this reason that it is plausible to suggest, in our definition of "reprehensible," that something can be reprehensible only if it would not have occurred but for a defect of character.

CONSCIENTIOUSNESS

Many people have thought that conscientiousness is central among traits of character. Some think, in fact, that conscientiousness is just all that there is to good character. Others think that the conscientiousness shown in an act is the only thing that affects whether the act is admirable or reprehensible in a "distinctively moral sense." In order to assess these views, it is necessary to get clear what conscientiousness is.

It may be helpful first to consider what we mean by "conscience." We often speak of having a "bad conscience" about something and of "consulting our conscience." What does such talk mean? When a person has a bad conscience about something, he cannot now justify to himself (by whatever means he uses) what he did; he can find no fully satisfactory excuse for it; when he reflects on the matter he feels guilty or remorseful ("conscience-smitten") about it.

Again, when a person "consults his conscience," what he does is reflect about the courses of action open to him and their compatibility with valid moral principles; perhaps he reconsiders what are the valid principles relevant to the issue. Or, he may consider whether he feels obligated to do one thing rather than another, and whether he will probably feel remorse afterwards if he does do it. There is another pair of phrases. One is: "He has *no* conscience." What this means is that the person in question is not given to appraising his past conduct morally or caring about whether contemplated conduct is morally acceptable, that he feels no guilt or shame when he thinks of his misconduct and does not allow moral considerations to affect his plans. Conversely, we sometimes say of someone, "He has a conscience." We assert thereby the opposite state of affairs.

Webster defines "conscientious" as meaning "governed by, or conformed to, a strict regard to the dictates of conscience, or by the known or supposed rules of right and wrong." A conscientious person, then, is one strongly motivated to avoid doing anything he thinks wrong, and who is willing to make considerable sacrifice to do what he thinks is right. He is also one who is scrupulously careful to be sure that his conduct *is* right; he is constantly on the alert about the moral justifiability of what he does or plans to do. By implication, then, he is a person who stands ready to behave in ways obviously required by moral principle: he will do his fair share, will be respectful of the rights of others, and so on.

Let us keep to the core meaning of "conscientious," as strong motivation to do one's duty. Let us ask ourselves what is the relation to conscientiousness in this sense to the other virtues, like unselfishness, kindness, generosity, thrift, prudence, self-control, honesty, and truthfulness. Since language contains all these many different terms, there is prima facie reason for thinking there are corresponding differences between these concepts, and that conscientiousness is not the only virtue, or lack of it the only vice. But then exactly what is the difference between it and the other virtues? (1) The other virtues are tendencies to act in rather more specific ways. For instance, honesty is essentially scrupulous regard for moral principles in certain areas, particularly property relations, and unwillingness to deceive in order to gain advantage. Conscientiousness is broader and less definite; it is scrupulousness about conforming to moral principle in general. (2) A person having one of the more specific traits is a person who is disposed to act in a certain way *from habit,* that is, without necessarily reflecting on whether a certain sort of action is morally required. A generous person, for instance, "instinctively" inclines to certain forms of behavior, without noticing that moral principle requires him to do so. Being conscientious is not a settled "habit" of behaving in some specific way.

These differences between conscientiousness and the other virtues explain why conscientiousness is *not* the whole of good character, for we approve of being moved to generous, sympathetic acts independently of the thought of duty, and we think there is something lacking in a person who does not have a direct impulse to do certain things in response to the plight of other human beings but does them only because he thinks he ought to. Why should we feel this way? Possibly one reason is that a man can be conscientious and still act wrongly. He may be unintelligent and come to strange conclusions about what is his duty; or he may be imperceptive, not responsive to the welfare of others, particularly in its subtler aspects. On the other hand, if he has the other virtues, he is much less likely to come to mistaken conclusions about his duty, and he will not be imperceptive. Clearly, to be courteous, generous, kind, modest, reasonable, sympathetic, tolerant, truthful, and uncomplaining—to be any of these is in some particular way to have developed a sensitivity and responsiveness to some aspect of human beings or human relations, or something worthwhile, that can be counted upon to make one's judgments about one's obligations more sensitive and reliable.

In saying this we should not forget, however, that conscientiousness is supremely important. If a person had all the other virtues but failed in conscientiousness, it would be unfortunate, indeed, for the very thing that we think distinctively good about some of the virtues other than conscientiousness is also a defect. Take generosity. We suggested that we value an immediate responsiveness to the plight of others, unmediated by any feeling of obligation. But such generosity can be misplaced: impulsive generosity may lead to action in conflict with the best interests, or the long-range interests, not only of the donor but the recipient of bene-factions. Generosity needs to be directed by knowledge of the facts, by intelligent application of sound moral principles. Impulsive generosity may suffer from defects of thoughtlessness.

Conscientiousness, then, is highly important but not the whole of good character. It might still be held, however, that behavior is never reprehensible (or admirable) "in the specifically moral sense" except as it manifests defect (or perfection) of conscientiousness. However, to hold this is a mistake. We must concede that serious faults of behavior are rare, when there is no deficiency of conscientiousness. Nev-ertheless, a conscientious man may be blind to the problems of others; he may be insensitive and mistaken on some moral principles. Hence, he may, for instance, make harsh demands of uprightness and not spare his condemnation when others fail; he may fail in modesty or in tolerance; and so on. And such behavior is rep-rehensible in the "specifically moral sense."

NOTES

1. We do not always speak in this way. When we say that somebody is a "man of character," what we mean is that he is a man with markedly *good* traits of character (in our sense). We are not using "character" in this sense.
2. We can define "virtue" as a "desirable trait of char-acter" and "vice" as an "undesirable trait of character."
3. In most cases such behavior is "within our voluntary control" in a stronger sense than that "we could have . . . if our desires had been different," as the remainder of this paragraph makes clear. Not in all, however. Consider un-selfishness. Can we now, if we wish, behave in all the ways typical of unselfishness, even if we are not unselfish? No: for instance, we cannot produce on order the ideas that would occur to a really unselfish person, or the feelings which a really unselfish person would have. What is the difference, then, between unselfishness and intelligence? The answer is that unselfishness is more within our "voluntary control" in the sense that *most* behavior characteristic of unselfishness is open to us even as we are, and that *all* of it would be possible for us if our *interests* were different.

41. *MORAL WORTH AND MORAL CREDIT*[1]

Elizabeth L. Beardsley

Judgments of moral praise and blame have al-ways occupied a central place in the study of ethics. In these metaethical times interest cen-ters in analyses of the meaning of such key terms as "praiseworthy" and "blameworthy."[2] Al-though the present paper will not contribute directly to the formulation of such an analysis, I hope that its results may be of service indirectly to this undertaking and can perhaps be assimi-lated in a variety of different analyses. My con-cern here is not with any phenomenal constitu-ents that judgments of moral praise and blame may have but rather with the standards which govern moral appraisals of this kind. I shall maintain that the terms "praiseworthy" and "blameworthy" are in ordinary usage applied to agents for two significantly different kinds of reason.[3] I shall also try to show that these two kinds of reasons point to the operation of two different standards for moral praise and blame. The alternative view, that only one standard governs our judgments of moral praise and blame, has some plausibility and apparently has been widely held; but it has not been very rig-orously examined. I shall claim that the two-standard interpretation is more successful in ac-

From E. L. Beardsley, "Moral Worth and Moral Credit," *The Philosophical Review,* Vol. 66 (1957), pp. 304–328. Re-printed by permission of *The Philosophical Review.*

counting for certain key features of our moral appraisals as they now stand. And I shall argue also that our moral appraisals will gain in clarity, flexibility, and above all in simple justice, if the distinction between the two standards involved is drawn more sharply than is sometimes the case at present.

I shall not deal here with the question whether there is an ambiguity in the actual meaning of the terms "praiseworthy" and "blameworthy" or whether we should say rather that the terms have the same meaning in all contexts but are applied in accordance with two different standards. In order to avoid intolerably complicated locutions, I shall sometimes speak of two different "attributes" of blameworthiness and of two different "attributes" of praiseworthiness, as well as of two different "kinds" of judgments of moral praise and blame. But it should be understood that my basic intention is to leave open fundamental questions of analysis of meaning.

In what follows I shall first describe one standard for applying the terms "praiseworthy" and "blameworthy," a standard which is in essentials familiar, having been described in recent ethical literature. Necessary and sufficient conditions for the presence of blameworthiness and praiseworthiness judged by this standard will be given. I shall then try to show that the terms "praiseworthy" and "blameworthy" are also very commonly applied in a second way, a way which involves the use of a different standard of appraisal; again, necessary and sufficient conditions for the presence of blameworthiness and praiseworthiness judged by the second standard will be given. I shall maintain that to distinguish carefully between the two standards will enable us to avoid ethical confusions of some seriousness and to explore certain features of our moral appraisals in a fruitful way.

One further preliminary remark should be made. It may be that a careful examination of expressions using the term "praise" and expressions using the term "blame" would reveal that these terms are not always exact antonyms.[4] In this paper, however, they will be treated as such. At times it will not be necessary to make explicit parallel comments for both praiseworthiness and blameworthiness; at such times, for the sake of brevity, comments pertaining to only one of them will be made. But, although I

may not always say that corresponding comments could be made about the other, this should be understood to be the case wherever no explicit assertion to the contrary is added.

I

I shall begin by proposing a set of necessary and sufficient conditions for the presence of blameworthiness and a set of necessary and sufficient conditions for the presence of praiseworthiness, as judged by one familiar standard.[5] An agent X is blameworthy to some degree for his act A if and only if: (1) act A is a breach of a moral rule, (2) act A was performed voluntarily, (3) agent X, in performing A, was not acting in ignorance of relevant facts, and (4) the desire felt by X which was dominant in causing him to commit act A was in that situation a bad desire.[6] And an agent X is praiseworthy to some degree for his act B if and only if: (1) act B is an exemplification of a moral rule or injunction, (2) act B was performed voluntarily, (3) agent X in performing B was not acting in ignorance of relevant facts, and (4) the desire felt by X which was dominant in causing him to commit act B was in that situation a good desire. For convenience, I shall refer to this set of conditions for the presence of blameworthiness as the "B_1 set," or "B_1 conditions," and to the corresponding set of conditions for the presence of praiseworthiness as the "P_1 set," or "P_1 conditions." The moral attribute which is present in an agent under B_1 conditions will be called 'B_1 blameworthiness"; agents who have B_1 blameworthiness will be called "B_1 blameworthy"; and judgments of blame which ascribe B_1 blameworthiness to an agent will be called "B_1 judgments." A similar terminology will be used for the moral attribute which is present in agents under P_1 conditions.

That many of the judgments of moral praise and blame made every day are made by the standard just described, that is, are B_1 and P_1 judgments, seems to me quite undeniable. We say, "Certainly John is to blame for that tactless remark: he knew perfectly well that it would hurt Ruth's feelings, and as a matter of fact he wanted to hurt her." Again, we say, "George deserves praise for his contribution to that fund for needy students—you know he really doesn't want to be thanked in public, he just wants to help boys who are having trouble in making ends meet." Judgments of this kind are entirely familiar to everyone.

Our P_1 and B_1 sets of conditions have been introduced as conditions for praiseworthiness and blameworthiness in agents on account of acts; but they can also be regarded as constituting a characteristic of value attaching to acts themselves. I shall call this general characteristic "moral worth," and shall say that the statement "Act A has positive moral worth to some degree" ("is morally worthy to some degree") means "The P_1 conditions for act A and its agent are satisfied." Similarly, "Act B has negative moral worth to some degree" ("is morally unworthy to some degree") means "The B_1 conditions for act B and its agent are satisfied." These definitions establish a usage only for ascribing moral worth to acts.

It is clear that we often make comparative judgments of praise and blame on grounds that introduce no factors other than those already included in the B_1 and P_1 conditions. We say, for example, that Anne deserves more blame for cheating in school than Sarah does, because Anne's actuating desire was to make trouble for her teacher, whereas Sarah's was simply to avoid trouble for herself. Those comparative judgments of blame which are made on grounds that do not go beyond the factors involved in the B_1 conditions are based on considerations of three kinds. These are: (1) the seriousness of the breach of a common moral rule (e.g., grand larceny as compared with petty larceny), (2) the stringency of the moral rule broken (e.g., a broken promise as compared with a lie), and (3) the badness of the actuating desire in its situation (e.g., the desire to hurt another as compared with the desire to avoid pain for oneself). Corresponding considerations govern the presence of degrees of P_1 praiseworthiness. All these factors are at the same time, of course, factors which determine the presence of different degrees of moral worth (positive or negative) in acts. It will be convenient to speak of them as "worth-determining factors."

Let us now see how we can formulate conditions for the presence of degrees of B_1 blameworthiness and P_1 praiseworthiness. It will not be necessary to work this out for both attributes. We can say that an agent X is more B_1 blameworthy for his act A than is agent Y for his act B if the following conditions hold: (1) X is B_1 blameworthy to some degree for act A; (2) Y is B_1 blameworthy to some degree for act B; and (3) one of the following is the case: either (a) A and B are equally serious breaches of their respective moral rules (these rules may of course coincide), and the rules broken are equally stringent, but A is committed from a desire worse in its situation than the desire from which B is committed; or (b) A and B are breaches of equally stringent moral rules and committed from desires equally bad in their respective situations, but A is a more serious breach of its moral rule than B is; or (c) A and B are equally serious breaches of their moral rules and committed from desires equally bad in their respective situations, but A breaks a more stringent moral rule than does B. This set of conditions will be referred to as the "extended B_1 conditions," and the corresponding set for degrees of P_1 praiseworthiness will be called the "extended P_1 conditions." Judgments ascribing degrees of praiseworthiness or blameworthiness on the basis of the extended P_1 conditions or the extended B_1 conditions will be called 'P_1 judgments of degree" and "B_1 judgments of degree." The expression "Act A has a greater degree of positive moral worth than act B" ("is morally more worthy than act B") means "The extended P_1 conditions for acts A and B and their agents are satisfied." The expression "Act C has a greater degree of negative moral worth than act D" ("is morally more unworthy than act D") means "The extended B_1 conditions for acts C and D and their agents are satisfied."

It will have been noted that the extended B_1 conditions are only sufficient conditions for the presence of a higher degree of B_1 blameworthiness in one agent for his act than in another agent for his act. They are not necessary conditions. They do not cover cases in which one act, A, is morally more unworthy than another, B, with respect to one of the worth-determining factors, say the stringency of the rule broken, while B is more unworthy than A with respect to a different worth-determining factor, say the badness of the actuating desire. Although the badness of the actuating desire carries more weight than the other worth-determining factors, it does not seem possible to lay down a general rule by which we decide comparative degrees of B_1 blameworthiness for agents in cases in which the various worth-determining factors for their acts point in different directions. Nevertheless, I should maintain that decisions are usually reached in actual instances of such cases and that these decisions command a high degree of general acceptance. If this is true, there is no reason to regard the various worth-determining factors as incommensurable in principle.

II

We have seen that many judgments of moral praise and blame are P_1 and B_1 judgments or P_1 and B_1 judgments of degree, that is, judgments made with reference to the standard of appraisal involved in the P_1 and B_1 sets of conditions, either in their original or in their extended form. I shall now try to show that many judgments of moral praise and blame are not P_1 or B_1 judgments at all but are judgments ascribing praiseworthiness or blameworthiness to agents on other grounds. I shall maintain also that there are reasons why these other grounds should not be regarded as combining with our P_1 or B_1 conditions to constitute a single more complex standard of appraisal. The facts that will be cited here are among the most commonplace in our moral experience; but they are facts which have seldom received serious consideration or detailed treatment in moral theory.

Our extended B_1 conditions are sufficient conditions for the presence of a greater degree of blameworthiness in one agent for his act than in another agent for his act. We saw that they do not as they stand cover all kinds of cases; but it was maintained that in cases of acts for which the worth-determining factors point in different directions, comparative judgments of B_1 blameworthiness can nevertheless be made, without bringing in any additional factors. But there is another group of cases which do not fit into the picture thus far outlined at all. These are cases in which two agents have committed acts that are equally serious breaches of the same moral rule (or of equally stringent rules) because of equally bad desires. We frequently make comparative judgments of blame in just such cases. We say, for example, that John is more to blame for his

vindictive, sarcastic remark than Peter for his equally vindictive and equally sarcastic remark, on the ground that Peter has been unwell and under an emotional strain for some time recently. These special factors in Peter's case are examples of the so-called "mitigating circumstances" that theoretical discussions of these matters so often mention and so seldom dwell on. The true significance of "mitigating circumstances," I think, is nearly always missed.

Insofar as ethical theorists give any real thought to these mitigating circumstances at all, the assumption made seems to be this. Mitigating circumstances are factors which may affect the degree of blameworthiness but not its presence or absence. Whether an agent is blameworthy at all is governed by conditions such as our original B_1 conditions, or some variants of these. After it has been determined that an agent is blameworthy to *some* degree, mitigating circumstances are (in some cases) among the factors taken into account in judging just *what* the degree of blameworthiness is. The degree of blameworthiness in such cases is determined partly by such things as the worth-determining factors described earlier but partly also by the presence in the agent's situation of additional special circumstances that made it unusually difficult for him to refrain from committing his act. Certainly the exact role of the mitigating circumstances, in this view, is anything but clear. Those who appear to adopt this position do not tell us just how mitigating circumstances are related to the other factors that are held to determine degrees of blameworthiness, or why these mitigating circumstances are sometimes brought into the picture and sometimes not, or whether analogous special circumstances are also taken into account in judging praiseworthiness. Nevertheless, it is evident that mitigating circumstances are regarded, in this view, as somehow pertaining to the same standard of appraisal as our extended B_1 set of conditions for degrees of blameworthiness already set forth. Accordingly, the account in question may conveniently be called the "single-standard" account of blameworthiness. It is by no means without plausibility; but there are some features of moral appraisals which indicate that this account is decidedly misleading. Let us see what these features are.

In the first place, as we have already seen, judgments are very often made which assign, not just "some" degree of blameworthiness to an agent for his act but a high degree or a low degree of blameworthiness to him, on the grounds of only the worth-determining factors for that act, without any consideration of the presence or absence of mitigating circumstances. And judgments of this sort, B_1 judgments of degree, stand on their own feet. As we shall see in a moment, observers sometimes feel that judgments of this kind do not tell the whole moral story about agents and their acts; but this is not to say that the judgments themselves are all as a group incompletely justified. We do not say that no decision concerning the degree of blameworthiness of an agent should ever be reached until the special circumstances of his individual case have been investigated. We do not condemn the entire class of B_1 judgments of degree as having been made on incomplete evidence. Many of our B_1 judgments of degree are made about agents whose special circumstances could be ascertained but have not been ascertained. And many of them are made about agents living in the past concerning whom this knowledge will never be available to anyone. In neither case do we feel obliged to throw such judgments out of court en masse as resting on insufficient grounds. On the contrary, the worth-determining factors are treated as constituting a unitary and coherent standard, one that can operate independently of any consideration of mitigating circumstances. B_1 judgments of degree are self-contained and can be well-grounded.

On the single-standard view, all this is very puzzling. If mitigating circumstances sometimes determine the degree of blameworthiness and if they belong to the same standard of appraisal as the worth-determining factors, how is it that the latter so often seem to operate without the former? If we ever take mitigating circumstances into account in assigning degrees of blameworthiness, should we not always at least ask whether such circumstances are present? The fact that we do not always ask this and (much more) the fact that we do not believe that we always need to ask this are not easy for the single-standard view to assimilate and account for.

The single-standard account of blameworthiness, then, finds a difficulty in our failure to appeal with any consistency to mitigating circumstances in judging degrees of blameworthiness. This difficulty is increased when we reflect that mitigating circumstances are, after all, only one subclass of a larger class. This larger class comprises all those special circumstances in the situations of individual agents which either promote or hamper the performance of their acts. Just as there are mitigating circumstances which reduce blameworthiness somehow, are there not other special circumstances which increase it? And are there not some special circumstances which reduce praiseworthiness, while others increase it? Moral judgments are sometimes made which ascribe degrees of blameworthiness and praiseworthiness on just these grounds. But if these factors belong to the same standard of appraisal as the worth-determining factors, why do we not believe that these considerations should *always* be brought to bear on *all* judgments of moral praise and blame? Why do we so often leave them out entirely, even where we have or could get the requisite information concerning the individual agent?

These questions are much easier to deal with if we regard all these special circumstances in the situations of individual agents as determining degrees of blameworthiness and praiseworthiness judged by a different standard of appraisal. The single-standard view faces a dilemma. Either it must maintain that there is something unaccountably missing from the evidence for those judgments of praise and blame that are simply B_1 and P_1 judgments of degree, so that this large and important class of moral judgments are all incompletely justified, or it must somehow formulate a standard of appraisal which will show exactly when special circumstances are to be taken into account and when they are not. Neither of these alternatives is really acceptable. But if the special circumstances bear on the determination of degrees of blameworthiness and praiseworthiness judged by a different standard, the difficulties we have just been examining largely disappear. We may still think that people are often rather quixotic in their moral appraisals, and we may wonder why those moral appraisals which are not B_1 or P_1 judgments of degree but which take into account special circumstances in individual cases are not made more frequently, more carefully, and above all more systematically than is the case. But this is a different matter.

The single-standard account of blameworthiness and praiseworthiness finds its chief strength in a certain kind of experience which is admittedly familiar. This is the experience of feeling dissatisfied with a B_1 or P_1 judgment of degree and of wishing to substitute for it a judgment of praise or blame which takes the special circumstances in the agent's situation into account. Those who have this experience often feel that what they want to do is to "correct" the original P_1 or B_1 judgment of degree, and this lends plausibility to the single-standard account. But let us examine a case of this kind a little more closely.

P_1 and B_1 judgments of degree often seem appropriate to those who observe an agent and his act from a certain psychic distance, while they fail to satisfy either the agent himself or those who know him more intimately. As agents, we are often convinced that acts eliciting a considerable amount of praise from outsiders were somehow for us unusually "easy," and in these cases we do not seem to ourselves to deserve high praise. Correspondingly (and doubtless far more often) we are convinced as agents that certain acts eliciting considerable blame from outsiders were for us such that acts alternative to them would have been somehow unusually "difficult," and here we feel that we do not deserve much blame. Furthermore, as any parent knows with a special poignancy, those who know an agent particularly well are often similarly dissatisfied with judgments of degrees of praise and blame made by outsiders. Thus Charles, a child who is gifted academically but not musically, has, from a conscientious desire to do assigned work well, prepared a laborious book report. This is a morally worthy act, certainly, and one which acquaintances praise highly; but Charles's parents praise him with more fervor for having worked, from the same kind of desire, on his piano exercise. The act of working in the two cases has the same degree of positive moral worth, and outsiders judge Charles to be equally praiseworthy for both.

The parents would say, if asked about this, that Charles is more praiseworthy for having

worked conscientiously along lines that he finds uncongenial to his aptitudes than for having worked just as conscientiously along lines that he does find congenial. Charles's parents here may very well feel that they are "correcting" the judgment of praise made by outsiders. On reflection, however, they would have to concede that the original P_1 judgment of degree made by the outsiders on the basis of the worth-determining factors alone was perfectly true and that it conveyed significant moral information about Charles and his two jobs of work. And they could then admit that what they want to do is more accurately understood as *supplementing* the P_1 judgment of degree by a second judgment of praise based on other factors rather than as *correcting* the P_1 judgment by substituting the second judgment for it.

Similar comments may be made concerning the alleged "correction" of judgments of B_1 blameworthiness in the light of mitigating circumstances. What is it, then, that mitigating circumstances mitigate? They do not reduce the degree of B_1 blameworthiness already ascribed to an agent; they reduce the degree of blameworthiness ascribable to him by a different standard. The situation here is not analogous to giving a student a low grade for his essay and then proceeding to raise that grade somewhat. It is comparable, rather, to giving the student one grade for his essay as judged for its clarity of organization and another grade for the essay as judged for its spelling and syntax. Two different appraisals, and two different standards, are involved.

Those who find it difficult to relinquish the single-standard account of these matters should consider a further point. This is the question whether the special circumstances in the situations of individual agents can legitimately be regarded as commensurable with the worth-determining factors. If two acts committed by two agents are equal in negative moral worth and the situation of one agent includes more mitigating circumstances than the situation of the other, there may seem to be little objection to saying that the former is less "blameworthy" than the latter. But how shall we make comparisons for cases in which the worth-determining factors point in one direction and the special circumstances in another? Mary has told a malicious lie,

Jane has told a careless lie; there are several strongly mitigating circumstances in Mary's case and scarcely any in Jane's. Which agent is the more "blameworthy"? It seems to me that the only satisfactory answer here is that Mary is more blameworthy by one kind of standard (her act is morally more unworthy) but that Jane is more blameworthy by a different standard, in terms of a set of conditions that we have not yet articulated. Even though we may have to decide to punish one agent here more severely than the other, for various complicated practical reasons, this does not indicate that the moral values or disvalues of their acts are commensurable. Nor does the fact that legal penalties are sometimes reduced because of mitigating circumstances necessarily support the commensurability of worth-determining factors with our "special circumstances," for punishments depend on many considerations, and most of these are tied to questions of utility.[7] A claim that the severity of legal penalties can be regarded as a reliable index of appraisals of the moral blameworthiness of the penalized agents would be a difficult one to defend; but to explore this complex matter adequately is not possible here. We saw earlier that, although it may not always be easy to arbitrate among the various worth-determining factors themselves when they point in different directions, these factors can still be regarded as fundamentally commensurable. I do not believe that such a conclusion can be defended where the relation between the worth-determining factors on one side and the special circumstances on the other is concerned.

I have tried to show that there are reasons for maintaining that two different standards for determining praiseworthiness and blameworthiness govern our common moral appraisals. On this assumption we may now proceed to set up conditions for the presence of praiseworthiness and blameworthiness as judged by the second standard. Before we can do this, however, we must be a little more precise in characterizing acts as "unusually easy" or "unusually difficult." What is intended by these rather casual phrases is a reference, not to subjective feelings of "effort," but rather to circumstances which are favorable or unfavorable to a certain event, here of course the performance of a certain act. It will be assumed that the concept of a "favorable" or "unfavorable" circumstance does not require rigorous analysis in order to be sufficiently clear for our present purposes. What is meant is roughly what is meant in such statements as these: "Getting one's feet wet is a favorable circumstance for catching cold" and "Having grown up in a politically liberal household is an unfavorable circumstance for voting conservatively." To say that C is a favorable circumstance for an event E is to say that, other things being equal, E is more likely to occur in the presence of C than in its absence. If E is more likely to occur in the absence of C than in its presence, C is then of course an unfavorable circumstance for event E. It is not possible for E to occur in the presence of a majority of unfavorable circumstances; but it is clearly possible for E to occur even though a majority of the known circumstances are reasonably judged to be unfavorable.

Let us now set up conditions for the presence of praiseworthiness and blameworthiness judged in relation to special circumstances in the individual agent's case: these attributes will be referred to as "P_2 praiseworthiness" and "B_2 blameworthiness." I propose to say, to begin with, that an agent has B_2 blameworthiness (is B_2 blameworthy) to some degree for an act only if that act has negative moral worth to some degree. The conditions which are both necessary and sufficient for the presence of some degree of B_1 blameworthiness are necessary but not sufficient for the presence of some degree of B_2 blameworthiness. That is to say, agents have the characteristic of B_2 blameworthiness for the same kinds of acts for which they have B_1 blameworthiness: acts which are breaches of moral rules, voluntary, not done in ignorance of relevant facts, and performed because of desires which in their situations are bad. But when we have established that an act belongs to this class, we do not yet know whether its agent has B_2 blameworthiness. An agent X is B_2 blameworthy to some degree for his act A if and only if the following conditions hold: (1) act A has negative moral worth to some degree and (2) X's situation at the time of performing A included among the known circumstances a preponderance of circumstances (other than the amount of "effort" put forth by X) which are reasonably judged to be unfavorable to the performance of A. It is thus possible for X to have some degree of B_1 blameworthiness for A but no B_2 blameworthiness for A, and it is also possible for X to have a low degree of blameworthiness for A on one ground and a high degree of blameworthiness for A on the other.

A few clarifications are now in order. The reference to "X's situation at the time of performing A" should not be interpreted as excluding past events or states of affairs, even quite distant ones; these may be part of an agent's "situation" in the broad sense here intended. The somewhat awkward expression "a preponderance of circumstances" is used because the situations of most agents will naturally include among the known circumstances not only circumstances reasonably judged to be unfavorable to the performance of their acts, but also other circumstances reasonably judged to be favorable to their acts, and still others reasonably judged to be neutral in that connection. What we do here is essentially this: we consider an agent as a member of all the classes of which we know him to be a member and then attempt to judge whether, on balance, we can reasonably say that people of his sort are more likely not to commit his act than to commit it. If we can say this, then the second condition set forth above has been met. It is important, however, to understand that the agent's circumstances are considered collectively and not distributively. This means that if we know, for example, that only about 25 per cent of those belonging to the class of C's commit acts like act A but that 75 per cent of those belonging to the class of CD's do so and that our agent is a CD, we cannot artificially select his being a C and count this as an unfavorable circumstance in judging our preponderance. If being a D is a circumstance in itself neutral to the performance of A and relevant only through having counteracted the effect of being a C, it would have been possible to overlook D entirely in our calculations if the circumstances had been evaluated separately. Here our moral appraisals are tied closely to our knowledge; and perplexing problems of moral judgment may, indeed, arise in cases in which we suspect that a usually unfavorable circumstance was not in fact unfavorable for a particular agent, even though we do not know how to specify any factors which counteracted its unfavorable effect in this instance. Suspicions of this kind,

arising in a context of moral appraisal, may in fact be fruitful in leading us to track down such counteracting factors and in thus improving the accuracy of our causal generalizations regarding human acts: here ethics becomes of service to psychology. In cases where we feel uncertain regarding the unfavorable status of a certain circumstance in a particular agent's situation, it is certainly legitimate to examine his behavior for signs of "effort" or "strain," and even to question him regarding these matters. Nevertheless, it seems more satisfactory, if it is at all possible, to avoid formulating our B_2 conditions in terms of such subjective and elusive concepts.[8]

Necessary and sufficient conditions for an agent's having some degree of P_2 praiseworthiness are parallel to those given for B_2 blameworthiness. An agent X is P_2 praiseworthy to some degree for his act B if and only if the following conditions hold: (1) act B has positive moral worth to some degree, and (2) X's situation at the time of performing B included a preponderance of known circumstances (other than the amount of "effort" put forth by X) which are reasonably judged to be unfavorable to the performance of B. The conditions for B_2 blameworthiness and P_2 praiseworthiness are called the "B_2" and "P_2 conditions"; and judgments ascribing B_2 blameworthiness and P_2 praiseworthiness are called "B_2" and "P_2 judgments."

The B_2 and P_2 conditions can also be regarded as constituting a characteristic of value attaching to acts. This general characteristic will be called "moral credit": like moral worth, it can be present in either a positive or a negative form. The statement "Act A has positive moral credit to some degree" ("is morally creditable to some degree") means "The P_2 conditions for act A and its agent are satisfied." Correspondingly, "Act B has negative moral credit to some degree" ("is morally discreditable to some degree") means "The B_2 conditions for act B and its agent are satisfied." Acts having moral credit are, as we have seen, a subclass of acts having moral worth. This notion of moral credit, or at all events something like it, has been a stepchild in ethical theory, alluded to by many writers in various offhand ways but seldom seriously examined.

We must now set up conditions for the presence of degrees of B_2 blameworthiness and P_2 praiseworthiness; but since it will be necessary to do this explicitly for only one of these attributes, let us confine our attention to B_2 blameworthiness. An agent X is more B_2 blameworthy for his act A than is agent Y for his act B if and only if: (1) X is B_2 blameworthy to some degree for A; (2) Y is B_2 blameworthy to some degree for B; and (3) the preponderance of known circumstances reasonably judged to be unfavorable to X's performing A is greater than the preponderance of known circumstances reasonably judged to be unfavorable to Y's performing B. If X is more B_2 blameworthy for A than Y for B, this will entail that each is B_1 blameworthy for his act to some degree; but the possibility is left open that X may nevertheless be less B_1 blameworthy for A than Y for B. We shall call the conditions for greater degrees of B_2 blameworthiness and P_2 praiseworthiness the "extended B_2 and P_2 conditions," and judgments ascribing degrees of these attributes will be called "B_2 and P_2 judgments of degree." The expression "Act A has a greater degree of positive moral credit than act B" means "The extended P_2 conditions for acts A and B and their agents are satisfied." The expression "Act C has a greater degree of negative moral credit than act D" means "The extended B_2 conditions for acts C and D and their agents are satisifed." Finally, circumstances favorable and unfavorable to the performance of a given act may be called "credit-determining factors" (potential or actual) for that act.

III

Certain features of the attribute of moral credit and of the relation between this and the attribute of moral worth must now be explored in more detail. I think that we can see quite clearly what the basic difference is between moral worth and moral credit. Moral worth is ascribed to an act regarded for the most part as a finished product, without reference to most of the specific conditions that produced it, whereas moral credit is ascribed to an act viewed in relation to a much wider context of causally relevant circumstances. It is of course important to remember that in ascribing moral worth to acts we do take account of *some* of the causally relevant circumstances: the voluntariness of the fact, the absence of factual ignorance on the part of the agent, the desire actuating the agent. Tremen-

dous moral progress is involved in the shift to praising and blaming agents for acts viewed in this context from praising and blaming them for acts that are merely taken as right or wrong. Nevertheless, the contextual factors that are taken into account in judgments of moral worth, however significant, are still a unified and relatively stable set of minimal considerations. It is often desirable to examine morally worthy and unworthy acts in relation to wider contexts of causally relevant circumstances, so that we can arrive at moral appraisals that are more successful (never wholly successful) in doing justice to the complexity of human behavior and to the enormous variations among individuals. The situation that presents to one man a moral challenge provides another with a moral sinecure. Judgments of moral credit take this into account.

Insofar as the presence of two standards of appraisal for praise and blame is recognized at all, it is widely assumed, more or less implicitly, that judgments of degree made by one standard do not conflict with judgments of degree made by the other. That is to say, it is assumed that any act which has a high degree of positive moral worth also possesses a high degree of positive moral credit and that any act that is to a high degree morally unworthy is to a high degree morally discreditable. Certainly a correspondence of this sort will often occur; but it is also possible, both logically and causally, for moral worth and moral credit to vary inversely. An act which is morally very worthy cannot of course be morally discreditable, as our conditions have been set up; but such an act can be morally creditable to only a very low degree, or even not at all. Unless we are alive to these possibilities, some very unjust moral appraisals will result. The tendency to regard moral worth as implying moral credit, and great moral worth as implying great moral credit, is strong and has been accentuated by the fact that the language of praise and blame has been used to convey approval and disapproval of agents on both kinds of grounds. This has enabled the terms "praiseworthy" and "blameworthy" to carry the suggestion that any agents to whom these terms are applied are not only B_1 blameworthy or P_1 praiseworthy for their acts but also B_2 blameworthy or P_2 praiseworthy. Doubtless the original tendency in our thinking to regard moral worth as implying moral credit was not created by language, but language has reinforced it. This consideration helps to explain the kind of dissatisfaction which, as we have seen, is often felt with B_1 and P_1 judgments of praise and blame. If Charles's parents had been able to feel assured that the P_1 judgment of those who said that he was equally praiseworthy for doing his book report and for doing his piano exercise carried no implication of equal moral credit, they would have felt quite differently about this judgment. They would then have seen it as failing to tell the whole truth, but not as being simply wrong.

A thorough investigation of the relation between moral worth and moral credit would reveal complexities that cannot be adequately treated here. For example, it would be found that in some cases certain facts that must be taken into account in making a judgment of moral credit for an act had already been considered in making a judgment of moral worth for that act. The fact that Charles wanted very much to do something else at the time when he was writing his book report, for example, is evidence for the conclusion that this job was done from a conscientious desire to do assigned work well. This actuating desire (a desire good in its situation) then satisfies one of the conditions for the presence of positive moral worth in Charles's act. But when we come to appraise the positive moral credit of the act, Charles's desire to do something else when he was writing his book report must be considered again: here as a circumstance unfavorable to his writing the report. As such, it enters directly into the calculation to decide whether a preponderance of such unfavorable circumstances was present. The existence of Charles's conscientious desire does not depend on the existence of a coexisting desire to do something else;[9] but the existence of a preponderance of circumstances unfavorable to his writing the report does depend (in part) on this latter desire. The relation between a desire in conflict with an actuating desire, on the one hand, and the moral credit of an act, on the other, is thus much more direct than is the relation between such a conflicting desire and the moral worth of an act. The bearing of these considerations on Kant's moral philosophy may be of interest, though the point cannot be pursued here.

We have spoken, rather loosely, of moral credit as ascribed to an act viewed in a relatively wide context of causally relevant circumstances. Thus far nothing has been said of the possible limits of such a context. Can *any* factor related causally to an agent's performance of an act be legitimately regarded as a credit-determining factor for that act? And if so, will this not involve us in what H. Rashdall (in a somewhat different connection) once called "extravagances"? As an example of such extravagances, Rashdall cited the decision that one ought not to condemn Cesare Borgia because factors "sufficient under favorable circumstances to have made a Socrates or a Saint Paul were wholly prevented from taking actual effect because the poor man chanced to be the illegitimate son of a Renaissance Pope, and to have breathed the most polluted moral atmosphere that social evolution has ever generated."[10] As a matter of fact, the ambivalent attitude set up in Borgia's moral judges, who will almost inevitably feel that he should be condemned and that he should not be condemned, can be effectively assuaged by a distinction between moral worth and moral credit.

True extravagances in judging moral credit, however, must indeed be avoided. Unfortunately, they cannot be avoided by referring to a rule that will tell us in advance just how relevant our causally relevant factors must be. Plainly, the more direct the causal connection between factor and act, the more significant is the factor for a judgment of moral credit. Equally plainly, factors both external and internal to the agent himself should be taken into account. Considerations of health, fatigue, mood, personal relationships, beliefs, intellectual and emotional makeup, previous behavior, special talents, training—any of these can enter into the judgments required for an appraisal of moral credit, of either the positive or negative sort. Nor, as we saw earlier, is there any statute of limitations to set a general chronological limit on the factors in an agent's past to be considered. Some of these factors in an agent's past may be acts of his own, or acts of others, which may themselves in turn become the objects of *other* judgments of moral credit. But dicta so general as these afford little real guidance.

Studies of the reasoning that is actually used to back up ascriptions of moral credit to acts of different kinds (i.e., to support judgments that their agents are blameworthy or praiseworthy on B_2 or P_2 grounds) would prove helpful here. Certainly those who would appraise the moral credit of acts are not required to know everything about the circumstances under which those acts are committed.[11] But several circumstances must be taken into account in judging a "preponderance," and up to a far-distant point at least, the more we know, the more satisfactory our appraisals of moral credit will be. Our knowledge here can of course be deficient in two ways: we can fail to have a knowledge of relevant causal generalizations concerning certain acts, or we can fail to have the knowledge of an individual agent which would tell us whether a given generalization applied in his case. Although judgments of moral credit based on material which is strikingly deficient in either of these respects are plainly of little or no value, such judgments are often made. At present, discussions of the acts of various juvenile delinquents abound in judgments of this sort. Statements like "Arthur comes from such a good home" or "Paul has never had real discipline" are very loosely tossed about in attempts to determine the moral credit of such acts. It may even be that there is an analogue in moral development to Toynbee's concept of challenge and response, so that more than a certain number of "favorable" factors in the background of a growing individual actually constitute an unfavorable circumstance.

The most serious obstacles to making well-grounded judgments of moral credit lie in the deficiencies of our knowledge and not in an inability to decide how far to push our investigations into factors known to be causally relevant. Given a knowledge of such factors and of their applicability to a given case, one may wager that there will be little disagreement in practice over the selection of factors sufficient to determine the moral credit of a certain act. All of the circumstances reasonably judged to be favorable or unfavorable to an agent's performance of an act are potential credit-determining factors for that act; but not all of the potential credit-determining factors for an act need to be considered in order to arrive at a reasonably well-founded judgment concerning that act's moral credit.

In any event, it is clear that factors which are irrelevant to a determination of moral worth may be entirely relevant to a determination of moral credit. Thus a statement like "I am not to blame for lying yesterday, because I am a dishonest person," which P. H. Nowell-Smith tells us is the kind of plea that can never exculpate,[12] is seen in a new light when the moral credit of the lie is being estimated. Certainly such a plea has no force at all against a judgment of negative moral worth. Nor will it be of any significance for the question of moral credit unless we define "dishonest" in such a way that it does not mean simply "having a tendency to lie." If, however, we can identify a more general pattern of behavior and show that it has been set up in a certain individual, and that repeated acts according to this pattern make it progressively more difficult to break, then we shall have a factor that is genuinely relevant for a judgment of negative moral credit for this act. To some, this way of looking at the matter will seem paradoxical, if not downright immoral. "What," they will cry, "are you actually proposing to excuse someone who tells a lie on the ground that he has told many lies and done other dishonest things before?" The answer is that if "excuse" means "remove or reduce the degree of negative moral worth attaching to an act," then obviously we cannot allow that having told previous lies can excuse the telling of a fresh one. But if "excuse" means "remove or reduce the degree of negative moral credit attaching to an act," then we do have here a circumstance that must be taken into account in the case of our liar's latest lie, though this circumstance may of course not be decisive.

Those who object to "excusing" a lie on the ground that its perpetrator has told lies before seem to fear that if we deny that a given lie is morally discreditable this will imply a denial that it is morally unworthy. This is a manifestation of the tendency referred to earlier to assume that moral worth implies moral credit. Actually, of course, where P does not imply Q in the first place, the denial of Q leaves P quite unaffected. But in the difficulty of disentangling moral worth and moral credit we may have an explanation of the fact that acts "out of character" have been variously appraised as more and less "blameworthy" than acts "in character." Writers who were primarily concerned with moral credit may have regarded those agents who performed acts out of character as the more blameworthy,[13] while writers who were primarily concerned with moral worth, especially if they judged this in reference to an agent's traits rather than his desires, may have adopted the opposite view.[14] A distinction between judgments of moral worth and judgments of moral credit enables us to do justice to the elements of truth in both positions.

Before we leave this part of our discussion, one further point should be made clear. This concerns the value of making both judgments of moral worth and judgments of moral credit. It is possible that someone might draw the conclusion, from what has been said here, that judgments of moral worth are all very well if they are all that we can have, but that they should be replaced, wherever our information permits, by judgments of moral credit. Judgments of moral worth, that is to say, are to be regarded as incomplete, as judgments of moral credit *manqués;* since judgments of moral credit take into account more of the circumstances of a given case, these appraisals must be morally more adequate and more significant, somehow, than mere judgments of moral worth can ever be. This impression is quite mistaken. Although the "discovery" of the importance of considerations of moral credit was perhaps a kind of landmark in the moral evolution of the human race, this does not at all imply that other kinds of moral judgments thereby became outmoded. Judgments of the rightness and wrongness of acts are not superseded by judgments of the moral worth of the acts, and judgments of moral worth are not superseded by judgments of moral credit. Many kinds of rewards and punishments are based on moral worth rather than on moral credit, just as other kinds of rewards and punishments are based on the rightness and wrongness of acts, or their utility, rather than on moral worth. The most significant difference in function between judgments of moral worth and judgments of moral credit, however, may lie in the fact that they have different roles to play in building up moral ideals of action and of general character. We enjoin persons (including ourselves) not only to perform right acts but also to develop in themselves dispositions to perform right acts from good motives, to do those things which are morally worthy. But we do not enjoin anyone to perform morally creditable acts, for this would mean saying to him, "Perform morally worthy acts against unfavorable circumstances." If unfavorable circumstances are present, we shall hold up the ideal of performing morally worthy acts *in spite of* such odds, of course; and this is one of our most highly valued character ideals. But if morally creditable acts as such were directly commanded or enjoined, agents would be under an obligation to set up such odds for themselves in order that these might then be overcome. Many writers have commented on the moral absurdity of such an ideal.

Throughout this paper moral worth and moral credit have been dealt with as characteristics of acts. The question whether there are features of our moral appraisals that make it desirable to extend the usage developed here so as to provide for the ascription of moral worth and moral credit to persons as well is one which I believe to have some interest for ethical theory. In fact, the value of distinguishing between our two standards emerges most clearly when moral praise and blame are directed toward persons for their general characters rather than for particular acts which they have performed. The distinction between moral worth and moral credit also has some importance for the issue between determinism and libertarianism in ethics. But these are points which I shall develop and defend in another paper.

It was pointed out at the beginning of the present paper that the problem of analyzing possible phenomenal constituents of judgments of praise and blame would here be bypassed completely. Whether there are such constituents in both B_1 and P_1 judgments on the one hand and B_2 and P_2 judgments on the other, and whether, if so, the elements in B_1 and B_2 judgments on the one hand and in P_1 and P_2 judgments on the other are the same elements, are questions avoided here. In the absence of answers to these questions a final recommendation concerning the usage of the terms "praiseworthy" and "blameworthy" cannot be made. But if the argument of this paper is correct, two different moral standards for praiseworthiness and blameworthiness are used, often without being at all clearly distinguished, and the failure to distinguish them clearly is responsible for some unfortunate moral confusions. In view of these conclusions (if the conclusions themselves are justified), it would seem desirable to adopt a linguistic usage which would always make the difference in standards clearly evident. One way of doing this would be to mention the grounds on which blameworthiness or praiseworthiness is judged in every context in which these attributes are mentioned: to say, for example, "Henry is praiseworthy for that act on the grounds of its moral worth," or "Susan is highly blameworthy for her act on the grounds of its moral worth, though not on the grounds of its moral credit." A second way would be to substitute another pair of terms either for "B_1 blameworthy" and "P_1 praiseworthy" or for "B_2 blameworthy" and "P_2 praiseworthy." If this latter alternative were to be adopted, a good procedure, I think, would be to substitute the terms "commendable" and "censurable" for "P_1 praiseworthy" and "B_1 blameworthy" respectively, while retaining "blameworthy" and "praiseworthy" for "B_2 blameworthy" and "P_2 praiseworthy." A thorough examination of the merits of this proposal, however, would take us beyond the limits of the present paper. Meanwhile, such terms as "moral worth" and "moral credit" are useful, the more useful in that they make a distinction unmarked by the terms "blameworthy" and "praiseworthy" in their present usage. I have tried to show that the distinction is one worth marking.

NOTES

1. This is a shortened and slightly altered version of a paper read before the Fullerton Club on Nov. 10, 1956.
2. For such an analysis, see Richard B. Brandt, "Blameworthiness and Obligation," to be published in A. I. Melden, ed., *Essays in Moral Philosophy* (University of Washington Press, 1957). I am indebted to this paper for help in clarifying certain of my own ideas; and I am also indebted to Mr. Brandt for his critical comments on the present paper.
3. These terms are used here and throughout this paper in the sense of "morally praiseworthy" and "morally blameworthy."
4. On this point, see Brandt, *op. cit.*
5. In this connection, see P. H. Nowell-Smith, *Ethics* (London, 1951). chs. xvii and xviii. Although I have departed from Nowell-Smith's treatment in certain respects, my account of this first standard owes much to his book.
6. Thorough clarification of the term "bad desire" is impossible here; but the affinity between this condition for blameworthiness and certain features of W. D. Ross's concepts of moral goodness and moral badness will be recognized. The present account is closer to that given in *The Foundations of Ethics* (Oxford, 1939) than to that in *The Right and the Good* (Oxford, 1930).
7. On this point, see Nowell-Smith, *op. cit.,* p. 299.
8. Some of the difficulties attaching to these concepts are brought out in Nowell-Smith, *op. cit.,* pp. 285–287.
9. This general point is of course familiar in the writings of Ross (see, e.g., *The Right and the Good,* p. 159).
10. H. Rashdall, *The Theory of Good and Evil* (Oxford, 1924), II, 323–324.
11. Indeed, it can be argued, as I shall do in a later paper, that they are required *not* to know everything.
12. Nowell-Smith, *op. cit.,* ch. xviii.
13. See, e.g., H. D. Lewis, "Moral Freedom in Recent Ethics," reprinted in W. Sellars and J. Hospers, *Readings in Ethical Theory* (New York, 1952), pp. 576–596.
14. See, e.g., A. K. Stout, "Free Will and Responsibility," reprinted in Sellars and Hospers, *op. cit.,* pp. 537–548.

42. SERVILITY AND SELF-RESPECT

Thomas E. Hill, Jr.

Several motives underlie this paper.[1] In the first place, I am curious to see if there is a legitimate source for the increasingly common feeling that servility can be as much a vice as arrogance. There seems to be something morally defective about the Uncle Tom and the submissive housewife; and yet, on the other hand, if the only interests they sacrifice are their own, it seems that we should have no right to complain. Secondly, I have some sympathy for the now unfashionable view that each person has duties to himself as well as to others. It does seem absurd to say that a person could literally violate his own rights or owe himself a debt of gratitude, but I suspect that the classic defenders of duties to oneself had something different in mind. If there are duties to oneself, it is natural to expect that a duty to avoid being servile would have a prominent place among them. Thirdly, I am interested in making sense of Kant's puzzling, but suggestive, remarks about respect for persons and respect for the moral law. On the usual reading, these remarks seem unduly moralistic; but, viewed in another way, they suggest an argument for a kind of self-respect which is incompatible with a servile attitude.

My procedure will not be to explicate Kant directly. Instead I shall try to isolate the defect of servility and sketch an argument to show why it is objectionable, noting only in passing how this relates to Kant and the controversy about duties to oneself. What I say about self-respect is far from the whole story. In particular, it is not concerned with esteem for one's special abilities and achievements or with the self-confidence which characterizes the especially autonomous person. Nor is my concern with the psychological antecedents and effects of self-respect. Nevertheless, my conclusions, if correct, should be of interest; for they imply that, given a

common view of morality, there are non-utilitarian moral reasons for each person, regardless of his merits, to respect himself. To avoid servility to the extent that one can is not simply a right but a duty, not simply a duty to others but a duty to oneself.

I

Three examples may give a preliminary idea of what I mean by *servility*. Consider, first, an extremely deferential black, whom I shall call the *Uncle Tom*. He always steps aside for white men; he does not complain when less qualified whites take over his job; he gratefully accepts whatever benefits his all-white government and employers allot him, and he would not think of protesting its insufficiency. He displays the symbols of deference to whites, and of contempt towards blacks: he faces the former with bowed stance and a ready 'sir' and 'Ma'am': he reserves his strongest obscenities for the latter. Imagine, too, that he is not playing a game. He is not the shrewdly prudent calculator, who knows how to make the best of a bad lot and mocks his masters behind their backs. He accepts without question the idea that, as a black, he is owed less than whites. He may believe that blacks are mentally inferior and of less social utility, but that is not the crucial point. The attitude which he displays is that what he values, aspires for, and can demand is of less importance than what whites value, aspire for, and can demand. He is far from the picture book's carefree, happy servant, but he does not feel that he has a right to expect anything better.

Another pattern of servility is illustrated by a person I shall call the *Self-Deprecator*. Like the Uncle Tom, he is reluctant to make demands. He says nothing when others take unfair advantage of him. When asked for his preferences or opinions, he tends to shrink away as if what he said should make no difference. His problem,

From Thomas E. Hill, Jr., "Servility and Self-Respect," *The Monist*, Vol. 57, No. 1 (January, 1973), pp. 87–104. Reprinted from *The Monist*, Vol. 57, No. 1 (1973), La Salle, Illinois, with the permission of the author and publisher.

however, is not a sense of racial inferiority but rather an acute awareness of his own inadequacies and failures as an individual. These defects are not imaginary: he has in fact done poorly by his own standards and others'. But, unlike many of us in the same situation, he acts as if his failings warrant quite unrelated maltreatment even by strangers. His sense of shame and self-contempt make him content to be the instrument of others. He feels that nothing is owed him until he has earned it and that he has earned very little. He is not simply playing a masochist's game of winning sympathy by disparaging himself. On the contrary, he assesses his individual merits with painful accuracy.

A rather different case is that of the *Deferential Wife*. This is a woman who is utterly devoted to serving her husband. She buys the clothes *he* prefers, invites the guests *he* wants to entertain, and makes love whenever *he* is in the mood. She willingly moves to a new city in order for him to have a more attractive job, counting her own friendships and geographical preferences insignificant by comparison. She loves her husband, but her conduct is not simply an expression of love. She is happy, but she does not subordinate herself as a means to happiness. She does not simply defer to her husband in certain spheres as a trade-off for his deference in other spheres. On the contrary, she tends not to form her own interests, values, and ideals; and, when she does, she counts them as less important than her husband's. She readily responds to appeals from Women's Liberation that she agrees that women are mentally and physically equal, if not superior, to men. She just believes that the proper role for a woman is to serve her family. As a matter of fact, much of her happiness derives from her belief that she fulfills this role very well. No one is trampling on her rights, she says; for she is quite glad, and proud, to serve her husband as she does.

Each one of these cases reflects the attitude which I call servility.[2] It betrays the absence of a certain kind of self-respect. What I take this attitude to be, more specifically, will become clearer later on. It is important at the outset, however, not to confuse the three cases sketched above with other, superficially similar cases. In particular, the cases I have sketched are not simply cases in which someone refuses to press his rights, speaks disparagingly of himself, or devotes himself to another. A black, for example, is not necessarily servile because he does not demand a just wage; for, seeing that such a demand would result in his being fired, he might forbear for the sake of his children. A self-critical person is not necessarily servile by virtue of bemoaning his faults in public; for his behavior may be merely a complex way of satisfying his own inner needs quite independent of a willingness to accept abuse from others. A woman need not be servile whenever she works to make her husband happy and prosperous; for she might freely and knowingly choose to do so from love or from a desire to share the rewards of his success. If the effort did not require her to submit to humiliation or maltreatment, her choice would not mark her as servile. There may, of course, be grounds for objecting to the attitudes in these cases; but the defect is not servility of the sort I want to consider. It should also be noted that my cases of servility are not simply instances of deference to superior knowledge or judgment. To defer to an expert's judgment on matters of fact is not to be servile; to defer to his every wish and whim is. Similarly, the belief that one's talents and achievements are comparatively low does not, by itself, make one servile. It is no vice to acknowledge the truth, and one may in fact have achieved less, and have less ability, than others. To be servile is not simply to hold certain empirical beliefs but to have a certain attitude concerning one's rightful place in a moral community.

II

Are there grounds for regarding the attitudes of the Uncle Tom, the Self-Deprecator, and the Deferential Wife as morally objectionable? Are there moral arguments we could give them to show that they ought to have more self-respect? None of the more obvious replies is entirely satisfactory.

One might, in the first place, adduce utilitarian considerations. Typically the servile person will be less happy than he might be. Moreover, he may be less prone to make the best of his own socially useful abilities. He may become a nuisance to others by being overly dependent. He will, in any case, lose the special contentment that comes from standing up for one's rights. A submissive attitude encourages exploitation, and exploitation spreads misery in a variety of ways. These considerations provide a prima facie case against the attitudes of the Uncle Tom, the Deferential Wife, and the Self-Deprecator, but they are hardly conclusive. Other utilities tend to counterbalance the ones just mentioned. When people refuse to press their rights, there are usually others who profit. There are undeniable pleasures in associating with those who are devoted, understanding, and grateful for whatever we see fit to give them—as our fondness for dogs attests. Even the servile person may find his attitude a source of happiness, as the case of the Deferential Wife illustrates. There may be comfort and security in thinking that the hard choices must be made by others, that what I would say has little to do with what ought to be done. Self-condemnation may bring relief from the pangs of guilt even if it is not deliberately used for that purpose. On balance, then, utilitarian considerations may turn out to favor servility as much as they oppose it.

For those who share my moral intuitions, there is another sort of reason for not trying to rest a case against servility on utilitarian considerations. Certain utilities seem irrelevant to the issue. The utilitarian must weigh them along with others, but to do so seems morally inappropriate. Suppose, for example, that the submissive attitudes of the Uncle Tom and the Deferential Wife result in positive utilities for those who dominate and exploit them. Do we need to tabulate *these* utilities before conceding that servility is objectionable? The Uncle Tom, it seems, is making an error, a moral error, quite apart from consideration of how much others in fact profit from his attitude. The Deferential Wife may be quite happy; but if her happiness turns out to be contingent on her distorted view of her own rights and worth as a person, then it carries little moral weight against the contention that she ought to change that view. Suppose I could cause a woman to find her happiness in denying all her rights and serving my every wish. No doubt I could do so only by nonrational manipulative techniques, which I ought not to use. But it this the only objection? My efforts would be wrong, it seems, not only because of the techniques they require but also because the resultant attitude is itself objectionable. When a

person's happiness stems from a morally objectionable attitude, it ought to be discounted. That a sadist gets pleasure from seeing others suffer should not count even as a partial justification for his attitude. That a servile person derives pleasure from denying her moral status, for similar reasons, cannot make her attitude acceptable. These brief intuitive remarks are not intended as a refutation of utilitarianism, with all its many varieties; but they do suggest that it is well to look elsewhere for adequate grounds for rejecting the attitudes of the Uncle Tom, the Self-Deprecator, and the Deferential Wife.

One might try to appeal to meritarian considerations. That is, one might argue that the servile person *deserves* more than he allows himself. This line of argument, however, is no more adequate than the utilitarian one. It may be wrong to deny others what they deserve, but it is not so obviously wrong to demand less for oneself than one deserves. In any case, the Self-Deprecator's problem is not that he underestimates his merits. By hypothesis, he assesses his merits quite accurately. We cannot reasonably tell him to have more respect for himself because he *deserves* more respect; he knows that he has not *earned* better treatment. His problem, in fact, is that he thinks of his moral status with regard to others as entirely dependent upon his merits. His interests and choices are important, he feels, only if he has earned the right to make demands; or if he had rights by birth, they were forfeited by his subsequent failures and misdeeds. My Self-Deprecator is no doubt an atypical person, but nevertheless he illustrates an important point. Normally when we find a self-contemptuous person, we can plausibly argue that he is not so bad as he thinks, that his self-contempt is an overreaction prompted more by inner needs than by objective assessment of his merits. Because this argument cannot work with the Self-Deprecator, his case draws attention to a distinction, applicable in other cases as well, between saying that someone deserves respect for his merits and saying that he is owed respect as a person. On meritarian grounds we can only say 'You deserve better than this', but the defect of the servile person is not merely failure to recognize his merits.

Other common arguments against the Uncle Tom, et al, may have some force but seem not to strike to the heart of the problem. For example, philosophers sometimes appeal to the value of human potentialities. As a human being, it is said, one at least has a capacity for rationality, morality, excellence, or autonomy, and this capacity is worthy of respect. Although such arguments have the merit of making respect independent of a person's actual deserts, they seem quite misplaced in some cases. There comes a time when we have sufficient evidence that a person is not ever going to *be* rational, moral, excellent, or autonomous even if he still has a capacity, in some sense, for being so. As a person approaches death with an atrocious record so far, the chances of his realizing his diminishing capacities become increasingly slim. To make these capacities the basis of his self-respect is to rest it on a shifting and unstable ground. We do, of course, respect persons for capacities which they are not exercising at the moment; for example, I might respect a person as a good philosopher even though he is just now blundering into gross confusion. In these cases, however, we respect the person for an active capacity, a ready disposition, which he has displayed on many occasions. On this analogy, a person should have respect for himself only when his capacities are developed and ready, needing only to be triggered by an appropriate occasion or the removal of some temporary obstacle. The Uncle Tom and the Deferential Wife, however, may in fact have quite limited capacities of this sort, and, since the Self-Deprecator is already overly concerned with his own inadequacies, drawing attention to his capacities seems a poor way to increase his self-respect. In any case, setting aside the Kantian nonempirical capacity for autonomy, the capacities of different persons vary widely; but what the servile person seems to overlook is something by virtue of which he is equal with every other person.

III

Why, then, is servility a moral defect? There is, I think, another sort of answer which is worth exploring. The first part of this answer must be an attempt to isolate the objectionable features of the servile person; later we can ask why these features are objectionable. As a step in this direction, let us examine again our three paradigm cases. The moral defect in each case, I suggest, is a failure to understand and acknowledge one's own moral rights. I assume, without argument here, that each person has moral rights.[3] Some of these rights may be basic human rights; that is, rights for which a person needs only to be human to qualify. Other rights will be derivative and contingent upon his special commitments, institutional affiliations, etc. Most rights will be prima facie ones; some may be absolute. Most can be waived under appropriate conditions; perhaps some cannot. Many rights can be forfeited; but some, presumably, cannot. The servile person does not, strictly speaking, violate his own rights. At least in our paradigm cases he fails to acknowledge fully his own moral status because he does not fully understand what his rights are, how they can be waived, and when they can be forfeited.

The defect of the Uncle Tom, for example, is that he displays an attitude that denies his moral equality with whites. He does not realize, or apprehend in an effective way, that he has as much right to a decent wage and a share of political power as any comparable white. His gratitude is misplaced; he accepts benefits which are his by right as if they were gifts. The Self-Deprecator is servile in a more complex way. He acts as if he has forfeited many important rights which in fact he has not. He does not understand, or fully realize in his own case, that certain rights to fair and decent treatment do not have to be earned. He sees his merits clearly enough, but he fails to see that what he can expect from others is not merely a function of his merits. The Deferential Wife *says* that she understands her rights vis-à-vis her husband, but what she fails to appreciate is that her consent to serve him is a valid waiver of her rights only under certain conditions. If her consent is coerced, say, by the lack of viable options for women in her society, then her consent is worth little. If socially fostered ignorance of her own talents and alternatives is responsible for her consent, then her consent should not count as a fully legitimate waiver of her right to equal consideration within the marriage. All the more, her consent to defer constantly to her husband is not a legitimate setting aside of her rights if it results from her mistaken belief that she has a moral duty to do so. (Recall: "The *proper* role for a woman is to serve her family.") If she believes that she has a *duty* to defer to her husband, then, whatever she may say, she cannot fully understand that she has a *right* not to defer to him. When she says that she freely gives up such a right, she is confused. Her confusion is rather like that of a person who has been persuaded by an unscrupulous lawyer that it is legally incumbent on him to refuse a jury trial but who nevertheless tells the judge that he understands that he has a right to a jury trial and freely waives it. He does not really understand what it is to have and freely give up the right if he thinks that it would be an offense for him to exercise it.

Insofar as servility results from moral ignorance or confusion, it need not be something for which a person is to blame. Even self-reproach may be inappropriate; for at the time a person is in ignorance he cannot feel guilty about his servility, and later he may conclude that his ignorance was unavoidable. In some cases, however, a person might reasonably believe that he should have known better. If, for example, the Deferential Wife's confusion about her rights resulted from a motivated resistance to drawing the implications of her own basic moral principles, then later she might find some ground for self-reproach. Whether blameworthy or not, servility could still be morally objectionable at least in the sense that it ought to be discouraged, that social conditions which nourish it should be reformed, and the like. Not all morally undesirable features of a person are ones for which he is responsible, but that does not mean that they are defects merely from an esthetic or prudential point of view.

In our paradigm cases, I have suggested, servility is a kind of deferential attitude towards others resulting from ignorance or misunderstanding of one's moral rights. A sufficient remedy, one might think, would be moral enlightenment. Suppose, however, that our servile persons come to know their rights but do not substantially alter their behavior. Are they not still servile in an objectionable way? One might even think that reproach is more appropriate now because they know what they are doing.

The problem, unfortunately, is not as simple as it may appear. Much depends on what they tolerate and why. Let us set aside cases in which a person merely refuses to *fight* for his rights, chooses not to exercise certain rights, or freely waives many rights which he might have insisted upon. Our problem concerns the previously ser-

vile person who continues to display the same marks of deference even after he fully knows his rights. Imagine, for example, that even after enlightenment our Uncle Tom persists in his old pattern of behavior, giving all the typical signs of believing that the injustices done to him are not really wrong. Suppose, too, that the newly enlightened Deferential Wife continues to defer to her husband, refusing to disturb the old way of life by introducing her new ideas. She acts as if she accepts the idea that she is merely doing her duty though actually she no longer believes it. Let us suppose, further, that the Uncle Tom and the Deferential Wife are not merely generous with their time and property, they also accept without protest, and even appear to sanction, treatment which is humiliating and degrading. That is, they do not simply consent to waive mutually acknowledged rights; they tolerate violations of their rights with apparent approval. They pretend to give their permission for subtle humiliations which they really believe no permission can make legitimate. Are such persons still servile despite their moral knowledge?

The answer, I think, should depend upon why the deferential role is played. If the motive is a morally commendable one, or a desire to avert dire consequences to oneself, or even an ambition to set an oppressor up for a later fall, then I would not count the role player as servile. The Uncle Tom, for instance, is not servile in my sense if he shuffles and bows to keep the Klan from killing his children, to save his own skin, or even to buy time while he plans the revolution. Similarly, the Deferential Wife is not servile if she tolerates an abusive husband because he is so ill that further strain would kill him, because protesting would deprive her of her only means of survival, or because she is collecting atrocity stories for her book against marriage. If there is fault in these situations, it seems inappropriate to call it *servility*. The story is quite different, however, if a person continues in his deferential role just from laziness, timidity, or a desire for some minor advantage. He shows too little concern for his moral status as a person, one is tempted to say, if he is willing to deny it for a small profit or simply because it requires some effort and courage to affirm it openly. A black who plays the Uncle Tom merely to gain an advantage over other blacks is harming them, of course; but he is also displaying disregard for his own moral position as an equal among human beings. Similarly, a woman throws away her rights too lightly if she continues to play the subservient role because she is used to it or is too timid to risk a change. A Self-Deprecator who readily accepts what he knows are violations of his rights may be indulging his peculiar need for punishment at the expense of denying something more valuable. In these cases, I suggest, we have a kind of servility independent of any ignorance or confusion about one's rights. The person who has it may or may not be blameworthy, depending on many factors; and the line between servile and nonservile role playing will often be hard to draw. Nevertheless, the objectionable feature is perhaps clear enough for present purposes: it is a willingness to disavow one's moral status, publicly and systematically, in the absence of any strong reason to do so.

My proposal, then, is that there are at least two types of servility: one resulting from misunderstanding of one's rights and the other from placing a comparatively low value on them. In either case, servility manifests the absence of a certain kind of self-respect. The respect which is missing is not respect for one's merits but respect for one's rights. The servile person displays this absence of respect not directly by acting contrary to his own rights but indirectly by acting as if his rights were nonexistent or insignificant. An arrogant person ignores the rights of others, thereby arrogating for himself a higher status than he is entitled to; a servile person denies his own rights, thereby assuming a lower position than he is entitled to. Whether rooted in ignorance or simply lack of concern for moral rights, the attitudes in both cases may be incompatible with a proper regard for morality. That this is so is obvious in the case of arrogance; but to see it in the case of servility requires some further argument.

IV

The objectionable feature of the servile person, as I have described him, is his tendency to disavow his own moral rights either because he misunderstands them or because he cares little for them. The question remains: why should anyone regard this as a moral defect? After all,

the rights which he denies are his own. He may be unfortunate, foolish, or even distasteful; but why *morally* deficient? One sort of answer, quite different from those reviewed earlier, is suggested by some of Kant's remarks. Kant held that servility is contrary to a perfect nonjuridical duty to oneself.[4] To say that the duty is perfect is roughly to say that it is stringent, never overridden by other considerations (e.g. beneficence). To say that the duty is nonjuridical is to say that a person cannot legitimately be coerced to comply. Although Kant did not develop an explicit argument for this view, an argument can easily be constructed from materials which reflect the spirit, if not the letter, of his moral theory. The argument which I have in mind is prompted by Kant's contention that respect for persons, strictly speaking, is respect for moral law.[5] If taken as a claim about all sorts of respect, this seems quite implausible. If it means that we respect persons only for their moral character, their capacity for moral conduct, or their status as "authors" of the moral law, then it seems unduly moralistic. My strategy is to construe the remark as saying that at least one sort of respect for persons is respect for the rights which the moral law accords them. If one respects the moral law, then one must respect one's own moral rights; and this amounts to having a kind of self-respect incompatible with servility.

The premises for the Kantian argument, which are all admittedly vague, can be sketched as follows:

First, let us assume, as Kant did, that all human beings have equal basic human rights. Specific rights vary with different conditions, but all must be justified from a point of view under which all are equal. Not all rights need to be earned, and some cannot be forfeited. Many rights can be waived but only under certain conditions of knowledge and freedom. These conditions are complex and difficult to state; but they include something like the condition that a person's consent releases others from obligation only if it is autonomously given, and consent resulting from underestimation of one's moral status is not autonomously given. Rights can be objects of knowledge, but also of ignorance, misunderstanding, deception, and the like.

Second, let us assume that my account of servility is correct; or, if one prefers, we can take it as a definition. That is, in brief, a servile person is one who tends to deny or disavow his own moral rights because he does not understand them or has little concern for the status they give him.

Third, we need one formal premise concerning moral duty, namely, that each person ought, as far as possible, to respect the moral law. In less Kantian language, the point is that everyone should approximate, to the extent that he can, the ideal of a person who fully adopts the moral point of view. Roughly, this means not only that each person ought to do what is morally required and refrain from what is morally wrong but also that each person should treat all the provisions of morality as valuable—worth preserving and prizing as well as obeying. One must, so to speak, take up the spirit of morality as well as meet the letter of its requirements. To keep one's promises, avoid hurting others, and the like, is not sufficient; one should also take an attitude of respect towards the principles, ideals, and goals of morality. A respectful attitude towards a system of rights and duties consists of more than a disposition to conform to its definite rules of behavior; it also involves holding the system in esteem, being unwilling to ridicule it, and being reluctant to give up one's place in it. The essentially Kantian idea here is that morality, as a system of equal fundamental rights and duties, is worthy of respect, and hence a completely moral person would respect it in word and manner as well as in deed. And what a completely moral person would do, in Kant's view, is our duty to do so far as we can.

The assumptions here are, of course, strong ones, and I make no attempt to justify them. They are, I suspect, widely held though rarely articulated. In any case, my present purpose is not to evaluate them but to see how, if granted, they constitute a case against servility. The objection to the servile person, given our premises, is that he does not satisfy the basic requirement to respect morality. A person who fully respected a system of moral rights would be disposed to learn his proper place in it, to affirm it proudly, and not to tolerate abuses of it lightly. This is just the sort of disposition that the servile person lacks. If he does not understand the system, he is in no position to respect it adequately. This lack of respect may be no fault of his own,

but it is still a way in which he falls short of a moral ideal. If, on the other hand, the servile person knowingly disavows his moral rights by pretending to approve of violations of them, then, barring special explanations, he shows an indifference to whether the provisions of morality are honored and publicly acknowledged. This avoidable display of indifference, by our Kantian premises, is contrary to the duty to respect morality. The disrespect in this second case is somewhat like the disrespect a religious believer might show towards his religion if, to avoid embarrassment, he laughed congenially while nonbelievers were mocking the beliefs which he secretly held. In any case, the servile person, as such, does not express disrespect for the system of moral rights in the obvious way by violating the rights of others. His lack of respect is more subtly manifested by his acting before others as if he did not know or care about his position of equality under that system.

The central idea here may be illustrated by an analogy. Imagine a club, say, an old German dueling fraternity. By the rules of the club, each member has certain rights and responsibilities. These are the same for each member regardless of what titles he may hold outside the club. Each has, for example, a right to be heard at meetings, a right not to be shouted down by the others. Some rights cannot be forfeited: for example, each may vote regardless of whether he has paid his dues and satisfied other rules. Some rights cannot be waived: for example, the right to be defended when attacked by several members of the rival fraternity. The members show respect for each other by respecting the status which the rules confer on each member. Now one new member is careful always to allow the others to speak at meetings; but when they shout him down, he does nothing. He just shrugs as if to say, 'Who am I to complain?' When he fails to stand up in defense of a fellow member, he feels ashamed and refuses to vote. He does not deserve to vote, he says. As the only commoner among illustrious barons, he feels that it is his place to serve them and defer to their decisions. When attackers from the rival fraternity come at him with swords drawn, he tells his companions to run and save themselves. When they defend him, he expresses immense gratitude—as if they had done him a gratuitous favor. Now one might argue that our new member fails to show respect for the fraternity and its rules. He does not actually violate any of the rules by refusing to vote, asking others not to defend him, and deferring to the barons, but he symbolically disavows the equal status which the rules confer on him. If he ought to have respect for the fraternity, he ought to change his attitude. Our servile person, then, is like the new member of the dueling fraternity in having insufficient respect for a system of rules and ideals. The difference is that everyone ought to respect morality whereas there is no comparable moral requirement to respect the fraternity.

The conclusion here is, of course, a limited one. Self-sacrifice is not always a sign of servility. It is not a duty always to press one's rights. Whether a given act is evidence of servility will depend not only on the attitude of the agent but also on the specific nature of his moral rights, a matter not considered here. Moreover, the extent to which a person is responsible, or blameworthy, for his defect remains an open question. Nevertheless, the conclusion should not be minimized. In order to avoid servility, a person who gives up his rights must do so with a full appreciation for what they are. A woman, for example, may devote herself to her husband if she is uncoerced, knows what she is doing, and does not pretend that she has no decent alternative. A self-contemptuous person may decide not to press various unforfeited rights but only if he does not take the attitude that he is too rotten to deserve them. A black may demand less than is due to him provided he is prepared to acknowledge that no one has a right to expect this of him. Sacrifices of this sort, I suspect, are extremely rare. Most people, if they fully acknowledged their rights, would not autonomously refuse to press them.

An even stronger conclusion would emerge if we could assume that some basic rights cannot be waived. That is, if there are some rights that others are bound to respect regardless of what we say, then, barring special explanation, we would be obliged not only to acknowledge these rights but also to avoid any appearance of consenting to give them up. To act as if we could release others from their obligation to grant these rights, apart from special circumstances, would be to fail to respect morality. Rousseau,

held, for example, that at least a minimal right to liberty cannot be waived. A man who consents to be enslaved, giving up liberty without *quid pro quo*, thereby displays a conditioned slavish mentality that renders his consent worthless. Similarly, a Kantian might argue that a person cannot release others from the obligation to refrain from killing him: consent is no defense against the charge of murder. To accept principles of this sort is to hold that rights of life and liberty are, as Kant believed, rather like a trustee's rights to preserve something valuable entrusted to him: he has not only a right but a duty to preserve it.

Even if there are no specific rights which cannot be waived, there might be at least one formal right of this sort. This is the right to some minimum degree of respect from others. No matter how willing a person is to submit to humiliation by others, they ought to show him some respect as a person. By analogy with self-respect, as presented here, this respect owed by others would consist of a willingness to acknowledge fully, in word as well as action, the person's basically equal moral status as defined by his other rights. To the extent that a person gives even tacit consent to humiliations incompatible with this respect, he will be acting as if he waives a right which he cannot in fact give up. To do this, barring special explanations, would mark one as servile.

V

Kant held that the avoidance of servility is a duty to oneself rather than a duty to others. Recent philosophers, however, tend to discard the idea of a duty to oneself as a conceptual confusion. Although admittedly the analogy between a duty to oneself and a duty to others is not perfect, I suggest that something important is reflected in Kant's contention.

Let us consider briefly the function of saying that a duty is *to* someone. *First,* to say that a duty is *to* a given person sometimes merely indicates who is the object of that duty. That is, it tells us that the duty is concerned with how that person is to be treated, how his interests and wishes are to be taken into account, and the like. Here we might as well say that we have a duty *towards,* or *regarding* that person. Typically the person in question is the beneficiary of the fulfillment of the duty. For example, in this sense I have a duty to my children and even a duty to a distant stranger if I promised a third party that I would help that stranger. Clearly a duty to avoid servility would be a duty to oneself at least in this minimal sense, for it is a duty to avoid, so far as possible, the denial of one's own moral status. The duty is concerned with understanding and affirming one's rights, which are, at least as a rule, for one's own benefit.

Second, when we say that a duty is *to* a certain person, we often indicate thereby the person especially entitled to complain in case the duty is not fulfilled. For example, if I fail in my duty to my colleagues, then it is they who can most appropriately reproach me. Others may sometimes speak up on their behalf, but, for the most part, it is not the business of strangers to set me straight. Analogously, to say that the duty to avoid servility is a duty to oneself would indicate that, though sometimes a person may justifiably reproach himself for being servile, others are not generally in the appropriate position to complain. Outside encouragement is sometimes necessary, but, if any blame is called for, it is primarily self-recrimination and not the censure of others.

Third, mention of the person to whom a duty is owed often tells us something about the source of that duty. For example, to say that I have a duty to another person may indicate that the argument to show that I have such a duty turns upon a promise to that person, his authority over me, my having accepted special benefits from him, or, more generally, his rights. Accordingly, to say that the duty to avoid servility is a duty to oneself would at least imply that it is not entirely based upon promises to others, their authority, their beneficence, or an obligation to respect their rights. More positively, the assertion might serve to indicate that the source of the duty is one's own rights rather than the rights of others, etc. That is, one ought not to be servile because, in some broad sense, one ought to respect one's own rights as a person. There is, to be sure, an asymmetry: one has certain duties to others because one ought not to violate their rights, and one has a duty to oneself because one ought to affirm one's own rights. Nevertheless, to dismiss duties to oneself out of hand is to overlook significant similarities.

Some familiar objections to duties to oneself, moreover, seem irrelevant in the case of servility. For example, some place much stock in the idea that a person would have no duties if alone on a desert island. This can be doubted, but in any case is irrelevant here. The duty to avoid servility is a duty to take a certain stance towards others and hence would be inapplicable if one were isolated on a desert island. Again, some suggest that if there were duties to oneself then one could make promises to oneself or owe oneself a debt of gratitude. Their paradigms are familiar ones. Someone remarks, 'I promised myself a vacation this year' or 'I have been such a good boy I owe myself a treat'. Concentration on these facetious cases tends to confuse the issue. In any case the duty to avoid servility, as presented here, does not presuppose promises to oneself or debts of gratitude to oneself. Other objections stem from the intuition that a person has no duty to promote his own happiness. A duty to oneself, it is sometimes assumed, must be a duty to promote one's own happiness. From a utilitarian point of view, in fact, this is what a duty to oneself would most likely be. The problems with such alleged duties, however, are irrelevant to the duty to avoid servility. This is a duty to understand and affirm one's rights, not to promote one's own welfare. While it is usually in the interest of a person to affirm his rights, our Kantian argument against servility was not based upon this premise. Finally, a more subtle line of objection turns on the idea that, given that rights and duties are correlative, a person who acted contrary to a duty to oneself would have to be violating his own rights, which seems absurd.[6] This objection raises issues too complex to examine here. One should note, however, that I have tried to give a sense to saying that servility is contrary to a duty to oneself with presupposing that the servile person violates his own rights. If acts contrary to duties to others are always violations of their rights, then duties to oneself are not parallel with duties to others to that extent. But this does not mean that it is empty or pointless to say that a duty is to oneself.

My argument against servility may prompt some to say that the duty is "to morality" rather than "to oneself". All this means, however, is that the duty is derived from a basic requirement to respect the provisions of morality; and in this sense every duty is a duty "to morality". My duties to my children are also derivative from a general requirement to respect moral principles, but they are still duties *to* them.

Kant suggests that duties to oneself are a precondition of duties to others. On our account of servility, there is at least one sense in which this is so. Insofar as the servile person is ignorant of his own rights, he is not in an adequate position to appreciate the rights of others. Misunderstanding the moral basis for his equal status with others, he is necessarily liable to underestimate the rights of those with whom he classifies himself. On the other hand, if he plays the servile role knowingly, then, barring special explanation, he displays a lack of concern to see the principles of morality acknowledged and respected and thus the absence of one motive which can move a moral person to respect the rights of others. In either case, the servile person's lack of self-respect necessarily puts him in a less than ideal position to respect others. Failure to fulfill one duty to oneself, then, renders a person liable to violate duties to others. This, however, is a consequence of our argument against servility, not a presupposition of it.

NOTES

1.   An earlier version of this paper was presented at the meetings of the American Philosophical Association, Pacific Division. A number of revisions have been made as a result of the helpful comments of others, especially Norman Dahl, Sharon Hill, Herbert Morris, and Mary Mothersill.

2.   Each of the cases is intended to represent only one possible pattern of servility. I make no claims about how often these patterns are exemplified, nor do I mean to imply that only these patterns could warrant the labels "Deferential Wife", "Uncle Tom", etc. All the more, I do not mean to imply any comparative judgments about the causes or relative magnitude of the problems of racial and sexual discrimination. One person, e.g. a self-contemptuous woman with a sense of racial inferiority, might exemplify features of several patterns at once; and, of course, a person might view her being a woman the way an Uncle Tom views his being black, etc.

3.   As will become evident, I am also presupposing some form of cognitive or "naturalistic" interpretation of rights. If, to accommodate an emotivist or prescriptivist, we set aside talk of moral knowledge and ignorance, we might construct a somewhat analogous case against servility from the point of view of those who adopt principles ascribing rights to all; but the argument, I suspect, would be more complex and less persuasive.

4.   See Immanuel Kant, *The Doctrine of Virtue,* Part II of *The Metaphysics of Morals,* ed. by M. J. Gregor (New York: Harper & Row, 1964), pp. 99–103; Prussian Academy edition, Vol. VI, pp. 434–37.

5.   Immanuel Kant, *Groundwork of the Metaphysics of Morals,* ed. by H. J. Paton (New York: Harper & Row, 1964), p. 69; Prussian Academy edition, Vol. IV, p. 401; *The Critique of Practical Reason,* ed. by Lewis W. Beck (New York: Bobbs-Merrill, 1956), pp. 81, 84; Prussian Academy edition, Vol. V, pp. 78, 81. My purpose here is not to interpret what Kant meant but to give a sense to his remark.

6.   This, I take it, is part of M. G. Singer's objection to duties to oneself in *Generalization in Ethics* (New York: Alfred A. Knopf, 1961), pp. 311–18. I have attempted to examine Singer's arguments in detail elsewhere.

SUGGESTIONS FOR FURTHER READING

A. WHY BE MORAL?

Baier, Kurt, *The Moral Point of View* (Ithaca, N.Y.: Cornell University Press, 1958), Chapters 11, 12.

Bradley, F. H., *Ethical Studies* second edition (New York: Oxford University Press, 1927; first edition, 1876), Essay 2.

Hospers, John, *Human Conduct* (New York: Harcourt, Brace & World, Inc., 1961), Chapter 4, Section 11.

Nielson, Kai, "Why Should I Be Moral?" *Methodos,* Vol. 15 (1963), pp. 275–306.

Plato, *The Republic,* various editions, especially Books II–VII.

Prichard, H. A., *Duty and Interest* (Oxford: Clarendon Press, 1928).

———, *Moral Obligation, Essays and Lectures* (Oxford: Clarendon Press, 1949), especially the title essay, written in 1937.

Sharp, Frank C., *Ethics* (New York: Appleton-Century, 1928), Chapters 22, 23.

B. PSYCHOLOGICAL EGOISM

Brandt, Richard B., *Ethical Theory* (Englewood Cliffs, N.J.: Prentice-Hall, Inc., 1959), Chapter 14.

Broad, C. D., *Five Types of Ethical Theory* (New York: Harcourt, Brace & Co., 1930), pp. 60–83, 184–192.

Garvin, Lucius, *A Modern Introduction to Ethics* (Boston: Houghton Miflin, 1953), Chapter 2.

Hobbes, Thomas, *Human Nature* (Various editions; first published London, 1650), Chapters, 7, 8, 9.

———, *Leviathan* (Various editions; first published, London, 1651), Part I, Chapters 15, 16.

———, *Of Liberty and Necessity* (Various editions; first published, London, 1654).

Hospers, John, *Human Conduct* (New York: Harcourt, Brace & World, Inc., 1961), Chapter 4, Section 9.

James, William, *The Principles of Psychology* (New York: Henry Holt, 1892), Vol. II, Chapter 26.

Locke, John, *An Essay concerning Human Understanding* (Various editions; first published, 1690; fourth edition revised by author, 1700), Book II, Chapter 28.

Mandeville, Bernard, "An Inquiry into the Origin of Moral Virtues," *The Fable of the Bees* (Various editions; first published, London, 1723).

Pratt, James B., *Reason in the Art of Living* (New York: Macmillan, 1949), Chapter 11.

Rashdall, Hastings, *The Theory of Good and Evil* (London: Oxford University Press, 1924), Vol. I, Chapter 2.

La Rouchefocauld, *Maximes* (Various editions), 83, 264.

Schlick, Moritz, *The Problems of Ethics* (Englewood Cliffs, N.J.: Prentice-Hall, 1939), Chapter 2.

Sidgwick, Henry, *Methods of Ethics,* 7th edition (New York and London: Macmillan, 1907), Book I, Chapter 4.

Slote, Michael Anthony, "An Empirical Basis for Psychological Egoism," *Journal of Philosophy,* Vol. 61, No. 18 (October 1, 1964).

C. ETHICAL EGOISM

Baumer, W. H., "Indefensible Impersonal Egoism," *Philosophical Studies,* Vol. 18 (1967), pp. 72–75.

Brandt, Richard B., *Ethical Theory* (Englewood Cliffs, N.J.: Prentice-Hall, Inc., 1959), Chapter 14.

Gauthier, D. P. (editor), *Morality and Rational Self-Interest* (Englewood Cliffs, N.J.: Prentice-Hall, 1970).

Hospers, John, *Human Conduct* (New York: Harcourt, Brace & World, Inc., 1961), Chapter 4, Section 10.

Milo, Ronald D. (editor), *Egoism and Altruism* (Belmont, Calif.: Wadsworth Publishing Company, Inc., 1973).

Moore, G. E., *Principia Ethica* (Cambridge: Cambridge University Press, 1903), Chapter 3.

Nagel, Thomas, *The Possibility of Altruism* (Oxford: Clarendon Press, 1970).

Pratt, James B., *Reason in the Art of Living* (New York: Macmillan, 1949), Chapter 10.

Schlick, Moritz, *Problems of Ethics* (Englewood Cliffs, N.J.: Prentice-Hall, Inc., 1939), Chapter 3.

Sidgwick, Henry, *The Methods of Ethics,* 7th edition (New York and London: Macmillan, 1907), Book II.

Williams, Gardner, "Individual, Social and Universal Ethics," *Journal of Philosophy,* Vol. 45 (1948), pp. 645–655.

D. DUTIES TO ONESELF

Baier, Kurt, *The Moral Point of View* (Ithaca, N.Y.: Cornell University Press, 1958), pp. 107–17, 188–90, 214–30.

Falk, W. D., "Morality, Self, and Others," in H. Castaneda and G. Nakhnikian (eds.) *Morality and the*

Language of Conduct (Detroit: Wayne State University, 1963), pp. 25–68.

Fotion, N., "Can We Have Moral Obligations to Ourselves?", *Australasian Journal of Philosophy*, Vol. 43 (1965), pp. 27–34.

Mabbott, J. D., "Prudence," *Proceedings of the Aristotelian Society,* Supp. Vol. 36 (1962), pp. 51–64.

Singer, M., "On Duties to Oneself," *Ethics,* Vol. 69 (1959), pp. 202–5.

von Wright, Georg, *The Varieties of Goodness* (London: Routledge and Kegan Paul, 1963), chapter 7, esp. pp. 149–54.